BEHIND THE FAÇADE
OF
Tantric

Buddhism

VOLUME 2

Master Xiao Pingshi

Translated by Ellen Lu

WHOLESOME VISION PUBLICATIONS

BEHIND THE FAÇADE
OF
Tantric

Buddhism

VOLUME 2

Wholesome Vision ™

Contents

ABOUT THE AUTHOR

Xiao Pingshi [蕭平實] was born in 1944 in a small town in Central Taiwan, into a family of farmers who had been engaged in agriculture for generations, with his father and grandfather both being disciples of the Triple Gem. His grandfather was an advanced graduate of the Qing Dynasty, and his maternal grandfather left behind many ancient books. In his early years, the author dabbled in worldly affairs and was averse to superstition. In middle age, he took refuge in the Triple Gem and explored the truth, was determined to seek the Path, and developed the skill related to the signless mindfulness of the Buddha. Soon after, he accomplished a task as difficult as grabbing a pearl from under the dragon's chin, which is to personally realize the reality-suchness and manifest the wisdom related to the sign of reality. He rapidly mastered the enlightenment of the Three Vehicles, brought forth compassion as well as fierce courage, and made the vow to save sentient beings and protect the correct Dharma seen by the wisdom-eye. Therefore, he established the Taipei Buddhist True Enlightenment Practitioners' Association and the True Enlightenment Education Foundation, as well as multiple True Enlightenment Lecture Halls throughout Taiwan. He has published more than a hundred books, such as *Signless Mindfulness of the Buddha, Commentary on the Śūraṅgama Sūtra*, and *Detailed Explanation of the Laṅkāvatāra Sūtra*, which are widely known in the Buddhist community.

TRANSLATOR'S NOTES

TO help readers better differentiate the different elements in the book, the main body texts written by the author are typeset in Calibri font while quoted texts (including quotes within quotes) are typeset in Comic San MS font. Annotations and explanations made by this author to help readers better understand the meanings of important words and phrases in the quotations as well as obscure words and phrases in the quoted excerpts of tantric sūtras and tantras are typeset in Calibri font enclosed with parentheses () while notes inserted by the original authors in the quoted sources are typeset in Comic San MS also enclosed with parentheses (). Notes inserted by this translator are enclosed with square brackets [] in Calibri while notes inserted by the translators of the quoted sources are typeset in Comic San MS and are also enclosed with square brackets []. All footnotes in this translation are from this translator to help readers better comprehend the content. Citations provided by this author in the original Chinese texts are also listed and translated in the footnotes based on the original Chinese sources. For Buddhist and tantric terminologies that are translated into English, alternative translations (Alt.) are provided in Sanskrit (S.), Tibetan (T.), or Chinese (C.), and explanations are also given to certain technical terms in the footnotes by the translator. All boldfaces in the text are added by this author. These conventions aim to help readers better comprehend the meaning of the tantric texts upon reading.

PREFACE

Those who practice the Buddha Dharma attain the doctrinal path by entirely relying on and strictly adhering to the Buddha's teachings, which have been compiled into sūtras to express His tenets. More specifically, all Buddhist disciples personally attain the Path to Buddhahood only by relying on the Buddha's empowerment to personally realize prajñā with sudden insight. Anyone who aspires to cultivate the Buddha Dharma and realize the Path to Buddhahood without following the World-Honored One and who endeavors to attain in this fashion the enlightenment of Buddhahood is just ignorant. By contrast, the views, practices, deeds, and fruitions in Esoteric Buddhism all comply with the guidelines of the yab-yum Buddha established by the leaders of this religion. Indeed, Esoteric Buddhists regard the yab-yum "Buddha" who constantly takes in sexual pleasure while embracing a woman as a reward body Buddha (in fact, this form of reward body Buddha is not a true manifestation of a reward body Buddha, but rather a deceptive appearance of a ghost, deity, or yaksha). Furthermore, these Esoteric Buddhists seek the Path to Buddhahood through the method of the yab-yum sexual union acquired from the non-Buddhist Sect of Shaktism and view this method as the correct way to cultivate the Buddha Dharma. Instead of following the World-Honored One Śākyamuni, the founder of Buddhism, they surprisingly follow Guru Padmasambhava, a mundane common being, and consider him the leader of Esoteric Buddhism in an attempt to rival Exoteric Buddhism without following the Buddha. Such behavior is the opposite of what the correct teachings urge us to do.

Padmasambhava was not a true incarnation of the lotus but was essentially a non-Buddhist ordinary being born from a womb who later married and had children. In order to establish the leader of their religion, Esoteric Buddhist gurus amplified, put together, and disseminated the contrived story that Padmasambhava had incarnated from a lotus. As later generations blindly and mistakenly

v

spread this rumor, Padmasambhava came to be officially recognized within Esoteric Buddhism as an incarnation of the lotus and was therefore called Lotus Born. Not only was the Lotus Born just an ordinary being, but the doctrines that he propagated also entirely consisted of the erroneous path of mundane sexual pleasure drawn from the non-Buddhist Sect of Shaktism. This practice results from the ignorance consisting of the love for the desire realm, which the Buddha has repeatedly condemned and refuted in the sūtras, saying that it should be eliminated by all Buddhist disciples of the Three Vehicles. Surprisingly, Padmasambhava exhorts people to crave the most intense blissful contact among the various forms of sexual desire, which is the complete opposite of what the Buddha has told us to do. How then could Padmasambhava be known as the "leader of the Esoteric Branch of Buddhism"? Therefore, Buddhist learners should rely on Buddha Śākyamuni instead of following Guru Padmasambhava, a non-Buddhist who is just a common being.

Furthermore, after knowing that one should rely on the Buddha instead of a non-Buddhist who is an ordinary being, one should understand the correct principle of following the correct Dharma instead of an individual (the principle of relying on the Dharma instead of an individual). The Dharma taught by the Buddha only comprises the Path to Liberation and the Path to the Enlightenment of Buddhahood. These two doctrines can, in a nutshell, be subsumed under the Path to the Enlightenment of Buddhahood. The practice and realization of the Path to Liberation are attained by eliminating self-view and self-attachment. Self-view consists of insisting that the mind that sees, hears, feels, and cognizes is the "permanent and indestructible self," firmly believing that this conscious mind has transmigrated from the previous life and can travel to the next life after death, and misapprehending this mind as the foundational consciousness of cyclic existence; such is self-view. This self-view is precisely the scope within which the teachings about the thoughtless mind with lucid awareness imparted by Guru Padmasambhava of Esoteric Buddhism after he "achieved both enlightenment and

Buddhahood" have fallen. After establishing Padmasambhava as their leader, those Esoteric Buddhists designated their eternalist non-Buddhist doctrines with Buddhist terms and claimed that these doctrines correspond to the Buddha Dharma. They further elevated these non-Buddhist doctrines above the Dharma of the Exoteric School in Buddhism and called these doctrines the wondrous path that leads to the attainment of Buddhahood with one's immediate body. In reality, these teachings entirely contradict the Buddha Dharma and are therefore non-Buddhist.

One must abandon one's self-attachment after eliminating one's self-view. Those who have eradicated their-attachment are known as arhats or solitary realizers worthy of receiving offerings from all humans and celestial beings in the three realms. Such is the correct way to cultivate the Path to Liberation. In contrast, all Esoteric Buddhist gurus—from the leader Padmasambhava at the top level down to all the contemporary gurus and Dharma-kings—regard the mind with lucid awareness amidst bliss and emptiness as well as the thoughtless mind with lucid awareness as the reality-suchness of the Ground of Buddhahood, thereby falling within the confines of the mental consciousness. Furthermore, those gurus mistakenly believe that the emptiness of shape and form observed in sexual pleasure as well as the emptiness of shape and form observed in the mind of feeling and cognition that takes in bliss correspond to the emptiness-nature, thereby misconstruing the Buddha's thoughts in the prajñā sūtras. Due to these two misunderstandings, those gurus are ordinary beings who have yet to abandon their self-view. The doctrines propagated based on such misapprehension are eternalist non-Buddhist doctrines that are no different from the soul-related folk beliefs, with the only distinction being the fact that the former is cultivated thoughtlessly whereas the latter is not. If these eternalist non-Buddhist doctrines were reliable, then all non-Buddhist doctrines could be relied upon as if they were the Buddha Dharma.

Not only do the doctrines taught by ancient and modern

Esoteric Buddhist gurus all consist of eternalist non-Buddhist methods, but they also revolve around the core philosophy of the Shaktist yab-yum practice transmitted by ghosts, deities, and yakshas. How could anyone adhere to such doctrines? The wise should observe and ponder carefully and subsequently be able to make the right choice to follow the correct Dharma instead of a guru. The correct way to cultivate the Path to the Enlightenment of Buddhahood is to comply with the following teaching from the Buddha: First, one personally realizes the tathāgatagarbha—the eighth consciousness—before proceeding to the personal intake based on the tathāgatagarbha that one has realized—one personally and directly takes in the properties of the tathāgatagarbha and thereby generates the fundamental knowledge within the wisdom of prajñā (the knowledge-of-general-aspect of prajñā) and the subsequently-attained knowledge within the wisdom of prajñā (the knowledge-of-specific-aspects and the knowledge-of-all-aspects of prajñā). It is by realizing this consciousness that one can understand the sign of reality. It is also by realizing this consciousness that one can give rise to a small portion of the knowledge-of-all-aspects within the subsequently-attained knowledge, which is known as the knowledge-of-the-aspects-of-paths, and become a Bodhisattva of the First Ground. This is the only correct way to cultivate the Path to the Enlightenment of Buddhahood.

Esoteric Buddhists, however, have not been able to generate the wisdom of prajñā due to their failure to realize the tathāgatagarbha—the eighth consciousness. They have therefore separately invented the existence of drops that appear through visualization in their central channel, have regarded these drops as the ālaya consciousness—the tathāgatagarbha—set forth by the Buddha, and have been deceiving followers by counterfeiting the tathāgatagarbha with these drops and by pretending that the cultivation of these drops corresponds to the practice and realization of the wisdom of prajñā. Furthermore, those Esoteric Buddhists have concealed this cultivation to prevent Exoteric Buddhists from knowing that the ālaya consciousness—the tathāgatagarbha—realized in Esoteric Buddhism is in fact the aforementioned drops. In addition, those Esoteric Buddhists consider the valid knowledge of non-Buddhist doctrines consisting of the penetrative ability to move the drops through the five vertically-aligned cakras in the central channel to be the valid knowledge attained by the Bodhisattvas of the First Ground at the stage of the penetrative understanding of the Buddhist wisdom of prajñā, thereby fooling both monastic and lay Bodhisattvas in Exoteric Buddhism as well as novice learners in Esoteric Buddhism and fueling their worship to the extent that they do not dare to question these teachings.

Ancient and modern Esoteric Buddhist gurus have strived to realize the Buddha Dharma in this fashion by following the non-Buddhist Padmasambhava and by adhering to the non-Buddhist method of visualizing the central channel and the drops. These endeavors, which are as futile as one's efforts to obtain cooked rice by boiling sand, are in fact disconnected from the Buddha Dharma and are the opposite of what the correct teachings urge us to do. Therefore, all Buddhist learners should, for their cultivation of the Buddha Dharma, follow the World-Honored One Śākyamuni instead of the non-Buddhist Padmasambhava; they should abide by the correct Buddhist Dharma instead of the non-Buddhist tantric doctrines; and they should follow the Buddhist sangha instead of the non-Buddhist gurus—lamas—of Esoteric Buddhism; otherwise, their thoughts and practices will stand in complete opposition to the correct teachings.

Furthermore, Esoteric Buddhists consider the method of the yab-yum sexual union between a male and a female to be the correct way to practice the Buddha Dharma. They equate the state of one-pointedness without distracting thoughts in orgasm with the state of meditative absorption and regard sexual intercourse as the correct way to cultivate meditative concentration. These views contradict the Buddha's teachings about the four concentrations and four formless absorptions cultivated and attained by non-Buddhists and Bodhisattvas. They also contradict the contents of the Path to Liberation set forth by the Buddha and completely oppose and veer in the opposite direction of the teachings about the Path to the Enlightenment of Buddhahood imparted by the Buddha. Esoteric Buddhists have elevated these methods of mundane sexual pleasure preached by the non-Buddhists of the Hindu Sect of Shaktism to the status of supreme doctrines that exceed Buddhist teachings. In fact, those who practice according to these tantric methods will definitely end up transmigrating endlessly and suffer immeasurable agony in the three evil paths for long kalpas during their future lives. How then could the cultivation of these methods be considered the correct way to cultivate the Buddha Dharma? Therefore, all those who practice the Buddha Dharma should abide by the doctrines taught by the Buddha instead of the non-Buddhist methods set forth by Esoteric Buddhist gurus.

The concurrent rise of Esoteric Buddhism and demise of Buddhism constitute a historical event that transpired in ancient India. The flourishing of Esoteric Buddhism inevitably triggers the downfall of the Buddha Dharma. In other words, Esoteric Buddhism will definitely annihilate Buddhism once it completely supplants Exoteric Buddhism at the culmination of its expansion. The reason is that Esoteric Buddhist doctrines do not correspond to the true Buddha Dharma. Despite their Buddhist veneer, they are essentially eternalist non-Buddhist mundane methods related to the enjoyment of sexual union, which demonstrates that Esoteric Buddhism is a religion whose monastics perform laic methods. Therefore, Buddhism will be extinguished once Esoteric Buddhism has completely replaced Exoteric Buddhism. There will be nothing left of Buddhism other than Buddhist monasteries and monastics and Buddhism will essentially be turned into a non-Buddhist faith that revolves around and depends on ghosts and deities.

Esoteric Buddhist gurus and Dharma-kings concur on the fact that all individuals entirely rely on the Buddha's empowerment for their cultivation of Esoteric Buddhist doctrines. However, those gurus also unanimously advocate that "one must principally follow the guru and secondarily the Buddha." Furthermore, they assert that "one must abide by the tantras composed by the gurus instead of the sūtras taught by Buddha Śākyamuni given that the tantras are superior to the Exoteric Buddhist sūtras." Similarly, Tsongkhapa advocates that "one must base one's practice on the great craving aroused through the yab-yum method and that the abandonment of this craving constitutes an infraction of the Samaya vows." In fact, the cultivation and attainments of ancient and contemporary Dharma-kings and gurus have all fallen within the confines of eternalist non-Buddhist doctrines. Moreover, all the sūtras and tantras among esoteric texts are the collective works of Esoteric Buddhist leaders compiled over a long period and their contents were not taught by the Buddha. The doctrines preached in those tantric texts are furthermore non-Buddhist. How can those gurus realize the Buddha Dharma when they claim in this fashion that one should follow the gurus instead of the Exoteric Buddhist sūtras and that one should rely on the yab-yum Buddhas, who are manifestations of the ghosts and deities worshipped in Esoteric Buddhism, instead of the authentic Buddha in Exoteric Buddhism? This demonstrates that the contents stated by those Esoteric Buddhist gurus and set forth in the tantras are the opposite of the correct teachings.

I composed this book for many different reasons. Esoteric Buddhist learners are generally unaware of the essence of their religion and have therefore been deceived and misled. Furthermore, a great number of renowned Exoteric Buddhist masters in Taiwan have in recent years scrambled to cozy up to the Esoteric Buddhist Dalai Lama, hoping to use his widespread fame to raise their own status. Such behavior has caused many within the two groups of monastics [translation note: bhikṣus and bhikṣunīs] in Exoteric Buddhism, who do not know that the intention of the reputable masters who pander to Esoteric Buddhism is to build themselves up, to mistakenly believe that Esoteric Buddhism truly corresponds to Buddhism. Furthermore, given the extreme difficulty to realize prajñā, as evidenced by the fact that many people have been unable to personally realize it despite practicing Buddhism for a long time, and given that the Esoteric Buddhist gurus whom they come across all have "valid knowledge"—those lamas all boast "an extremely high level" of valid knowledge, easily reaching the First Ground or Buddhahood—those two groups of monastics have turned to Esoteric Buddhism to seek the Dharma as they do not know its background. Lastly, as the general public is largely unaware that Esoteric Buddhism does not correspond to Buddhism, it has concluded that the sex scandals that erupted at the cultivation centers that propagate esoteric teachings were instances of sexual misconduct committed by masters of Buddhist cultivation centers and has accused Buddhism for these misdeeds, frequently dragging it through the mud and harming it on myriad occasions. Due to the above reasons, I had to compose this book to rectify the erroneous knowledge and protect Buddhism.

In fact, the first and foremost reason that led to the writing of this book is my observation that Esoteric Buddhists have substituted Buddhist doctrines with non-Buddhist ones and have claimed that the latter exceeds the Exoteric Buddhist Dharma-gate of the ultimate attainment of Buddhahood in all respects. Esoteric Buddhists have thus counterfeited the Buddha Dharma with non-Buddhist doctrines. In addition, the lamas have, in their capacity as non-Buddhists, disguised themselves as Buddhist monastics. Furthermore, they have been gnawing and devouring Buddhist resources through the tactic of exalting Esotericism and suppressing Exotericism, thereby gradually and peacefully exterminating Buddhism without Buddhist disciples realizing it. We will then see a historical recurrence of the eradication of Buddhism in ancient India at the hands of Tantric followers. In the modern age, the most prominent exponents of Esoteric Buddhist doctrines are the Dalai Lama and Master Yinshun. The former openly propagates the view of "dependent arising coupled with an empty nature"—the Theory of Uncausedness—and negates the vijñaptimātra sūtras of the third turning of the Dharma wheel by labeling the doctrines taught therein as non-definitive based on Tsongkhapa's assertions. Furthermore, the Dalai Lama secretly disseminates the yab-yum practice, asserting that it is a method that leads to the ultimate attainment of Buddhahood. As for Master Yinshun, he willingly took over the erroneous Esoteric Buddhist doctrines in his capacity as an Exoteric Buddhist master and vigorously propagates the view of Prāsaṅgika Madhyamaka—the Theory of Uncausedness—preached by the Gelug School in Tantric Buddhism. He is openly against Esoteric Buddhism (he has denounced and refuted the yab-yum practice in this religion), but in reality defends and supports Esoteric Buddhism by widely disseminating the Theory of Uncausedness—the view of Prāsaṅgika Madhyamaka—thereby negating the wondrous doctrine of the tathāgatagarbha set forth by the Buddha in the sūtras of the third turning of the Dharma wheel and granting the yab-yum method in Esoteric Buddhism room for survival. Thus, the current dissemination of the fallacious Esoteric Buddhist doctrines by two prominent masters of Esoteric and Exoteric Buddhism—one overtly and the other covertly—has allowed Esoteric Buddhism to expand its power and caused Buddhist learners to mistakenly believe that Esoteric Buddhism truly is Buddhism. In view of the detrimental and far-reaching influences of these deeds, I have no choice but to reveal the truth as it is.

Due to the above reasons, it is necessary to fully demonstrate the secrets related to Esoteric Buddhist doctrines and thoroughly distinguish the right and wrong of these doctrines so that all Buddhist disciples and the general public can be aware of these secrets and errors—hence the composition and publication of this book. The purpose is to protect authentic Buddhism by informing the public about the non-Buddhist essence of Esoteric Buddhism and its discrepancies with authentic Buddhism.

My rectification of Esoteric Buddhist doctrines aims to cause their followers to revert to Exoteric Buddhist doctrines and to expulse the non-Buddhist erroneous methods worshipped by those followers from Buddhism. I, therefore, wrote this book in the hope of helping Buddhist doctrines recover the purity that they had at the time of the Buddha, when they were not interspersed with the non-Buddhist doctrines of Esoteric Buddhism. May all learners and renowned masters of Buddhism understand the true colors of Esoteric Buddhism, so that Esoteric Buddhism can dissociate itself from non-Buddhist doctrines and revert to the correct Dharma set forth by the Buddha in the Exoteric Buddhist sūtras and so that Buddhism can grow purer every day. The objective is to prolong the wisdom-life of the Buddha Dharma until the arrival of Bodhisattva Candraprabha in this world. If Esoteric Buddhists refuse to correct their non-Buddhist doctrines, then Esoteric Buddhism should be detached from Buddhism so that the two religions become unrelated. Only then will the World-Honored One's exalted teachings be able to live on in peace without being perturbed again by the non-Buddhist doctrines of Esoteric Buddhism.

Despite witnessing my rectification of the Esoteric Buddhist doctrines, tantric gurus have refused to correct their erroneous doctrines. Instead, they want to maintain their mistaken methods in order to save these non-Buddhist tantric doctrines from the brink of extinction and ensure the longevity of these fallacious tantric methods. To achieve this goal, they deliberately assumed the identities of Exoteric Buddhist learners on the Internet and used fake names to vilify me as a non-Buddhist who leeches off the Buddha Dharma. Their objective is to confuse and mislead the public—to cause people to mistakenly believe that the criticism against me originates from Exoteric Buddhist learners. This lowly and undignified behavior is no different from that of a thief who yells: "Catch the thief!" Despite being furious with me, as evidenced by the fact that they impudently defamed me as a non-Buddhist, those tantric gurus can only tell their disciples the following excuse in private: "The lay Buddhist Pinghi is an amateur when it comes to esoteric doctrines; we do not want to condescend to him either for discussions or debates." However, in the face of my statements, they neither have the courage nor the ability to propose a Buddhist doctrinal debate by disclosing their real names and addresses and can only make evasive statements as well as assertions that conceal the truth.

The reason behind this attitude is that the lamas—gurus— who have practiced Esoteric Buddhism for over thirty years are in fact aware that tantric doctrines merely result from the designation of mundane methods that their leaders have learned from non-Buddhists with the terminology of the Buddha Dharma, while these methods are in essence absolutely non-Buddhist. Those gurus are indeed also aware that they have never attained prajñā, have not realized the tathāgatagarbha, and have yet to enter the Dharma of Bodhisattvas. However, if they told the truth, they would inevitably be assailed by hordes of Esoteric Buddhists, and therefore none of them are willing to speak truthfully. In addition, as those lamas are reluctant to relinquish fame and material welfare, they continue to rely on Esoteric Buddhist doctrines to receive offerings, refuse to break out of their old habits, and just live on. Due to these reasons, Esoteric Buddhist gurus have been heavily silent in response to my statements about the contents of their doctrines. They neither dare to defend their views openly under their real names nor have the courage to come forward to debate the doctrines with me in private. They are all aware that Esoteric Buddhist doctrines are just non-Buddhist mundane methods coated with various terms of the Buddha Dharma and are not presentable in any formal context.

Furthermore, Esoteric Buddhist doctrines are associated from beginning to end with the method of the fourth joy—the yab-yum sexual pleasure—the cultivation of which is displayed as the ultimate objective of the practice that leads to the attainment of Buddhahood. Therefore, all the obscure terms in the Tibetan Esoteric Buddhist tantras unequivocally allude to this method. To explicate each and every tantra of the various tantric schools individually would inevitably entail repeating the same discussions throughout this book, which would make this writing tedious to read and would have no practical significance. Consequently, I have only cited representative tantras of tantric schools and have provided just sufficient annotations in brackets to help readers understand the meanings of those tantras.

Furthermore, the wording in this book must be simple and

clear; common and colloquial terms and proverbs are even used instead of formal ones for reasons that should also be explained here. Esoteric Buddhist doctrines do involve sexual misconduct and are indeed preposterous. This fact must be kept from the knowledge of outsiders and therefore these doctrines are propagated with evasive and opaque terms—hence the extensive use of obscure words in the tantras. If these obscure terms are not explained plainly, then learners will not be able to understand their meanings upon reading them. If they do not comprehend these meanings, then they will not be able to distinguish the right and wrong of the tantric doctrines. This will enable Esoteric Buddhist gurus to continue to divert people's attention and conceal their mistakes with evasive statements, which means that my endeavors to protect and uphold the correct Buddhist Dharma will come up short. Therefore, the wording in this book must be simple and unambiguous so that all readers can grasp the meanings of the obscure terms and Esoteric Buddhist gurus will not be able to distort these meanings and conceal their mistakes. Furthermore, given that novice practitioners of Tantric Buddhism are **mostly** less educated, the wording in this book must be plain and the use of uncommon vocabulary must be avoided as much as possible so that these practitioners can truly understand the meanings highlighted in my book upon reading them.

Furthermore, the terms from the Sūtra and Tantra Divisions of Esoteric Buddhism cited in this book have mostly been annotated in parentheses behind those words. The reasons are as follows: To explain every single paragraph individually would lengthen the book significantly. Therefore, I have adopted the simpler and more convenient method of providing annotations in parentheses to avoid lengthening the book. Readers will understand those annotations upon reading them and will be able to analyze according to the truth and understand the right and wrong of Esoteric Buddhist doctrines. They will then be able to return to the right path and abandon those incorrect doctrines, which means that my objective will be achieved. Therefore, I have provided annotations through this simpler and more convenient method.

Furthermore, the original plan was for each volume of this book to be approximately 400 pages long. However, since Esoteric Buddhist doctrines **completely** deviate from the truth and are **entirely** erroneous, a critique of these doctrines requires a massive and irreducible word count. Given the final book length of over 550,000 words, three extra lines have been added to each page of the body text, bringing the total number of lines per page to 17. Even by fitting in this fashion as many lines as possible to every page, this book still needs to be divided into four volumes in order to be entirely printed. Therefore, the more cluttered layout may make it harder for elderly readers to peruse this writing, which actually goes against my will, and I hereby present my apologies.

Furthermore, in order to prevent some blind followers of Tantric Buddhism from gathering and burning this publication in large quantities—in the same way that some people in the past collected and incinerated *Treasury of the Correct Dharma Seen by the Wisdom-Eye: Collection of Protecting the Dharma*—this publication will not be disseminated in the form of free printed material, but will instead be distributed as a payable publication. However, given that our goal is not to make a profit, this book will be distributed below cost—at a token "cost price." The related losses will be covered by the profits made from the other writings published by our company. The purpose is to protect the correct Buddhist Dharma by widely disseminating this writing and extensively benefiting learners.

Right before the publication of this book, I have described the reasons for its composition and the general idea of the editing as above. May all Exoteric and Esoteric Buddhist practitioners read this book carefully and distinguish right from wrong by verifying each of my statements in order to protect themselves and save others. May everyone avoid the grievous misdeed of destroying the correct Buddhist Dharma and refrain from perfunctorily following the erroneous tantric doctrines deep down a devious path.

Buddhist disciple and holder of the Bodhisattva Precepts

Lay Buddhist Pingshi

Spring, 2002

At the Residence of Clamor

JIANGBA LUOJIE'S FOREWORD

From Dzi Beads to Tantric Buddhism

Prostrating myself before the omniscient Bhagavān,
And offering my body, speech, and mind to the Triple Gem.

More than ten years ago, the New Age movement in Europe and the US, coupled with the unique social customs on Taiwan Island, gave rise to a craze for dzi beads in Taiwan. Originally a family heirloom for Tibetan women, these gemstones were either intentionally or unintentionally hyped as treasures that fell from the sky, that did not previously exist in the human world, and that anyone who carried them would definitely attain Buddhahood in the future without the need for practice. Later, modern scientific testing confirmed that these stones were merely processed products of whitened ancient agates. Today, Taiwan has even become the world's largest exporter of ancient dzi beads—it actually sells them to Tibet to satisfy collectors worldwide. The revelation of the aforementioned hard fact upended the beautiful but dissonant myth surrounding dzi beads.

From an anthropological perspective, the Buddha Dharma has often undergone cultural substitution based on temporal and geographical conditions as it spread to other regions throughout history, with the environment even being a determining factor of the restructured cultural elements. Mr. Li Yuansong [李元松] of the Modern Chan Society has thus said: "Esoteric Buddhism is essentially a pile of gilded trash surrounding a diamond." But is the sparkling diamond amidst the trash truly the intrinsic ground that the World-Honored One touched with His cottony hand as well as the bright star that He beheld with His clear purple-blue eyes at night? Or is it just a zircon that simulates a diamond—but just because its glare is too strong, tantric practitioners cannot and will not see its essence clearly?

Generally speaking, China inherited the Mahāyāna Buddhism that existed in ancient India before the Tang Dynasty in its entirety, whereas Tibet took over the subsequent non-Buddhist faith into which Indian Buddhism developed. After thriving in India, Mahāyāna Buddhism gradually assimilated a plethora of cultural elements from Hinduism and evolved through this transculturation into Tantric Buddhism, which became the predominant philosophy of the Indian Buddha Dharma. These facts are attested by the archaeological records uncovered at the ruins of the Nālandā Monastery and are also well evidenced by the bibliographies found in Master Xuanzang's [玄奘] and Master Yijing's [義淨] writings.

During the reign of Songtsän Gampo (around the early Tang Dynasty), Tibet officially entered the era of writing and massively imported new cultural elements from India and China. The most impactful development was certainly the official establishment of the Buddha Dharma as Tibet's state religion. After the Dark Age, Tibet adopted Tantric Buddhism from India almost in its entirety and incorporated therein some elements from the Tibetan religion Bön. The dissemination of this faith by translation masters such as Rinchen Zangpo during the latter period of the propagation of Buddhism in Tibet helped establish the main structures of Tibetan Buddhism, which primarily include the following stages of practice: Hīnayāna, followed by Mahāyāna, then Vajrayāna (Esoteric Buddhism), and finally the attainment of Buddhahood with one's immediate body.

From the perspective of their philosophical background, the various schools of Tibetan Buddhism that have existed since ancient times can be subsumed under two different systems: the Tathāgatagarbha Madhyamaka and the Prāsaṅgika Madhyamaka. The former encompasses the Nyingma, Kagyu, Sakya, and Jonang traditions and includes teachings related to the tathāgatagarbha,

Svātantrika Madhyamaka, the view of vijñaptimātra, the view of the non-duality of saṃsāra and nirvāṇa, the Great Madhyamaka, the view of other-emptiness, and so forth. These contents are all based on the principle of "the non-existence of conventional truth and the existence of the ultimate truth," with each tradition delineating its own thoughts about the ultimate truth, which differ drastically from and even completely oppose one another. As for the view of Prāsaṅgika Madhyamaka, it was popularized by Tsongkhapa from the later-established Gelug tradition as well as by his disciples over many generations. Leaning on its newly-acquired political supremacy, the Gelug tradition hindered the propagation of the tathāgatagarbha-based thoughts and triggered a loss of talent in the lineages that disseminated these thoughts. Meanwhile, Prāsaṅgika Madhyamaka remains up to this day the predominant thought within the Tibetan Buddhist philosophy.

In the Tibetan Esoteric Buddhist philosophy, Highest Yoga Tantra is regarded as the supreme and most difficult path as well as the only path that enables practitioners to instantaneously bypass all grounds and attain Buddhahood with one's immediate body (even without going through the intermediate state). Practitioners who are equipped with both merit and wisdom can attain the three exalted bodies and fulfill the fruition of Buddhahood through this path. With respect to the cultivation of this path, the initial first and second initiations serve as a basis for the subsequent third and fourth initiations. Practitioners then reach a higher level by achieving the meritorious activities related to the third initiation, before attaining the perfect fruition of Buddhahood by cultivating the more advanced fourth initiation. They may, during this process, skip the wisdom initiation and proceed directly to the cultivation of the more advanced name initiation, but only under the condition that they do not violate the spirit of the first three initiations.

I began to practice Esoteric Buddhism in 1984 and devoted an extensive amount of time to receive the complete set of initiations and teachings. I then set aside all worldly affairs and made my religious practice a full-time occupation. I read and reflected upon the sūtras by day—I had perused more than half of all the books kept in the Buddhist library—and cultivated esoteric doctrines at night for eleven long years. It was very difficult back then to get a hold of any information related to esoteric doctrines, and those who came upon such materials treated them as prized treasures. I remember how I always journeyed throughout the country, in search of gurus and visiting friends just to obtain fragmentary pieces of tantric literature. To receive tantric teachings, I traveled back and forth between India and Nepal and visited elders and meritorious practitioners from various traditions. Over the years, I witnessed firsthand the expansion of Esoteric Buddhism in Taiwan.

While I was able to personally experience most of the individual paths of cultivation and attainment trodden by my predecessors, the doubts that I harbored kept growing stronger. Although the propagation of esoteric doctrines is reputed to be the true transmission of the Dharma outside the scriptures, these doctrines contradict the World-Honored One's teachings in the sūtras in all respects. The discrepancies are so flagrant that they can no longer be encompassed with the conventional expressions "expedient teachings" and "occasional explanations." Worst yet, whenever I asked those renowned vajra gurus "endowed with both knowledge and attainments" to elucidate the unresolved blind spots in my mind, they just distorted the truth with deceptive tactics.

When the craze for dzi beads faded in Taiwan, the "iron meteorite" took over as the new obsession. The owner of a Buddhist arts and crafts store near the Bouddhanath Stupa in Nepal once unintentionally placed a pestle made of celestial iron in its doorway. The sun heated the pestle and a Taiwanese burnt his hand while picking it up. He immediately shouted that the iron rod was blessed by the Buddhas and Bodhisattvas and eventually paid a hefty sum of money to "respectfully purchase" this iron pestle "with psychic connections with the ghosts and deities." After that, every owner of a Buddhist arts and crafts store displayed iron products in his storefront under the sun to attract Taiwanese pilgrims. The generous donations from Taiwanese Buddhist disciples largely financed the tangible and intangible assets of "Buddhist monasteries" in Tibet, India, and Nepal. In those foreign lands, I frequently came across pious Buddhist disciples who had given up their families and careers to follow an Esoteric Buddhist guru in those countries, but what they achieved remained related to nonsensical and fallacious thoughts within the confines of arising-and-ceasing phenomena. They neither lacked devotion nor assiduity, but ended up falling within the scope of erroneous thoughts, which is truly pitiful.

The cultivation of the four initiations of Highest Yoga Tantra entirely consists of engaging in imaginative thinking and taking in various sensations on the plane of one's conscious mind. It even requires the performance of self-insinuation and self-anesthesia. This practice sometimes involves psychic connections with ghosts and deities and is associated with the nature related to the properties of erroneous thinking. As stated by Guru Norlha: "Being able to converse with meditational deities is only the first step of the practice." Tantric practitioners are unaware that their miraculous abilities have been conferred on them by external forces consisting of ghosts and deities and that they may, in the worst case, be degraded to the position of spokesperson or agent of these ghosts and deities. No matter how solid their accomplishments in deity yoga are, once they enter an operating room, one dose of anesthesia suffices to obliterate all their attainments. How then can this cultivation be called yoga that leads to the achievement of a deity's celestial form body?

As for the contents of the second and third initiations, they actually consist of the repeated cultivation of the winds, channels, and drops in the subtle body, which is a practice drawn from the Tantric School of Hinduism. The so-called accomplishment of the subtle body is based on Hindu contents coated with the terminology related to the samādhis in the Buddha Dharma and has in fact nothing to do with the cultivation and realization of the Buddha Dharma. Practitioners of Hindu traditions also cultivate the channels, winds, drops, and union; many of them have also been rumored to have attained the rainbow body; and a great number of renowned gurus in the history of Esoteric Buddhism also served as reputable masters in the lineage of Hinduism. Since the emergence of the hippy movement in Europe and the US, a plethora of publications about the philosophy of the subtle body has been translated into English, which enables us to easily verify that the Tibetan and the Hindu Dharma gates of practice related to the subtle body simply originate from the same source and that the actual stages of practice in these two Dharma gates are exactly identical, with the only difference being that Tantric Buddhists have designated their teachings with the terminology of the Buddha Dharma. However, Esoteric Buddhist practitioners are both unable and unwilling to admit this fact given that most of them are reluctant to extensively study the sūtras of the Buddha Dharma or even worldly doctrines. Moreover, the five essential Dharma teachings such as *Great Perfection* and *Vajrakīlaya* cultivated in the Bön religion are identical to the actual contents transmitted in Esoteric Buddhism. Historically, the excavators of the treasures in the Bön religion and the Nyingma School have always exchanged thoughts and feelings. In addition, many "renowned gurus" hold the position of esteemed religious masters in both Buddhism and Bön. Thus, one cannot help but wonder: What sets the Buddha Dharma apart from non-Buddhism?

The cultivation of the name initiation denotes the end of the tantric practice. However, if we take a closer look at the statements found in the unsurpassed and extremely confidential mind essentials of the Four Major Schools, we will notice that the scope within which they have fallen is similar to that of the preposterous and imaginary "great ease pervading the empty space" set forth by Master Yuexi [月溪] of Hong Kong, where practitioners endeavor to obtain cooked rice by steaming sand or strive to live on like a ghost in a dark cave on the plane of the conscious mind. Those practitioners have presumptuously proclaimed to have realized the reality-suchness of the Ground of Buddhahood when they still do not have the ability to directly observe the functions of their own seventh and eighth consciousnesses. How can they transform their consciousnesses into wisdom when they actually remain entrapped within the confines of the properties and functions of the sixth consciousness? They have in fact committed the misdeed of grievous false speech without knowing it.

The practice and attainment of Highest Yoga Tantra are irrelevant to the cultivation of the Triple Training in the Buddha Dharma, as they comply with the same tenets as those of the other religions and merely possess the veneer of the Buddha Dharma. This is precisely the reason why we can say that Buddhism in ancient India was essentially extinguished during the process where it evolved into Tantrism, well before its extermination by heretics, considering that the Buddha Dharma had already lost its core teachings.

In short, the Esoteric Buddhist philosophy is not the true Buddha Dharma and contradicts the World-Honored One's scriptural teachings in every way. As its followers neither possess the knowledge-of-the-aspects-of-paths nor understand Buddha Śākyamuni's real intent, they do not have the ability to inspect whether the practices and attainments highlighted in the tantric teachings are correct and therefore all abide by their gurus' guidelines without being able to distinguish right from wrong. While early generations of followers misunderstood those teachings in this fashion, later generations were even more bewildered without being aware of it. As time went by, Esoteric Buddhism has developed into a religion that merely possesses terminology of the Buddha Dharma and whose practitioners essentially perform non-Buddhist methods. The inability of Esoteric Buddhist practitioners to examine those teachings themselves, coupled with the fact that they idolize the Esoteric Buddhist Dharma-kings and gurus for their fame, authority, and so forth, has prevented them from facing the truth as it is and from analyzing which principles are correct. All they can do is numb themselves emotionally and convince themselves to believe the following: The gurus are Buddhas; the celestial bodies that these practitioners imagine will one day become real; the states that they visualize will turn into reality once the conditions ripen; the states manifested by deity sky-travelers are real; the visualizer and the visualized will become one; the teachings imparted by the deity sky-travelers embodied by ghosts and deities relate to the definitive meaning; the states perceived during meditative concentration are real; the Shambhala Pure Land truly exists; the pure lands that these practitioners have imagined will eventually become real; one will obtain a Buddha's body by accomplishing the cultivation of the channels and winds; the yab-yum practice is an unsurpassed great method that is absolutely not obscene; the thoughtless omniscience of bliss and luminosity is a state of the intrinsic mind of nirvāṇa; the one hundred peaceful and wrathful deities inside and outside one's body will transform, after one's death, into a Buddha that is about to enter the non-duality of saṃsāra and nirvāṇa; and so forth.

Today's Tibetan Esoteric Buddhism has developed into a colossal institution. In Taiwan alone, over one hundred Esoteric Buddhist centers have emerged one after another, likely attracting hundreds of thousands of devotees and amassing incalculable resources. On the surface, the Buddha Dharma seems to be flourishing; in reality, tantric gurus have been steering these followers towards non-Buddhist doctrines and heretical methods, and even doctrines that entail the grievous sin of violating the precepts. This is a recurrence of the historical decline and annihilation of Buddhism in ancient India. The deeper underlying reason for these phenomena is that for several decades, the Buddhist institutes in Taiwan have used Master Yinshun's writings as a template for almost all of their teachings. However, Yinshun's philosophy essentially continues the thought of Prāsaṅgika Madhyamaka transmitted by the Gelug School of Tibetan Tantrism. Moreover, he extensively insinuates in his writings that the Buddha Dharma of the Great Vehicle was not taught by the Buddha; Buddha Amitābha and His pure land do not exist; Buddha

Śākyamuni's reward body does not permanently reside in a palace of the Highest Heaven of the Form Realm to teach the Dharma; there are no such things as Bodhisattvas or hell; and so forth. Yinshun's disciples can only seek the true doctrines in either one of the following two extremes if they want to advance in their cultivation: Theravāda Buddha Dharma or Tibetan Buddha Dharma. It is therefore no exaggeration to say that Yinshun "dons a monastic robe but destroys the World-Honored One's correct Dharma." The elders at the major monasteries either believe and accept Yinshun's doctrines as they do not have the ability to check the correctness of these doctrines due to their lack of the knowledge-of-aspects, or pander to Esoteric Buddhist devotees for their wealth and fame and therefore scramble to follow them and to rely on them. One cannot help but worry about what lies ahead for the correct Dharma.

All disciples of the Three Vehicles should frequently undergo an in-depth self-reflection: What was my original motivation to learn Buddhism? Am I increasingly able to perceive the darkness in my mind? Have I expelled some of the confusion in my mind and generated the wisdom related to the Buddha Dharma since I started to learn Buddhism? Do I conduct myself based on wisdom or by following someone? Do my deeds truly benefit sentient beings? Have I truly been acting according to the correct Dharma taught by the Buddha? Have I personally attained enlightenment—the sign of reality of definitive meaning? Furthermore, the Buddha has said that the seventh and the eighth consciousnesses of sentient beings are unceasing; then do I know how our seventh and eighth consciousnesses function every instant without interruption during all twelve dual hours in a way that can be directly witnessed? If one does not even know about the ālaya (translator's note: ālaya consciousness) that all individuals inherently possess and that forever exists at all times or the Manas (translator's note: Manas consciousness) that constantly makes decisions, then one is just fooling oneself and others by proclaiming how marvelous the other samādhis are.

In the winter of 1996, I had the good fortune to learn from my master Mr. Pingshi, perhaps owing to the slight amount of meritorious quality that I had accumulated in my former lives. I was then able to get an in-depth glimpse into the Buddha Dharma. On the one hand, I rectified my knowledge and view of the Buddha Dharma. The vessels connecting the various parts of the correct Dharma surfaced one by one, whereas the haziness of queries and objections resulting from learning Esoteric Buddhism dissipated step by step, which enabled me to realize my past prejudices and self-limiting mindset. Only then did the various levels and trails connecting the grounds of ordinary beings to the grounds of Bodhisattvas and finally to the Ground of Buddhahood become clear in my mind. I gradually acquired the knowledge-of-the-aspects-of-paths and the wisdom-eye to select the correct doctrines from the incorrect ones and was therefore able to know the sphere within which each cultivation center had fallen as clearly as if I was looking at a fruit on my palm. On the other hand, I embarked on my practice through the Dharma-gate of the mindfulness of the Buddha and enhanced my meditative concentration skill through the prostration to the Buddha with the signless mindfulness of the Buddha. When my meditative concentration skill became continuous, I was well aware that I had every chance of taking rebirth in the Western Pure Land without having to wait for Buddha Amitābha to manifest prior to my death. I realized with surprise the reason why a great number of ancient and modern meritorious practitioners had regretted the fact that although they were hopeful of being reborn in the Western Pure Land, they painfully lacked the confidence to do so. When the causes and conditions ripened, I was able to see the sign of reality, which is the pedestal on which all the sūtras of definitive meaning in the Three Vehicles are established. Even the deities and ghosts do not know about this sign of reality—reality-suchness. It is only based on this realization that I have been able to advance ground by ground. This realization marked the beginning of my post-enlightenment practice, during which I have been cultivating the more advanced knowledge-of-all-aspects and have been correctly practicing the samādhis in accordance with the Buddha's words and with the teachings imparted by my benevolent master. All these internal matters should only be known by internal persons. I am no longer the mayfly or the frog at the bottom of the well which is clueless about the coiled dragon flying in the sky.

My benevolent master Mr. Pingshi has a personality that befits his name. Although he was indeed a religious leader in many of his former lives and his past teachings are still frequently worshipped today, he resolutely left behind the illusory fame of the past. He disdains the worldly masters' use of gimmicks to attract attention, always conducts himself and teaches others in a plain and down-to-earth manner, and is indeed a role model for sentient beings—as he never senselessly engages in fancy story-telling about the valid knowledge that he has attained, many arrogant learners have ill intentions towards him and look down upon him. My master invariably protects the longevity of the correct Dharma with his own life and his determination to protect the Dharma has not budged despite people's contempt and trampling. Owing to his compassion, he cannot bear seeing sentient beings commit hell-bound deeds despite acting out of good intentions. Therefore, in keeping with the ethos of the Tathāgata's lineage, he made the lion roar with the hope of rescuing and protecting sentient beings by awakening them from ignorance with such an outcry. Those who do not understand the reasons behind his behavior often regard him as arrogant, which is a serious mistake.

Having been an attendant by my master's side for years, I have come to know that he is easy-going and respectful of karmic conditions in his dealing with people and circumstances. He is extremely compassionate, teaches the Dharma with infinite solicitude, and benefits everyone with a total disregard for himself. To widely save and protect Buddhist disciples, to radically reform the current state of the Buddha Dharma, and to ensure the longevity of the correct Dharma, my master can neither turn a blind eye to the current situation nor continue to approve of others out of fear of creating discord. He has no choice but to resort to a strong cure in order to effectively treat a serious illness. Therefore, he composed this monumental work titled *Behind the Façade of Tantric Buddhism* by extensively collecting esoteric sūtras and tantras, thoroughly exposing the lines of thought of pseudo-Buddhism, and demonstrating the mani jewel of the knowledge-of-aspects in order to purify the defiled and obstruct learners from entering the gates of hell in their future lives. Only a reincarnated Bodhisattva can accomplish such an amazing task.

My master entrusted me with the composition of this Foreword despite my obtuseness and undeserved role as his student. I wrote these words with great respect, hoping that all readers can set aside their prejudices for a moment, carefully examine and compare the esoteric sūtras and tantras, and then repeatedly reflect upon and thoroughly validate the contents of this book to save themselves from any downfall. This is my sincere wish!

A holder of the Bodhisattva Precepts,

Qiuji Jiangba Luojie

Chinese New Year, 2002

At the Shuanghe Residence

CHAPTER 7

THE MADHYAMAKA OF PRAJÑĀ: A DELINEATION OF THE MAHĀMUDRĀ OF CLEAR LIGHT IN TANTRIC BUDDHISM

1. The Mahāmudrā of Clear Light: The Madhyamaka of Prajñā in Tantric Buddhism

The method of Highest Yoga Tantra[1] in Tantric Buddhism comprises two different parts: the Mahāmudrā[2] of the Path of Desire, and the Mahāmudrā of the Path to Liberation (also known as the Mahāmudrā of clear light[3] or the Mahāmudrā of luminosity and emptiness). These two parts are also called "Mahāmudrā of the Path of Desire" and "Mahāmudrā of the Path to Nirvāṇa":

> Those who contemplate the state of this profound secret meaning must rely on the teachings and guidance of a guru of the Highest Yoga Tantra found in the Mantra Vehicle. A practitioner can, by obtaining the essence, validate in accordance with the truth the state of a Bodhisattva's complete no-self that he has always been seeking. When he practices to the point where he is capable of learning these contents, his guru will bestow upon him these essential and wondrous teachings, which are briefly as follows: "You should now observe that **all existences in the three realms are issued from sexual union**. The function of these existences is embodied by the masculine entity of the Buddha-father, whereas their wisdom is embodied by the feminine entity of the Buddha-mother; the two unite into one inseparable entity (original note: the fusion of compassion and wisdom) of two bodies. **One achieves the ultimate path, also known as Mahāmudrā, through this entity of two bodies.**" When the practitioner reaches this level, his guru will impart to him the

---

1   Highest Yoga Tantra: S. *anuttarayogatantra*; T. *rnal 'by or bla na med pa'i rgy ud*; C. *wushang yuqie* 無上瑜伽.
2   Mahāmudrā: In Sanskrit, lit. "great seal"; T.phy ag rgy a chen po; C. da shouyin 大手印.
3   Clear light: S. *prabhāsvara*; T. *'od gsal*; C. *guangming* 光明.

3

condensed teachings of Mahāmudrā as follows: "First, the sign of reality is devoid of verbalization and name and do not consist of two extremes. This sole property is indistinguishable. One must understand this truth to realize the unsurpassed bliss of perfect bodhi. Those who have validated this truth can naturally bring forth measureless great compassion from their bodhicitta of great perfection. Feeling empathy for all those who are still entrapped in the bitter sea of ignorance, they will eagerly strive to lift those sentient beings up so that each and every one of them could join them on the luminous path of enlightenment," and so forth. Therefore, those who possess this measureless great compassion, which encompasses everything in the three realms, are the ones who have entered the Path to Enlightenment of the Great Vehicle.[4]

The Mahāmudrā of the Path of Desire teaches about the yab-yum practice between a man and a woman. This method will be extensively illustrated in Chapter 9, Highest Yoga Tantra, of this book as well as in Volume 3. In addition, Chapter 9 will explain why this practice is called Highest Yoga Tantra. Therefore, we will not elaborate further on this topic and will instead just focus on the tantric Mahāmudrā of the Path to Liberation, which is also known as the Mahāmudrā of the Path to Nirvāṇa due to its relationship with prajñā.

The view highlighted by a tantric guru in the above passage contains egregious mistakes. For instance, the statement **"all existences in the three realms are issued from sexual union"** is completely false. Although the celestial beings in the six heavens of the desire realm still perform acts of love, the higher heaven they reside in, the less desire they exhibit. In contrast to the celestial beings of the third heaven and above, who no longer engage in sexual intercourse, those in the second heaven and below—the

---

[4]   Lü Tiegang 呂鐵鋼, *Zangmi xiufa midian* 藏密修法密典 [*A Secret Book on the Practices of Tibetan Tantra*], Vol. 4 (Beijing: Beijing Huaxia Publisher 北京華夏出版社, 1995), 641-43. Translated into English from Chinese.

Heaven of Four Great Kings and the Heaven of Divinities of the Thirty-Three—still copulate; nonetheless, they are not, as claimed by Tantric Buddhists, **"issued from sexual union,"** but instead took rebirth in those heavens due their performance of the ten wholesome deeds, coupled with the fact that they had not eliminated sexual desire.

Furthermore, celestial beings of the form realm take rebirth in the lower thirteen heavens of this realm purely due to the power of their meditative concentration, while those who take rebirth in the upper five heavens of no return of this realm are able to do so purely due to their elimination of afflictions—the upper five heavens are exclusively reserved for the exalted ones of the Three Vehicles, and the non-Buddhists who have not eliminated their afflictions, as well as ordinary people, have no access to these five heavens. The highest heaven of the realm of subtle materiality is only accessible to those who have attained the knowledge-of-the-aspects-of-paths.[5] Therefore, none of the celestial beings in the eighteen heavens of the form realm are **"issued from sexual union"** as Tantric Buddhists have alleged. Furthermore, celestial beings in the four heavens of the formless realm do not have a form body; instead, they purely consist of the state of meditative concentration—the states of the sixth, seventh, and eighth consciousnesses. Would a bodiless state of meditative concentration need to be **"issued from sexual union"**? How utterly ignorant of tantric gurus to claim that **"all existences in the three realms are issued from sexual union"**! It is, therefore, no surprise that the reward body "Buddhas" and the Dharma body[6] "Buddhas" of Tantrism are all "Buddhas" of the desire realm who take in various types of sexual pleasure during the yab-yum copulation and cannot transcend the states of the desire realm. This demonstrates that the tantric theory and Dharma-gate of practice to "attain

---

5   Knowledge-of-the-aspects-of-paths: Alt. exalted-wisdom-of-paths, exalted-wisdom-of-the-aspects-of-paths, the partial knowledge-of-all-aspects, the wisdom of the bodhisattvas who have attained the stage of the First Ground or above; S. *mārgakārajñatā*; T. *lam shes*; C. *dao zhongzhi* 道種智.

6   Dharma body: S. *dharmakāya*; T. *chos sku*; C. *fashen* 法身.

Buddhahood" are all based on erroneous thoughts and are utterly preposterous.

Tantric Buddhism regards the constant intake of sexual pleasure in the yab-yum copulation, in which the male embodies expedient compassion and the female embodies wisdom, as the reward of attaining Buddhahood. Consequently, all tantric "Buddhas" permanently dwell in the state of sexual pleasure during the yab-yum copulation, and this state is called the "union of compassion and wisdom." Such is the tantric Dharma-gate of "attaining Buddhahood" in one's current body through the Path of Desire. To distinguish this Dharma-gate from the Mahāmudrā of luminosity and emptiness, tantric gurus assert that one has attained the reality-suchness of the "Ground of Buddhahood" if one is able to attain through sitting meditation the state where the mind of feeling and cognition can cognize various states while being thoughtless. Such is the Dharma-gate for "the attainment of Buddhahood" through the Mahāmudrā of clear light or the Mahāmudrā of luminosity and emptiness.

C. M. Chen [Chen Chienming 陳健民] has made similar statements:

> The Division of Highest Yoga Tantra comprises two paths: (1) the expedient path, also known as the Path of Desire, in which one must practice the action seal[7] (the deeds of sexual pleasure experienced through the yab-yum method) and (2) the Path to Liberation, also known as Mahāmudrā or the Mahāmudrā of clear light. The expedient path (the path of the yab-yum method) merges with Mahāmudrā once the practitioner reaches the stage of the fourth initiation.[8] As for the Path to Liberation, its main practice differs from the expedient path in that one can directly cultivate it according to Mahāmudrā without having to go through the third initiation.[9]

---

[7]   Action seal: S. *karmamudrā*; T. *las ky i phy ag rgy a*; C. *shiye shouyin* 事業手印.

[8]   Initiation: Alt. empowerment; S. *abhiseka*; C. *guanding* 灌頂.

[9]   Yogi C. M. Chen (Chen Chien-ming 陳健民), *Qugongzhai quanji* 曲肱齋全集 [*The Complete Works of Yogi Chen*], vol. 1-5, ed. Xu Qinying 徐芹庭 (Taipei: Puxianwang

In other words, the Mahāmudrā of clear light is a method to achieve the realization of the clear light of liberation. In contrast, the action seal is a Dharma-gate of sexual pleasure based on the actual cultivation of the yab-yum method with a person of the opposite sex. It involves worldly acts between a male and a female—hence the term "action seal." Since the action seal is related to sexual desire, it is called the Path of Desire, meaning that this method adopts sexual desire as its path. This Dharma-gate of practice is also known as the expedient path given that the cultivation thereof relies on sexual desire as an expedient means.

The Mahāmudrā of clear light is the commonly known Mahāmudrā in Tantric Buddhism. Yogi C. M. Chen and the other tantric gurus have misconstrued what the prajñā of Exoteric Buddhism is all about:

> The statement "to abide without mental applications [10] throughout the three times" on pp. 27-28 of the aforementioned *Ocean of Definitive Meanings* [*Liaoyihai* 了義海] (*Jusheng qihe shendao liaoyihai xinyao* 俱生契合深導了義海心要) refers to a method in the Vehicle of Prajñā—see the Diamond Sūtra. If this method is not experienced based on the emptiness-nature, then it will be no different from the practice of "abiding without mental applications throughout the three times" cultivated by non-Buddhists during meditative concentration. There is no harm in performing Mahāmudrā as a preparatory practice in the Vehicle of Prajñā, but it must not be confused with the main practice. If Mahāmudrā was made into the main practice, then the practitioners who adopt it in the Vehicle of Prajñā will definitely need three terms of asaṃkhya kalpas to attain Buddhahood, whereas those who apply it in the Tantra Vehicle can become Buddhas in a single lifetime, which would not make

---

rulai fojiaohui 普賢王如來佛教會, 1991), vol. 3, 699. Translated into English from Chinese.

[10] Mental application: Alt. mental engagement, or attention; S. *manaskāra*. (alt. *manasikāra*); T. *yid la byed pa*; C. *zuoyi* 作意.

any sense.[11]

The above passage misunderstands the teachings of prajñā in Exoteric Buddhism. "To abide without mental applications throughout the three times," as mentioned on pp. 27-28 of *Ocean of Definitive Meanings [Liaoyihai]*, is absolutely not a correct way to practice the prajñā of the Great Vehicle. Unaware of what prajñā is and having failed to realize it, those gurus have been trying to grasp it based on their own speculation: They have equated the mental consciousness (mind of feeling and cognition) that abides in a state of thoughtlessness and without any mental applications with the non-abiding mind [12] illustrated in the prajñā sūtras. According to them, those who are able to dwell in this fashion have attained the fundamental non-conceptual meditative concentration. Furthermore, they assert that those who "abide without mental applications throughout the three times" are sages who have realized nirvāṇa.

In fact, the non-abiding mind set forth in the prajñā of Exoteric Buddhism refers to the mind consisting of the eighth consciousness, a mind that "has abided without mental applications" for immeasurable kalpas. This mind has, throughout immeasurable kalpas, never had one single thought of mental application—it has never had any desire to see, hear, feel, or cognize anything. In other words, it has never brought forth any type of mental function of desire on the states of the six sense-objects. However, tantric gurus mistakenly believe that the mental consciousness that does not bring forth any mental function of desire amidst the six sense-objects and that abides in a state of thoughtlessness corresponds to the non-abiding mind set forth in the prajñā of Exoteric Buddhism. Consequently, they teach their followers "to abide without mental applications throughout the

---

[11]   Yogi C. M. Chen (Chen Chien-ming 陳健民), *Qugongzhai quanji 曲肱齋全集 [The Complete Works of Yogi Chen]*, vol. 1-5, ed. Xu Qinying 徐芹庭 (Taipei: Puxianwang rulai fojiaohui 普賢王如來佛教會, 1991), vol. 3, 698. Translated into English from Chinese.

[12]   Non-abiding mind: C. *wuzhu xin* 無住心.

three times," thinking that this is the correct way to practice the Buddha Dharma. Based on such a misapprehension of the "Buddha Dharma," they have disparaged Exoteric Buddhists by asserting that it will take Exoteric Buddhists three great terms of asaṃkhya kalpas to attain Buddhahood given their way of practice. Furthermore, those gurus have proclaimed that, in contrast, the Esoteric Buddhist way of cultivation coupled with the method of the union of bliss and emptiness (the yab-yum practice between a male and a female) enables its followers to achieve Buddhahood in their current bodies. Such statements merely stem from those tantric gurus' misunderstandings and do not reflect the truth about the practice and realization of prajñā in Exoteric Buddhism.

Based on their misapprehension of the prajñā in Exoteric Buddhism, those tantric gurus have denounced the inefficiency of the practice of prajñā in this religion. Not only have they vaunted that their non-Buddhist Shaktist practice that is based on sexual cravings and has in fact absolutely nothing to do with the Buddha Dharma—a Dharma-gate of practice that will never lead to the achievement of Buddhahood—is a method that enables followers to attain Buddhahood in their current bodies, but they have also used this method to deprecate the correct practices of Exoteric Buddhism. What a total reversal of the truth!

Such condemnations of Exoteric Buddhism due to the misapprehension of its doctrines as well as such self-glorifying and erroneous views and teachings that reverse the truth are, to an alarming degree, extensively seen in all the writings authored by ancient and contemporary tantric gurus—not only are they seen in every single publication, but they are even seen in every single page of those publications. As the tantric Mahāmudrās all fall within the scope of the conscious mind, they have not even been able to touch upon the level of the seventh consciousness—the manas consciousness—let alone that of the eighth consciousness—the mind of reality. Moreover, these Tantric practitioners believe that if one's conscious mind is able to dwell without mental applications, then one has realized the mind of reality that "abides without mental applications throughout the three times." After wrongly branding this method as an Exoteric Buddhist Dharma-gate of practice of prajñā, they have disparaged Exoteric Buddhism as being an inefficient and inferior way of practice based on this misunderstanding. It is truly pitiful that they reverse the truth to such an extent.

2. The View of Prajñā Found in the Tantric Svātantrika Madhyamaka

The view of Svātantrika Madhyamaka in Tantric Buddhism refers to the view of Madhyamaka propounded by the Nyingma, Kagyu, and Sakya schools. Such a view of Madhyamaka is a view of the Middle-Way based on a mental consciousness that neither abides in two extremes nor clings to any phenomena. These schools believe that if one's mental consciousness is able to dwell in a state in which it "does not conceptualize" any phenomena, then one has realized the non-conceptual mind or attained the fundamental non-conceptual wisdom of prajñā—the fundamental meditative concentration. Such a realization of the fundamental non-conceptual wisdom stands in conflict with the teachings of Exoteric Buddhism. In Exoteric Buddhism, those who have truly attained the Path of Vision have used their mental consciousness to realize the eighth consciousness—the tathāgatagarbha—which is intrinsically without conceptualizations; next, their mental consciousness has, based on this practice and realization, attained "the wisdom that the eighth consciousness—the tathāgatagarbha—has been dwelling in non-conceptuality since the beginningless time"; the ability to abide in this wisdom is called the realization of the fundamental non-conceptual wisdom.

Tantric gurus have completely misapprehended what prajñā is all about. Indeed, they believe that one has realized the fundamental non-conceptual wisdom when one's mental consciousness is able to remain immovable and without conceptualizations—hence the statement: "Through the power of continual practice, one gradually reduces conceptuality and increases non-conceptuality." This demonstrates that the non-conceptual nature realized by tantric followers is attained through practice. For instance, *Path with the Result—Compendium of the Esoterics of the*

11

Mahāyāna Main Path—Commentary on the Vajra Lines [Daoguo— dasheng yaodao miji—bensong jingang juji zhu 道果一大乘要道密集一本頌金剛句偈註]¹ says:

> "The advance and retreat of primordial awareness." This is how meditative concentration arises. For a beginner, at times such as the first gathering of the essential constituents, even though a nonconceptual meditative concentration may arise, it is unstable. Thoughts are in control; so, even when primordial awareness arises, it [soon] retreats and is of little benefit, like the sun in the midst of clouds.²
>
> However, through the power of continual practice, one gradually reduces conceptuality and increases non-conceptuality, causing the object of manifestation to grow, like a dark shadow that progressively becomes clearer.³

While the three major schools such as Ningma and so forth have always adhered to the Madhyamaka view of the tantric Svātantrika, the Gelug School stands out as the only lineage that does not concur with this view. The truth is, none of those tantric practitioners are aware that the eighth consciousness (ālaya) corresponds to the tathāgatagarbha. Furthermore, those followers do not understand the concept that the ālaya-consciousness is neither real nor unreal—a principle that was taught by the Buddha—and instead maintain that this consciousness is purely unreal. Given that sentient beings undergo cyclic existence based on the ālaya-consciousness, they believe that this ālaya-consciousness must be purely unreal, and therefore, practitioners must absolutely not identify it as the real mind. Due to this erroneous view, those followers do not enjoy reading or hearing about the ālaya-consciousness, do not aspire to realize it, and even formulate all kinds of falsities to refute the fact that it is the real

---

1   Daoguo 道果 is the Chinese translation of the Tibetan word lamdré (lam 'bras), meaning the "path with the result."

2   Stearns, Cyrus (trans. and ed.), *Taking the Result as the Path: Core Teachings of the Sakya Lamdré Tradition* (Boston: Wisdom Publications, 2006), 72.

3   Virūpa, *Daoguo* 道果, 467. Translated into English from Chinese.

mind.

Little do those people know that sentient beings undergo cyclic existence due to the seeds of the dependent-arising of ālaya found in the ālaya-consciousness. However, it is also due to the existence of this dependent-arising of ālaya that sentient beings can achieve the ultimate Path to Buddhahood by practicing progressively based on this dependent-arising of ālaya. Without the seeds of the dependent-arising of ālaya, sentient beings would not have any future lifetimes; in addition, all the virtuous meritorious quality and pure deeds accumulated in this lifetime would just be futile, for they would not be carried into the future lifetimes. How then could those sentient beings possibly advance in their pure practice of the Buddha Dharma and achieve the ultimate path to Buddhahood? One should know the following concept with respect to the dependent-arising of the reality-suchness: One becomes an exalted one who has attained the fruition of liberation by eliminating the manifestation of the afflictive seeds of delimited existence stored in the eighth consciousness (ālaya), thus transforming the eighth consciousness into the ninth consciousness—the maturational consciousness. Without the dependent-arising of ālaya found in the eighth consciousness, all Bodhisattvas would, upon attaining the fruition of liberation, definitely enter the remainderless nirvāṇa after death—by failing to forsake the remainderless nirvāṇa, they would not be able to transmigrate into future lifetimes in order to advance in their cultivation of the fruition of Buddhahood. Consequently, Bodhisattvas must, during the process in which they practice and realize the knowledge-of-all-aspects of Buddhahood, rely on the function of the dependent-arising of ālaya found in the ālaya consciousness to make the vow to be reborn and not enter the remainderless nirvāṇa after attaining the fruition of liberation; by having future existences, they can progressively cultivate the fruition of Buddhahood in the right sequence until they finally achieve the ultimate Path to Buddhahood. Given that Buddhahood can only be achieved through the dependent-arising of ālaya, which exists in dependence upon the ālaya-consciousness, how could those tantric practitioners speak about the practice and realization of the Buddha Dharma while refuting that the ālaya-consciousness is the real mind? How could they discuss the cultivation and attainment of the fruition of Buddhahood outside the context of the ālaya-consciousness and without having realized this ālaya-consciounesss? Their behavior is just senseless.

Furthermore, given that Bodhisattvas have, upon attaining the fruition of liberation, eliminated the manifestation of afflictive hindrances but not the latent habitual seeds of afflictive hindrances, they must further rely on the dependent-arising of ālaya, which is inherent to the eighth consciousness, to take rebirths in the human world and thereby eradicate their latent habitual seeds of afflictive hindrances by repeatedly facing different situations through experiencing various conditions. Those who aspire to achieve the fruition of Buddhahood must, in addition, realize all the seeds stored in the eighth consciousness also through a long process of facing different situations through experiencing various conditions, in order to extirpate bit by bit the innumerable afflictions of beginningless ignorance.[4] The functional potentialities[5] in the eighth consciousness will manifest gradually as they realize bit by bit all the seeds stored in the eighth consciousness. It is only by gradually extinguishing their innumerable afflictions and by manifesting all the seeds in the eighth consciousness during three great terms of incalculable kalpas that they can attain the ultimate Buddhahood. In this process, they must rely on the dependent-arising of ālaya found in the eighth consciousness to proceed with their practice through future rebirths until attaining Buddhahood.

Once a practitioner has realized the fruition of liberation, his dependent-arising of ālaya is renamed "dependent-arising of maturation" and his cyclic existence in the three realms is known as "result of maturation." Indeed, his dependent-arising of ālaya is

---

[4] Innumerable afflictions of beginningless ignorance: C. *wushiwuming chenshahuo* 無始無明塵沙惑.

[5] Functional potentiality: Alt. potentiality, distinct functional potentiality; C. *gongneng chabie* 功能差別.

renamed as "maturation" given that he has eliminated the function that stores delimited existences—at this stage, all manifestations of a Bodhisattva's form body and mental factors arise from the result of maturation rather than from the retribution of karmic seeds; hence, the dependent-arising of ālaya is no longer called "dependent-arising of ālaya," but still exists in dependence upon the eighth consciousness. If the eighth consciousness was not endowed with the natures of meritorious quality such as the dependent-arising of ālaya, the dependent-arising of maturation, and so forth, then after attaining the fruition of liberation, one would not have future lifetimes and would not be able to advance on the Path to Buddhahood. In that case, no Buddha would ever appear in the three realms—there would only be arhats and no Buddha. Given that both the dependent-arising of ālaya and the fruition of maturation exist in dependence upon the eighth consciousness, and given that the knowledge-of-all-aspects of the Buddha Dharma is obtained from the cultivation and realization of the seeds in the eighth consciousness, all practices of the Buddha Dharma must be based on the eighth consciousness. How then could those tantric followers speak about the practice and realization of the Buddha Dharma outside the context of the eighth consciousness while refuting that this eighth consciousness is the real mind? Their behavior does not make any sense.

Clearly, all ancient and contemporary tantric gurus have been speaking about the practice and realization of the Buddha Dharma outside the context of the eighth consciousness, have posited the existence of a tathāgatagarbha other than the eighth consciousness, and have established the mental consciousness (mind of feeling and cognition) in a state of thoughtlessness as the tathāgatagarbha. How could such concepts, which have absolutely nothing to do with the Buddha Dharma, be hailed as superior to Exoteric Buddhism? How could those gurus proclaim their practice as the Dharma-gate that "leads to the attainment of Buddhahood with one's immediate body"? The truth is, their practice is essentially based on the erroneous thinking that stems from non-Buddhist views and is therefore wholly unrelated to the Buddha

Dharma. Such assertions, teachings, and realizations cannot help anyone enter or attain the Path of Vision in the Buddha Dharma in the Three Vehicles; they constitute nothing but a Dharma-gate of practice that does not correspond to the Buddha Dharma.

The view, meditation, behavior, and fruition taught by the three major schools of Tibetan Tantrism—Nyingma, Kagyu, and Sakya—in their Dharma-gates of practice are all based on the view of Svātantrika Madhyamaka. According to this view, "the self" consisting of the mental consciousness in a state of thoughtlessness and lucid awareness can remain unceasing across the three times (past, present, and future) to practice the Buddha Dharma. Such teachings, actualizations, and practices of the "Buddha Dharma," which are all based and centered on "the self" consisting of the mental consciousness, are actually unrelated to the Buddha Dharma; instead, they constitute non-Buddhist eternalist doctrines underpinned by the view of Svātantrika Madhyamaka.

According to the view of Svātantrika Madhyamaka, "Madhyamaka" can be realized through two different methods. The first one consists of striving, during sitting meditation, to attain a state of clarity called "union of luminosity and emptiness," in which the mental consciousness abides in thoughtlessness—a state in which it is able to discern the five sense objects "without clinging" to them. Within this union of luminosity and emptiness, one observes that such a state is actually generated by the mind of feeling and cognition (which, in this state, is regarded by Tantric Buddhists as the tathāgatagarbha); therefore, "the union of luminosity and emptiness" and "the mental consciousness that brings forth this union" are non-dual. The mental consciousness thus remains thoughtless yet is able to discern all six sense objects distinctly and without obscuration; all the while, one observes at all times that this mind of feeling and cognition is empty of shape and sign and is therefore just empty. The state in which one maintains an inseparable union of such natures of "emptiness" and "luminosity" is called "union of luminosity and emptiness," which corresponds to "the Mahāmudrā of the Path to Liberation" set forth in Tantric Buddhism. Those who are able to carry out such observations have achieved, through practice, the ultimate Path to Buddhahood in their current bodies—they have ultimately become Buddhas—hence the assertion that there exists a method in Tantric Buddhism that allows practitioners to attain Buddhahood in this lifetime.

The second method consists of maintaining the blissful sexual contact experienced during the yab-yum practice for an extended period of time (eight dual hours[6] every day, as stipulated by Tsongkhapa) while making the following observations: (1) The mind of feeling and cognition that experiences this blissful contact is "empty" of form and shape; (2) the mind of feeling and cognition that experiences this blissful sensation and the blissful sensation itself are non-dual; (3) the mind of feeling and cognition that experiences this blissful contact is known as the "emptiness-nature of the great bliss" for being empty of form and shape; and (4) this "emptiness-nature of the great bliss" and the sexual pleasure are non-dual and undifferentiable, for the emptiness of great bliss is generated by the mind of feeling and cognition that takes the bliss in. Those who have directly observed the above are said to have obtained "the view of the non-duality of bliss and emptiness," meaning that they have become "ultimate Buddhas" in their current fleshly bodies.

The proponents of Svātantrika Madhyamaka perform the deed-contemplation of "prajñā" based on the aforementioned Dharma-gate of practice and thereby observe that "luminosity and emptiness" as well as "bliss and emptiness" and the mind of feeling and cognition are neither identical nor different (the followers of Prāsaṅgika Madhyamaka observe the non-duality of bliss and emptiness in a similar fashion; in fact, both lineages propound the same view with respect to the attainment of Buddhahood through

---

6   Dual hour: A traditional Chinese unit of time that is roughly double the modern hour; C. *shichen* 時辰.

the current body based on the non-duality of bliss and emptiness as well as the union of bliss and emptiness)—hence the term "view of the Middle Way." Tantric practitioners further observe the following: Given that "luminosity and emptiness" as well as "bliss and emptiness" coexist with the mind of feeling and cognition, and given that the mind of feeling and cognition "abides permanently" without interruption, the mind of feeling and cognition is able to dwell in the state of "the union of luminosity and emptiness" or "the union of bliss and emptiness" at any place and time; therefore, "luminosity and emptiness" as well as "bliss and emptiness" are said to be neither coming nor going—hence the term "view of the Middle Way." As those followers observe that the union of luminosity and emptiness or the union of bliss and emptiness is a state endowed with various natures of the "Middle Way," they equate the "view of Madhyamaka based on the union of luminosity and emptiness" with the "Madhyamaka of prajñā" practiced and realized in Exoteric Buddhism throughout three great terms of asaṃkhya kalpas. In addition, those followers assert that the union of bliss and emptiness is a Dharma-gate leading to the ultimate attainment of Buddhahood—which enables one to achieve the fruition of Buddhahood of the reward-body in one's current fleshly body—that has never been taught by the Buddhas in Exoteric Buddhism. They further hail the Dharma-gate cultivated by both a male and a female based on the union of bliss and emptiness as an unsurpassed esoteric method that is unknown to and cannot be realized by the Buddhas of Exoteric Buddhism.

This fundamentally lustful view of Madhyamaka deviates from the truth and is completely unrelated to the Buddha Dharma. Even if one practices assiduously in this fashion during three great terms of asaṃkhya kalpas, one can neither connect with any of the Dharma-gates found in the Buddha Dharma of the Three Vehicles nor attain the Path of Vision in the Buddha Dharma of any of the Three Vehicles, not to mention ultimately become Buddhas— "achieve, through cultivation, the ultimate fruition of Buddhahood in the current body." Those followers are trying to obtain cooked rice by boiling sand; they will never achieve their goal even after trying for numerous kalpas, for sand is not rice to begin with. Hence, the view of Svātantrika Madhyamaka stems from the erroneous thinking of ordinary people and has nothing to do with the Buddha Dharma. Those who do not believe in my statements and proceed further in their practice by adhering to this view are forever secluding themselves from the Buddha Dharma of the Three Vehicles. How ignorant and pitiful of those tantric followers to boast that their "practices and realizations" of the Buddha Dharma "pertain to the Fruition Ground," while they have in fact excluded themselves from the Buddha Dharma!

3. The View of Prajñā Found in Prāsaṅgika Madhyamaka

The followers of the Gelug School worship the tantric view of Prāsaṅgika Madhyamaka, take immense pride in this view of Madhyamaka, and hail it as the ultimate teaching in the Buddha Dharma. Master Yinshun [印順], who also adulates this view, has gushed in his writing: "Prāsaṅgika Madhyamaka is the pride of Tibetan Tantric Buddhism," lauding its elaborate structure and thorough rationale and proclaiming it as the most ultimate doctrine in the Buddha Dharma. He has made the following prediction, as he expects this view to definitely flourish as a result of correct and perfect propagation:

> The Tibetan philosophy of Madhyamaka is allegedly comprised of the Prāsaṅgika doctrines conveyed by Buddhapālita and Candrakīrti as well as the Svātantrika doctrines imparted by Śāntarakṣita and Bhāvaviveka. Although each of these schools was introduced into Tibet under different circumstances, the Prāsaṅgika tradition of Buddhapālita and Candrakīrti has, after a long period of propagation, prevailed as the legitimate Madhyamaka. Some Tibetan tantras of Madhyamaka have recently been translated into Chinese. At the same time, the discovery of the Sanskrit *Treatise on the Middle Way [Zhong lun 中論]* has enabled the Japanese to widely expand their understanding of this view through textual research. Cross-references among the Tibetan, Chinese, and Sanskrit versions **will definitely allow** the characteristics of Madhyamaka **to flourish as a result of correct and perfect propagation.**[1]

The view of Prāsaṅgika Madhyamaka, however, has been extensively refuted by Bodhisattva Xuanzang [玄奘] in his *Cheng*

---

[1] Yinshun, *Zhongkuan Jinlun 中觀今論*,], (Taiwan: Zhengwen chubanshe 正聞出版社, 1950), 4. Translated into English from Chinese.

Weishi Lun [成唯識論] and even earlier by Bodhisattva Nagarjuna [龍樹] in his *Treatise on the Middle Way [Zhong lun]*. Master Yinshun has misconstrued what this *Treatise on the Middle Way* is all about, mistakenly claiming that it teaches the doctrine of "the emptiness of all phenomena outside the context of the tathāgatagarbha." His errors will not be discussed here but will be discussed separately in books authored by direct Dharma teachers[2] of our Association. In fact, the erroneous view of Prāsaṅgika Madhyamaka has also been extensively rebutted by the brothers Asaṅga [無著] and Vasubandhu [世親] in their treatises. However, Master Yinshun has declared that the tantric view of Prāsaṅgika Madhyamaka is the ultimate doctrine because he has failed to understand and realize the correct meaning of Madhyamaka taught by the Buddha and because he has been beguiled by the Tibetan tantric view of Prāsaṅgika Madhyamaka. How unwise!

I have, in many of my writings (including *Detailed Explanation of Laṅkāvatāra Sūtra [Lengqie jing xiangjie 楞伽經詳解]*, *Self and No-Self [Wo yu wuwo 我與無我]*, *Mastering and Skillfully Articulating the Essence of Buddhist Enlightenment [Zongtong yu shuotong 宗通與說通]*, *False Views versus the Buddha Dharma [Xiejian yu fofa 邪見與佛法]*, *The Real Tathāgatagarbha [Zhenshi rulaizang 真實如來藏]*, and so forth) systemically identified and corrected Master Yinshun's statements about the erroneous view of Prāsaṅgika Madhyamaka, indicated the fallacies of this view, demonstrated that Master Yinshun's thought is entirely based on Prāsaṅgika Madhyamaka, and highlighted the various errors related to the theme "Buddha Dharma and Madhyamaka" in Yinshun's works. In fact, Master Yinshun is himself well aware of his mistakes after he read my books, but has been incapable of justifying himself. Moreover, he can neither step forward to defend and justify his assertions, nor admit the fallacies in his publications such as *The Collection of Wonderful Clouds [Miaoyunji 妙雲集]* and

---

2   Direct dharma teacher: S. *upādhyāya*; T. *mkhan po*; C. *qinjiao shi* 親教師.

so forth, for fear of losing face; he is hence stuck in a position from which there is no retreat (his disciples would disapprove of any acknowledgment of errors, for such a move would adversely impact their fame as well as the material welfare that they receive). His only option is to remain silent, as there is nothing else he can do. Eventually, he will die with regrets and suffer the retribution of pain for many future lifetimes to come.

The Inheritors of Master Yinshun's incorrect teachings have been poisoned by his erroneous views but lack the correct knowledge and views to distinguish between right and wrong. As a matter of act, they are paving the way for their inevitable downfall after death, as they continue to adhere to Yinshun's misconceptions and to propagate the fallacious view of Prāsaṅgika Madhyamaka for fear of losing face. To maintain their fame reputation and material welfare, as well as the status within the Buddhist community that they have achieved in this lifetime, those inheritors have made various assertions to conceal the truth, such as pretending that Master Yinshun disdains to debate the Dharma with me. By objecting to the idea that Master Yinshun should admit his errors in public and hindering him from doing so, they are making him bear the grievous sin of incorrigibles[3] **for slandering the Bodhisattva repository;** how unmerciful of them! The endeavors of those disciples to cover up their faults with embellished statements reflect their selfishness and inability to seek the truth. Such persons do not accept criticism gracefully, do not seek the true meanings quickly, and do not examine their errors with respect to the Buddhist doctrine; instead, they formulate all kinds of pretexts and embellished statements to hide their faults. As such, they are not true learners of the Path of Bodhisattvas, for they do not act like Bodhisattvas.

Another example is that of Professor Jiang Cantong [江 燦騰].

---

3   Robert E. Buswell Jr. and Donald S. Lopez Jr., "icchantika" in *The Princeton Dictionary of Buddhism* (NJ: Princeton University Press, 2014). Incorrigible; a person who has severed all his wholesome faculties; S. *icchantika*; T. *'dod chen*; C. *yichanti ren* 一闡提人.

He has declared, in a response letter to the lay Buddhist Li Yuansong [李元松; 1957-2003] posted on the Modern Chan Society's website, that he disdains to have a dialogue with me despite the compliment that I have given him and the respect that I have shown him. In fact, his untruthful words are just an excuse to avoid me. I recall that I once lauded him with great respect after reading in his writing about the forthright admonitions that he bravely expressed with respect to the anomalies found in today's Buddhist community. I gifted him two of my books, including *The Dharma Eye of the Chan School [Zongmen Fayan 宗門法眼]*. In return, he gave me a copy of his *The Debate on and Development of the Chinese Modern Buddhist Thought [Zhongguo jindai fojiao sixiang de zhengbian yu fazhan 中國近代佛教思想的諍辯與發展]*. Under these circumstances, I gave him my opinion on the debate between Xiong Shili [熊十力] and Lüzheng [呂澂] about "the noumenon's quiescence vs. the noumenon's enlightenment," which was highlighted in his book. Given that Professor Jiang did not understand the explanation that I had given in my letter with respect to the meaning of "the noumenon's quiescence vs. the noumenon's enlightenment," had not attained the Path of Vision in any of the three vehicles, and had yet to break the bad habit of mutual belittling among peers seen in Chinese scholars, he suggested that I should read Buddhaghoṣa's *The Path of Purification [Qingjing daolun 清淨道論]*, a work of Theravada Buddhism, implying that he had the ability to act as my teacher and to guide me towards more advanced study.

Professor Jiang has written the following:

As a scholar, I believe that you should step out of the Chan School's traditional thinking model. Buddhaghoṣa's *The Path of Purification*, Vasubandhu's *A Treasury of Abhidharma, with Commentary [Jushe lun 俱舍論; Abhidharmakośa-bhāṣya]*, and Tsongkhapa's *The Great Treatise on the Stages of the Path to Enlightenment [Putidao cidi guanglun 菩提道次第廣論; Lamrim Chenmo]* (the section on tranquility and insight) can all broaden your vision. (See Jiang Canteng's letter on October 14, 1998.)

However, Vasubandhu composed *A Treasury of Abhidharma, with Commentary [Jushelun; Abhidharmakośa-bhāṣya]* before learning and realizing the doctrinal theory of the Great Vehicle when he was still cultivating the sound-hearer Dharma in the Lesser Vehicle. Professor Jiang should be aware that some of the reasonings in this treatise are in fact disputable despite the fact that its teachings accord with the true principle of the Path to Liberation in the Two Vehicles and that this writing is not completely correct from the perspective of the Path to the Enlightenment of Buddhahood in the Great Vehicle.

As for the statements found in Buddhaghoṣa's *The Path of Purification*, a work of the Theravada Buddha Dharma, they do not conform to the Path to Liberation that is based on the consciousness in "the name-and-form conditions the consciousness—the eighth consciousness, tathāgatagarbha" set forth by the Buddha, contradict the Buddha's teachings, and also contradict the valid knowledge through direct perception that I have attained from my practice and realization of the Path to Liberation. Not only have the doctrines set forth by Buddhagosa failed to touch upon the sign of reality—the truth of the foremost meaning—but they have also misconstrued the Path to Liberation of the Two Vehicles found in the Theravada Buddha Dharma of his own school. Entrapped within the self-view of the mental consciousness, he has never attained the ground of vision related to the first fruition of sound-hearer—he simply has not eliminated his self-view and is still stuck in the stage of non-Buddhist ordinary people.

As for the teachings in Tsongkhapa's *The Great Exposition of Secret Mantra [Mizongdao cidi guanglun 密宗道次第廣論], The Great Treatise on the Stages of the Path to Enlightenment [Putidao cidi guanglun 菩提道次第廣論, Lamrim Chenmo], The Medium Treatise on the Stages of the Path to Enlightenment [Putidao cidi luelun 菩提道次第略論]*, and so forth, they are all steeped in errors and stand at odds with scriptures and reasonings. Readers can get an idea of Tsongkhapa's erroneous views through the examples cited in this book. In his discussion about **the practice and realization** of "tranquility and insight" in *The Great Treatise on the Stages of the Path to Enlightenment*, he makes no mention whatsoever of **the practice and realization** of this method. As he has not even attained the first concentration, his illustration of the principle of meditative absorption and the correct principle of meditative concentration completely oppose one another and also contradict the valid knowledge attained through my practice and realization of meditative concentration. As a matter of fact, he does not understand in any way the correct meanings of meditative equipoise, meditative absorption, or meditative stabilization.

Except for *A Treasury of Abhidharma, with Commentary [Jushelun; Abhidharmakośa-bhāṣya]*, which was composed by Vasubandhu in a period of this life when he was still propagating the sound-hearer Dharma, all the above treatises have misapprehended the Buddha Dharma to an extent of completely contradicting it. This proves that neither Buddhaghoṣa nor Tsongkhapa understands the correct principles of the Buddha Dharma in any way, with the former still in the stage of ordinary people, and the latter simply a heretic. As a result, their treatises are extremely misleading, for they are imbibed in self-view and erroneous view; how could they be readable or credible in any way? Nevertheless, Professor Jiang has been vigorously promoting them, which demonstrates how misinformed he is! Consequently, all I did after reading his letter was to add the following annotation in red as a reminder, before setting this letter aside forever: "Just mail him *Pingshi's Letter [Pingshi shuqian 平實書箋]*; no need to reply."

The doctrines that I expound are not just based on the traditional thinking model of the Chan School. The teachings found in my writings, from my early publications including *The Real Tathāgatagarbha [Zhenshi rulaizang 真實如來藏]*, *Treasury of the Wisdom-Eye that Sees the Correct Dharma [Zheng fayanzang 正法眼藏]*, and *Perfect Harmony between Chan and Pure Land [Chanjing yuanrong 禪淨圓融]*, through to recent works such as *Mastering and Skillfully Articulating the Essence of Buddhist*

Enlightenment [*Zongtong yu shuotong* 宗通與說], *False Views versus the Buddha Dharma [Xiejian yu fofa* 邪見與佛法], *The Nectar Rain of the Dharma Teaching [Ganlu fayu* 甘露法雨], *Self and No-Self [Wo yu wuwo* 我與無], *and Detailed Explanation of the Laṅkāvatāra Sūtra [Lengqiejing xiangjie* 楞伽經詳解], encompass the Buddha Dharma of all Three Vehicles—sound-hearer, Solitary-Realizer, and Mahāyāna—connect the correct doctrines found in the sūtras of Āgama, Prajñā, and Vijñaptimātratā, which are set forth in the first through to the third turning of the Dharma Wheel, and also refute the fallaciousness of the Mantra Vehicle. Thus, by no means do my teachings just stem from the thinking model of the traditional Chan School. Such a full integration of the Buddha Dharma found in the Three Vehicles is seen in all my early writings and can be easily verified given the accessibility of the evidence. However, Professor Jiang could not grasp this fact given his narrow view and made those superficial comments after assessing my wisdom based on his speculation. This just reflects how ill-informed he is.

The reason I set Professor Jiang's letter aside forever without responding to it is that I had observed his haughtiness and extreme lack of knowledge and views about the Buddha Dhama of the Three Vehicles and therefore knew that he did not possess the conditions to connect with either the truth of the foremost meaning or the Path to Liberation of the Two Vehicles. If he thinks that I still hold him in high esteem and therefore acts arrogantly, then he would be ignorant of the truth and totally mistaken. In fact, he has continued to assimilate Master Yinshun's fallacious views up to this day without knowing that they are to be abandoned, which clearly demonstrates that he is an opinionated and self-righteous person who has no idea of the real meanings of the Buddha Dharma of the Three Vehicles. Furthermore, due to such ignorance and his adulation of Master Yinshun, he makes various excuses to conceal the latter's faults, showing that he is not an upright person without flattery. Based on such ignorance as well as opinionated and self-righteous mindset, he even dared to wrongly criticize my doctrines:

With respect to Mr. Xiao Pingshi's vehemently calling into question Yinshun's teachings, Mr. Lan and I myself have simply not responded. The reason is not that Yinshun's theory should not be questioned, but that Xiao is simply uninitiated and does not deserve our time. As for Xiao himself, he holds me in high regard, but this does not mean that I should agree with whatever he says. (See Mr. Jiang's response letter to the lay Buddhist Li Yuansong posted on the Modern Chan Society's website.)

Professor Jiang Canteng's statements are, however, untruthful. How unwise of him to try to conceal his errors but end up exposing them and to deviate from the correct Dharma! Why is that? In his response letter to the lay Buddhist Li Yuansong, Professor Jiang is only able to comment the deeds related to the body, speech, and mind of the Modern Chan Society's members, but is incapable of providing a correct critique of this society based on its Buddhist doctrine. Such personal attacks should not have come from a practitioner of the Buddha Dharma; hence, Professor Jiang cannot be regarded as such, but only as an academic researcher of Buddhism. If Professor Jiang were wise—"an initiated" as he claims—then he should have identified and corrected the erroneous doctrines of the Modern Chan Society in writing instead of drawing criticism for **making personal attacks** on the deeds related to the body, speech, and mind of its members. In addition, with respect to the expositions in my writings—*The Real Tathāgatagarbha [Zhenshi rulaizang]*, *False Views versus the Buddha Dharma [Xiejian yu fofa]*, *Detailed Explanation of the Laṅkāvatāra Sūtra [Lengqiejing xiangjie]*, *Mastering and Skillfully Articulating the Essence of Buddhist Enlightenment [Zongtong yu shuotong]*, and so forth—that specifically comment on "Master" Yinshun's mistaken views and provide pieces of evidence on his destruction of the correct Buddhist Dharma and so forth, Professor Jiang should respond by publishing a book that gives a detailed critique about the right and wrong of my teachings, so as to obliterate the "uninitiated Xiao Pingshi's erroneous statements." (I hereby suggest that Professor Jiang ask Yinshun to revise this book before its publication, so as to avoid completely losing face once people discover the plethora of errors in this writing; such a revision will also prevent Professor Jiang from complaining that I did not warn him beforehand and from dragging Master Yinshun further down and "harming" him further by arguing in favor of his doctrines.)

After reading Professor Jiang's work, I will ask one of my disciples, "who is even less initiated than myself," to publish a book in reply to his comments, so that the members of the Buddhist community can examine with their Dharma-eye [4] whether Professor Jiang "understands the Buddha Dharma" as he proclaims and whether he is truly "initiated." (However, given that most of the practitioners in our Association hold a daily job and have limited time, it will take approximately one and a half years after Professor Jiang publishes his book or text to see the completion and release of a work that responds to Profession Jiang's comments; readers will just need to be patient.)

I wrote the above provoking statements in an attempt to vex Professor Jiang and incite him to write and print a book where he provides constructive criticism of my doctrines. If he is incapable of doing what an "initiated" should do and instead asserts, "Xiao is simply uninitiated and does not deserve our time," then we can conclude that he is merely using these insincere excuses to feign strength. Going forward, he should refrain from speaking about the persons and affairs of the Buddhist community as well as about the right and wrong of the Buddha Dharma. Why do I say this? The affairs of the Buddhist community consist of internal matters among Buddhist practitioners—those practitioners do not need suggestions from "academic researchers" like Professor Jiang who specialize in the "academic research of Buddhism" but do not practice according to the Buddha's words in the sūtras. The doctrinal debates within the Buddhist community suffice to restore the purity of the tenets and ensure the longevity of the true

---

[4]   Dharma-eye: S. *dharmacakṣus*; T. *chos kyi mig*; C. *fayan* 法眼.

Dharma without the help of an outsider. It is also pointless for "academic researchers of Buddhism" like Professor Jiang, who have yet to become Buddhists who engage in the true practice and realization of the paths, to preach the Dharma to Buddhist prctitioners. Professor Jiang and Master Yinshun as well as Yinshun's disciples all conduct research on the Buddha Dharma instead of truly practicing and realizing it. In essence, they are by no means authentic Buddhists—Yinshun is merely a destroyer of the Dharma donning a monk's robe, who has centered his philosophy on the erroneous tantric view of Prāsaṅgika Madhyamaka and used it to uproot the basis of Buddhism, namely the Dharma of the eighth consciousness—the tathāgatagarbha. Yinshun's deeds have indeed relegated the true Buddhist Dharma to the realm of metaphysics and conceptual proliferations.

My provoking statements will certainly infuriate Professor Jiang (we can expect such a reaction from him in light of the language he used in his response letter to the lay Buddhist Li Yuansong and in his attacks on Master Rushi [如石]). If, after his outburst, he still does not write any book to comment in detail on the errors of my teachings, then we can conclude that he is just a hypocrite who does not understand the Buddha Dharma and the public will be able to determine whether his words have any credibility. If, instead of debating the Buddhist doctrine, Professor Jiang chooses to comment on me based on groundless and malicious slander found on the Internet in my regard, then he will simply be engaging in personal attacks, which have nothing to do with doctrinal debates. If so, then the public can draw conclusions about his "valid knowledge" of the Buddha Dharma and can ignore all his speeches and deeds going forward, for they are wholly meaningless and totally unrelated to the Buddhist community.

Professor Jiang should no longer state: "The reason is not that Yinshun's theory should not be criticized, but that Xiao is simply uninitiated and does not deserve our time." Why is that? Master Yinshun and his followers are in no way magnanimous, as evidenced by the case involving the lay Buddhist "Zhong Qingji [鍾

慶吉]," who is completely unknown to the Buddhist community and is even less "initiated" than me. In an article written for the Sunday column "Zili Podium [自立講台]" of the *Zili Morning Post [自立早報]*, Zhong Qingji used satirical wording to admonish Master Yinshun for his erroneous views, with the hope that Yinshun could correct them and possibly avoid atrocious retribution in the future. Although Zhong's statements were rather out of the norm, his intention was good. Master Yinshun, despite being hospitalized due to an illness, as well as his "disciple" Master Zhaohui [昭慧] reacted immediately by each publishing a letter to refute Zhong's statements in the following week's Zili Podium. The release of a text by this unknown person, who is less initiated than me, sufficed to elicit a prompt rebuttal from both the master and his disciple, who took this matter with care and solemnity. By contrast, with respect to my persistent and incessant discussions about Yinshun's errors over the years and up until this day through books and texts dedicated to this purpose—*The Real Tathāgatagarbha [Zhenshi rulaizang], False Views versus the Buddha Dharma [Xiejian yu fofa], Detailed Explanation of the Laṅkāvatāra Sūtra [Lengqiejing xiangjie], Mastering and Skillfully Articulating the Essence of Buddhist Enlightenment [Zongtong yu shuotong]*, and so forth—Professor Jiang has surprisingly asserted: "Master Yinshun and his followers disdain to hold discussions with Xiao Pingshi," implying that Yinshun refuses to condescend to a debate out of magnanimity. Obviously, Professor Jiang cannot see the forest for the trees and his statements do not make any sense.

Clearly, Professor Jiang's declaration "Master Yinshun and his followers disdain to hold discussions with Xiao Pingshi" is an untruthful excuse to conceal their weakness. They are merely trying to cover up the embarrassment caused by their inability to debate the Dharma and the dilemma in which they are mired. Why is that? If the Dharma that they preach contains any errors, then it will inevitably be corrected by a wise person, who will, upon reading Professor Jiang's reasoning and analysis with respect to the Buddhist doctrine, immediately understand the fallacies and will not be duped by Professor Jiang's excuses and cover-ups.

If Professor Jiang actually had some attainments and truly understood the Buddha Dharma, then the first thing he should do with respect to the books that I composed for the purpose of critiquing Yinshun's doctrines—*The Real Tathāgatagarbha [Zhenshi rulaizang], False Views versus the Buddha Dharma [Xiejian yu fofa], An Exposition on the Laṅkāvatāra Sūtra [Lengqiejing xiangjie], Mastering and Skillfully Articulating the Essence of Buddhist Enlightenment [Zongtong yu shuotong]*, and so forth—is to argue **from the perspective of the Dharma** and defend Yinshun's doctrines one by one to prove that his doctrines are correct and demonstrate that my doctrines are incorrect and that my statements are those of an "uninitiated" person. Only after he has thus proven his capability to refute me is he qualified to declare that he "disdains to hold discussions" with me; otherwise, his statements would just be untruthful excuses to conceal his faults. If Professor Jiang could argue from the perspective of the doctrines, then he could choose either the Path to Liberation in the Hīnayāna Buddha Dharma or the truth of the foremost meaning in the Mahāyāna Buddha Dharma as his topic of debate and openly question, through texts published under his real name, the improper or uneducated aspects of my discussions; he could also write a series of books to debate the doctrines. Another option would be to subdue me and turn me into his disciple through a doctrinal debate either in public or in private. A person who is able to tame me **with respect to the doctrines** must truly be a practitioner with great attainments; he will be precisely the great master that I have been seeking. There is no difficulty for me to prostrate before him and ask him to be my teacher upon meeting him, for I have spent years ardently searching, without success, for such a great master from whom I can learn.

The reality is that Professor Jiang has neither the ability nor the courage to debate, either in writing or in person, the doctrines found in my books. Therefore, he chose to assimilate Master Yinshun's erroneous views and came up with evasive statements and excurses to justify and conceal his faults. He even put feathers in his cap by proclaiming that I revered him—in fact, I once lauded him for constructively criticizing the absurd behavior of a renowned Buddhist master—but did not mention the fact that I later set aside his letter without ever replying to it. This example demonstrates that he is not an honest person.

In the past, I respected and praised Professor Jiang for his audacity to speak out about the drawbacks of the Buddhist community. Given that he now thinks Xiao Pingshi is uninitiated in the Buddha Dharma and therefore my teachings must be "misleading," he should draw on the same fearlessness and conscience that previously spurred him to point out the malpractices in the Buddhist community and rescue learners by publishing a book to extirpate my "incorrect" statements." Only then will he be worthy of the compliment that I gave him in the past for his virtue and courage. He should not have used excuses such as "Xiao Pingshi is an amateur," "I have no time," and so forth to avoid **debating the Dharma** with me—he would not need to extirpate my teachings or debate the Dharma with me if he agreed with my doctrines.

If Professor Jiang believes that Yinshun's views are correct, then he should step forward to defend his "teacher" Yinshun's doctrines in order to prove that they are correct and truthful—such would be the proper way to act. However, he has failed to do so by shunning from arguing in favor of his "teacher's" wrong views and by turning a blind eye to my persistent admonishment of Yinshun over the years—he has failed to save Yinshun as he has constantly avoided giving any constructive criticism of my "erroneous assertions." Moreover, he has surprisingly made various embellished statements to conceal Yinshun's mistakes in his response letter to the Modern Chan Society, which has been posted on this Society's website, and is obviously unworthy of the compliment that I gave him in the past. Therefore, I hereby "retract" my compliment to reflect the truth as it is.

The fact that Professor Jiang's response letter to the lay Buddhist Li Yuansong highlights my respect towards him but deliberately fails to mention that I later ignored him by not replying to his letter demonstrates that he is not an honest person, but a mundane being devoid of wisdom and courage, preoccupied with his reputation, and afraid of losing face. It does not make any sense to view such a mundane person whose occupation is an academic researcher of Buddhism as a Buddhist disciple who cultivates the Buddha Dharma. In other words, how could such an person, who is merely a mundane being who panders to Master Yinshun for his fame and uses the academic study of Buddhism as a livelihood, deserve to be regarded as a Buddhist who truly practices the Buddha Dharma?

What is the reason for me to state the above? If Professor Jiang Canteng deems that I am an amateur and that the doctrines taught in my writings do not correspond to the true Buddha Dharma, then he should, as a merciful, wise, and courageous Buddhist, rebut them with a sound argument to obliterate my "erroneous views" and steer learners as well as myself back onto the right path. While the Buddhist community has gradually come to acknowledge the doctrines that I teach as the correct Buddhist Dharma, if Professor Jiang Canteng is well aware that my statements are "misleading" and "do not conform" to the Buddha Dharma, then he should, out of mercy and compassion, rescue all learners and myself and prevent the Buddhist community from being misled onto the "erroneous path" by an "uninitiated" person like me. Only would such behavior be worthy of a wise, merciful, and brave Buddhist.

Professor Jiang has, however, no intention to act in this way. Instead, he has declared that he disdains to discuss with Xiao Pingshi and has made various excuses and embellished statements to defend the mistaken views of Master Yinshun. Such pretense of strength, which is of no benefit to himself or others, actually constitutes the grave and evil sin of slandering a sage. Preoccupied with the reputation and image that he has achieved in this life, he completely disregards the real Buddhist doctrines and the excruciating retribution that awaits him for countless lifetimes to come. Such unwise acts are not those of a Buddhist who deeply believes in the law of cause and effect.

As Yinshun does not believe in the existence of hell, the Pure Land of the Ultimate Bliss, the Pure Land of Lapus Lazuli Light, the worlds in the ten directions, and so forth, which are set forth in the sūtras of the Three Vehicles, he is convinced that those places are merely expedient teachings from sages—there are, for him, no such things as entering hell or undergoing the retribution of suffering in hell in future lives. Consequently, he dares to deny the true existence of hell and the various Buddha lands and so forth in the ten directions, which are set forth in the four Āgamas. Clearly, Yinshun does not believe in the teachings found in the four Āgamas of Early Buddhism; it can also be inferred that, deep down, he does not believe in the law of cause and effect of future lifetimes. Since Professor Jiang adulates the statements in Yinshun's writings, he must adhere to Yinshun's mistaken view that there is no such thing as undergoing the retribution—due to the law of cause and effect—of hell in future lifetimes. Therefore, he dares to teach the Buddha Dharma of the Three Vehicles without conforming to the sūtras or relying on any valid knowledge and dares to refute the truthfulness of the correct Dharma based on "Master" Yinshun's erroneous tantric view of Prāsaṅgika Madhyamaka. How could such a person be said to deeply believe in the law of cause and effect? Could the statements made by an academic researcher who does not believe in the law of cause and effect and who has no valid knowledge be regarded as the Buddha Dharma? Aren't the learners very ignorant to believe everything he says without distinguishing between right and wrong? How regretful!

I have always refuted, with stern words and without any leniency, the statements of any renowned master who champions the tantric view of Prāsaṅgika Madhyamaka. I have no choice but to do so, for I have clearly witnessed the extent to which the erroneous view of Prāsaṅgika Madhyamaka has ravaged the fundamental doctrines of Buddhism. Given that Professor Jiang thinks that I am an amateur and that my teachings do not correspond to the correct Dharma, he should, out of mercy and compassion, step forward to save the lineage of the correct Buddhist Dharma and rescue me from being entrapped in an irremediable state for countless kalpas. I would be infinitely grateful if he could help me realize my errors by elaborating on the Buddha Dharma in accordance with the truth; how would I ever dare to conceal my mistakes and formulate any fake excuses? I would repent and correct my faults in public right away to avoid the excruciating retribution that I would otherwise have to undergo for long kalpas in future lifetimes.

It is not difficult for me to repent in public; in fact, I have done it frequently in the past. I do not dare to conceal my errors in the slightest, as evidenced by some of the statements in my writings. Bodhisattvas should not fear losing face, for repentance is a virtuous deed from someone with shame and embarrassment and also a virtuous dharma cultivated by Bodhisattvas—the Bodhisattvas who have realized the emptiness-nature and aligned their behavior with the mode of this emptiness-nature have long discarded all concerns about losing face. I hereby call on anyone who has detected that my doctrines are misleading and do not correspond to the Buddha Dharma to save me by promptly publishing a book that refutes my teachings so that I can avoid future errors by being aware of and rectifying my current mistakes and by subsequently repenting in public. However, if I do not have any faults, then please do not blindly criticize me out of selfishness if you do not wish to undergo excruciating retribution in future lifetimes. May my sincere suggestions be heard and accepted by the Buddhist community; if so, then current and future learners as well as all of Buddhism stand to benefit tremendously.

Master Yinshun (he in fact should not be addressed as a Buddhist master given that his doctrines have destroyed the foundation of the Buddha Dharma—the dharma of the eighth consciousness, the tathāgatagarbha. He is merely a person donning a Buddhist monastic robe who transmits the doctrine based on the theory of uncausedness set forth by nihilistic non-Buddhists) has been demolishing the fundamentals of the Buddha Dharma in every respect by preaching the erroneous view of Prāsaṅgika Madhyamaka, turning the essence of the Buddha Dharma of the Three Vehicles into the nihilistic emptiness outlined in the theory of uncausedness. The harm of this fault far exceeds the great harm caused by the infiltration of the tantric yab-yum practice into Buddhism due to the following reasons: (1) The propagation of the erroneous tantric view of Prāsaṅgika Madhyamaka justifies the non-Buddhist Dharma-gate of sexual misconduct cultivated by a male and a female through the tantric yab-yum practice and ensures its continued existence within "tantric Buddhism," even allowing it to gradually infiltrate into authentic Buddhism; (2) Prāsaṅgika Madhyamaka regards the mental consciousness in the state of thoughtless and lucid awareness as the reality suchness of the Buddha Ground; and (3) the blissful sensation resulting from the lustful contact between a male and a female during the yab-yum practice falls into the sphere of the mental consciousness consisting of a mind in a state of thoughtlessness and lucid awareness but not into the sphere of the eighth consciousness—the tathāgatagarbha.

After denying the existence of the eighth consciousness, Yinshun feared that people might criticize his Prāsaṅgika Madhyamaka teachings for falling into the view of nihilism, and as a result, he contradicted the Buddha's tenets by establishing the narrative about an "unknowable and unrealizable subtle mind consisting of the mental consciousness" in many of his writings. He has used this mind to replace the "knowable and realizable tathāgatagarbha" taught by the Buddha and has regarded this subtle mental consciousness as the mind that connects the cyclic existences in the three times in an attempt to save his doctrines from falling into the view of nihilism or the theory of uncausedness. However, the Buddha states in the four Āgamas that all kinds of mental consciousness, whether coarse or subtle, are knowable and realizable—there is no subtle mental consciousness that can neither be known nor realized. Yinshun's establishment of this unknowable and unrealizable subtle mind consisting of the mental consciousness clearly contradicts the Buddha's tenets and is merely an attempt to save the Prāsaṅgika Madhyamaka teachings, which he adulates, from falling into the view of nihilism. Yinshun's deeds, which contradict the scriptures and correct reasonings, are no different from the deeds of Candrakīrti and others in ancient India, because they all help justify the yab-yum practice, which tantric Buddhists have acquired from non-Buddhists, since the yab-yum practice revolves around the mind of feeling and cognition— the mental consciousness. Thanks to Yinshun's acts, Tantric Buddhists can rationalize the fact that they have turned a method of sexual cravings drawn from non-Buddhist Shaktism into the core practice of tantric Esoteric Buddhism, thus enabling Tantric Buddhism to infiltrate true Buddhism and, unbeknownst to all Buddhists, gradually take over the legitimacy of true Buddhism. Yinshun's behavior has also caused all practitioners of Tantric Buddhism who adhere to Tantrism to fall into both the nihilist view and eternalist view and to regard the mental consciousness—be it the coarse mind or subtle mind—as a permanent and indestructible dharma.

Once Tantrism has completely supplanted Exoteric Buddhism, no learners will ever be able to realize the true meaning of the Buddha Dharma of the Three Vehicles, and the Buddhist doctrine will be downgraded to metaphysics—it will be turned into a mundane philosophy. As a result, the Buddhist doctrine will definitely become shallow and will no longer feature the wondrous teachings that drastically differentiate it from the various non-Buddhist methods; as such, the Buddhist doctrine will be disparaged by worldly beings. The fact that the Buddha Dharma is belittled by worldly beings will inevitably cause Buddhism to also be looked down upon by worldly beings, which means that the Buddhist path of practice will be disparaged by worldly beings. They will no longer cultivate the path due to a lack of reverence and adulation and will merely consider the Buddhist doctrine to be a philosophy—they will study it but will not actually practice it. What ensues is that the monastic masters of Buddhism will be despised by worldly beings, for they will no longer be viewed as persons with practice and attainments or as the inheritors of the Buddha's true, profound, and supreme doctrine. If this is to occur, then in future lifetimes people will view Buddhist masters as ordinary beings and will no longer show any reverence towards them.

In future lifetimes, the endeavors of the monastics—the saṃgha—who have truly realized the eighth consciousness—the tathāgatagarbha—and brought forth the wisdom of prajñā and who appear in this world to uphold and propagate the Buddha's correct Dharma will be condemned and thwarted by the novice disciples of Master Yinshun and others, making it tougher for those who have realized the path to uphold and propagate the correct Dharma. Before long, the saṃgha will be eliminated or ostracized as a result of the immense power of mistaken views and erroneous doctrines. No Buddhist master should ever turn a blind eye and neglect the likelihood of such events given the extensive harm that those fallacies might cause and given the enormity of the stakes for the Buddhist monastic masters in the present and future as well as the lineage of the correct Buddhist Dharma in the future. If the Buddhist masters keep ignoring this danger, then the entirety of Buddhism will fall into the erroneous doctrine based on the theory of uncausedness related to the view of Prāsaṅgika Madhyamaka in twenty years and will be exterminated soon after.

Based on his mistaken view of Prāsaṅgika Madhyamaka, Yinshun has negated the correct Dharma of the tathāgatagarbha and further refuted the authenticity of the Mahāyāna sutras, asserting that they are a mere fabrication of later generations. Therefore, he dared to assert that hell, the Pure Land of the Ultimate Bliss, and the Pure Land of Lapus Lazuli Light do not exist and are merely expedient designations established for the sake of the trainees. The reason Yinshun has refuted the veracity of the Mahāyāna sūtras and refused to acknowledge that their contents were truly taught by the Buddha is that he has been unable to realize, according to the Mahāyāna scriptures, the eighth consciousness—the tathāgatagarbha. Consequently, he has outright refuted the authenticity of these sutras to avoid the embarrassment of having to give a negative answer when people ask him whether he is enlightened. However, Yinshun's denial of the existence of the eighth consciousness due to the aforementioned selfishness, his assertion that neither the seventh consciousness nor the eighth consciousness is set forth in the Original Buddha Dharma, and his declaration that the contents of the Buddhist sūtras of the Great Vehicle were not taught by the Buddha in person have caused the Dharma of the Three Vehicles to fall into the view of nihilism, have caused the Buddha Dharma of the Great Vehicle to lose its foothold, stripped the Buddhist sūtras of the Great Vehicle of their function to uphold the Early Buddha Dharma, caused the Early Buddha Dharma to lose its profundity, and prompted a large number of learners to doubt or not believe in the authenticity of the sūtras of the Great Vehicle, leading to their refusal to practice in accordance with the Buddha's words in those sūtras. These are the egregious faults caused by Yinshun and his followers. Such behavior consists of directly uprooting the basis of the Buddha Dharma from within Buddhism. If this could be regarded as "the propagation—rather than the destruction—of the Buddha Dharma," then the burning down of monasteries and the killing of the saṃgha by non-Buddhists should not be considered to be acts that destroy Buddhism, for those misdeeds are far less destructive than the destruction of the Dharma by Yinshun and his followers, who have been extirpating the basis of the Buddha Dharma of the Three Vehicles directly from within Buddhism.

Furthermore, in many of his writings such as *The Collection of Wonderful Clouds [Miaoyun chi 妙雲集]*, Yinshun advocates that only the contents of the four Āgamas were truly taught by the Buddha in person He believes that the contents of the sūtras of the Great Vehicle were not taught by the Buddha in person, but were instead created collectively by the Buddha's disciples after the Buddha's passing and later compiled into books—hence, he believes that these contents were not imparted by the Buddha in person. Owing to this erroneous view, Yinshun does not believe the Buddha's words in the sūtras of the Great Vehicle that the Buddha's body will, after ceasing [translation note: after its manifested ceasing], transform into a reward-body that will permanently dwell in the Highest Heaven of the Realm of Subtle Materiality to teach the knowledge-of-all-aspects. Instead, Yinshun has asserted in his publications that, after Śākyamuni's passing, His body has disintegrated, like the evaporation of dust and smoke, and that there is in fact no reward-body Buddha who is still preaching the Dharma in Heaven. This statement completely contradicts the teachings of the Āgamas Sūtras. The Āgama Sūtras mention the Buddha's "form of liberation," saying that all Buddhas have a permanent and indestructible "form of liberation" that endlessly benefits sentient beings. The Mahāyāna sūtras also state that all Buddhas have three types of mind-made body and a magnificent reward body, which permanently reside in the three realms of the ten directions to benefit sentient beings. Such a form of liberation is an uncontaminated conditioned dharma because (1) it has realized the four nirvāṇas—the nirvāṇa with remainder, the remainderless nirvāṇa, the nirvāṇa that is primordially and naturally pure, and the non-abiding nirvāṇa—and (2) not only has it eliminated all delimited existences, but it has also extinguished all transformational existences. This form of liberation is known as "the ultimate nirvāṇa," "the great nirvāṇa," or "permanence, bliss, self, and purity."

Such a form of liberation is recorded in all the sūtras of the Three Vehicles; among them, the Āgama Sūtras are readily accessible. Why does Yinshun not believe in its existence? Why does he refute the valid knowledge through exalted teachings that the Buddha's body is permanent and indestructible? Why does he wrongly claim that the non-cessation of the Buddha's body is merely a fictitious fact asserted by the Buddha's disciples of later generations to express their perpetual yearning for the Buddha? It is, therefore, no surprise that Yinshun declares in his writings that, after Śākyamuni's passing, His body disintegrated like evaporated dust and smoke, and therefore, there is in fact no reward body that is still preaching the Dharma in Heaven. It is obvious that the person who came up with this statement does not comprehend the Buddha Dharma—he is clearly neither fully equipped with the basic knowledge and view of the Buddha Dharma nor has complete faith in the Buddha-jewel and the Dharma-jewel. Such a declaration will shatter all faith and reverence that the learners of future generations might exhibit towards Buddha Śākyamuni. Moreover, Yinshun's statement is incorrect; in this lifetime, I have sometimes been summoned by the World-Honored One and have beheld Him in person, which proves that He did not evaporate like dust and smoke, as claimed by Yinshun. How then could we believe the "Buddha Dharma" preached by Yinshun? However, his disciples do not possess the wisdom-eye and adhere to his assertions with adamant faith; they promote Yinshun's teachings while falsely condemning my statements, which accord with the truth. They are people who make random criticism without any concern for the truth

Furthermore, Master Yinshun does not believe any of the contents related to the Western Pure Land of the Ultimate Bliss found in the Three Sūtras of the Pure Land, nor does he believe any of the contents related to the Eastern Pure Land of Lapus Lazuli Light found in the Mahāyāna sūtras. He asserts that the sūtras were fabricated by the Buddha's disciples to express their yearning for Him after His passing. Owing to this erroneous view, Yinshun has refuted the true existence of the Pure Land of the Ultimate Bliss and the Pure Land of Lapus Lazuli Light and wrote down this view in his books. In addition, he has distorted the meanings of the Buddha's words about the tathāgatagarbha in the subtle, wondrous, profound, and extensive *Laṅkāvatāra Sūtra [Lengqie jing 楞伽經]* by declaring that the tathāgatagarbha does not exist. In his *The Discourse on the Summary of Mahāyāna [Shedasheng lun jiangji 攝大乘論講記]*, Yinshun **strenuously distorts** Bodhisattva Asaṅga's explicit contents in the treatise *Summary of Mahāyāna [Shedasheng lun 攝大乘論]* about the existence of the tathāgatagarbha by affirming that the tathāgatagarbha does not exist to corroborate his erroneous tantric view of Prāsaṅgika Madhyamaka. In doing so, Yinshun's intention is to prevent people from respecting and believing in the ultimate and definitive Vijñaptimātratā sūtras of the third turning of the Dharma Wheel as well as in the treatises of the correct meaning composed by

Bodhisattvas. Such refutation of the existence of the dharma of the eighth consciousness—the tathāgatagarbha—has pushed the correct doctrine of the tathāgatagarbha—the basis of the Buddha Dharma of the Three Vehicles—to the brink of extermination and deterred many contemporary learners from cultivating the dharma of the tathāgatagarbha due to doubt or disbelief. This situation results from Yinshun's refutation of the existence of the tathagatagarbha through decades of systemic writing.

Furthermore, Master Yinshun does not believe any of the contents related to hell set forth by the World-Honored One in the Āgamas and disbelieves even more all the contents related to hell in the Mahāyāna sūtras. He has widely disseminated such disbelief by writing about them in his publications. As a result of the statements found in those works, the students of Buddhist academies in today's China neither believe in the law of cause and effect nor the existence of hell, and their after-school activities include eating meat and drinking alcohol, and even seeking prostitutes and so forth. These behaviors are also seen in some of the monastics. Those people state:

> The masters and teachers of the Buddha Dharma in our Buddhist academy told us in class that neither hell nor the Pure Land of the Ultimate Bliss exists and that there is no such thing as Buddha Śākyamuni still preaching the Dharma in Heaven. Such teachings are based on *The Collection of Wonderful Clouds [Miaoyun chi 妙雲集] and The Collection of Flower and Rain [Huayu chi 華雨集]* authored by the Venerable Great Master Yinshun according to the sūtras. Therefore, there is simply no such thing as retribution of cause and effect or hell where one suffers the retribution of future lifetimes. How foolish of you to fritter your life away by eschewing good foods, nice drinks, and great entertainment while observing the precepts.

The students who graduated from Buddhist academies will mostly become monastics. The fact that they surprisingly harbor such profoundly mistaken views raises grave concerns about the future of Buddhism in China. The culprits are Yinshun's works such as *The Collection of Wonderful Clouds [Miaoyun chi], The Collection of Flower and Rain [Huayu chi]*, and so forth, which are all based on the erroneous view of Prāsaṅgika Madhyamaka. Given that Buddhism in China is already suffering from the dire consequences of Yinshun's fallacious views, how could the elders and meritorious ones of the Taiwan Buddhist community who worry about the future of Buddhism still deliberately turn a blind eye to this situation and bury their heads in the sand in this crucial moment? How could they passively allow Yinshun's mistaken view of Prāsaṅgika Madhyamaka as well as the fallacious views in his *The Collection of Wonderful Clouds, The Collection of Flower and Rain*, and so forth to continue to poison the students of Buddhist academies—the future pillars of Buddhism? Are they truly insensitive to this predicament? I earnestly call on the elders and meritorious ones of the various Buddhist groups to confront the severity of this problem as quickly as possible and promptly devise a plan to save the correct Buddhist Dharma; otherwise, how will they face the World-Honored One when He greets them after death?

The right thing for Jiang Canteng to do now would be to visit China and investigate and discuss the abominable influence exerted by Yinshun's writings on the Buddhist community in that country. Only then will he live up to the good conscience and duty of an "academic researcher in Buddhism" and exhibit the strength of character—the audacity to make criticism and give advice— emblematic of Chinese literati. He should not shun away from the truth like an ostrich burying its head in the sand while invariably making various excuses for and arguing unreasonably in favor of Yinshun's mistaken views—such behavior has helped the erroneous views contained in Yinshun's publications to continue to poison the minds of the students in both Taiwanese and Chinese Buddhist academies. If Mr. Jiang is willing to perform this investigation, he must first seek to attain the true meaning of the Mahāyāna Dharma. To do so, he must first realize the eighth consciousness, confirm its existence, personally experience its truly existent properties, and verify the multitudes of seeds stored in it.

Only then will he truly understand the supremacy and wondrousness of the knowledge-of-all-aspects set forth in the Mahāyāna sūtras, validate the extensive harm caused by the multifarious poisonous teachings found in Yinshun's writings, and obtain the capacity to observe and investigate the fact that Chinese Buddhism is being damaged by Yinshun's books. One must possess the knowledge-of-the-aspects-of-the-path to make truthful observations without being deluded by false appearances; otherwise, it is impossible to fully grasp the perniciousness of Yinshun's writings.

If Mr. Jiang had any wisdom, then he should first rid of the literati's bad habit of belittling their peers and instead reason calmly and investigate the truth based on the facts; otherwise, his writings will inevitably be refuted by enlightened persons and his lifelong reputation will be shattered. The loss of lifelong reputation is trivial compared to the excruciating retribution of sheer pain that will plague him after death for countless future lifetimes over many kalpas. Why is that? Because the true existence of hell and of the retribution resulting from the law of cause and effect is not contingent upon Mr. Jiang's belief or disbelief in such existence. Sentient beings' belief or disbelief in the existence of hell does not determine the existence or inexistence of hell and of the retribution resulting from the law of cause and effect. Instead, both hell and such retribution will continue to exist, so that those who perform evil deeds will suffer the related retribution in hell after death. Indeed, neither hell nor the aforementioned retribution will vanish just because sentient beings do not believe in their existence. I have personally witnessed the dire retribution that I had to endure due to a verbal misdeed that I committed in a past life as a novice Buddhist learner. If Mr. Jiang had any wisdom, he should contemplate the truth calmly, unless he agrees with the statements in Yinshun's books and does not believe in the existence of an eighth consciousness that automatically records all the karmic deeds of this life or the existence of hell and of the law of cause and effect—unless he would rather endure excruciating sheer agony for long kalpas in future lives than lose the illusory fame gained in this life.

The proponents of Prāsaṅgika Madhyamaka should be lauded for their enthusiastic rebuttal of non-Buddhist teachings. However, their refutation of the Vijñaptimātratā doctrines is a great fault, because it shows that they have seriously misunderstood what the knowledge-of-the-aspects of Vijñaptimātratā is all about and because making such criticism is an act that destroys the Buddha Dharma. For instance, the tantric "Bodhisattva" Śāntideva in ancient India specifically repudiated the Vijñaptimātratā School by refuting the self-witnessing portion:

> The Protector of the World stated that the mind does not perceive the mind. Just as a sword cannot cut itself, so it is with the mind.[5] (The mental faculty is as sharp as a sword, but it cannot cut itself.) . . .
> [Yogacarin:] It is said that a lamp illuminates once this is cognized with awareness. The mind is said to illuminate once this is cognized with what?
> [Madhyamika:] If no one perceives whether the mind is luminous or not, then there is no point in discussing it, like the beauty of a barren woman's daughter.[6]

The above criticism on the training in higher wisdom—the knowledge-of-the-aspects of Vijñaptimātratā—are made from the perspective of an ordinary person.

Why do I say so? The teaching **"the mind does not perceive the mind"** found in the knowledge-of-the-aspects of Vijñaptimātratā refers to the eighth consciousness—the ālaya mind—and not the mental consciousness—the mind of feeling and cognition. Given that the ālaya-consciousness is invariably devoid of the mental functions of seeing, hearing, feeling, and cognition

---

5   Shantideva, *Annotation of Bodhisattvacaryāvatāra [Rupusaxing yizhu* 入菩薩行譯 注*]*, trans. Chen Yujiao 陳玉蛟, (Zanghai Publisher 藏海出版社, 1992), 322-26. Translated into English from Chinese.

6   Santideva, *A guide to the bodhisattva way of life: Bodhicaryavatara*, translated from the Sanskrit and Tibetan by Vesna A. Wallace and B. Alan Wallace., 1st ed. (Snow Lion Publications, Ithaca, New York, 1997), 120.

and never observes itself amidst all the phenomena consisting of the six sense objects in the three realms, it is without a self-witnessing portion or an awareness of self-witnessing portion amidst those phenomena. The Buddha's statement "without a self-witnessing portion or an awareness of self-witnessing portion—the mind does not perceive the mind" refers to the mind consisting of the eighth consciousness and not the mental consciousness consisting of the mind of feeling and cognition—as claimed by the tantric proponents of Prāsaṅgika Madhyamaka—or the mental consciousness consisting of a subtle mind—as asserted by Yinshun. After misapprehending the correct dharma of the knowledge-of-the-aspects of Vijñaptimātratā, the proponents of Prāsaṅgika Madhyamaka wrongfully condemned the correct Dharma preached by the Vijñaptimātratā School. How ignorant! Unaware of the egregious mistakes contained in Prāsaṅgika Madhyamaka, Master Yinshun untruthfully extolled this erroneous tantric view, willfully took over this view (see the Preface of *Zhongguan jinlun* 中觀今論 [*Contemporary Opinion of the Middle-Way View*]), and propagated it vigorously. How unwise!

In the third turning of the Dharma Wheel, the Buddha always stated that the eighth consciousness is without a self-witnessing portion or an awareness of self-witnessing portion. In contrast, the Buddha declared that the mental consciousness has a self-witnessing portion and an awareness of self-witnessing portion. Indeed, He has extensively said that the conscious mind—the mental consciousness consisting of the mind of feeling and cognition—can ascertain various phenomena and observe itself and is endowed with the determinative mental concomitants. Given that none of the proponents of Prāsaṅgika Madhyamaka—Yinshun, the Dalai Lama, and so forth in the modern days and Atiśa, Śāntideva, Candrakīrti, and so forth in ancient times—have been able to comprehend and realize the mind consisting of the eighth consciousness, they have squarely denied its existence. Furthermore, they have ascribed the properties of the mind consisting of the eighth consciousness set forth by the Buddha to the sixth consciousness—the mind of feeling and cognition—and have stated the opposite of the Buddha's teachings by wrongly affirming that, according to the Buddha, this mind of feeling and cognition is without a self-witnessing portion or an awareness of self-witnessing portion. Having misunderstood the correct meaning of the knowledge-of-the-aspects of Vijñaptimātratā, they have condemned the Vijñaptimātratā School for preaching that the mental consciousness has an awareness of self-witnessing portion, which, according to them, is a non-definitive teaching that contradicts the Buddha's statements. Moreover, they have denounced the sūtras of the third turning of the Dharma Wheel expounded by the Buddha for being non-definitive. This demonstrates that the proponents of the Prāsaṅgika Madhyamaka School are ignorant people who state the opposite of the truth and specialize in groundless and unreasonable argumentation. In fact, given that the mental consciousness is endowed with determinative mental concomitants, it can definitely observe whether it itself is dwelling amidst the six sense objects, whether it itself is experiencing pain or happiness amidst the six sense-objects, and whether it itself is currently amidst the sensation of pain or happiness in a given state. This teaching is not just imparted by the Buddha in the sūtras of Vijñaptimātratā, but is also set forth by the Buddha in the Āgamas Sūtras. One should not wrongfully affirm that the Āgamas Sūtras make no mention of it.

The mental consciousness—the mind of feeling and cognition—is without a self-witnessing portion or an awareness of self-witnessing portion only when it ceases (in the five states such as deep sleep, unconsciousness, and so forth), for the mental consciousness itself no longer exists when it ceases. Indeed, whenever the mental consciousness arises, it necessarily has a self-witnessing portion and an awareness of self-witnessing portion, and the five determinative mental concomitants will necessarily arise. Therefore, the mental consciousnsess—the mind of feeling and cognition—is necessarily endowed with an awarenesss of self-witnessing portion. Anyone can directly validate this fact, which is asserted by all sūtras and treatises of the Vijñaptimātratā School. Those texts all state that the mental consciousness is endowed with a self-witnessing portion and an awareness of self-witnessing portion and have never claimed that the eighth consciousness has a self-witnessing portion. How could the proponents of Prāsaṅgika Madhyamaka—ancient and contemporary alike—wrongfully condemn the tenets of the Vijñaptimātratā School for being "erroneous" after misconstruing them? How could they lie through their teeth? How could they wrongfully reprimand the Vijñaptimātratā School after distorting its doctrines?

Any ordinary person can ascertain the existence of the mental consciousness' awareness of self-witnessing portion. The reason is that anyone can, whenever his mental consciousness (including his thoughtless lucid mind) arises, cognize, within the states of the six sense objects, the states of the sense objects in which he himself currently is. Due to the cognition that he is himself currently in the states of the six sense objects, his mind experiences pleasurable or unpleasurable sensations; hence, there are sensations of pain, happiness, worry, joy, indifference, and so forth. This proves that the conscious mind is indeed endowed with a self-witnessing portion. Due to the possession of this self-witnessing portion, the mental consciousness—the mind of feeling and cognition—can also cognize—can observe and validate—whether it itself currently is in a pleasurable or unpleasurable state. This proves that the conscious mind is indeed endowed with an awareness of self-witnessing portion. By contrast, the proponents of Prāsaṅgika Madhyamaka in today's Taiwan—they are currently experiencing anger, hate, resentment, and distress due to my stern criticism of their ignorance but, like a person in a vegetative state, do not cognize that they themselves are in such an unpleasurable state at this moment can be said to be without an awareness of self-witnessing portion. Thus, contrary to the erroneous assertion made by the proponents of Prāsaṅgika Madhyamaka that the mental consciousness—the mind of feeling and cognition—does not possess an awareness of self-witnessing portion, this mental consciousness can, within all states of the six sense objects, cognize whether it itself currently is in a pleasurable or unpleasurable state, and is, therefore, endowed with an awareness of self-witnessing portion.

Even ordinary persons can thus understand that the mental consciousness—the mind of lucid awareness—is endowed with the function of the awareness of self-witnessing portion; the proponents of Prāsaṅgika Madhyamaka, who view themselves as having achieved the highest levels of practice, valid cognition, and wisdom, surprisingly cannot discern that their mental consciousness itself is endowed with an awareness of self-witnessing portion. They are indeed people who inverse the truth and point to a deer while saying that it is a horse. The truth is, all proponents of Prāsaṅgika Madhyamaka have long understood the mental consciousness' awareness of self-witnessing portion, but have deliberated asserted the opposite of the truth in an attempt to defend the fallacious reasonings of Prāsaṅgika Madhyamaka.

The Buddha has thus stated in the sūtras of the third turning of the Dharma Wheel that the mind consisting of the eighth consciousness does not have an awareness of self-witnessing portion and that the conscious mind does have such an awareness of self-witnessing portion. Given that the proponents of Prāsaṅgika Madhyamaka have denied the existence of the eighth consciousness, their only option is to use the statement **"the mind does not perceive the mind"**—the words used by the Buddha to expound the eighth consciousness—to explain the sixth consciousness—the mind of lucid awareness—and to wrongfully claims that, according to the Buddha, the mental consciousness does not have an awareness of self-witnessing portion. They clearly know that their assertion is inconsistent with their experience in daily life, but still forcefully argue that the conscious mind is without an awareness of self-witnessing portion. They have been using the Buddha's words about a property of the eighth consciousness to wrongfully condemn the Vijñaptimātratā School for being mistaken in saying that the conscious mind is endowed with an awareness of self-witnessing portion. In reality, the Vijñaptimātratā School speaks in accordance with the Buddha's words when it asserts that the eighth consciousness does not have an awareness of self-witnessing portion and that the sixth consciousness—the mind of feeling and cognition—does have such an awareness. This proclamation is consistent with the Buddha's words but contradicts the statement of the Prāsaṅgika School. Therefore, the Prāsaṅgika School has deliberately misinterpreted the Buddha's words and has disparaged the assertion of the Vijñaptimātratā School by claiming that it is inconsistent with the Buddha's teachings. The truth is, the proponents of Prāsaṅgika Madhyamaka have, after misquoting and misinterpreting the Buddha's words, wrongfully accused the assertion of the Vijñaptimātratā School, which propagates the correct Dharma, for contradicting the Buddha's words while in fact, the Prāsaṅgika School is the one that contradicts the Buddha's words.

Furthermore, the Buddha's statement "**Just as a sword cannot cut itself, so it is with the mind** [the mental faculty is as sharp as a sword, but it cannot cut itself]" refers to the seventh consciousness—the mental faculty—which is also known as the manas-consciousness. According to the Buddha, this seventh consciousness is called mental faculty for being the activating power that causes the seeds of the mental consciousness to arise from within the eighth consciousness—the mental consciousness arises only in dependence upon the mental application of the manas-consciousness; once it has arisen, it operates also in dependence upon the mental application of the mental faculty—the manas-consciousness. Hence, the manas-consciousness is said to be the faculty of mental consciousness. Endowed with an extremely obtuse mental concomitant of wisdom, this mental faculty only performs very basic discernment on the mental object of the five sense objects, such as whether this mental object is undergoing a significant change. Unlike the mental consciousness—the mind of feeling and cognition—which operates astutely through the five determinative mental concomitants, the seventh consciousness is devoid of the four mental concomitants of desire, determination, recollection, and concentration. Even its function of mental concomitant of wisdom (determinative wisdom) is extremely obtuse, as it can only perform extremely basic discernment on the changes related to the mental object.

How could the manas-consciousness have the ability to observe itself when it is thus unable to even perform any discernment on the five sense objects and must arouse the mental consciousness so that it can subsequently make decisions concerning various states in dependence upon the mental consciousness' mental concomitant of wisdom? How could it have the ability to ponder over various doctrines? How could it have the ability to correct its own mental deeds and predispositions? Therefore, although the manas-consciousness is extremely astute for being able to pervasively observe all phenomena, and although it can make decisions in all places and at all times in dependence upon the conscious mind's mental concomitant of wisdom and can decide about various mental deeds, there is nothing it can do without the mental consciousness' mental concomitant of wisdom. Given such properties, the Buddha states: "The mental faculty (the manas-consciousness) is as sharp as a sword (this is a metaphor for the mental faculty's astuteness—its ability to pervasively observe all phenomena; in contrast, the mental consciousness is endowed with the mental concomitant of wisdom, yet is unable to pervasively observe all phenomena), but it cannot cut itself (this is a metaphor for the fact that the manas-consciousness is without an awareness of self-witnessing portion of the mental concomitant of wisdom and is, therefore, unable to adjust or rectify its virtuous or non-virtuous deeds). In other words, this consciousness needs to rely on the mental consciousness' determinative wisdom and thinking wisdom in order to amend its defiled nature and transform into a pure mental faculty—it is unable to eliminate the afflictive emotions with which it is connected by just relying on its own functions. For this reason, the Buddha states: "**Just as a sword cannot cut itself, so it is with the mind** (the mental faculty is as sharp as a sword, but it cannot cut itself)." However, the proponents of Prāsaṅgika Madhyamaka have wrongfully condemned the correct principles of the knowledge-of-the-aspects set forth by the Vijñaptimātratā School after misconstruing the Buddha's tenets. How then could their doctrines be said to be the real Buddha Dharma? How do they dare to wrongly criticize the correct Dharma of the Vijñaptimātratā School by branding it as incorrect Dharma? How could they have refuted the wondrous Dharma of the Vijñaptimātratā knowledge-of-the-aspects based on their mistaken views? Clearly, they have inverted the truth to a large extent.

The statement made by the proponents of the Vijñaptimātratā School and cited by tantric followers, "if the self-witnessing portion did not exist, how could the mental consciousness remember anything?" means that sentient beings must rely on the self-witnessing portion to remember the states experienced in the past. However, Śāntideva maintains that it is possible to recall past events without the self-witnessing portion for the following reason: "Due to the connection between the mind and all states, the mind is able to cognize, for instance, a rat's poisoning." This assertion means that, although the conscious mind sometimes ceases, this mind of feeling and cognition possesses the function of knowing successive occurrences and can therefore recollect past events. Such a concept, however, contradicts the Buddha's teachings as well as what we actually experience in our daily lives.

As we all know, if we can bring forth the correct ascertainment for either a state that we have never experienced but have heard someone else speak about or a state that we have personally experienced, then this state becomes an experienced state (those who have heard about it regard the state understood through hearing as an experienced state, whereas those who have personally experienced it regard the state that they have experienced as their "personally experienced state"). Only then can we, henceforth, recollect this state repeatedly—bring forth the memory of the state that we have heard someone speak about or the state that we have personally experienced. Consequently, it is necessary to have a correct ascertainment of a state to recall it in the future.

One cannot have a correct ascertainment of an experienced state without one's self-witnessing portion (for instance, a person has no awareness of a given state when he is drowsy while hearing about it or experiencing it—he has no-self-witnessing portion related to this state), which means that one will, in the future, be unable to recollect the details related to this state. This principle is extremely easy to understand; any ordinary person will comprehend it and can personally verify it upon hearing about it. However, the proponents of Prāsaṅgika Madhyamaka forcefully and unreasonably argue: "Due to the connection between the mind and all states, the mind is able to cognize, for instance, a rat's poisoning."

This statement means the following:

Due to the connection between the mind and all states, the recollection of external states **experienced** in the past brings forth the memory of the **mind that experienced** those states. For instance, a person, who had no clue that he was poisoned when he was bitten by a rat in winter, eventually finds out about the poisoning only when the poison breaks out during a spring thunder. Therefore, recollection is possible without one's self-witnessing portion.[7]

However, this explanation does not address the problem. Indeed, Śāntideva has admitted that the recollection of external states **experienced in the past** allows one to **bring forth the mind that experienced those states.** This demonstrates that this person already had, at the time, a correct ascertainment of **the personally experienced state.** The existence of the personally experienced state proves that the self-witnessing portion existed at the time of the experience because there was, at the time, sufficient cognition of the state. Given the existence of sufficient cognition, the one that cognized that state was precisely the self-witnessing portion. Those who, despite this fact, claim that the mental consciousness— the mind of feeling and cognition—does not have a self-witnessing portion are the ones who make forceful and groundless

---

7 Shantideva, *Annotation of Bodhisattvacaryāvatāra [Rupusaxing yizhu 入菩薩行譯 注]*, trans. Chen Yujiao 陳玉蛟, (Zanghai Publisher 藏海出版社, 1992), 325. Translated into English from Chinese.

argumentation. Therefore, it is incorrect—and completely senseless—for the proponents of Prāsaṅgika Madhyamaka to refute the Vijñaptimātratā School's assertion that the mental consciousness is endowed with a self-witnessing portion.

Furthermore, Śāntideva's statement, "due to the connection between the mind and all states, the mind is able to cognize, for instance, a rat's poisoning" contains egregious mistakes. Indeed, given that the mind of feeling and cognition ceases every night, its feeling and cognition—and hence its recollection of past occurrences—must be reactivated the following morning from within the tathagatagarbha based on the mental application of the mental faculty. How could such a phenomenon, which undergoes cessations and must rely on other consciousnesses (the mental faculty and the seeds of the mental consciousness stored in the ālaya-consciousness) to arise the following morning, possess itself the function of recollection? How could it be said, with respect to the conscious mind, that there is **"connection between the mind and all states"**? Indeed, this conscious mind ceases during deep sleep. It turns into nothingness once it ceases, and nothingness can definitely not re-arise on its own. How could there be **"connection between the mind and all states"** yesterday and today with respect to a nothingness that cannot re-arise on its own? Those gurus' assertions just do not make any sense.

Only the mind that never ceases can be said to possess the meritorious quality of **"connection between the mind and all states"** yesterday and today as well as in the past kalpa and the current kalpa. Anyone can witness that the mental consciousness—the mind of feeling and cognition—ceases every night and must rely on others (the four dharmas of simultaneous support[8]) to arise the following morning—it cannot even arise on its own. How then could the tantric proponents of Prāsaṅgika Madhyamaka falsely speak, with respect to the mental consciousness—a phenomenon that ceases every night—about the fact that **"due to the connection**

---

[8]   Simultaneous support: S. *saha-bhūtāśraya; sahabhv-āśraya;* C. *juyou yi* 俱有依.

between the mind and all states, the mind is able to cognize, for instance, a rat's poisoning" and assert that this mental consciousness can recollect on its own personally experienced states? Those gurus' statements do not make any sense.

Furthermore, if the mental consciousness—the mind of feeling and cognition—was able to know past occurrences based on the connection between the mind and all states and without the eighth consciousness holding any seeds, then all the seeds of past occurrences would be held by the mental consciousness' own mind. In that case, the mental consciousness would be able to recollect everything it has experienced. However, it is clear that the mental consciousness is unable to fully remember everything it has experienced: Sometimes it tries to but is unable to recall a particular event that it has personally experienced, the name of a particular person, or a place where a particular object has been left; it is only after the mental faculty's touching from within the eighth consciousness that the mental consciousness—the mind of feeling and cognition—will suddenly remember that particular event or item. If the mental consciousness was a mind that connects with all states, then it must be the seed-holder and must be able to think at will and without error about anything that it wishes to think about—anything that transpired in a given month of a given year of a given lifetime—this is, however, clearly not the case. Therefore, Śāntideva's statement, **"due to the connection between the mind and all states, the mind is able to cognize, for instance, a rat's poisoning"** does not apply to the mental consciousness in any way, for the mental consciousness definitely ceases in the five states such as deep sleep and so forth and therefore cannot be the mind in **"the connection between the mind and all states."** If it is not the mind that connects with all states before and after, then we can conclude that it is definitely not the seed-holder and must rely on another dharma to hold seeds. How could the mental consciousness—the mind of feeling and cognition—be said to be the mind in **"the connection between the mind and all states"** when it is not an unceasing dharma and when it itself cannot act as the mind that connects with all states before and after? Clearly, those gurus' assertions do not make any sense.

Śāntideva has also mistakenly claimed that it is possible to feel and cognize without one's self-witnessing portion:

> The manner in which something is seen, heard, or cognized is not what is refuted here, but the conceptualization of its true existence, which is the cause of suffering, is rejected here.[9]

The author indicates through this statement that the conscious mind is real and indestructible. He further questions the Vijñaptimātratā School in the following way:

> If the mind were free of any apprehended object, then all beings would be Tathagatas. Thus, what good is gained by speculating that only the mind exists?[10]

This is yet another example of calling into question and refuting the doctrines of the Vijñaptimātratā School after misconstruing its true tenets.

According to the Vijñaptimātratā School, the reason sentient beings cannot free themselves from cyclic existence and transcend the three realms is that they insist that the mental consciousness—the mind of feeling and cognition—is the real and indestructible mind; therefore, it is necessary for these sentient beings to first eliminate the self-view consisting of believing that the mental consciousness is permanent and indestructible and traverses the three times. In contrast, Śāntideva claims that his Prāsaṅgika Madhyamaka School does not refute the natures of seeing, hearing, feeling, and cognition. According to him, what is refuted in the above clarification of the Dharma is the cause of all sufferings—the insistence that all phenomena truly exist (see the above passage). We can see from the above argument that Śāntideva has not yet eliminated his self-view. According to the proponents of Prāsaṅgika Madhyamaka such as Śāntideva, and Candrakīrti as well as Yinshun,

---

9   Santideva, *A guide to the bodhisattva way of life: Bodhicaryavatara*, translated from Sanskrit and Tibetan by Vesna A. Wallace and B Alan Wallace, (Snow Lion Publications Ithaca, New York, 1997), 121.
10   Ibid., 121.

and others, the Buddha has only taught about the existence of six consciousnesses. They have denied the existence of the seventh and the eighth consciousnesses, as they are totally unaware that the Buddha has implicitly and explicitly taught about the secret meanings of these two consciousnesses in the sūtras of the Three Vehicles.

Once the proponents of Prāsaṅgika Madhyamaka have denied the existence of the seventh and the eighth consciousnesses, the "remainderless nirvāṇa" that they attain is inevitably reduced to a nihilistic state. As a result, they have unwaveringly disapproved of the Buddha's negation of the conscious mind and have wholeheartedly established the teaching that **the mental consciousness has a subtle mind that is indestructible.** They adamantly disagree with the following teaching from the Buddha: "**The mental consciousness arises upon the conditions of the mental faculty and mental object; the mental consciousness is unreal and cannot traverse the three times.**" Therefore, they deliberately distorted the Buddha's tenets and misquoted the sūtras, claiming that the mental consciousness is indestructible. Consequently, they do not refute the unreal mind consisting of the mental consciousness and aspire to enter the remainderless nirvāṇa with this mind. Owing to this reason, Śāntideva states in the above passage from *A Guide to the Bodhisattva Way of Life* that what is refuted is not the cognizing nature of the mental consciousness, but only the mental consciousness' insistence that all phenomena truly exist.

Such an assertion, however, totally contradicts the Buddha's tenets. Indeed, the practice and realization of the fruition of liberation set forth by the Buddha consist of eliminating one's self-view—the belief that the mental consciousness is permanent and indestructible and traverses the three times. The Buddha has further indicated the following: "All coarse and subtle mental consciousnesses arise in dependence upon the conditions of the mental faculty and mental object." The goal of these teachings is to help disciples eliminate their self-view, which consists of believing that the mental consciousness is permanent and indestructible and traverses the three times, and subsequently help these disciples eradicate the self-attachment of their mental faculty so that they can become arhats who have transcended the delimited existence within the three realms—they will, upon death, eliminate their self consisting of the eighteen elements, leaving no element behind and leaving no opportunity for the appearance of the self in future lifetimes. This is known as the remainderless nirvāṇa, which is the true doctrine of the no-self in the Two Vehicles.

A Bodhisattva with the full mind of the First Ground can, upon death, extinguish the afflictions associated with mentation and thereby attain liberation through wisdom and enter nirvāṇa in the state of intermediate existence. As for the Bodhisattva with the full mind of the Third Ground or above, after realizing such a doctrine of the no-self, he can, upon death, extinguish the afflictions associated with mentation and thereby become the one who has attained the twofold liberation and directly enter nirvāṇa. However, to pursue their own achievement of the ultimate Path to Buddhahood and extensively benefit sentient beings, Bodhisattvas do not transcend cyclic existence through extinguishment despite their ability to enter the remainderless nirvāṇa. Instead, they make the vow of rebirth and, based on a mental consciousness and a Manas-consciousness that have both been purified through alignment [translation note: alignment with the properties of the tathagatagarbha], undergo future existences in the human world through mind-made bodies. Without ever eliminating these two purified consciousnesses, they take rebirth in the three realms in each and every life in order to advance in their cultivation of the Path to Buddhahood and benefit sentient beings, thus progressing step by step towards the Buddha Ground. In other words, instead of entering the remainderless nirvāṇa by eliminating their mental consciousness and manas-consciousness, these great Bodhisattvas take rebirth in the three realms in every life in order to learn the Buddha Dharma. The prerequisite, however, is that they must have eradicated their self-view and realized the mind of the sign of reality consisting of the eighth consciousness—the tathagatagarbha—through the practice of Prajñā-Chan; otherwise, Bodhisattvas would be no different than ordinary people—how then could there be any valid knowledge of the Buddha Dharma and fruition of liberation to speak of?

Therefore, the non-elimination and non-refutation of the mind of feeling and cognition by the Bodhisattvas of the First Ground and those with the full mind of the Third Ground and above differ drastically from the non-refutation of the mind of feeling and cognition by the proponents of Prāsaṅgika Madhyamaka (for instance, Master Yinshun as well as Tsongkhapa, the Dalai Lama, and so forth do not conform to the Buddha's teachings by separately establishing a subtle mind of the mental consciousness that is permanent and indestructible and by regarding it as the main consciousness with which sentient beings undergo cyclic existence throughout the three times). After having realized the eighth consciousness—the tathāgatagarbha—as well as all the seeds stored therein, Bodhisattvas bring forth the knowledge-of-the-aspects-of-the-path, actually witness the non-reality of the mind of feeling and cognition, and use the self consisting of the mind of feeling and cognition as a tool to practice the Buddha Dharma and to transform the self-attachment of the mental faculty—the Manas-consciousness—in order to attain the liberation fruition realized in the Three Vehicles and the knowledge-of-all-aspects of the Buddha Ground. The proponents of Prāsaṅgika Madhythea from the Gelug School have intentionally ignored the teaching from the Buddha that "the mental consciousness arises upon the conditions of the mental faculty and mental object." Instead, they hold that the mental consciousness is a permanent and indestructible dharma that exists intrinsically by itself and that this mental consciousness, contrary to the Buddha's teaching, does not arise in dependence upon the conditions of the mental faculty and mental object. This concept precisely falls within the scope of self-view and blatantly contradicts the Buddha's teachings. While those gurus have not yet eliminated their self-view, they proclaim that they have extinguished it along with self-attachment; in fact, their statements, practices, and realizations all fall within the scope of the non-Buddhist eternalism and self-view. Those gurus have not entered the doctrine of the Path of Vision of the Three Vehicles, as they are still entrapped in the self-view of non-Buddhist ordinary people. Therefore, the knowledge and views of the proponents of Prāsaṅgika Madhyamaka such as Yinshun, the Dalai Lama, Tsongkhapa, Śāntideva, Candrakirti, Atiśa, and so forth all deviate from the truth, differ drastically from the views, practices, and realizations of Bodhisattvas, and contradict the Buddha's words—the valid knowledge through the exalted teachings.

Those with such mistaken views and self-view of Prāsaṅgika Madhyamaka insist that the mental consciousness is permanent and indestructible and traverses the three times—they believe that the mental consciousness is the main consciousness that undergoes cyclic existence. Based on such non-Buddhist eternalist views, they have refuted the extremely profound knowledge-of-all-aspects propagated by the Vijñaptimātratā School, which conforms perfectly to the Buddha's tenets. They have wrongfully criticized the correct statements made by the Vijñaptimātratā School—such as "the mental consciousness is endowed with a self-witnessing portion, whereas the ālaya-consciousness is not endowed with an awareness of self-witnessing portion," and so forth—by asserting that they do not conform to the Buddha's teachings. While the Buddha has said that "the ālaya-consciousness does not have an awareness of self-witnessing portion and the mental consciousness does have such an awareness," those proponents of Prāsaṅgika Madhyamaka have inverted this correct statement by asserting that, according to the Buddha, "the mental consciousness neither has an awareness of self-witnessing portion nor a self-witnessing portion." They have, based on such an inversion, wrongfully criticized the doctrines preached by the Vijñaptimātratā School as being incorrect. The fact that the knowledge and views of the proponents of Prāsaṅgika Madhyamaka—Atiśa, Śāntideva, Yinshun, the Dalai Lama, and so forth—are the complete opposite of the truth simply reflects their limited and superficial knowledge and ignorance.

Surprisingly, those ignorant people without attainments have reprimanded the Vijñaptimātratā School in the following way, "If the mind were free of any apprehended object, then all beings would be Tathagatas. Thus, what good is gained by speculating that only the mind exists?" Clearly, those proponents of Prāsaṅgika Madhyamaka have misunderstood what the Vijñaptimātratā School meant by asserting that **"one can become an ultimate Tathagata if one's mind is free from the apprehending subject and apprehended object"**—they do not understand how the mind of feeling and cognition can realize wisdom—prajñā—when this mind is free from the apprehending subject and apprehended object, which would mean that this mind is, like inanimate objects such as wood and stone, without any function and use. Hence, they question the Vijñaptimātratā School about what the point is of thus speaking about the achievement of the ultimate Path to Buddhahood.

As a matter of fact, the Vijñaptimātratā School's statement **"one's mind is free from the apprehending subject and apprehended object"** refers to the following: Once a Bodhisattva has realized that the eighth consciousness—the ālaya mind—is primordially devoid of apprehending subject and apprehended object, he aligns his mind of feeling and cognition as well as his manas-consciousness, which is constantly making evaluations and decisions, with the intrinsic pure property of his eighth consciousness and thereby (1) eliminates the self-view consisting of holding that the mind of feeling and cognition is permanent and indestructible and (2) has no apprehension for himself as he gets rid of the self-attachment consisting of apprehending himself. He further severs all attachment to the phenomena of the three realms—thus, his mind is known as being free from the apprehending subject and apprehended object. A Bodhisattva practices in this fashion and once he has reached the Buddha Ground after going through step-by-step cultivation and is ultimately without attachment, he is known as being ultimately free from the apprehending subject and apprehended object and has therefore become a Tathagata. However, the mind of feeling and cognition on the Tathagata Ground, despite being without the slightest attachment, still distinguishes all phenomena. Therefore, the Buddhas distinguish and refute all types of erroneous views held by non-Buddhists with mistaken views in the human world, devoting their entire lives to rebut the fallacious teachings while upholding the correct ones to save sentient beings. They do not cause their minds of feeling and cognition to lose their feelings and cognition; it is not that their minds of feeling and cognition do not cognize the six sense objects.

The proponents of Prāsaṅgika Madhyamaka have misconstrued the main tenets of the Vijñaptimātratā knowledge-of-aspects, as they mistakenly believe that the Vijñaptimātratā School teaches the following: "One must cause the mind of feeling and cognition to become free from the apprehending subject and apprehended object—to never cognize the six sense objects." If this were to happen, then all Buddhas would become idiots who cannot distinguish between right and wrong and the form bodies that they manifest in the human world would not feel pain or itch. What is the point of declaring that one has achieved such Buddhahood? Such a rebuke is a rightful rebuke. In contrast, the proponents of Prāsaṅgika Madhyamaka have misconstrued the correct meaning of the knowledge-of-aspects set forth in the Vijñaptimātratā School, and have rebuked this School after misunderstanding the doctrines taught by this School and asserting the opposite of these doctrines. Such a rebuke is a wrongful rebuke. Those gurus do not even qualify as upright and wise in the mundane context, let alone being regarded as persons with attainments and wisdom in the Buddha Dharma.

Although the proponents of Prāsaṅgika Madhyamaka also advocate **the necessity to behold the emptiness-nature,** they mistakenly believe that the emptiness-nature refers to the following: "All phenomena are dependent arising and with an empty nature; the mind of feeling and cognition—the mental consciousness—that cognizes this fact is empty of shape and form and is precisely the mind of the emptiness-nature." Based on this reasoning, Śāntideva states:

> Without the mind of the emptiness-nature,
> The temporarily-extinguished afflictions will arise again,
> Just like the equipoise of non-perception,
> And therefore, one should meditate on the emptiness-nature.
> To save those who suffer from ignorance,
> Bodhisattvas abide in cycle existence with compassion and
> wisdom,
> And without cravings or fear,
> Such is the fruition of realizing emptiness.
> The aforementioned mode of the emptiness-nature,
> Should not be refuted wrongly;
> Meditate on the emptiness-nature in accordance with the
> true principle,
> And make sure you do not have any doubt.[11]

Such is the view of the emptiness-nature held by the proponents of Prāsaṅgika Madhyamaka: The fact that all phenomena beyond the confines of the mind are dependent arising and with an empty nature corresponds to the emptiness-nature; the mind of feeling and cognition is also empty of shape and form and is therefore the mind of the emptiness-nature. Śāntideva further exhorts tantric practitioners to cultivate the emptiness-nature in this fashion—to try to eliminate both the afflictive and the cognitive hindrances[12] through this practice and realization of the "emptiness-nature." However, such a practice of the Buddha Dharma thoroughly falls within the sphere of the conscious mind and has never touched in any way upon the sign of reality of the dharma-realm—the eighth consciousness (the tathāgatagarbha) and the seeds stored therein.

Through such a practice, the proponents of Prāsaṅgika

---

[11] Shantideva, *Annotation of Bodhisattvacaryāvatāra [Rupusaxing yizhu 入菩薩行譯注]*, trans. Chen Yujiao 陳玉蛟, (Zanghai Publisher 藏海出版社, 1992), 329. Translated into English from Chinese.

[12] Cognitive hindrances: Robert E. Buswell Jr. and Donald S. Lopez Jr., "jñeyāvaraṇa" in *The Princeton Dictionary of Buddhism* (NJ: Princeton University Press, 2014). Cognitive hindrance; S. *jñeyāvaraṇa*; T. *shes bya'I sgrib pa*; C. *suozhi zhang* 所知障.

Madhyamaka have precisely fallen into both the afflictive and the cognitive hindrances, but, surprisingly, they have presumptuously proclaimed that such cultivation allows them to eradicate both hindrances. To eliminate the afflictive hindrances, the top priority is to extirpate one's self-view through the recognition that the mind of feeling and cognition is dependent arising and with an empty nature and relies on others to exist, and that it has never had a permanent and indestructible nature. Those who insist that the mind of feeling and cognition is permanent and indestructible, such as the proponents of Prāsaṅgika Madhyamaka, are ordinary people with self-view—the Buddha states in the four Āgamas that such a belief constitutes the self-view of eternalist non-Buddhists. In contrast, the proponents of Prāsaṅgika Madhyamaka believe that the mind of feeling and cognition becomes the mind of the emptiness-nature after cognizing that it itself is empty of shape and form. Based on this "mind of emptiness-nature," those gurus neither fear the sufferings of cyclic existence nor crave mundane phenomena; this allows them to bring forth compassion and "wisdom" and to abide in this world to save sentient beings. Hence, it is said: "To save those who suffer from ignorance, Bodhisattvas abide in cyclic existence with compassion and wisdom and without carvings or fear; such is the fruition of realizing emptiness." However, the term "wisdom" in "compassion and wisdom" here merely refers to mundane wisdom; it does not correspond to the "mundane and supramundane" wisdom of Bodhisattvas—the wisdom based on the understanding of the eighth consciousness— the mind of emptiness-nature—as taught by the Buddha. After those gurus bring forth compassion based on a "wisdom" that is nothing but the self-view of ordinary people, they steer the sentient beings that they aim to save into such self-view; at the same time, they all commit the grievous sin of false speech by proclaiming their elimination of self-view and their realization of the mind of the emptiness-nature.

The reason why the proponents of Prāsaṅgika Madhyamaka have all fallen within the scope of the conscious mind and have mistaken this conscious mind for the mind of the emptiness-nature is because their adherence to the erroneous view of Prāsaṅgika Madhyamaka has caused them to deny the existence of the eighth consciousness and to look for another mind of the emptiness-nature. Tsongkhapa states:

> Second—thus, also in the periods during the breaks, when you have left a previous session and have not yet begun the next [session], you spend your time doing virtuous activities. So the way of [doing] that is [to do] the yoga of thoroughly purifying your enjoyments: having recollected the pride of whichever is your principal [deity], when your sense faculties are engaged with objects, you see the objects as having the nature of deities, and you visualize that they are making offerings [to your senses visualized as deities].
>
> In terms of purification in general, you should view **everything** as having the form of Vajradhara[13] who **has the nature of the intuition of nonduality**. Regarding specific purifications, you view [visual] forms as Vairochana, sounds as Akṣhobhya, scents as Ratnasambhava, tastes as Amitābha, and tangibles as Amoghasiddhi—that is the art-purification. In terms of the wisdom-purification, you view the five objects as the five goddesses such as Rūpavajrā [Matter Vajra], etc., and then you should offer [them].
>
> Moreover, conjoining [all activities] with the wisdom that does not objectify the three sectors [of an action][566]—and cultivating mindfulness of this at all times—is the art that easily perfects the two stores [of merit and intuition].[14]

Due to their inability to realize the mind consisting of the eighth consciousness, the proponents of Prāsaṅgika Madhyamaka have denied that this mind is the tathāgatagarbha and have refused to acknowledge that there exists such a mind which corresponds to

---

[13] Vajradhara: a principal deity or buddha in Tantric Buddhism; Alt. vajra-holder; S. *vajradhara*; C. *jingangchi* 金剛持.

[14] Tsong Khapa Losang Drakpa, Great Treatise on the Stages of Mantra (sngags rim chen mo): Critical Elucidation of the Key Instructions in All the Secret Stages of the Path of the Victorious Universal Lord, Great Vajradhara. Chapters XI–XII (The Creation Stages), introduction and translation by Thomas Freeman Yarnall, (AIBS, CBS & THUS, New York, 2013), 277.

the tathāgatagarbha. As a result, they have fallen into the states of the mental consciousness and have been seeking the entity of prajñā based on the various states with which the mental consciousness connects with. Therefore, they regard the "wisdom of the non-duality of bliss and emptiness" attained during the yab-yum practice as the entity of prajñā. From this concept, those gurus have derived the erroneous view that consists of pairing the five sense objects with the five Buddhas, thus falling into an erroneous view. They have, in this fashion, considered the wisdom of the non-duality of bliss and emptiness in the dharma-realm of the five sense objects to be the entity of prajñā, which is a view that differs drastically from the concept taught by the Buddha that one should regard the intrinsicality, nature, purity, and nirvāṇa of the eighth consciousness—"the mind that is not a mind", "the mind without the signs of an ordinary mind"—as the entity of prajñā. How then could those gurus' assertions be regarded as the Buddha Dharma? Furthermore, they have disparaged the correct Dharma propagated by Exoteric Buddhists and have elevated their doctrines above those of Exoteric Buddhists. The fact is that neither those gurus nor their disciples can extricate themselves from the quagmire of non-Buddhist fallacious views; how are they superior in any way?

The tantric gurus do not eliminate their self-view because they do not base their practice on the eradication of the mistaken view that the mind of feeling and cognition is permanent, everlasting, and indestructible. In addition, they do not exterminate their self-attachment because they do not base their practice on the elimination of the fallacious view that the mind of feeling and cognition is permanent, everlasting, and indestructible. Instead, they regard the act of loving others while renouncing the self as the elimination of self-attachment. Therefore, they have made the following assertion, which contradicts the Buddha's thoughts in the Dharma of the Lesser Vehicle:

> Due to habituation, there is a sense that "I" exists in the drops of blood and semen that belong to others, even though the being in question does not exist.

> Why do I not also consider another's body as myself in the same way, since the otherness of my own body is not difficult to determine?
>
> Acknowledging oneself as fault-ridden and others as oceans of virtues, one should contemplate renouncing one's self-identity and accepting others.[15]

The above statements from Śāntideva refer to the practice of switching the self and others with a loving mind towards sentient beings, a process through which one gradually eliminates self-attachment. However, our World-Honored One has taught in the Two-Vehicle Dharma that self-attachment is severed by directly observing, amidst the four deportments, that each of the eighteen elements (including the mind of feeling and cognition—the mental consciousness—and the decision-making manas-consciousness) is unreal and falsely-existing. Such elimination of self-attachment through direct observation differs from the teachings found in the Dharma-gate of the deed-contemplation of switching the self and others invented by Tibetan Buddhists. Indeed, the door of the practice of switching the self and others requires at all times the presence of the conscious mind—"the permanent and indestructible 'self' consisting of the mind of feeling and cognition"; as a result, its practitioners cannot eliminate their self-view, not to mention their self-attachment. Therefore, those gurus' statements are senseless.

In the Mahāyāna Dharma, not only must one directly observe the falsity of the two selves consisting of the mind of feeling and cognition and the decision-making manas-consciousness, but one must also directly realize the eighth consciousness and directly observe how the mind consisting of the eighth consciousness generates the first seven consciousnesses, how it generates the form body, how it generates the sentient beings' mental deeds of seeing, hearing, feeling, and cognition, as well as the relationship

---

[15] Santideva, *A guide to the bodhisattva way of life: Bodhicaryavatara,* translated from the Sanskrit and Tibetan by Vesna A. Wallace and B. Alan Wallace., 1st ed. (Snow Lion Publications, Ithaca, New York, 1997), 103.

between the eighth consciousness and various afflictive emotions. After one has extinguished one's self-view by witnessing in this fashion that the first seven consciousnesses are unreal, one must further eradicate one's self-attachment through the same direct observation, thereby bringing forth the knowledge-of-specific-aspects and the knowledge-of-all-aspects of prajñā.

There is absolutely no way that Tantric practitioners could eliminate their self-attachment through the deed-contemplation of switching the self and others. While they believe that they have severed their self-attachment, they are in fact unable to truly do so, for their method is not a correct practice of the true Buddha Dharma. The reason the proponents of the tantric Gelug School have fallen into this erroneous view is mainly that they have denied the existence of the eighth consciousness. As a result, they no longer have the causes and conditions to realize the mind consisting of the eighth consciousness and can only pursue a Buddha Dharma beyond this real mind, thus becoming non-Buddhists who seek the Dharma beyond the real mind. All Buddhist learners should be mindful of these causes and conditions, which will eventually lead to their degradation, and should, unlike those gurus, refrain from calumniating the correct Dharma of Vijñaptimātratā if they do not want to hinder their causes and conditions of realizing the wisdom of prajñā in the future.

The followers of the tantric Gelug School are entrapped in the nihilistic theory of the no-self—the theory of uncausedness—due to their denial of the eighth consciousness' existence, eventually becoming tenet holders who refute the law of cause and effect. Śāntideva claims:

> [Objection:] Without the Self, the relationship between an action and its result is not possible, for if the agent of an action has perished, who will have the result?
> [Madhyamika:] When both of us have agreed that an action and its result have different bases and that the Self has no influence in this matter, then there is no point in arguing about

this.[16]

Śāntideva holds that the mind of feeling and cognition can definitely proceed into future lifetimes, and therefore, he believes that a mode of retribution would make sense only if the mind of feeling and cognition that is the deed-performer in this lifetime undergoes the related retribution in a future lifetime. In other words, Śāntideva is unwilling to accept the mode of retribution whereby the deed-performer (conscious mind) in this lifetime cannot proceed to a future lifetime after performing a deed, and therefore, the related retribution will be borne by a brand new mental consciousness of a future lifetime. He does not know that both the manas-consciousness and the eighth consciousness—the tathāgatagarbha—will proceed into future lifetimes and will generate a brand new mental consciousness that will undergo he retribution. *Sūtra on Upāsaka Precepts [Pusa youposai jie jing 菩薩 優婆塞戒經]* speaks of such retribution as "neither self-created and self-borne nor other-created and other-borne." This means that, since the mind of feeling and cognition of this lifetime will not proceed into a future lifetime to bear the retribution of its deeds, the mind of feeling and cognition of a future lifetime that bears this retribution will have no clue as to why it is undergoing such retribution, hence the statement "neither self-created and self-borne." Nonetheless, the manas-consciousness and eighth consciousness will proceed into future lifetimes and will generate a brand new mind of feeling and cognition to receive the aforementioned retribution, hence the statement "nor other-created and other-borne." How could the proponents of Prāsaṅgika Madhyamaka comprehend and realize this correct principle when they do not even have the conditions to hear about it? How could they have the causes and conditions to realize and understand the aforementioned principle after they have denied the existence of the seventh and eighth consciousnesses thereby depriving them of the causes and conditions to realize them? All

---

[16] Ibid., 128.

Buddhist learners should remember this lesson and refrain from negating at will the dharma of the eighth consciousness—the tathagatagarbha; otherwise, such negation will inevitably become the causes and conditions that hinder their practice on the Path. This issue should by no means be taken lightly.

Tantric gurus have drastically misunderstood the truth of the emptiness-nature of prajñā, as they interpret this emptiness-nature with the statement, "all phenomena are impermanent and empty; the mind of feeling and cognition is shapeless and formless like space" :

> When all phenomena are empty in this way, what can be gained and what can be lost?
> Who will be honored or despised by whom?
> Whence comes happiness or suffering?
> What is pleasant and what is unpleasant?
> When investigated in its own nature, what is craving and for what is that craving?
> Upon investigation, what is the world of living beings, and who will really die here?
> Who will come into existence, and who has come into existence?
> Who is a relative, and who is a friend of whom?
> May those who are like me apprehend everything as being like space.[17]

These verses are quoted from "Illustration of the Real Meaning" of "Exhortation on the Practice of the Emptiness-Nature" which is found in "Bodhisattva" Śāntideva's *A Guide to the Bodhisattva Way of Life*. They regard nihilistic emptiness, a state in which all phenomena are unreal and impermanent and will eventually become empty, as the mode of the emptiness-nature of prajñā. In addition, they view the impermanence, and hence the emptiness, of one's five concealments, family, friends, and so forth as the "emptiness-nature"; hence the statement "everything as

---

17   Ibid., 148.

being like space," a state that they equate with the "emptiness-nature." Such is Śāntideva's understanding of the emptiness-nature.

The emptiness-nature set forth by the World-Honored One, however, does not refer to the impermanence, and hence emptiness, of the five concealments and all phenomena. Instead, this emptiness-nature refers to the mind of the eighth consciousness, which is intrinsically found within every sentient being. This mind is known as "emptiness-nature" for being eternally devoid of the functions of seeing, hearing, feeling, and cognition, being always free from greed and defilement, being detached from all phenomena of the three realms, and having a pure nature. The above teaching from Śāntideva about the emptiness-nature is inconsistent with the meaning of the emptiness-nature set forth by the Buddha. Such "exhortation on the practice of the emptiness-nature" and "illustration of the real meaning" do not correspond to the Buddha Dharma, because such "emptiness-nature" does not correspond to the emptiness-nature taught by the Buddha and because such "real meaning" differs from the real meaning of the Buddha Dharma.

By looking through Śāntideva's assertions in *A Guide to the Bodhisattva Way of Life*, we can clearly see that among the ten knowledges[18] of the liberation fruition, he is only able to realize the first one—the mundane knowledge.[19] He has not yet attained the dharma knowledge[20] or the subsequent knowledge[21] and is even less likely to realize the knowledge of destruction[22] or the knowledge of non-arising,[23] which are the last two of those ten knowledges. In other words, Śāntideva is only able to realize the impermanence of the form body, just like ordinary people, and remains unaware that the mind of feeling and cognition is also

---

18 Ten knowledges: S. *daśa jñānāni*; C. *shi zhi* 十智.
19 Mundane knowledge: S. *sajvrti-jñāna*; C. *shisu zhi* 世俗智.
20 Dharma knowledge: S. *dharma-jñāna*; C. *fa zhi* 法智.
21 Subsequent knowledge: S. *anvaya-jñāna*; C. *lei zhi* 類智.
22 Knowledge of destruction: S. *kṣaya-jñāna*; C. *jin zhi* 盡智.
23 Knowledge of non-arising: S. *anutpāda-jñāna*; C. *wusheng zhi* 無生智.

impermanent. He still insists that the mind of feeling and cognition is permanent and indestructible and can proceed into future lives. Therefore, although he asserts in his treatise that the five concealments of the human body are impermanent, he does not truly understand their signs of impermanence, as he holds that the consciousness aggregate (one of the five concealments) is the reality-suchness and that the sixth consciousness (the mind of feeling and cognition, which is also one of the five concealments) is a permanent and indestructible phenomenon, which means that his view is no different than that of eternalist non-Buddhists.

Śāntideva is even less likely to attain the Path of Vision in the Mahāyāna Dharma. Why is that? Because one must, in order to attain the Mahāyāna Path of Vision, realize the eighth consciousness—the tathāgatagarbha—before being able to generate the Dharma knowledge and the subsequent knowledge of the knowledge of prajñā. One must, along with these two knowledges of prajñā, generate the following knowledges pertaining to the ten knowledges of the fruition of liberation: the knowledge of suffering,[24] the knowledge of origin,[25] the knowledge of cessation,[26] the knowledge of the path,[27] and the knowledge of others' minds[28] (this should not be mistaken for the knowledge of others' mind consisting of the ability to read other people's minds). Śāntideva has not yet fulfilled these knowledges of liberation; how could an ordinary person like him, who still insists that the mental consciousness is indestructible and is therefore mired in his self-view, know anything about the subsequently-acquired knowledge of destruction or knowledge of non-arising? Someone with the a **wisdom of a lower Ground** has no clue about the **wisdoms of higher Grounds**; therefore, those who have not eliminated their self-view—who still hold that the mental consciousness is indestructible—are unable to realize and comprehend the Dharma

---

[24] Knowledge of suffering: S. *duḥkha-jñāna*; C. *ku zhi* 苦智.
[25] Knowledge of origin: S. *samudaya-jñāna*; C. *ji zhi* 集智.
[26] Knowledge of cessation: S. *nirodha-jñāna*; C. *mie zhi* 滅智.
[27] Knowledge of the path: S. *mārga-jñāna*; C. *dao zhi* 道智.
[28] Knowledge of others' minds: S. *para-citta-jñāna*; C. *taxin zhi* 他心智.

knowledge and the subsequent knowledge pertaining to the **wisdom of liberation.** Even if they had attained all ten knowledges pertaining to this sound-hearer wisdom of liberation, they still would not have the slightest clue about the knowledge-of-general-aspect of prajñā realized by the Bodhisattvas of Mahāyāna, not to mention the knowledge-of-specific-aspects and knowledge-of-aspects that are acquired after one has attained the knowledge-of-general-aspect.

Clearly, Śāntideva has neither attained the Path of Vision of Mahāthe nor has he been able to understand the Path to Liberation realized in the Two Vehicles. The cultivation and realization of the emptiness-nature depicted in his works do not exceed the scope of the first of the ten knowledges pertaining to the wisdom of liberation. Furthermore, he has not been able to realize the tathāgatagarbha and mistakenly believes that one has realized the emptiness-nature when one's sixth consciousness—the mind of feeling and cognition—can abide without distracting thoughts and without clinging to any phenomena. He has absolutely no idea what the correct meaning of the emptiness-nature taught in the prajñā sūtras is all about and mistakenly regards the mental consciousness as the mind of the emptiness-nature set forth in those sūtras. This demonstrates that his view simply remains that of an eternalist non-Buddhist and an ordinary person. It is obvious that Śāntideva has indeed never realized the eighth consciousness—ālaya—given that he has denied its existence and does not acknowledge that it truly exists. Moreover, his unawareness of the fact that the ālaya-consciousness is precisely the tathāgatagarbha—the reality-suchness of the Buddha Ground that one will attain in the future—demonstrates that he simply does not understand and has not realized the wisdom of prajñā in the Mahāyāna Buddha Dharma; he is not yet a Bodhisattva of the Seventh Abiding in the Distinct Teaching given that he has not realized the tathāgatagarbha. In addition, he is also not a Bodhisattva of the Sixth Abiding, for he has not eliminated his self-view and still regards the mind of feeling and cognition as the tathāgatagarbha. Thus, he has not cultivated the four preparatory practices[29] of Exoteric Buddhism and has therefore not eliminated his self-view. In other words, he is not a Bodhisattva of the Sixth Abiding since such a Bodhisattva must have realized the emptiness of both the apprehending-subject and the apprehended-object through the cultivation of the aforementioned four preparatory practices—the mind of feeling and cognition is precisely the mind consisting of the apprehending-subject and inevitably connects with the states of the apprehended-objects—the six sense-objects.

How could Śāntideva be blindly hailed as a Bodhisattva of the First Ground when he has realized neither the Dharma knowledge and other types of knowledge of sound-hearer nor the Dharma knowledge and other types of knowledge of Mahāyāna and has not yet entered the Bodhisattva stage of the Sixth Abiding? Furthermore, Bodhisattvas of the First Ground have partially realized the acquiescence to the non-arising of dharmas. [30] To obtain the acquiescence to the non-arising of dharmas, one must attain the knowledge-of-the-aspects-of-paths, which denotes a partial realization of the knowledge-of-all-aspects. As for the knowledge-of-the-aspects-of-paths, one attains it by progressing step by step after realizing the eighth consciousness—ālaya. Therefore, the attainments of the knowledge-of-general-aspect, the knowledge-of-specific-aspects, and the knowledge-of-all-aspects, which all pertain to the knowledge-of-aspects of prajñā, are all based on the realization of the eighth consciousness—ālaya—which acts as the cause of these attainments. How could Śāntideva have realized the eighth consciousness—ālaya—given that he has denied and does not acknowledge its existence? As someone who has not realized the eighth consciousness, he is simply unable to directly observe the functioning of the tathāgatagarbha, which implies that he cannot possibly possess the knowledge-of-general-aspect of prajñā of the Bodhisattvas of the Seventh Abiding, let alone the knowledge-of-specific-aspects or

---

29   Four preparatory practices: C. *sijiaxing* 四加行.

30   Acquiescence to the non-arising of dharmas: S. *anutpattikadharmakṣānti*; T. *mi skye ba'i chos la bzod pa*; C. *wushengfaren* 無生法忍.

even the knowledge-of-aspects. Still unaware that the secret meaning set forth in prajñā relates to the properties of the eighth consciousness, Śāntideva has denied the existence of this consciousness in his treatise and acknowledged the existence of only six consciousnesses. Furthermore, he has misapprehended the Madhyamaka of prajñā by regarding the emptiness of all phenomena as the emptiness-nature and has, based on this misconstrued view of Madhyamaka, negated the knowledge-of-aspects of the eighth consciousness—the tathāgatagarbha—which must be cultivated by all those who have truly realized Madhyamaka as they advance on the path. In addition, based on his misapprehension of the meaning of Vijñaptimātratā, he has deprecated the correct meaning of the true Vijñaptimātratā, as well as criticized and destroyed the various doctrines of the Vijñaptimātratā knowledge-of-aspects. How could he be said to have attained the Path of Vision? It does not make any sense to view him as a Bodhisattva of the First Ground when he is not even a Bodhisattva of the Seventh Abiding who has just entered the Path of Vision. Therefore, although Śāntideva's lifelong dissemination of the mistaken view of Prāsaṅgika Madhyamaka is reputed as the propagation of the true Dharma, he has in essence been destroying the correct Dharma due to his adherence to the erroneous view of Prāsaṅgika Madhyamaka.

Śāntideva was not the only proponent of Prāsaṅgika Madhyamaka. For instance, Atiśa also believes that the view of Madhyamaka consists of regarding all phenomena as being dependent arising and with an empty nature after having denied the existence of the tathāgatagarbha. He said the following in *The Quintessence of Madhyamaka [Zhongguan yaojue 中觀要訣]*:

> 1. Fundamental view of Madhyamaka: We must first understand that, conventionally and from the perspective of short-sighted ordinary people, all phenomena—all establishments such as cause and effect and so forth—are as real as they appear. However, ultimately or from the viewpoint of reality, all phenomena that appear conventionally are unobtainable even for the minimal quantity of one percent of

a hair tip, if we analyze them through every great correct cause.

2. Contemplative practice: Subsequently, sit on a comfortable meditation cushion in the crossed-legged sitting posture [original note: and practice the following contemplation]: There are two types of compounded phenomena: forms and non-forms. Among those, forms are aggregates of extremely tiny particles.[31] Furthermore, if one analyzes them with the division method of parts, then there will be nothing left, not even the tiniest substance. Non-forms refer to the mind and are as follows: The past mind has ceased and perished; the future mind has not yet arisen; and the current mind is in this way extremely difficult to observe: It is shapeless and formless, is a nothingness like space, is free from singularity and plurality for some reason, is non-arising for some reason, is the natural clear light for some reason, and so forth. If we observe and analyze this mind through the sharp tool of the correct reasoning, we will understand that it is not established. . . .

3. Practicing the non-conceptualizing wisdom at the fundamental stage: Eliminate all faults such as drowsiness, restlessness, and so forth. During the intervals in which there is neither drowsiness nor restlessness, the mental consciousness should neither proceed to any ideation nor cling to any image—it should eliminate all mindfulness and mental applications. Try your best to ensure that your mental consciousness abides in this state before the enemy or the robber consisting of image or conceptuality emerges.

4. Practicing illusion-like virtues at the stage of subsequent attainment: If you wish to exit from meditative stabilization, get up slowly after releasing your cross-legged posture and perform, with an illusion-like mindset, as many virtuous deeds of body, speech, and mind as possible.

5. The benefits of practicing emptiness: Those with

---

31 Robert E. Buswell Jr. and Donald S. Lopez Jr., "paramāṇu" in *The Princeton Dictionary of Buddhism* (NJ: Princeton University Press, 2014). Particle: S. *paramāṇu*; T. *rdul phra rab*; C. *jiwei/weichen* 極微/微塵.

wholesome faculties who practice in this fashion respectfully, incessantly, and for an extended period of time will witness the truth in this lifetime and will manifestly realize the following: "All phenomena are similar to the moon disc in the sky; one can attain the siddhi without striving and without practicing diligently."

6. Attaining Buddhahood through the path: What is obtained (original note: the wisdom of subsequent attainment) after exiting from this (original note: fundamental meditative stabilization) is the understanding that all phenomena are illusion-like and so forth. After manifestly realizing the vajra meditative stabilization, one will no longer possess the wisdom of subsequent attainment and will abide in the state of samahita—meditative equipoise—at all times. Otherwise, what difference would there be between (original note: Buddhas) and Bodhisattvas? The related teachings will not be expounded here.[32]

As far as the true Madhyamaka is concerned, the four Āgamas, the prajñā sūtras of the second turning of the Dharma Wheel, and the Vijñaptimātratā sūtras of the third turning of the Dharma Wheel all regard the Middle-Way natures of the tathāgatagarbha as the main entity of the view of the Middle Way. The so-called prajñā consists of engaging in deed-contemplation based on the natures of the Middle Way of the eighth consciousness— tathāgatagarbha—as well as realizing and understanding these natures. The fulfillment of the knowledge-of-all-aspects is also based on the realization and comprehension of all the seeds stored in the eighth consciousness—tathāgatagarbha.

In contrast, Atiśa regards the "direct observation" that the five aggregates and so forth are empty as the realization of the emptiness-nature. In addition, he has misapprehended the five concealments, as he views the fact that the mental consciousness

---

[32] Chen Yujiao 陳玉蛟 (ed.), *Adixia yu putidao dengshi* 阿底峽與菩提道燈釋 *[Atiśa and Commentary on the Lamp for the Path to Enlightenment]* (Dongchu Publisher 東初出版社, 1991), 281-82. Translated into English from Chinese.

(the mind of feeling and cognition)—which is a component of the concealment of consciousness—is empty of shape and form as the emptiness-nature. As such, he is not truly able to directly observe that the five concealments are impermanent and therefore empty. In fact, in the sūtras of the Three Vehicles, the Buddha speaks of this emptiness as the "emptiness-signs" of the five concealments— the fact that the five concealments are dependent arising and have therefore an empty nature—and regards the mind consisting of the eighth consciousness as the emptiness-nature. The reasons are as follows: The mental consciousness—the mind of feeling and cognition—is an unreal consciousness that arises in dependence upon other dharmas; the prajñā sūtras state that the mental consciousness is a phenomenon with signs; and the mental consciousness connects with the six sense objects. Moreover, the four Āgamas even assert that the mental consciousness—the mind of feeling and cognition—is the "permanent and indestructible mind" set forth by the eternalist non-Buddhists. The fact that Atiśa regards the mental consciousness' emptiness of shape and form as the indestructible emptiness-nature demonstrates that Atiśa has not yet eliminated his self-view and has not realized the eighth consciousness—the ālaya. This proves that he has not attained the meritorious quality related to the Path of Vision in any of the Buddha Dharma of the Three Vehicles and that he is still at the stage of the Fifth Abiding of the Distinct Teaching and has not attained the validation of the emptiness of both the apprehending-subject and the apprehended-object—a realization of the Bodhisattvas of the Sixth Abiding.

Furthermore, Atiśa believes that one has attained the fundamental meditative concentration if one is able to achieve the state of thoughtlessness in sitting meditation and abide therein without torpor and restlessness and without being mindful of any phenomena. He equates this meditative concentration with the definite wisdom in the fundamental non-conceptual wisdom, which is a clear misapprehension of the correct meaning of the fundamental non-conceptual wisdom in the Buddha Dharma. In fact, one attains the fundamental non-conceptual wisdom in the

Buddha Dharma only by realizing the eighth consciousness and by directly seeing that, in all conditions consisting of various states, it functions spontaneously according to various conditions and without conceptualizing. It is only by abiding in this definite view unwaveringly and without any doubt that one can be said to have attained the fundamental meditative concentration—the fundamental meditative concentration of the non-conceptual wisdom is not achieved by keeping the mental consciousness—the mind of feeling and cognition—immobile.

Atiśa further believes that one attains the **vajra meditative concentration** by reaching the state of thoughtlessness in sitting meditation. According to him, if one is able, post-meditation, to observe that all phenomena are illusion-like, to dismiss all wisdoms such that **one no longer possesses even the wisdom of subsequent attainment**, and to thus abide post-mediation without conceptualizing any phenomena, then one will be abiding in the state of meditative equipoise, which means that one has achieved the ultimate Path to Buddhahood. However, the practitioners who have attained such a state have never been able to eradicate the self view into which eternalist non-Buddhist's have fallen, for they have always considered the mental consciousness to be the indestructible mind of the emptiness-nature and have never been capable of realizing the eighth consciousness. One who has not realized the eighth consciousness is unable to understand the knowledge-of-general-aspect of prajñā, not to mention the knowledge-of-specific-aspects of prajñā or the knowledge-of-all-aspects of prajñā. It does not make any sense to proclaim one's attainment of the Path to Buddhahood when one does not comprehend and has not realized the knowledge-of-all-aspects. The entity of the wisdom of prajñā consists of the non-conceptual nature, the Middle-Way nature, and the nirvana nature of the eighth consciousness; no deed-contemplation of the mode of the Middle-Way is possible outside the context of the eighth consciousness.

Not only did the fundamental non-conceptual wisdom of the

Path of Vision stay with all the Buddhas and Bodhisattvas after they had entered this Path in the Causal Stage, but those Buddhas and Bodhisattvas kept, during the Stage of the Path of Cultivation—which follows the Path of Vision—this fundamental non-conceptual wisdom, which they had attained upon entering the Path of Vision, and also maintained this wisdom of the Path of Vision throughout all the Stages that take place after the start of Path of Cultivation, including after the achievement of Buddhahood, thus allowing the fundamental non-conceptual wisdom of the Path of Vision to coexist without conflict with the non-conceptual wisdom of subsequent attainment obtained from the Path of Cultivation. This contradicts Atiśa's assertion that **if one no longer possesses even the wisdom of subsequent attainment** and thus abides post-meditation without conceptualizing any phenomena, then one will be abiding in the state of meditative equipoise, which means that one has achieved the ultimate Path to Buddhahood.

If the dwelling of all Buddhas and Bodhisattvas in the meritorious quality of the Buddha Ground were determined, as claimed by Atiśa, by whether they abide in the state of meditative equipoise, then all Buddhas and Bodhisattvas would sometimes be Buddhas and Bodhisattvas and other times ordinary people, depending on whether they abide in the state of meditative equipoise of Chan concentration. If the Buddhist Dharma were as taught by Atiśa, then the view, meditation, conduct, and fruition of Buddhism would not be in any way valuable for the following reasons: Such view, meditation, conduct, and fruition would be identical to the methods of concentration cultivated by non-Buddhists; those who "have become Buddhas" would not be Buddhas forever; the Bodhisattvas who have reached the "stages of the Path of Vision and the Path of Cultivation" would not always be Bodhisattvas of those stages; their possession of the fundamental wisdom and the wisdom of subsequent attainment would be determined by whether they abide in meditative equipoise; and their dwelling in the wisdom of Buddhahood would also hinge on whether they abide in the state of meditative equipoise. Hence, I hereby state that Atiśa's statement is egregiously mistaken. Whether all Buddhas and Bodhisattvas abide in the state of meditative equipoise, the fundamental non-conceptual wisdom and the non-conceptual wisdom of subsequent attainment that they have attained will appear at all times and without interruption whenever their mental consciousness manifests; not abiding in the state of meditative equipoise will not prevent those two wisdoms from arising, and abiding in the state of meditative equipoise after "becoming Buddhas" will not cause those Buddhas to **no longer possess even the wisdom of subsequent attainment.**

The reason why the proponents of Prāsaṅgika Madhyamaka attain nothing from their assiduous practice and therefore have no choice but to negate the tathāgatagarbha—the eighth consciousness—and the sūtras of the third turning of the Dharma Wheel, fall into non-Buddhist erroneous views, and commit the hell-destined sins of grievous false speech and destroying the correct Dharma is because of their negation of the eighth consciousness from the onset; they do not believe in the Buddha's statements about the existence of the eighth consciousness, are unaware that the Buddha has taught about such an existence in the sūtras of the three turnings of the Dharma Wheel, and do not understand that, with respect to the Path of Vision of the Great Vehicle taught by the Buddha, the contents of this Path consist of the realization of the eighth consciousness—the tathāgatagarbha. Instead, they mistakenly believe that the contents of the Path of Vision and the Path of Cultivation involve remaining thoughtless after entering and abiding in meditative concentration and experiencing the view and understanding that the mind of feeling and cognition and the state of meditative concentration where this mind abides are "neither identical nor distinct." As a result, not only have those erroneous statements from Atiśa persisted until today, but the gurus and learners of Tantric Buddhism all regard the ability of the mind of feeling and cognition to abide in a state of thoughtlessness as the realization of the fundamental non-conceptual wisdom and consider the attainment of this state followed by the ability to cognize, post-meditation, all phenomena without clinging to any of them to be the obtention of the non-conceptual wisdom of subsequent attainment. In the above teaching, Atiśa further equates the state devoid of all feelings, cognition, and conceptualizations with the state of Buddhahood and therefore he believes that **one has achieved the ultimate fruition of Buddhahood** if one abides in the state of meditative equipoise and thereby **no longer possesses even the wisdom of subsequent attainment**. Due to this erroneous view, which consists of not knowing that the natures of the eighth consciousness constitute the entity of the wisdom of prajñā, those tantric gurus negate the Dharma of the Vijñaptimātratā knowledge-of-aspects as well as the eighth consciousness and therefore practice the Buddha Dharma outside the context of the eighth consciousness and become followers who seek the Dharma outside the context of the mind, and even commit the great sin of grievous false speech. How pitiful! All wise learners should absolutely refrain from emulating them if they do not wish to hinder their own cultivation path and suffer from excruciating retribution in future lives.

Atiśa is not the only one who has negated the seventh and the eighth consciousnesses; Tsongkhapa, a Tibetan tantric proponent of Prāsaṅgika Madhyamaka, also asserts that the "wisdom" of the yab-yum practice is the entity of the Dharma and that the seventh and the eighth consciousnesses are therefore unnecessary:

> Both the support and what is supported are purified; Yoga Tantra teaches that dharmas of meritorious quality such as faith and so forth are purified. Highest Yoga Tantra professes that both the path and the aggregates and so forth are purified. In order to negate the erroneous attachment to the support and what is supported, such as the attachment to the distinct entities of animate beings and inanimate objects that are not yet purified, the palace is said to be purified. In order to negate the erroneous attachment to the distinct entities of the deities, the heaven is said to be purified. In this fashion, bring forth the signs of maṇḍala of the support and of what is

supported (the signs of maṇḍala belonging to the pudendum of the support and of what is supported) solely in dependence upon the portion of the signs of the main deity's wisdom. There is no entity to speak of beyond these signs of maṇḍala; therefore, wisdom constitutes the entity of them all (the wisdom of the non-duality of bliss and emptiness experienced during the yab-yum practice constitutes the entity of all those wisdoms). [33]

Thus, after establishing the purity of the aggregate of forms, the mind of feeling and cognition, the Path of Desire, the observed palace, the observed deities, the maṇḍala of the ḍākinī used in the co-practice (the maṇḍala of the consort's lower body), and so forth, practitioners must regard the wisdom of the non-duality of bliss and emptiness experienced in the yab-yum practice as the entity of prajñā. In this fashion, they will be able to attain Buddhahood in their current bodies based on the non-duality of bliss and emptiness; such is the establishment of the tantric Dharma-gate of practice of the Fruition Ground that allows for the achievement of the ultimate Buddhahood in one's current body. While this method is in fact based on erroneous thinking, the tantric gurus use it to disparage the Exoteric Buddhist Dharma-gate, which consists of real practices and attainments of the path, as being composed of inferior doctrines of the Causal Ground. What an utter inversion of the truth!

Tsongkhapa views the seventh and the eighth consciousnesses as unnecessary given that he regards the bliss of the yab-yum practice as the true nature of the Dharma. Such an assertion can be seen in many different places throughout his writings. Let's cite another example to prove this fact. Tsongkhapa says in *The Great Exposition of Secret Mantra [Mizong daocidi guanglun 密宗道次第廣論]*:

Abandon in this fashion the left and the right winds and cause it to enter the central channel[34] and to remain motionless,

---

[33] Tsongkhapa, *Mizong daocidi guang lun 密宗道次第廣論*, 393. Translated into English from Chinese.

[34] Central channel: S. *avadhūtī*; T. *rtsa dbu ma*; C. *afudi/zhongmai* 阿嚩底 / 中脈.

thereby perfecting the functions of vitality.[35] After that, one should practice withholding because it is only through withholding that one can achieve the goal of "firmly stabilizing the fruition of non-vitality in the central channel." Next, if the wind enters and abides in the central channel, then rely on the fierce yoga power of subsequent mindfulness to ignite a scorching fire and dissolve the realms (dissolve the seeds—semen); cause these realms to descend to the vajra tip (the glans penis) without discharging them (without ejaculating), and achieve the innate, immutable, and wondrous bliss (the innate, immutable, and wondrous bliss of the fourth joy can be achieved through this descent and withholding of ejaculation). . . . Dissolve the mind of enlightenment (dissolve the material mind of enlightenment—semen) and withhold it without ejaculating to practice the immutable wondrous bliss. Through the sixth branch, the forms that result from the cultivation of the first two branches naturally become the bodies of empty forms of the father and the mother in the heaven of the desire realm; attain the immutable bliss through the Mahāmudrā of subsequent love (withhold ejaculation at the glans penis and cultivate the sexual pleasure consisting of the ultimate bliss of the fourth joy) and gradually enhance it (gradually enhance the bliss by practicing eight dual hours a day). At last, extinguish all coarse aggregates of forms and so forth; your body will become a vajra body of empty forms (through this practice of visualization, the form body becomes a phenomenon of empty forms without physicality and is known as a vajra body) and your mind will become the immutable wondrous bliss (the mind of feeling and cognition will become a mind of immutable wondrous bliss consisting of the ultimate bliss of the fourth joy); you will abide in the real nature of Dharma at all times and will attain the body of the union (you will abide in the "real nature" of the "Dharma" in this fashion at all times—you will dwell in this property of the ultimate bliss that allows you to take in this fourth joy—this is known as attaining the body of the union of

---

35   Vitality: Alt. life force, life faculty; S. *jīvita/jīvitendriya*; T. *srog/ srog gi dbang po*; C. *ming gen/mingli* 命根/命力.

emptiness and bliss).[36]

The **Tantric Path** taught by Tsongkhapa in the above passage consists of the path to "the achievement of Buddhahood in one's current body," of which Tantric Buddhists are extremely proud. Its content is as follows: Once a tantric practitioner has successfully visualized a deity's divine body, he should further visualize the image of this divine body embracing a female consort and enjoying sexual pleasure while copulating with her. After the completion of this visualization, he should practice the visualization of channels[37] and drops,[38] the vase breathing technique, and the inner fire.[39] Subsequently, based on his skills of the vase breathing technique and of the inner fire, he should visualize that the white mind of enlightenment (white drops) at the crown cakra[40] dissolves (drips down) and descends into the vajra tip (descends into the glans penis), inducing sexual pleasure. The practitioner must withhold ejaculation while he takes in the pleasure; this will enable him to enhance this sexual bliss and to take it in for a long stretch of time—Tsongkhapa stipulates that "one must engage in this practice eight dual hours a day." When one practices in this fashion and reaches the point where one is able to take the bliss in permanently without ever ejaculating, one has attained the non-leakage (uncontamination) of the mind of enlightenment, which is known as the realization of "uncontamination," the achievement of the "fruition of liberation." By observing in such "uncontaminated meditative concentration" that the sexual pleasure is permanent and immutable, one realizes that this bliss is the immutable great bliss. By thus visualizing that the divine bodies of the father and the mother meditational deities fuse with one's own body and take sexual pleasure in for a long stretch of time and without regression,

---

36 Tsongkhapa, *Mizong daocidi guang lun* 密宗道次第廣論, 564. Translated into English from Chinese.
37 Channel: S. *nāḍī;* T. *rtsa;* C. *mai* 脈.
38 Drop: S. *bindu;* T. *thig le;* C. *mingdian* 明點.
39 Inner fire: Alt. inner heat, psychic heat, fierce woman; S. *caṇḍālī;* T. *gtum mo;* C. *zhantuoli/ zhuohuo/dantian huo* 旃陀利/拙火/丹田火.
40 Cakra: also spelled as "chakra" and is commonly translated as "wheel" in the context of Tantric Buddhism; T. *'khor lo;* C. *lun* 輪.

one attains "the Mahāmudrā of subsequent love—one obtains the immutable wondrous bliss."

If one can, through the assiduous cultivation of the aforementioned yab-yum practice, gradually enhance the sexual pleasure, forever abide (abide for a long stretch of time) in the aforementioned state in which one takes in the bliss without ejaculating and ensure that the utmost sexual bliss of orgasm remains uninterrupted, then one has attained the "immutable wondrous bliss." In other words, "[one's] mind [has] become the immutable wondrous bliss; [one abides] in the real nature of Dharma at all times and [has attained] the body of the union," meaning that one has achieved the "ultimate Path to Buddhahood." One who has realized such a form body of wondrous bliss of union has attained the fruition of the reward body Buddha set forth in Tantrism—all reward body Buddhas in Tantrism have the reward of taking bliss in through the yab-yum copulation between a male and a female— meaning that one has become an "ultimate Buddha." For this reason, the tantric Dharma-gate of practice is said to be a method that allows for the "attainment of Buddhahood on the Fruition Ground."

The above passage proves that Tsongkhapa, a proponent of Prāsaṅgika Madhyamaka, regards the immutable great sexual bliss consisting of the sexual pleasure between a male and a female as the entity of wisdom, and therefore, he does not need the eighth consciousness to act as the entity of the "prajñā of the Buddha Dharma" that he has attained. As a result, he has negated the mind consisting of the eighth consciousness, does not acknowledge that this mind truly exists, and has intentionally misinterpreted the Buddha's words in the Vijñaptimātratā sūtras of the third turning of the Dharma Wheel, falsely claiming the following: "The Buddha's statement about the existence of the eighth consciousness is just an expedient means; it does not truly mean that there exists a mind consisting of the eighth consciousness." Such misrepresentations of the Buddha's words in the scriptures can be seen throughout Tsongkhapa's publications, most notably in *Illumination of the Thought: An Extensive Explanation of Chandrakirti's "Supplement* to the 'Middle Way'" [Ru zhonglun shanxian miyi shu 入中論善顯密意疏], which contains distorted statements in almost every single page, followed by *Essence of Eloquence on the Provisional and Definitive [Bian liaobuliaoyi shanshun zanglun 辨了不了義善說藏論]* and *The Great Exposition of Secret Mantra [Mizong daocidi guanglun]*, where distorted statements appear frequently, although not in every page.

Tsongkhapa not only regards the sexual pleasure experienced during the yab-yum practice as the intrinsic entity of the emptiness-nature, but sometimes he also views the drops that result from visualization as the emptiness-nature set forth in the prajñā sūtras, calling them "limit of reality." As a result, the proponents of Prāsaṅgika Madhyamaka are able to establish their theory of the "Buddha Dharma" without the seventh and eighth consciousnesses:

> The mode of withdrawing (the illusionary body) into the clear light is as set forth in *A Lamp to Illuminate the Five Stages*:[41]
> (Cause the visualized white drops at the crown to travel) from the head to the foot, traveling as far as the heart, the yogi **entering the limit of perfection** is known as held-as-a-whole. The animate and the inanimate at first become the clear light (of the drops), after which, in similar fashion, is the subsequent dissolution. Just as breath dissolves on a mirror, likewise the yogi **enters, again and again, the limit of perfection.**[42] . . .
> This treatise has a similar teaching. Therefore, what evolves without distinction with the five-colored wind is the mind's empty drops (the drops). Given that wind, fire, water, and so forth arise from them (the drops) during birth, they must return into them (the drops) during withdrawal. The mode whereby one enters the clear light of samādhi (the clear light

---

[41] Tsongkhapa, *Mizong daocidi guang lun* 密宗道次第廣論, 555. Translated into English from Chinese.

[42] Je Tsongkhapa, *A Lamp to Illuminate the Five Stages: Teachings on Guhyasamāja Tantra*, ed. Thupten Jinpa, trans. Gavin Kilty (Boston: Wisdom Publication, 2013), 453.

of the drops) after having practiced the three-stacked sattva in concordance with the purified things conforms to what is asserted in the Ārya tradition.[43]

Tsongkhapa has thus established the visualized drops as the limit of perfection [also rendered as "limit of reality"] of the "prajñā" of the Buddha Dharma. In other words, those who frequently enter and abide in the states of the drops are yogis; furthermore, frequently entering and abiding in the states of the drops without observing external phenomena is **entering again and again the limit of perfection.** Given that the proponents of Prāsaṅgika Madhyamaka have established the drops as the true mind of enlightenment, it is not necessary for them to cultivate and realize the eighth consciousness—the ālaya mind—set forth by the Buddha; in fact, they equate the realization of the drops with the realization of the "ālaya-consciousness." Once they have thus established the drops as the ālaya-consciousness, they claim that the ālaya-consciousness set forth by the Buddha is an establishment, an expedient teaching, as there is not truly a mind called ālaya-consciousness, and that therefore, the teaching about the eighth consciousness is merely an expediency. Such is asserted by all the proponents of Prāsaṅgika Madhyamaka, the most elevated Dharma-gate within Tantric Buddhism. If anyone expresses the view—which differs from theirs—that, based on the Buddha's teachings, the eighth consciousness is precisely the tathāgatagarbha, the entity of prajñā, they will assail this person and even exterminate him (for instance, after wrongfully denouncing the Jonang School as a non-Buddhist destroyer of the Buddha Dharma, they misrepresented the Jonang School's doctrines before exterminating this lineage). How could those people be called Buddhist practitioners when they have, due to their incapacity to realize the mind consisting of the eighth consciousness, intentionally misinterpreted the Buddha's tenets in the sūtras and have separately established the contact and

---

[43] Tsongkhapa, *Mizong daocidi guang lun* 密宗道次第廣論, 555. Translated into English from Chinese.

sensation of sexual pleasure and the drop as the mind of enlightenment in order to replace the esoteric Dharma-gate of practice found in the original Buddha Dharma? Therefore, the tantric Prāsaṅgika Madhyamaka is just an erroneous view based on the theory of uncausedness, a non-Buddhist doctrine that has replaced the ālaya-consciousness of the Buddha Dharma with the visualized drops.

Tsongkhapa, who is a proponent of Prāsaṅgika Madhyamaka, has wrongly proclaimed in his *The Great Exposition of Secret Mantra [Mizong daocidi guanglun]* that the sexual pleasure consisting of the fourth joy is the immutable wondrous bliss and that one can eliminate one's self-view and self-attachment through the cultivation of sexual pleasure in the yab-yum practice. As a result, tantric followers practice the Buddha Dharma beyond the Path to Liberation and the Path to the Enlightenment of Buddhahood set forth by the Buddha and advocate that the sexual pleasure experienced during the yab-yum practice is an immutable and indestructible dharma and that the "wondrous bliss" experienced amidst the sexual pleasure consisting of the fourth joy is the entity of prajñā. Hence, it is not necessary for them to regard the tathāgatagarbha set forth by the Buddha as the entity of prajñā.

Based on the erroneous views of Prāsaṅgika Madhyamaka, Tsongkhapa holds that the aforementioned cultivation of sexual pleasure also allows one to attain the fruition of Buddhahood and fulfill the wisdom of Madhyamaka:

> The word "immutable" in "immutable wondrous bliss" does not imply that it cannot be generated by causes and conditions. The previous paragraphs have repeatedly stated that the discharge of basic constituents (the term "basic constituent" in Tantrism refers to the semen seed) is called disintegration; hence, such **binding of basic constituents without leakage** (such binding of the semen seeds without leakage) is called **immutable**. The bliss generated from this practice does not refer to the generation, through the binding of basic constituents in the body, of the blissful sensation of the body from the "pleasant contact" within the body, nor does it

correspond to the blissful sensation pertaining to the mind's agreeable signs of uninterrupted-conditions, nor does it point to the non-conceptual meditative concentration induced by blissful sensation. Instead, it is **the wondrous bliss of thoroughly understanding reality** (the real wondrous bliss obtained from thoroughly understanding the skill of never ejaculating—such a skill enables one to abide permanently in the great bliss) **that arises from (1) the right view consisting of thoroughly understanding that all phenomena are natureless as a direct-cause-condition, and (2) binding basic constituents without leaking them as a contributory-condition** (binding the semen seeds without leaking them as a contributory-condition). For this reason, this sūtra says that contrary to the empty form, **bliss cannot be attained** [translaton note: It cannot be attained because it is innate]. As stated in Chapter 5 of *The Great Explanatory Notes [Dashu 大疏]*:"Emptiness refers to the fact that all phenomena are neither arising nor ceasing and are manifested by one's own mind; wisdom points to the realization of its immutable bliss." This teaching shows a thorough understanding of the fact that, **based on the meaning of reality, empty forms are empty of the nature of arising-and-ceasing and the nature of non-abiding is the immutable bliss**. . . . The assertion that self-attachment constitutes the basis of cyclic existence is a common knowledge of Mahāyāna and Hīnayāna as well as of Exoteric Buddhism and Esoteric Buddhism. Therefore, the assertion that realizing the wisdom of no-self allows one to eliminate the basis of the bounds of cyclic existence is the most obvious. Hence, Chapter 4 of *The Great Explanatory Notes [Dashu]* states: "Next, one should be mindful of the three bases, namely generating the great mind of enlightenment, having a pure zeal, and eliminating the attachment to the self and the belongings of the self." This assertion constitutes a path that can help eliminate self-attachment, given that realizing the wisdom of no-self constitutes the basis of the path. In addition, it is said that the proponents of Madhyamaka cultivate the immutable non-dual wisdom also through the door of the two no-selves.[44]

According to Tsongkhapa, if tantric male practitioners can, amidst the sexual pleasure of the yab-yum practice, abide permanently in the highest orgasm of blissful contact without discharging the basic constituents in their bodies (Tantric followers have borrowed the term "basic constituent"—seed—from the Vijñaptimātratā teachings; in this context, "basic constituent" means "seed" and refers to the male's semen), then they can maintain their erection and permanently dwell in the bliss of contact amidst the sexual pleasure consisting of the fourth joy. According to Tsongkhapa, this bliss is precisely the immutable bliss—this type of blissful sensation is not one of those impermanent and mutable pleasures and is therefore called immutable bliss. Furthermore, Tsongkhapa believes that one is able to eliminate one's self-view and self-attachment by abiding for a long stretch of time in the tactile perception of sexual pleasure without ejaculating, by observing that the divine body that one has visualized is devoid of coarse physical forms and hence is empty of its own nature, and by further observing that "the immutable blissful sensation" of sexual contact can arise in a state that is empty of forms and that the mind of feeling and cognition amidst this blissful sensation is non-abiding—detached from all phenomena.

Such statements are based on forceful and unreasonable argumentation. No blissful sensation of sexual contact is possible beyond the impermanent coarse form body in the desire realm. Furthermore, without such a coarse form body, it is also impossible to achieve the practices of the divine body, of the drops in the central channel, and of the vase breathing technique. Indeed, the minds of feeling and cognition of the sentient beings in the desire realm could not even manifest if those sentient beings were without their impermanent coarse form bodies; how then would the central channel and drop within their bodies, the vase

---

44   Ibid., 565-66.

breathing technique, and the visualized divine body be in any way attainable? How could there be any "wondrous bliss of empty forms" or "permanent" and immutable bliss to speak of? What an utter inversion of the truth!

Don't the tantric practitioners find it too exhausting to strive to permanently abide in the aforementioned way in the wondrous bliss of sexual contact and enjoy the blissful contact generated by constantly embracing a woman? How could this pleasure be called the bliss of liberation? How could those practitioners proclaim themselves to be without any attachment when such clinging to the permanent and non-regressive characteristic of the blissful contact is precisely an attachment to the phenomenon of the blissful contact experienced on the five sense objects, an evidence that they are bound by the love for the desire realm? How could they eliminate their self-view and self-attachment by negating or exterminating their self consisting of the mind of feeling and cognition when they still hold onto the tangible object beyond their minds of feeling and cognition? How could they eliminate their self-view when they do not even know that they are thus entrapped in it? How could they claim to be able to sever their self-attachment through sexual pleasure when they cannot even eliminate their self-view? How could Tsongkhapa be considered to be a great practitioner when his assertions are the opposite of the truth and when he firmly holds onto and does not get rid of his self-view and self-attachment? How could the tantric followers hail him as "the Most Honorable"?

The proponents of Prāsaṅgika Madhyamaka have negated the eighth consciousness and believe that the emptiness-nature consists of **"the emptiness of all phenomena as well as the fact that the mind of feeling and cognition is without the coarse shapes and forms of the human world and is therefore empty."** This concept has caused Buddhist disciples to mistake the mental consciousness for the real mind and has helped establish the theory of the yab-yum practice set forth in Highest Yoga Tantra—the method whereby the mind of feeling and cognition connects with sexual contact and remains permanent and indestructible. As a result, the proponents of Prāsaṅgika Madhyamaka do not need to regard the eighth consciousness as the entity of prajñā. In this fashion, thinking that they have overcome the predicament of inevitably veering into nihilistic emptiness due to their negation of the eighth consciousness, tantric practitioners have been extensively propagating the Path of Desire of the yab-yum practice and have been destroying the originally pure Buddhism. These egregious faults can all be ascribed to Prāsaṅgika Madhyamaka. In fact, anyone can directly witness the easily-arising and easily-ceasing characteristic of the mind of feeling and cognition, for it temporarily ceases when one falls into a deep sleep every night and disappears in the states of unconsciousness, thorough death, absorption of non-perception, and absorption of cessation. Hence, establishing the mind of feeling and cognition as a permanent and indestructible dharma entails various mistakes and was in fact extensively refuted and identified long ago as a non-Buddhist view of eternalism by the Buddha in the four Āgamas long ago. Therefore, Tsongkhapa's establishment of the mind of feeling and cognition as the indestructible mind of the emptiness-nature in the dharma-realm, the drops as the ālaya-consciousness, and the sexual pleasure consisting of the fourth joy as the entity of prajñā contradict the Buddha's sacred teachings as well as the mundane truth known to all; therefore, such establishment from Tsongkhapa does not correspond to any correct doctrine.

For instance, Tsongkhapa speaks about the emptiness-nature in the following manner:

> Furthermore, in the generation stage, when you gradually withdraw the animate and the inanimate into the emptiness-nature, extinguish all coarse states such as color and so forth and clearly abide in mind-only. Subsequently, exit from this meditative concentration; you will be able to manifest the divine body as well as the pure and the unhindered even

without mental application. [45]

Tsongkhapa's view and knowledge are clearly reflected in the above teaching. With respect to all the phenomena that one has visualized—divine body, drops, and so forth—one must, at last, visualize that they enter the moon disc after being dissolved; furthermore, one must dissolve the moon disc and so forth and cause it to enter the mind of feeling and cognition; this is called "withdrawing the animate and the inanimate into the emptiness-nature." Next, only the self consisting of the mind of feeling and cognition subsists, abiding alone without moving and without observing any phenomena with images; this is called "dwelling in the state of mind-only." However, these contents all consist of various states of the conscious mind and do not correspond to the correct doctrine, taught by the Buddha in the Mahāyāna sūtras, "all three realms are mind-only." Indeed, in those tantric contents, the mental consciousness—the mind of feeling and cognition—is regarded as the permanent and indestructible mind, whereas in the Buddha's teaching, "all three realms are mind-only," the mind refers to the eighth consciousness—the tathāgatagarbha. Hence, the aforementioned view of Prāsaṅgika Madhyamaka is precisely the view of eternalist non-Buddhists. Nowadays, however, the mind of feeling and cognition set forth in the view of eternalist non-Buddhists held by the Prāsaṅgika School—a view which has been propagated by Tsongkhapa and inherited by Yinshun—is widely identified by exoteric and esoteric learners as the true mind. In light of the difficulties to rectify this erroneous view, the current era is said to be the Dharma-ending age.

The Buddha's statements in the sūtras of the Three-Vehicles about the fact that all phenomena are empty are all based on one important premise: **All phenomena are said to be dependent arising and with an empty nature in dependence upon the eighth consciousness.** In the four Āgamas, which are mainly about the

---

45   Tsongkhapa, *Mizong daocidi guang lun* 密宗道次第廣論, 549. Translated into English from Chinese.

doctrines of the Two Vehicles, the Buddha preaches, in dependence upon the nirvāṇa consisting of "the limit of intrinsicality," "the limit of reality," "the reality-suchness," "the consciousness," and "the true self" that all phenomena consisting of the aggregates, the sense-fields, the elements, and so forth are dependent arising and with an empty nature. In *Eight Thousand Stanza Perfection of Wisdom Sūtra [Mahā-prajñāpāramitā Sūtra, Dapin boruo jing 大品般若經]* and *Twenty-Five Thousand Stanza Perfection of Wisdom Sūtra [Aṣṭasāhasrikā Prajñāpāramitā, Xiaopin boruo jing 小品般若經]*, the Buddha preaches, in dependence upon "the mind that is not a mind," "the mind without the signs of a mind," "the unmindful mind," and "the non-abiding mind," that all phenomena are dependent arising and with an empty nature. In the Vijñaptimātratā sūtras of the third turning of the Dharma Wheel, the Buddha teaches, in dependence upon the ālaya-consciousness, about the Path to Buddhahood as well as the fact that the mental consciousness—the mind of feeling and cognition—is an easily-arising and easily-ceasing mind with an other-dependent nature and is therefore an evolving consciousness and not a real mind. The Buddha also preaches that the mental faculty—the manas-consciousness—arises and possesses an imputational nature—it observes all phenomena pervasively and without omission—in dependence upon the ālaya-consciousness. Therefore, by emptiness-nature, the Buddha refers to the eighth consciousness and not the nihilistic emptiness in the emptiness of all phenomena. Neither Tsongkhapa or Yinshun are aware of this fact and have cunningly and forcefully argued that the Buddha's teachings about the eighth consciousness are just an expediency. As such, they are destroyers of the Dharma.

Why is the eighth consciousness not an expedient teaching, as claimed by Tsongkhapa and Yinshun? The reason is that the Buddha has preached in the sūtras of **all three** turnings of the Dharma Wheel that the ālaya-consciousness is a dharma that generates the mental consciousness, the manas, and the eighteen elements because it is a permanent and unceasing dharma. As Tsongkhapa believes that the mental consciousness, which ceases every night, can act as the permanent and indestructible dharma, how then could the ālaya-consciousness, which generates the mental consciousness, possibly be a dharma of expediency? How could the ālaya-consciousness be said to not be a real dharma? The reason that I raised those questions is as follows: Would it be possible that the produced mental consciousness is a real dharma, while the ālaya-consciousness, which produces the mental consciousness, is an unreal, established dharma consisting of a fake denomination? Does such reasoning make any sense, mundanely or supramundanely speaking? It is surprising that Tsongkhapa has made statements that invert the truth to such an extent and that none of the masters and disciples of the Gelug school, from the ancient gurus through to today's Dalai Lama, Yinshun, and so forth, have had the wisdom to identify his errors. It is surprising that there exists such a bizarre religion in the world, which hails the utterly preposterous Prāsaṅgika Madhyamaka as the unsurpassed Madhyamaka. What an utmost pity!

As the Buddha has frequently taught in the sūtras, those who falsely claim that all phenomena are empty will definitely fall to hell. We will cite the Buddha's words in Volume 8 of the *Śūraṅgama Sūtra*—a scripture of the esoteric division—to prove this fact:

> There were also King Virūḍhaka and Bhikṣu Sunakṣatra. King Virūḍhaka exterminated the Gautama clan, and Sunakṣatra persisted in making false statements about the emptiness of phenomena. These two also fell alive into the Unrelenting Hell .... If, in this submerged state of mind, they **have spoken ill of the Mahāyāna teachings** or of the Buddhas' precepts; if they have **recklessly propounded false doctrines which they present as being in accord with Dharma**; if they have greedily sought the offerings of the faithful under false pretenses; if they have shamelessly accepted undeserved reverence from others; or if they have committed the five unnatural crimes or the ten major offenses, **they will be reborn in the Unrelenting Hell in one world after another throughout the**

ten directions. [46]

In the *Śūraṅgama Sūtra*, the Buddha has thus extensively taught that the concealments, sense-fields, and elements are unreal and that the natures of seeing, hearing, cognition, and feeling, and so forth all arise from the tathāgatagarbha according to causes from past lifetimes such as karmic seeds, greed, love, and so forth. Based on the neither-arising-nor-ceasing nature of the tathāgatagarbha, those natures of seeing, hearing, cognition, and feeling, and so forth disappear every night and reappear the next morning, disappear after every lifetime and reappear the next lifetime; hence, the natures of seeing, hearing, feeling, cognition, and so forth are said to be "neither arising-and-ceasing nor non-arising-and-non-ceasing," for they are **"intrinsically the tathāgatagarbha's wondrous nature of the reality-suchness"**— they can always re-arise after they cease in dependence upon the tathāgatagarbha. Outside the context of the dharma of the tathāgatagarbha and purely from the perspective of the natures of seeing, hearing, cognition, and feeling, those natures are arising-and-ceasing phenomena. However, from the perspective of the fact that the tathāgatagarbha's permanence always allows the natures of seeing, hearing, and so forth to re-arise after they cease, those natures can also be said to have a non-arising-and-non-ceasing nature—those natures are said to be permanent and unceasing given that the tathāgatagarbha is permanent and unceasing. Consequently, the nature of seeing, hearing, cognition, and feeling cannot be said to be permanent and unceasing outside the context of the tathāgatagarbha, and the natures of the concealments, elements, entries, and so forth are said to be a part of the properties stored in the tathāgatagarbha—these properties of the seven evolving consciousnesses are all stored in the tathāgatagarbha and constitute a part of the tathāgatagarbha's properties. Based on this correct doctrine, the *Śūraṅgama Sūtra*

---

[46] *The Śūraṅgama Sūtra*: A New Translation, with Excerpts from the Commentary by Venerable Master Hsüan Hua (Burlingame, CA: Buddhist Text Translation Society, 2009), 347-52.

tells learners that the tathāgatagarbha is to be sought—**cognizing and seeing that which does not see; this is precisely nirvāṇa, uncontamination, and true purity**—learners must, in the midst of seeing, hearing, feeling, and cognition, seek the tathagatagarbha, which is at all times forever free from all seeing, hearing, feeling, and cognition; anyone who is truly able to cognize and personally see "the mind that never sees" has attained the nirvāṇa, the uncontamination, and the true purity—"the intrinsicality, the nature, the purity, and the nirvāṇa."

The tantric learners of Prāsaṅgika Madhyamaka, however, do not understand the Buddha's thoughts upon hearing His teachings. They have extracted passages of the prajñā sūtras out of their contexts, have dismissed the Buddha's words about the tathāgatagarbha such as "the mind that is not a mind," "the mind without the signs of a mind," "the unmindful mind," and so forth, and have claimed that all phenomena such as the aggregates, sense-fields, elements, and so forth are empty. According to those learners, once those phenomena are empty, their "nothingness" will exist permanently, and therefore, the nature of "nothingness" is neither arising nor ceasing. Consequently, those people regard the concept that "all phenomena are empty" as a correct doctrine taught by the Buddha. After veering in this fashion into nihilistic emptiness, they have wrongfully denounced the teachings about the tathāgatagarbha, which have realized the Buddha's true doctrines as being identical to the non-Buddhist philosophy of the Self and Divine Self, and have even resorted to political means to exterminate other sects and schools. Such is the erroneous view of Prāsaṅgika Madhyamaka held by the Gelug School in Tantric Buddhism, which is the so-called most ultimate view that towers over the views held by all the other schools.

The gurus of Prāsaṅgika Madhyamaka such as Candrakīrti, Ye-Shes-sDe, and so forth in ancient India; Atiśa, Tsongkhapa, Khedrup Je, Thuhu in ancient Tibet; and the Dalai Lama, Yinshun, and so forth in modern times—have all vigorously refuted the eighth consciousness—the tathāgatagarbha—in this fashion, falsely claiming that it is an expedient imputation and wrongfully affirming that it has never been taught by the Buddha. Having thus negated the eighth consciousness—the tathāgatagarbha—they have falsely asserted that the emptiness of all phenomena is what prajñā is all about. As a result, Tsongkhapa as well as the successive Dalai Lamas and so forth have even proclaimed that the Vijñaptimātratā sūtras of the third turning of the Dharma Wheel are non-definitive teachings (see Tsongkhapa's writings such as *Essence of Eloquence on the Provisional and Definitive [Bian liaobuliaoyi shanshun zanglun* 辨了不了義善說藏論*], The Medium Treatise on the Stages of the Path to Enlightenment [Putidao cidi lüelun* 菩提道次第略論*],* and so forth). Master Yinshun has also extensively professed the same contents in his publications, fully adopting the tantric view of Prāsaṅgika Madhyamaka as his core philosophy. Therefore, it can be said that, although Yinshun seems to belong to exoteric Buddhism by all appearances, he belongs in essence to Tantric Buddhism, just like the other gurus because his doctrines solely consist of the erroneous tantric view of Prāsaṅgika Madhyamaka—his philosophy would have nothing left without this view.

Having inherited the erroneous view of nihilism passed down through many generations from Candrakīrti, Śāntideva, and so forth in ancient India, the proponents of Madhyamaka from the Prāsaṅgika School in Tantric Buddhism are all entrapped in the belief that all phenomena are empty. While they do not establish their own school tenets, they refute all the doctrines from the other schools and sects, thinking that their own school tenets are the most ultimate doctrines in Buddhism. Their thoughts are, for instance, reflected in the following statements from Atiśa:

> Candrakīrti advocates the following: The truth is devoid of expressions; although it can be exemplified by metaphors, it does not have any cause that can be established. Therefore, our school does not establish specific inferences, but only expediently borrows the views of adversarial schools as causes in order to refute adversaries with argumentation and cause

them to realize the stances of their own schools.[47]

In fact, all the proponents of Madhyamaka from the Prāsaṅgika School have veered into the erroneous view that all phenomena are empty, which is exactly the view held by the non-Buddhist nihilists. Unaware that they have fallen into a mistaken view, those proponents of Madhyamaka boast that their school tenets are the most ultimate and, when they engage in Dharma debates with the other schools, they refute the other party's doctrines on the spot upon hearing them. They even rebut the true, ultimate, and definitive Dharma of the eighth consciousness, firmly believing that this Dharma is non-Buddhist. Such behavior consists of destroying the true Buddha Dharma with Buddhist terminology and non-Buddhist views. As a matter of fact, the mistaken view of Prāsaṅgika Madhyamaka has managed to poison Buddhist practitioners for as long as one thousand years only because no knowledgeable great mentor who has truly realized the knowledge-of-the-aspects-of-paths was to be found in Exoteric Buddhism during this timespan. Now that someone knows the truth, he must identify and analyze the erroneous aspects of the tantric doctrines and inform the public of those falsities, so as to prevent the learners of future generations from falling—just like the learners of past and current generations have done—into the Theory of the Rabbit Without Horns, a doctrine of Prāsaṅgika Madhyamaka about the emptiness of all phenomena.

The contemporary Master Yinshun has even less wisdom than the aforementioned tantric gurus. Not only is he unaware of the fallacies of Prāsaṅgika Madhyamaka, but he willfully took on, as an exalted Exoteric saṃgha-jewel, the legacy of the erroneous view of Prāsaṅgika Madhyamaka, which, among the various non-Buddhist tantric misconceptions, has destroyed the Buddha Dharma to the largest extent. Based on this erroneous view, Yinshun has misinterpreted, in *The Collection of Wonderful Clouds [Miaoyunji]*

---

[47]   Chen Yujiao 陳玉蛟 (ed.), *Adixia yu putidao dengshi* 阿底峽與菩提道燈釋 [*Atiśa and Commentary on the Lamp for the Path to Enlightenment*] (Dongchu Publisher 東初出版社, 1991), 52. Translated into English from Chinese.

as well as in all his other publications, the Buddha's tenets in the prajñā sūtras, falsely claiming that prajñā is about "the emptiness of the noumenon coupled with the mere existence of terminology": Prajñā is only about the fact that all phenomena are empty while there is no real noumenon—prajñā is merely about terminology. Yinshun has thus turned prajñā into conceptual proliferations of metaphysics with "mere terminology" and "no real noumenon" as well as into a doctrine of unreal signs; consequently, prajñā is no longer a true teaching and scriptural doctrine about the sign of reality of the Dharma-realm. Based on such behavior, Master Yinshun is said to be, by all appearances, an Exoteric Buddhist master who propagates the Buddha Dharma, but in fact he has been extirpating the doctrine of the sign of reality found in the Buddha Dharma from its fundamentals, replacing it with the Theory of Uncausedness of the tantric Prāsaṅgika Madhyamaka. Yinshun cannot be viewed as belonging to Exoteric Buddhism, for his core philosophy wholly consists of the doctrines of the tantric Prāsaṅgika Madhyamaka. Taking on the appearance of an Exoteric Buddhist, Yinshun has been replacing the correct Dharma of Exoteric Buddhism with tantric doctrines in an attempt to exterminate the correct Dharma of Exoteric Buddhism before the public gains knowledge of it; in fact, his tactics are so skillful that they cannot be easily detected. If no one steps forward to correct those fallacies with the true doctrines and to widely inform the learners about them, then soon the correct and definitive Dharma of Buddhism will forever disappear from the human world due to the propagation of Yinshun's tantric philosophy and its devastating effects.

The proponents of the tantric Prāsaṅgika Madhyamaka have all been incorrectly preaching about the emptiness of all phenomena outside the context of the tathāgatagarbha. Given that their sin far exceeds that of falsely enlightened persons such as Master Weijue [惟覺], Master Shengyan [聖嚴], and so forth, who have misapprehended the natures of seeing, hearing, cognition, and feeling as the permanent and indestructible mind, and given that such negation of the eighth consciousness—the tathagatagarbha—directly extirpates the fundamentals of the Buddha Dharma of the Three Vehicles, the Buddha has taught that those who falsely proclaim in this fashion that all phenomena are empty will fall into hell and endure therein the retribution of anguish for long kalpas, before having to transmigrate to the hells in the other directions in order to further undergo the grave retribution of sheer agony for long kalpas (see the Buddha's teachings in *Mahāyāna Vaipulya Dharani Sūtra [Dasheng fanfguang zongchi jing 大乘方廣總持經]*). Given the extreme gravity of this sin, no learners should ever emulate the acts of the Dalai Lama, Yinshun, and so forth that consist of negating the eighth consciousness and proclaiming that all phenomena are empty if they do not wish to undergo the grave retribution of sheer anguish for long kalpas in their future lifetimes. In brief, **it makes sense to affirm, in dependence upon the eighth consciousness— the tathagatagarbha—that all phenomena consisting of the aggregates, sense-fields, elements, mind of feeling and cognition, and so forth are empty; however, it is senseless to say so outside the context of the eighth consciousness or after denying the existence of this consciousness.** All learners should be mindful of this teaching.

While the proponents of the Prāsaṅgika School of Tantric Buddhism have always negated the eighth consciousness—the tathāgatagarbha—Master Yinshun has gone even further by asserting that the Dharma of the tathagatagarbha is a resurrection of the non-Buddhist philosophies of the Brahma Self and Divine Self." He has thus falsely denounced the eighth consciousness—the tathāgatagarbha—as being identical to the mind consisting of the sixth consciousness in the form of the non-Buddhist Brahma Self and Divine Self, causing practitioners to believe that there is no tathāgatagarbha to be realized and therefore leading to the perpetual extinction of the profound, wondrous, and correct Buddhist Dharma and forever preventing it from being passed down to future generations. Master Yinshun's views and knowledge are not just distorted and mistaken, as highlighted above, but they have also seriously damaged the Buddha Dharma of the Three Vehicles, causing it to fall in essence into nihilism, converting it into the Theory of the Rabbit Without Horns and into the Theory of Uncausedness, which are both based on "the emptiness of the noumenon coupled with the mere existence of terminology" and transforming it into a philosophy of metaphysics consisting of conceptual proliferation. In other words, Master Yinshun is a destroyer of the correct Dharma of Buddhism. All learners should make a joint effort to forsake such fallacious views so as to avoid perpetuating the erroneous views that wreck the correct Dharma of Buddhism and poison the current and future generations of followers of the Buddha Dharma.

4. Examples of the View of Prajñā Found in Svātantrika Madhyamaka

The view of Svātantrika Madhyamaka refers to the view of prajñā preached by the Nyingma, Kagyu, and Sakya Schools of Tantric Buddhism. The holders of this view acknowledge the existence of the tathāgatagarbha, but do not know that the tathāgatagarbha corresponds to the eighth consciousness, the ālaya mind. Therefore, they regard the mind of feeling and cognition—the mental consciousness—in a state of thoughtlessness as the tathāgatagarbha; in some cases, they downright consider this conscious mind to be the reality-suchness of the ultimate Ground of Buddhahood. Based on a theory of the Svātantrika School, its proponents firmly believe that **the self consisting of the mind of feeling and cognition** has the ability to move on to the next lifetime as well the capacity to come to the current lifetime from the past one, hence the name "Svātantrika." Contrary to the holders of the view of Prāsaṅgika Madhyamaka, the holders of the view of Svātantrika Madhyamaka acknowledge the existence of the tathāgatagarbha. Both schools (together, they encompass the Four Major Traditions of Tibetan Tantric Buddhism), however, regard the fact that "all phenomena are dependent arising and with an empty nature outside the context of the tathāgatagarbha" as the emptiness-nature set forth in prajñā; furthermore, they both consider the conscious mind's emptiness of shape and form to be the emptiness-nature within prajñā taught by the Buddha; therefore, the view of the emptiness-nature within prajñā held by the proponents of Madhyamaka from the Prāsaṅgika School does not differ in any way from that held by the proponents of Madhyamaka from the Svātantrika School.

For instance, C. M. Chen, a highly renowned contemporary tantric guru, says:

We must realize that emptiness is no different from form and form is no different from emptiness. In "all variants of the emptiness-nature," emptiness and form are completely unified (original note: including everything related to the "self" such as feelings and so forth). The five aggregates and the emptiness-nature are neither identical nor different. **In the "external sphere," the emptiness-nature pervades all locations and all signs of phenomena are empty.** Some believe that emptiness is attained through analysis, but the true emptiness-nature is not obtained in this fashion. Such an endeavor only allows one to understand the compounded emptiness—the emptiness of conditioned, aggregated phenomena. Such an analysis is very popular in the Gelug School, but it can only be used as an expedient to explain key concepts.[1]

According to the above passage, the emptiness-nature pervades all external phenomena—this impermanent—and therefore empty—nature eternally pervades all external phenomena given that all phenomena will eventually disintegrate due to their impermanence. This tantric guru is unaware that the emptiness-nature taught by the Buddha actually refers to the fundamental mind of the Dharma-realm—the eighth consciousness, the ālaya mind. This is an instance where the emptiness-nature is misconstrued.

Such misunderstandings are rampant within Tantric Buddhism, as evidenced by Tsongkhapa's statements:

Next, one should ascertain the meaning of the no-self by refuting, with the correct principle, the self of persons imputed by the non-Buddhists and the self of phenomena imputed by the two factions of the inner path. Bring forth the ultimate mind of enlightenment with the power of practice— this is how you should first seek the view of the no-self. Such

---

[1] *Fojiao chanding* 佛教禪定 [*Buddhist Meditation*], vol. 1, narrated by C. M. Chen, recorded by Kangdi Paulo 康地保羅, and translated by Wuyouzi 無憂子, (Taipei: Puxianwangrulai yinjinghui 普賢王如來印經會, 1991), 73. Translated into English from Chinese.

is the principle articulated by Vairocana in explaining the mind of enlightenment set forth by each of the six Tathāgatas in *Guhyasamāja [Jimi 集密]*:

Having abandoned all things,
And eliminated the aggregates, sense-fields, elements,
As well as the apprehending subject and the apprehended object,
All phenomena are selfless and equal,
One's own mind is intrinsically non-arising,
The emptiness-nature is the nature.

Therefore, this work is named the explanation of the bodhicitta. Hence, Bodhisattva Longmong [龍猛] has thus stated that the meditation on the ultimate bodhicitta consists of negating the two selves with the correct reasoning and of practicing the ascertained view of the no-self; bodhisattvas who cultivate the secret mantra should also practice in this fashion. The aforementioned text also wisely refutes the views that delineate the observations of practice and of wisdom; these are stipulations of Exoteric Buddhism, not Tantric Buddhism. *Ornament of the Vajra Tantra* [*Vajrahṛdayālaṃkāra, Jingang zhuangyanxu 金剛莊嚴續*] also says:

The mind has observed the six parts of fine
particles, And dissolved them
Into the ten directions;
Through this understanding of the doctrine,
The mind is purified and the most undefiled.
Past and future minds,
Are thus without obtainment,
Neither dual nor non-dual,
The empty space is also non-abiding.
Having thus observed,
All sentient beings are empty,
This is the undefiled yoga,
Which consists of thinking that one's own mind has
no entity.
The above statements suggest that observing minute

particles and analyzing them in the ten directions constitute the meditation on the emptiness-nature. In *Explanation of the Vajra Sky-Traveler [Jingang kongxingshi 金剛空行釋]*, Bafubatuoluo [跋縛跋陀羅] has, just like in *Ornament of Madhyamakā [Madhyamakālaṃkāra, Zhingguan zhuangyanlun 中觀莊嚴論]*, ascertained the emptiness-nature by observing minute particles in each of the ten directions.[2]

Tsongkhapa is in fact not qualified to refute the view of the self of persons held by non-Buddhists. Indeed, he has not yet eliminated his own view of the self of persons and is not aware that the mind of feeling and cognition, which he regards as permanent and indestructible, is precisely the self set forth by those eternalist non-Buddhists; how then could he have the ability to refute the view of the self of persons held by eternalist non-Buddhists? As someone who has not yet extinguished his own view of the self of persons, he has presumptuously proclaimed his intention to go one step further by extinguishing the view of the self of phenomena, which even the Buddhists (those who have entered the Path of Vision in Buddhism) have not yet been able to eliminate. How extremely arrogant and ignorant!

Furthermore, the Emptiness-nature set forth by the Buddha refers to the limit of reality—the eighth consciousness, the tathāgatagarbha—of all sentient beings' lives and the limit of reality of the remainderless nirvāṇa. In contrast, Tsongkhapa wrongly regards the post-disintegration emptiness that results from the impermanence—and therefore inevitable destruction—of the form body as the emptiness-nature; he also misapprehends the fact that all form objects outside the body do not have a real nature as the emptiness-nature; therefore, he has quoted some tantras to validate his own assertions. Furthermore, he has cited *Ornament of the Vajra Essence Tantra [Vajrahṛdayālaṃkāra, Jingang zhuangyanxu 金剛莊嚴續]*: "After having observed in this

---

2 Tsongkhapa, *Mizong daocidi guang lun* 密宗道次第廣論, 606-07. Translated into English from Chinese.

fashion and ascertained that all sentient beings are empty, one has achieved the non-defiled yoga, which consists of thinking that one's own mind has no real essence," thinking that the mind of feeling and cognition corresponds to the emptiness-nature because it itself is formless and shapeless. This all results from Tsongkhapa's unwillingness to acknowledge the existence of the mind consisting of the eighth consciousness and his complete adherence to the fallacious view of Prāsaṅgika Madhyamaka, which means that he will never be able to realize and apprehend the eighth consciousness—the mind of the emptiness-nature. Consequently, he has made those absurd statements and proclaimed that those erroneous views correspond to the view of the emptiness-nature transmitted by the Buddha.

Tsongkhapa further says:

When by means of the individuating wisdom you have determined that all the things of saṃsāra and nirvana are not established ultimately, then even though [this analytic determination in itself] does not reverse the dualistic perception with respect to the objects which appear to that mind, still, since the [very] import of [such determined] certain knowledge [does entail] the reversal of dualistic perception, you do not need [to develop some] further additional apprehension of the thorough pacification of dualistic perception. Accordingly, you should develop certainty, thinking 'All things are free of the two extremes, they have the characteristic of lacking intrinsic reality, they are the reality realm free of all [mental] elaborations'; so, as [Śāntideva] states in *Engaging in the Bodhisattvas' Way of Life*, **all things have a non-objectifiable nature and are radically immersed in emptiness:**

When neither something nor nothing
Remains before the mind
Then, since there is no other alternative,
There is radical peace, free of objectification.

[IX.34].[3]

According to the above excerpt, one enters the emptiness-nature by observing that the mental consciousness—the mind of feeling and cognition—is without obtainment amidst all phenomena. The truth is, the mind of feeling and cognition is not without obtainment amidst all phenomena because it inevitably brings forth sensations of pain, of happiness, and of neither-pain-nor-happiness amidst those phenomena. Given its connections with those sensations, it is obviously not truly without obtainment; indeed, there ends up being an emptiness due to impermanence after the obtainment, but it is not that the mental consciousness is originally without obtainment. The so-called "without obtainment" taught by the Buddha refers to the fact that the eighth consciousness functions spontaneously in accordance with various conditions amidst all phenomena, free from all seeing, hearing, feeling, and cognition and without connecting with any sensations of pain, of happiness, and of neither-pain-nor-happiness amidst the six sense objects; such is being originally without obtainment. It is based on this fact that the mental consciousness—the mind of feeling and cognition—can be said to be without obtainment. The various sensations that it obtains are impermanent and will eventually disintegrate. In other words, one cannot assert outside the context of the eighth consciousness—the mind of the sign of reality—that the mental consciousness will eventually be without obtainment after taking in the sensations of pain and happiness. This example demonstrates that Tsongkhapa has mistaken the emptiness-nature within prajñā for an emptiness that results from impermanence, whereas the Buddha has taught that the eighth consciousness—the tathāgatagarbha—corresponds to the emptiness-nature of prajñā.

---

[3]   Tsong Khapa Losang Drakpa, *Great Treatise on the Stages of Mantra (sngags rim chen mo): Critical Elucidation of the Key Instructions in All the Secret Stages of the Path of the Victorious Universal Lord, Great Vajradhara. Chapters XI–XII (The Creation Stages),* introduction and translation by Thomas Freeman Yarnall, (AIBS, CBS & THUS, New York, 2013), 207-08.

Based on the aforementioned eternalist view, Tsongkhapa has further proclaimed his intention to extinguish the view of the self of phenomena still possessed by Buddhists—the Bodhisattvas who have realized the emptiness-nature and eliminated their self-view through entering the Path of Vision. Little do people know that Tsongkhapa has never even entered the Path of Vision—he has never even extinguished the view of the self of persons. However, he aspires to teach the Bodhisattvas who have entered the Path of Vision how to eliminate their view of the self of phenomena when he himself has not entered the Path of Vision and still holds onto his eternalist non-Buddhist view of the self of persons. Thus, he is acting like an elementary school student who does not understand middle-school algebra, yet proclaims his intention to teach college students about calculus. Such an attitude is as arrogant and ignorant as Śāntideva's composition of *A Guide to the Bodhisattva Way of Life* is illusory.

Not only has the Gelug School misconstrued in this fashion the emptiness within prajñā and the emptiness of all phenomena, but such misunderstandings of the emptiness within prajñā and the emptiness of all phenomena also exist within the view of Svātantrika Madhyamaka held by the other three Major Schools:

> All of you should know that all phenomena have an empty nature and that the eighteen elements are not truly obtainable even in the slightest. All seeing, hearing, feeling, and cognition are empty and illusory, like a mirage projected from an aggregation of causes and conditions. If one constantly bears this in mind, then naturally one's greed will not arise. The arising of greed entails serious karmic sins. However, is this a nihilistic state? Absolutely not! **This is not the non-existence of all phenomena, but rather the emptiness of their nature.** One must be aware that both the eternalist view and the nihilistic view must be avoided; otherwise, one will fall into a stubborn emptiness and hinder oneself severely. **One should think that all phenomena have an empty nature and that there is no such thing as "truly produced" in the world; it is good enough to have this though.** . . . It is very difficult to

understand such a mode of emptiness, and it would be even more wonderful to be able to truly see the emptiness of all phenomena. **The so-called emptiness does not entail not seeing form nor not hearing sound, but only not clinging to them.** For example, do a sentient being and the five aggregates constitute one entity? Or two entities? Choosing between "one" and "two" just reflects one's erroneous attachment. All phenomena in this world consist of false denominations given that their nature is intrinsically empty, and therefore, they do not truly exist. Which one of them does not arise upon the aggregation of causes and conditions and cease upon the dispersal of those causes and conditions? A detailed contemplation of the twelve links of dependent arising will enable one to easily grasp the mode of emptiness of all phenomena as well as the principle whereby causes and conditions aggregate and disperse.[4]

With respect to the emptiness within prajñā delineated above, **the emptiness of nature of all phenomena** is regarded as the emptiness-nature within prajñā, which contradicts the Buddha's teachings. In fact, the statement **"One should think that all phenomena have an empty nature and that there is no such thing as 'truly produced' in the world; it is good enough to have this thought"** still falls within the sphere of the conscious mind and does not reflect any penetrative understanding of the secret meaning related to the emptiness-nature within prajñā. Moreover, the assertion **"The so-called emptiness does not entail not seeing form nor not hearing sound, but only not clinging to them"** further equates the ability of the conscious mind to remain detached from all phenomena with the realization of the emptiness-nature set forth in the prajñā sūtras. This fault is common to all tantric gurus. Since they have been unable to realize the eighth consciousness—the tathāgatagarbha—they cannot understand the true signs of the

---

[4]   *Naluo liufa 那洛六法 [The Six Yogas of Nāropa]*, narrated by Blo-Bzan-Grags-Pa Zam Lam [Daoran baluobu cangsangbu 道然巴羅布倉桑布], recorded by Lu Yizhao 盧以炤 (Taipei: Chenxi Wenhua Gongsi 晨曦文化公司, 1994), 240-41. Translated into English from Chinese.

properties of the dharma-realm and have therefore misconstrued all the prajñā sūtras and misled sentient beings based on those misunderstandings.

Blo-Bzan-Grags-Pa Zam Lam further says:

> Yesterday, we spoke about the fact that all phenomena are empty and that all sentient beings are illusory-like; therefore, any attempt to find reality in them will be in vain. We undergo in this lifetime the retribution of virtuous and evil deeds performed in past lifetimes. **If we cultivate in this lifetime the emptiness of all phenomena, then we will be able to eradicate cyclic existence and will never enter it again. If the true mind comes by, then we will see all sentient beings as transformed Buddhas** and all inanimate objects as maṇḍalas. By practicing frequently in this fashion—one-pointedly and without any doubt—bliss will arise as soon as the empty mind comes by, which will result in the non-duality of emptiness and bliss; at this point, the practitioner will see everything as Buddha. At the beginning of the practice, one abides in this state for only tens of minutes but will gradually be able to dwell longer; with the passage of time, one will eventually abide in this state not only when one is awake but also in dreams.
>
> At this moment, the mind of virtuous deeds is very important, and one must absolutely avoid evil deeds. It is thus recommended to accumulate as many virtuous deeds as possible in this lifetime. This practice is no longer necessary once the emptiness of phenomena and the emptiness of the self are attained.
>
> At this stage, wherever one finds oneself to be, whatever one's six sense faculties come into contact with will be apprehended as emptiness. **Such is the realization of the Path.**[5]

Anyone who cultivates the emptiness of all phenomena in

---

5.   *Naluo liufa 那洛六法 [The Six Yogas of Nāropa]*, narrated by Blo-Bzan-Grags-Pa Zam Lam [Daoran baluobu cangsangbu 道然巴羅布倉桑布], recorded by Lu Yizhao 盧以炤 (Taipei: Chenxi Wenhua Gongsi 晨曦文化公司, 1994), 243. Translated into English from Chinese.

this fashion will be precisely making a false speech if he proclaims that he has eliminated his self-view while in fact he has not. Those who have eliminated their self-view are known as srotaāpannas. The tantric gurus involved in the aforementioned method of practice; however, all regard the mental consciousness—the mind of feeling and cognition—as the shapeless and formless emptiness-nature—they have all mistaken the conscious mind for the reality-suchness—and are therefore no different than eternalist non-Buddhists. As they have not yet eliminated their self-view, how could they speak about **eradicating cyclic existence and never entering it again?** Even the practitioners of the first fruition with obtuse faculty still need to undergo rebirths in the human and the celestial worlds to and fro seven times in order to sever cyclic existence; how then could ordinary people, who have not eliminated the self-view related to the mental consciousness and who have not entered the Path of Vision, possibly never enter cyclic existence again? Clearly, those gurus' statements do not make any sense.

Furthermore, tantric gurus generally believe that a person has eliminated both his self-view and self-attachment if he is able to observe that the six external sense objects are impermanent and therefore empty and that the form body is also empty. Furthermore, they regard the mind of feeling and cognition that makes this observation as the true mind—they assert that the person who can make this observation already has the capacity to **see all sentient beings as transformed Buddhas** and that **such is the realization of the Path.** In fact, not only have they misunderstood the definition of "transformed Buddha," but they have also misconstrued the true mind. One should know that the mental consciousness of all sentient beings remains a mental consciousness even after those sentient beings have practiced for long kalpas; it will never become the true mind. Therefore, the mental consciousness of the Ground of Buddhahood remains a mental consciousness and has not been transformed into the true mind. Similarly, the eighth consciousness—the consciousness of true signs—which is possessed by all sentient beings, was already a consciousness of true signs before one's practice; it is intrinsically a consciousness of true signs—the true mind—and did not become the true mind after one's practice. However, most of the tantric gurus do not understand this principle and have always strived to convert the unreal mind—the mental consciousness—into the true mind through practice. Such endeavors are all based on erroneous thoughts and views. Why is that? Because if the mental consciousness could be converted into the true mind, then enlightened sentient beings would have no mental consciousness and would have become vegetables who cannot distinguish between pain and itchiness because their mind of feeling and cognition—mental consciousness—would have become the true mind and the true mind is free from all seeing, hearing, feeling, and cognition. However, all ancient as well as contemporary enlightened worthies [6] and sages are seen to possess all eight consciousnesses—they possess each of the eight consciousnesses without missing any of them. Based on the records in the sūtras, the Buddha was still able to make all kinds of distinctions after He became enlightened; not only was He not without a mind of feeling and cognition—mental consciousness—but He was also fully endowed with the eighth consciousness—the reality-suchness—which at this stage of Buddhahood is renamed "immaculate consciousness." Hence, the statements made by those tantric gurus about transforming the mental consciousness into the true mind are based on erroneous thinking, which is issued from their own speculation. Those assertions are nothing but preposterous for the wise.

Blo-Bzan-Grags-Pa Zam Lam has also said the following:

> If such evidence for death does not come by, then one should mull over the idea of dissolving one's life into the central channel. During the exit of life, all phenomena are empty should lead the way. What do I mean by all phenomena are empty should lead the way? One will see a pale-yellow light

---

[6]   Worthy: a bodhisattva at the Three Stages of Worthiness (*sanxian wei* 三賢位) on the Path to Buddhahood; C. *xianren* 賢人.

upon the arrival of the fourth emptiness; "light is emptiness and emptiness is light." All phenomena are empty should lead the way refers to the fact that this pale-yellow light will appear as if it was leading the way ahead of you. Thereafter, one's Buddha-like appearance will arise. One will go to bed after practicing in this fashion. Once asleep, one will be aware of the emergence of one's transformation body even in one's dreams. It would be excellent to attain this state. . . . (At death,) upon the arrival of the fourth all-emptiness, darkness will abruptly open up and one will suddenly see a beam of red light akin to lightning, which will vanish in a split second. Once the red light has vanished, one will see a pale yellow light akin to the first light of the morning. By then, one's spirit will have exited; the pale yellow light that you will see will be the light in "emptiness," the so-called clear light. These are the states that will appear upon the arrival of the fourth all-emptiness (original note: The syllable *ham* [亨] found at the end of the *Mantra of the Contemplation on Emptiness*, which is recited during one's practice, signifies emptiness and refers precisely to this fourth emptiness). All of the above will come by through practice; they will not appear without practice. The aforementioned clear light is the true "fundamental clear light," the basis of all.[7]

Unlike in previous passages, the emptiness of all phenomena highlighted in this teaching refers to the form object of clear light; such a concept differs from those articulated previously. The statement "light is emptiness and emptiness is light" also stands in contrast to previous assertions because here the author neither regards the fact that the mind of feeling and cognition is empty of shape and form as the emptiness-nature nor considers the impermanence of all to be the emptiness-nature. Such inconsistencies related to the delineation of the emptiness-nature

---

[7] *Naluo liufa* 那洛六法 *[The Six Yogas of Nāropa]*, narrated by Blo-Bzan-Grags-Pa Zam Lam [Daoran baluobu cangsangbu 道然巴羅布倉桑布], recorded by Lu Yizhao 盧以炤 (Taipei: Chenxi Wenhua Gongsi 晨曦文化公司, 1994), 285-86. Translated into English from Chinese.

have left tantric practitioners wondering which statements are correct. In fact, the emptiness-nature thus delineated has nothing to do with the emptiness-nature within prajñā, because it is not practiced and realized in dependence upon the eighth consciousness set forth by the Buddha in the prajñā sūtras.

With respect to the emptiness-nature, the same publication further says:

> What is being discussed here is the dissolving of one's life into the central channel in the awake state; skill will come if one practices frequently in this fashion. Later on, if one can practice in the same way during sleep, then one's power will come by. All kinds of states will naturally come by along with power. First, one will internally see a mirage akin to water or fire emerge as if it was right before one's eyes. At this moment, one will lose one's concentration and will be muddle-headed. Subsequently, one will internally see a green smoke engulf one's eyes and appear as if it arises massively from fire. Next, one will see a light of firefly dance and scintillate in the sky, followed by a bean-sized fire burning steadily like a clear lamp in a closed room. Afterward, one will internally see a white color that resembles—but is actually not—the moon; it has a white surrounding, which is not the moonlight, but rather a function that arises from the mind. Everything that one will see at this moment will take on this shape, like the full moon of the night (the fifteenth night of the lunar calendar)—extremely bright and all-pervasive; this is the manifestation of emptiness.[8]

The same publication also says:

Now let us further speak about the fact that one will see a large number of circles upon the arrival of "emptiness." A white color will vaguely seem to appear beyond the circles; it is neither as red as the sun nor as white as the moon when one looks at it closely. But when one looks at it again, it will appear

---

[8]   Ibid., 307.

red like the sunlight. The "extreme emptiness" will arrive when you see this red color. The red color and the extreme emptiness will arrive simultaneously, and great emptiness will arrive once the red color has dissolved. One will then internally see darkness; not only will the sun or the moon be non-existent, but the mind will also not exist. In the darkness, there will seem to be at first countless circles; upon closer inspection, these circles will also be non-existent, and only darkness will remain. Within this period of darkness, one's mind will be foggy during the first half of this period but will gradually awaken in the second half. At this moment, one will see a clear light coming from afar; it will progressively become obvious and will then become blue like the sky and extremely bright. These are the states that will appear upon the arrival of "the emptiness of all phenomena." The light at this moment will be similar to the light of dawn, while the empty space in the sky will be cloudless and exceptionally bright; this is exactly the clear light. At this moment, although the practitioner's body will remain in its usual sitting posture, his life will have exited from within his heart's "union." He will then think: "My death denotes impermanence; all phenomena are empty; I will become a deity above the sky," and so forth. One should always practice in this fashion without interruption. . . . Those who practice sitting meditation well will obtain the fourth clear light. What is the fourth clear light? Don't you remember the five paths taught earlier? They are as follows: (1) quiescence of both the body and speech, (2) quiescence of the mind, (3) illusory body, (4) clear light, and (5) immense, unparalleled bliss obtained from copulating with and embracing a wisdom mother (female consort). During the fourth clear light, the yin and the yang copulate (engage in the yab-yum practice), causing bliss to arise. When the bliss arises, the practitioner should think, "My death denotes impermanence; all phenomena are empty." When he meditates on the clear light together with the emptiness of all phenomena, his mind should be completely immobile and he should be impassible to all the forms that he sees and all the sounds that he hears as he sits single-mindedly in meditation. This is the non-dual and indivisible emptiness and bliss found in the unsurpassed Esoteric School, which is the foremost wondrous thought.[9]

In the above statements about emptiness, clear light—and not the mental consciousness (the mind of feeling and cognition)—is regarded as the entity of emptiness. Such teaching differs from previous assertions. However, there is only one emptiness-nature within prajñā, not two or three different ones because it is absolute dharma. We can, therefore, conclude that Tantric followers have no idea whatsoever about the emptiness-nature within prajñā and have not been able to realize it.

Although the Nyingma, Kagyu, and Sakya traditions in the Svātantrika School acknowledge the existence of the tathāgatagarbha, they do not comprehend the Buddha Dharma—they do not know that the tathāgatagarbha is precisely the eighth consciousness—the ālaya mind. Nonetheless, they are aware that the practitioners of the Gelug tradition are skillful in debates, but deficient when it comes to religious practice:

> Fazun (法尊) did not dare to publish his translation of Tsongkhapa's *The Great Exposition of Secret Mantra [Mizong daocidi guanglun, (Guang jingang dao 廣金剛道)]*; in fact, this work has already been printed and is currently in circulation among veteran practitioners of Tibetan Tantric Buddhism). In my view, the worst mistakes in this text are as follows: equating the emptiness of the no-self of persons in the Two Vehicles with the ultimate luminous emptiness in the Secret Mantra Vehicle; and citing the deeds of the six perfections as the only cause of Buddhahood. There is a particular emphasis on the collection of merits; this resonates well with the practitioners in Tibet but is the complete opposite of what people believe in China. It is only fitting that he did not dare to publish this text. Although the reasonings are sound, one will obtain nothing if one is not **skillful** in the methods (if one is not skillful in the cultivation method of the yab-yum practice), just as the

---

9   Ibid., 309-10.

Gelug practitioners are skillful in debates, but deficient when it comes to religious practice.[10]

In Rangjung Dorje's (the teacher of a Ming Dynasty emperor) *The Profound Inner Reality [Shenshen neiyi 甚深內義]*, although the commentator Rinpoche Palpung Khyentse, Guru Gangkar, and Guru C.M. Chen have all commended the enlightenment set forth in the Chan School—Guru Chen has even expounded the doctrines of the Chan School as a self-deemed enlightened person—none of them actually understand the prajñā realized in the Chan School:

> An ocean wave can carry a boat as well as overturn it—the ocean is a metaphor for thoughts. If the boatman sails along the waves, then the boat will move firmly downwind; therefore, the teacher's (Rinpoche Palpung Khyentse) ocean of benevolence, the Buddha's ocean of enlightenment, and one's own ocean of nature will all be in perfect concordance. However, some people might still exhibit aversion [towards these teachings]; I will tell them that simple and straightforward skills will eventually become effective, whereas fragmented actions and deeds will eventually cause one to be submerged. These people then proclaim that they are definitely superior to me; in that case, I will tell them that the Great Esoteric School (original note: Guru Norlha refers to the Chan School as the great esoteric school) originally existed in China; it is intrinsically the fundamental entity of the Dharma treasury characterized by the infinite waves of the ocean of benevolence.[11]

Why do I assert that C. M. Chen—just like the other gurus—does not understand the prajñā realized in the Chan School? Because what is touched upon and realized by a truly enlightened person in the Chan School is the mind consisting of the eighth consciousness, which is exactly the consciousness of true signs

---

10   Yogi C. M. Chen (Chen Chien-ming 陳健民), *Qugongzhai quanji 曲肱齋全集 [The Complete Works of Yogi Chen]*, vol. 1-5, ed. Xu Qinying 徐芹庭 (Taipei: Puxianwang rulai fojiaohui 普賢王如來佛教會, 1991), vol. 3, 322. Translated into English from Chinese.
11   Ibid., 323.

taught by the Buddha in the sūtras of the Three Vehicles. In contrast, the statements made by Guru C. M. Chen of Tantric Buddhism relate to the "treasury consciousness set forth by the proponents of Tantrism based on their own interpretations;" this consciousness differs drastically from the eighth consciousness taught by the Buddha:

> With respect to the winds, channels, and drops of the three bodies, the dharma-realm of the ultimate great bliss is the Dharma body, also known as the most profound body (original note: According to the teacher [Rinpoche Palpung Khyentse], this refers to the body of nature); its support—the causally concordant cause in conventional truth—is the reward body or emanation body. The reward body is obtained by transforming the mind and vitality in dependence upon dreams and the purification of the eight consciousnesses. The emanation body arises from the purification of the first six consciousnesses in ordinary states and on all phenomena. The channels, winds, and drops are the vajras of body, speech, and mind; the purity of those three leads to the achievement of vajras, and hence they constitute the fundamental entity of all Buddhas' three deeds. The four bodies arise in the four states respectively. *Great Commentary on the "Kālacakra Tantra"*: *Stainless Light [Wugouguang lun 無垢光論]* (original note: According to the teacher, this is a commentary on the *Kālacakra Tantra*) says: In deep sleep, that which abides in thoughtlessness is the Dharma body; in dreams, that which "appears only sporadically" through vitality is the reward body; in the awake state, all manifested objects are the emanation body; in the state of greed, that which is difficult to tame and obscured by defilements is the wisdom body. These are the four bodies of defiled sentient beings, which stand in contrast to the Buddhas' four bodies of undefiled fruition.[12]

---

[12] Yogi C. M. Chen (Chen Chien-ming 陳健民), *Qugongzhai quanji 曲肱齋全集 [The Complete Works of Yogi Chen]*, vol. 1-5, ed. Xu Qinying 徐芹庭 (Taipei: Puxianwang rulai fojiaohui 普賢王如來佛教會, 1991), vol. 3, 329. Translated into English from Chinese.

The prajñā sūtras do not regard the "ultimate great bliss (the non-duality of bliss and emptiness in the yab-yum practice)" set forth in Tibetan Tantric Buddhism as the dharma-body; instead, they consider the eighth consciousness to be a sentient being's dharma body on the Causal Ground. After entering the Path of Vision, one eliminates through practice the latent seeds of afflictive hindrances and all latencies of beginningless ignorance, all of which are stored in one's eighth consciousness, thereby achieving the dharma body of the ultimate Ground of Buddhahood. In this process, the eighth consciousness is invariably regarded as the dharma-body—the prajñā sūtras have never equated the "ultimate great bliss" as the dharma-body. In fact, "the ultimate great bliss" set forth in Tibetan Buddhism is merely a state of the mental consciousness and has completely nothing to do with the eighth consciousness—the dharma body. Clearly, the assertions made by those gurus are the total opposite of the Buddha's teachings.

5. The Other Views of the Emptiness-Nature in Tantric Buddhism

Many disparities exist among the views of the emptiness-nature propounded by the various gurus of Tantric Buddhism; as a matter of fact, their teachings all differ from one another. In some cases, the assertions made by the same guru also show inconsistencies. We will now list some of the teachings about the emptiness-nature other than the ones highlighted in previous sections to illustrate this fact.

Some tantric practitioners regard the attainment of emptiness and bliss in the yab-yum practice set forth in Highest Yoga Tantra as the realization of the emptiness-nature:

> Yesterday, we spoke about the fact that there are three possible ways to practice the illusory path: (1) practicing in the awake state, (2) practicing in dreams, and (3) practicing in the intermediate state. There are four emptinesses related to the first way of practice—practicing in the awake state. What are the four emptinesses? They are the emptiness,[1] the great emptiness,[2] the wondrous emptiness,[3] and the emptiness of all phenomena.[4] It is indispensable to clearly understand all four emptinesses. The cultivation of the fourth one, the emptiness of all phenomena, consists of thinking that all phenomena have an empty nature. The union of this emptiness with bliss gives rise to the non-duality and indivisibility of emptiness and bliss. One's mind must remain in equipoise amidst the non-duality and indivisibility of emptiness and bliss. One can certainly practice by embracing a consort mother if there is one available (if a female of the yab-yum practice is available); otherwise, it is also

---

[1]   Emptiness; T.123ac he*g pa*; C. *kong* 空.

[2]   Great emptiness; T. *shin tu*123ac *heg pa*; *dakong* 大空.

[3]   Wondrous emptiness; T.123ac he*g pa chen po*; C. *miaokong* 妙空.

[4]   Emptiness of all phenomena; C. *yiqiefakong* 一切法空.

fine to imagine embracing a consort mother (if there is no female consort, it is also fine to contemplate oneself practicing with a female consort through the method of visualization), as this will allow one to experience the bliss felt by those who actually embrace a female consort (as this can also induce the sexual pleasure enjoyed by practicing with a real female consort). Such a way of practice will become a habit if one adopts it in the long run. This will become a habit through long-term practice. The practitioner should abide one-pointedly in the non-duality and indivisibility of emptiness and bliss whether in meditation or post-meditation. At this stage, he should thoroughly abandon all previous mindsets of an ordinary person consisting of fussing about good or bad. Furthermore, he should one-pointedly and without any doubt in mind regard sentient beings as manifested Buddhas and empty places as maṇḍalas. Only those who can do so are realizers of the Path.[5]

It is certain that the tantric practitioners who engage in this tantric Dharma-gate of practice will obtain nothing despite cultivating the Buddha Dharma for a long time. Firstly, the concept that all phenomena are empty cannot be equated with the Buddha Dharma; those who ponder this concept do not actually understand it. To realize and understand that all phenomena are empty, one should begin by observing all phenomena beyond one's body and mind—by observing the fact that they are impermanent and mutable and will eventually disintegrate. Hence, all phenomena are empty. Furthermore, one should carefully observe one's body and mind—one should observe that one's body results from the illusory aggregate of the father's sperm, the mother's blood, and the four great elements.[6] Given that the body results from the illusory aggregate of various conditions, it is a dependent-arising phenomenon. All dependent-arising phenomena are

---

5   *Naluo liufa* 那洛六法 *[The Six Yogas of Nāropa]*, narrated by Blo-Bzan-Grags-Pa Zam Lam [Daoran baluobu cangsangbu 道然巴羅布倉桑布], recorded by Lu Yizhao 盧以炤 (Taipei: Chenxi Wenhua Gongsi 晨曦文化公司, 1994), 233. Translated into English from Chinese.

6   Great elements: S. mahābhūta; T. 'by ung124ac henn po; C. da[zhong] 大[種].

produced and have a beginning; phenomena that are produced and have a beginning will inevitably perish and cease in the future; phenomena that perish and cease are impermanent; impermanent phenomena are the emptiness-signs—they exist temporarily and will eventually disintegrate. Hence, our form body is also said to be empty.

One should, furthermore, observe that our mind of seeing, hearing, feeling, and cognition is also empty. Why is it empty? This mind consists of the first six consciousnesses. The properties of these six-consciousnesses—seeing, hearing, feeling, and cognition—arise and function only in dependence upon the five form sense faculties of the form body and upon the contact of the seventh consciousness—the mental faculty—with the mental object. If any one of these conditions is missing, then this person will fall into the state of deep sleep, or even coma or death. One does not need to personally experience each of those states one by one, but can directly validate them by observing, in the human world, the four deportments of oneself and others as well as the various accidents that occur to others or by observing those states in hospitals. Given that the mind of seeing, hearing, feeling, perceiving, cognition, thinking, and conceptualizing arises, as previously mentioned, only in dependence upon many conditions, it is a phenomenon that relies upon other dharmas to arise; a phenomenon that depends upon other dharmas to arise is necessarily an arising and ceasing phenomenon. All of us can also directly witness that the mind of feeling and cognition—which sees, hears, feels, cognizes, and conceptualizes—inevitably ceases in deep sleep every night and wakes up only when the mental faculty comes into contact with the mental object—the mind of feeling and cognition cannot wake up by itself (the ceasing of the mental consciousness gives way to nothingness; nothingness cannot possibly reappear on its own—it reappears only when it is produced by other conditions).

For instance, if one becomes unconscious after being severely hit, one will regain consciousness only after one's form body has gradually recovered. Another example is that of a person who undergoes surgery. The effect of an external factor (anesthetic) on his form body prevents the natures of his mind of seeing, hearing, feeling, and cognition from continuing to function normally. Although this person's decision-making manas-consciousness is present, it cannot cause him to wake up. Therefore, when those who have been anesthetized during surgery are about to wake up once the effect of the anesthetic has slightly subsided—when their manas-consciousness arouses the mind of feeling and cognition when these persons are about to wake up—given that the anesthetic has not completely dissolved, they will become drowsy and will fall back to sleep as soon as they open their eyes due to the impact of the anesthetic.

Clearly, the natures of the mind of seeing, hearing, feeling, cognition, thinking, and conceptualizing (the natures of the first six consciousnesses) do indeed arise in dependence upon other dharmas—they wake up only in dependence upon the normal functioning of the five form sense faculties and the mental application of the manas-consciousness to wake up. When the five form sense faculties are abnormal (for instance, when one is seriously ill or under the effect of an anesthetic), the anomalies of the five form sense-faculties will prevent the mind of feeling and cognition from appearing and functioning. This proves that the mind of seeing, hearing, feeling, cognition, thinking, and observation is a phenomenon that arises and ceases—it is indeed a phenomenon that arises and functions only in dependence upon other phenomena and various conditions, and it is not a phenomenon that has intrinsically existed by itself since beginningless time. Given that this mind is a phenomenon that arises and ceases, it is an impermanent, compounded, and mutable phenomenon; therefore, one cannot assert that the mind of feeling and cognition is the mind of the emptiness-nature set forth by the Buddha, which is neither arising nor ceasing and which has intrinsically existed since beginningless time. However, tantric Buddhists regard the following as the emptiness-nature: (1) the state in which the mind of feeling and cognition that takes in the blissful contact amidst the sexual pleasure induced by the yab-yum practice is able to remain thoughtless and without any cravings for the sexual pleasure(in fact, this is precisely a state in which the mind of feeling and cognition craves for the sexual pleasure because it is taking in the cognition and feeling related to the illicit contact experienced amidst the sexual pleasure), and (2) the emptiness of shapes and forms of the sexual contact as well as the emptiness of shapes and forms of the mind of feeling and cognition amidst this sexual contact. Those tantric followers thus observe that the sexual contact and the mind of feeling and cognition are neither one nor dual and call this state the non-duality of bliss and emptiness, the realization of the emptiness-nature. It is truly astonishing to misapprehend the Buddha Dharma to such an extent!

Tantric practitioners thus observe that all phenomena are empty, but surprisingly they neither know that their own mind of seeing, hearing, feeling, and cognition is precisely an impermanent and mutable phenomenon that is included among the five aggregates nor do they understand that this mind also counts among "all phenomena" in "all phenomena are empty." Surprisingly, they falsely assert that the mind of feeling and cognition is permanent and indestructible, thus falling into the erroneous view held by eternalist non-Buddhists. How could they be called the wise?

Another misapprehension of the emptiness-nature is as follows:

> Because our body is similar to the image in a mirror, it is entirely empty and false, completely devoid of real substance; this is the so-called "form is emptiness and emptiness is form." How could the phenomena outside the body be any different from this? It is a misconception to insist that they are real! If a practitioner can thoroughly realize the mode of emptiness and practice earnestly, then he will, with the passage of time, be able to attain the submergence of the earth, the emptiness of both the phenomena and the self. In the early stage of the practice, he might as well start with a smaller scope, in which only one or two phenomena are empty. Once he enters this

state, he can gradually enlarge the scope until reaching the point where all phenomena are empty. During the practice, he may hang a Buddha's image on the wall in front of him and then place two mirrors—one behind him and the other in front of him—so that the Buddha's image at the front can be projected into the mirror behind before being in turn projected into the mirror at the front. He may adjust the position of the Buddha's image so that it appears on top of his own image in the front mirror. Once everything is in place, he should visualize that the two images in the mirror are neither dual nor distinct. By frequently practicing in this way, he will realize in a wondrous fashion the mode of emptiness and illusion, and the mindset that "all phenomena are empty" will naturally gain tremendous strength.[7]

Such visualization, based on an image in the mirror, that oneself is empty will never enable one to eliminate the erroneous thought that the self consisting of the mind of feeling and cognition is real and permanent. While those practitioners have never been able to eliminate their self-view, it is surprising that they mistakenly believe to have done so by observing that their own form bodies are empty of shape and substance, like an image in the mirror. In fact, they are still convinced that the self consisting of the mind of feeling and cognition is real and indestructible and is permanent dharma; as such, they have precisely fallen into the eternalist self-view refuted by the Buddha in the four Āgamas. It is senseless to claim that one can realize the fact that all phenomena are empty with such a misapprehension of self-view and through a doctrine based on a mistaken way of cultivation. Indeed, those who insist that the self consisting of the mind of feeling and cognition is real and indestructible dharma have not realized the fact that all phenomena are empty and have inevitably fallen into the view of eternalism.

---

[7]   *Naluo liufa 那洛六法 [The Six Yogas of Nāropa]*, narrated by Blo-Bzan-Grags-Pa Zam Lam [Daoran baluobu cangsangbu 道然巴羅布倉桑布], recorded by Lu Yizhao 盧以炤 (Taipei: Chenxi Wenhua Gongsi 晨曦文化公司, 1994), 236. Translated into English from Chinese.

Tantric gurus have further taught a method to practice the emptiness of all phenomena:

> Practitioners must observe that "all phenomena are empty and are like dreams and illusions"; none of those phenomena are real. In fact, life is basically akin to a big dream and mundane affairs are similar to illusions. Those who do not believe this can go to some crossroads, raise their heads, and look around; after a while, they can mull over the following: Where have the carriages, humans, and objects that they have just seen all gone? Isn't all this like a dream? What truly existed has all vanished; if this is not emptiness, then what is? Therefore, if those who practice at home do not quite understand this concept, they can look around in the streets. Is there anything that does not disappear instantaneously? All arising and ceasing phenomena in this world basically follow this same pattern of arising upon the gathering of causes and conditions and ceasing upon the dispersion thereof; this also applies to a person's life and death. Practitioners of the Dharma should indeed frequently take a look at the deceased, for this will cause them to ponder deeply. Without looking at the deceased, they cannot bring forth "the fear of death." Without that fear, they will not diligently pursue the Path to Liberation. This is a definite and immutable principle.[8]

Instead of observing that their own eighteen elements are empty and illusionary, those tantric gurus observe the empty and illusory nature of external phenomena. As such, they will never eliminate their self-view, let alone their self-attachment and the belief that all phenomena are empty—none of the above will be eradicated. If tantric practitioners wish to truly exterminate their self-view, then they should first engage in the deed-contemplation of the falsity of their own mind of seeing, hearing, feeling, and cognition as well as the other powered nature of this mind. Those who can truly and directly observe the falsity of the self consisting of the mind of feeling and cognition will be able to eliminate their

---

8   Ibid., 237.

self-view. Only can such persons be called a realizer of the first fruition of Sound-Hearer. Those who are unable to directly observe the falsity of the self consisting of the mind of feeling and cognition will never cut off their self-view and will always abide in the view of eternalism. Although they claim to have severed their self-view, they are in fact no different from eternalist non-Buddhists. If they refuse to take my earnest advice and continue to regard the mind of feeling and cognition in a state of detachment from all phenomena as the permanent and indestructible reality-suchness and continue to proclaim that they have in this fashion eradicated their self-view, then they will be committing the deed of grievous false speech. How pitiful!

Tsongkhapa has also misconstrued the mode of the emptiness-nature and regards the emptiness of all phenomena as the emptiness-nature set forth in the prajñā sūtras:

> The prajñā sūtra says: "The Buddha is also like an illusion and a dream. If there is an dharma superior to nirvāṇa, then I would say it is also like an illusion and a dream." The Seven Preparatory Practices [Qijiaxing 七加行] says: "I shall teach the four preparatory practices given that practitioners are good at negating erroneous phenomena." It also says: "Among all phenomena, naturelessness is said to be the principal one. Indeed, it is through this practice that the princes of the Dharma achieve all the perfections of Buddhahood." Its naturelessness is the supreme emptiness-nature endowed with all aspects [or "all seeds"]. The emptiness epitomized by the flower in the sky and the horns of a rabbit is nothingness; it cannot be directly realized. *Ratnakūṭa Sūtra [Baoding jing 寶頂經]* says that the emptiness associated with giving or even with the Buddha Dharma is the supreme emptiness-nature endowed with all aspects [all seeds].[9]

Tsongkhapa has not only misconstrued the mode of the

---

[9] Tsongkhapa, *Mizong daocidi guang lun* 密宗道次第廣論, 564. Translated into English from Chinese.

emptiness-nature, but he has also misapprehended the true meaning of the expression "all aspects" taught by the Buddha. The emptiness-nature set forth in the prajñā sūtras corresponds to neither the impermanent emptiness in "all phenomena are empty" nor the nothingness found after disintegration. Instead, this emptiness-nature refers to the limit of reality of nirvāna—the neither arising nor ceasing mind of the sign of reality intrinsically possessed by sentient beings—which is the eighth consciousness of true signs. The Buddha has expounded the practice and realization of nirvāna based on the eighth consciousness and has spoken about the remainderless nirvāna based on the fact that the eighth consciousness takes no further rebirth; there is no nirvāna to speak of beyond the entity of the eighth consciousness. For this reason, "nirvāna" only results from an establishment of verbalization; the state of the remainderless nirvāna is taught based on the fact that the eighth consciousness no longer takes rebirth in the three realms.

The remainderless nirvāna, however, is not an ultimate dharma, for there remain latent seeds of afflictive hindrances that are not extinguished. The Buddha preaches that only the mahaparinirvāna is ultimate, because all habitual seeds of afflictive hindrances as well as all latent cognitive hindrances are extinguished in this state.

The nirvāna realized by all sages of the Three Vehicles in Buddhism is the ultimate dharma of the three realms; there is no phenomenon to speak of beyond it. In the state of the remainderless nirvāna, the first seven consciousnesses are all extinguished and none of the eighteen elements manifest; there is neither the one that feels and cognizes (the mental consciousness) in the awake state nor the decision-maker (manas-consciousness) in deep sleep—as all phenomena are extinct, what phenomenon is there to speak of? Hence, the Buddha says: "If there is any dharma superior to nirvāna, then I also say it is also like an illusion and a dream." This is because the various selves do not exist in the state of the remainderless nirvāna—the self consisting of the mind of feeling and cognition and the self consisting of the decision-making mind are both extinguished.

If the mental consciousness did not cease and was able to travel throughout the three times as well as enter and abide in the remainderless nirvāṇa, then the mind of feeling and cognition and the decision-making mind would still exist in the state of nirvāṇa; there would still be phenomena in that state; and all the phenomena that continue to appear, exist, and function in that state would be superior to and more wondrous than the dharma of nirvāṇa. Does this reasoning not make sense? Indeed, given that all phenomena in the state of nirvāṇa manifest the great functions of supramundane dharmas based on nirvāṇa, they should be superior to the dharma of nirvāṇa. If this were the case, then the Buddha's words would be false, and we should thus request the Buddha to teach and re-write the contents of the prajñā sūtras. Is Tsongkhapa's claim true or false? All wise persons should think about this carefully.

The emptiness-nature set forth by the Buddha refers to the mind consisting of the eighth consciousness. The Buddha has further taught, based on the natures of the Middle-Way of the mind consisting of the eighth consciousness, about the emptiness-signs of all phenomena consisting of the five aggregates—the fact that the form body and the mind of seeing, hearing, feeling, and cognition are both unreal. Therefore, He has not just preached about the emptithes-signs of all phenomena consisting of the five aggregates. Tantric gurus such as Tsongkhapa and so forth have misinterpreted these teachings due to their failure to understand their meanings upon reading them; having misconstrued the Buddha's statements about the emptiness of the form body and all phenomena outside the body, they regard the emptiness of all phenomena as the emptiness-nature of prajñā.

Furthermore, the words "all aspects" do not refer to "all aspects of phenomena" as stated by Tsongkhapa, but rather to all the seeds stored in the mind of sentient beings consisting of the eighth consciousness. The term "seed" is also known as "realm" or "functional potentiality"; all the seeds stored in the eighth consciousness correspond to all the functional potentialities stored in this consciousness. Having failed to comprehend the Buddha's tenets, Tsongkhapa has misinterpreted them based on his own understanding and has misled sentient beings with teachings issued from such misinterpretations. However, none of the tantric gurus have, since ancient times, been aware of Tsongkhapa's errors; by perpetuating those mistakes, those gurus will continue to mislead present and future learners—exoteric and esoteric learners alike—unless someone refutes those fallacies based on the true doctrines and exposes them to the public.

Within Tantric Buddhism, there are instances where the mode of the emptiness-nature is misapprehended more gravely than in the examples highlighted above. There is even the case of tantric practitioners, who after incorporating the Shaktist method of Hinduism into Buddhism, have hailed the "emptiness-nature" attained through this non-Buddhist method as being superior to the emptiness-nature realized in Buddhism—those practitioners have claimed that the tantric "emptiness-nature" are supreme than the mode of the emptiness-nature propagated in the original Buddhism:

> In the context of the aforementioned basis of empowerment, the emphasis is on the fact that the mind of enlightenment must be real. Then what is the emphasis in the context of the basis of achievement? The emphasis is on the fact that the no-self of the emptiness-nature must be real and on the ability to utilize the emptiness-nature. Emptiness-nature is cultivated in Exoteric Buddhism: Practitioners of Hīnayāna cultivate the no-self of persons, which is about the emptiness-nature; practitioners of Mahāyāna practice until entering the Path of Vision, which is also about the emptiness-nature. The emptiness-nature is also cultivated in Tantric Buddhism. Then what are the differences among these practices of the emptiness-nature? One should know that there are four levels of profundity within the emptiness-nature—namely, external, internal, secret, and extremely secret. The emptiness-nature

emphasized in the basis of achievement pertains to the secret level. Therefore, practitioners generally select Heruka[10] as their deity (see the tantric wrathful form engaged in the yab-yum copulation in standing position) because this will conform to the requirement of the basis of achievement. **With emptiness on one side and bliss on the other side, there is union of emptiness and bliss. One should cultivate the practice of the winds and maintain the non-duality of mind and winds. This practice is not emphasized in the emptiness-nature cultivated by Bodhisattvas.**[11]

Such methods have been unanimously enacted and taught by all ancient and contemporary gurus of Tantric Buddhism. None of those gurus have been able to realize and comprehend the enlightenment of the Two Vehicles for the following reasons: They have always failed to realize the emptiness of the self of persons; they have invariably regarded the mind of feeling and cognition as the permanent and indestructible mind of the reality-suchness; the mind of feeling and cognition has invariably been said by the Buddha in the four Āgamas to correspond to the Divine Self and the Brahma Self found in eternalist non-Buddhism; and the Buddha has always referred to the aforementioned concept as self-view. Those gurus, who have not yet eliminated their self-view, sought the Shaktist Theory found in Hinduism and brought it into Buddhism, and claimed that this theory is superior to the doctrines found in the original Buddha Dharma. Fearing that the learners might not believe them, those gurus fabricated *The Vairocanābhisaṃbodhi Sūtra* and untruthfully claimed that it was preached by the Buddha Mahāvairocana of the *Flower Garland Sūtra*. However, if we take a look at the assertions in *The Vairocanābhisaṃbodhi Sūtra*, we will notice that they are entirely based on the Shaktist Theory found in Hinduism and are the complete opposite of the doctrines of the

---

10   Heruka: wrathful deity; C. *heiluga/ heluge* 黑魯嘎／赫魯噶.
11   Yogi C. M. Chen (Chen Chien-ming 陳健民), *Qugongzhai quanji* 曲肱齋全集 [*The Complete Works of Yogi Chen*], vol. 1-5, ed. Xu Qinying 徐芹庭 (Taipei: Puxianwang rulai fojiaohui 普賢王如來佛教會, 1991), vol. 1, 396. Translated into English from Chinese.

enlightenment of the Three Vehicles set forth in the Buddha Dharma and differ drastically from the Dharma of great Bodhisattvas taught in the *Flower Garland Sūtra*. The fallacies of the tantric mode of the "emptiness-nature" related to Heruka's sexual contact mentioned in the above text will be treated in detail in Chapter 9, which is mainly about the Highest Yoga Tantra of bliss and emptiness. Readers will then gain a clear understanding of this topic.

Having misunderstood what the prajñā sūtras are all about, Tsongkhapa regards the emptiness of nature as the emptiness-nature. He has thus been teaching and misleading sentient beings. Such errors do not occur just once or twice, but can be seen throughout his writings:

> Regarding that yoga in which the mind that has the pattern of the circle [of a mandala] engages with the thatness of no-self: according to Shrī Phalavajra's explanation, [such a nondual mind] is generally operative in all three meditative stabilizations, and this also is Jñānapāda's (the guru's) thought. Thus, although it is indeed the case that in the context of the first stage one principally meditates the circle of deities that is the perception side, nonetheless one does train oneself in everything arising as an illusion by developing intense certitude about the import of the intrinsic identitylessness of all things. So, [1] [first there is] the meditation on [building up] the circle of deities; then having visualized the objective deity, after that [one engages in] [2] the yoga of the nonduality of the profound and the vivid in which the subjective mind that is certain about the import of the intrinsic identitylessness of [that deity] form—[which mind has] a habit-pattern involving certain knowledge—while engaging in emptiness, arises as the objective form of the habitat and the deities who are the inhabitants. So you should perform the practice, by alternating [2] [this yoga of the nonduality of the profound and the vivid] with [1] evocation meditation.
>
> Having seen the power of this import, the root *Tantra of the Hevajra* says:
>
> With the yoga of the creation stage,

The ascetic should meditate an elaborated [world].
Making [this] elaborated [world] dreamlike,
With this very elaboration he should make it un-
elaborative.
And the explanatory Tantra on that, The [Vajra]
Pavilion, says:
For example, the moon [reflected] in water,
Oh friends, is neither true nor false.
Likewise here, the wheel of the mandala
Has a nature which is transparent and vivid.

Therefore, since meditation on emptiness is necessary in the contexts of both stages, in the context of Mantra it is not the case that all meditations on any emptiness are the perfection stage. On the other hand [on the perception/body side], since in the context of the creation stage there is an extreme development of the yoga of a deity body—which [body] is like the moon [reflected] in water, or a rainbow in the sky, like an illusion which though perceived is yet identityless—one must distinguish that [highly developed creation stage illusory deity body] from the illusion body of the self-consecration [stage of] the perfection stage. [12]

The freedom from conceptual proliferations, as taught by the Buddha, has however nothing to do with such false thinking from tantric gurus. Tsongkhapa believes that one has realized the emptiness-nature of all phenomena if, after completing the generation stage of the tantric path, one is able to observe and understand the fact that the nature of all phenomena "is empty of shape and substance" and is able to subsequently acknowledge this fact. Based on this realization, tantric practitioners do not frequently engage in deeds of verbalizations anymore; instead, they often abide in the state of thoughtlessness and observe that the verbalizations used to explicate these various practices all

---

[12] Tsong Khapa Losang Drakpa, *Great Treatise on the Stages of Mantra (sngags rim chen mo): Critical Elucidation of the Key Instructions in All the Secret Stages of the Path of the Victorious Universal Lord, Great Vajradhara. Chapters XI–XII (The Creation Stages)*, introduction and translation by Thomas Freeman Yarnall, (AIBS, CBS & THUS, New York, 2013), 195-96.

consist of conceptual proliferations. Those who are able to comprehend and realize this concept have become "free from conceptual proliferations" in the tantric sense. However, **the "freedom from conceptual proliferations" set forth by the World-Honored One** does not refer to the freedom from all verbalizations, but instead points to the true realization of the eighth consciousness; thanks to the realization of this mind, the ground of vision that arises from one's mind of feeling and cognition and all the verbalizations that one uses to teach others will be associated with the true and correct doctrine of the foremost meaning; the state in which one abides and the speeches that one makes will all be based on mental applications that accord with the correct mode and will all be associated with the truth of the foremost meaning; the speeches that one makes will all result from one's actual realization of the foremost meaning and will not be some conceptual proliferations issued from the erroneous thinking stemming from one's own understanding; such is the meaning of "freedom from conceptual proliferations" set forth by the World-Honored One. As none of the ancient and contemporary tantric gurus such as Tsongkhapa and so forth have been able to grasp what the World-Honored One's sūtras are all about, they have been misleading sentient beings with their misinterpretations. It just does not make any sense for them to proclaim that their statements can free people from conceptual proliferations while those statements do not touch upon the truth of the foremost meaning and have always consisted of conceptual proliferations.

6. The Misunderstandings of the Path to Liberation and the Path to the Enlightenment of Buddhahood in Tantric Buddhism

Tantric gurus, ancient and modern alike, have absolutely no idea about the differences between the practice and realization of an arhat and those of a Buddha due to their inability to understand the Path to the Enlightenment of Buddhahood and the Path to Liberation:

> Tsongkhapa also believes that arhats and Buddhas differ in that Buddhas have accumulated more meritorious quality than arhats have. In addition, he holds that arhats do not have the wisdom that it takes to realize the emptiness-nature. **With respect to the realization of the emptiness-nature, he sees no difference between Hīnayāna and Mahāyāna.**[1]

The above teaching demonstrates that tantric gurus are totally unable to understand and realize the Path to Liberation and the Path to the Enlightenment of Buddhahood. The meritorious quality accumulated by a Buddha certainly exceeds those of an arhat to an immeasurable, and even unknowable, extent. Furthermore, a Buddha and an arhat do not just differ with respect to the actual contents that they have realized in the Path to Liberation (the difference lies in the elimination or not of habitual seeds). Their biggest difference lies in the practice and realization or not of the Path to the Enlightenment of Buddhahood. Having failed to grasp this principle, all ancient and modern tantric gurus (including Master Yinshun, who is a proponent of Prāsaṅgika Madhyamaka) have falsely claimed that they can teach learners the

---

1   *Fojiao chanding* 佛教禪定 [*Buddhist Meditation*], vol. 1, narrated by C. M. Chen, recorded by Kangdi Paulo 康地保羅, and translated by Wuyouzi 無憂子, (Taipei: Puxianwangrulai yinjinghui 普賢王如來印經會, 1991), vol. 1, 167. Translated into English from Chinese.

Path to Liberation and *The Path to Buddhahood* [this is the title of a publication authored by Master Yinshun]—such assertions are nothing but falsities and overblown statements. Based on such elementary and erroneous thinking, those tantric gurus have further proclaimed that their path is superior to that of Exoteric Buddhism. Their behavior is akin to that of an elementary school student bragging that he is better versed in Chinese literature than a university professor in Chinese. It is very difficult to engage in a dialogue with those tantric gurus given the immense gap between the levels of our knowledge and view of the Buddha Dharma.

The first difference between a Buddha and an arhat relates to the practice and realization of the Path to Liberation. An arhat has only eliminated the manifestation of afflictive hindrances (self-view and self-attachment)—he does not eradicate the habitual seeds of afflictive hindrances stored in his eighth consciousness. A Buddha had, in contrast, gradually been eliminating all the habitual seeds of afflictive hindrances stored in His eighth consciousness starting from the First Ground, which was two great terms of asaṃkhya kalpas before He became Buddha. By the time He attained Buddhahood, He had completely extinguished even the extremely subtle habitual seeds of afflictive hindrances, without leaving any seed behind. For this reason, a Buddha does not have any predispositions left, whereas an arhat still has predispositions that he has not even started to eliminate. Therefore, the fruition of liberation attained by a Buddha differs drastically from that achieved by an arhat.

The second difference between a Buddha and an arhat concerns the practice and realization of the Path to the Enlightenment of Buddhahood. Three great terms of asaṃkhya kalpas ago, the Buddha fulfilled the Ten Faiths and entered the stage of Bodhisattva for the first time, where He extensively cultivated countless deeds of the six pāramitās outside the door [translation note: before enlightenment] until He gradually reached and entered the Sixth Abiding. He stumbled upon the teachings of a virtuous mentor and therefore realized the mind consisting of the eighth consciousness; He brought forth the wisdom of prajñā and entered and abided in the Seventh Abiding, thus becoming a Bodhisattva of non-regression from the stage. He then studied the prajñā sūtras and realized the knowledge-of-specific-aspects of prajñā. He saw the Buddha-nature with his physical eyes at the stage of the Tenth Abiding. Next, He eliminated the non-exalted nature of ordinary people and brought forth the vajra mind. Having no fear for the great power of all humans and celestial beings, He appeared in this world to refute the incorrect doctrines while manifesting the correct ones. Based on this meritorious quality, He advanced in his practice by cultivating the knowledge-of-all-aspects, thereby gradually heading towards the First Ground. He achieved the acquiescence to the non-arising of dharmas pertaining to the First Ground and attained the knowledge-of-the-aspects-of-paths pertaining to the First Ground.

Based on the knowledge-of-the-aspects-of-paths pertaining to the First Ground, a Buddha proceeded further in His practice by cultivating, in the correct sequence and during two great terms of asaṃkhya kalpas, the acquiescence to the non-arising of dharmas pertaining to every Ground and brought forth all the seeds in the eighth consciousness that must be realized in each Ground. He gradually completed the realization of the knowledge-of-all-aspects and perfected the ten pāramitās. Thereafter, He cultivated excellent marks over a period of one hundred kalpas, during which He could sacrifice his body, life, and wealth in any place and at any time. Having extensively accumulated meritorious quality in this fashion, He exterminated, in the Final Stage of Bodhisattva, the extremely subtle residual of latent cognitive hindrances and attained the ultimate fruition of Buddhahood. Such destruction and extinguishment of cognitive hindrances as well as such practice and realization of the wisdom related to all the seeds of the eighth consciousness do not exist in the cultivation of sound-hearer arhats. As the sound-hearer arhats cannot even apprehend the knowledge-of-general-aspect pertaining to prajñā brought forth by the Bodhisattvas of the Seventh Abiding through the realization of the eighth consciousness, how could those arhats be said to have ever realized the correct mode of the emptiness-nature expounded in the Mahāyāna prajñā? Those gurus' statements do not make any sense.

Indeed, the fruition of the enlightenment of the Two-Vehicles attained by sound-hearer arhats merely consists of the realization of the emptiness-signs—the realization of the "emptiness of the self of persons" through the direct observation and cognition that all phenomena consisting of the aggregates, sense fields, and elements are impermanent and therefore empty and through the direct observation and cognition that the mind of feeling and cognition is impermanent and therefore empty and that the decision-making mind—the mental faculty—is not the mind that exists on its own and is therefore empty. Contrary to tantric practitioners, sound-hearer arhats do not insist that the emptiness of shape and form observed in the mind of feeling and cognition and in the sensation of sexual pleasure corresponds to the emptiness-nature. Therefore, sound-hearer arhats do not understand and do not strive to realize the emptiness-nature set forth in prajñā. As for all the ancient and modern gurus of Tantric Buddhism, not only do they not understand and not strive to realize the correct doctrine of the emptiness-nature of prajñā, just like sound-hearer arhats, but they also do not understand the enlightenment of the Two-Vehicles realized by sound-hearer arhats—the correct doctrine about the emptiness-signs related to the aggregates, sense fields, and elements—hence their untruthful statements.

The complete lack of knowledge and comprehension about the differences between an arhat and a Buddha exhibited by tantric gurus can be attributed to their total ignorance of the correct doctrine of the emptiness-nature preached by the Buddha in the prajñā sūtras as well as their complete ignorance of the enlightenment of the Two-Vehicles. Those gurus have always regarded the emptiness of all phenomena as the emptiness-nature of prajñā and are unaware that the emptiness-nature of prajñā set forth by the Buddha actually refers to the eighth consciousness—the mind of the sign of reality. They believe that one understands and has realized the emptiness-nature of prajñā if one knows that the form body is impermanent and therefore empty. In addition, unaware that the Buddha has, in the Āgamas, extensively refuted the mind of feeling and cognition by pointing out that it is an unreal phenomenon, those tantric gurus insist that the mind of feeling and cognition in a state of thoughtlessness corresponds to the mind of the sign of reality—the reality-suchness—thus precisely falling into self-view. While they are thus unable to realize the Path to Liberation and the Path to the Enlightenment of Buddhahood, they have disparaged Exoteric Buddhism by proclaiming the superiority of their practices and realizations. What a total inversion of the truth!

Such misapprehensions of the emptiness-nature of prajñā and the Path to Liberation pervade Tsongkhapa's publications. Not only do they pervade Tsongkhapa's writings, but they can also be seen throughout the works of the Gelug School's followers. Not only can such misunderstandings be seen throughout the publications of the Gelug School's followers, but they can also be found throughout the writings of all ancient and contemporary gurus from the other three major tantric schools. It is impossible to list all those misinterpretations; all learners can validate this fact themselves by searching through those works with a little attention. It would be pointless for me to cite all those misunderstandings, as such an endeavor would bore readers.

Those who do not believe my statements can take a look at the following assertions by the great tantric practitioner, C. M. Chen:

> Yamāntaka is an important deity in the Gelug School. . . . The witnessing portion in *The Philosophy of the Witnessing Portion of Yamāntaka* [*Daweide zhengfenlunzheli* 大威德證分論哲理] lies in the "basis" found in the doctrines of basis, path, and fruition. . . . but its basic philosophy asserts that both

Hīnayāna and Mahāyāna teach the same emptiness-nature and that their only difference lies in their methods. This assertion seems arbitrary. Please see this chapter for the details.[2]

C. M. Chen's criticism of the Gelug School is well-founded. In fact, the Nyingma, Kagyu, and Sakya Schools have also fallen into the same view, as their proponents believe that the sages of both Hīnayāna and Mahāyāna realize the same "emptiness-nature"; therefore, those proponents only make judgments on whether those sages possess skillful methods or have attained different levels of valid knowledge of realization. However, those tantric practitioners do not know the differences between the contents of the Path to Liberation realized by a Buddha and those attained by an arhat. Furthermore, they have never been aware of the fact that the arhats of Hīnayāna who do not turn to Mahāyāna are completely ignorant of the enlightenment of Buddhahood because they have never realized the eighth consciousness. Thus, those tantric practitioners do not understand and have not realized the Path to Liberation and the Path to the Enlightenment of Buddhahood. Surprisingly, they introduced the view of eternalist non-Buddhists as well as the Dharma-gate of fallacious religion consisting of the non-Buddhist Shaktism into Buddhism and hailed them as being superior to the two principal Paths preached by Buddha Śākyamuni. They have declared that their false views of ordinary people and non-Buddhists allow people to attain Buddhahood in their current bodies and are therefore superior to the views of Exoteric Buddhism. It is difficult to engage in a dialogue with them given the extent to which they have inverted the truth.

Tantric gurus are all unaware of the meaning of prajñā and have explained the tenets of prajñā based on their understanding. There is a tantric guru who believes that one has eliminated one's self-view and self-attachment if one is able to attain the state of

---

2   Yogi C. M. Chen (Chen Chien-ming 陳健民), *Qugongzhai quanji 曲肱齋全集 [The Complete Works of Yogi Chen]*, vol. 1-5, ed. Xu Qinying 徐芹庭 (Taipei: Puxianwang rulai fojiaohui 普賢王如來佛教會, 1991), vol. 3, 116. Translated into English from Chinese.

the cloudless and sunny sky in sitting meditation:

My explanation of the "cloudless and sunny sky," based on my own experience, differs from the descriptions found in most of the books. There is not just a state of cloudless and sunny sky above one's head, nor is there a "self" beholding this cloudless and sunny sky. **There is in fact a state of nothingness, in which the cloudless and sunny sky pervades all places, including the center, all sides, the four directions, and so forth**. In this state, not only does the practitioner have no self-attachment in his mind, but he no longer has a physical body. This is all from my personal experience and not from some rumors or plagiarized contents among book authors. However, it is difficult to prolong this experience indefinitely; the reason is because one cannot often remain concentrated in this fashion due to the insufficiency of concentration power. **If one can often remain concentrated in this fashion, then one has already realized the Dharma body Buddha**. Therefore, this is the pivot of all practices. If you can abandon everything and solely focus on this method, then you will not go astray because this is the most reliable shortcut. The clear entity of Mahāmudrā is it; the Great Perfection[3] and the ground of vision in the Chan School are also it. The so-called Śūraṅgama Samādhi, Lotus Samādhi, and the Profound Gates of the *Avataṃsaka Sūtra* are all it. . . . The so-called meritorious quality of supernatural power also stems from this; if it does not manifest now, it will certainly do so in the future. The so-called profound gates all stem from this because there is profundity only when there is emptiness. If you can consider the dharma-realm to be the entity, then you will become selfless; you will always benefit others and will not hurt anyone. Only with emptiness can one

---

3   Great Perfection: T. *rdzogs chen* (*dzokchen*); C. *da yuanman* 大圓滿, also known as atiyoga (utmost yoga), is a tradition of teachings in Indo-Tibetan Buddhism aimed at discovering and continuing in the ultimate ground of existence; Pettit, John Whitne, *Mipha''s beacon of certainty: illuminating the view of Dzogchen, the Great Perfection*, (Wisdom Publications, 1999).

benefit others because emptiness leads to the no-self. How could there be no-self without emptiness? The no-self and the emptiness of all phenomena are in fact two sides of the same coin. Those who taught "emptiness" earlier did not bother to teach the "no-self," thinking that the two are unrelated, but actually they are the same. Once you understand the immensity of the dharma-realm, you will not be attached to the small selfish self; once you realize the boundlessness of the three times—past, present, and future—you will not focus on just one instant or one tiny thing. It is painful to consider things by singling out the time period in which those things occurred; if one can prolong or shorten the time period, then there will be no pain. Therefore, this is determined by the first two sentences: "The ten directions are broad and boundless, and the three times flow endlessly." It is imperative to first achieve the following: You can imagine that there is a dot in your mind; on that dot exists a horizontal line extending infinitely leftward and rightward; the ten directions are broad and boundless, without anything within them. With respect to the statement, "The three times flow endlessly," time's death signs cannot be detected within myriad pasts, nor can we detect time's rebirth signs within myriad futures. The upper and the lower sides of the aforementioned line also extend upward infinitely, without a beginning or an ending. If you were a geometrician, you could draw a sphere on this cross; this sphere would be your dharma-realm. Just imagine for a short while the infinite vastness of this dharma-realm; how exhilarating. . . . Regarding the word "mind" in the scriptures, "the wondrous mind of the reality-suchness; this mind becomes Buddha; and this mind is Buddha," one should not regard it as an ordinary mind. **In our statement about the fundamental meditative concentration of the dharma-realm, we have replaced the mind with the dharma-realm;** dharma refers to all phenomena, including the mind and the physical objects. . . . The statement "The ten directions are broad and boundless, and the three times flow endlessly" constitutes a basis that is similar to the pillars of the dharma-realm. The dharma-realm is measureless; there is no center in yu (space) and zhou (time). [The term "yu zhou" in Mandarin means "universe."] In other words, every dot constitutes a center. During visualization, we can, for the time being, regard our own mind as the center—the place of practice and withdrawal. However, this is just for the sake of expediency; do not forget that the object of our practice is the "selfless" great meditative concentration of the dharma-realm. We should forget ourselves completely—we are not the ones practicing the meditative concentration, but instead it is the dharma-realm itself manifesting the great meditative concentration of the dharma-realm. Therefore, the state of "the self losing the self" does indeed exist. [4]

The cloudless and sunny sky in the upward, downward, forward, backward, leftward, and rightward directions is actually a state of the mental consciousness—the mind of feeling and cognition—a state visualized by the mental consciousness and in which it abides. Although those who abide in this state proclaim that there is no state to speak of and that there is not a "self" dwelling in this state, there is in fact the "self" consisting of the mind of feeling and cognition "abiding" in the state of cloudless sunny sky, because there is a "self" cognizing that it itself "abides" in this state. How could one speak of no-self when there exists a "self" cognizing this state, a state in which one abides, and a "self" abiding in this state? Although the mind of feeling and cognition abiding in this state does not perform the function of seeing, this state is still being taken in by a mind that can cognize and feel. It is senseless to claim that there is no-self when there exists a mind taking in the "cloudless and sunny sky." In fact, the abiding in this state is in fact associated with self-view. Indeed, the one that cognizes and abides is the aggregate of consciousness (one of the five aggregates)—the conscious mind (one of the phenomena

---

4   Yogi C. M. Chen (Chen Chien-ming 陳健民), *Qugongzhai quanji* 曲肱齋全集 *[The Complete Works of Yogi Chen]*, vol. 1-5, ed. Xu Qinying 徐芹庭 (Taipei: Puxianwang rulai fojiaohui 普賢王如來佛教會, 1991), vol. 3, 924-31. Translated into English from Chinese.

consisting of the eighteen elements).

In the true view of the no-self, the no-self does not involve entering a state where there is neither feeling nor cognition. Instead, the true view of the no-self consists of exterminating the view that the self consisting of the mind of feeling and cognition is permanent and indestructible by directly observing with one's mind of feeling and cognition—when one's mind of feeling and cognition manifests—that the self consisting of the mind of feeling and cognition is unreal. This is the elimination of self-view. Such deed-contemplation is extensively preached by the Buddha in the four Āgamas. All realizers of the first fruition in the sound-hearer Dharma have all performed the following direct observation amidst the four deportments: They have personally observed that their self consisting of the mind of feeling and cognition is unreal and have exterminated the self-view that this self in the desire realm is permanent and indestructible. It is through this deed-contemplation that they became sound-hearer realizers of the first fruition—stream-enterers, who are pre-counted within the stream of exalted ones.

With respect to the arhats in the sound-hearer Dharma who have attained the meritorious quality of exterminating their self-attachment, they further performed, based on the aforementioned elimination of the self-view of the desire realm, various deed-contemplations that enabled them to abandon the self-view of the form realm and then the self-view of the formless realm in the correct sequence, thereby extinguishing their self-attachment and becoming realizers of the fourth fruition, who are also known as "the ones worthy of receiving offerings from the worlds" or "thief killers" for having exterminated the mental thieves that are the self-view of the three realms and the clinging to the self. However, none of the realizers of the first fruition through to the fourth fruition eliminated their self-view or self-attachment by entering and abiding in the state of the "cloudless and sunny sky" or in the state without feeling and cognition of the "dim awareness of access concentration." Remaining in a bustling environment did not prevent them from attaining the view of the no-self or abandoning their self-attachment.

Similarly, Bodhisattvas search for the mind consisting of the eighth consciousness—which has always been free from all seeing, hearing, feeling, and cognition—in the conditions consisting of bustling states, without entering and abiding in a state devoid of feeling and cognition or the state of the "cloudless and sunny sky." Once they have found the eighth consciousness, they directly observe and validate the fact that its entity never arises and therefore never ceases. They directly observe and validate the fact that the entity of this eighth consciousness never has any verbal thought, has never slept or dreamt, has never been mindful of any phenomenon, never abides in any state of meditative concentration, never exhibits greed, anger, joy, or repugnance, and never has mental activities that are either pure or defiled. Only can such a state of one's own mind where the eighth consciousness abides be called great meditative concentration of the dharma-realm—the aforementioned state of the "cloudless and sunny sky" set forth in Tantric Buddhism cannot be dubbed great meditative concentration of the dharma-realm.

While the eighth consciousness—the tathāgatagarbha—has, in this fashion, always been free from all states, it can, within the bodies of all sentient beings of the three realms and with perfect accuracy, manifest various objects according to the conditions and illuminate with both astuteness and lucidity. Even when sentient beings are in states of deep sleep, unconsciousness, and death, the eighth consciousness continues to function in this manner without interruption; sentient beings cannot live an instant without it, yet they are unable to realize or understand it. Furthermore, Bodhisattvas directly observe, based on the natures of the mind consisting of the eighth consciousness, that the mind of seeing, hearing, feeling, and cognition as well as the decision-making mind in deep sleep both arise from the eighth consciousness. Based on this direct observation and validation, Bodhisattvas can realize and comprehend that the mind of feeling and cognition is indeed endowed with an other-powered nature and cannot exist by itself—it cannot exist alone without the eighth consciousness even for an instant. Due to this direct observation and validation, they can eliminate the view that the self consisting of the mind of feeling and cognition is permanent and indestructible as well as the view that the self consisting of the decision-making mind can abide by itself permanently and is indestructible, thereby becoming those who have eliminated their self-view. Consequently, they can bring forth the wisdom of prajñā. Even if the arhats who do not turn to the Mahāyāna Dharma exhaust their ten knowledges of sound-hearer liberation, they will not even slightly understand this wisdom of prajñā realized by the Bodhisattvas of the Seventh Abiding.

If Bodhisattvas can, based on this ground of vision, further eradicate their self-attachment, then they will be able to achieve the meritorious quality of liberation attained by arhats while also possessing the wisdom of the enlightenment of Buddhahood, which cannot be apprehended by arhats. Bodhisattvas do not realize of such an eighth consciousness free from all seeing, hearing, feeling, and cognition—the limit of reality of the remainderless nirvāṇa—by entering and abiding in the "cloudless and sunny sky" through the practice of meditative concentration or by pretending to have realized "the "reality-suchness free from all verbalizations" while dwelling without seeing, hearing, feeling, or cognition in meditative concentration. As a matter of fact, one realizes the mind consisting of the eighth consciousness, which is free from all verbalizations and all states consisting of the six sense objects, without dissociating oneself from any verbalizations or from within any states consisting of the six sense objects and without eliminating any verbalizations or any states consisting of the six sense objects. The mind consisting of the eighth consciousness—which has always been free from all verbalizations and all states—co-exists with the mind of feeling and cognition. Therefore, after one's enlightenment, it is perfectly fine that while one's mind of feeling and cognition connects with verbalizations and various states, there is separately a wondrous mind consisting of the reality-suchness—which is intrinsically free from all verbalizations and all states—that functions in tandem with the mind of feeling and cognition. Only those who can perceive and witness this fact have truly realized the enlightenment of Buddhahood; their wisdom cannot be apprehended by the arhats who do not turn to Mahāyāna.

We can observe that after all Buddhas and Bodhisattvas became enlightened, they all still have two minds—the mind of feeling and cognition and the fundamental mind consisting of the eighth consciousness, which is free from feeling and cognition— that function in tandem. They are neither said to be enlightened because they entered the state of the cloudless and sunny sky, nor are they said to be unenlightened because they did not enter this state. All learners who wish to pursue such enlightenment of Mahāyāna should thus understand, thus practice, thus realize, and more importantly thus gradually advance towards the Ground of Buddhahood.

The empty space in the ten directions, furthermore, does not correspond to the dharma-realm. "Empty space" purely results from the establishment of a denomination, as there is no such a dharma as "empty space": It is just a terminology with no dharma behind it. The denomination "empty space" is established based on the area devoid of objects beyond the edge of a form dharma. Given that the denomination "empty space" is established based on the absence of objects, it should be known that the denomination "empty space" is actually established based upon the edge of a form dharma—it exists in dependence upon a form dharma. Hence, *Abhidharma Treasury Treatise [Jushelun 俱舍論]* speaks of empty space as "form dharma beyond form"[5]—it is just a terminology with no actual dharma behind it. How could "empty space," which is a terminology with no dharma behind it—without

---

[5]   Form dharma beyond form: Alt. the form dharma beyond the edge of physical
form, a term defined based on the existence of physical form. C. *sebianse* 色邊色.

any single dharma behind it—be called dharma-realm? To speak of "dharma", there must be a "dharma" that can be personally taken in by sentient beings—both exalted and ordinary people—in the three realms. In addition, this "dharma" must have its specific functional potentiality—a functional potentiality to which other dharmas do not have access—and what sentient beings can take in from each dharma is limited to the specific functional potentiality of each dharma, hence the term "realm" and consequently the term "dharma-realm." However, having misconstrued the true meaning of the dharma-realm—just like C. M. Chen—all ancient and contemporary tantric gurus regard the non-existence of dharmas in the empty space in the ten directions as the dharma-realm and consider this empty space to be the life source of all sentient beings. C. M. Chen has further established the aforementioned "great meditative concentration of the dharma-realm," urging learners to practice in the aforementioned fashion. As a matter of fact, his teachings are all based on erroneous thinking that stems from his own understandings and have nothing to do with either meditative concentration or the dharma-realm and are even more unrelated to the wisdom of the enlightenment of Buddhahood.

"The dharma-realm in the ten directions" refers to the fact that there are immeasurable and countless lands in the empty space of the ten directions; there are immeasurable and countless sentient beings in those immeasurable and countless lands; given that there are immeasurable and countless sentient beings, there must be immeasurable and countless dharmas; as there are immeasurable and countless dharmas, there must be immeasurable and countless dharma-realms. The existence of immeasurable and countless dharma-realms implies that there are immeasurable and countless sentient beings of the four births and twenty-five existences and that there must be all sentient beings such as myriad sound-hearer exalted beings as well as Buddhas, Bodhisattvas, and so forth. Therefore, the statement "the dharma-realms in the ten directions" refers to countless exalted and ordinary sentient beings in countless lands in the empty space in the ten directions—the empty space in the ten directions cannot be said to be the dharma-realm. We can conclude that the tantric method consisting of visualizing "the dharma-realm of the empty space in the ten directions" is based on erroneous thinking and has nothing to do with the Buddha Dharma. Even if one is able to achieve such visualization, this practice remains useless, as it does not allow one to connect with the Path to Liberation or the Path to the Enlightenment of Buddhahood. Therefore, those who aspire to learn Buddhism must, before embarking on their cultivation, clearly understand the reasonings of the Buddha Dharma and truly comprehend the similarities and differences between the Path to Liberation and the enlightenment of Buddhahood. They should not blindly adhere to fallacious teachings and recklessly abide by erroneous doctrines imparted by falsely virtuous mentors; otherwise, their practice and training will all be futile and they will inevitably end up impeding others' progress due to their own mistakes and suffer from grave consequences.

Furthermore, some misinformed and ignorant persons who do not understand the prajñā of the Path to the Enlightenment of Buddhahood and who blindly believe in the false knowledge and views found in Tantric Buddhism believe that the so-called "Chan" in the Chan School consists of a **shock therapy**. For instance, Chen Chunlong [陳淳隆] (Miaozhan[妙湛]), and Ding Guangwen [丁光文] have posted the following falsities on their website with respect to The Sudden Teaching of Great Perfection in the Chan School and the Esoteric School:

> The Sudden Teaching consists of relying on various means such as Deshan's Blow, Linji's Shout, Beholding the Blooming of Flowers, Listening to Bird Sounds, and so forth in order to spark off the religious experience of the sixth consciousness and use it as an impact to destroy the attachments to the self and to the dharmas in the seventh [or the eighth] consciousness and to achieve enlightenment—to enter the Path of Vision. These are all very personal issues: Those with strong attachments to the self and to the dharmas need to destroy

those attachments with high-intensity impact, whereas those with weak attachments to the self and to the dharmas can destroy those attachments just with an impact of ordinary intensity. This in fact corresponds to the "shock therapy" found in western psychology. Such a practice indeed differs substantially from the method to attain enlightenment highlighted in Buddhist sūtras, which consists of using the peaceful mindset of entering meditative concentration to gradually dissolving the attachments to the self and to the dharmas. . . . This demonstrates that some practitioners who have committed the deed of grievous false speech by proclaiming their enlightenment become furious when they are criticized by people with discrepant views and therefore openly request in their publications to hold Dharma debates. They even declare in those publications that both sides must sign an affidavit before the debate: "The loser of this debate must assume his defeat by taking his own life." Such vindictive mindset, which consists of being content only after having successfully inflicted the threat of death on the other party, clearly contradicts the state of liberation consisting of the "union of compassion and wisdom" experienced by Buddhas and Bodhisattvas. Therefore, these practitioners have obviously not achieved enlightenment, and their speeches and assertions can certainly be disregarded.[6]

Chen Chunlong and Ding Guangwen are indeed outsiders when it comes to the Buddha Dharma. Unable to understand the Buddha Dharma, they have been deceiving tantric learners with the aforementioned falsities, thereby exposing their shortfalls. Why is that so? Although the sudden teaching of the Chan School causes learners to achieve enlightenment with various means such as Deshan's Blow, Linji's Shout, Beholding the Blooming of Flowers, Listening to Bird Sounds, and so forth, this method—contrary to

---

[6]   Chen, Chunlong 陳淳隆 (Miaozhan 妙湛) and Ding Guangwen 丁光文, *Kongxing jian xinjiaodu de chanshi* 空性見新角度的闡釋 《上下集》 *[An Explanation of the New Perspective on the View of Emptiness, vols. 1 & 2]*, retrieved from http://city080.mydreamer.com.tw/. Translated into English from Chinese.

Chen and Ding's assertions—does not **"spark off the religious experience of the sixth consciousness and use it as an impact,"** nor does it **"destroy the attachments to the self and to the dharmas in the seventh [or the eighth] consciousness"** in order **"to achieve enlightenment—to enter the Path of Vision."** In fact, the sudden teaching in the Chan School consists of using various sharp prods[7] in order to cause people to realize on the spot the eighth consciousness—the mind consisting of the sign of reality—and thereby bring forth the wisdom of prajñā. Upon realizing the eighth consciousness, one can cognize on the spot that this eighth consciousness is the source of all dharma-realms consisting of sentient beings—both ordinary and exalted people—in the worlds of the ten directions; that is, one will cognize that this eighth consciousness—tathāgatagarbha—constitutes the source of the properties of all dharma-realms. Consequently, one will realize the wisdom of the properties of the dharma-realm and understand what the prajñā sūtras are all about without anyone's teaching.

To **"destroying the attachments to the self and to the dharmas in the seventh [or the eighth] consciousness"** is a task that comes after enlightenment (after the realization of the eighth consciousness). By realizing the intrinsic, natural, pure, and nirvāṇic natures of the eighth consciousness and directly observing the intrinsicality, nature, purity, and nirvāṇa of this eighth consciousness, one cognizes that the dharma-realms consisting of all sentient beings—ordinary people and exalted beings— correspond to this property; this is, therefore, called enlightenment. Based on this enlightenment, one becomes a Buddha after one has gradually eliminated through practice the concomitant and intermittent self-attachment [8] and the concomitant and intermittent dharma-attachment[9] of the sixth

---

[7]   Sharp prod: an acute stimulus given at the right moment to help one attain sudden enlightenment; C. *jifeng* 機鋒.

[8]   Concomitant and intermittent self-attachment: C. *jusheng duanxu wozhi* 俱生斷續 我執.

[9]   Concomitant and intermittent dharma-attachment: C. *jusheng duanxu fazhi* 俱生斷

consciousness and after one has further eliminated the concomitant and continuous self-attachment [10] and the concomitant and continuous dharma-attachment[11] of the seventh consciousness. One does not **"achieve enlightenment—enter the Path of Vision"** after one has **"destroy[ed] the attachments to the self and to the dharmas in the seventh [or the eighth] consciousness."** Indeed, how could anyone **"destroy the attachments to the self and to the dharmas in the seventh [or the eighth] consciousness"** without first becoming enlightened— without first realizing the seventh and the eighth consciousnesses—and without knowing the properties of these two consciousnesses? Chen Chunlong and Ding Guangwen do not understand and have not realized the seventh and the eighth consciousnesses. They do not comprehend the Buddha Dharma, yet they refuse to remain silent—they make those false assertions to defend Tantric Buddhism. However, the more they speak, the more faults they reveal and the more they inform people about their lack of knowledge and skills.

Furthermore, there is no attachment to the self or attachment to the dharmas in the eighth consciousness, as these two attachments are found in the sixth and the seventh consciousnesses. How could Chen and Ding claim that the eighth consciousness possesses these two attachments? They are just outsiders who forcefully speak like insiders, thereby all the more exposing their ignorance of the Buddha Dharma.

Furthermore, the so-called "Chan" in the Chan School does not consist of relying on various means such as Deshan's Blow and so forth in order **"to spark off the religious experience of the sixth consciousness and use it as an impact"** **"to achieve enlightenment— to enter the Path of Vision."** Instead, it is about using sharp prods

---

續法執.

[10] Concomitant and continuous self-attachment: C. *jusheng xiangxu wozhi* 俱生相續我執.

[11] Concomitant and continuous dharma-attachment: C. *jusheng xiangxu fazhi* 俱生相續法執.

to cause the natures of seeing, hearing, cognition, and feeling of the sixth consciousness to touch upon and realize the mind consisting of the eighth consciousness. Subsequently, these natures of the sixth consciousness can experience the intrinsicality, nature, purity, and nirvāṇa as well as the various Middle-Way natures of the mind consisting of the eighth consciousness, experience the fact that this eighth consciousness generates one's self consisting of the mind of seeing, hearing, feeling, and cognition, directly contemplate that this self is unreal and therefore cognize that this self is unreal, which creates an impact. Indeed, one has, since beginningless time, always believed that the self that sees, hears, feels, and cognizes is real and permanent; now, all of a sudden, one validates that one's self is unreal and that the eighth consciousness, which coexists with one's self, is instead the real self. This eighth consciousness is, in contrast, free from all seeing, hearing, feeling, cognition as well as the nature of decision-making, has always dwelled in intrinsicality, nature, purity, and nirvāṇa and without awareness of itself—hence the statement "the mind itself does not see the mind"—this mind is not attached to itself—hence the statement "intrinsically and naturally pure"—as it has never died, it is said to be intrinsically without birth; since this mind has never had any birth, it is said to intrinsically be nirvāṇa, and therefore one does not need to pursue the practice and realization of nirvāṇa.

The practice and realization of the remainderless nirvāṇa is a task of the self consisting of the mind of feeling and cognition; it is this self that realizes the remainderless nirvāṇa: The remainderless nirvāṇa is when there will be noself of future lifetimes after this self eliminated self-attachment and then exterminated itself during death. The eighth consciousness is intrinsically without birth and death; it is intrinsically nirvāṇa, and therefore, we do not need to practice and realize nirvāṇa on its behalf.

The sixth consciousness is greatly impacted by such a realization of nirvāṇa: Before enlightenment, one had always believed that the self that sees, hears, feels, and cognizes was the one that entered nirvāṇa after one's death; however, one learns after enlightenment that the so-called remainderless nirvāṇa is when one has exterminated oneself after death and what remains is only the eighth consciousness existing alone, free from all seeing, hearing, feeling, and cognition—when there is truly no "self." Such realization and cognition generate a great impact, as one discovers that the remainderless nirvāṇa is completely different from what one has previously imagined: After eliminating one's self-attachment, one has not realized the remainderless nirvāṇa but has only exterminated oneself (see my publication *False Views versus the Buddha Dharma [Xiejian yu fofa]*). Therefore, one does not become enlightened by sparking off the religious impact of the sixth consciousness; on the contrary, it is the attainment of enlightenment that generates an impact on the sixth consciousness. Chen and Ding's statements are the complete opposite of the truth, which demonstrates that those two persons are by no means enlightened. By speaking according to their imagination as they are wholly ignorant of the contents and the ground of vision related to enlightenment, all they do is reveal even more of their shortcomings and all they can achieve is duping unenlightened persons.

Furthermore, the attachments to the self and to the dharmas are not destroyed by the impact of the sixth consciousness. Instead, one must directly observe that the self consisting of the mind of seeing, hearing, feeling, and cognition is unreal and that it is indeed generated by the mind consisting of the eighth consciousness and is not a mind that originally existed by itself. The fact that this self is brought forth every day after deep sleep from the eighth consciousness based on a decision by the everlasting and unceasing mind consisting of the seventh consciousness—this is, therefore, called "waking up"—proves that this self is unreal. Based on this direct observation and realization, one eliminates the self-view that the mind of seeing, hearing, feeling, and cognition is permanent and indestructible and thereby become a stream-enterer of the first fruition. Owing to such view and knowledge, this stream-enterer is able to ascertain whether the great masters in various directions have eradicated their self-view and is therefore regarded as having eliminated his skeptical doubt.[12] Still unaware that the self consisting of the mind of seeing, hearing, feeling, and cognition is unreal, Chen and Ding refuse to accept the following ground of vision set forth in my publications: **"The eighth consciousness has been free from all seeing, hearing, feeling, and cognition since beginningless time."** They falsely believe that the eighth consciousness has feeling and cognition and erroneously regard the mind of feeling and cognition in a thoughtlessness as the mind consisting of the eighth consciousness, clearly falling into the scope of the conscious mind's natures—mistaking the conscious mind in thoughtlessness for the eighth consciousness. This demonstrates that neither of them has abandoned their self-view. It just does not make any sense for anyone to proclaim his ability to teach others how to eliminate their self-view when he has not done so himself.

Furthermore, how could Chen and Ding destroy their attachments to the self and to the dharmas when they do not even know the contents thereof? In fact, there are two types of attachment to the self: the self-attachment of the mental consciousness and the self-attachment of the manas-consciousness. How could those two persons eliminate these two self-attachments without understanding them? And how could they teach others to abandon them? Moreover, it is a lie to pretend that they can extinguish their attachment to the dharmas and teach others to do so when they have no idea what the attachment to the self is.

The self-attachment of the sixth consciousness arises from self-view. It is not necessary to re-explain self-view here as it has already been illustrated in previous sections and readers can understand this concept by pondering over those teachings themselves. With respect to the self-attachment of the sixth

---

12 Skeptical doubt: S. *vicikitsā*; C. *yijian* 疑見.

consciousness, although a practitioner has eliminated his self-view by comprehending and realizing that his self consisting of the mind of feeling and cognition is unreal, his mental consciousness constantly exhibits a self-centered habit that has been formed due to the continuous permeation of this habit since beginningless time; this is known as the self-attachment of the mental consciousness. Novice Bodhisattvas (those who have achieved their first ever enlightenment in this lifetime—they have never been enlightened in any of their previous lifetimes) and so forth must eliminate, through gradual practice after enlightenment, such self-attachment associated with the mental consciousness. It is called "self-attachment," as those Bodhisattvas are unable to fully exterminate it upon enlightenment. Moreover, such self-attachment is called "concomitant self-attachment" because it appears concomitantly with the mental consciousness of this lifetime; it does not come into existence through a process of seed-transformation after one's birth. This self-attachment is called "concomitant and intermittent self-attachment," because it disappears temporarily when the mental consciousness ceases every night and reappears concomitantly with the mental consciousness when it arises after one wakes up—it is distinct from the "concomitant and continuous self-attachment of the seventh consciousness."

This concomitant and intermittent self-attachment associated with the mental consciousness is also called "conceptual and intermittent self-attachment." Indeed, the self-attachment associated with the mental consciousness arises because of the conceptual nature of the mental consciousness—this self-attachment inevitably exists every instant the mental consciousness appears. There is cognition whenever the mental consciousness appears, and the existence of cognition implies that there is conceptualization. Therefore, the mental consciousness can discern, without going through any verbalization, all phenomena consisting of the six sense objects; this is the conceptual nature—the cognition—of the mental consciousness. Whenever this nature of cognition appears, the aforementioned self-attachment of the mental consciousness appears concomitantly and simultaneously with the nature of cognition and feeling of the mental consciousness; therefore, the mental consciousness is in every instant aware of the existence of a self—such cognition is the self-attachment of the mental consciousness. The Bodhisattvas who are not yet truly enlightened will not understand this principle until they hear the related explanations from a truly virtuous mentor. How could novice learners like Chen and Ding practice and learn based on this principle when they do not even believe it upon hearing it?

Given that the cognition and conceptualization of the mental consciousness cease every night and reappear when one wakes up, the conceptual self-attachment is not everlasting and continuous. For this reason, this concomitant and intermittent self-attachment associated with the mental consciousness is also known as conceptual and intermittent self-attachment. Novice Bodhisattvas cannot exterminate it upon enlightenment; they must gradually eliminate it by facing different situations through experiencing various conditions.

Veteran Bodhisattvas are able to exterminate their concomitant and intermittent self-attachment associated with the mental consciousness at the same time as they attain enlightenment in this lifetime. Indeed, they eliminated their self-view upon achieving enlightenment in many of their past lifetimes; in addition, they also gradually eliminated the manifestation and predispositions of their self-attachment by facing different situations through experiencing various conditions after becoming enlightened in many past lifetimes. Since these Bodhisattvas are still unable to avoid the loss of past-life memories, their mental consciousness of the previous lifetime ceased forever when they took rebirth in this lifetime; their concomitant and intermittent self-attachment associated with the mental consciousness re-emerged while their newly-produced mental consciousness of this lifetime had not yet become enlightened (this is the reason why sound-hearer arhats are unwilling to make great vows for the sake of sentient beings—they fear that their self-attachment will re-emerge after they take rebirth in future lifetimes). However, when these veteran Bodhisattvas became enlightened, the meritorious quality resulting from their elimination of self-attachment by facing different situations through experiencing various conditions in past lifetimes will manifest in this lifetime concomitantly with their extermination of self-view upon enlightenment. Therefore, veteran Bodhisattvas do not need to gradually trim their self-attachment post-enlightenment by facing different situations through experiencing various conditions but can eliminate it after their sudden enlightenment.

Such elimination of self-attachment can only be achieved—after attaining enlightenment in this lifetime or in past lifetimes—through the practice of tranquility and insight carried out by facing different situations through experiencing various conditions. Such a practice of tranquility and insight consists of bringing forth the mental application to eliminate one's own body and mind after observing that they are unreal; the goal is not to destroy them through the Chan School's impact of blows and shouts, as claimed by Chen and Ding. The purpose of blows and shouts is not to create any impact on learners, but only to cause them to realize the mind consisting of the eighth consciousness. Wholly unaware of the principles of enlightenment in Mahāyāna and of the elimination of self-view and self-attachment in Hīnayāna, those two persons have become a laughing stock in the Buddhist community with the false claim that **those with strong attachments to the self and to the dharmas need to destroy those attachments with a high-intensity impact, whereas those with weak attachments to the self and to the dharmas can destroy those attachments with just an impact of ordinary intensity.**

If the attachments to the self and to the dharmas could be destroyed through the impact of the sixth consciousness, then it would be unnecessary for Chen and Ding to practice Chan and tantra. All they would need to do is ask others to create an impact on them every day with unexpected blows and shouts. They would definitely have a chance to become enlightened given that a year contains three hundred and sixty-five days; if they were not able to attain enlightenment in one year, then they would definitely achieve this goal after ten years—approximately after three thousand six hundred and fifty days. Why do they not resort to this method? Why are they still submerged by their self-view up to this day? I have illustrated the correct principle of the true elimination of one's self-view in my publications; why is it that those two persons still do not believe or understand this principle and still insist that the mind of seeing, hearing, feeling, and cognition is the real and indestructible mind?

All Buddhist practitioners must be equipped with the right knowledge and view before embarking on their cultivation. They must not practice and train blindly by following the false views of Tantric Buddhism; otherwise, they will inevitably obtain the opposite of what they pursue—while seeking liberation and the Buddha's wisdom, they will fall into false views and wind up transmigrating within the three evil paths without ever having a chance to escape; how utterly heart-wrenching!

The concomitant and continuous self-attachment consists of self-ignorance, self-arrogance, self-view, and self-love, all of which are associated with the manas-consciousness—the mental faculty. All sentient beings are endowed with the mental faculty—the seventh consciousness, the manas-consciousness. The self-view of the manas-consciousness is as follows: This consciousness has been unaware, since beginningless time, of its own falsity. Due to the permeation of self-view and erroneous view undergone by the mental consciousness, the manas-consciousness has been holding, since beginningless time and through the conceptual nature of the mental consciousness, onto the fact that it itself (the decision-making mind) is a real and indestructible dharma that is everlasting, is the sole truth, and can make decisions; it believes that it itself is permanent and indestructible and that it is the dominator that produces the aggregates, sense-fields, and elements. Such is the self-view of the manas-consciousness.

With respect to self-arrogance, the manas-consciousness functions according to the cognition of the mental consciousness and elevates the mind that it itself is in all conditions consisting of various states, believing that it is superior to all other sentient beings and all phenomena. As for self-love, it consists of the greed and attachment exhibited by the manas-consciousness in all conditions consisting of various states and based on the cognitive nature of the conscious mind, towards the self consisting of the natures of seeing, hearing, feeling, and cognition as well as towards the worldly natures of the eighth consciousness (this statement can only be understood by those who are truly enlightened; those who are not yet enlightened cannot truly grasp the meaning of this assertion upon hearing it). Such is the self-love of the manas-consciousness. Self-ignorance refers to the fact that the manas-consciousness cannot understand the mode of the eighth consciousness manifested on things and therefore abides, purely based on the afflictions such as self-view, self-love, and so forth that are associated with the still unenlightened mental consciousness of ordinary people, in the beginningless ignorance and the ignorance in a single thought and is unable to extinguish the afflictive hindrances. This is called self-ignorance.

These four afflictions associated with the manas-consciousness constitute the concomitant and continuous self-attachment. As the manas-consciousness—the mental faculty—has, since beginningless time, manifested everlastingly and without interruption, the four afflictions associated with it have continuously manifested concomitantly with it; hence, they are called continuous self-attachment. In other words, these four afflictions are known as concomitant and continuous self-attachment given that they exist based on and concomitantly with the manas-consciousness—the mental faculty—and given that the manas-consciousness has, since beginningless time, never ceased—not even for an instant.

With respect to these four afflictions of self-attachment, one must first experience and realize the aforementioned seventh consciousness before being able to experience the manifestation of these four afflictions and then exterminate them through one's cultivation—by facing different situations through experiencing various conditions. In ancient times, all arhats realized this seventh consciousness based on the Buddha's teachings and called it "mental faculty." Due to their ability to realize and comprehend the seventh consciousness, those arhats were able to eliminate the concomitant and continuous self-attachment associated with the seventh consciousness by facing different situations through experiencing various conditions, which enabled them to attain the fruition of liberation.

Still unable to realize and understand the location of this seventh consciousness and having no idea about how to engage in the deed-contemplation of the self-attachment related to this consciousness, Chen and Ding wrongly claim that the impact from **"the religious experience of the sixth consciousness" can "destroy the attachments to the self and to the dharmas in the seventh [or the eighth] consciousness . . . ."** Given their complete ignorance of the Buddha Dharma, it is wholly impossible for them to have the view and knowledge needed to judge whether the virtuous mentors in the various directions are enlightened.

Furthermore, Chen and Ding have slandered me in the following way: **"Such a vindictive mindset, which consists of being content only after having successfully inflicted the threat of death on the other party, clearly contradicts the state of liberation consisting of the 'union of compassion and wisdom' experienced by Buddhas and Bodhisattvas. Therefore, such persons have obviously not achieved enlightenment, and their speeches and assertions can certainly be disregarded."** What Chen and Ding mean is that to level any word of criticism against my statements would be a waste of their time; why then do they attack me on their website when they proclaim that my assertions can be disregarded? Such contradictory statements and insincere attitudes demonstrate that they are just hypocrites.

Furthermore, those two persons' accusations against me,

"such a vindictive mindset, which consists of being content only after having successfully inflicted the threat of death on the other party," was made by **maliciously taking some statements out of their context**. Indeed, I have separately provided an expedient alternative that offers people such as Chen, Ding, and so forth who do not dare to step forward to seek the truth and debate the Dharma in public out of fear of death the possibility to explore the truth through a private debate. In this option, they would not need to die or recognize the other party as their master with a prostration after acknowledging their defeat. However, those two persons have not had the audacity to come forward for a public or private doctrinal debate; instead, they framed me and deprecated me with untruthful accusations: They deliberately omitted the passage in my letter about a private debate while making biased assertions by focusing exclusively on the passage about a public debate; thus, they wrongfully disparaged me for having "such a vindictive mindset, which consists of being content only after having successfully inflicted the threat of death on the other party"; they deliberately omitted, in an attempt to mislead the public and conceal the truth, the section in which I separately offered a way out for them through a private debate. Hence, I have said that those two persons are **dishonest and that they maliciously took some statements out of their context**.

Furthermore, with respect to Chen and Ding's statement, "the state of liberation consisting of the 'union of compassion and wisdom' experienced by Buddhas and Bodhisattvas," how could they have the wisdom to teach others about this state when they would not even know it in their wildest dreams? Upon seeing that sentient beings are being misled, all Buddhas and Bodhisattvas will definitely appear in this world in order to make the lion's roar out of great compassion—they will subdue the erroneous teachings in order to save sentient beings, fearless of the great masters in all directions while performing this great deed. It is only by behaving in this fashion that one can be said to have attained "the state of liberation consisting of the 'union of compassion and wisdom.'" Those who cannot behave in this fashion can be said to be in a state of fetters devoid of compassion and wisdom of ordinary sentient beings who fear death and the loss of fame.

After the World-Honored One had realized the Path and had appeared in this world to propagate the Dharma, He unrelentingly refuted the eternalist and the nihilist non-Buddhists, and even all ninety-six types of non-Buddhists. He went as far as refuting each of the Six Non-Buddhist Masters by following each of their footsteps throughout all the big cities in India back then. Only those who are able to refute in this fashion the false teachings and manifest the correct doctrines without fear have truly attained "**the state of liberation consisting of the 'union of compassion and wisdom.'**" Such refutation of the non-Buddhists is recounted in the four Āgamas, in the prajñā sūtras, and even more in the Vijñaptimātratā sūtras of the third turning of the Dharma Wheel. Neither Chen nor Ding has the slightest idea about all this.

Furthermore, there have always existed two types of Buddhist doctrinal debates in China and India since ancient times: public and private. The private debates are held either just between the two parties or by inviting a third party to attend, depending upon the agreement between the two parties. In contrast, the public debates are governed by a determined set of rules: The main debater must propound an assertion related to the foremost meaning and ask the local king to make regular announcements to inform the public about the event. During the debate, all persons are allowed to take the stage to debate the doctrines in public—except for those who agree with the main debater's assertions—and under no circumstances can the main debater reject anyone's request to do so. Hence, such events are called "**unhindered** assemblies of doctrinal debate."

All those who go on stage to debate the doctrines must sign an affidavit with the main debater: The party who ends up losing the debate must recognize the winner as his master with a prostration; if he refuses to do, he must take his own life on the spot. The king will act as a witness of this affidavit and will enact it, ensuring that no one breaks the rules by resorting to trickery. Enlightened practitioners in ancient India often took part in such debates, which still exist nowadays in that country and are recognized by academics. Back then, Bodhisattva Xuanzang traveled to all the kingdoms in India after completing his studies. In every kingdom, he asked the king to hold the aforementioned unhindered great assembly in an attempt to subdue the false views and manifest the correct doctrines, as well as to widely help the public understand the differences between the correct and the incorrect doctrines. Although the assemblies did not always take place as he had hoped, such endeavors did lead to the revival of Indian Buddhism.

Such publicly-held, unhindered great assemblies of doctrinal debates were widespread in ancient India; I am only replicating them in a different space and time. Just because misinformed persons like Chen and Ding have not heard about them, they calumniated me by asserting that I have **"such a vindictive mindset, which consists of being content only after having successfully inflicted the threat of death on the other party,"** deliberately concealing and omitting the fact that I had kindly offered them the alternative of a "private doctrinal debate." Such groundless slander demonstrates that they are neither candid nor forthright.

Those persons are tough on the outside but weak on the inside. How could they be viewed as forthright and brave when they do not even dare to participate in a private debate? If they are convinced that I am truly an unworthy debate opponent, then they would certainly not have slandered me on their website. Having ascertained the necessity to debate the Dharma but not having the slightest confidence to do so, they exhibited hypocrisy by deprecating me on their website with statements taken out of their context. Hypocrites are not qualified to practice the two principal paths of the true Buddha Dharma and can merely learn the tantric Dharma-gate of the erroneous path.

Furthermore, although a main debater is confident and well-prepared when he requests the organization of an unhindered great assemby of doctrinal debate, **no one knows for sure who will come out victorious**. The outcome will only be known after the two parties have debated on the spot during the actual unhindered great assembly. Will the main debater end up winning? No one knows for sure. Thus, the person who must kill himself or recognize the other party as his master with a prostration might turn out to be the main debater himself, who requested to hold the unhindered great assembly. All main debaters are well-aware of the inevitable consequences of a potential loss and will certainly consider such a possibility before requesting to hold an unhindered great assembly of doctrinal debate. For this reason, in ancient times, no one in central India dared to assert that the main debater Xuanzang had *"such a vindictive mindset, which consists of being content only after having successfully inflicted the threat of death on the other party."* Instead, everyone was eager to sing his praises.

Why is that? Anyone who reprimands someone else with the aforementioned words before taking part in a debate will be deemed by the public as an unwise coward with erroneous views who speaks untruthfully. Chen and Ding will certainly be derided by the Buddhist community given that they have openly made the aforementioned rebuke on their website but do not dare to come forward for a public debate or even for **a private debate for which they will not be held accountable**. How unwise! It is only fitting that they slump further down the wrong path by holding onto the erroneous views of Tantric Buddhism without being willing to make any changes. While they do not understand the Buddha Dharma, they have untruthfully declared that they are able to comprehend the doctrines of the Chan School and have falsely claimed that the blows and shouts of the Chan School constitute a shock therapy, which consists of eliminating the attachments to the self and to the dharmas through a shock impact. How are these mistaken assertions and views credible in any way? It is surprising that the multitudes of disciples who learn the Dharma from them do not have the wisdom to distinguish between right and wrong and believe in them unwaveringly.

7. The Misunderstandings of the Emptiness-Nature of prajñā in the Tantric text The Vairocanābhisaṃbodhi Sūtra

*T*he Vairocanābhisaṃbodhi Sūtra [Dari jing 大日經], the principal text of Tibetan Buddhism, is fully known as *Mahāvairocana Abhisaṃbodhi Vikurvita Adhiṣṭhāna Tantra [Da piluzhena chengfo shenbian jiachi jing 大毘盧遮那成佛神變加持經].* Even the "Buddha Mahāvairocana" in this text has misconstrued the emptiness-nature set forth in the prajñā sūtras, as he regards the emptiness-signs of the aggregates, sense-fields, and elements—the fact that all phenomena are dependent arising and are without their own nature—as the emptiness-nature. Consequently, none of his teachings touch upon the sign of reality of the mind consisting of the foremost meaning. For example, "Buddha Mahāvairocana" says in Volume 1:

> The Buddha said, "Lord of Mysteries, it is in one's own mind that one seeks bodhi and omniscience. Why? Because its original nature is pure. The mind is neither within nor without, nor can the mind be apprehended between the two. . . .
>
> [Because] the mind, which has the characteristic of empty space, is free from all differentiation and nondifferentiation. Why is that? That whose nature is the same as empty space is identical to the mind, and that whose nature is the same as the mind is identical to bodhi. In this manner, Lord of Mysteries, the three entities of mind, the realm of empty space, and bodhi are without duality. . . .
>
> Lord of Mysteries, if a man of [good] family or a woman of [good] family wishes to know bodhi, they should know their own mind in this manner. Lord of Mysteries, how is one to know one's own mind? It cannot, namely, be apprehended by seeking it in distinctions, or colors, or shapes, or external objects; or in form or sensation, ideation, volition, or consciousness; or in

'I' or 'mine'; or in the grasper (i.e., subject) or the grasped (i.e., object); or in the pure; or in the [eighteen] elements [of existence] or [the twelve] sense fields; or in any other distinctions.[1]

Although the *Śuraṃgama Sūtra* 楞嚴經 [Lengyan jing] contains a similar teaching, that teaching is actually about the natures of the unreal mind consisting of the first seven consciousnesses, the fact that the natures of seeing, hearing, . . . , and even cognizing manifested by this unreal mind are indeed its functions, and the fact that this mind and those functions cannot exist without various conditions or the eighth consciousness (tathāgatagarbha). Based on the permanence of the tathāgatagarbha, the mind consisting of the six consciousnesses and those functions of seeing, hearing, and so forth can, after ceasing every night, re-arise the next morning—hence, those functions are said to be neither ceasing nor permanent. The *Śuraṃgama Sūtra* explicitly states that those functions cannot be said to be permanent outside the context of the tathāgatagarbha because the natures of seeing, hearing, and so forth, which "result from causes and conditions," all exist in dependence upon the tathāgatagarbha. However, given that the "tantric Buddha Mahāvairocana" in *The Vairocanābhisaṃbodhi Sūtra* has misconstrued the meanings of the *Śuraṃgama Sūtra*, he regards the properties of the unreal mind consisting of the six consciousnesses set forth in the *Śuraṃgama Sūtra* as those of the real mind, and wrongly considers this unreal mind, which is other than the tathāgatagarbha, to be the mind of the sign of reality illustrated in the prajñā sūtras. Such concepts differ drastically from the Buddha's teachings and cannot be viewed as the true Buddha Dharma. Clearly, *The Vairocanābhisaṃbodhi Sūtra* was by no means preached by Buddha Mahāvairocana and was instead fabricated and compiled over a long period of time by a group of

---

1   *The Vairocanābhisaṃbodhi Sūtra*, translated by Rolf W. Giebel (Berkeley, CA: Numata Center for Buddhist Translation and Research, 2005), 6. [CBETA, T18, no. 848, 21c23-22a21.]

unenlightened tantric gurus in the old days, who falsely claimed that it was taught by the Buddha Mahāvairocana of the *Flower Garland Sūtra [Huayan jing 華嚴經]*.

Although the "tantric Buddha Mahāvairocana" of *The Vairocanābhisaṃbodhi Sūtra* has stated that the real mind is the ālaya-consciousness, he takes the properties of the mind consisting of the mental consciousness and the mind consisting of the manas for the properties of the ālaya-consciousness. Although he has declared in Volume 1 that the mind has fifty-nine signs, the signs of the mind that he has delineated all consist of taking the signs of the mind consisting of the mental consciousness and the mind consisting of the Manas for the signs of the mind consisting of the ālaya-consciousness. Having thus mistaken the unreal minds for "the real, supramundane mind," this "Buddha" said:

> Lord of Mysteries, multiplying by two once, twice, three times, four times and five times, there are altogether one hundred and sixty minds. When one transcends the mundane three false attachments, the supramundane mind is born. That is to say, having thus understood that there are only the [five] aggregates and no-self, one lingers on in cultivation [associated with] the [six] sense organs, [six] sense objects, and [six] elements (i.e., six consciousnesses), pulls out the stumps of karma and mental afflictions and the seeds of ignorance whence are born the twelve causes and conditions [of dependent arising], and dissociates oneself from the schools of established [purity] and so on. Such deep serenity cannot be known by any non-Buddhists, and previous buddhas have proclaimed it to be free from all faults.
>
> Lord of Mysteries, with this supramundane mind dwelling in the [five] aggregates, such wisdom may arise correspondingly. If one is to give rise to freedom from attachment to the aggregates, one should observe foam, bubbles, a plantain tree, a mirage, and an illusion, thereby attaining liberation. That is to say, the [five] aggregates, [twelve] sense fields, [eighteen] elements, and the grasper and the grasped are all removed from the noumenon, and when one realizes the realm of

quiescence in this manner, it is called the supramundane mind.[2]

In this passage, the mind is illustrated in the same way as in the modern day teachings of Master Yinshun and the Dalai Lama. Those errors stem from those people's misapprehension of the Buddha's tenets in the prajñā sūtras and the *Śūraṃgama Sūtra*, which has caused them to explain the mind of the sign of reality with the concept of "dependent arising and with an empty nature" outside the context of the tathāgatagarbha and to further claim that the mind of feeling and cognition that abides in a state of deep serenity is the mind of reality, the supramundane mind. Those people all regard the pure mental consciousness that does not observe any phenomena as the supramundane consciousness of reality.

Those who disagree with my explanation of the above passage from *The Vairocanābhisaṃbodhi Sūtra* and insist that it does not refer to the mind of feeling and cognition may take a look at the following text to get an idea of the truth:

> Then the Bhagavān, the Buddha Vairocana, addressed Vajrapāṇi:
>> Listen carefully to the characteristics of the Dharma!
>> The Dharma is free from differentiation and all false conceptions.
>> **If one eliminates false conceptions and the workings of the mind and thought,**
>> **The supreme and perfect awakening that I attained is ultimately like empty space,**
>> But unknown to ordinary foolish beings, who are wrongly attached to the objective realm.
>> That they hanker after [auspicious] times, directions, signs, and so on is because they are enveloped by ignorance,
>> And it is in order to liberate them that these are taught in conformity with them as an expedient.[3]

---

2   Ibid., 13.
3   Ibid., 20.

According to this passage, one becomes free from the nature of differentiation after one's mental consciousness (mind of feeling and cognition) has eliminated all verbalizations and false conceptions, thus allowing all workings to come from a clear and pure mental consciousness devoid of verbalizations. This passage further states that those who are able to frequently abide in this state have attained the ultimate Buddhahood. The "tantric Buddha Mahāvairocana" of *The Vairocanābhisaṃbodhi Sūtra* has called the mind consisting of the mental consciousness that, in this fashion, does not bring forth any verbalizations or false conceptions "true mind," thereby falling into the self-view of the mind consisting of the mental consciousness. Moreover, this "Buddha" has called the state in which one observes that all phenomena other than the mind of feeling and cognition are empty "the mental equipoise of Perfectly Awakened Ones." Hence, after hearing the "Buddha" preach the Dharma, "Bodhisattva" Vajrapāṇi replied:

> The Buddha has taught that all is empty and that this is the mental equipoise of Perfectly Awakened Ones.
> Samādhi is knowing the mind by direct witness, and it is not obtained from anything else.
> Such a state is the concentration of all Tathāgatas.
> Therefore, it is explained as great emptiness and consummates sarvajna [jnāna].[4]

Thus, after regarding the thoughtless mind of feeling and cognition as the real and indestructible mind, the "tantric Buddha Mahāvairocana" of *The Vairocanābhisaṃbodhi Sūtra* and Bodhisattva Vajrapāṇi have further established "empty space" as the source of all dharma-realms:

> Thereupon the World-honored One again gazed upon the entire great assembly and, wishing to fulfill all wishes, again expounded Dharma-phrases for the consummation of knowledge determined by immeasurable gateways throughout

---

4   Ibid., 38.

the three ages.
Empty space is unsullied, without own-nature, and bestows various kinds of skillful knowledge;
Because its own-nature is originally always empty, it is dependently arisen, most profound, and difficult to see,
And in special progress over a long period of time it grants the unsurpassed result as desired.
For example, just as dwellings in all destinies, although dependent on empty space, are not attached to it,
So too is this pure Dharma like that, and the three existences without exception are born pure.[5]

The above statements contradict each other. Given that a previous passage regards the thoughtless mind of feeling and cognition as the real, permanent, and undestructible dharma, it ensues that all phenomena such as the body, mind, and so forth of sentient beings are generated by this mind of feeling and cognition. However, in the above passage, this "Buddha" views empty space as the source of all phenomena, **"Empty space is unsullied, without own-nature, and bestows various kinds of skillful knowledge,"** which stands at odds with his previous assertions and clearly shows that his statements are self-contradictory. How could there possibly be such a Buddha in the world? Aren't those tantric practitioners deceitful when they hail him as the "Buddha Mahāvairocana" of the Dharma body and of the reward body? This proves that *The Vairocanābhisaṃbodhi Sūtra*, which is worshipped by Tantric Buddhists, is in fact a product that was created over a long period of time by a group of unenlightened ordinary people based on their imagination and that has been falsely labeled as the teachings of the Buddha Mahāvairocana mentioned in the *Flower Garland Sūtra*. Therefore, *The Vairocanābhisaṃbodhi Sūtra* is by no means an authentic sūtra taught by a Buddha and can only beguile the Bodhisattvas without the knowledge-of-the-aspects-of-paths. Those with the knowledge-of-the-aspects-of-paths have definitely enough wisdom to refute this text and can explain and analyze its

---

5   Ibid., 71.

fallacies to the Buddha's sons.

What does the "Buddha Mahāvairocana"—a "Tathāgata of the reward-body"—in *The Vairocanābhisaṃbodhi Sūtra* say about seeing the truth? Please take a look at the following passage:

> In *dharmas* originally quiescent and always without own-nature,
> He rests like [Mount] Sume[ru]: this is called seeing the truth.
> This emptiness corresponds to the ultimate reality, and it is not false words;
> What is seen [by him] is like [that which is seen by] the Buddha, and previous buddhas have [also] seen thus.
> The *siddhi*[6] of attaining the *bodhi*-mind is quite unsurpassed;[7]

According to the above verses, one "has attained the vision of the path" in the tantric sense if one's mind of feeling and cognition can abide in the thought that "all phenomena are empty"—if one can observe the following: All phenomena are impermanent, mutable, and with an intrinsically empty nature, whereas the mind of feeling and cognition is permanent and indestructible.

Furthermore, the "Buddha Mahāvairocana"—a "Tathāgata of the reward body"—in *The Vairocanābhisaṃbodhi Sūtra* has also taught the following:

> The *samādhis* of the Great Seer, perfectly awakened, and of the multitudes of the Buddha's sons
> Are pure and dissociated from thought; those associated with thought are mundane.
> In the acquisition of results through action, there is maturation[8] and a time for maturation;

---

6   Siddhi: T. *dngos grub*; C. *xidi/chengjiu* 悉地/成就.
7   *The Vairocanābhisaṃbodhi Sūtra*, translated by Rolf W. Giebel (Berkeley, CA: Numata Center for Buddhist Translation and Research, 2005), 133. [CBETA, T18, no. 848, 21c23-22a21.]
8   Maturation: Alt. ripening, fruition, or result; S. *vipāka*; T. *rnam par smin pa*; C.

If one achieves *siddhi,* one performs actions freely.
Because the mind has no own-nature, it is far removed from cause and result,
And liberated from karma and [re]birth, one's birth is commensurate with empty space.[9]

The tantric text *The Vairocanābhisaṃbodhi Sūtra* speaks extensively of the six evolving consciousnesses—the mind of feeling, cognition, and so forth—as the basis of all phenomena and as the mind that produces all phenomena. Having thus asserted, this text also indicates, however, that the natures of seeing, hearing, feeling, and cognition—the six evolving consciousnesses— as well as the decision-making mind consisting of the Manas are devoid of real and indestructible property: **"Because the mind has no own-nature, it is far removed from cause and result."** This means that the mind of feeling, cognition, and so forth is free from cause and result because it is without its own nature. It is based on this "naturelessness" that this text speaks about liberation from karmic retribution and about the fact that continued cyclic existence in future lifetimes is similar to empty space. Thus, the statements in the same sūtra contradict one another.

However, the Buddha has clearly expounded in the *Laṅkāvatāra Sūtra* that the eighth consciousness (the ālaya mind) is endowed with seven intrinsic natures, which enable it to produce all phenomena such as the five aggregates, the seven consciousnesses, and so forth. After producing all these phenomena, the eighth consciousness transmigrates within the three realms along with the unreal mind consisting of the seven consciousnesses, yet it manifests, within the cyclic existence in the three realms, that it has neither birth nor death and is free from causes and effects. Therefore, the *Laṅkāvatāra Sūtra* teaches that the mind consisting of the eighth consciousness is the intrinsic

---

guobao/yishu 果報/異熟.

[9] *The Vairocanābhisaṃbodhi Sūtra,* translated by Rolf W. Giebel (Berkeley, CA: Numata Center for Buddhist Translation and Research, 2005), 135. [CBETA, T18, no. 848, 21c23-22a21.]

entity of all phenomena, unlike *The Vairocanābhisaṃbodhi Sūtra*, which regards the mind of feeling and cognition as the intrinsic entity of all phenomena and asserts in the aforementioned passage that **"because the mind has no own-nature, it is far removed from cause and result."** In fact, the mind of feeling, cognition, and so forth is unavoidably subject to the law of cause and effect and the retribution of pain and happiness, because it connects with all phenomena consisting of the six sense objects and does not undergo the the retribution of pain and happiness only when it temporarily ceases in the five states including deep sleep and so forth. How could such "Buddha Dharma" set forth in *The Vairocanābhisaṃbodhi Sūtra* be said to be the true Buddha Dharma when it differs drastically from the doctrines imparted by the Buddha in the sūtras of the Three Vehicles? How could such "Buddha Dharma" be ascribed to a Buddha? It merely consists of false teachings created by a group of ancient tantric gurus based on their self-view and eternalist view.

The "Great Sun Tathāgata" in *The Vairocanābhisaṃbodhi Sūtra* equates, based on visualized states, the essence of mantras with a Buddha's true Dharma body and a Tathāgata of the Dharma body. According to this text, those who have attained such an essence of mantras have achieved abandonment and realization, have become Buddhas, and so forth:

> Thereupon the vajradhara [Vajrapāṇi] next further asked
> the World-honored One Mahāvairocana about the essence of
> the mantras of the *maṇḍalas*, uttering these verses:
> "What is the essence of all mantras, or true speech?
> What should one understand so as to be called an *ācārya*?"[10]
> Then the Bhagavān Mahāvairocana
> Exhorted Vajrapāṇi, [saying,] "Excellent, Mahāsattva!"
> And making his heart rejoice, he further addressed him with
> these words:
> "How to understand the most secret of secrets, the great

---

10   Ācārya: In Sanskrit, lit. "teacher" or "master"; T. *slob dpon*; C. *asheli* 阿闍黎.

essence of the knowledge of mantras—
I shall now explain it for you: with singlemindedness you
should listen attentively!
The letter A is the essence of all mantras,
And from it there issue forth everywhere immeasurable
mantras;
All frivolous arguments cease, and it is able to produce
skillful wisdom.
Lord of Mysteries, why is [the letter A] the essence of all
mantras?
The Buddha, honored among two-legged beings, has taught
that the letter A is called the seed.
Therefore, everything is like this, [having the letter A as its
seed,] and it rests in all the limbs;
Having allocated it as appropriate, bestow it everywhere in
accordance with the rules.
Because that primordial letter (i.e., A) pervades the
augmented letters,
The letters form sounds, and the limbs arise from this.
Therefore, this pervades all bodies and produces various
virtues.
I shall now explain where [the letters] are to be distributed:
listen singlemindedly, Son of the Buddha!
**Assign the essence (i.e., A) to your heart and allocate
the remaining [letters] to your limbs.**
**If you do everything in this manner, then you will be
identical to my person.**
Resting in the *yoga* posture, think of the Tathāgatas.
If one comprehends this vast knowledge in these teachings,
The Perfectly Awakened One, of great virtue, has taught
that [such a person] is an *ācārya*.
He is a Tathāgata and is also called a Buddha.[11]

The syllable A (*ah*, 阿) is thus viewed as the essence of all

---

[11] *The Vairocanābhisaṃbodhi Sūtra*, translated by Rolf W. Giebel (Berkeley, CA:
Numata Center for Buddhist Translation and Research, 2005), 159-160. [CBETA,
T18, no. 848, 21c23-22a21.]

mantras and is therefore said to generate all phenomena. However, the above-quoted "Buddha's words" from the same sūtra describe empty space in the following manner: **"Empty space is unsullied, without own-nature, and bestows various kinds of skillful knowledge; Because its own-nature is originally always empty, it is dependently arisen, most profound, and difficult to see."** In this case, "empty space" should be the real mind, as this "Buddha" claims that it **"bestows various kinds of skillful knowledge"** and that **"its own-nature is originally always empty."** Thus, the statements in various parts of *The Vairocanābhisaṃbodhi Sūtra* fail to follow a consistent line of thought, do not delineate the same doctrine, and even contradict one another. Furthermore, the authors of this text had clearly not attained the wisdom of prajñā, as they did not comprehend and had not realized the tathāgatagarbha—the sign of reality of all dharma-realms. We can conclude that this sūtra was definitely not taught by the Buddham but is instead a compilation, over a long period of time, of the teachings imparted by the gurus of the various tantric schools.

According to the above passage from *The Vairocanābhisaṃbodhi Sūtra*, one should recite the mantra, practice the method of visualization, and distribute the seed syllables; those who have achieved this visualization have become ultimate Buddhas and are no different than the Buddhas. Not only does this teaching contradict previous statements, but it is also preposterous and groundless. Indeed, *The Vairocanābhisaṃbodhi Sūtra* variously regards the mind of feeling and cognition, empty space, and the syllable *A* as the real entity of all phenomena. In brief, it is false to assert that one can become a Buddha through the visualization of seed syllables, without realizing the tathagatagarbha—the consciousness consisting of the intrinsic entity of all phenomena.

"Buddha Mahāvairocana"—a tantric "Buddha of Dharma body and the reward body"—has surprisingly committed some errors that even a Bodhisattva of the First Ground would not commit if he were to formulate or "create" a Buddhist sūtra on his own. The doctrines that this "Buddha" teaches are shockingly steeped in mistakes and self-contradictory. It is senseless to claim that "the Great Sun Tathāgata" in *The Vairocanābhisaṃbodhi Sūtra* corresponds to the Great Sun Tathāgata, a Buddha of the Dharma body, set forth in the *Flower Garland Sūtra*, when he is incapable of identifying—either explicitly or implicitly—the location of the mind consisting of the eighth consciousness, which is the real entity of prajñā.

Tsongkhapa's mistaken view about "the achievement of Buddhahood through the practice of the Madhyamaka of prajñā," which stems from his misapprehension of prajñā, is equally absurd. He believes that one has attained Buddhahood if one is completely thoughtless with respect to all phenomena:

> In order to briefly expound the meaning, the World-Honored One thus speaks. What does He speak about? About practicing the thoughtless wisdom of a Tathāgata. What are those statements for? For the **achievement of Buddhahood**. Which sūtra speaks about this? The Prajñā Sūtra says: "To cultivate existence and non-existence, emptiness and non-emptiness, and so forth is to course on signs and not on prajñā pāramitā"; some people have misapprehended the above scripture. **Those with thoughts cannot practice the profound path to Buddhahood because to think is to conceptualize:** One becomes bound by cyclic existence by conceptualizing, by being carried away by desirable or undesirable signs, and by bringing forth "greed" and "anger without greed." **Therefore, one can, through complete thoughtlessness, eliminate desirable and undesirable signs as well as the conceptuality that results from being carried away by those signs. Because of this elimination, one can exterminate cyclic existence and become a Buddha. Therefore, the Path to Buddhahood is purely about being completely thoughtless and does not consist of any conceptual meditative concentration.** The Tathāgata's wisdom here refers to the Path to Buddhahood (the Path to Buddhahood on the Causal Ground found in Exoteric Buddhism) and not the wisdom of the Fruition Ground (not the wisdom of Buddhahood on the Fruition

Ground taught in Tantric Buddhism—indeed, according to Tibetan Tantrism, one must realize the state of the union of bliss and emptiness to attain Buddhahood on the Fruition Ground). It derives its designation from the fact that it allows one to practice the Tathāgata's wisdom. In *The Great Commentary [of Stainless Light]*, there is one passage about refuting attachment and another one about responding to objections. The first passage is further divided into two parts.

First, with respect to the refutation through the right reasoning, as stated in *The Great Commentary*: "If one can attain Buddhahood with the thoughtless wisdom, then how come not all sentient beings have become Buddhas? Their thoughtless wisdom functions in the state of profound sleep, and therefore, they do not exhibit greed with respect to desirable things and also do not shun from greed with respect to undesirable things." In other words, "If Buddhahood could be attained solely through the practice of abiding in thorough thoughtlessness, then since this state arises when sentient beings are in profound sleep and has existed since beginningless time, all sentient beings should have become Buddhas by now." In summary, if one does not practice the no-self that is ascertained by the correct view, but claims that the non-conceptuality of Buddhahood can be attained by solely abiding without attachment to any extremes, then this state is no different from that of profound sleep. The non-attachment to any extremes is also a state that exists in profound sleep. **However, one does not abide in the correct view during profound sleep.** Such non-attachment to any extremes is not the same as the freedom from all extremes. With this crucial point in mind, we can conclude that those people's assertion is erroneous.[12]

According to Tsongkhapa's teaching, one has achieved the Path to Buddhahood if one's mind of feeling and cognition can

---

12 Tsongkhapa, *Mizong daocidi guang lun* 密宗道次第廣論, 568. Translated into English from Chinese.

abide in a thoughtless and non-conceptual state. In response to the objection that if this could be called achieving Buddhahood, then given that there is neither thought nor conceptuality during sleep— which means that one has non-conceptual wisdom in that state— all people should have achieved the path to Buddhahood during sleep. Tsongkhapa argued the following: During sleep, sentient beings do not possess the "correct view" that all phenomena are dependent arising and with an empty nature, because their nature of feeling and cognition does not arise; therefore, although sentient beings "possess" the non-conceptual wisdom during sleep, they cannot be said to have achieved the Path to Buddhahood given that, in this state, they do not have the correct view related to the concept of "dependent arising and with an empty nature."

In order for Tantric practitioners to attain the "non-conceptual wisdom" and "achieve the Path to Buddhahood," all they need to do is abide, while awake, in a thoughtless state without exhibiting discriminations of greed or aversion towards phenomena that are "desirable," "undesirable," and so forth, while maintaining the "correct view" that all phenomena are dependent arising and with an empty nature. In other words, those who adhere to the view of Prāsaṅgika Madhyamaka such as Tsongkhapa and so forth believe that a person "has achieved Buddhahood" if, in the awake state, his mind remains thoughtless and non-conceptual, while he does not cling to any extremes and possesses the view that all phenomena are dependent arising and with and empty nature. They believe that their stance differs from those who achieve the Path to Buddhahood by dissociating themselves from all extremes during sleep, as those people do not have the "correct view" that all phenomena are dependent arising and with an empty nature"—as their minds are deeply asleep and therefore cannot bring forth this "correct view."

Such is the so-called "Path to the Achievement of Buddhahood through the Mahāmudrā of Luminosity and Emptiness with One's Current Body" taught by the proponents of Prāsaṅgika Madhyamaka, a school whose practitioners boast the highest level of practice and attainment within Tantric Buddhism. If the state attained through this path could be called Buddhahood, then the learners in our True Enlightenment Practitioners Association would all have achieved the Path to Buddhahood with just the completion of a two-and-a-half-year course—without having to realize the eighth consciousness (tathāgatagarbha) through Chan contemplation. Why is that so? Because the students in our Association can acquire the skill to dwell in thoughtlessness within six months or one year of learning. Some students are not just able to dwell in thoughtlessness but can acquire the skill to abide in a continuous pure thought, which is a more difficult achievement than dwelling in thoughtlessness, and can, by the time they complete their two-and-a-half year course, maintain this state of concentration amidst their four deportments.

In our Association, the teachers provide, during the course of the joint cultivation of Chan and Pure Land, a meticulous analysis of each of the phenomena consisting of the eighteen elements. Not only do they explain in detail that the coarse and subtle minds consisting of the mental consciousness are unreal as well as dependent arising and with an empty nature, but they also elaborate on the seventh consciousness—the mental faculty, which Tsongkhapa has been unable to realize—thus allowing the students to directly witness and observe it. The students can, through such a direct observation, comprehend the emptiness-signs of the five aggregates and directly contemplate that all phenomena are dependent arising and with an empty nature in a far more profound and subtle way than Tsongkhapa was ever able to do. As Tsongkhapa has not been able to realize the mind consisting of the seventh consciousness—the mental faculty—he has denied its existence and therefore knows nothing about it. Furthermore, as he is unaware that the mind of feeling and cognition—the mental consciousness—is dependent arising and with an empty nature, he insists that this mental consciousness is a permanent and indestructible dharma; hence, he must only have a rudimentary knowledge of—he does not fully understand—the correct view that the five aggregates are dependent arising and with an empty nature. As a result, he is definitely unable to understand, in accordance with the truth, the correct principles of "being detached from all extremes" and "dependent arising and with an empty nature," definitely holds the mental consciousness—the mind of feeling and cognition—as a permanent and indestructible dharma, is definitely unable to touch upon the seventh consciousness and experience the fact that it is unreal, and is incapable of fully comprehending that the eighteen elements are unreal. As such, Tsongkhapa's insight of the Buddha Dharma is far less penetrating than that of the learners in our Association. Therefore, if Tsongkhapa's words were to be believed, then the correct view related to the concept of "dependent arising and with an empty nature" attained by the learners in our Association upon the completion of their two-and-a-half year course must be far more profound and subtle than Tsongkhapa's view, and those learners must all have become Buddhas! However, I have never said that those learners have achieved the Path to Buddhahood nor have I even affirmed that they have all entered the Bodhisattva stage of the Seventh Abiding. They must have personally realized the eighth consciousness (the tathāgatagarbha) to obtain my certification that they have entered the Bodhisattva stage of the Seventh Abiding.

Based on the above passage from Tsongkhapa, we can conclude that his so-called "without attachment to any extremes" is a state that is shallower than that attained by the learners of our Association. Moreover, his understanding of the correct principle of "dependent arising and with an empty nature" is far more elementary than that of our learners. If Tsongkhapa could thus be hailed as the Most Honorable, then all the learners of our Association could be dubbed "the Most Honorable among the Most Honorable" upon completing their two-and-a-half year course and before realizing the eighth consciousness—the tathāgatagarbha— because their correct view related to the concept "dependent arising and with an empty nature" is far more profound and subtle than Tsongkhapa's view. Thus, we need to ask the gurus of Tibetan

Tantric Buddhism if Tsongkhapa's attainment of Buddhahood makes any sense at all.

One should know that the Path to Buddhahood is not achieved by having one's mind of feeling and cognition dwell without conceptuality or by ensuring that this mind possesses the correct view related to the concept of "dependent arising and with an empty nature." Instead, one must use one's conceptual mind of feeling and cognition to find a non-conceptual mind—the eighth consciousness (tathāgatagarbha)—that operates in tandem with this conceptual mind. Next, one must realize and comprehend all the seeds of this eighth consciousness to obtain the knowledge-of-all-aspects—to fully realize the knowledge-of-all-aspects in its entirety, without leaving any seed behind. Only then can one become a Buddha. Those tantric gurus proclaim that they can grasp the Buddha's tenets in the Exoteric Buddhist sūtras and can therefore achieve the Path to Buddhahood, while in fact they only understand those thoughts partially. They believe that they can "become Buddhas" if their conscious mind does not cling to any extremes while it abides in the state in which it remains thoughtless but holds the correct view related to the concept of "dependent arising and with an empty nature." As such, they are nothing but ordinary people who remain entrapped in the view and knowledge of eternalist non-Buddhists. While those gurus are completely ignorant of both the Path to Liberation and the Path to the Enlightenment of Buddhahood due to such views and knowledge that fully pertain to ordinary beings, they have disparaged the practice of Exoteric Buddhism—which allows learners to cultivate and realize these two paths—as elementary and have proclaimed that their false tantric doctrines, which are based on the non-Buddhist view of ordinary beings, enable them to become Buddhas in their current bodies. How extremely preposterous!

Tsonghapa has, based on such eternalist non-Buddhist view and knowledge, deprecated the Mahāyāna Dharma for not truly being a doctrine of no-self because it does not instruct learners to abandon the self-view with respect to phenomena. In fact, he has himself failed to eliminate the self-view with respect to the person in which the eternalist non-Buddhists are entrapped. Indeed, instead of eliminating—as exhorted by the Buddha—the self-view consisting of considering the self that is the conscious mind to be permanent and indestructible, Tsongkhapa regards the conscious mind that does not cling to any phenomena or any extremes and that does not engage in any mental activities of thinking as the mind of Buddhahood, thereby falling into the sphere of the mental consciousness. Furthermore, his misapprehension of the clear light as the real and permanent dharma (see previous citations) has also caused him to fall into the scope of the mental consciousness. Although he has, in this fashion, fallen into eternalist non-Buddhist view and knowledge, he unscrupulously boasts that he can refute "the self of phenomena imputed by the two factions of inner path and ascertain the meaning of selflessness"[13] (we will not elaborate on this topic, as readers may see Section 4 of Chapter 7 for further details). How could the tantric gurus and disciples of the Gelug School hail such a person devoid of shame and embarrassment as "the Most Honorable"?

Tsongkhapa asserts that neither his view nor his doctrines have veered into nihilistic emptiness. However, he has avoided nihilistic emptiness not because he has realized the mind consisting of the eighth consciousness—as the Buddha has taught us to do—but has done so through the cultivation and attainment of a visualized state consisting of a deity body of "indivisible emptiness and form." Tsongkhapa believes that the image of the "deity form body" that he has successfully visualized is by all means permanent and indestructible and therefore regards this "deity body" as the permanent and indestructible "Dharma body." Next, he merges this "deity body" with the mind of feeling and cognition—which understands the emptiness of all phenomena—into one single dharma. He views this single dharma as the support of all phenomena that connects the three times and therefore claims

---

13 Tsongkhapa, *Mizong daocidi guang lun* 密宗道次第廣論, 606-07. Translated into English from Chinese.

that he has not veered into nihilistic emptiness:

> One can become a wisdom body through practicing the indivisibility of body and mind with both the wisdom that ascertains the emptiness-nature and the manifested emptiness and form. Indeed, the body aggregated by fine particles cannot become a wisdom body. Given that such refutation of emptiness does not consist of refuting all emptiness-natures, one will regard all as the nihilistic emptiness of nothingness if one does not observe well. . . . Thus, one cannot refute the profound meanings cultivated by adversary schools if one does not determine whether the view of no-self should be practiced or not. In summary, one will be ridiculed by the wise if one asserts to have directly realized the meaning of no-self when one has not eliminated self-attachment in the slightest. Hence, the non-exalted ones do not exhibit no-self. How could the path harm self-attachment if one does not ascertain no-self through the general aspect?[14]

In fact, the mind of feeling and cognition, which is a phenomenon that arises and ceases easily, has been extensively denounced by the Buddha in the sūtras of the Three Vehicles as being the permanent and indestructible "self" set forth by eternalist non-Buddhists. The permanent and unbreakable "deity body" established by Tsongkhapa is an unreal phenomenon visualized by the easily-arising and easily-ceasing mind of feeling and cognition (mental consciousness). How could such a "deity body" be established as real given that it is visualized by the intrinsically unreal mind of feeling and cognition (mental consciousness) and given that this "deity body" is an unreal state issued from visualization instead of a truly achieved deity body?

Even if one has true attainments in meditative concentration and is able to achieve a real deity body through the practice of supernatural powers in meditative equipoise, this deity body remains a phenomenon issued from causes and conditions and

---

14   Ibid., 572.

therefore cannot be viewed as permanent. How then could it be established as a permanent and indestructible dharma? Even a real deity body cannot be established as a permanent and indestructible dharma, let alone the "deity body" issued from the visualization of Tantric Buddhists—it is even more of an unreal dharma of causes and conditions that is issued from visualization and is even less of a permanent and indestructible dharma, which means that it is not intrinsically existent. As such, how could it be forcefully established as a permanent and indestructible dharma?

The mind of feeling and cognition and the visualized "deity body" inevitably disappear in the five states such as deep sleep and so forth. As Tsongkhapa can validate this fact himself, how could he unreasonably argue that such a mind and deity body are permanent and indestructible dharmas? How could he establish them as the origin of all dharma-realms? What a complete inversion of the truth! A lay "Buddhist learner" in China called Shangping [上平] has even publicly insisted on the internet that the "self" consisting of the mind of feeling and cognition in a thoughtless and lucid state corresponds to the permanent and indestructible mind that is the reality-suchness—he has asserted that the thoughtless conscious mind is everlasting and indestructible. Such utterly unreasonable behavior is typical of someone from the Dharma-ending era.

The gurus and disciples of the Gelug School such as Tsongkhapa and so forth have furthermore misapprehended the clear light as the limit of reality:

> The principle of withdrawing (the illusory body) into the clear light is described in *A Lamp to Illuminate the Five Stages*:
> > From the head to the feet, traveling as far as the heart,
> > the yogi entering the limit of perfection is known as
> > held-as-a-whole. The animate and the inanimate
> > at first become the clear light (of the drop), after
> > which, in similar fashion, is the subsequent dissolution.
> > Just as breath dissolves on a mirror, likewise the yogi

enters again and again the limit of perfection.[15]

Tsongkhapa futher says:

The Innate Practice [Jusheng xiufa 俱生修法] states:
Its intent is vast,
The flow of compounded conceptual proliferations;
Those who frequently practice in this fashion
Should be subsequently mindful of the clear light.
The variegated lotus and the sun,
Vajrabhairava and kālī,
Lord of loving mother and empty treasure,
Below the five Tathāgatas,
The body and the supreme limbs,
The moon, the drop, nada, and so forth
Cause this to gradually disappear.[16]
Just as breath dissolves on a mirror,
Likewise the yogi **enters again and again
the limit of perfection.**[17]

Similarly, A Lamp to Illuminate the Five Stages: Teachings on
the *Guhyasamāja Tantra [Jimi wucidi lun 集密五次第論]*
asserts that **the vast deity body enters the clear light in
the various stages of subsequent dissolution.**[18]

The theories in Tsongkhapa's *The Great Exposition of Secret
Mantra [Mizong daocidi guanglun]* contain contradictory ideas.
Some of those theories regard the emptiness of shape and
substance in the mind of feeling and cognition as the emptiness-
nature; other theories consider the visualized deity body together

---

15   Je Tsongkhapa, *A Lamp to Illuminate the Five Stages: Teachings on Guhyasamāja Tantra,* ed. Thupten Jinpa, trans. Gavin Kilty (Boston: Wisdom Publication, 2013), 453.

16   Tsongkhapa, *Mizong daocidi guang lun* 密宗道次第廣論, 579. Translated into English from Chinese.

17   Je Tsongkhapa, *A Lamp to Illuminate the Five Stages: Teachings on Guhyasamāja Tantra,* ed. Thupten Jinpa, trans. Gavin Kilty (Boston: Wisdom Publication, 2013), 453.

18   Tsongkhapa, *Mizong daocidi guang lun* 密宗道次第廣論, 579. Translated into English from Chinese.

with the visualizing mind of feeling and cognition to be the emptiness-nature—the limit of reality; and still other theories view the clear light that appears during visualization as the emptiness-nature and equate this clear light with the limit of reality.

The Buddha has preached in the four Āgamas that the consciousness in "the name-and-form conditions the consciousness" refers to the limit of reality in the remainderless nirvāṇa and is also known as the intrinsic limit, suchness, the reality-suchness, the self, or the tathāgatagarbha. He has expounded in the prajñā sūtras that the limit of reality is precisely "the mind that is not a mind," "the mind without the signs of a mind," "the unmindful mind," or "the non-abiding mind." In the vijnaptimatra sūtras of the third turning of the Dharma Wheel, the Buddha has taught that the limit of reality corresponds to the ālaya-consciousness, the immaculate consciousness, the maturational consciousness, the undefiled consciousness, the tathāgatagarbha, the reality-suchness, the reality-suchness of transmigration, the reality-suchness of the sign of reality, the reality-suchness of vijnaptimatra, the reality-suchness of establishment, the reality-suchness of the wrong conduct, the reality- suchness of the proper conduct, the reality-suchness of purity, and so forth—all these different names designate the entity of the eighth consciousness. Moreover, each of the six uncompounded dharmas is established based on the various states of liberation in which the eighth consciousness abides: empty space, motionlessness, analytical cessation, non-analytical cessation, cessation of cognition and sensation, and reality-suchness. Outside the context of the entity of the eighth consciousness, there are neither uncompounded phenomena, nor sentient beings in the dharma-realms of the ten directions, nor any other phenomena.

In contrast to the above teaching, Tsongkhapa uses the mind of feeling and cognition, which is produced by the eighth consciousness, to visualize the state of the clear light, regards the clear light generated (by the eighth consciousness) through the visualization of the mental consciousness as the limit of reality, and exhorts learners to dissolve the visualized deity body into the visualized clear light—a process which he calls "entering the limit of reality." Such reasoning is similar to that of a person who clenches his fist, releases and spreads his fingers wide, and calls his fist's disappearance "emptiness-nature." Likewise, having fallen into the aforementioned mistaken view and thought, the proponents of Prāsaṅgika Madhyamaka claim that they possess the most supreme and wondrous doctrines within Buddhism. How utterly preposterous! However, the vast majority of tantric learners cannot distinguish between right and wrong; they believe in those teachings unwaveringly and are misled by those faulty gurus into erroneous views. In response to my attempts to rescue them from the abyss of misconceptions, they vituperated me, reviled my doctrines in every way, and even assailed me with all kinds of personal attacks. How extremely sad!

In ancient times, the Gelug School of Tibetan Tantric Buddhism deprecated, based on its fallacious views, the Jonang School by branding it as a destroyer of the Dharma and later instructed the Sakya School and the Dabu School to either slay the disciples of the Jonang School or expel them from Tibet by way of combat. Subsequently, the Gelug School took various initiatives to distort the tenets of the Jonang School, misinterpreting its view of other-emptiness by rewriting and recarving the printing plates of books that it had stored. Furthermore, the Gelug School resorted to political means to coerce the disciples of the Jonang School who did not follow their Dharma-king Tāranātha in exile as well as their monasteries into converting to the Gelug School tenets. Such complete extermination of the Jonang School has obliterated all chances for the Tibetans to learn the definitive Dharma and has caused them to fall into the mistaken views of the Four Major Tibetan Tantric Schools up to this day.

Tsongkhapa and all the other ancient and contemporary tantric gurus and followers have, unbeknownst to themselves, gone astray due to their blind faith in the mistaken knowledge and false views found in *The Vairocanābhisambodhi Sūtra*. This text regards the fact that all phenomena are dependent arising and with an empty nature outside the context of the tathāgatagarbha as the emptiness-nature set forth in the prajñā sūtras. Such an "emptiness-nature" differs drastically from the emptiness-nature taught by the Buddha in the prajñā sūtras—the mind that is not a mind, the unmindful mind, and the mind without the signs of a mind—the eighth consciousness, the tathāgatagarbha. Furthermore, the aforementioned "emptiness-nature" in the tantric sense differs even more from the eighth consciousness— the consciousness of real signs, the ālaya consciousness—set forth by the Buddha in the vijnaptimatra sūtras of the third turning of the Dharma Wheel.

Not only are the assertions made by tantric gurus with respect to the permanent and indestructible dharma inconsistent within the same writings, but they also show great discrepancies when we compare them across various publications, leaving tantric learners at a loss about what to do. What is even more absurd is the fact that those gurus regard the mental consciousness—the mind of feeling and cognition—which is said by the Buddha to be a dependently arising phenomenon with an other-dependent nature, as the permanent and indestructible true mind. They publicly assert that this mental consciousness is permanent and indestructible, thus openly contradicting the Buddha's intent to extensively refute the non-Buddhist eternalism in the four Āgamas. Surprisingly, this erroneous doctrine based on non-Buddhist misconceptions is hailed as superior to the Exoteric Buddhist Dharma-gate of practice and widely used to eclipse and denigrate the latter. Another surprising fact is that the renowned masters in today's major Exoteric Buddhist monasteries have been turning a blind eye to this situation and have been scrambling to flatter the tantric doctrines in an effort to raise their own status. Master Yinshun even took the initiative to inherit the misconceptions of Prāsaṅgika Madhyamaka—the most preposterous tantric view, which openly contradicts Buddha Śākyamuni's tenets—and has been destroying the true Dharma by dedicating his entire life to the extensive propagation of this fallacious view through the composition of erroneous Prāsaṅgika Madhyamaka writings such as *The Collection of Wonderful Clouds [Miaoyunji 妙雲集], The Collection of Flower and Rain [Huayuji 華雨集], Research on Tathāgatagarbha [Rulaizang zhiyanjiu 如來藏之研究], Exploration of Emptiness [Kongzhi tanjiu 空之探究], Xingkongxue tanyuan Exploring the Theory of the Emptiness-Nature [性空學探源]*, and so forth. What an unwise and demonic monk of the Dharma-ending era!

In my past lifetime, I was vexed at my inability to fix such inversions of the truth, which had persisted for a long time, and to rescue tantric practitioners out of the mistaken views that cause people to commit the grievous sin of destroying the Dharma because the Jonang School was exterminated by the Sakya School and the Dabu School under the order of the Fifth Dalai Lama. It is now time to face up to this issue, as the false tantric views have flooded Taiwan, a precious island, and are even being gradually propagated to the entire world. Therefore, I hereby aim to identify and correct each of the erroneous tantric views. By revealing those falsities to the world, I hope that, once and for all, current and future Buddhist learners will no longer be tormented by the false tantric views and will be able to practice the path without fear, and that Buddhism will no longer be plagued by those mistaken views, thus allowing the pure and the defiled to go their separate ways without interfering each other. Then, all current and future Buddhist learners will be able to progress on the path without being misled and disturbed by the fallacious tantric views.

8. The Fragmentation of the Buddhist Doctrines by the Erroneous Views in Tantric Buddhism

The egregious views found in Tantric Buddhism have fragmented the Buddha Dharma, causing the components in each of the following pairs to become dual: Madhyamaka and Vijñaptimātratā, Madhyamaka (tantric gurus wrongly regard the mental consciousness that is free from two extremes as the sign of reality of Madhyamaka) and prajñā (they have misapprehended the emptiness of all phenomena as prajñā), Exoteric Buddhism and Esoteric Buddhism, and the tathāgatagarbha and the ālaya. Given that none of the ancient and contemporary tantric gurus (most notably the Madhyamaka proponents of the Prāsaṅgika School such as Yinshun, the Dalai Lama, Tsongkhapa, and so forth) have been to understand the principle that Madhyamaka, prajñā and Vijñaptimātratā are non-dual as well as the principle that Exoteric Buddhism and Esoteric Buddhism are non-dual, and given their inability to realize the eighth consciousness—the ālaya consciousness—the tathāgatagarbha set forth in the vijñaptimātratā sūtras, they have rejected the tenets of the Vijñaptimātratā School, have wrongly branded those tenets as non-definitive doctrines, and have incorrectly denounced that the Buddha's ultimate and definitive words in the Vijñaptimātratā sūtras of the third turning of the Dharma Wheel consist of expedient teachings and non-definitive doctrines.

All Buddhist disciples who aspire to understand prajñā and truly enter Buddhism should first seek the entry point by abiding by the Chan School (although Tantric Buddhists also commend the Chan practice, the enlightenment in the Chan School has actually nothing to do with the so-called clear entity in Tantric Buddhism); next, they should advance in their practice by cultivating the knowledge-of-specific-aspects within prajñā taught in the prajñā sūtras; and finally, they should progress further by cultivating the knowledge-of-all-aspects set forth in the Vijñaptimātratā sūtras. It is only by advancing step-by-step in this fashion that they can gradually fulfill the practice and realization of the Path to Buddhahood. They must not emulate the tantric gurus' behavior that consists of wrongfully slandering the knowledge-of-all-aspects within Vijñaptimātratā, so as to avoid committing the grave misdeed of wrongfully deprecating the ultimate Dharma. Indeed, the training in the knowledge-of-aspects within Vijñaptimātratā corresponds to the knowledge-of-all-aspects that all Bodhisattvas must practice and learn after their enlightenment and to the training in higher wisdom cultivated by the Bodhisattvas of each Ground.

For instance, the tantric text *Essential Teachings about the Path of Nirvāṇa and the Mahāmudrā Yoga [Niepandao dashouyinyuqie fayao 涅槃道大手印瑜伽法要]* says:

> Contemplation of single and plural dharmas: The question is whether the mind is a single or plural dharma? If it is a single dharma, then how can it generate various dharmas? If it is a plural dharma, then all those various dharmas should be endowed with this same property of true emptiness. Based on this observation, one can well abide in neither the extreme of single nor the extreme of plural. It is to be known that the dharma that does not abide in either of the two extremes is precisely the Mahāmudrā, i.e., this very mind, which is the unique great true mind that abides without having any absolute place where to abide. It is only by knowing this fact that yogis can enter samadhi correctly. In that state, they will, in all certainty, perfectly achieve the perceptive, lucid, astute, and bright "faculty of the wisdom of individual analysis" and will attain the unsurpassed, pure, and correct wisdom. There is not a single sign beyond this. Therefore, the Mahāmudrā of innate wisdom corresponds to the unique sign of reality devoid of all signs.[1]

---

[1]   Lü Tiegang 呂鐵鋼, *Zangmi xiufa midian 藏密修法密典 [A Secret Book on the*

According to the above statements, one must use the mind
of feeling and cognition to observe whether this mind itself is single
or plural; next, one must use this mind to bring forth the mental
application of not abiding in either of two extremes; those who are
able to do so have achieved the freedom from two extremes—they
do not abide in either of two extremes. However, the concepts
"freedom from two extremes" and "not abiding in either of two
extremes" set forth by the Buddha are related to the realization, by
the mind of feeling and cognition, of an eighth consciousness that
functions in tandem with this mind of feeling and cognition and
that is always free from two extremes and never abides in either of
two extremes. The mind of feeling and cognition then dwells
according to this eighth consciousness' pure property of never
abiding in either of two extremes—the mind of feeling and
cognition dwells according to the wisdom related to the eighth
consciousness' property of being free from two extremes. In
contrast, tantric gurus abide in the mental application of "being
free from two extremes" brought forth by the entity of the mind of
feeling and cognition. Such a practice does not make sense because
the mind of feeling and cognition is always amidst two extremes as
it is never dissociated from the six sense objects.

In the Tantric Buddhists' explication of the Path to Liberation
with the aforementioned view and understanding set forth in
*Essential Teachings about the Path of Nirvāṇa and the Mahāmudrā
Yoga [Niepandao dashouyinyuqie fayao]*, the view of Madhyamaka
is achieved by using the mind of feeling and cognition to bring forth
the mental application of being free from two extremes. This text
has furthermore established its own view of the signs of reality
within prajñā:

> Manifestation of the sign of reality: As a result of the
> aforementioned practice of the correct contemplation of the
> yoga of no-birth, it is necessary to extirpate all conceptual

---

Practices of Tibetan Tantra], Vol. 4 (Beijing: Beijing Huaxia Publisher 北京華夏出版
社, 1995), 638-30. Translated into English from Chinese.

proliferations and false views related to the misapprehension of the illusory existence as reality and understand that all illusory existences are in essence similar to a show put on by a magician. If this can be achieved, then the unique sign of reality will manifest. As stated by the verses:

I can see the unique great sign of reality
In front of me, behind me, and in the ten directions;
All illusory views have vanished according to my guru's teachings.
What else is there for me to seek from other people?[2]

The sign of reality delineated above does not correspond in any way to the true sign of reality. In fact, the sign of reality set forth by the Buddha in the prajñā sūtras refers to the mind consisting of the eighth consciousness that intrinsically exists in all sentient beings. According to these sūtras, given that this eighth consciousness is the source of all dharma-realms, it is the sign of reality of all sentient beings and all phenomena in the dharma-realms of the ten directions and is therefore called sign of reality. In contrast, tantric gurus regard the fact that all phenomena are dependent arising and have an empty nature—all phenomena are impermanent and have an empty nature—as the sign of reality set forth in the prajñā sūtras. However, the Dharma taught in this fashion is that of the signs of non-reality. Indeed, all dharmas that are dependent arising and with an empty nature are dharmas that disintegrate and within which there is no real and indestructible entity. Consequently, they are not dharmas of the sign of reality, because they do not have the eighth consciousness' real, permanent, and indestructible entity and because all these dharmas are impermanent and therefore empty; hence, they are called dharmas of the signs of non-reality.

Due to this mistaken view, tantric gurus stripped away the deed-contemplation performed on the Middle-Way mind-natures

---

[2] Ibid., 639.

of the eighth consciousness (Madhyamaka) from within the eighth consciousness, thereby dissociating the deed-contemplation on the Middle-Way mind-natures from the eighth consciousness and turning this deed-contemplation into some kind of metaphysics. Furthermore, they stripped away the doctrine of the eighth consciousness consisting of the emptiness-nature—the sign of reality—set forth in the prajñā sūtras from the eighth consciousness, thereby dissociating the emptiness-nature and the eighth consciousness and creating some other kind of metaphysics. Next, they separated Madhyamaka and the sign of reality, turning them into two different kinds of metaphysics. The Buddha Dharma has thus been cut off and fragmented by tantric scholars.

With respect to the contemplation based on the limit of reality, however, Madhyamaka is the deed-contemplation that consists of observing the Middle-Way natures of the eighth consciousness; there are no Middle-Way natures to contemplate beyond the Middle-Way natures of the eighth consciousness. Given that all deed-contemplation of the Middle-Way natures directly or indirectly arises from and exists because of the mind consisting of the eighth consciousness, no deed-contemplation of the Middle Way is possible beyond the eighth consciousness. As for the sign of reality, one must observe the real nature of the eighth consciousness and directly observe how the eighth consciousness produces one's five aggregates and eighteen elements, how it stores the seeds of all karmic deeds that one has performed in this and previous lifetimes, how it allows sentient beings to realize the fruition of liberation, how it enables sentient beings to eliminate their habitual seeds based on its pure property, and how the various realms of the eighth consciousness allow people to extinguish all latent beginningless ignorance and thereby achieve Buddhahood. It is only by achieving these observations that one can be said to have attained the Middle-Way view of the sign of reality.

Both Madhyamaka and the sign of reality thus exist in dependence upon the natures of the eighth consciousness. The

Buddha has taught Madhyamaka and the sign of reality based on such Middle-Way natures of the mind consisting of the eighth consciousness. Therefore, the correct way for Buddhist disciples to practice prajñā is to rely on the conceptual nature of the mind of feeling and cognition—the mental consciousness—to observe the Middle-Way natures of the eighth consciousness amidst the four deportments. As those tantric gurus neither know nor see this principle, they have misinterpreted Madhyamaka as "the non-observation of two extremes by the mind of feeling and cognition" and have misconstrued the sign of reality as the fact that "all phenomena are dependent arising and with an empty nature," thus breaking up Madhyamaka and the sign of reality into two distinct doctrines and fragmenting the Buddha Dharma that consists of the non-dual and non-distinct Madhyamaka and sign of reality, which both manifest and exist in dependence upon the same mind consisting of the eighth consciousness. This egregious mistake can be ascribed to the proponents of Prāsaṅgika Madhyamaka in Tantric Buddhism.

Tantric Buddhists have also broken up the reality-suchness and Vijñaptimātratā into two distinct doctrines—they have broken up the Buddha Dharma, which is in essence one single doctrine, and which has been expediently taught in separate ways for the sake of sentient beings, into two distinct doctrines:

> The objective of the dependent arising based upon the reality-suchness is to complement the fact that Vijñaptimātratā leans towards inanition and to explain the basic source of the non-duality of the mind and matter. All form phenomena and mental phenomena originally abide in the fundamental entity of the reality-suchness, without the distinction of the mind and matter. Having primordially formed a harmonious unity, the mind and matter are neither identical nor different, neither defiled nor pure, and neither arising nor ceasing. The deluded activities of the ignorance in a single thought of sentient beings triggers deluded activities; this is called "ignorance conditions formations." Formations and consciousness seem to be a dichotomy. In fact, formations do not correspond to the

practice of the Path while consciousness cannot be equated with the correct view—hence formations condition consciousness. After this consciousness falsely established name-and-form, the distinction between the mind and matter gradually emerged from this name-and-form, causing the various contemporary scientific and philosophical schools to make false assertions and to stray away from the fundamental entity of the reality-suchness. This has resulted in the cyclic existence of the twelve links of dependent arising, with the universe being precisely the environment for this unreal cyclic existence. The lives of ordinary people are entities that are plagued by the sufferings of cyclic existence. As Mahāyāna practitioners are aware that the fundamental entity of the reality-suchness is originally endowed with the Buddha-nature and that it is not impossible to convert the Sahā World into a Pure Land, they assiduously educate others, commend the teachings of the Pure Land, and bring forth their mind of enlightenment. They accumulate the collection of compassion through the mental deeds of individual karma; moreover, it is possible to build a Pure Land in this human world by transforming collective karma. This is to be done by the Bodhisattvas of the Great Vehicle. By cultivating both the no-self of the person and the no-self of phenomena, one does not lean towards Vijñaptimātratā or materialism; this is the correct Madhyamaka path of the Great Vehicle.[3]

Such statements, which have broken up Vijñaptimātratā—the training in higher wisdom—and the dependent arising based upon the reality-suchness into two distinct doctrines, clearly come from someone who has misapprehended the knowledge-of-aspects within Vijñaptimātratā; truly enlightened people will never make such declarations. In other words, those tantric gurus do not understand the principle of the dependent arising based upon the

---

3   Yogi C. M. Chen (Chen Chien-ming 陳健民), *Qugongzhai quanji* 曲肱齋全集 *[The Complete Works of Yogi Chen]*, vol. 1-5, ed. Xu Qinying 徐芹庭 (Taipei: Puxianwang rulai fojiaohui 普賢王如來佛教會, 1991), vol. 3, 25. Translated into English from Chinese.

reality-suchness, whose meaning is as follows: Although the mind consisting of the eighth consciousness in the Causal Ground is the mind of an ordinary person, its nature is intrinsically pure; when the eighth consciousness is together with sentient beings amidst the six sense objects, it reflects various matters and objects according to conditions, making things easy for those sentient beings. However, as it manifests its functions when it is together with sentient beings, it remains completely undefiled by the six sense objects, is invariably free from all greed and aversion, and always functions according to its pure nature. Given that this eighth consciousness is endowed with a permanent and indestructible nature that exists independently without depending on any phenomena, people can turn this eighth consciousness into the reality-suchness of the Ground of Buddhahood by thoroughly purifying the defiled seeds of the first consciousness through to the seventh consciousness stored in this eighth consciousness. Therefore, this nature of the eighth consciousness is called dependent arising based upon the reality-suchness. With respect to the principle of the dependent arising based upon the reality-suchness, we can conclude that there is no dependent arising based upon the reality-suchness to speak of beyond the eighth consciousness.

The principle taught in Vijñaptimātratā is precisely the correct principle of the dependent arising based upon the reality-suchness. How could those tantric gurus deprecate Vijñaptimātratā based on their misapprehension by branding it as a doctrine that "leans towards inanition"? Furthermore, the knowledge-of-aspects in the training of Vijñaptimātratā is not just about the principle of the dependent arising based upon the reality-suchness, but it is also about the origin of sentient beings' mind of feeling and cognition, the origin of sentient beings' form body, the origin of the world's arising, and the origin of sentient beings' cyclic existence within the three realms. In addition, the knowledge-of-aspects elaborates on the knowledge-of-specific-aspects, which is encompassed by the eight negations of the Middle Way[4] and is set forth in prajñā and explains in detail its subtle and wondrous contents through to the ultimate Ground, which cannot be fully grasped by the Bodhisattvas under the First Ground. Consequently, the gate of dependent arising based upon the reality-suchness definitely does not represent the entirety of knowledge-of-aspects within Vijñaptimātratā—the training in higher wisdom—but only accounts for a small portion of the doctrine of this knowledge-of-aspects.

Dubbed by the Buddha as the training in higher wisdom of the Great Vehicle, the training of the knowledge-of-aspects within Vijñaptimātratā is precisely what all Bodhisattvas on or above the First Ground should learn. Unaware that the doctrine of the dependent arising based upon the reality-suchness only accounts for a small portion of the Vijñaptimātratā knowledge-of-aspects, those tantric gurus surprisingly held onto this small portion of the doctrines of Vijñaptimātratā, misinterpreted those contents, and then asserted the opposite of those contents in order to wrongfully revile the tenets of Vijñaptimātratā. After breaking up the doctrine of the reality-suchness and the doctrine of Vijñaptimātratā into two distinct entities, they misrepresented those teachings and elevated one doctrine above the other. How could Tantric Buddhism be regarded as a Buddhist school when they misconstrue the Buddha Dharma so gravely?

The elementary learners of Tantric Buddhism have further broken up Madhyamaka and Vijñaptimātratā into two distinct doctrines. For instance, as Chen Chunlong and Ding Guangwen are unable to understand the correct doctrine of Vijñaptimātratā—the tathāgatagarbha—and have misapprehended the main thoughts of Madhyamaka, they have broken up the tathāgatagarbha and Madhyamaka, both of which are set forth in Vijñaptimātratā, into two different doctrines:

---

4   Eight negations of the Middle Way: S. *aṣṭānta*; C. *babuzhongdao* 八不中道.

In fact, "the attainment of Buddhahood denotes the everlasting elimination of the afflictive and the cognitive hindrances." This is what gave rise to the philosophy about the permanent nature and eternality of "the tathāgatagarbha and Buddha-nature." Furthermore, this has enabled a vast number of Buddhists to feel that their cultivation is indeed meaningful; otherwise, if even the attainment of Buddhahood was impermanent, then everyone's efforts would be futile. . . . The contention among various Buddhist schools since ancient times has not been a good thing. The sectarian debates between Madhyamaka and Vijñaptimātratā persisted for one thousand years, leading to the extinction of the Buddha Dharma in India.[5]

By making such statements, the Tantric Buddhists Chen Chunlong and Ding Guangwen behaved like robbers who have murdered someone but wrongfully accuse others of being the robbers. The Buddhism in ancient India was not extinguished as a result of sectarian debates between Madhyamaka and Vijñaptimātratā but was instead destroyed at the hands of Tantric Buddhists—in the same way that today's Buddha Dharma is currently being replaced by non-Buddhist doctrines under the initiatives of Chen and Ding—through a process analogous to the grafting of a plum tree onto a peach tree. How could the Tantric Buddhists Chen and Ding denounce the sectarian debates between Madhyamaka and Vijñaptimātratā as meaningless?

In ancient times, the sectarian debates between Madhyamaka and Vijñaptimātratā occurred in essence among the unenlightened members of both Schools. Never would such sectarian debates have taken place among the truly enlightened members. Given that no sectarian debate has ever occurred among the enlightened members, there is naturally no documentation on this topic for the later generations to read. In contrast, the

---

[5] Chen, Chunlong 陳淳隆 (Miaozhan 妙)) and Ding Guangwen 丁光文's *Kongxing jian xinjiaodu de chanshi* 空性見新角度的闡釋《上下集》 *[An Explanation of the New Perspective on the View of Emptiness, vols. 1 & 2]*, retrieved from http://city080.mydreamer.com.tw/. Translated into English from Chinese.

occurrence of sectarian disputes among the unenlightened members of both Schools must have caused a plethora of related information to be passed down to the later generations. Given that the debates occurred among unenlightened persons, the points of argumentation that have gone down to later generations must all have been statements consisting of conceptual proliferations. As the academic researchers in Buddhism of the later generations are unenlightened and do not know that the principles of Madhyamaka and Vijñaptimātratā are in fact non-dual, they are unaware of the mistakes related to the conceptual proliferations resulting from the debates among the unenlightened members of both Schools and therefore have certainly been conducting research based on those conceptual proliferations. In that case, how could the findings from their research have anything to do with the Buddha Dharma? The Buddhist researchers in Europe, the U.S., and Japan have all fallen into this trap. This is also true of the elderly Master Yinshun in Taiwan, who had followed in those researchers' footsteps and was unable to avoid this error. Wholly unaware of this principle, Chen and Ding adhered to the arguments put forth by a handful of unenlightened Chinese and foreign academic researchers in Buddhism and drew conclusions from those arguments. Ignorant of the fact that the Buddhism in ancient India was actually extinguished at the hands of Tantric Buddhists, Chen and Ding made comments and conducted research based on the analysis resulting from the debates among the unenlightened members of the Madhyamaka and the Vijñaptimātratā Schools. Consequently, their publications merely contain imaginary and speculative assertions and their statements have absolutely no true meaning to speak of.

All truly enlightened persons are aware that Madhyamaka refers to the Madhyamaka within prajñā and that Vijñaptimātratā designates the Vijñaptimātratā within prajñā—they know that both Madhyamaka and Vijñaptimātratā fall entirely within the scope of prajñā. Indeed, prajñā encompasses the entirety of the Buddha Dharma, starting with semblance prajñā, which practitioners must conceive by coming into contact with the Dharma in a process of seed-transformation; followed by the knowledge-of-general-aspect within prajñā, which is encompassed by the eight negations of the Middle-Way properties of the true mind and which is known by practitioners upon their realization of the eighth consciousness; next, the knowledge-of-specific-aspects, which is set forth in the prajñā sūtras and which is practiced post-enlightenment in a process of seed-transformation based on the knowledge-of-general-aspect; and finally the knowledge-of-all-aspects, which is expounded in the sūtras of the third turning of the Dharma Wheel and which is cultivated in a process of seed-transformation by the Bodhisattvas on or above the First Ground. All these teachings are known as prajñā. Madhyamaka includes the knowledge-of-general-aspect and the knowledge-of-specific-aspects that must be practiced and realized by unenlightened persons and also falls within the category of prajñā. Vijñaptimātratā designates the partial knowledge-of-all-aspects to be further cultivated by those who have attained the knowledge-of-specific-aspects through post-enlightenment practice. This partial knowledge-of-all-aspects is only fully perfected on the Ground of Buddhahood—only then will it be known as the knowledge-of-all-aspects. The knowledge-of-all-aspects possessed by all Bodhisattvas on or above the First Ground, who have not yet perfected their cultivation and who have not yet attained the Ground of Buddhahood, is called knowledge-of-the-aspects-of-paths.

The wisdom of Madhyamaka only encompasses the knowledge-of-general-aspect and the knowledge-of-specific-aspects found in the wisdom of prajñā. Those who have realized these two wisdoms are still unable to attain the knowledge-of-all-aspects within prajñā. In order to realize the knowledge-of-all-aspects, they will still need to learn personally from the Buddha (or from the Vijñaptimātratā sūtras) after they become enlightened. Vijñaptimātratā, on the other hand, is about the knowledge-of-all-aspects—the doctrine found in the Vijñaptimātratā sūtras, which was taught by the Buddha during the third turning of the Dharma Wheel, the knowledge-of-the-aspects-of-paths that must be cultivated by the Bodhisattvas who have attained the knowledge-of-specific-aspects within prajñā as they advance in their practice. Hence, the doctrines of Madhyamaka and Vijñaptimātratāare in fact non-dual and only differ in profundity and scope. Why do tantric gurus argue about the doctrines of Madhyamaka and Vijñaptimātratā? And why have they broken up Madhyamaka and Vijñaptimātratā into two distinct doctrines? Their behavior does not make any sense.

Therefore, all disputes among the scholars of Madhyamaka and Vijñaptimātratā throughout the history of Buddhism consist of conceptual proliferations among unenlightened persons, because the statements made by those contenders certainly do not touch upon the truth of the foremost meaning and because no contention would ever occur among the truly enlightened proponents of these two Schools given that they share the same view of the truth. Wholly unaware of this principle, Chen and Ding adhered to the arguments put forth by a handful of unenlightened academic researchers in Buddhism and asserted that the extermination of Buddhism in ancient India resulted from the debates between Madhyamaka and Vijñaptimātratā.

Madhyamaka consists of observing the Middle-Way natures of the tathāgatagarbha. The tathāgatagarbha is the fundamental entity of Madhyamaka—Madhyamaka exists in dependence upon the Middle-Way natures of the tathāgatagarbha. For this reason, it is impossible to dissociate Madhyamaka and the tathāgatagarbha into two distinct doctrines. There is no way that Chen and Ding can grasp the contents of the afflictive and the cognitive hindrances, which the Buddha has eliminated. How could they grasp the contents of the cognitive hindrances when they still do not know the location of the tathāgatagarbha? How could they understand and eradicate their afflictive hindrances when they still have no idea about the contents thereof? How could they have the wisdom to help others eliminate these hindrances when they do not even comprehend them and have not exterminated them? Indeed, as they remain entrapped within the sphere of the conscious mind's natures and insist that the mind of feeling and cognition corresponds to the reality- suchness, they still do not understand the meaning of the "non-Buddhist view of eternalism" frequently mentioned by the Buddha in the sūtras of the Three Vehicles. How could such people who are unable to relinquish their non-Buddhist view of eternalism grasp the principle whereby sound-hearers eliminate their afflictive hindrances? How could they teach the Buddha Dharma and presumptuously assert on their website the principles whereby one achieves Buddhahood—such as eliminating the afflictive and the cognitive hindrances and so forth—when they neither understand nor have realized the principle whereby one eliminates these two hindrances? Clearly, their behavior does not make any sense.

Furthermore, Chen and Ding have claimed: "The occurrence of sectarian disputes within Buddhism since ancient times has not been a good thing." I concur with these truthful words. However, this assertion was not made out of good intentions. What those two persons have been trying to do is use those words to thwart my endeavors to identify and rectify the mistaken tantric thoughts and doctrines. Another objective is to deliberately trick learners into equating doctrinal debates with sectarian disputes. How malicious! Sectarian contention within Buddhism inevitably leads to the diversion of Buddhist resources and thereby gives non-Buddhist sects that rely on the Buddha Dharma to exist—such as Tibetan Buddhism and so forth—the opportunity to take advantage of the situation. In fact, sectarian contention exclusively occurs among unenlightened persons and never among their enlightened peers.

Marked differences exist between sectarian disputes and doctrinal debates, yet Buddhist learners in general are unable to detect them. In a sectarian dispute, both parties compete for the superiority of their lineage, i.e., they vie for the prestige of having a superior lineage and would rather die than admit their mistakes— they will argue to the bitter end even if they are aware that their doctrines contain errors. In a doctrinal debate, on the other hand, both parties argue about the doctrines based on what the doctrines actually are, regardless of personal relationships and potential gains and losses for their own school and the other party's school and purely in dependence upon the Buddha's doctrines. Therefore, when an enlightened person comes across someone who pretends to be enlightened when he is not, who affirms he has attainments when he does not, and who misleads sentient beings with mistaken views and knowledge, he will immediately step forward to identify right from wrong and manifest what is right—except in the case where that falsely enlightened person has not propagated the Dharma in public. This will allow the falsely enlightened person who has propagated the Dharma in public to know his errors upon hearing the statements made by the enlightened person; he will then rectify those errors right away and will acknowledge his faults and show repentance openly without hiding anything.

Enlightened persons will definitely identify and rectify any erroneous doctrines when they see that sentient beings are being misled by a false master. Those who are attached to their own school will, in all certainty, wrongfully brand the statements made by these virtuous mentors to identify and rectify the erroneous doctrines as words of sectarian dispute in an effort to confuse the public and foil those virtuous mentors' endeavors to defend the true Dharma and rescue sentient beings. By creating confusion, those false masters aim to stop the virtuous mentors from identifying and correcting the fallacious doctrines so that those false masters can perpetuate their erroneous teachings. This will allow them to continue to mislead sentient beings and to maintain their fame and current levels of income.

For instance, with respect to my identification and correction of wrong doctrines through various publications, false tantric masters such as Chen and Ding will certainly brand my **correct deeds to identify and rectify false doctrines** as acts of sectarian contention and will assert that such behavior does not benefit Buddhism in any way. The truth is, my behavior is immensively beneficial to Buddhism and also extremely detrimental to the tantric gurus who preach erroneous doctrines and the renowned masters who are falsely enlightened. For this reason, those people will, in all certainty, wrongfully equate my **identification and correction of wrong doctrines** with acts of sectarian dispute. Those who are unaware of the gravity of this issue and who cannot distinguish between right and wrong will be beguiled by those masters; they will promote those masters' achievements and will urge me to stop all deeds of identifying and rectifying erroneous doctrines. This will prevent non-Buddhist methods from being expelled from Buddhism and will allow various non-Buddhist doctrines to remain within Buddhism and to continue to nibble and devour Buddhism—to continue to progressively turn Buddhist doctrines into non-Buddhist teachings. If I do not expose and put an end to those people's misdeeds, then we will eventually see a recurrence of the historic event whereby the Buddhism of ancient India was in essence exterminated by Tantric Buddhism. All Buddhist disciples who aspire to protect the correct Dharma of Buddhism and all benevolent persons who wish to benefit current and future learners of the Buddha Dharma should not neglect the importance of identifying and rectifying erroneous doctrines **nor allow the false tantric gurus to forcefully misrepresent such behavior as "acts of sectarian dispute between the exoteric and the esoteric schools."**

Why do I say so? Indeed, how could I have any sectarian bias given that I realized prajñā in this lifetime without benefiting from any enlightened mentor's transmission? I achieved enlightenment on my own, based on my experience of enlightenment in past lifetimes and without relying on the transmission from a specific master, school, or tradition. Since there was neither transmission from a master of exoteric tradition nor transmission from a guru of esoteric tradition, I do not need to dispute the Dharma on behalf of any school or tradition; hence, there is no sectarian contention to speak of. Furthermore, my practice and realization relates to the all-encompassing Buddha Dharma, which includes both exoteric and esoteric doctrines—the doctrines explicitly set forth by the Buddha in the sūtras as well as the secret meanings of the Buddha

Dharma implicitly preached by the Buddha in those sūtras. Given that such Buddha Dharma is not from a purely exoteric or purely esoteric school or tradition, it is not necessary for me to vie for any exoteric or esoteric lineage.

All tantric gurus will undoubtedly aspire to misrepresent my identification and rectification of fallacious doctrines as acts of sectarian dispute between the exoteric and the esoteric schools, in an effort to stop me from commenting on the tantric Dharma-gate, which is based on false knowledge, views, and practices. However, the public should know that if Tantric Buddhism were indeed Buddhism, then I would be committing the grievous sin of deprecating the correct Dharma and would, after death, inevitably fall into hell, where I would suffer excruciating, sheer anguish for many long kalpas. How would I dare to commit such a grievous deed given my profound faith in the law of cause and effect—my extreme fear of retribution? One should know that my behavior is by no means groundless and should observe whether the plethora of comments that I have made with respect to the tantric doctrines are justified and in accord with the scriptures. One will then know that I am telling the truth. Therefore, before gaining the ability to distinguish between authentic and fake, one should not promote the non-Buddhist tantric doctrines and had better not support Tantric Buddhism; otherwise, how could one remedy, upon death, the collective deed of helping Tantric Buddhism destroy the correct Dharma of Buddhism?

The public should know that the Madhyamaka and the Vijñaptimātratā doctrines were both pronounced by the Buddha and are in fact non-dual. They only differ in profundity, subtleness, and scope. Any truly enlightened person who has advanced to the stage of cultivating the knowledge-of-all-aspects will unequivocally agree with my statements. Only unenlightened ordinary persons will dispute over Madhyamaka and the knowledge-of-aspects within Vijñaptimātratā, misconstruing them as two different Dharma-gates of practice. In fact, the main entities of these two doctrines are non-dual: These two doctrines both have the eighth consciousness—the tathāgatagarbha—as their main entity. Therefore, there is no point to argue about them relentlessly given that their differences only lie in the order sequence in which their contents must be practiced and in the profundity of these contents. Why not make better use of one's time by contemplating and searching for the mind consisting of the eighth consciousness? Having realized the mind consisting of the eighth consciousness, one will understand the veracity of my statements after respectfully seeking and studying the sūtras preached by the Buddha in the second and the third turnings of the Dharma Wheel and comparing one's realization with the contents of those sūtras. Thereafter, one will by all means no longer follow the mistaken views propounded by the ordinary sentient beings of ancient times who engaged in sectarian arguments—one will never regard Madhyamaka and the Vijñaptimātratā as two distinct doctrines and dispute over which one is superior. If this can happen, then the impact of the Tantric Buddhists' misdeeds that consist of taking the liberty to break up the doctrines of prajñā found in Buddhism and thereby shattering these subtle and wondrous doctrines of prajñā will dissipate in the present and future.

Another egregious defect of Tantric Buddhists is to break up Exoteric Buddhism and Esoteric Buddhism into two distinct doctrines. Furthermore, unaware of the true esoteric meaning in Buddhism, they have established mundane methods of sexual pleasure, the method of visualizing the deity body, and so forth, all of which are transmitted orally and covertly by non-Buddhists, as the ultimate, supreme, and wondrous doctrines within Buddhism, thereby shattering the correct meaning of prajñā in the Buddha Dharma. For example, Tsongkhapa says:

> Well then, you may wonder, what is the meaning of saying that according to whether something is or is not measured in terms of place and time it is magnificent or paltry?
>
> When you meditate deity yoga in terms of its being of one taste with the thatness of things and [in terms of the deity circle] having just that [nondual] nondeceptive quality, you are meditating in terms of its totality—without determining from

a limited perspective the extent of the excellences, places,
and times of the form bodies, etc., of all the transcendent
buddhas—and thus it is magnificent. But if you lack that kind
of deity yoga, then although you may have the profound yoga
of being nondifferentiated from the suchness of all things, you
are not meditating without discriminating a [particular] extent,
in terms of [ordinary] qualities, and thus it is paltry.[6]

In the above passage, Tsongkhapa indicates that, although
the Exoteric Buddhists are able to cultivate and realize **"one taste
with the thatness of things,"** they do not have the capacity to
generate a large deity body given that they do not practice deity
yoga (given that they do not perform the visualization of a large
deity body—the practice of deity yoga consists of visualizing the
main deity's large deity body). As a result, their "reward body" of
Buddhahood is paltry—it does not exceed the size of the fleshly
body in the human world. Hence, Tsongkhapa asserts that the
Dharma-gate of Exoteric Buddhism is "limited" and "not large."

However, those Tibetan Buddhists' belief that their
visualization of a large deity body will enable them to obtain a
reward body when they achieve Buddhahood in the future is
nothing but false thinking. Indeed, the magnificent reward body
that Buddhist disciples will obtain upon attaining Buddhahood is
not attained in the slightest from the practice of visualization but is
instead a fruition attained through the wisdom of prajñā and
meditative concentration. Buddhist disciples enter the First Ground
by realizing the knowledge-of-the-aspects-of-paths within the
wisdom of prajñā. Those who have additionally attained the fourth
concentration can certainly take rebirth in the highest heaven of
the realm of subtle materiality after death if they wish to do so.
Once they are reborn in that heaven, they will naturally obtain the

---

6   Tsong Khapa Losang Drakpa, Great Treatise on the Stages of Mantra (sngags rim
chen mo): Critical Elucidation of the Key Instructions in All the Secret Stages of the
Path of the Victorious Universal Lord, Great Vajradhara. Chapters XI–XII (The
Creation Stages), introduction and translation by Thomas Freeman Yarnall, (AIBS,
CBS & THUS, New York, 2013), 283.

largest body in the three realms without having to practice any visualization. This is a maturational fruition that results from their knowledge-of-the-aspects-of-paths, their eternal suppression of dispositional hindrances, and their ten inexhaustible vows. [7] In contrast, although tantric practitioners cultivate the method of "visualizing a large deity body," given that they are not even able to realize the knowledge-of-general-aspect within prajñā—they misapprehend the mental consciousness (the mind of feeling and cognition) as the reality-suchness—they definitely cannot cultivate the more advanced knowledge-of-all-aspects, and therefore, it will be impossible for them to enter the First Ground by realizing the knowledge-of-the-aspects-of-paths and to take rebirth in the highest heaven of the realm of subtle materiality, which means that they will not be able to obtain the largest deity body in the three realms.

Even if those tantric followers visualize that their own deity body is boundlessly large, they cannot confer any properties or functions to this visualized deity body, for it is merely a portion of signs in their own minds. How could they bring forth, after death, the largest body—the body of the highest heaven of the realm of subtle materiality—when they are unable to even take rebirth in the heaven of the first-dhyāna and obtain a form body that is taller and larger than the form body of the celestial beings in the desire realm? A large body issued from the visualization performed by one's own mind of feeling and cognition is nothing more than a portion of signs within this mind and therefore does not have any meritorious quality that can be used in the three realms after one's death, because this method of visualization does not generate any maturational fruition of future lives—any maturational fruition of future lifetimes results from its correct cause, and the method of visualization is not the correct cause of any such maturational fruition. Moreover, given that those tantric practitioners have not realized the wisdom of prajñā, they cannot be reborn in a heaven

---

[7]   Ten inexhaustible vows; C. *shiwujinyuan* 十無盡願.

of the desire-realm, let alone take rebirth in a heaven of the form realm and obtain the fruition of a deity body. Therefore, they cannot possibly obtain a tall and large deity body. Those tantric Buddhists' belief that they can achieve, through the practice of visualization, "a large deity body" that will serve as their Buddha body is nothing but false thinking.

Furthermore, those who aspire to obtain a deity body of the desire realm must forsake the mistaken tantric practice of pursuing sexual bliss, reduce their sexual desires, observe the five precepts, and on top of the above benefit sentient beings by extensively performing the ten wholesome deeds. For those who are able to extensively perform the ten wholesome deeds and observe the precepts, the lesser their sexual desires, the higher the heaven (among the six heavens of desire) where they will take rebirth, and the taller and larger the deity body that they will obtain. It is unnecessary for them to practice the visualization of deity bodies, because the tall and large deity bodies of the desire realm are not attained through the method of visualization—the method of visualizing a deity body is not the correct cause of the maturational fruition consisting of rebirth in a heaven of the desire realm. Furthermore, the method of visualizing a deity body is futile, because it is impossible to increase the size of the body that one will obtain when one takes rebirth in a heaven of the desire realm by assiduously practicing this method.

The way to obtain a taller and larger deity body of the form realm is to practice meditative concentration; one takes rebirth in one of the heavens of the form realm based on the level of meditative concentration that one has attained. In other words, the higher one's level of meditative concentration, the more elevated the heaven of the form realm where one can take rebirth, and consequently the taller and larger one's deity body. Therefore, one will not obtain a deity body just because one has practiced the visualization of a deity body before death, and the characteristics of the deity body that one will obtain does not depend upon whether one has visualized a deity body before death.

The celestial beings in the highest heaven of the realm of subtle materiality are the sentient beings in the three realms with the tallest and largest body. Only Bodhisattvas on or above the First Ground can take rebirth in that heaven based on their knowledge-of-the-aspects-of-paths, their eternal suppression of dispositional hindrances, their performance of pure deeds such as rescuing sentient beings by steering them back onto the correct path, and the fact that they have bravely made the ten inexhaustible vows. These four conditions must be met for those Bodhisattvas to take rebirth in that heaven. sound-hearer arhats do not have the capacity to be reborn there (because they will definitely enter the remainderless nirvāṇa and do not possess the knowledge-of-the-aspects-of-paths); the exalted ones of the third fruition are also unable to take rebirth in that heaven. Tantric practitioners are even less likely to be reborn in take rebirth there because not only are they unable to reduce their sexual desires, but they even seek the greatest blissful sensation consisting of the fourth joy amidst sexual desires due to their adherence to the mistaken tantric views—they even pursue the most enduring blissful sensation amidst sexual desires. Although they claim that they are without any attachment amidst such blissful sensation, their mindset and conduct show the opposite: They have in fact stronger attachment—sexual desires— than others. This will definitely cause them to forever fall to the lowest ranks in the desire realm, becoming peers with the libidinous men and women of the human world. How could those tantric followers have less desires than the celestial beings in the six heavens of the desire realm when those followers' desires actually exceed those of most people in the human world?

Thus, the view, meditation, conduct, fruition, and so forth of tantric practitioners will not enable them to take rebirth in any of the six heavens of the desire realm. Indeed, how could they be reborn in a heaven of the desire realm when the maturational fruition of their next lifetime is to be reborn again with the short and small fleshly body of the human world? How could they be reborn in a heaven of the form realm when they do not have the capacity to take rebirth in any of the heavens of the desire realm?

How could they be reborn in the highest heaven of the realm of
subtle materiality and obtain the tallest and largest deity body in
the three realms when they are unable to take rebirth in any of the
heavens of the form realm? How could those tantric practitioners
wrongly claim that the method of visualization allows one to obtain
the tallest and largest deity body when one achieves Buddhahood
in the future? All these statements are based on erroneous thinking.
Unaware of the correct principle to obtain a tall and large deity
body, tantric practitioners such as Tsongkhapa and so forth
mistakenly believe that the practice of visualization will allow them
to attain a tall and large deity body that will serve as their Buddha
body. How unwise! Endowed with the so-called "most superior
faculty," tantric learners surprisingly practice the most
preposterous and vulgar methods. Their assertion that only those
with the most superior faculty are fit to practice the esoteric
doctrines is the opposite of the truth and is certainly senseless.

Tsongkhapa further says:

Therefore, (the tantric) Shāntipa says [in his Commentary on
Dīpaṅkarabhadra's] *The Four Hundred and Fifty [Verses]:*
On the strength of your meditation on the stage of the
extreme purity of the manifestations of [your ultimate]
nature and on their [nondually] having a transcendent [empty]
nature, you completely perfect in every mental instant your
own transcendences, etc., through the transcendences, etc.,
of all the buddhas; and even when making offerings to yourself
or to others you make offerings to all the buddhas; and you
even can make a superlative offering out of inferior things.
Thus it is easy to reach enlightenment, and this therefore,
comes to be the nature of the path to enlightenment.
Therefore, by such expressions, it is shown how there is
special distinction [in the Mantra Vehicle] of causing the
attainment of enlightenment exclusively with extreme speed—
as [Vajradhara] said:
Oh yogins, by only mis very very [path],
You will achieve buddhahood swiftly!
And so, as explained above, the way of purifying the bases

of purification, and meditating after visualizing the actuality of the infinite qualities of a buddha, are the means for developing the roots of virtue which give rise to the entire the stage of perfection. Therefore, although the three lower classes of Tantra also have meditations on emptiness and on a mere deity body, it [the Unexcelled Yoga creation stage methodology being described here] is extremely distinctive, and thus it is different from those [lower three]. From this perspective, the superlative magnificence brings us to the occasion of the perfection stage.

Although the Transcendence Vehicle has meditation on a path which accords with the truth body, it lacks meditation on a path which accords with the form body, which is the counter-agent to the perception of an ordinary body; therefore, [in this Vehicle] it takes an extremely long time to complete the stores which are the cause of the form body. Since the Mantra Vehicle does have these, it is said that it easily complete the stores; . . .[8]

Tsongkhapa is in fact wholly ignorant of the Buddha Dharma. Not only is he completely clueless about the Path to the Enlightenment of Buddhahood realized in the Great Vehicle, but he is also totally ignorant of even the elementary contents of the Path to Liberation in the Two Vehicles, because he insists that the mental consciousness and the drops, as well as the mind of feeling and cognition and the wisdom of the non-duality of bliss and emptiness attained amidst the sexual pleasure, with which the mind of feeling and cognition connects, are indestructible phenomena. This topic will not be elaborated here, but will be illustrated in Chapters 8 and 9. We will hereby focus on rectifying the fallacies found in the above teaching from Tsongkhapa.

According to Tsongkhapa, those who practice according to

---

[8] Tsong Khapa Losang Drakpa, Great Treatise on the Stages of Mantra (sngags rim chen mo): Critical Elucidation of the Key Instructions in All the Secret Stages of the Path of the Victorious Universal Lord, Great Vajradhara. Chapters XI–XII (The Creation Stages), introduction and translation by Thomas Freeman Yarnall, (AIBS, CBS & THUS, New York, 2013), 283-84.

the doctrines set forth in Tibetan Buddhism will not only obtain all the meritorious qualities realized in Exoteric Buddhism, but they will also attain enlightenment by making offerings with inferior objects due to the superiority of the esoteric doctrines. Therefore, unlike Exoteric Buddhists, tantric practitioners do not need to realize the tathāgatagarbha and perform immeasurable deeds of giving. In other words, they can swiftly attain the fruition of enlightenment and become a Buddha through the tantric practice of offering to "Buddhas" the five nectars and the five meats, coupled with the offering of the contact within their bodies—such as sexual pleasure and so forth—and the visualization experienced during the yab-yum practice. Owing to this wondrous offering— "the supreme and wondrous method of the sexual pleasure consisting of the fourth joy"—Tsongkhapa has denigrated the Dharma-gate of Exoteric Buddhism by asserting that it is slow in yielding results and inefficacious when it comes to the attainment of the fruition of Buddhahood.

This, however, is the complete opposite of the truth. Those who practice according to the Dharma-gate set forth by Tsongkhapa will neither become a Buddha nor realize the wisdom of prajñā attained on every Ground or the following wisdoms of the Ten Abidings, which are below the First Ground: the wisdom of prajñā of the Seventh Abiding and even the wisdom of emptiness obtained from "validating the emptiness of both the apprehending-subject and the apprehended-object" and attained by the Bodhisattvas of the Sixth Abiding. Indeed, upon validating the emptiness of both the apprehending-subject and the apprehended-object, the Bodhisattvas of the Sixth Abiding will firmly resolve to never identify the mind of feeling and cognition as the indestructible mind and to even less identify the mind of feeling and cognition in the union of bliss and emptiness experienced during the yab-yum practice as the permanent and indestructible mind. They will even negate this mind of feeling and cognition and will speak of it as the mental consciousness with a dependent-arising nature. Furthermore, they will directly observe that this mind of feeling and cognition, which takes bliss in, is the "permanent and indestructible self" set forth in eternalist non-Buddhism, will directly observe that this mind is a phenomenon generated by a combination of conditions, and will directly observe that the sexual pleasure with which this mind comes into contact is precisely the basis of cyclic existence within the desire realm undergone by the sentient beings of this realm and that this sexual pleasure also arises from many different conditions. Due to these observations, these Bodhisattvas are said to be the ones who have directly observed the emptiness of both the apprehending-subject and the apprehended-object—they have gained resolve from validating the emptiness of both the apprehending-subject and the apprehended-object and will not back down from this view. As such, they are known as Bodhisattvas who have attained the full mind of the Sixth Abiding.

In contrast, Tsongkhapa and all the other ancient and contemporary gurus of the Four Major Tantric Schools have all identified the drops as the ālaya-consciousness, the mind of feeling and cognition in the union of bliss and emptiness as the reality-suchness of the Ground of Buddhahood, and the thoughtless mind of feeling and cognition in sitting meditation also as the reality-suchness of the Ground of Buddhahood. This clearly indicates that the ancient and contemporary gurus of Four Major Tibetan Tantric Schools all regard the mind of feeling and cognition that takes bliss in one-pointedly and without any distracting thoughts as "the reality-suchness of the reward body in the Ground of Buddhahood," and therefore, they believe that they have achieved siddhi, i.e., they have attained Buddhahood in their current bodies.

Those who thus view the mental consciousness as the reality-suchness of the Ground of Buddhahood have in fact not yet attained the wisdom of the emptiness-signs of all phenomena related to the validation of the emptiness of both the apprehending-subject and the apprehended-object, which is realized by the Bodhisattvas of the Sixth Abiding. Indeed, the thoughtless mind of feeling and cognition is precisely the mind consisting of the mental consciousness that apprehends all phenomena as well as "the permanent and indestructible mind" onto which the eternalist non-Buddhists hold. Those Dharma-kings of Tantric Buddhism cannot even realize the wisdom of the emptiness related to the concept of "dependent arising and with an empty nature" attained by the practitioners of the Two-Vehicles; how then could they understand the wisdom of the emptiness-nature within prajñā—the eighth consciousness' intrinsicality, nature, purity, and nirvāṇa as well as its Middle-way properties of the eight negations—realized at the Seventh Abiding in Mahāyāna Buddhism? How could they grasp the knowledge-of-the-aspects-of-paths of the First Ground when they do not comprehend and have not realized the wisdom of the emptiness-signs or the wisdom of the emptiness-nature attained by the Bodhisattvas of the Sixth Abiding and Seventh Abiding (the wisdom related to the fact that the aggregates, sense-fields, and elements are dependent arising and with an empty nature and the wisdom of prajñā attained from realizing the origin of all phenomena—the mind of the emptiness-nature, the eighth consciousness)? How could they comprehend the wisdom of the Ground of Buddhahood without understanding or having realized the knowledge-of-the-aspects-of-paths of the First Ground? Surprisingly, such tantric gurus—ordinary people who do not comprehend and have not realized the wisdom of the Mahāyāna Path of Vision—dare to denigrate the practice and realizations achieved by the Bodhisattvas of Exoteric Buddhism as being elementary and superficial and the practice and realizations attained by the Buddhas of Exoteric Buddhism as being elementary, superficial, and inferior to the attainments of the tantric "Buddhas" who engage in sexual misconduct, while boasting that the practice and realizations of Tantric Buddhists are superior to those of Exoteric Buddhists, for they allow practitioners to achieve the states of "the reward body Buddha and Dharma body Buddha in their current bodies." Are they not the most foolish and arrogant people in the world? Strangely, the renowned masters of Exoteric Buddhism are unaware of those gurus' errors and scramble to pander to the Dalai Lama and other persons who propagate teachings of sexual misconduct. Are those masters not utterly ignorant? For instance, **the Dalai Lama regards the mind in a state of thoughtlessness and lucid awareness during orgasm as the reality-suchness of the Ground of Buddhahood:**

> Dalai Lama: Among these four, fainting is very strong, but the one that you experience at the time of orgasm is the strongest. That is one of the reasons why the practice of bliss (the Dharma-gate that allows for the attainment of Buddhahood in this body, which consists of realizing the reality-suchness of the Buddha Ground through the union of bliss and emptiness in the yab-yum practice) comes into the highest yoga tantra. There is a lot of misunderstanding of the sexual and other imagery associated with the Anuttara yoga tantra. The actual reason for this sexual imagery is precisely because among these four ordinary occasions in which the clear light appears, orgasm is the strongest. Thus this imagery is used in meditation to extend the experience of the arising of clear light and also to clarify it or make it more vivid. This is the point. During the event of orgasm because the experience of clear light is longer in duration, already you have a greater opportunity to utilize it.[9]

Given that the Dharma-gate preached by the Dalai Lama is based on orgasm, he has definitively fallen within the sphere of the conscious mind.

Unaware that the eighth consciousness—the ālaya—corresponds to the tathāgatagarbha, tantric gurus have misconstrued the visualized drops in the central channel as the consciousness of the tathāgatagarbha and have separately established another dharma—the mind of feeling and cognition (the mental consciousness) that takes bliss in one-pointedly amidst the union of bliss and emptiness—as the tathāgatagarbha.

---

[9]   Jeremy W. Hayward, The Dalai Lama & Francisco J. Varela, *Gentle Bridges: Conversations with the Dalai Lama on the Sciences of Mind* (Shambhala Publications, Inc. 1992), 81-82.

Therefore, they have broken up the tathāgatagarbha and the eighth consciousness into two distinct doctrines. According to them, those who aim to realize the "tathāgatagarbha" through practice must either cultivate and attain the skill of thoughtlessness in sitting meditation or cultivate the fourth joy of the yab-yum practice with a guru of the opposite sex. The objective is to abide "permanently" and thoughtlessly in the greatest blissful contact of sexual pleasure and to bring forth "the view of the emptiness-nature" consisting of acknowledging that "the mind of feeling and cognition amidst sexual pleasure is empty of shape and form and is therefore the emptiness-nature" and that "the contact and sensation amid the sexual pleasure consisting of the fourth joy is also shapeless and formless and is therefore the emptiness-nature." In Tantric Buddhism, those who have attained this state "have realized the tathāgatagarbha" and achieved the reward body and the Dharma body.

For this reason, all tantric practitioners who aspire to realize the tathāgatagarbha—the ālaya-consciousness—through practice must visualize, in sitting meditation, the central channel and the drops. Those who can successfully visualize the drops have "indeed" realized the eighth consciousness—the ālaya. Furthermore, those who can move the drops up and down freely between the crown cakra and the root cakra within the central channel are exalted ones who have attained the tantric "fruition of the Bodhisattvas of the First Ground." Indeed, Tantric Buddhists assert that such "exalted ones" have achieved the same valid knowledge as the Bodhisattvas of the First Ground in Exoteric Buddhism (in reality, those "exalted ones" can absolutely not be identified with such Bodhisattvas). Consequently, those tantric followers claim that the tantric doctrines are the most supreme doctrines that involve cultivation and realization on the Fruition Ground, for it enables practitioners to attain the fruition of the First Ground in one lifetime and therefore supersedes the Exoteric Buddhist practice, through which the fruition of the First Ground can only be achieved after one great term of asaṃkhya kalpas.

225

Due to this mistaken view, the ālaya-consciousness—the tathāgatagarbha—which is in essence one single doctrine, has been dismantled and arbitrarily established as two distinct doctrines by Tantric Buddhists. Owing to the erroneous establishment of these two doctrines, the correct Dharma, which in essence is one single doctrine, has been transformed into the false practice of two different doctrines, fragmenting the true Buddhist doctrines and making it difficult for learners to realize the wisdom related to the sign of reality of prajñā. As a result, the Tibetan tantric non-Buddhists can fool the learners of Exoteric Buddhism by proclaiming that they have become Bodhisattvas of the First Ground and so forth.

Unaware that the Dharma body is in fact the eighth consciousness, the ālaya (on the Causal Ground, it is named "ālaya-consciousness" or "maturational consciousness," or generically called "tathāgatagarbha"; on the Ground of Buddhahood, it is no longer designated as "tathāgatagarbha" and is only known as "immaculate consciousness"—"reality-suchness"), tantric gurus falsely claim that by visualizing the immensity and magnificence of a deity body, one will, during the union of bliss and emptiness, be able to attain the mind of feeling and cognition of this union and to transform it into the reality-suchness of the Ground of Buddhahood—one will be able to regard the mind of feeling and cognition that takes bliss in and that understands the non-duality of bliss and emptiness and bliss as the Dharma body of the reality-suchness of the Ground of Buddhahood. Furthermore, one will conceive the visualized deity body as the perfect reward body of the Dharma body. In fact, those gurus do not know that the perfect reward body of the Ground of Buddhahood results from one's knowledge-of-general-aspect, knowledge-of-specific-aspects, and knowledge-of-all-aspects within prajñā, for the perfect reward body is a maturational fruition issued from the knowledge-of-all-aspects.

Those practitioners with erroneous thoughts have forcefully positioned their non-Buddhist methods atop the doctrines of the

Three Vehicles, vaunting that the former is more supreme and more wondrous than the latter and euphemistically dubbing their methods as a Dharma-gate that allows for "the attainment of Buddhahood in one's current body" and that enables one to become a "Dharma body Buddha." However, the "wisdom" that those followers cultivate and attain consists of non-Buddhist erroneous views, and the various states that they practice and realize are nothing but non-Buddhist mundane states that are completely unrelated to the Buddha Dharma. Despite holding such non-Buddhist mistaken views, those tantric followers dare to unabashedly deprecate the practice and realizations of the Exoteric Buddhist Bodhisattvas, degrade the correct Dharma of the Three Vehicles transmitted by the World-Honored One by branding it as an "inferior vehicle," and disparage Exoteric Buddhists by declaring them unfit for the practice of the esoteric doctrines due to their "inferior faculty."

However, the fundamental scripture of Tantric Buddhism, *The Vairocanābhisaṃbodhi Sūtra*, has long acknowledged that the Dharma-gate of practice of the esoteric doctrines is an expediency established to entice sentient beings "of inferior intelligence" who crave for sensual pleasures and phenomena with signs ("characteristics") into the "path to Buddhahood":

> The Dharma without [differentiating] characteristics, most profound, is unsuitable for those of inferior intelligence.
> In order to cater for them there also exists the teaching of that which has [differentiating] characteristics.[10]

In reality, the various doctrines set forth in *The Vairocanābhisaṃbodhi Sūtra* are nothing but conceptual proliferations that do not touch upon the true meaning. They only teach about the emptiness of the aggregates, sense fields, and elements based on the emptiness-signs of all phenomena—the

---

10   *The Vairocanābhisaṃbodhi Sūtra*, translated by Rolf W. Giebel (Berkeley, CA: Numata Center for Buddhist Translation and Research, 2005), 250. [CBETA, T18, no. 848, 38a26-b13.]

principle of "dependent arising and with an empty nature"—and do not touch upon the truth of the foremost meaning of the emptiness-nature consisting of the sign of reality—the tathāgatagarbha. The Bodhisattvas who had truly attained the enlightenment of Buddhahood could not accept this sūtra when it first appeared in this world. However, the statement "The Dharma without [differentiating] characteristics, most profound, is unsuitable for those of inferior intelligence. In order to cater for them there also exists the teaching of that which has [differentiating] characteristics," made it difficult for those Bodhisattvas to criticize this sūtra and therefore ensured the continuous existence and dissemination of this text among sentient beings who cling to signs. Later, the Dharma-ending era gradually approached and enlightened Bodhisattvas seldom came to the human world; most of them were aware that the faculties of the people worsened by the day and that it was very difficult to free them from cyclic existence. For this reason, the number of Bodhisattvas who could identify the true colors of this sūtra progressily dwindled, and eventually no one in the world was able to see through its non-Buddhist nature, allowing Tantric followers to propagate the non-Buddhist doctrines of this sūtra unabashedly while engulfing Buddhist resources. Today, those followers have even elevated those non-Buddhist tenets above the doctrines of the Three Vehicles, which shows how skillful they are at inverting the truth.

Long before the future birth of Bodhisattva Candraprabha in this world, Buddhism was exterminated by Tantric practitioners in ancient India. Today, tantric practitioners are deploying the same tactics in Taiwan and across the world. If we do not devise a plan rapidly to tackle this issue, then the frightening truth is that we may assist in thirty years to a recurrence of the historical event whereby the Buddhism of ancient India was extinguished at the hands of Tantric followers. This time around, true Buddhism will never be revived if Tantric followers exterminate it again worldwide. Thereafter, all Buddhist practitioners will believe that the non-Buddhist doctrines transmitted by Tantric practitioners teach the correct practice of the Buddha Dharma. My strategy to save the

Buddhist lineage from the brink of extinction is to expose the true picture of Tantric Buddhism to the general public. I also hope that my deed can help extend the Buddhist lineage until the arrival of Bodhisattva Candraprabha in this world. If this can happen, then future Buddhist learners will benefit immensely.

The above examples demonstrate that tantric gurus do not understand the principle of the non-duality of Exoteric Buddhism and Esoteric Buddhism and have established **Esoteric Buddhism** based on various secrets that **are not easily transmittable to outsiders** such as secret mantra, body mudrā, hand mudrā, visualization, winds, the sexual pleasure experienced in the yab-yum practice, and so forth. However, for the Buddhas and Bodhisattvas in the ten directions, the "esoteric doctrines" refer to the esoteric meaning of prajñā. In order to prevent sentient beings with insufficient meritorious quality from falling to hell by committing the sin of slandering this meaning, the Buddhas and Bodhisattvas do not allow it to be transmitted explicitly and therefore conceal it amidst various words, lines, and statements and speak of it as "esoteric." Clearly, such an "esoteric meaning" differs completely from the esoteric doctrines set forth in Tantric Buddhism.

As a matter of fact, there are in essence no esotericism within the doctrines of the Three Vehicles. The term "esoteric" only results from the fact that learners all have different levels of attainment and that the esoteric meaning cannot be explicitly revealed to unenlightened persons. In other words, the exoteric and the esoteric doctrines are in essence non-dual within the true Buddhist doctrines, as they consist in essence of the Path to Liberation of the Two Vehicles and the Path to the Enlightenment of Buddhahood of the Great Vehicle transmitted by the same Buddha. There is no Buddha Dharma aside from these two paths. In these two paths, the esoteric meaning is shown through explicit assertions; it is in essence in the assertions and has never been beyond them. Hence, the exoteric and the esoteric doctrines are in essence non-dual, and therefore, it is unnecessary for Tantric

Buddhism to separately create Esoteric Buddhism and establish some Buddha Dharma with mundane methods of the desire realm drawn from the Shaktist non-Buddhist practice.

Despite all the efforts made by Tantric Buddhists to fancify and embellish the aforementioned non-Buddhist mundane methods of sexual pleasure, which they proudly claim to be superior to the Exoteric Buddhist doctrines, those tantric methods remain non-Buddhist in nature; the wise Buddhist disciples will eventually see through their falsity and fallacy. In the true Buddhist doctrines, the exoteric and the esoteric doctrines are in essence non-dual. Given those tantric gurus's unawareness of this principle, they established the esoteric doctrines with a licentious practice drawn from the non-Buddhist Sect of Shaktism and euphemized those doctrines with the expression "taking sensual desire as the path." Next, they hailed those doctrines as the most ultimate Dharma within "Buddhism," thereby dividing Buddhism into the Exoteric and the Esoteric Schools. Those gurus have thus destroyed the essence of the correct Buddhist doctrines though their erroneous deeds.

Furthermore, as none of the tantric gurus are aware that the tathāgatagarbha corresponds to the eighth consciousness—the ālaya—they have incorrectly broken up the tathāgatagarbha and the ālaya-consciousness into two different doctrines. Moreover, as they do not know the location of the ālaya-consciousness, they have directly designated the drops issued from their visualization as the ālaya-consciousness set forth by the Buddha, which is the complete opposite of the truth and an utter nonsense. Those gurus have thus shattered the Buddha Dharma into pieces by breaking up the tathāgatagarbha and the ālaya-consciousness. This will prevent the Buddhist learners of later generations from establishing the correct knowledge and views and will forever obliterate their conditions of entering the Path of Vision. Those tantric gurus will then become destroyers of the Dharma and grievous sinners in Buddhism.

The Buddha has spoken of the tathāgatagarbha with various

names, and it is difficult to list them all. In brief, those different names all designate the mind consisting of the eighth consciousness. Before one has extinguished the afflictions associated with unwhosome views and the afflictions associated with mentation, one's mind consisting of **the eighth consciousness** is generically called "ālaya-consciousness." After the thorough elimination of these two afflictions, the generic name of this consciousness becomes "maturational consciousness"; the term **"ninth consciousness"** has been separately established in order to help learners comprehend—when needed—that there exists a difference. One's eighth consciousness is called tathāgatagarbha before one attains the ultimate Ground of Buddhahood. After one has become a Buddha, one's eighth consciousness is named reality-suchness or immaculate consciousness; again, the term **"tenth consciousness"** has been separately established to help learners understand that there is a difference. Before one attains Buddhahood, one's eighth consciousness is sometimes said to be the reality-suchness, but this is just an expedient verbal establishment; its correct names should be reality-suchness of wrong conduct, reality-suchness of transmigration, reality-suchness of establishment, reality-suchness of proper conduct, and so forth, all of which are categorized as the reality-suchness on the Causal Ground. Through the process of eliminating afflictions, cultivation, and achieving attainments, one gradually advances from the stage of sentient beings to the Ground of Buddhahood, causing the eighth consciousness to become the reality-suchness on the Ground of Buddhahood. Given that the various attainments in this process are all achieved in dependence upon the eighth consciousness, this process is called "dependent arising based upon the reality-suchness." The correct principles, process, and contents related to the dependent arising based upon reality-suchness, whereby one eliminates afflictions, advances in the practice, and achieves various attainments have been extensively illustrated in some of my other publications—*Mastering and Skillfully Articulating the Essence of Buddhist Enlightenment*

[Zongtong yu shuotong 宗通與說通], *Treasury of the Wisdom-Eye that Sees the Correct Dharma—Collection of Protecting the Dharma [Zhengfayanzang—hufa ji 正法眼藏—護法集]*, and *Self and Non-Self [Wo yu wuwo 我與無我]*. Hence, I will not elaborate further on this topic, as readers may directly refer to those writings.

Tantric gurus (including Master Yinshun) have all types of erroneous thoughts due to their unawareness that the eighth consciousness and the ālaya-consciousness both correspond to the tathāgatagarbha. Having failed to realize the tathāgatagarbha, they have identified and established the drops that they visualize as the ālaya-consciousness and have separately established another pure mind born from their imagination as the tathāgatagarbha or have regarded the thoughtless mental consciousness—the mind of feeling and cognition—as the tathāgatagarbha, and so forth. All those mistaken views related to the misapprehension of prajñā stem from those gurus' misunderstandings of the eighth consciousness—the tathāgatagarbha. For instance, C. M. Chen says:

> Also, the word "mind" has the broadest meanings. The fleshly mind is physiological; the mind of erroneous thinking is psychological; the conscience, the virtuous mind, and the evil mind are ethical; the nine mental abidings are religious and philosophical; the mind of collection is from the Buddhist School of Vijñaptimātratā; the last one is called the "mind of the tathāgatagarbha," the "wondrous mind of perfect enlightenment," the "naturally pure mind," the "wondrous mind of the reality- suchness," or the "wondrous mind of nirvāṇa," all of which belong to the Dharma body on the Fruition Ground of Buddhism. The mind set forth in Mahāmudrā refers to the last type of mind and therefore should not be confused with the other types of mind that are enumerated.[11]

In the above passage, the mind of Mahāmudrā is equated with

---

[11] Yogi C. M. Chen (Chen Chien-ming 陳健民), *Qugongzhai quanji 曲肱齋全集 [The Complete Works of Yogi Chen]*, vol. 1-5, ed. Xu Qinying 徐芹庭 (Taipei: Puxianwang rulai fojiaohui 普賢王如來佛教會, 1991), vol. 3, 701. Translated into English from Chinese.

the tathāgatagarbha. However, Yogi C.M. Chen neither knows that the mind consisting of the tathāgatagarbha is precisely the eighth consciousness—the ālaya—nor understands that the mind of collection—the ālaya-consciousness—set forth in the Vijñaptimātratā School corresponds to the tathāgatagarbha. This has caused him to misconstrue the mind consisting of the tathāgatagarbha:

> The words "entity, nature, and emptiness" refer to Mahāmudrā, the entity of the mind of clear light illustrated in the fourth sentence. Therefore, the term "mind" is the most likely to be confused. The term "clear entity" is especially emphasized here in order to distinguish it from the others. . . . The word "clear" refers to the compassionated wisdom of both mind and matter, while the word "entity" points to the fundamental entity of both mind and matter. Given that this term has not been used in the Exoteric Buddhist teachings and terminology, I suggest to replace the terms "wondrous mind of the reality-suchness," "wondrous mind of nirvāṇa," and so forth with the words "clear entity," so as to facilitate the explanation of the Mahāmudrā of dependent arising based on the six elements.[12]

If the clear entity in this passage refers to the drops in the central channel issued from one's visualization, then such drops should not be the tathāgatagarbha. Indeed, the tathāgatagarbha is not a produced phenomenon and therefore should not be issued from the visualization of the mental consciousness—the mind of feeling and cognition—otherwise, the tathāgatagarbha set forth in Tantric Buddhism would become a compounded phenomenon that arises and ceases. However, tantric gurus often assert that the tathāgatagarbha corresponds to the clear entity and that the clear entity is precisely the mind of feeling and cognition that can perform visualizations despite being thoughtless. If the clear entity were the mind of feeling and cognition that is capable of performing visualizations, then given that the mind of feeling and

---

12   Ibid., 704-705.

cognition is in fact the mental consciousness, which is generated by the tathāgatagarbha based on the contact of the mental faculty and the mental object, we can conclude that this clear entity consisting of the mind of feeling and cognition is a produced phenomenon that arises in dependence upon other dharmas. Since the clear light is a produced phenomenon, the "clear entity consisting of the tathāgatagarbha" set forth in Tantric Buddhism would be a phenomenon that arises and ceases—in contrast to the tathāgatagarbha realized by Exoteric Buddhists, which exists at all times, such a clear entity only appears in the mind of feeling and cognition during visualizations

Those tantric gurus' perception of the clear entity as the tathāgatagarbha entails many egregious faults. Therefore, one should not contradict the Buddha's thoughts by establishing the clear entity as the tathāgatagarbha. Instead, one should, in accordance with His teachings in the sūtras of the Three Vehicles, recognize both the eighth—the ālaya—and the "consciousness" in the principle "the name-and-form conditions the consciousness" as the tathāgatagarbha, and then proceed in one's practice to realize the tathāgatagarbha through assiduous Chan contemplation. Once one has realized the eighth consciousness—the ālaya—one can directly witness the true meanings of the tathāgatagarbha and understand the meanings of the prajñā sūtras without anyone's help. If one has the opportunity to encounter a truly virtuous mentor and follow in his footsteps in learning the knowledge-of-all-aspects, expanding the collection of meritorious quality, sparing no effort in protecting the Buddha's definitive correct Dharma, and making the ten inexhaustible vows, then one will be able to enter the First Ground in one lifetime, which means that one will have already gone through the first great term of asaṃkhya kalpas. How wonderful! If one breaks up the ālaya-consciousness and the tathāgatagarbha into two different doctrines, as all ancient and contemporary tantric gurus have done, and further misleads sentient beings by causing them to misconstrue the true doctrine of the tathāgatagarbha, thereby shattering the Buddhist doctrines into pieces, then one's efforts to cultivate the path will all be futile even if one dedicates an entire life to the assiduous practice of this path. Worse yet, one will commit the grievous misdeed of wrecking the Dharma—by wrongly asserting that the clear entity or the mind of feeling and cognition that is free from distracting thoughts corresponds to the tathāgatagarbha, one becomes a destroyer of the Buddha's correct Dharma, thereby planting the seeds for immeasurable atrocious retribution that one will suffer in future lifetimes for long kalpas to come. How heart-wrenching!

Therefore, learners should not adhere to the mistaken views of ancient and modern tantric gurus—they should not break up the tathāgatagarbha and the ālaya-consciousness into two different doctrines and then seek a tathāgatagarbha beyond the true tathāgatagarbha—the ālaya-consciousness. If they can avoid such errors, then they will have a chance to realize prajñā in this lifetime. Conversely, if they search for the tathāgatagarbha beyond the eighth consciousness, then they will never attain enlightenment and will eventually fall into non-Buddhist erroneous views—not only will they forever remain entrapped in the sea of cyclic existence, but they will also fall into hell by perpetrating the grievous sin of destroying the Dharma.

All ancient and modern tantric gurus have failed to understand the true principle of the non-duality of Madhyamaka and prajñā, of Madhyamaka and Vijñaptimātratā, and of Exoteric Buddhism and Esoteric Buddhism. While their understanding of the doctrines related to Buddhist terminology is merely superficial, they believe that they have grasped the Buddha's tenets and proclaim their comprehension of the correct Vijñaptimātratā doctrines based on their misunderstandings of the Vijñaptimātratā tenets. Because of such misapprehension and even more, because of the fact that the following tantric views will inevitably be entirely exposed if people understand the Vijñaptimātratā tenets, those gurus repelled and wrongfully vilified those tenets by branding them as non-definitive doctrines. Their stategem is to cause people to detest the profound, subtle, wondrous, and correct meanings of Vijñaptimātratā and to stay away from and refuse to cultivate its wondrous doctrines. In that way, tantric Buddhism will no longer be unrestrained by the doctrines of the Vijñaptimātratā knowledge-of-aspects; in addition, all those who have attained "siddhi" within the Dharma-gate of Tantric Buddhism will no longer engage in introspection based on the Vijñaptimātratā doctrines consisting of the knowledge-of-all-aspects. This will prevent the falsity of the tantric doctrines as well as the faults that they entail from being exposed. However, such deeds by tantric Buddhists are self-contradictory, for they conflict with their original motive to practice the wisdom of prajñā of the Buddha Dharma and will inevitably be cited as counter-examples and refuted by the wise.

For instance, Tsongkhapa says:

> The path of these persons is the Mahayana proceeding to **omniscience**, and **the general body of the path is just this for Mahayanists of the Perfection Vehicle.**[13] However, when Mahayanists of the Perfection Vehicle are divided by way of their view of emptiness, there are Madhyamikas and Chittamatrins. Even so, they are not explained as having different vehicles; both are one vehicle. Since there is a difference of whether or not they have penetrated the depth of suchness, Madhyamikas are said to be of sharp faculties and Chittamatrins are said to be of dull faculties. Furthermore, Madhyamikas are the main special trainees for whom the Perfection Vehicle (according to Tsongkhapa, the Prajñā Perfection Vehicle includes those who engage in the cultivation and realization of Mahāyāna) was taught; Chittamatrins are subsidiary or secondary trainees of that Vehicle. . . .
>
> The Chapter of the *True One Sūtra [Saktyakaparivarta]* expresses it clearly:
>
>> Manjushri, if the Tathagata taught Mahayana to some beings, the Solitary Realiser Vehicle to some, and the Hearer Vehicle to others, the Tathagata's mind would be very impure and without equanimity, with the fault of attraction, partial compassion and different

---

13   Perfection Vehicle: S. *Pāramitāyāna*; C. *boluomiduo sheng* 波羅蜜多乘.

discriminations. I would also then be miserly with regard to the doctrine.

Manjushri, all the doctrines that I teach to sentient beings **are for the sake of attaining omniscient wisdom. Flowing into enlightenment and descending into the Mahayana, they are means of achieving omniscience, leading completely to one place. Therefore, I do not create different vehicles.**[14]

The above passage demonstrates that Tsongkhapa does not know anything about the Buddha Dharma. Indeed, the knowledge-of-all-aspects is the most ultimate wisdom realized by all Buddhas; only those who have perfected this wisdom can enter the ultimate stage of Buddhahood. No mundane or supramundane dharma transcends this wisdom; both the Madhyamaka prajñā and the Vijñaptimātratā prajñā are fully encompassed by this wisdom and do not exceed its scope. The wisdom of Madhyamaka only corresponds to the knowledge-of-general-aspect and the knowledge-of-specific-aspects within prajñā; this is the wisdom that results from directly observing the Middle-Way natures of the eighth consciousness—the ālaya mind—based on the realization of this consciousness. As for the knowledge-of-all-aspects, it can only be cultivated and realized based on the wisdom of the Madhyamaka prajñā that arises after the realization of the tathāgatagarbha; in other words, ordinary people who have not attained the wisdom of Madhyamaka can neither practice nor realize the knowledge-of-all-aspects.

Why is that? Because the wisdom of Madhyamaka is as follows: The wisdom that results from directly observing the Middle-Way natures of the mind consisting of the eighth consciousness is precisely the wisdom of Madhyamaka. Nonetheless, this wisdom is rudimentary and therefore does not

---

14   Tsongkhapa, *Tantra in Tibet: The Great Exposition of Secret Mantra*, vol. 1, trans. & ed. Jeffrey Hopkins, with introduction by H.H. Tenzin Gyatso, the Fourteenth Dalai Lama (London: George Allen & Unwin, 1975), 100–102.

enable one to understand all the seeds (also called realms or functional potentialities) stored in the eighth consciousness. It is not until the conditions ripen that one can advance in one's practice by cultivating the knowledge-of-all-aspects under the guidance of a great, virtuous mentor. The knowledge-of-all-aspects is the wisdom obtained from personally realizing all the seeds—all the functional potentialities—stored in the eighth consciousness. Consequently, all those who aspire to realize the knowledge-of-all-aspects must first attain the Madhyamaka prajñā; otherwise, they will not be able to cultivate and realize the knowledge-of-all-aspects.

As for the knowledge-of-all-aspects, it is the wisdom that is cultivated by the practitioners of the Vijñaptimātratā School after they achieve enlightenment; unenlightened persons are unable to truly practice it. If one engages in the contemplation and cultivation of the Madhyamaka within prajñā without having realized the mind consisting of the eighth consciousness through the doctrines of the Chan School and without having subsequently engaged in the contemplation and cultivation of the Madhyamaka consisting of the knowledge-of-specific-aspects set forth in the prajñā sūtras, then one is merely practicing the so-called "semblance prajñā" or "semblance Madhyamaka" instead of the real prajñā or real Madhyamaka. Those who work on the contemplation and cultivation of the knowledge-of-aspects within Vijñaptimātratā without having realized the tathāgatagarbha are not truly cultivating and have not truly realized this knowledge-of-aspects, but are merely engaged in a process of seed-transformation in relation to this wisdom.

The training in Vijñaptimātratā corresponds to the training in higher wisdom set forth in the sūtras of the third turning of the Dharma Wheel. Therefore, the true tenets of Vijñaptimātratā can only be cultivated by the practitioners of Madhyamaka who have genuinely attained enlightenment and fulfilled the contemplation and cultivation of the knowledge-of-specific-aspects within prajñā; such is the right sequence of practice on the path. How could Tsongkhapa claim that the teachings of Madhyamaka are for those with sharp faculties while the tenets of Vijñaptimātratāare for those with dull faculties? Is it possible that the practitioners endowed with the wisdom of higher Grounds possess dull faculties, while those endowed with the wisdom of lower Grounds have sharp faculties? Clearly, Tsongkhapa's statements do not make any sense.

With respect to Tsongkhapa's "valid knowledge," we can conclude that he has simply not yet attained the knowledge-of-general-aspect within the Madhyamaka prajñā given his inability to realize the eighth consciousness (this is obvious from his negation of the eighth consciousness—the ālaya). Indeed, the wisdom of the Madhyamaka prajñā is based on the realization of the natures of the eighth consciousness. How could Tsongkhapa understand the knowledge-of-specific-aspects set forth in the prajñā sūtras when he has not yet realized the knowledge-of-general-aspect within the Madhyamaka prajñā? It is, therefore, no surprise that Tsonghkapa has always expounded the emptiness-nature within prajñā through the doctrine of the emptiness-signs of the aggregates, sense-fields, and elements—the principle that all phenomena are dependent arising and with an empty nature outside the context of the tathāgatagarbha. Such a concept differs markedly from the Buddha's teachings. Given that Tsongkhapa has not realized the knowledge-of-general-aspect—the emptiness-nature—within prajñā, we can conclude that he has definitely not attained the knowledge-of-specific-aspects and certainly does not comprehend the knowledge-of-all-aspects. It is difficult to imagine that such an ordinary person, who does not understand the knowledge-of-general-aspect, the knowledge-of-specific-aspects, or the knowledge-of-all-aspects within prajñā, can comment on the correct principles of Madhyamaka and the knowledge-of-aspects within Vijñaptimātratā. Clearly, his assertions do not make any sense.

How can we believe Tsongkhapa when he asserts that he is able to validate and has indeed validated the truthfulness of some unsurpassed esoteric doctrines that are superior to the teachings of Mahāyāna when he has in fact not yet realized the true meanings of the prajñā in the Great Vehicle of Perfection? If such unsurpassed esoteric doctrines were superior to all the Mahāyāna doctrines, then these esoteric doctrines would be doctrines of an upper Ground; a person who has realized the doctrines of an upper Ground should definitely understand the doctrines of a lower Ground. However, Tsongkhapa and all the other tantric gurus and disciples have noticeably misconstrued the wisdom of prajñā in the Perfection of the Great Vehicle, which is of a "lower Ground." As they claim to have realized some doctrines that are superior to the Mahāyāna doctrines when they do not even understand those "lower-ranked" Mahāyāna doctrines, we can conclude that their unsurpassed esoteric doctrines are definitely not the Buddha Dharma. If the unsurpassed esoteric doctrines of Tantric Buddhism were the true Buddha Dharma and if they were, on top of that, superior to the Mahāyāna doctrines, then those tantric gurus should not have misapprehended the Mahāyāna doctrines to the point of being completely ignorant about them. This demonstrates that the "Mahāyāna doctrines" set forth by Tantric Buddhists are absolutely not the Mahāyāna doctrines taught by the Buddha, but are just some "Mahāyāna doctrines" that they believe they have understood.

However, my statements do not mean that the true proponents of Madhyamaka are persons with dull faculties. In fact, only the practitioners of prajñā who are able to genuinely realize the eighth consciousness and attain the wisdom of Madhyamaka are true proponents of Madhyamaka. Such persons are definitely not of dull faculties given that they are endowed with a profound and astute wisdom that cannot be grasped by sound-hearer arhats. However, those who can realize the knowledge-of-all-aspects within Vijñaptimātratā (this wisdom is known as the knowledge-of-the-aspects-of-paths in the stage of Bodhisattva) in this lifetime are even less endowed with dull faculties, as their wisdom far exceeds that of the truly enlightened proponents of Madhyamaka. Fully unaware of these correct principles, Tsongkhapa is no different from ordinary, mundane beings; hence, I say that his assertions are untruthful and non-credible.

The ultimate purpose of the Buddha's appearance in this human world and education of sentient beings is to cause them to enter a Buddha's wisdom. The knowledge-of-all-aspects represents the overall Buddha's wisdom—it encompasses the wisdom of liberation of mahaparinirvāṇa and the four wisdoms such as the wisdom of great perfect mirror and so forth; none of the mundane and supramundane wisdom can transcend it. Owing to the fact that sentient beings are endowed with different faculties and given that the wisdom of the enlightenment of Buddhahood is extremely profound and difficult to understand and attain, the Buddha established the sound-hearer wisdom of liberation in order to cause disciples to first attain the fruition of liberation. Once they have attained it and have gained full faith in the Buddha, the Buddha can then steer them into the Mahāyāna Dharma, so that they can gradually advance on the Path to the Great Enlightenment, which is fulfilled by Bodhisattvas only after long kalpas. Such was the Buddha's intent to teach the Dharma of the Two Vehicles; it was not out of selfishness, miserliness, or partiality that He only taught the Dharma of the Two Vehicles to the practitioners of the first turning of the Dharma Wheel.

As stated in the scripture cited by Tsongkhapa, "All the doctrines that I teach to sentient beings are for the sake of attaining **omniscient wisdom**. Flowing into enlightenment and **descending into the Mahayana, they are means of achieving omniscience, leading completely to one place**," the Buddha's initial teaching of doctrines such as the Path to Liberation and so forth that are cultivated in the Two Vehicles was in fact an expedient means to introduce disciples into Mahāyāna, so that they could progressively enter the wisdom of prajñā consisting of the knowledge-of-all-aspects. This wisdom of prajñā is precisely the wisdom about all the seeds related to the mind-kings consisting of the eight consciousnesses set forth in Vijñaptimātratā. The statement that the Buddha's objective was to cause all disciples to cultivate the wisdom of the knowledge-of-aspects within Vijñaptimātratā and to **"achiev[e] omniscience, leading completely to one place"** demonstrates that the knowledge-of-aspects within Vijñaptimātratā is the most ultimate and supreme doctrine within the Buddha Dharma, unsurpassed by any other teachings. As Tsongkhapa is ignorant of the knowledge-of-all-aspects and does not understand the knowledge-of-general-aspect within prajñā due to his inability to realize it, he has misconstrued and negated the Buddha's words in this passage after reading them. His citation of those words in this writing substantiates the fact that has not realized prajñā.

Furthermore, based on the Buddha's words in the following scriptural passage quoted by Tsongkhapa, "All the doctrines that I teach to sentient beings are for the sake of attaining omniscient wisdom. Flowing into enlightenment and descending into the Mahayana, **they are means of achieving omniscience, leading completely to one place**. Therefore, I do not create different vehicles," the Buddha has clearly stated that there is no Buddha Dharma other than the Path to Liberation of the Two Vehicles and the Path to the Enlightenment of Buddhahood of the Great Vehicle. Why is that? Because the Buddha has said in this scriptural passage that He **does not create any vehicles** other than omniscience (the knowledge-of-all-aspects). Given that omniscience is the most ultimate doctrine and that the Buddha **does not create any vehicles** other than this omniscience, we can conclude that the following assertion from Tsongkhapa contradicts the correct teachings and doctrines and are the opposite of the Buddha's statements, "Madhyamikas are said to be of sharp faculties and Chittamatrins are said to be of dull faculties." This also tells us that the tantric gurus' claim that there exists an unsurpassed secret vehicle above the Mahāyāna Madhyamaka and Vijñaptimātratā is untruthful. Based on the aforementioned Buddha's words, we can conclude that Tantric Buddhism was definitely not transmitted by the World-Honored One Śākyamuni—indeed, the Buddha has stated that He **does not create any vehicles other than omniscience**.

Not only do the doctrines propagated by the tantric gurus of ancient India and by Guru Padmasambhava, the founder of Tibetan Tantric Buddhism, fall within the scope of the view of eternalist non-Buddhism in every respect, but they also induce the cravings for the lingering sensation of the sexual pleasure in the desire realm—they are associated with the greed for the phenomena of the desire realm. How could such doctrines, which fully come from ordinary people, be credible in any way? The wise might think about this fact for a while. They can ascertain it without having to think for too long. Based on this true principle, we can conclude that the practitioners of the various tantric schools who have rejected the Vijñaptimātratā tenets and have branded them as non-definitive do not understand and have not realized prajñā. Why is that? Because all truly enlightened persons will, without exception, gradually comprehend the Vijñaptimātratā tenets and progressively advance toward the correct path that consists of cultivating the training in higher wisdom—the knowledge-of-all-aspects within Vijñaptimātratā. No enlightened persons would, in their right minds—while they are aware that they must advance in their practice by cultivating the knowledge-of-aspects within Vijñaptimātratā—emulate Tsongkhapa by vehemently negating Vijñaptimātratā and by falsely declaring that Vijñaptimātratā consists of non-definitive doctrines.

These facts tell us that the correct doctrines of Madhyamaka and Vijñaptimātratā both correspond to the wisdom of prajñā and do not constitute two distinct doctrines, as they both exist in dependence upon the realization and experiencing of the eighth consciousness. In reality, they both relate to the same dharma that is the mind consisting of the eighth consciousness and only differ in the sequence in which they are cultivated and in their profundity and scope. Therefore, there is no need to call into question the assertion that the tantric proponents of Prāsaṅgika Madhyamaka such as Yinshun, Tsongkhapa, and all other persons who negate the knowledge-of-all-aspects within Vijñaptimātratā, as well as those who falsely claim that "Madhyamaka is the ultimate definitive

Dharma, whereas Vijñaptimātratā is not so," are all unenlightened.

All Buddhist disciples who aspire to understand prajñā should abide by the Chan School to seek the entry point. The "great practitioner and living Buddha Norlha" of Tantric Buddhism also commends the Chan School:

> **The Chan School,** which is regarded by the Chinese as Exoteric Buddhism, **is validated by the late Guru Norlha as the Great Esoteric School** because its practices are superior to all other methods and are identical to the Great Perfection of the Nyingma School. In my view, the way this school transmits its tradition is not to grasp ordinary words of prajñā or to use ordinary expressions to describe the ultimate meaning. Instead, the patriarchs transmit their tradition directly through their valid knowledge, while the disciples receive it also directly through their valid knowledge, **which puts this method one notch above "the translated text of the Great Perfection."** This topic is discussed in detail in my discourses titled *A Discussion about the Moon in the Locust Tree's Shadow* [*Huaiyin huayuelu* 槐 陰 話 月 錄] and *Differentiating the Emptiness School, the Great Perfection, Mahāmudrā, and the Chan School* [*Kongzong dashouyin dayuanmon chanzong bianwei* 空宗大手印大圓滿禪宗辨微].[15]

However, the contents of the so-called "sudden enlightenment" in Tantric Buddhism relate to the clear entity consisting of the drops and the mind of feeling and cognition amidst the non-duality of luminosity and emptiness—tantric followers regard the mind of feeling and cognition in this state as the reality-suchness. By contrast, what is realized by the truly enlightened persons in the Chan School is neither the so-called clear entity in Tantric Buddhism, nor the mind of feeling and cognition in the state of "the union of luminosity and emptiness"

---

[15] Yogi C. M. Chen (Chen Chien-ming 陳健民), *Qugongzhai quanji* 曲肱齋全集 [*The Complete Works of Yogi Chen*], vol. 1-5, ed. Xu Qinying 徐芹庭 (Taipei: Puxianwang rulai fojiaohui 普賢王如來佛教會, 1991), vol. 3, 778. Translated into English from Chinese.

set forth in Tantric Buddhism. Although some tantric gurus are aware of the supremacy and wondrousness of the Chan School, their knowledge thereof is entirely based on their own speculation and is substantiated by the assertions about the conscious mind made by the falsely enlightened persons in the Chan School. Those gurus do not even comprehend the wisdom of prajñā attained by truly enlightened ones; how then could they understand the knowledge-of-specific-aspects and the knowledge-of-all-aspects attained through post-enlightenment practice? Having failed to grasp the fact that the knowledge-of-all-aspects is precisely the training in the knowledge-of-aspects within Vijñaptimātratā that one must cultivate post-enlightenment, those gurus have misconstrued Vijñaptimātratā and have even denigrated it based on mistaken views issued from their imagination. They have thus perpetrated the grievous misdeed of deprecating the correct Dharma, for the knowledge-of- aspects within Vijñaptimātratā is the most ultimate doctrine within the Buddha Dharma and corresponds to the knowledge-of-all-aspects cultivated by the Bodhisattvas on or above the First Ground.

Those who negate the eighth consciousness (tathāgatagarbha) are called "incorrigibles" by the Buddha in the *Laṅkāvatāra Sūtra*. The incorrigibles are those who have renounced all wholesome faculties. According to the Buddha, those who have deprecated the eighth consciousness by denying its existence "have, after making such a statement, eradicated all their wholesome faculties and become incorrigibles." Given that anyone who negates the eighth consciousness is an incorrigible, people like those tantric gurus who have replaced the dharma consisting of the eighth-consciousness with unreal phenomena, thereby causing others to misapprehend unreal, established phenomena for the eighth consciousness—the tathāgatagarbha—are also incorrigibles who have destroyed the Dharma.

The gurus of Tibetan Tantric Buddhism have committed the grievous sin of incorrigibleness by substituting their non-Buddhist doctrines for the correct Buddhist Dharma. Therefore, no learner should emulate the behavior of those tantric gurus and Yinshun, which consists of wrongfully denigrating the eighth consciousness—the mind consisting of the tathagatagarbha—by branding it as **"a phenomenon that is a mere denomination without any substance"** and that is established for the sake of expediency, and no learner should follow in those tantric gurus' footsteps by replacing the eighth consciousness—the tathāgatagarbha—set forth in Buddhism with the drops issued from visualization drop. Otherwise, he will commit the grievous misdeed of destroying the definitive an`d correct Buddhist Dharma and become one who has eradicated all wholesome faculties; it will then be too late for him to show remorse upon death.

CHAPTER 8

INITIATIONS

1. Overview of Initiations

This section briefly discusses the various initiations. Initiations constitute the basis of the practice and learning of the secret doctrines, and therefore, all tantric learners must be initiated before embarking on such a practice. As Tsongkhapa says in *The Great Exposition of Secret Mantra [Mizong daocidi guanglun]*:

> The ones with exactly the right capacity for Highest Yoga Tantra (the yab-yum practice based on the union of bliss and emptiness) are, as mentioned previously, those who have practiced the common path and who have purified the continuum of the Mahāyāna disposition; they are the greatly capable ones in Mahāyāna fully endowed with the supreme disposition. The intention brought forth from their great compassion has fueled intense cravings as well as the vow to attain Buddhahood swiftly. In order to enter the Dharma-gate of Highest Yoga and quickly achieve Buddhahood, they must correctly understand the meanings of the tantras and proficiently study the two stages and the various esoteric practices.[1]

According to Tsongkhapa, those who aspire to learn the tantric path must first "purify the continuum of the Mahāyāna disposition" by receiving initiation from their gurus; only then can they cultivate the yab-yum method of Highest Yoga Tantra transmitted in Tantric Buddhism. Hence, initiations are said to be the basis of the path to cultivate the secret doctrines, just as undergoing a health examination and completing the registration process are the requirements for school entry.

Before the initiation, a guru and his disciple must observe each other to find out whether they have good chemistry and whether they can connect with the secret doctrines; only then can

---

[1] Tsongkhapa, *Mizong daocidi guang lun* 密宗道次第廣論, 154. Translated into English from Chinese.

they proceed to the initiation:

> If a guru does not observe whether the disciples are Dharma-vessels and confers initiation on any persons, then given that non-Dharma-vessels are unable to uphold the samaya precepts (they are unable to safeguard the secret meaning of the "meditative absorption" experienced during the yab-yum practice), current and future damages will ensue. Therefore, teaching (everything related to initiations) to non-vessels entails myriad faults, constitutes a violation of the samaya precepts, keeps the guru away from all achievements, and brings about harm from demons. On the other hand, if a disciple does not observe the characteristics of the guru, receives initiation from any person, and is deceived by this false guru, then his inability to uphold the samaya precepts set forth in the scriptures and transmitted by the guru will destroy his achievements, will bring about harm from demons, and will entail many faults. Therefore, the guru and the disciple must observe each other well.[2]

According to this passage, the guru who wishes to bestow initiation on a disciple must first observe this disciple's faculty to find out whether he is fit to learn the tantric path. If he confers initiation on a disciple without making any prior observations, and if this disciple does not possess the correct capacity for Tantrism, then he may, in the future, fail to safeguard the "secret doctrine" of the tantric yab-yum practice and may divulge it. This will hinder the propagation of the tantric path, wreaking havoc on both the guru and the disciple in the present as well as in the future. Therefore, the guru must first observe whether the disciple is suitable to practice the tantric path. If the answer is negative, then he must not confer the initiation on this disciple. Similarly, the disciple must, before receiving the initiation, observe whether the guru is a true tantric master; otherwise, he may be deceived by an unlearned and incompetent person and may end up learning false tantric doctrines. Therefore, it is said that before the relationship

---

2   Ibid., 160-163.

of guru and disciple is established, both parties must first observe each other before deciding whether they should perform the initiation ceremony.

In traditional Tantric Buddhism, initiations are sometimes handled with extreme care. For instance, it may take up to twelve years to observe a disciple's capacity:

> Chapter 2 of *Vajra Rosary Tantra* [*Jinkangman jing* 金剛鬘經] states: "Just as one should observe precious jade with polishing skill or gold with refining expertise, so one should carefully observe one's disciple for twelve years. Both should thus observe each other at all times; otherwise, there will be hindrances from demons and destruction of achievements." Chapter 54 further states: "Just as the lion's milk should not be poured in earthenware, so such a great yoga should not be transmitted to non-vessels. Otherwise, the disciple will die instantaneously, causing current and future damage. By imparting the teachings to unfit ones, the guru will wreck his achievements."[3]

Such solemnity can be attributed to the desire to keep the "secret method" consisting of the tantric yab-yum practice away from public knowledge and to thereby prevent the tantric path from being repudiated by the true realizers of the path. In reality, the tantric path does not contain any profound, wondrous Buddha Dharma, but merely encompasses methods of mundane sensual pleasure cloaked in Buddhist terminology. Not only has this path been subsequently inflated and extolled as the secret practice and realization of the unsurpassed Buddha Dharma, but it has also been hailed as the Buddha Dharma of the highest level, the most ultimate Buddha Dharma, in an effort to dupe and beguile sentient beings. Since this path is devoid of actual practices and realizations of the Buddha Dharma, its proponents prohibit its disclosure so as to avoid all repudiation by outsiders like myself. For this reason, tantric gurus must, in order to prevent the secret doctrines from

---

3   Ibid., 160-161.

being divulged and rebutted, carefully observe whether their disciples are suitable for the tantric practice and can guard its secrets.

However, the initiations conferred by contemporary Tantric Buddhists in Taiwan—no matter whether those initiations are performed by gurus coming from Nepal, the Dalai Lama flying in from India, or gurus sent by other traditions or coming from other locations—have become a formality: During the ceremony, the guru merely upholds the ritual instrument for the initiates to behold, and then the initiation is considered completed. For example, during the conferral of the throne initiation, vajra-pestle initiation, bell initiation, vase initiation, and so forth, after the recitation of the mantras and so forth, the guru upholds the ritual instrument and displays it to the left and the right sides for the throng of initiates to see. The initiation is thus deemed as having been achieved. Such initiations have become standardized procedures—**initiations deceptively stripped of key elements** and devoid of real substance, which are not performed "properly" according to the secret doctrines. The initiations mentioned henceforth in this book refer to those that follow the "proper" procedures highlighted in the tantras. Any tantric practitioner in Taiwan who has been initiated through rituals that differ from those described below should know that he was not initiated "properly" and should regard the proceedings presented in this publication as the rightful ones, for they are depicted in complete accordance with the tantras.

There are primarily five types of initiation, the first one being causal initiation. The gurus who wish to confer the causal initiation must be aware of all the related details before being allowed to perform it. Tsongkhapa says:

> With respect to the subdivisions of the initiation rituals, you should understand the rituals of fire offering and resource cakra, as well as the characteristics of the mantra chanter, the bell, the pestle, the big and small dippers, the skeleton stick, and so forth needed to cultivate these rituals—you

should know how to make them and then how to use them and so forth. **Thus, these tools become ritual instruments through the power of the initiation. By being skillful at the samaya precepts, coming into contact with and pondering over the teachings, and ascertaining the right practice, those with superior faculty will attain Buddhahood in this lifetime, those with mid-level faculty will attain Buddhahood after generating an intermediate state from** [the subtle discrimination of the body of] **other sentient beings, and those with inferior faculty will attain Buddhahood in the next rebirth.**[4]

The contents of the so-called "attaining Buddhahood" in this passage deviate drastically from those set forth in Exoteric Buddhism; they are merely states of "attaining Buddhahood" uniquely found in Tantric Buddhism and are in fact issued from false thinking. This topic will be elaborated later. Before receiving initiation, a disciple must first delight his guru by serving him; only then will the guru confer the initiation on him.

Nowadays, most of the tantric Dharma-kings and gurus who travel to Taiwan do not perform the initiations with such solemnity. They simply confer initiation on the attendees as scheduled, after the host in Taiwan has arranged the ceremony and the maṇḍala has been set up. During the initiations, those gurus neither observe whether the initiates have a faculty suited for the tantric practice, nor explain the purport of the initiations to them, nor indicate to them the gist of the cultivation of the secret method—the yab-yum practice—in which they should engage after being initiated, nor do they bestow initiation according to the stipulations of the tantras. Hence, the main objectives of the contemporary tantric gurus who travel to Taiwan to perform initiations are to build good relationships and to collect offerings in order to support their overseas cultivation centers. Stripped of the significance of real initiations, the majority of such events can merely be called

---

[4] Ibid., 156..

"bonding initiations."

In a formal causal initiation, the guru must explain the meaning of the initiation and briefly illustrate the "supremacy" of the Dharma-gate that allows for the attainment of Buddhahood in this body, so that the learners can bring forth joy as well as the delight of believing in this practice. Once the disciples have brought forth such joy and delight, the guru must succinctly highlight the main significance of the yab-yum Dharma-gate that allows for the attainment of Buddhahood in this body; only then can he formally bestow the initiation on these disciples.

The second type of initiation is vase initiation, the third is secret initiation, the fourth is wisdom initiation, and the fifth is fourth initiation. The following sections will elaborate on each of these initiations. The tantric text *Samputa Tantra [Jiehe jing* 結合 經*]*, however, only enumerates four kinds of initiation: "There are four types of initiation: (1) vase initiation, (2) secret initiation, (3) wisdom initiation, and (4) all of the above."

The causal initiation and the vase initiation pertain to the generation stage and involve a sequence of rituals. These two initiations are sometimes performed together. Below is a brief depiction of the formal and proper performance of such initiations.

It is important to note three key topics related to the causal initiation: (1) the maṇḍala, (2) the contents of the initiation; and (3) a discussion about "which defilements are purified" during this initiation.

First, one must build the maṇḍala and establish the perfect and remainderless seats of the deities:

> Based on the initial vase initiation, the seats of the Buddhas are in the center and the seats of the Bodhisattvas are in the inner circle. With respect to the two female consorts, the seat of the female consort of wisdom is in the center and the seat of the actual female consort is to the left of this seat. The seats of the celestial ladies are, in the manner of being of one taste, in the inner circle; the seats of wrathful males and

wrathful females are in the outer circle. One should know that the above is just like the establishment of the thirty-seven deities in the *Glorious Chakrasaṃvara Tantra* and the thirty-two deities in the *Guhyasamāja Tantra*.[5]

Next, one should build the painted maṇḍala, in which the guru confers the eleven factors on the disciples:

> The eleven factors that allow for the obtention of the vase initiation include the first seven, which are water, crown, pestle, bell, name, prohibited acts, and the vajra guru. Furthermore, the guru must consent to perform the following: blessing, identification, exhortation, and praise (original note: comfort, prediction, rejoicing, and teaching). These are the supplemented four empowerments.[6]

The causal initiation is commonly known as water initiation. Tsongkhapa has delineated the rituals that take place after one has built a maṇḍala, made offerings to the guru, invoked the guru, bathed, recited the nectar mantra, made a fire offering, and so forth:

> Next, the guru (visualizes that he) emits light from the seed of his own mind to invite the Buddhas and female consorts in boundless places (these "Buddhas" and consorts take on the form of taking in bliss during the yab-yum copulation) to abide in the empty space in front of him. After making offerings to those Buddhas and consorts, the guru asks them to bestow initiation on the disciple and says:
>> "In order to save sentient beings,
>> Buddha Vajradhara,
>> Bestows initiations that generate meritorious quality,
>> He thus bestows this initiation. . . .
> The sequence of visualizations that must be performed before the water initiation: The guru must visualize that Tathāgatas and Lochanā consorts pervade the empty space, holding parasols, banners, and clothes above the disciple,

---

5   Virūpa, *Daoguo* 道果, 181-96. Translated into English from Chinese.
6   Ibid., 192.

singing, dancing, having fun, and sprinkling wondrous flowers. They hold a slightly tilting white vase filled with bodhicitta nectar (sexual fluid) just obtained from the lotus of the Buddha-mother (from the female consort's sexual organ) and pour the nectar onto the disciple's crown. At the same time, the Vajravārāhī and so forth chant an auspicious mantra as follows:

> All auspiciousnesses abide in the minds of sentient beings,
> The supreme lineage lords of all properties,
> Bring about great bliss for all sentient beings,
> And now pouring [the nectar] onto your crown is the most auspicious.
> The perfect meritorious qualities are similar to a golden mountain,
> They can be relied upon throughout the three times to purify the three defilements;
> The Buddha's eyes are long and broad like a lotus flower,
> And now your quiescence is the most auspicious.
> He preaches the wondrous Dharma that is immovable,
> Extensively propagates it throughout the three times while receiving offerings from humans and celestial beings;
> The supreme Dharma always pacifies sentient beings,
> And now your quiescence is the most auspicious.
> The more true Dharma one hears the more auspicious,
> That is the source to which the offerings of humans, celestial beings, and āsuras should be directed;
> The monastics admit to the Honorable Ones that they are ashamed of their insufficient virtues,
> And now your quiescence is the most auspicious.[7]

The *Vairocanābhisaṃbodhi Sūtra* only enumerates three types of initiation instead of four:

---

[7] Tsongkhapa, *Mizong daocidi guang lun* 密宗道次第廣論, 356-58. Translated into English from Chinese.

There are three kinds of consecration—listen
wholeheartedly, Son of the Buddha!
The expedient means with secret seals is dissociated from
[other] actions;
It is called the first excellent method, and one is
consecrated by the Tathāgata.
That which is called the second gives rise to the performance
of many [ritual] deeds.
The third is conferred by the mind and is completely
dissociated from time and place;
In order to please the honored [ācārya], one should perform
it as explained,
And one will be consecrated directly by the Buddha: this is
the most excellent.[8]

In the Sakya School, the secret initiation, wisdom initiation, and fourth initiation all pertain to the completion stage instead of the generation stage. These three types of initiation are said to belong to the completion stage, for the proponents of this school believe that the performance and cultivation thereof allow practitioners to attain the fruition of Buddhahood. As stated by the Sakya School's *Path with the Result [Daoguo]*, the vase initiation enables practitioners to realize the meritorious quality associated with the fruitions of emanation body from the First Ground through to the Sixth Ground; the secret initiation enables them to realize the meritorious quality associated with the fruitions from the Seventh Ground through to the Tenth Ground; the wisdom initiation enables them to realize the meritorious quality associated with the fruitions from the Eleventh Ground through to the Twelfth Ground; and the fourth initiation enables them to achieve the ultimate Buddhahood and attain the body of the properties of the dharma-realm. Those contents will not be cited here, readers may refer to pp. 188-194 of *Path with the Result [Daoguo]* for further details. As a matter of fact, the meritorious

---

8   *The Vairocanābhisaṃbodhi Sūtra*, translated by Rolf W. Giebel (Berkeley, CA: Numata Center for Buddhist Translation and Research, 2005), 132. [CBETA, T18, no. 848, p. 33a15-22.]

quality associated with the fruitions of the various Grounds and of Buddhahood taught by Tantric Buddhists as well as the reward of the three bodies—emanation body, reward body, and dharma body—and so forth that they have obtained are nothing but their own fabrication; they all differ from the sabda found in the Exoteric Buddhist sutras and are by no means set forth in Buddhism. This topic will be discussed later.

There exist four types of guru as a result of the four initiations: (1) the gurus who have externally eliminated superimpositions, (2) the gurus who have internally manifested the self-arisen wisdom, (3) the gurus who have secretly manifested the innate wisdom, and (4) the gurus who have ultimately manifested the extremely pure reality of all phenomena. The level of the initiations that a guru can perform varies according to the depth of his attainments within the Dharma-gate of Tantric Buddhism. For this reason, some gurus can confer the causal initiation and vase initiation, some can bestow the wisdom initiation, while others can give all four initiations. Hence, the gurus are also said to exhibit four distinct levels.

Generally speaking, the gurus who confer the water initiation and vase initiation are called external gurus, given that those two initiations pertain to the generation stage. By contrast, the gurus who confer the later three types of initiation are known as internal gurus, for those three types of initiation belong to the completion stage. Internal gurus are further categorized as internal, secret, and ultimate. The gurus of the secret initiation are able to visualize, within the channels of their bodies, channel syllables and images of deities, female consorts, and so forth in the yab-yum practice that are subtler and more occult than those visualized by the aforementioned external gurus—hence the appellation "internal gurus."

The gurus of the wisdom initiation are known as secret gurus, for the seed syllables and the purified portions (also known as pure appearance portions; see Section 2 of this chapter) of the "essential constituent (which means "semen")" that they cultivate and attain in their channel syllables are extremely occult, like a secret that is difficult for people in general to decipher—hence the term "secret." Separately, The gurus of the fourth type of initiation—secret initiation—are also called "ultimate gurus" for the following reasons: The seed syllables and so forth that they visualize within their central channel can pervade their entire bodies; "the stored wind of wisdom that pours the nectar rain of the three realms is the ultimate of their basis of purification, and they are endowed with the meanings that purify each of the four layers of all initiations, paths, views, tenets, fruitions, and so forth"; and they have penetrative understanding of the ultimate—hence the appellation "ultimate gurus."

The path of the secret doctrines cultivated in the Sakya School consists of twenty methods, which are divided into four categories: vase initiation, secret initiation, wisdom initiation, and fourth initiation. Each of these initiations comprises five methods—path, view, tenet, dying, and fruition—which add up to a total of twenty methods. This topic will not be illustrated here; readers may refer to the *Path with the Result* [Sakya School's *Daoguo*] for more details. In brief, receiving initiation is a mandatory requirement for all those who embark on the cultivation of the secret doctrines within Tantric Buddhism. Anyone who learns such doctrines without having been initiated in the maṇḍala will not attain any achievements from his cultivation; hence, finding a guru and asking him or her to confer initiation are an inevitable process that all learners of the secret doctrines must go through.

2. The Vase Initiation

The vase initiation, which belongs to the class of causal initiation, is further divided into internal initiation and external initiation. The previous section dealt with external initiation. With respect to internal initiation, the guru visualizes that the seed syllable in his mind emits light in order to invite the Buddhas to each embrace a female consort (such is the form taken on by the reward body Buddhas in Tibetan Buddhism—they always appear in the form of embracing a female consort and taking in bliss during the yab-yum copulation) and to abide in the empty space in front of the guru. Furthermore, after the guru visualizes that he offers all kinds of mundane enjoyments to those Buddhas, he must visualize nectar as well as his conferring of initiation on his disciple with this visualized nectar:

> Summon the wisdom deity inward after Buddha Akshobhya has arisen from the water. According to Ratnavarman *[Baokai* 寶 鎧*]*, after he transforms into water, the water in the vases first becomes the syllable *hum* [吽] for purification; the syllable *hum* then transforms into a magnificent vajra syllable *hum*, from which arises Buddha Akshobhya. Next, emit light from the seed in your mind in order to summon the intuition hero[1] inward; the intuition hero also transforms into water after having received an offering. Furthermore, according to *Abhaya's Vajra Rosary [Manlun* 鬘論*]*, after the dissolution of the Tathāgata, summon the disciple into your mouth and confer initiation on him. Although the sequence articulated by Baokai is different, it is easier to implement, and therefore, you should follow his instructions. First, summon the disciple into your mouth; the disciple exits through the vajra route (through your urethra) and abides in the female consort's lotus

---

[1]   Intuition hero: Alt. intuition being, knowledge being, wisdom deity; S. *jñānasattva*; T. *ye shes sems dpa'*; C. *zhihui saduo* 智慧薩埵.

(in the female consort's vulva). Next, visualize that after the disciple disappears instantaneously, he first becomes a syllable *hum* and then transforms into a vajra; the magnificent syllable *hum* becomes the Honorable Akshobhya and a female consort. The wisdom deity is summoned inward because he is identical to the intuition hero. Next, all Tathāgatas and their female consorts enter meditative absorption (all "Tathāgatas" and the female consorts that they embrace engage in sexual intercourse, experience sexual pleasure, and achieve orgasm; this is called entering meditative absorption), causing the great craving (the craving for the sensation of the orgasm of ejaculation or for the fourth joy) to dissolve and to pour into (your) crown from its aperture. The bodhicitta exits along the vajra route (the bodhicitta—the semen that has blended with the consort's sexual fluid—flows outward from your urethra) onto the lotus and becomes a disciple with a deity body (this disciple is issued from visualization) who receives the initiation.[2]

The above initiation is entirely performed through visualization and therefore does not exhibit an outer shape—there is no water initiation with outer shape to be seen. This type of initiation is specifically designated as "internal initiation" despite being classified at the same level as the vase initiation. It is in fact the visualization method performed by gurus during an internal initiation of Tantric Buddhism and is generally regarded by tantric practitioners as being superior to the usual water initiation.

The term "guru with a pure appearance portion" points to the pure appearance portion of body, speech, and mind—the three uncontaminated and magnificent wheels—at the stage of Tathāgata. This epithet is established from the perspective of the fruition. From the perspective of the Causal Ground, there are four distinct types of sugata[3] based on their different levels of

---

[2] Tsongkhapa, *Mizong daocidi guang lun* 密宗道次第廣論, 356-57. Translated into English from Chinese.

[3] Robert E. Buswell Jr. and Donald S. Lopez Jr., "sugata" in *The Princeton Dictionary of Buddhism* (NJ: Princeton University Press, 2014). (T. *bde bar gshegs pa*; C. *shanshi*; J. *zenzei*; K. *sŏnsŏ* 善逝). In Sanskrit and Pāli, lit., "well gone," one in a standard list

meritorious quality:

(1) Sugatas of outer shape:

When the practitioners who strive to become sugatas through the path of the two collections first cultivate the vase initiation, its related path, and the outer shape of the generation stage, those with inferior faculty emit light from the seed syllables in their minds in order to invite the deity whose shape is non-distinct from that of the guru to abide in the empty space in front of them, so that they can make offerings to this deity; those with superior faculty abide as the one hundred and fifty-seven deities endowed with a luminous shape of the outer and the inner generation stages; what is between the initiations and the validation of the lord of lineage is their collection of merit, and the meditative concentration that arises from their support is their collection of wisdom. In brief, this is the generation of the supreme emanation body from the cultivation of the generation stage of outer shape.[4]

(2) Sugatas of inner mantra:

When the practitioners who strive to become sugatas through the path of the short syllable *ah* in the inner central channel cultivate the secret initiation, its related path, and the self-empowered inner fire, those with inferior faculty implement three types of pure antidotes; the mental winds of those with superior faculty blend at the location of the short syllable *ah* in the channel cakra at the navel and move upward in the reverse direction through their central channel. In brief, this is the generation of the perfect reward body through the cultivation of the self-empowerment of Chandali fire.[5]

(3) Sugatas of the secret initiation:

When the practitioners who strive to become sugatas from the palace of the Buddha-father and Buddha-mother cultivate the wisdom initiation, its related path, and the maṇḍala cakra, those with inferior faculty empower their own and others'

---

of epithets of the Buddha.

[4]   Virūpa, *Daoguo* 道果, 164. Translated into English from Chinese.

[5]   Ibid., 165.

seals; the mental winds of those with superior faculty gather and operate in the lotus palace of the Buddha-mother (in the female consort's sexual organ). In brief, this is the realization of the dharma body through the cultivation of others' body.[6]

(4) Sugatas of the ultimate reality:

When the practitioners who strive to become sugatas through the path of the three gates of liberation cultivate the fourth initiation, its related path, and the path of the vajra wave, those with inferior faculty hold the lady endowed with the lotus (see Chapter 9 for more details about "the lady endowed with the lotus") after empowering her; the mental winds of those with superior faculty gather at the supreme pistil of the lady endowed with the lotus (those with superior faculty gather their mental winds at the cervix or clitoris of the lady endowed with the lotus), purifying the continuum of method, purifying the continuum of wisdom, and purifying on the instant of the individual, as well as solidifying their right holder, left holder, and the three-wave path of the non-duality of the apprehended and the apprehender in the central channel and thereby becoming sugatas through the path of the three gates of liberation. In brief, this is the realization of the body of properties through the cultivation of the vajra-wave path.[7]

These four states of pure appearance portion (purified portion) encompass four different ways to achieve Buddhahood in Tantric Buddhism, starting from the attainment of Buddhahood with the method of "sugata of outer shape" through to the achievement of the state of Buddhahood—the ultimate Ground—with the method of "sugata of the ultimate reality." However, none of these states of Buddhahood involve the realization of the eighth consciousness or the true understanding of the knowledge-of-general-aspect and the knowledge-of-specific-aspects within prajñā, not to mention the knowledge-of-the-aspects-of-paths exclusively possessed by the Bodhisattvas on or above the First

---

[6]   Ibid., 165.

[7]   Virūpa, *Daoguo* 道果, 165-66. Translated into English from Chinese.

Ground and the knowledge-of-all-aspects pertaining to the Buddha Ground. It is utterly preposterous of those gurus to vaunt that they have attained Buddhahood and can help practitioners attain Buddhahood in this body when they are completely ignorant of and have not realized prajñā.

Given the belief in Tantrism Buddhism that such initiations can purify one's defilements, some practitioners are keen to receive initiation from their gurus multiple times. However, the afflictions associated with unwholesome views, the afflictions associated with mentation, and even all the other afflictions and so forth, which, according to the tantric gurus, can be eliminated during the initiations, have different meanings in Tantrism than in the Buddha Dharma. Therefore, despite all the efforts to fancify the method of initiation and no matter how many times practitioners are initiated, this practice is unrelated to the elimination of afflictions and the realization of wisdom in the Buddha Dharma. All Buddhist learners must have a correct understanding of these facts.

There exist four other types of initiation: crown initiation, vajra initiation, bell initiation, and name initiation.

With respect to the crown initiation:

After invoking the guru, visualize that the disciple relies on the method of the three segments to transform into Buddha Ratnasambhava and even Buddha Vairocana from the syllable *am* [盎] and the treasure, the syllable *sa* [什] and the lotus, the syllable *kham* [康] and the sword, as well as the syllable *om* [嗡] and the cakra, just like in the previous practice. The objects of the initiation are also the same as those highlighted in the previous practice. The object used in the crown initiation is a five-Buddha crown made of gold, cloth, and so forth, at the center of which dwells the disciple's lineage lord. Wear this crown on your head after reciting the following five mantras in the right sequence—first at the the center of the head (at the forehead), then on the two sides of the head, at the vertex, and finally at the back of the head—"*Om vajrasattva abhisinca hum* [嗡斑捺達底穴日阿毗懇捺吽]," "*Om sarva tathagata aisvarya abhisekai var* [嗡薩縛達塔白達薩埵班即阿毗懇捴種]," "*Om ratna abhisinca trah* [嗡惹那班即阿毗懇捴阿]," "*Om padma abhisinca hrih* [嗡達摩班即阿毗懇捴什]," and "*Om karma abhisincaca ah* [嗡迦摩班即阿毗懇捴掌]."[8]

With respect to the vajra initiation:

First, recite the verses "The great vajra initiation." Next, recite the following:

> All Buddhas will now confer on you,
> The initiation of the pestle;
> As this is [the entity of] all Buddhas,
> You should practice and seek this vajra.
> Touch the disciple's heart, throat, and crown with the vajra pestle, before passing this vajra pestle over to the disciple's right hand.

Commentary on the Real Radiance [*Zhenshi guangminglun* 真實光明論] explains the meaning of these verses as follows: All Buddhas will now confer the vajra initiation on you, and therefore, you should seek and receive this vajra. Given that the bodhicitta is the pestle (the penis) and that the wisdom is the bell (the vulva), the vajra initiation corresponds to the initiation of the vajra wisdom (the vajra initiation corresponds to the wisdom initiation of the yab-yum practice). This vajra initiation is the initiation of all Buddhas, as it is the nature of bodhicitta that is inseparable from the emptiness-nature. The reason you should receive this vajra initiation is that this vajra is the entity of all Buddhas, and therefore, you should cultivate it in order to obtain it.[9]

With respect to the bell initiation:

Pass the bell over to the disciple's left hand and cause him to hold the bell and the pestle in an embracing posture (in the sitting sex posture of the Buddha-father and Buddha-mother). First, recite "The great vajra initiation" and so forth, before

---

8   Tsongkhapa, *Mizong daocidi guang lun* 密宗道次第廣論, 359. Translated into English from Chinese.
9   Ibid., 360.

reciting the following lines from Volume 4 of *The Tent Tantra* [*Mujing* 慕經]: "*Om vajradhipati tvam* [嗡班拶阿底跋底當], *Abhisencami* [阿毗懇拶彌], *Tistha vajra samayas tvam* [底叉 班拶三昧耶當]." Next, make the disciple recite "*Om vajra ghante hum hum* [嗡班拶根枳痛痛]; the World-Honored One guides and teaches me; may He thoroughly come close to me."[10]

With respect to the name initiation:

Hold a bell and a pestle and place them on the disciple's crown. First, recite "The great vajra initiation" and so forth as well as the following lines from Volume 4 of *The Tent Tantra* [*Mujing*]: "*Om vajra-satvatvam* [嗡班拶薩埵當], *Abhisincami* [阿毗懇拶彌], *Vajra-namabhisekatah* [班拶那摩阿毗克迦達]." Next, based on the name of the deity lineage on which the tossed flower lands, invoke either the anger Vajra or the ignorance vajra and so forth and confer the initiation of Vairocana's nature. Establish the names of the males and females according to the six divisions; you should know that this is extensively explained in *Abhaya's Vajra Rosary* [*Manlun*].[11]

Finally, during the vajra initiation and bell initiation, most gurus will also transmit the texts of vajra samaya, the prohibited acts of vajra, and bell samaya, which constitute the prohibited acts of the vajra ācārya. After the bell initiation and before the name initiation, some gurus will transmit "the mudrā samaya," while others will perform the ācārya initiation.

After these four initiations, some gurus will separately transmit the water initiation for the following reasons:

All of these are associated with vases and are therefore called vase initiations. *Abhaya's Vajra Rosary* [*Manlun*] also says that, in all of them, a Tathāgata and a female consort confer initiation by holding a vase; therefore, the six initiations ranging from water initiation through to ācārya initiation are

---

all known as vase initiations.[12]

With respect to the visualization and rituals related to initiation, there are three types of water initiation. Tsongkhapa says:

> Next, there are in brief three types of water initiation. The first one consists of performing the water initiation by pouring a small amount of water from the vases of the supreme deity and so forth (see the sections of Chapter 9) into a cup made of human skull or shell. Another type consists of conferring initiation with the vase of the supreme deity, then with the vase of the four Tathāgatas, followed by the vase of the four celestial ladies, and finally with all the vases in the maṇḍala: If there is only one vase of initiation available, then grab the flowery branch above the vase of the supreme deity with your right hand, which holds the pestle, use the flowery branch to pick up a small quantity of the nectar of bodhicitta with an immutable property contained in the vase of the supreme deity, and bestow initiation by allowing the liquid to drip along the tip of the vajra. Recite the following:
>
> The great vajra initiation,
> Is worshipped by the three realms;
> The vajra is generated by three secrets,
> Conferred in front of the Buddhas.
> Om ah vajra-udaka [嗡啊班拶鄔答迦],
> Abhisinca hum [阿毗懸拶吽],
> Surata tram aham [蘇惹達當阿吭].[13]

All learners who aspire to receive a tantric initiation must first grasp the meaning of the vase initiation before being allowed to be initiated. They should by no means ask to be initiated or follow other people in receiving initiation before understanding the contents of the vase initiation; otherwise, they will sow the seeds of an unwanted Dharma connection with erroneous teachings:

---

[12]   Ibid., 362.
[13]   Tsongkhapa, *Mizong daocidi guang lun* 密宗道次第廣論, 358. Translated into English from Chinese.

Speaking of the water in the vase of the first initiation, exactly what kind of water is contained in that vase? And what does it signify? During the great initiation, it takes the guru an entire day—the entire first day of the initiation—to handle just the content of this vase. He needs to convert (through visualization) all the water inside the vase into the deity's nectar (the sexual fluid generated by the deity amid sexual pleasure). A little pestle should be placed on the top of the vase; this pestle is connected to the guru's heart via five-colored threads. The guru should steer (through visualization) the light in his heart as well as the light on the fruition of all Buddhas into this vase. Next, the guru should drink the nectar. He himself should see the deity and obtain his permission to perform the initiation: "I hereby allow you to confer the initiation." . . . This is how the water in the vase should be empowered at the beginning of the first initiation. One should think of this empowered water as nectar. In Highest Yoga Tantra, you will need the Buddha-father and Buddha-mother to perform the union inside the vase (you will need the "Buddha" and the female consort to copulate inside the vase), so that nectar will drip out (so that the sexual fluid will flow out and serve as the nectar for the initiation). If one does not believe in this, then one will simply be unable to receive the initiation. For example, there is a very famous German who pretends to be a lama—he is Lama Govinda, a renowned person who has written some books. He has not even heard about the five meats and the five nectars. I explained the five nectars to him by telling him that the great fragrance refers to feces and the little fragrance designates urine. He replied doubtfully: "Oh! Why should one eat such filthy things?" I told him: " You have simply not been actually initiated and do not even know the important significance of the five meats and the five nectars. How could you write books without ever been actually initiated? How could you teach any principle? How could you say 'Why should we add such filthy things"? You have simply not gained faith!" By all means he should (he must) think that the Buddha-father and Buddha-mother are the ones performing intercourse inside the vase and that the nectar (sexual fluid) issued from their sexual act is called red bodhi and white bodhi. With these red bodhi and white bodhi, the initiation can then be performed. Human beings are engendered from the father's semen and the mother's blood. **We can create a Buddha with the nectars of white bodhi and red bodhi!**[14]

Therefore, the guru must first perform the method of visualization with respect to the water in the vase used during the initiation. Indeed, he must visualize that a reward body Buddha (a "Buddha" in the yab-yum form and the female consort that he embraces) engages in sexual intercourse inside the vase, experiences sexual pleasure, and ejaculates a blending of the sexual fluids issued from both parties; this liquid falls into the vase and is known as nectar. After completing this visualization, the guru collects the water and uses it to bestow initiation on the tantric practitioner. Only then is this practitioner actually initiated; otherwise, he cannot become a practitioner who has entered the Dharma-gate of Tantric Buddhism. All Buddhist learners should understand the significance of initiations before deciding whether they want to receive a tantric initiation. Based on the above theory, it is clear that the union of bliss and emptiness acts as the fundamental belief for the attainment of Buddhahood throughout the entire tantric practice. Upon hearing this fact, the wise should be able to distinguish between right and wrong and make the correct choices.

The aforementioned initiations are performed by a guru. Those who practice self-initiation must pick the right time:

> The time to practice self-initiation depends on the type of initiation performed. If the self-initiation involves a Dharma-protector, then the proper time is at night; if it involves a guru, then the appropriate time is in the early morning; if it involves

---

14 Yogi C. M. Chen (Chen Chien-ming 陳健民), *Qugongzhai quanji* 曲肱齋全集 *[The Complete Works of Yogi Chen]*, vol. 1-5, ed. Xu Qinying 徐芹庭 (Taipei: Puxianwang rulai fojiaohui 普賢王如來佛教會, 1991), vol. 1, 298-99. Translated into English from Chinese.

a deity, then the proper time is in the morning; and if it involves a ḍākinī, then the proper time is in the afternoon.[15]

The above explanations relate to the vase initiation in general. The path initiation will be discussed in the next section.

---

15   Ibid., 261.

3. The Path Initiation

There are four types of path initiation: vase initiation, secret initiation, wisdom initiation, and fourth initiation.

3.1 The Vase Initiation

Those who aspire to perform the path initiation should first cultivate the body maṇḍala:

> Those who practice the body maṇḍala should first perfect the branch of tranquil reflection: Visualize that the seed syllable in your mind emits light to invite Vajra Heruka (the wrath deity) to abide in the empty space in front of you, appearing exactly like the guru. Make various offerings to Vajra Heruka—external, internal, secret (for more details about secret offerings, see "The Tantric Actions of Power" illustrated in Chapter 13), reality (for more details about reality offering, see "The Tantric Actions of Power" expounded in Chapter 13), and so forth—and intensively pay homage to him, and so forth. Furthermore, absorb him into your body. Just as a lamp is upheld to fend off darkness, so the body maṇḍala is clearly established and the support is also distinctly established.[1]

Having thus visualized, one must cultivate the protection cakra:

> Visualize that there are various vajra pestles on your crown aperture, the feet are a vajra foundation, the ribs are a vajra wall, the skin is a vajra curtain and luxurious umbrella, the capillaries are an arrow net, and the fingernails are fiercely blazing flames. In the palace beyond all measures, with respect to their habitat consisting of the body, there is wind below the feet, the palace of life is of fire, the abdomen is of water,

---

[1] Virūpa, *Daoguo* 道果, 200. Translated into English from Chinese.

the heart is of earth, and the spine is Mount Sumeru. The body maṇḍala is a square, the four channels at the heart are four doors, the eight joints are eight pillars, the eyes are five-colored eaves, the nose is a tile made of gemstones, the teeth are half a garland, the lips and tongue are for enjoyments, and the ears are a memorial arch. The habitat consisting of the maṇḍala appears clearly and luminously.[2]

One can obtain the three views of property by practicing the following path:

> The three views of property issued from the path of actual practice are as follows: the view of property of the apparent aspect, the view of property of the empty aspect, and the view of property of the union. . . . Below is its actual method of cultivation. The inhabitant and the habitat consisting of the body maṇḍala are luminously established. The right sequence of practice is as follows: Obtain the face maṇḍala of the deity in the mind-vajra palace at the heart or visualize that the red third wisdom-eye moves slowly; observe what is above it with focus and in a relaxed manner. Extinguish these contents whether they are obvious or obscure. Next, practice as instructed previously. When you concentrate your mind on the wisdom-eye with one-pointed lucid awareness, transform and expel your ignorance with the wisdom-eye; when you hold it clearly with lucid awareness, this is "the existent dharma inverted by the appearance of ignorance." At that moment, do not enter either one of the two discriminations—either the luminosity [exhibited by the body maṇḍala seen] by the wisdom-eye or [visualized discriminations such as] other deities, maṇḍalas, and so forth. This method negates all discriminations of "saṃsāra and nirvāṇa"; such is "the characteristic of being free from the imputational mind." This is neither the ascertainment to become free from the noumenon that does not generate aspects such as one and so forth, nor the intrinsically and naturally pure noumenon; it is "the noumenon consisting of the yogi's consciousness of non-

---

2   Ibid., 200.

discriminative sensation that manifests clearly." This method refutes, through negation, the two discriminations consisting of the characteristic of ignorance and of the imputational mind and establishes, through the Dharma-gate of elimination and antidote, the existent dharma and the noumenon. Moreover, the so-called "holding the existent dharma of lucid awareness to generate the non-discriminative noumenon" is also established through the Dharma-gate of the establishing subject and established object. Furthermore, the generation of non-discrimination by solely holding onto lucid awareness, along with the view that the sole generation and manifestation of non-discrimination is lucid awareness, is called "unity of property." The so-called "differing in their functions" refers to establishing existent dharmas by holding onto the Dharma-gate of lucid awareness while realizing emptiness through other discriminative observations; this is the establishment of the noumenon through the Dharma-gate that generates non-discrimination. Given that it (the view of property of the apparent aspect) can be held easily, if one can wholly generate, in the right sequence, the external and the internal maṇḍala deities of the habitat and inhabitant, or if one can thoroughly generate the wisdom related to the aforementioned ground of vision among all effective things, which include the appearances of both sentient and inanimate worlds, then it is "the view of property of the apparent aspect." The view of property of the empty aspect is as follows: One abides without fascination for any paired objects of the eyes and so forth; the only thing that remains is a lucid and luminous sensation of emptiness. This is called holding the noumenon and so forth by way of the lucid awareness of empty aspect, which is as previously illustrated. The view of property of the union is as follows: When one's mind abides in the eyes and so forth, neither the state that is cultivated nor the sensation of emptiness arises; when the sensation of smoke, mirage, or Tathāgata arises in front of oneself, there is "union." As this view is neither achieved from external states nor obtained from the thought of desire, it is not real. However, given that the appearance of awareness generated is not unreal either, this view is said to be neither real nor unreal. As there is union with the observed paired object, the person who understands this observed object is said to possess"the property of the union."[3]

The above passage defines the view of property of the apparent aspect as follows: During the practice of visualization, if the mind of feeling and cognition can abide in the state of lucid awareness without any distracting thoughts, can hold onto the fact that this mental entity of lucid awareness can generate the state of lucid awareness, and can dwell without discriminating any phenomena, then at this moment the mind of feeling and cognition and the state of lucid awareness are one and their properties are non-dual; this is called having realized the view of property of the apparent aspect—having brought forth "the ground of vision." According to the tantric path, those who have brought forth "the ground of vision" are "Bodhisattva of the First Ground." The truth is that such Bodhisattvas have absolutely no idea what a ground of vision is. The ground of vision associated with the First Ground is corresponds to the wisdom consisting of the knowledge-of-aspects of the eighth consciousness (tathāgatagarbha). To achieve this wisdom, one must first obtain the knowledge-of-general-aspect by realizing the entity of the eighth consciousness at the stage of the Seventh Abiding. Next, one must generate the knowledge-of-specific-aspects by cultivating, in a process of seed-transformation, the teachings of the prajñā sūtras or by practicing, also in a process of seed-transformation, the knowledge-of-specific-aspects within prajñā under the guidance of a truly virtuous mentor. After perfecting the wisdom of prajñā pertaining to the stage of the sages, one must practice, under the guidance of a virtuous mentor, the knowledge-of-aspects—the doctrine of the mind-kings consisting of the eight consciousnesses, the seven foremost meanings, the natures of the seven properties, the five doctrines, the three natures, and the doctrine of the two types of no-self, all of which are set forth in the *Laṅkāvatāra Sūtra*. Once all these practices are

---

[3]   Virūpa, *Daoguo* 道果, 204-206. Translated into English from Chinese.

fulfilled, one will attain the ground of vision associated with the stage of unimpeded penetrating understanding. By contrast, the wisdom attained by tantric practitioners through "the view of property of the apparent aspect" does not involve in any way the understanding of the natures of the eighth consciousness or the realization through contact of the entity of the eighth consciousness. It just does not make any sense for them to claim that they can attain the ground of vision through such "view of property of the apparent aspect."

Furthermore, "the view of property of the empty aspect" merely refers to the situation in which one's mind of feeling and cognition, devoid of all fascination for sense objects, just abides in the sensation of "emptiness" and remains in the empty and luminous state of lucid awareness and solitary self-reflection. In fact, such an actual "practice and realization" has never enabled those tantric proponents to realize through contact the mind consisting of the eighth consciousness—the emptiness-nature—which means that they cannot claim to have gained the meritorious quality associated with seeing the Path of Vision in Mahāyāna. In addition, they do not possess the meritorious quality associated with seeing the Path of Vision in the sound-hearer doctrine, as they have not yet eliminated the self-view consisting of holding that "the mind of feeling and cognition is permanent and indestructible."

To describe "the view of property of the union" as "neither real nor unreal" is in fact a misapprehension of the Buddha Dharma. The mind of feeling and cognition has never been anything else than the mental consciousness, which is intrinsically an unreal phenomenon. In the four Āgamas, the Buddha says that this mind is "the permanent indestructible self" set forth by the eternalistic non-Buddhists; the prajñā sūtras speak of it as an unreal phenomenon with characteristics; in the vijñaptimātratā sūtras of the third turning of the Dharma Wheel, the Buddha identifies it as "a mind with an other-dependent nature," which still means that it is an unreal phenomenon. In contrast, Tantric Buddhists speak of this conscious mind as "the mind of the emptiness-nature" given that its entity is empty of physical substance; furthermore, they believe that one has attained the view of property of the union if one's conscious mind has united with the state of lucid awareness—they claim that, with this achievement, one can attain the fruitions and realizations of the First Ground through to the Sixth Ground as well as the rewards of emanation body pertaining to those Grounds (see pp. 523-535 of *Daoguo*). Such assertions are in fact completely groundless and do not accord with the Buddha Dharma. How could anyone possibly attain the wisdoms of the First Ground through to the Sixth Ground before realizing a wisdom of a lower level—the knowledge-of-general-aspect within prajñā of the eighth consciousness' nature, which is attained at the stage of the Seventh Abiding? It just does not make any sense. Therefore, the above statements about the meritorious quality associated with the practice and realization of the Buddha Dharma brought forth by the path initiation are all unfounded.

Those tantric gurus' assertions that the view of property of the apparent aspect, the view of property of the empty aspect, and the view of property of the union obtained through the path initiation allow their practitioners to realize the view of indivisible saṃsāra and nirvāṇa pertaining to the Sixth Ground also stems from erroneous thinking:

> The tenets (of the path initiation): When one has attained the view of indivisible saṃsāra and nirvāṇa during the six spiritual levels of the vase initiation in the supramundane, one is able to fit the three-thousandfold world systems into a mustard seed without problem of size, penetrate through walls without obstruction, cause rivers to flow upstream, hold the sun and the moon firmly, make many from one, one from many, and so forth.[4]

These statements do not conform to the truth: A plethora of tantric gurus have received the path initiation, but none of them

---

[4]   Virūpa, *Daoguo* 道果, 207. Translated into English based on Stearns, Cyrus (trans. and ed.), *Taking the Result as the Path: Core Teachings of the Sakya Path with the Result Tradition* (Boston: Wisdom Publications, 2006), 29.

have gained the ability to perform the various miraculous displays described in the above passage. We can, therefore, conclude that those assertions are untruthful. If those gurus can perform such displays only within their own minds of feeling and cognition, then they are merely engaging in imaginary visualization; those displays, which are devoid of actual substance, are purely their internal perceived-portions and are without any benefit for the cultivation and attainment of the Path to Buddhahood. What good is there to practice this method? Furthermore, the non-duality of saṃsāra and nirvāṇa is just the state in which the eighth consciousness (tathāgatagarbha)—and not the mind of feeling and cognition— abides. Indeed, since beginningless kalpas, the mind consisting of the eighth consciousness has never arisen because it has never ceased; it is thus referred to as the non-duality of saṃsāra and nirvāṇa for being neither arising nor ceasing.

Furthermore, as the mind consisting of the eighth consciousness has, since beginningless kalpas, never connected with any of the phenomena consisting of the six sense objects in the three realms, it has never exhibited greed or aversion towards any of those phenomena. Hence, this mind is referred to as the non-duality of saṃsāra and nirvāṇa, as there is neither saṃsāra nor nirvāṇa to speak of. On the contrary, the mind of feeling and cognition (mental consciousness) disappears every night and does not come from the previous lifetime; it exists for only one lifetime. Moreover, as it will never proceed to the next lifetime, it is said to be produced—it is produced by the tathāgatagarbha in dependence upon the form body of this lifetime as a condition. The mind of feeling and cognition is also said to be ceasing—it disintegrates along with the form body and forever ceases when one enters the embryo to take rebirth; it will never reappear in endless futures and therefore the mind of feeling and cognitions of future lifetimes will be brand new ones. Thus, the mind of feeling and cognition is said to be arising and ceasing. How could such an arising-and-ceasing mind of feeling and cognition be called the mind of the non-duality of saṃsāra and nirvāṇa? It just does not make any sense. Consequently, the eighth consciousness is the only mind that can be referred to as the non-duality of saṃsāra and nirvāṇa. Having all failed to comprehend and realize the mind consisting of the eighth consciousness, those tantric gurus— ancient and contemporary alike—have claimed that the mind of feeling and cognition can, through the method of the path initiation, attain the ground of vision associated with the First Ground and the fruition of emanation body pertaining to this Ground. How could their statements be credible in any way? Only the unwise would believe them.

3.2 The Secret Initiation

Before conferring the secret initiation, a guru must verify whether his disciples have achieved the practice of the winds. If the answer is negative, then the guru must not bestow the secret initiation on them. Those who are about to receive such an initiation must, before the initiation itself, offer a maṇḍala and visualize making offerings in order to eliminate their sins and accumulate their collection of meritorious quality:

> It is necessary to offer a maṇḍala in order to accumulate the collection of concordant conditions. The method is as follows: Visualize that there are a lotus and a moon on the throne adorned with miscellaneous treasures in the empty space in front of yourself and that your fundamental guru sits on the throne. The guru is endowed with the properties of body, speech, and mind of the Buddhas in the three times and is non-distinct from Vajradhara. The guru is surrounded by all the patriarchs of the lineage as well as by all Buddhas and Bodhisattvas, who abide with the characteristics that you find pleasurable. Offer seven piles of flowers on the maṇḍala vase as the support for the observed objects. On the vaiḍūrya foundation endowed with a fundamentally pure nature, the four continents, Mount Sumeru, the sun, the moon, human beings, and celestial beings are all readily available. Furthermore, the worldly realm is filled with all resources offered by yourself without any attachments. Vow to accumulate all wholesome roots of Īśvara's complete enjoyment body in the three times. Make offerings repeatedly without looking at any guests in front of you and ask for the empowerment that enables you to generate the continuum of manifest realization, meditative concentration, and endless meritorious quality. Reiterate this request a specific number of times.
>
> Furthermore, exhibit strong respect and faith with respect to the above; this is called "removing adverse conditions": Recite the one-hundred-syllable mantra and visualize that a vajrasattva with one face and two arms abides

on your crown, holding a pestle and a bell. The Buddha-mother—vajra-pride mother—holds a trowel and a vessel made of a skull. The two bodies, which are white and adorned with treasures and bone ornaments, embrace each other in the full-lotus vajra position. The white syllable *hum* on the moon disc's maṇḍala at your heart generates a continuum of nectar, which pervades the bodies of the Bhagavān vajrasattva Buddha-father and Buddha-mother. Furthermore, similar to the arising of clouds and rain (similar to the performance of sexual intercourse), their continuum of nectar flows into the crown aperture (the sexual fluids that flow out from their sexual organs continue to enter the practitioner's body from his crown aperture), thereby eliminating all aspects of darkness (all aspects of dark karmic actions). Once the continuum of nectar has purified the two defiled paths (after the nectar has continuously purified the urethra and the anus), it flows out from the center of the soles (the center of the practitioner's soles); the wisdom nectar (the sexual fluid bestowed by the Buddha-father and Buddha-mother) pervades the entire body. Furthermore, recite the one-hundred-syllable mantra of Heruka (the one-hundred-syllable mantra of Hevajra). Accumulate the collection [the collection of concordant conditions] as well as purify and eliminate joy in this fashion month after month, year after year. After performing these two practices a specific number of times, offer this total number to the guru. If this number differs from what the guru said, then great obstructions and lowly meditative concentration will ensue. If this number coincides with what the guru said, then wondrous meditative concentration and few obstructions will be generated.[1]

As readers can understand the meanings of the above quintessential instruction based on my annotations of the obscure terms, no further explanations are needed. The significance of the one-hundred-syllable mantra will be discussed later. Having thus accumulated the collection of meritorious quality, tantric

---

[1]   Virūpa, *Daoguo* 道果, 224-25. Translated into English from Chinese.

practitioners can formally practice the preparatory and main paths of the secret initiation.

With respect to the various steps related to the practice of the secret initiation, one must first cultivate the path of the stage of self-empowerment, which includes the preparatory and main practices. The preparatory practice is as follows:

> First practice the nine branches of tranquil reflection. Next, perform the three purifications. With respect to the purification of the body, rotate your head and neck, swing both arms, and shake your feet fiercely; this is the so-called purification of the five limbs. By practicing properly in this fashion, your body, speech, and mind will slack off once you are exhausted, and you will appear relaxed and slow. With respect to the purification of the speech, stop reciting sūtras, chattering, and so forth in order to eliminate the karma of speech. As for the purification of the mind, abandon temporarily all contemplative practices of tranquil reflection such as deity yoga and so forth; your mind must leave behind all karma and exhibit aversion towards them. You must perform these three purifications for months and even for years, which will definitely cause your meditative concentration to arise. If it does not arise, then perform the main practice of tranquil reflection.[2]

The so-called "tranquil reflection" in this preparatory practice does not correspond to the tranquil reflection consisting of meditative concentration set forth in Buddhism, but instead points to a Dharma-gate of tranquil reflection invented by Tantric Buddhists. Those who practice accordingly will not be able to achieve the meritorious quality associated with tranquil reflection such as meditative concentration and so forth or the various states of this tranquil reflection preached by the Buddha in the sūtras of the Three Vehicles, for this practice is nothing but a method of visualization—a Dharma-gate of "tranquil reflection"—established

---

[2]   Ibid., 226-27.

by tantric gurus based on their fallacious thinking with respect to the attainment of Buddhahood. All learners should be aware of the truth and should not mistakenly regard the "tranquil reflection" fabricated by Tantric Buddhists for the various methods found in the Dharma-gate of samādhi set forth by the Buddha. What follows is an illustration of this topic.

There are three "preparatory practices" of tranquil reflection:

Body essentials: Sit comfortably in the full-lotus position or a straight posture. However, you must straighten your spine and sit without back support, slightly lower your head, stare upward, place your tongue against the palate, and close your lips and teeth; this is the establishment of the body essentials, like building the wall of a house. Next, exhale forcefully three times, like sweeping away filthy objects inside a house; this is the establishment of the speech essentials. Next, with respect to the establishment of the mind essentials, keep the mind relaxed and distracted and exhale like a free galloping horse. With respect to the first of these three preparatory practices, vow to attain Buddhahood in order to benefit all sentient beings; this is the cultivation of the bodhicitta. Meditate that the guru abides at your crown aperture and exhibit ardent respect and faith towards him. The recitation of the syllable *hum* constitutes the protection wheel; practice deity yoga based on the recitation of the syllable *hum*. These nine methods of tranquil reflection constitute the preparatory practice of all tranquil reflections.[3]

The "main practice" of tranquil reflection is as follows:

Even if its wind yoga can cause one to be pure and perfectly awakened, it is said to be inconceivable. Moreover, its quintessential instructions comprise twenty-one thousand and six hundred instructions, which can be condensed into nine hundred instructions, further into two hundred and twenty-five instructions, further into ten instructions, and finally into

---

[3]   Ibid., 227-28.

four instructions—"releasing, taking-in, retaining, and dispersing." Once you gain control over your wind yoga, you can cultivate all paths with these four instructions—vitality and exertion or vajra recitation. There are four instructions related to releasing: releasing both vitality and exertion, stopping exertion and releasing vitality, releasing both vigor and life, and releasing sound from the mouth. There are two instructions related to filling-up: stopping exertion and filling up vitality, and not taking in sound into the mouth. (The quintessential instruction) related to retaining consists of the coinciding of the practice and the path. There are four essentials related to the actual practice of the above: (1) the expedients of the actual practice; (2) the valid knowledge of the ultimate; (3) what is the meritorious quality that is generated? and (4) which faults are removed?[4]

Furthermore, one must cultivate the five wheels of independence: "the feeding of the lamp flame, Brahmā's lightning, the channel yoga, the wheel of the fire drill, and the yoga of the drops." [5] In addition, one must cultivate the three wheels of dependence: sharpness, swiftness, and stability. Furthermore, there exist the quintessential instructions about the cultivation of the five wheels of independence and the three wheels of dependence, other quintessential instructions, and the seven observed methods: "red inner fire, fire blazing, the battle of drops, the cakra visualization, the blazing of fire more than that, the blazing of fire much more than that, and the blazing if everything on fire."[6] Through the cultivation of these methods, one can attain the "ground of vision" and thereby generate the four meditative concentrations: "the meditative concentration of naturally arisen affliction, the meditative concentration of naturally arisen thought, the meditative concentration of naturally arisen blankness, and the meditative concentration of naturally arisen lucidity, buoyancy, and

---

4   Virūpa, *Daoguo* 道果, 228-30. Translated into English from Chinese.
5   Stearns, Cyrus (trans. and ed.), *Taking the Result as the Path: Core Teachings of the Sakya Lamdré Tradition* (Boston: Wisdom Publications, 2006), 30.
6   Ibid., 34.

naturally arisen great primordial awareness."[7]

As for the actual cultivation of such "tranquil reflection" as well as the related quintessential instructions, learners must work on the practice of the winds, visualization of seed syllables, Dharma-gates related to various skills such as the ability to avoid the leakage of semen when one experiences the sexual pleasure induced by visualizing that the drops have been lowered to the tip of the sexual organ and so forth. Furthermore, the proponents of Tantric Buddhism claim that those who practice assiduously in this fashion will attain "the ground of vision" as well as achieve the four meditative concentrations and so forth. However, the contents of those meditative concentrations, wisdom, and so forth correspond to neither the tranquil reflection and meditative states cultivated in Buddhism, nor the wisdom of prajñā found in this religion. The endeavors of those tantric followers consist of "seeking the Dharma beyond the mind," for they have nothing to do with the main entity of the eighth consciousness set forth in the sūtras of the Three Vehicles. The assertion that those non-Buddhist methods enable practitioners to attain "the fruition of the spontaneous achievement of the perfect reward body and so forth" set forth in Buddhism (see pp. 230-269 of *Daoguo*; those teachings will not be cited here given their lengths) is erroneous, as those practices are completely unrelated to the elimination of afflictions and the realization of fruitions in the Buddha Dharma—the tantric path as well as the contents of the rewards realized by its followers are by no means the Buddha Dharma given their stark differences with the latter.

What tantric practitioners achieve by practicing assiduously and one-pointedly in this fashion is the clear light of death, which does not need to be cultivated secretly with other methods during death, as well as the ultimate attainment—**the fruition of the spontaneous achievement of the perfect reward body** (see p. 269 of *Daoguo*). However, their teachings and realizations constitute a

---

[7]   Ibid., 34.

Dharma-gate of practice that is based on non-Buddhist erroneous view and knowledge and have therefore absolutely nothing to do with the practice and realization of the Path to Liberation or the Path to Buddhahood set forth in the Buddhist sūtras—their so-called **"attaining the fruition of the spontaneous achievement of the perfect reward body"** is indeed unrelated to the fruition of the perfect reward body cultivated and attained in Buddhism. Unaware of the fallacy of their practice, tantric followers adhere to those mistaken views and methods and diligently engage in the erroneous cultivation thereof. The reward that they will attain is nothing but the false realization of non-Buddhist states; in addition, they will commit the severe sin of grievous false speech—which consists of untruthfully pretending that one is enlightened or has attained a given realization—and the pernicious karma of "wrecking the propagation of the true Buddhist Dharma." How heart-wrenching!

During the conferral of the secret initiation, the guru must visualize that the "Buddha-father and Buddha-mother" attain the union of bliss and emptiness by copulating inside the vase and subsequently discharge their sexual fluids—"nectar"—in this vase. Only then can this guru bestow initiation on tantric practitioners. Therefore, the secret initiation is also known as "the third initiation of visualization." The gurus who are unable to achieve such visualization are not allowed to confer the secret initiation; even if they perform it, the practitioners will not be truly initiated.

Before bestowing the secret initiation, the guru must have already received it himself, obtained the qualification of ācārya, become well-versed in the rituals of this initiation and the significance of its contents, and successfully performed the required visualization; only then is he allowed to confer this initiation. With respect to the ācārya initiation, Tsongkhapa illustrates the unique vajra ācārya initiation as follows:

> With respect to the proper way to perform the vajra ācārya *initiation, Holding Auspiciousness [Chixiang 持祥] says:*
> "Furthermore, the non-regressive initiation consists of

empowering the body with the samaya of the vajra and the bell." It also says: "This empowerment allows one to achieve the Mahāmudrā of the property of the desire-realm heavens (this empowerment allows one to achieve the Mahāmudrā of the property consisting of taking in the pleasure issued from the intercourse between a male and a female of the desire-realm heavens); this is the mudrā samaya." In other words, the main practice of the ācārya initiation is bestowed during the conferral of the mudrā samaya (during the conferral of the Mahāmudrā samaya related to the secret meanings of the yab-yum method). *The Permanently Abiding Vajra of Rāhula's Auspicious Friend [Luohouluo chixiangyou changzhu jingang 羅侯羅吉祥友常住金剛]* also says that the conferral of the mudrā samaya consists of performing the ācārya initiation while making the posture of a father and a mother of the desire-realm heavens embracing each other. In order to help practitioners realize such mudrā samaya, this text cites "the wisdom at just the age of sixteen (the wisdom mothers needed in the secret initiation are girls who have just turned sixteen)" and so forth. Guru Lawapa also says: "During this, the nature of Vajradhara in one's body of desire-realm heavens is empowered with the sequence of union, causing one to adopt an embracing posture; this is the Mahāmudrā samaya." This teaching causes learners to practice in this fashion based on the verses of mudrā samaya. . . . Why is the statement "the wisdom at just the age of sixteen" and so forth also cited? . . . Because transforming, through practice, one's body into a father and a mother of desire-realm heavens constitutes the causal branch of the ācārya initiation. It is necessary to practice the father and the mother of the desire-realm heavens in order to realize samaya—hence the citation of the statement "the wisdom at just the age of sixteen" and so forth. In other words, one should practice the wisdom seal in that posture. The statement "the union of the vajra and the bell" means that one should practice the embracing posture by holding a bell and a pestle. The commentator Ratnakarasanti also says: "The union of the vajra and the bell means using both hands." The statement "constitutes the guru initiation" refers to the generation, through embracing, of the samādhi of wondrous bliss. (During the performance of this secret initiation, one should attain the union of bliss and emptiness by embracing and copulating with a "wisdom mother" who has just reached the age of sixteen—one should ejaculate after bringing forth the samādhi of wondrous bliss consisting of the non-duality of bliss and emptiness, thereby producing a blending of the male and the female's sexual fluids—the red and white bodhicitta—which will be used for the initiation; only then can this secret initiation be effectively performed.) . . . *The Great Commentary on the Kālacakra Tantra [Shilundashu 時輪大疏]* says: "Next, bestow the bell and the pestle on the disciple's hands and confer the vajra ācārya on him." In other words, before the vase initiation, the guru confers an ācārya initiation based on the three samaya doors. . . . With respect to this first vase initiation, *Little Saṃvara Tantra [Lüexu 略續]* says:

> The first contact on the breasts of
> auspicious wisdom,
> Is the vase initiation.

Hevajra Tantra [Huanxijingang jing 歡喜金剛經] provides the following explanation with respect to the statement "the wisdom at just the age of sixteen" and so forth: Both the vase initiation and the ācārya initiation are taught in dependence upon a real female consort (an actual consort, not one who is issued from visualization); the second vase initiation refers to the wondrous bliss generated from embracing and coming into contact with nine female consorts. (In other words, this initiation requires the use of as many as nine female consorts; wondrous bliss is generated by copulating with each of these consorts, thereby producing large quantities of blendings—sexual fluids issued from the male and the females—which will be used for the initiation.) *The only difference lies in the number of female consorts; the rest is as previously highlighted.*[8]

As mentioned above, the only difference lies in the number of female consorts. Through this statement, Tsongkhapa's intent is to enable the gurus to have sexual intercourse with each of the nine female consorts during the "conferral of this unique guru initiation." In this fashion, those gurus can do an onsite demonstration to the disciples who receive the initiation and therefore help those disciples comprehend the differences in the sexual desire exhibited by the various consorts. As a result, the day when those disciples confer the secret initiation on their disciples of the opposite sex after having become vajra gurus themselves, they will know how to enable different categories of female disciples to achieve orgasm and experience the non-duality of bliss and emptiness amidst the sexual contact and so forth; in this manner, the disciples who are being initiated can obtain the secret initiation that qualifies them as ācāryas (gurus).

With respect to this secret initiation, Tsongkhapa advocates that one must use as many as nine actual female consorts and have each of them copulate with the guru in the maṇḍala of initiation; the sexual fluids thus collected will be used for the secret initiation. One must also ensure that the disciples understand the similarities and differences exhibited by the various categories of women when it comes to orgasm, so that these disciples will know which expedient and skillful means to use when they confer the secret initiation in the future. Most schools advocate the use of only one female consort in the ācārya initiation pertaining to the secret initiation, whereas the above passage from Tsongkhapa's *The Great Exposition of Secret Mantra*

---

[8]   Tsongkhapa, *Mizong daocidi guang lun* 密宗道次第廣論, 363-66. Translated into English from Chinese.

[Mizong daocidi guanglun] claims that nine consorts are needed. Apart from this discrepancy, the stipulations related to this initiation are roughly the same across the various schools. The above discussion concerns the secret initiation pertaining to the path initiation and the unique guru initiation.

Tsongkhapa says the following with respect to the designation "secret initiation":

> As far as its samaya is concerned, *Samputa Tantra [Jiehe jing]* says:
>
>> Based on the five nectars, one must neither harm sentient beings, nor abandon the female treasure, nor slander one's guru. This designation refers to the conferral of initiation with the secret object—bodhicitta—from the father and the mother (the semen from the male and the sexual fluid from the female)—hence the designation "secret initiation."
>
> The dharani[9] of the secret initiation says:
>
>> Offer a female consort and plead,
>> For a disciple of Amitābha to be born;
>> The guru and the Buddha-mother confer initiation,
>> With two secret objects (the guru ejaculates after copulating with a female consort; the semen that blends with the consort's sexual fluid is known as the nectar fully endowed with the red and the white bodhicitta—the two secret objects);
>> This is the pure conferral of initiation (only the initiations that are performed according to this stipulation are known as pure initiations).[10]

Therefore, a secret initiation must be performed with nectar, which is the blending of sexual fluids issued from the male and the female. Without these two secret objects (the white bodhicitta consisting of the male guru's semen and the red bodhicitta consisting of the

---

9   Dharani: In Sanskrit, lit. "mnemonic device," or "code"; Alt. overall summary; T. *gzungs*; C. *waduonan/zongchi* 嗢柁南/總持.

10   Tsongkhapa, *Mizong daocidi guang lun* 密宗道次第廣論, 397. Translated into English from Chinese.

female consort's sexual fluid), the secret initiation will not be valid and will not generate any meritorious quality of initiation—the initiation will not be considered to be "pure" and no one will be actually initiated.

3.3 The Wisdom Initiation

The following paragraphs will discuss about the wisdom initiation pertaining to the path initiation. In this initiation, the guru engages in Highest Yoga Tantra (the guru copulates with a person of the opposite sex in the maṇḍala of initiation and obtains nectar after ejaculating) and confers initiation on the disciples, while providing casual explanations to them. Hence, the wisdom initiation is also called the second initiation of performance—the guru only provides succinct explanations during this second initiation (detailed explications are given solely during the unique guru initiation; in contrast, the gurus only furnish brief explanations during the secret initiations other than the unique guru initiation). Having already received the unique ācārya initiation, the guru is aware of the true significance of the secret initiation and the wisdom initiation; as such, he is capable of bestowing these two initiations on the disciples.

In order to receive the wisdom initiation, a disciple must have achieved the practice of wind yoga under his guru's guidance, must have gained the capacity to move the drops upward and downward at will, and must be able to enjoy pleasure without ejaculating after having lowered the drops to the maṇi (a male's maṇi refers to his glans penis, whereas a female's maṇi points to her clitoris; the maṇi is also known as jewel cakra). Only then can this disciple receive this initiation. Furthermore, Practitioners who aspire to receive the wisdom initiation are strictly required to have received the secret initiation beforehand. In other words, before receiving the wisdom initiation, one must have understood the contents and meanings of both the secret initiation and the wisdom initiation. Indeed, those who are unaware of their meanings will definitely accuse the guru of sexual assault once the initiation is completed, which will harm the reputation and "the Dharma propagation business" of Tantric Buddhism—hence the establishment of numerous stringent rules.

With respect to the method of initiation, one must first find a female consort with proper characteristics. There are six categories of ladies with such characteristics:

1. The lady with the features of a beast: She has firm and perky breasts, a plump and tight lower body, and a slim waist; she walks with a relaxed gait and does not blink when she sees a male; her body and secret place emit the fragrance of musk.

2. The lady with the features of a conch: She has, on the whole, big bones as well as soft and silky flesh; her navel has lines that spiral to the right; her body is powerful and she moves swiftly; she has a clear, loud, and fast-speaking voice.

3. The lady with the features of an elephant: She has, on the whole, plump flesh, short limbs, great strength, small eyes, long and large ears; she emits an extremely nice fragrance when she sweats; she is intelligent and has few desire; she is frequently surrounded by bees.

4. The lady with lines: She has a rosy complexion; her navel is marked by three vertical lines and her glabella by one vertical line; she has long limbs, which are marked by many auspicious and glorious lines; she is caring about children. Those with such features deserve particular praise.

5. The lady with various characteristics: She is endowed with four types of meritorious quality, or with two or three types of meritorious quality.

Other teachings also mention about the lady with the features of a cow; she possesses the same characteristics as the lady with the features of an elephant. In addition, there are the ones who are so-called endowed with the lineage of the lady with the features of a lotus (their cervix—the opening located at the low end of the central channel—is distinct and can easily connect with the glans penis). . . . Regardless to which categories they belong, those females should be endowed with the following meritorious qualities: curly hair, attractive eyes, eyebrows without gaps; both their mouth and nose should emit the fragrance of musk; they should have a special front tooth as well as firm and perky breasts; their navel should be marked with three vertical lines and their forehead with one vertical line; their lower body should be plump and broad; their lotus (sexual organ) should be hairless; their cheeks should be chubby; they should emit the fragrance of dipterocarpaceae; they should be keen to perform the deeds and activities (the yab-yum practice) of the maṇḍala and so forth. Only those who are endowed with these meritorious qualities are fit to be the support (females) for the practitioners's achievements.[1]

Having thus found a female consort with proper characteristics, the guru must purify the produced one—the consort whom he has found—so that she can be used as a "Buddha-mother" for the yab-yum practice. The purification process begins with coming into contact with and pondering the "Buddha Dharma," before proceeding to the purification itself:

> When you come into contact with the four classes of tantras in Vajrayāna (when you come into contact with the yab-yum practice set forth in the four classes of tantras in Vajrayāna), bring forth the unique faith (believe in and accept this Dharma-gate of Vajrayāna, which is not shared by Exoteric Buddhism) in order to eliminate conceptual proliferations (abandon all statements that belittle the yab-yum method by fully believing in and accepting it) and fearlessly course in the very profound doctrine (do not be afraid of cultivating the very profound doctrine of this yab-yum method with a counterpart).[2]

Next, one must purify the female consort with the precepts—one must make her take the samaya precepts of Tantrism so that she will not divulge the secret:

> The upāsikās [3] who observe the ten wholesome precepts, extensively cultivate this method (assiduously cultivate this yab-yum method) and perform the poṣadha rituals to perfection must purify their minds through the continuum of the Precepts of Other-Liberation, the Precepts of Bodhicitta,

---

1   Virūpa, *Daoguo* 道果, 275-76. Translated into English from Chinese.
2   Ibid., 277.
3   Upāsikā: a female lay Buddhist disciple; T. *dge bsny en ma*; C. *youpoyi* 優婆夷.

the Precepts of Bodhisattvas, and so forth.[4]

Next, one must turn the female consort into a Vajrayāna disciple by bestowing initiation on her, before being allowed to cultivate the method of the union of bliss and emptiness with her and to thereby cause her to unwaveringly believe that the yab-yum practice constitutes the unsurpassed Buddha Dharma. Only then can one obtain "nectar" through this cultivation of the yab-yum method with the female consort and perform the wisdom initiation on the disciples who aspire to receive it: "Purity through initiation: Purify through the perfection of the four initiations."[5]

The female who has been thus purified still cannot be used as a consort. She must undergo a training that will enable her to achieve the meditative concentration of yoga (the vase breathing technique and the skill to cause the drops to ascend and descend). Only then will she be able, during this wisdom initiation, to assist the guru in his efforts to move the drop upward and downward and so forth amidst the union of bliss and emptiness—a process through which he generates the nectar for this wisdom initiation (the sexual fluid needed for this wisdom initiation, which is regarded by tantric Buddhists as the nectar of bodhicitta endowed with both the red and the white drops—the semen of the male guru is the nectar of white bodhicitta, whereas the sexual fluid of the female consort is the nectar of red bodhicitta):

> Purity through the meditative concentration of yoga:[6] Retain
> the wind through the power of yoga; this is achieved by those
> who can hold the bodhicitta (who can keep the drops—semen—
> from leaking out).[7]

In other words, the Sakya School has established stringent criteria for females to be used as consorts. Based on those rigorous standards, a female consort must also be able to control her

---

[4]   Virūpa, *Daoguo* 道果, 277. Translated into English from Chinese.
[5]   Ibid., 277.
[6]   Stearns, Cyrus (trans. and ed.), *Taking the Result as the Path: Core Teachings of the Sakya Lamdré Tradition* (Boston: Wisdom Publications, 2006), 36.
[7]   Virūpa, *Daoguo* 道果, 278. Translated into English from Chinese.

orgasm. This will enable her to experience the state of the union of bliss and emptiness by entering meditative absorption (orgasm) when the guru allows her to do so. The consort's red bodhicitta (sexual fluid) can thus be obtained—by attaining orgasm at the same time as the guru, the consort can help him obtain an equal amount of red and white bodhicitta (an equal amount of sexual fluid can be obtained from the male and the female by ensuring that both sides reach orgasm at the same time), which will be used to confer the wisdom initiation on tantric disciples. Therefore, it is difficult to find a qualified female consort as far as the practice of the Sakya School is concerned. Even if a suitable one is found, many tasks need to be completed before this third wisdom initiation can be performed on disciples.

The above stipulations relate to the criteria of a qualified female consort advocated by the Sakya School; they are more stringent than those established by the other schools. Once a suitable female consort is found and purified and has entered the maṇḍala of initiation, she must achieve the equanimity of speech, desire, and empowerment—the equanimity of body and speech, the equanimity of desired objects, and the equanimity of empowerment. Those are the tasks of which the guru must take care during the wisdom secret initiation; they will be illustrated with citations in the discussion about the actual cultivation of the yab-yum method in Chapter 9.

Opinions were already divided in ancient India as to whether one must use a female consort to cooperate with the guru during the wisdom initiation. **Tsongkhapa** says:

> Therefore, some of the seventeen schools in India claim that one must abide in the bliss of the maṇi during the third one (some schools assert that, during the third initiation, the guru must dwell in the great bliss induced from his glans penis); the bodhicitta thus generated (the great bliss induces ejaculation—the expulsion of the white bodhicitta (semen), which will be provided to the disciple, for tasting), constitutes the fourth one (the fourth initiation). Some schools assert that the third initiation is without interstice (the guru and the female consort

reach orgasm at the same time and contemplate the non-duality of bliss and emptiness; "without interstice" refers to the fact that the guru and the female consort simultaneously attain the union of blissful contact and of the contemplation of the emptiness-nature; the sexual fluid thus obtained is known as the red and the white bodhicitta); the tasting of (this) bodhicitta (by the disciple who is being initiated) constitutes the fourth one (the fourth initiation). Some other schools claim that the third one (the third initiation) is without interstice (consists of the tasting without interstice of the bodhicitta—sexual fluid); the use of other female consorts (if this refers to the case where it is necessary to use more than one female consort) constitutes the fourth one and so forth (the fourth initiation pertaining to the third initiation).[8]

Based on the above passage from Tsongkhapa, the various schools hold different opinions with respect to whether it is necessary to use a female consort during the third secret initiation in order to obtain the white bodhicitta (if no female consort is used, then the guru must bring forth bliss by relying on the method of visualization, which will enable him to ejaculate and obtain the bodhicitta—semen—he can also ejaculate by relying on masturbation) or whether numeous female consorts must be used in order to obtain a blending of the red and the white bodhicitta issued from the guru and those consorts—this blending will be used for the initiation of the disciples and provided to them for tasting. There is no definitive conclusion among the various schools given the wide spectrum of opinions, and therefore, different solutions are possible. One of the schools advocates that it is sufficient for the guru to explain verbally the contents of the initiation to the disciples:

> As previously indicated, when performing the fourth initiation, one has conferred initiation on the disciples by merely causing them to understand the contents through speech. The

---

8   Tsongkhapa, *Mizong daocidi guang lun* 密宗道次第廣論, 399. Translated into English from Chinese.

disciples are also deemed to have received the initiation merely through speech; this is the fourth initiation that turns them into Dharma-vessels.[9]

As for Tsongkhapa, he believes one should cooperate with a female consort in order to obtain the red and the white bodhicitta to be used during the secret initiation:

> With respect to the conferral of the last secret initiation bestowed for the purpose of preaching the sūtras and so forth, **the guru must enter meditative absorption with nine consorts who are aged from twelve to twenty** (the guru must copulate with each of the nine female consorts who are aged variously from twelve to twenty and must reach orgasm and contemplate the non-duality of bliss and emptiness simultaneously with each of them; he must then ejaculate into the sexual organ of each of the consorts and collect the sexual fluids) and must confer the initiation by pouring the vajra (this sexual fluid is called vajra bodhicitta) endowed with the seeds (endowed with the red and the white bodhi issued from the nine consorts—the blending of the sexual fluids from the guru and the consorts—endowed with the seeds of both the male and the females) into the disciple's mouth. Thus, the guru enjoys wondrous joy with one female consort during the former one— the third initiation. During the latter one, he immediately enters meditative absorption with nine consorts (during the latter one, he immediately reaches orgasm simultaneously with each of the nine consorts); it is from the wondrous joy thus generated (that they obtain the nectar needed to confer initiation on the disciple).[10]

Therefore, the various schools have not reached a definitive conclusion as to whether the guru should cooperate with a female consort in order to obtain the seeds consisting of bodhicitta? Or are the guru's seeds consisting of white bodhicitta sufficient for the initiation? Or should the guru work with several consorts in order

---

9   Ibid., 397.
10   Ibid., 399-400.

to obtain the seeds consisting of the red and the white bodhicitta needed to perform the secret initiation on disciples? **Tsongkhapa believes that it is necessary to enter "meditative absorption" simultaneously with nine female consorts in order to obtain "the innate seeds," which will then be poured into the disciple's mouth, so that he can bring forth sexual pleasure by tasting them. Only can such an initiation be regarded as a pure and proper one.**

The Sakya School asserts that one must cooperate with a female consort in order to confer the secret initiation on disciples:

> To obtain the third initiation, there are three types of discrimination consisting of investigation:
>
> 1. For those who investigate to a limited extent from the start, the objects for the secret initiation appear in the conch and the clam (appear in the vulva and the penis); they are placed on their tongues (on the disciples' tongues so that they can taste them).
>
> 2. For those who discriminate slightly: (This case concerns the disciples who slightly discriminate the impurity of this secret objects), the objects are seasoned with milk, liquor, and so forth before being bestowed on them for drinking.
>
> 3. For those who discriminate extensively: (This case concerns the disciples who extensively discriminate the impurity of the sexual fluid of this secret initiation), the objects must not be placed on their tongues (because those disciples will not dare to taste them); instead, just apply the drops on their throats (all you need to do is apply the drops on the disciples' throats).[11]

As there is mention of the conch and the clam, we can conclude that the Sakya School advocates the use of a female consort.

---

[11] Virūpa, *Daoguo* 道果, 193-94. Translated into English from Chinese.

With respect to the best way to request the vajra guru to confer this secret initiation, **Tsongkhapa** says:

> First, making a request with an offering: Having built a concealed area with a curtain and so forth, the disciple must thoroughly understand that "the guru is a vajrasattva" and must offer him wisdom mothers fully endowed with samaya—virgins whose genitals have no defection and who are aged twelve and so forth (the disciple must make an offering consisting of nine virgin girls who are aged from twelve to twenty and whose genitals have no defection to the guru for enjoyment. The words "and so forth" mean that one girl of every age from twelve to twenty is offered, adding up to a total of nine girls). As stated in Section 2 of *Mahāmudrā Drop Tantra* [*Dayin kongdian* 大印空點]:
>
>> Endowed with intelligence, long and thin eyes,
>> As well as stunning physical appearance (they must be beautiful),
>> They are aged twelve or sixteen (their ages must be between twelve and sixteen);
>> If they are difficult to obtain, then twenty is also acceptable (then one can please the guru by offering an unmarried female aged twenty for his enjoyment).
>> Those above twenty act as seals for other purposes (those aged above twenty are not suited for the secret initiation and must be used as other seals for other purposes),
>> For they will drive the siddhi away (they will prevent the practitioner from attaining the siddhi that should otherwise be obtained from secret initiation).
>> One can offer one's sisters, daughters, or wife to the guru.[12]

Thus, depending on one's financial means, one must please the guru by offering him either young girls with supreme beauty, young girls whose physical appearance is one notch below supreme,

---

[12] Tsongkhapa, *Mizong daocidi guang lun* 密宗道次第廣論, 376. Translated into English from Chinese.

or women whose age is approaching twenty. Those who cannot afford hiring girls that meet those criteria due to limited financial resources can please their gurus by offering their wives or sisters who are below the age of twenty, or their young daughters; only then will the gurus bestow the secret initiation on them. This is the method set forth by **Tsongkhapa** to request a guru to confer the secret initiation.

Tsongkhapa further says:

> With respect to cultivating "the objects of the secret initiation," the guru who is endowed with the pride of the main deity must then visualize the body of a mundane female as empty before generating (through visualization) the body of a celestial lady. He must first empower the vajra lotus (the female consort's vulva). Next, he must enter meditative absorption (at the same time as the female consort—the two must enter orgasm simultaneously) and recite (during orgasm):
>
> "*Om sarva tathagata anuragana* [嗡薩縛達塔伽達阿奴惹迦那],
>
> *Vajra svabhava* [班拶娑跋縛], and
>
> *Atma koh-hang* [阿摩郭吭]."

These verses are from *Tent Tantra [Mujing]* and *Guhyasamāja Tantra [Jimijing 集密經]*. (Next,) visualize that the seed syllable at your heart emits light to invite Buddha Vairocana (the reward body Buddha in the yab-yum form set forth in Tantric Buddhism) and Mother Lochana and so forth to enter meditative concentration (to enter orgasm and abide therein one-pointedly without distracting and discriminative thoughts); (further, visualize that the Vairocana Buddha-father and Buddha-mother experience great bliss during sexual intercourse and therefore discharge red and white bodhicitta—sexual fluid—which) enter your body through the Vairocana gate (through the gate of your crown), dissolve the great craving, and reach the vajra maṇi (reach the glans penis) through the avadhūtī (through the central channel), causing you to be firm and innate (causing your penis to be erect and firm and thereby bringing forth the innate joy unintermittedly). As stated in *Guhyasamāja Later Tantra [Jimi houxu 集密後續]*:

The vajra and the lotus are united (the male and the
female's sexual organs are united);
They collect the vajra of all existences (they collect the
vajra mind of all existences—the semen and the
female's sexual fluid);
The application of the body, speech, and mind (this
refers to the acts performed during sexual intercourse
such as the deeds of the body, speech, and mind,
striving, and so forth),
Is drawn into the mind (is drawn into the bodhicitta—
the sexual fluid from the male and female);
It exits from the vajra route (the semen is discharged
from the urethra),
And descends (pours) into the disciple's mouth.[13]

Tsongkhapa further says:

With respect to the method of conferring the secret initiation,
the next step is to extract the vajra out of the lotus (next,
extract the vajra mind—sexual fluid—out of the female consort's
sexual organ): Extract the maṇi jewel with the thumb and the
ring finger (collect with the fingers the semen that the guru has
ejaculated into the female consort's vagina) and thoroughly
understand that the fluid transformed from the Tathāgata
and your bodhicitta (semen) are non-dual. Given that the
disciple who holds the Amitabha pride of the speech vajra
might not believe it upon seeing it, cover the disciple's face, so
that his hands and eyes cannot come into contact with it (so
that the disciple cannot see it or touch it). Recite the following
verses from *Vajra Rosary Tantra* [*Jingangman jing* 金剛鬘經]:
    The Vajradhara of the past,
    Conferred initiation on the Buddha's son;
    With the wondrous bodhicitta (with this supreme
    bodhicitta—sexual fluid),
    I now confer initiation on the disciple.
Furthermore, recite the mantras of the main deity such as
"*Om ah vajra sattva hum* [嗡啊班撈枳吽]" and so forth, before

---

13   Ibid., 376-77.

placing it (the sexual fluid—vajra mind) into the disciple's mouth. At this moment, the disciple must visualize that it is the aggregate property of all Tathāgatas such as Buddha Vairocana and so forth, and must recite "*Ah mahasukha* [阿賀 摩訶蘇喀]" before swallowing it. This mantra signifies "rare great bliss." Next, the female consort arises from meditative concentration (the female consort leaves the state in which she takes in bliss one-pointedly and gets up), naked. She collects a few drops of nectar from the lotus (from her vagina) and thus places them into his mouth (into the mouth of the disciple who receives this secret initiation). He then drinks it as previously instructed (the disciple then drinks it as previously taught by the guru). The term "thus" refers to the fact that this is not an object of the eyes or of the hands (the disciple is not allowed to see it or touch it), that it should be collected with the thumb and the ring finger, and that one must recite the mantras and verses as previously mentioned (and then bestow the nectar on the disciple for tasting). The words "as previously highlighted" mean that one must collect the minds of all Buddhas (one must visualize that all Buddha-fathers and Buddha-mothers unite, copulate, and take the bliss in within the bodies of the guru and the female consort, thereby discharging red and white bodhicitta, which is then collected for the tantric practitioner). (The tantric practitioner) drinks it and also recites "Ah mahasukha" as previously mentioned. According to **Commentator Candrakīrti** and so forth, even if there is only one disciple (even if there is only one disciple who receives the initiation), **the secret initiation needs to be conferred by both a father and a mother** (the secret initiation needs to be bestowed by both the guru and the female consort after they perform sexual intercourse in the maṇḍala of the secret initiation)—**they are both indispensable** (the ceremony will not be proper without either the guru or the consort).[14]

Based on the above statements from Tsongkhapa as well as his citation of the assertions made by the tantric "Bodhisattva"

---

[14]   Ibid., 376-77.

Candrakīrti, it is clear that one needs to cooperate with a female consort in order to obtain both the red and the white bodhicitta. As stated by Candrakīrti, "Even if there is only one disciple, the secret initiation needs to be conferred by both a father and a mother—both of them are indispensable."

With respect to the initiation that follows, Tsongkhapa says:

> Thus, *A Lamp to Illuminate the Five Stages* [Wucidilun 五次第論] and *The Compendium of Practice* [Shexinglun 攝行論] also say, "Keep the bodhicitta (sexual fluid) in a bottle or a cup and confer initiation (on the disciples)." *Commentary on the Manifest Union* [Mingxian shuangyunlun 明顯雙運論] says, "Once the guru has bestowed it (sexual fluid) by placing it into the disciple's mouth with his thumb and ring fingers, he must keep the (remaining) bodhicitta (sexual fluid) in a shell cup and so forth and blend it with scented water, confer the initiation after chanting an auspicious verse, and cite *Tantra of the Moon Secret Drop* [Yuemi kongdian jing 月密空點經] as evidence." . . . With respect to the entity of the secret initiation, Section 2 of *Mahāmudrā Drop Tantra* [Dayin kongdian] says:
>
> > Due to the union of the thumb and ring finger,
> > The enjoyment enters the inner body;
> > Thereupon, the correct wisdom arises,
> > Similar to the bliss of a virgin girl.
>
> In other words, the guru father and the mother's empty drops must be placed on the disciple's tongue (this means that the guru and the consort's sexual fluids must be placed on the disciple's tongue); the tasting thereof generates the samādhi of wondrous bliss (the tasting of this sexual fluid induces sexual pleasure, which enables one to enter a state of wondrous bliss in which one abides one-pointedly without distracting thoughts). . . . Having received the secret initiation, the disciple must first make a request to his guru with texts such as "The Bodhi Vajra" and so forth. Next, the guru, pointing to the female consorts who were previously offered by the disciple and who are endowed with samaya and the precepts of conduct or to other females with wondrous looks (thereupon, the guru points to

several beautiful consorts who were just offered by the disciple receiving the initiation or to other consorts with wondrous looks), says the following (gives the following instruction to the disciple):

The Buddha has observed the following:

You should rely on these delightful appearances (based on His observations, "the Buddha" believes that you should cultivate the yab-yum method by relying on these consorts with wondrous looks);

The cakras fuse in the right sequence (the five cakras in your central channel must fuse with those of the female consort in the correct sequence—the two bodies must be tightly united; the male's drops, after entering the lower end of the consort's central channel through his sexual organ, must fuse and move together with the consort's drops within the five cakras of her central channel),

You should enjoy the supreme bliss (you should enjoy the supreme, wondrous bliss generated through this practice);

From the full-lotus vajra position (from performing sexual intercourse in a seated position and attaining the union of bliss and emptiness of the fourth joy),

The mind (the semen and the drops consisting of the mind of feeling and cognition) enters the maṇi (moves into the glans penis, inducing the great bliss consisting of the fourth joy).

After causing the disciple to understand this (this secret meaning),

The guru gives them (the female consorts) to the disciple. (Thereupon, the disciple cultivates the yab-yum method with these consorts.) . . .

Water (sexual fluid) is generated (within) the naked body of the female consort,

Which is perfumed with wondrous scents made of red flowers and so forth.

The female consort (points to her sexual organ and) instructs the disciple:

A rare, wondrous lotus (this is a rare and wondrous lotus),

Endowed with all blisses;
If you rely on it in accordance with the
Dharma,
I will permanently abide in front of it.
If you perform the deeds of the lotus (if
you engage in the activities of the lotus—the
yab-yum practice),
Then you are close to the Buddhas and so
forth;
The sovereign king of the great bliss (the
reward body Buddha set forth in Tantric
Buddhism, e.g. the tantric Samantabhadra
Raja "Tathāgata"),
Will always abide therein (will forever abide
in the lotus).
Benzan [奔拶, rely] *mucha* [木叉, mokṣa or
liberation], how exhilarating [賀]![15]

These are the contents of the secret initiation set forth by
Tsongkhapa of the Tibetan Tantric Gelug School.

What are the purposes of conferring this third secret
initiation? **Tsongkhapa** says:

(The purposes of) the secret initiation are to transform
(disciples) into fields of faith and wisdom, to protect the
samaya precepts, and to purify one's speech. Those who have
become "fields of faith" have adamant faith in the secret
mantra and the secret practice (yab-yum practice) and do not
harbor any erroneous doubts about them. **The mode of
transforming one into a Dharma-vessel of faith is as follows:
Offer a female consort to the guru and taste the two
realms of meditative absorption issued from the guru and
the female consort** (taste the sexual fluid that has been blended
with the semen ejaculated by the guru after enjoying the great
bliss of sexual intercourse); **bring forth the supreme bliss**

---

15   Tsongkhapa, *Mizong daocidi guang lun* 密宗道次第廣論, 377-82. Translated into
English from Chinese.

thanks to the power of the guru and the deity and expel all disbelief. . . . With respect to the empty essential constituent, according to Nareba [挐 熱 跋 , a tantric practitioner], the union between the vajra (penis) of the guru father (the guru is the "father") and the lotus (vulva) of the mother (the consort is the "mother") (is called) empty essential constituent. This empty essential constituent is actually composed of the two essential constituents (this empty essential constituent actually consists of the guru's seeds and the female consort's seeds, which are collectively called "the two essential constituents") and scented water (sexual fluid), the rest being the aggregate quintessence of its pure portions. With respect to the purification of speeches, the secret objects of the innate joy (the sexual fluid blended with the ejaculated semen, both of which result from the fourth joy) generated through the meditative absorption (the state in which one abides one-pointedly without distracting thoughts during orgasm) of the "guru father and mother," who are in fact no other than the "main deity father and mother," are indivisible from the property into which all Buddhas and Bodhisattvas of the ten directions have been requested to transform (all Buddhas are of this same property given that they are also born from these red and white bodhi seeds—hence the term "indivisible"). In light of their great power, the tasting thereof brings forth the virgin-like bliss set forth in *Mahāmudrā Drop Tantra [Dayin kongdian]*. When this bliss moves down to the tongue, throat, and so forth, it can purify the channels and winds of those locations and therefore the speech. The possibility to purify the speech by tasting and taking in the flavors of the bodhicitta (the possibility to cleanse the karma of the speech by way of tasting the flavors of the sexual fluid) results from the power of the secret initiation. The possibility to purify the mind (the possibility to cleanse the karma of the mind) by using one's body to take in and enter into contact with the tactile object consisting of the two essential constituents (by using one's form body to take in the tactile object issued from the blending of the sexual fluids generated from the sexual intercourse between the guru and the female consort) results from the power of the third initiation. Thus, owing to the empowerment of the channels, winds, and bodhicitta by the causes and conditions of those supreme objects, one becomes a yoga-vessel of the fierce practice of the channels, the winds, and so forth. Due to the practice thereof, one becomes a vessel of self-empowered illusory samādhi and therefore gains control over the practice of that path.[16]

The above statements from **Tsongkhapa** demonstrate that the main purpose of conferring the third initiation—the secret initiation—is to transform the disciples into "vessels of the path" fit for the yab-yum practice of Tantric Buddhism. The explanations about the theory and the contents of the secret initiation are to help the disciples prepare for the generation and practice of the yab-yum method by causing them to believe in and accept this method as well as to ensure that they understand it and do not have any doubts about it. Such is the primary purpose of the third initiation—the wisdom initiation.

The guru must teach the disciples the differences among the four joys when he bestows the third initiation—the secret initiation—on them, as stated by **Tsongkhapa**:

> With respect to the statement, "at this moment, the guru must teach the differences among the four joys," what are the four joys? As stated in *Clusters of Instructions* [*Suilun* 穗論]:
>
>> Based on bola [波拉] (based on the visualization of the drops and so forth as well as on the yab-yum practice), bring forth the first three joys from the secret lotus and the vajra maṇi (bring forth the first three joys from the secret vulva and the glans penis) as well as the innate joy from within the maṇi (lastly, bring forth the fourth joy, which is known as the innate joy, from within the glans penis). This is an establishment.

---

[16] Ibid., 416-18.

The text further quotes the Kālacakra School:
    The fluid flows from the turban,
    And becomes joy when it reaches the tip of the lotus,
    (visualize that the drops—the white bodhicitta, the
    semen—appears at the crown aperture and descends to
    the glans penis—the tip of the vajra—or to the vulva,
    thereby bringing forth the first joy);
    The supreme joy and the wondrous joy,
    Arise from the throat and the heart (the "supreme
    joy" and the "wondrous joy" are generated by moving
    the drops in the glans penis that brings forth sexual
    pleasure all the way up to the heart and the throat).
    The joy of absence arises at the navel (the "joy of
    absence" arises when the drops have been lowered to
    the navel cakra),
    And even at the secret lotus (it is also possible to bring
    forth the "joy of absence" when the drops are lowered
    further down into the secret vulva).
    The most secret vajra treasure,
    Is the innate joy without emission (the fourth joy—
    "the most secret vajra treasure"— is generated in the
    following way: When the drops descend into the glans
    penis or the vulva and induce the greatest blissful
    contact, if one is able to withhold ejaculation and abide
    long-lastingly in orgasm without interruption, then the
    joy—the greatest blissful contact in the world thus
    obtained—is the fourth joy, also known as the innate
    joy—hence the assertion that the most secret vajra
    treasure is the innate joy without ejaculation).

The first one arises from the vajra root (the first one arises
from the vajra practitioner's root—penis); before it reaches the
center of the maṇi (the center of the glans penis), three joys of
wisdom arise from the discriminations at different locations
(three joys of sexual contact consisting of "wisdom" arise from
the discriminations made at the locations reached by the drop).
The designations "joy, supreme joy, and wondrous joy" are
established based on the elimination of the three coarse
discriminations—the discriminations of the highest, high, and

middle levels. Although there is a subtle lower level, the "innate joy" is established due to the absence of the coarse one. (Although there exists a subtle lower level of discrimination consisting of "repugnance," the fourth joy is established as the innate joy given that there is no longer any extremely coarse discrimination consisting of repugnance.) . . . As stated in Abhaya's *Vajra Rosary* [Manlun]:

> The auspiciousness of the union of wisdom (the auspiciousness generated from the union of a male and a female through the wisdom related to the secret teachings),
> Correctly manifests reality (correctly manifests the sign of reality of the Dharma-realm);
> From the full-lotus vajra position (the realization of the sign of reality lasts from the moment when ultimate bliss is induced through the practice of sitting intercourse between a male and a female until the moment when this bliss causes breathing to cease temporarily; see the next few sentences in this passage),
> The mind enters the maṇi (bliss is brought forth by moving the red and the white bodhicitta into the glans penis).

This means that, among the four joys, the innate wisdom is established as this wisdom. (In other words, among the four joys, the "wisdom of the innate joy" realized during the fourth joy is established as the wisdom attained through this yab-yum practice.) The moment it arises is when the bodhicitta has reached the vajra maṇij, but has not yet been expulsed. (The moment when the innate bliss arises is when the semen has arrived at the glans penis and the practitioner is enjoying extreme bliss without having ejaculated.) The full-lotus vajra position refers to the moment when one abides in the maṇi and when nasal breathing ceases. (The full-lotus vajra position refers to the moment when one brings forth the extreme blissful contact by moving the drops and semen to the glans penis while withholding the semen and then long-lastingly enjoys the blissful contact of orgasm to the point that one can hardly endure, thereby causing nasal breathing to cease.) According to Guru Lawapa, the timing whereby the innate wisdom arises and its property are as previously mentioned (the timing, causes, and conditions whereby the innate joy arises as well as its property are the same as those of the first three joys—they all arise from sexual contact); all four joys arise from the supreme joy, the joy of absence, and the stages between them (all four joys arise from the first three joys, which are issued from sexual contact). Guru Saraha also says that the innate wisdom is the third initiation. If a guru confers initiation on female disciples, then the "vajra place" should be understood as the lotus (when a guru confers the third initiation on female disciples, he should make them understand that the term "vajra place" refers to the vulva). This is as stated in the section "The Third Initiation" of *Oral Teachings of Mañjuśrī [Miaojixiang koushoulun 妙吉祥 口授論]*:

> From the union of vajra in the realm of empty space
> (based on the visualization of the union between the
> main deity father and mother in the vajra realm and the
> union of the drop and sexual fluid issued from the
> intercourse between oneself and the female consort),
> Those endowed with the correct eyes can bring forth
> the great bliss (those endowed with the correct eyes—
> those who truly understand this doctrine—can therefore
> bring forth great bliss);
> If one can renounce the joy of desire amidst the
> correct joy (if one can renounce the joy consisting of
> the desire for ejaculation while taking in the joy of
> orgasm in the proper way),
> Then one will see the middle of two extremes and will
> become free and steadfast (then one will see the
> correct Middle Way that is free from two extremes and
> will therefore renounce the desire for ejaculation, thus
> allowing one's sexual organ to always remain firm while
> one takes in the utmost bliss permanently and
> unintermittedly).
> The lotus emptiness and vajra maṇi are treasures (the
> emptiness-nature of the vulva and the glans penis maṇi
> are treasures of Vajrayāna),
> The union of the lotus and treasure in the full-lotus

position (the moment when one enters the utmost bliss and when nasal breathing ceases temporarily due to the copulation of the vulva and the penis),

If, at that moment, one sees the mind enter the maṇi (if one can withhold ejaculation while witnessing, at that moment, the drop—semen—reach the glans penis),

Then one will understand that this bliss is precisely the wisdom (then one will comprehend that the path that enables one to take in the utmost bliss everlastingly—to take the bliss in without eventually ejaculating—is the wisdom of Vajrayāna).

This is the path that fulfills the various stages (This is the Dharma-gate that fulfills the various stages related to the ultimate practice and realization of the "Buddha Dharma"),

Preached in common by the supreme gurus (such a Dharma-gate is taught in common by the gurus who have realized the most supreme state).

Both the states of greed and without greed are without attainment (whether one is craving for sexual pleasure or free from the craving for ejaculation, one is in fact without attainment amidst the blissful contact and proper sensation experienced in those states—no material phenomena can be obtained in those states),

But the wondrous wisdom manifests for a brief instant therein (but the wondrous wisdom that arises during the brief instant of the union between the two sexual organs manifests during this sexual intercourse);

One must receive this wisdom (a tantric practitioner must receive this wisdom properly and incessantly amidst the sexual happiness of the fourth joy) for eight dual hours, a day, a month (for eight dual hours a day, for an entire day, or for an entire month),

A yeur, u kulpu, ur u Ihuusund kulpus.

While this is taken in for only a brief moment during a proper initiation, one must, during the main practice, take it in for long durations, such as eight dual hours and so forth. (During a proper reception of initiation, one only enjoys a brief happiness induced by tasting the sexual fluids issued from the guru and the female consort; after this initiation, when one enters the main practice consisting of the yab-yum method, one must take this bliss in for extended periods of time, such as eight dual hours per day. "And so forth" refers to the fact that one must take this bliss in for an entire day, an entire month, an entire year, an entire kalpa, or even as long as one thousand kalpas.)[17]

The innate bliss, innate joy, and so forth highlighted by **Tsongkhapa** in the above passage are all synonyms for sexual pleasure. The various designations of "joy" are established only to differentiate the locations where the sexual pleasure is induced as well as the intensity and duration of the blissful sensations. The purpose of teaching these four joys is to explain to tantric practitioners that each of the different levels of "joy" that they attain corresponds to a different level of "Buddhahood." In addition, this teaching aims to demonstrate that the duration of one's blissful sensations denotes the level of one's valid knowledge. Hence, it is said that one takes in bliss for only a short period of time during a proper third initiation—wisdom initiation—when one tastes the sexual fluids issued from the copulation between the guru and the female consort. However, when one proceeds to the yab-yum practice after the initiation, one must engage in sexual intercourse with a person of the opposite sex for long durations in order to take in the orgasm of sexual pleasure for as long as eight consecutive dual hours consecutively (in ancient times, a day was divided into twelve dual hours, as "the hour" was not established as a timekeeping unit). Those with the capacity to withhold ejaculation and enjoy the orgasm of sexual pleasure long-lastingly and without interruption are regarded as "grand practitioners" with "an extremely high level of valid knowledge," for they are able to comprehend the skills and the blissful contact related to this practice, as well as attain the non-duality of bliss and emptiness and the union of bliss and emptiness for extremely long durations. According to **Tsongkhapa**, it is necessary to confer this third initiation and explain the secret meaning of the yab-yum practice

---

[17]   Ibid., 383-84.

to tantric practitioners, so that they can gain mastery over this yab-yum practice—so that they can take sexual pleasure in long-lastingly by withholding ejaculation perfectly at will.

3.4 The Fourth Initiation

The fourth initiation consists of the first practice cultivated with one's vajra guru after one has completed the third secret initiation—wisdom initiation. This fourth initiation, along with the subsequent yab-yum practice of the non-duality of bliss and emptiness cultivated with one's wife, daughter, mother, aunt, or fellow tantric practitioner of the opposite sex, is categorized as "internal seal." By contrast, the third secret initiation—wisdom initiation—is classified as "external seal," for the disciple is unable to personally practice with a counterpart of the opposite sex and can only generate bliss by tasting the red and the white bodhicitta issued from the guru and the female consort— he does not take in, throughout his body, the bliss in "the non-duality of bliss and emptiness" by "practicing properly" on his own. For this reason, the third initiation—wisdom initiation—is called "external seal," as the bliss of tasting the sexual fluids is induced by an external phenomenon—it is not a self-generated internal phenomenon.

How do tantric disciples obtain "wisdom" when they do not personally get involved in the cultivation of the third initiation? **Tsongkhapa** says:

> With respect to the wisdom of the third initiation, the superior wisdom exists therein (the "supreme wisdom" exists because of this initiation); it is the external seal. "Wisdom" signifies that the non-discriminative mind that arises from it (the term "wisdom" refers to the wisdom generated from the third initiation that does not discriminate the impurity of the nectar—sexual fluid) induces the pure innate joy (induces the pure ultimate bliss consisting of the innate joy), as extensively explained. Based on the innate wisdom manifested by practicing the third initiation, one finally becomes free from all hindrances and attains pervasive purity; this is the fourth initiation. It is also called initiation, as these (these blisses) result from the cleansing of the thought by the taste of the

great bliss. (The innate bliss induced by the sexual union between the guru and the female consort in the maṇḍala of initiation triggers the expulsion of sexual fluid—nectar—thus allowing the disciple to understand, while tasting this fluid, that this is "the taste of the great bliss"; the wisdom of this bliss thus generated can cleanse the disciple's original thought that "the nectar—sexual fluid—is impure.") Therefore, apart from the previously established functions, it allows one to be unimpeded in the path and is established as initiation.[1]

We can conclude from **Tsongkhapa**'s explanations above that one must have received the wisdom initiation before being able to practice the fourth initiation. When the disciple performs sexual intercourse with his guru while receiving the fourth initiation from this guru, he will be taught by the guru in person about the mode of cultivation and realization of the yab-yum method; only then will this disciple be allowed to practice the union of bliss and emptiness set forth in Highest Yoga Tantra with other people. To directly cultivate the yab-yum method with others without having previously entered the maṇḍala of the fourth initiation to receive "onsite" guidance from the guru constitutes a violation of the precept of forbiddance, which is one of the fourteen tantric root infractions. According to the tantric teachings, such a person will definitively fall to the "vajra" hell.

Therefore, one must have received the fourth initiation from the guru before being allowed to "cultivate and realize" the yab-yum method and being able to attain, through the non-duality of bliss and emptiness, the "wisdom" related to the achievement of Buddhahood in this body. Henceforth, one will gain a penetrative understanding of all the tantras and become a vajra guru with veritable valid knowledge, because the fourth initiation is the basis for the actual practice of Highest Yoga Tantra, and because a penetrative understanding of the fourth initiation enables one to comprehend the secret meanings and the actual practices of all the Dharma-gates of Tantric Buddhism. Before receiving a proper

---

[1]   Ibid., 418.

fourth initiation, a disciple must find female consorts who will delight the guru. Next, this disciple must ask the guru to bring forth the bliss consisting of the fourth joy by performing sexual intercourse in the maṇḍala and to bestow the "nectar" endowed with "the flavors of superior bliss" for this disciple to taste. The disciple is then allowed to pick another date to receive the fourth initiation—to cultivate the yab-yum practice with his or her guru for the first time and thereby benefit from the guru's personal onsite guidance. For this reason, **Tsongkhapa asserts** that the fourth initiation is required in order to complete the initiation as well as the practice and realization pertaining to the tantric Dharma-gate that allows for the attainment of Buddhahood in this body:

> With respect to the conferral of the last secret initiation bestowed for the purpose of preaching the sūtras and so forth (with respect to the conferral of the last secret initiation to the disciple in order to enable him to preach all tantric sūtras and so forth), the guru must enter meditative absorption with nine consorts who are aged from twelve to twenty (the guru must copulate with each of the nine female consorts—one of every age from twelve to twenty—and must enter and abide in orgasm simultaneously with each of them) and must confer the initiation by pouring the vajra endowed with the seeds into the disciple's mouth. (The guru must bring forth the great bliss, ejaculate, and inject into the disciple's mouth the blending of the sexual fluids from the guru and the nine consorts that is endowed with the seeds of all ten persons; in other words, he must confer initiation with those seeds—nectar.) Thus, the guru enjoys wondrous joy with one female consort during the former one—the third initiation. (Thus, during the former one—the third initiation—the guru copulates and enjoys wondrous bliss with just one female consort.) During the latter one, he immediately enters meditative absorption with nine consorts (during the latter one—the fourth initiation—he should enter meditative absorption—orgasm—simultaneously with each of nine consorts according to the teachings of the tantric sūtras); it is from the wondrous joy thus generated (it is from the wondrous joy

generated by the guru and each of the female consorts that nectar is obtained; the guru confers the fourth initiation on the disciple with this nectar). What occurs before the fourth initiation: When the bodhicitta abides in the maṇi and does not leak out, the innate bliss (with respect to what is realized before the fourth initiation, only after one has received initiation in this way, one ensures that the semen and the drop abide simultaneously in the glans penis without leaking out; this is just the innate joy) is the conventional fourth initiation (this can only be said to be the fourth initiation of the conventional truth— it is not the fourth initiation of the ultimate truth). In the maṇḍala rituals of other mantras, this is said be to the third initiation. (This type of initiation is said to be merely the third initiation.) If one has just obtained it (if one has just obtained this type of initiation) but has not obtained the last one—the fourth initiation (and has never obtained the fourth initiation, which occurs last)—then one still cannot listen to or preach all the sūtras and so forth with unimpeded understanding (when listening to or preaching the tantric sūtras, one still does not have unimpeded understanding of all their teachings—one cannot truly understand their meanings). If one has received this initiation in the Kālacakra, one still cannot expound all the sūtras (one still cannot explicate all the tantric sūtras) despite being able to listen to them, given that one has not obtained the unsurpassed fourth initiation (given that one has never received the unsurpassed fourth initiation). To be able to preach all the sūtras, one must have obtained the second initiation— vase initiation—the secret initiation, the wisdom initiation, and the fourth initiation. (Only those who have obtained the second, the third, and the fourth initiations are able to teach all the secret meanings in the tantric sūtras.) The rituals found in the other sūtras have never taught [have never taught that one can preach all the sūtras with the obtention of] the first three. [To be able to preach all the sūtras,] one must have obtained the the last one—the fourth initiation—such an assertion is also found in all the other sūtras. The rest is easy to understand.[2]

---

[2]   Ibid., 399-400.

Tsongkhapa further says:

The fourth initiation of the ultimate meaning is also said to be supramundane because it is difficult to understand. I will explain it as follows. As stated in *The Great Commentary [of the Stainless Light] [Da shu 大疏]*:

> The four initiations consisting of laughing, gazing, holding hands, and coupling do not constitute the meaning of reality (the four initiations in which a male and a female practitioner laugh together, gaze into each other's eyes, hold hands, and copulate still do not constitute "the real meaning"). The real meaning here is as follows: If one does not embrace (if the two do not embrace each other or copulate), but only observes what arises from the action seal (if one only observes what arises from the action seal—female consort—and does not personally engage in sexual intercourse), then this is not the non-dual wisdom. The so-called "fourth initiation of the real meaning" or "fourth initiation of the ultimate meaning" here refers to the **non-dual wisdom**. The two items implied in "non-dual" have repeatedly been said to be "**bliss and emptiness**" (in the aforementioned conventional initiation, the two items implied in "non-dual" have repeatedly been said to be "bliss and emptiness"). A sūtra says:
>
> > The non-evolving bliss of nirvāṇa that
> > arises from it ("the non-evolving bliss of
> > nirvāṇa" that arises from the yab-yum
> > copulation),
> > Is the fourth, which is innate and
> > immutable (it is only by realizing the
> > uninterrupted and immutable wondrous bliss
> > by withholding ejaculation long-lastingly
> > during the motion of bliss and emptiness that
> > one can be said to have achieved the fourth
> > initiation).
>
> This means that the immutable bliss is called the fourth (the statement of this tantric scripture signifies that realizing the immutable wondrous bliss amidst the

non-duality of bliss and emptiness constitutes the true meaning of the fourth initiation). Therefore, not all blisses are valid (therefore, one cannot be said to have achieved the fourth initiation with the realization of just any kind of blissful contact in the yab-yum practice); it has to be a bliss that is equal to or above the branches of samādhi (one must attain the meditative absorption of samādhi by relying on the guru's guidance—the guru and the disciple must simultaneously enter and abide in the orgasm of the fourth joy—and directly observe "the non-duality of bliss and emptiness"; it is only by fully realizing a bliss equal to or above the seven branches of meritorious quality in this samādhi that one can be said to be fully endowed with the ultimate meaning of the fourth initiation).[3]

Why does **Tsongkhapa** advocate the necessity to confer the fourth initiation after the performance of the third initiation? The reasons are as follows: Although the disciple has completed the learning related to the third initiation, during which the guru has explained the principle of the yab-yum practice, the guru is worried that the disciple has not fully grasped the theory of Highest Yoga Tantra as well as the various skillful expedients related to the nuts and bolts of its actual practice. In addition, the blissful contact taken in by the disciple during the third initiation is minimal compared to the great bliss that can be taken in during the fourth initiation—those two blisses are indeed drastically different.

Furthermore, the disciple does not have the opportunity to take in the non-duality of bliss and emptiness during the third initiation—hence the necessity to confer the fourth initiation. Indeed, the guru will, during the fourth initiation, provide detailed explanations to the disciple while copulating with nine female consorts; he will then bestow those nine consorts on the disciple so that the disciple can personally practice with them under the guidance of the guru beside him. This will enable the disciple to

---

[3]   Ibid., 399-400.

take in the "supreme bliss" of the fourth joy while practicing with those nine consorts. Therefore, it is necessary to further perform the fourth initiation, so that the disciple can personally take part in the co-practice of this initiation by his vajra guru and the female consorts and subsequently engage in the practice of the fourth joy with those consorts himself. While the disciple experiences this method with the nine consorts, he will ask the guru to provide onsite guidance, i.e. thorough and precise explanations that will allow the disciple to comprehend all the details. For this reason, the third and the fourth initiations are said to be different. **Tsongkhapa** thus says:

> If the innate wisdom of the third initiation was established as the realization of reality then it would have no difference whatsoever from the innate wisdom of the indivisible bliss and emptiness attained in the fourth initiation. Those who do not realize it stand in contradiction with the statements in many treatises: "This initiation is conferred in order to demonstrate the meaning of reality to the disciple through a supreme expedient," and "the meaning expressed through the practice of the third initiation allows for the realization of reality." . . . One who receives initiation (the third initiation) only through the wisdom seal also needs to clearly visualize that oneself and the female consort become a father and a mother of desire-realm heavens, hold the divine pride, and so forth; one must thoroughly understand that the father and the mother enter meditative absorption and generate bodhicitta, which then moves into the maṇi (one must completely understand that the semen and the sexual fluid generated by the male and the female when they attain orgasm move into the glans penis) and induces bliss (the great bliss). Next, one must cause the disciple to recall the correct view and to abide in it and clearly inform him about the initiation (Next, one must cause the disciple to recall the correct view of the non-duality of bliss and emptiness and to abide in the great bliss; furthermore, one must, through these teachings, cause him to understand the true meaning of the secret initiation). The innate one of the Fruition Ground can be brought forth through the practice of the innate wisdom

expounded in this initiation. Therefore, one must realize the innate one of the real meaning during the initiation. (Therefore, one must realize the innate bliss and the innate wisdom of the real meaning during the secret initiation.)[4]

In tantric traditions other than the Gelug School, one must have realized the real meaning of the fourth initiation before being able to attain the innate wisdom of the Fruition Ground (the tantric Buddhahood). Therefore, it is necessary for the guru, during the process in which he practices with a disciple of the opposite sex, to provide comprehensive explanations so as to help this disciple gain a full understanding of this method. In addition, the guru must use his practice with the disciple as an opportunity to thoroughly educate this disciple about the innate wisdom of indivisible bliss and emptiness attained during the fourth initiation, to give him the tips that can prolong the blissful sensation experienced during this initiation, and to teach him the various expedients related to the deed-contemplation performed during this initiation. Therefore, it is indispensable for the guru and the disciple to practice together during the fourth initiation.

As for **Tsongkhapa** of the Gelug School, the previous citations have shown that he advocates the necessity to provide the guru with nine female consorts—one of every age from twelve to twenty—for sexual intercourse, so as to obtain the "nectar" with the "taste of the great bliss" that will be used for the fourth initiation. According to Tsongkhapa, the guru must then bestow all or some of the female consorts on the disciple, so that the disciple can, upon receiving the fourth initiation, personally practice with them under the guru's on-site guidance. The disciple will then be able to realize the innate wisdom of "the non-duality of bliss and emptiness" and thereby perfect the "meritorious quality" of the fourth initiation. He will, through this initiation, "achieve" the fruitions pertaining to the Dharma-kings of the Sixth Ground

---

[4]   Tsongkhapa, *Mizong daocidi guang lun* 密宗道次第廣論, 385-89. Translated into English from Chinese.

through to the Tenth Ground. These are the discrepancies between **Tsongkhapa's** assertions and the teachings of the other three major traditions.

After this fourth initiation of "unsurpassed wisdom," if one practices numerous times with a female vajra guru or with other female consorts—Buddha-mothers (tantric female practitioners should practice with male gurus or other male practitioners, who are also known as male consorts)—then one's cultivation no longer falls within the scope of initiations; instead, it pertains to the practice of Highest Yoga Tantra, which will be separately illustrated in Chapter 9.

The cultivation path of the fourth initiation conferred by the gurus comprises, in brief, three methods—the vajra-wave path of the body, the vajra-wave path of the speech, and the vajra-wave path of the mind. They correspond to the onsite teaching of the deeds related to the body, the speech, and the mind during the yab-yum practice:

> **The vajra-wave path of the body:** First, purify the "nine branches related to the preparatory practice of tranquil reflection" and so forth of the body and so forth; in addition, one must arouse and shake the lower wind through the seven preparatory practices of wind yoga such as vitality, exertion and so forth (arouse the sexual organ's winds and cause them to be stable and firm). With respect to the wave of the body (the drawing and thrusting motion of the body and the inducement of its bliss), practice the fusion of the winds (visualize that the winds in your central channel and the winds in the female consort's central channel fuse inside her sexual organ and so forth). . . . **The wave path of the speech:** Isolate yourself in a silent place, sit in the full-lotus position or an upright posture (sit in an embracing and copulating position, with the body upright), lower your head like in a prostration in order to steer the winds smoothly, and exhale the "*Ching hum* [琴吽]" sounds and so forth. The former syllable "*ji* [寂]" must be steered quietly, whereas the latter syllable "*fen* [忿]" must be steered loudly, with the throat releasing the winds so that

the sounds can be heard nearby, far away, and so forth. In the same way, shake the body through the steering of the speech, shake the channel through the shaking of the body, and shake the bodhicitta through the shaking of the channel, thereby inducing bliss. By following the natural direction of the winds and steering them upward, you will obtain a strong and healthy body as well as a radiant complexion and you will gain control over the descending winds (the words "gain control" mean that you will not ejaculate easily). **The wave path of the mind:** This is also a path of purification dependent on an actual seal or a wisdom seal (this is also a path of purification dependent on an actual female consort or a visualized female consort), which consists of three methods: the purification of the continuum of method, the purification of the continuum of wisdom, and the individual purification of the continuums of method and wisdom. With respect to the use of an actual seal (if one practices with a real female or male consort instead of a visualized one), each must perform the deeds individually and simultaneously (during sexual union, each must individually perform visualization as well as various deeds such as generating sexual bliss, moving the winds in the channel, and so forth) and then perform, with the other party, the union of method and wisdom (and then perform, with the other party, the union of the male embodiment of method and of the female embodiment of wisdom, whereby the two simultaneously enter meditative absorption—orgasm). With respect to wisdom (if the female acts as the main entity), then the deeds are performed by the method (then the male must perform various expedient deeds that will delight the female).

1. The purification of the continuum of method: Perform the three equanimities—body, speech, and so forth—just like in the third initiation. Furthermore, one must abide in the instant union of method (the male's semen) and wisdom (the female's sexual fluid). The purified portions of the essential constituents (seeds) that course within the father and the mother reach the supreme pistils (the cervix and glans penis) at the lower end of the central channel; they interconnect like a mountain and a mouth (the tip of the pestle at the lower

end of the male's central channel and the cervix at the lower end of the female's central channel interconnect) and like waters that converge in a pond (the fusion of the ejaculated semen and the female's sexual fluid represents the union of the red and the white bodhicitta, which is similar to the convergence of two kinds of water in a pond). (At this moment, visualize that) the white-colored drops, which are similar to mustard seeds, transform into rays of light that travel through the right channel to the navel cakra. At the navel cakra, the light is like a sun that comes up at dawn, rises slowly, becomes extremely bright, and then illuminates all places; it is also like lungs that expand with air. Again the rays of light travel through the right channel; observe that it is also endowed with three qualities at the heart cakra. Again they travel through the channel to the throat cakra, where they are also endowed with three qualities. Furthermore, they travel through the channel to the right ear, where they radiate and exit. A deity's mandala then appears amidst the light and performs the four initiations on the continuums of all sentient beings, transforming these sentient beings into deities. These sentient beings' deities and the light that they radiate blend into the essence of nectar, which abides at the central channel's opening outside the crown's Brahmā aperture. Again, be mindful that the crown cakra is endowed with three qualities. The light [of the nectar], which is red, descends to the throat cakra and possesses the brilliance of a thousand suns. Again it descends to the heart cakra, transforming your continuum into experimented signs of five bodies, while the light becomes five-colored. Given that the essential constituents aggregate easily (given that the seeds—semen and sexual fluid—are easy to collect and aggregate easily) below the navel cakra, the path of the purified channel emerges from the navel and abides in the form of a drop in the Buddha-mother's lotus palace, as previously mentioned (in the female consort's uterus, as previously mentioned). The wave solid (the purified portion that has taken shape from the drop) that is the apprehended-object at the right will gather perfectly in the right channel; you will then attain mastery over the breath of exertion. This will be the "gate to liberation consisting of emptiness," **which is** (the realization of) **the first fruit.** If the drop also moves through the left channel, then the wave solid that is the apprehending-subject will gather perfectly in the left channel; you will then attain mastery over the breath of vitality. This will be the "gate to liberation consisting of wishlessness," **which is** (the realization of) **the second fruit.** If the drop moves through the central channel, then the wave solid that is the apprehending-subject and the apprehended-object will purify the central channel; you will then attain mastery over the breath of abiding; this is the "gate to liberation consisting of signlessness," **which is** (the realization of) **the third fruit.**

2. The purification of the continuum of wisdom: You should understand, in the same fashion, the continuum of wisdom in relation to the drop. However, the rays of light do not radiate outward after reaching both ears through the left and right channels. You are free to choose whether you want to allow the light to move through the central channel and radiate outward from the Brahmā aperture at the crown cakra before you retract it. You should attain mastery over the three wave solids, the three purifications of channels, and the three deeds consisting of drawing-in, retaining, and releasing; **understand them along with the three gates to liberation as previously mentioned.**

3. The individual purification of the continuums of method and wisdom: Furthermore, in order to individually purify the continuums of method and wisdom, cause the purified portion of the essential constituent in the father's central channel to move with a luminous appearance (the purified portion of the seeds—semen—which was drawn upward during orgasm and has entered the central channel, ascends with a luminous appearance) and dissolves into the turban above the crown. The same applies to the mother (the female must engage in the same practice and realization).

Both the father and the mother should only be mindful of the spontaneous achievement of the five bodies. With respect to the drop, the purification of the continuum of method requires three instants, the purification of the continuum of wisdom requires three instants, and the individual purification requires one instant, which add up to a total of seven instants. Among these, it is not necessary to draw in and retain the winds, nor is it necessary to practice the ascertainment of the four seats. Also, the vajra is the bliss adorned with non-discrimination; the wave is the garland chain of discrimination; and the solid is the property of dissolving into the vajra non-discrimination. All sensations that it generates are not definite; however, it can easily keep whatever it generates.[5]

The methods cited above are those of the Sakya School.

According to the Kagyu School, the fourth initiation is also known as the ultimate initiation. Indeed, those who receive the secret wisdom initiation pertaining to the fourth initiation—those who cultivate the yab-yum practice with a guru of the opposite sex for the first time—can attain the Path of Vision and enter the First Ground:

Now you are about to attain the Path of Vision pertaining to the second term of asaṃkhya kalpas! How are you able to **attain the Path of Vision** so rapidly? Other people achieve it only during the second term of asaṃkhya kalpas, whereas you are able to attain it right away. Why? It is all because of the guru. The initiations that he performs are supreme; moreover, he has himself attained the Path of Vision and has steered Bodhisattvas who have attained the Path of Vision into your body. By steering into your body all the Bodhisattvas who have practiced for three great terms of asaṃkhya kalpas, a thousand great terms of asaṃkhya kalpas, a hundred great terms of asaṃkhya kalpas, and an inexpressibly large number

---

[5]   Virūpa, *Daoguo* 道果, 296. Translated into English from Chinese.

of asaṃkhya kalpas, he has caused your wisdom to grow thousands of times, and even tens of thousands of times, which allows you to attain the Path of Vision easily. Meanwhile, the so-called ultimate initiation, the fourth initiation, involves the attainment of the Path of Vision. In other words, **the obtention of the ultimate initiation denotes the attainment of the Path of Vision**, for the term "ultimate" in "ultimate initiation" refers to the final view and knowledge of Buddhahood at the final stage. The Dharma manifested from the wisdom of unsurpassed perfect enlightenment is said to be "ultimate"; hence, **the fourth initiation is the ultimate initiation.**[6]

After hearing from their gurus that the reception of the fourth initiation allows one to immediately obtain the meritorious quality associated with the attainment of the Path of Vision, and given that, according to the tantric teachings, one becomes a **Bodhisattva of the First Ground** by attaining the stage of the Path of Vision, many tantric practitioners have received the fourth initiation and cultivated the yab-yum method with a guru of the opposite sex for the first time. Thinking that they have become Bodhisattvas of the First Ground after engaging in the yab-yum method, they disparage the valid knowledges achieved by Exoteric Buddhist followers by branding them as elementary—such a view is based on the fact that the realization of the eighth consciousness by those Exoteric Buddhist followers only denotes their attainment of the stage of the Seventh Abiding. However, those tantric practitioners are not aware that **the attainment of the Path of Vision** in the fourth initiation of Tantric Buddhism is actually based on their gurus' erroneous thinking. From the perspective of the true Buddha Dharma, those gurus are common people with an eternalist view who have not even entered the stage of the Path of Vision

---

[6]   Yogi C. M. Chen (Chen Chien-ming 陳健民), *Qugongzhai quanji* 曲肱齋全集 *[The Complete Works of Yogi Chen]*, vol. 1-5, ed. Xu Qinying 徐芹庭 (Taipei: Puxianwang rulai fojiaohui 普賢王如來佛教會, 1991), vol. 1, 175-76. Translated into English from Chinese.

pertaining to the Seventh Abiding in Exoteric Buddhism.

Furthermore, the attainment of the Path of Vision consists of realizing the eighth consciousness (ālaya), which only corresponds to the stage of the Seventh Abiding. A Bodhisattva who has achieved this level must further practice and learn the knowledge-of-specific-aspects and the knowledge-of-all-aspects; they must fully understand the five doctrines, the three natures, the seven foremost meanings, the natures of the seven properties, and the two types of no-self, all of which belong to the mind-kings consisting of the eight consciousnesses, thereby bringing forth the wisdom of the acquiescence to the non-arising of dharmas, the possession of which is a feature of the mind that enters the First Ground. In addition, this Bodhisattva must forever subdue his dispositional hindrances like an arhat. He must also bravely make the ten inexhaustible vows and never regress from them—he must, in order to protect the true Dharma, be able to fearlessly refute all non-Buddhist doctrines without concern for his fame and benefits. He must bring forth his disposition of the path[7] by thus eliminating his non-exalted nature. Furthermore, he must, based on the aforementioned wisdom of the acquiescence to the non-arising of dharmas, have unimpeded penetrating understanding of the meaning of prajñā related to the Path of Vision. Only then will he able to enter the First Ground—he cannot be established as a Bodhisattva of the First Ground (the stage of unimpeded penetrating understanding) upon attaining the Path of Vision.

Why do I assert that the reception of the fourth initiation of Tantric Buddhism does not enable one to truly attain the Path of Vision? The reason is as follows: Although Tantric Buddhists claim that the fourth initiation is the ultimate initiation that enables one to attain the Path of Vision, it in fact falls within the sphere of the conscious mind set forth in the non-Buddhist view of eternalism and therefore does not allow for the attainment of the Path of Vision:

---

[7] Disposition of the path: C. *daozhongxing* 道種性.

One should, upon obtaining the ultimate initiation, be able to see the clear entity. At least one should see its contours, meaning that although you cannot see a cloudless sunny sky, you suddenly experience an interruption of thoughts; after this interruption, you suddenly feel the void of a sense of self, vastness, and looseness, as if your body was weightless—as if you had thrown away your weight or scrapped a heavy burden.[8]

The above statements about attaining the Path of Vision and becoming a Bodhisattva of the First Ground still fall within the states of obtention pertaining to the mental consciousness (mind of feeling and cognition). They do not touch upon the realization of the wisdom of prajñā set forth in Buddhism because, according to them, one attains the Path of Vision by experiencing the state in which one's thoughts are interrupted and by abiding, after this interruption of thoughts, in a state of serenity free from all preoccupations.

Not only do the gurus from the Nyingma, Kagyu, and Sakya schools propagate the above doctrines, but **Tsongkhapa** of the Gelug School is an even bigger exponent thereof. They all consider the state in which the mental consciousness experiences sexual pleasure to be the main entity of the attainment of the Path of Vision in Tantric Buddhism. Despite having thus failed to realize the Middle Way nature, the emptiness-nature, the nirvāṇic nature, the pure nature, and the permanent nature of the mind consisting of the eighth consciousness, they often teach about the attainment of the Path of Vision in the Mahāyāna Buddha Dharma and claim to have achieved the meritorious quality pertaining to the Bodhisattvas of the First Ground. In fact, such meritorious quality of the "First Ground" is merely an invention of Tantric Buddhists; such valid knowledge of the "First Ground" is merely validated by Tantric Buddhists themselves; and such wisdom of the "First

---

[8]   Yogi C. M. Chen (Chen Chien-ming 陳健民), *Qugongzhai quanji* 曲肱齋全集 *[The Complete Works of Yogi Chen]*, vol. 1-5, ed. Xu Qinying 徐芹庭 (Taipei: Puxianwang rulai fojiaohui 普賢王如來佛教會, 1991), vol. 1, 266. Translated into English from Chinese.

Ground" is merely proclaimed by Tantric Buddhists themselves. They have absolutely nothing to do with the meritorious quality as well as the valid knowledge, the wisdom, and so forth of the First Ground set forth in Exoteric Buddhism. Therefore, those gurus have, by making those assertions, committed the sin of grievous false speech.

Having all failed to realize the eighth consciousness, those tantric "Bodhisattvas of the First Ground" have not even attained the knowledge-of-general-aspect related to this consciousness and have therefore not been able to enter the stage of the Seventh Abiding, which corresponds to the initial stage of the Path of Vision in Mahāyāna Buddhism; how then could they have obtained the wisdom pertaining to the Bodhisattvas of the First Ground in Buddhism? Furthermore, "the wisdom of the Path of Vision" that they preach consists entirely of non-Buddhist erroneous views and is therefore wholly unrelated to the wisdom of prajñā found in the Buddha Dharma; how then could such wisdom be said to be the wisdom of the First Ground? Those tantric practitioners have, by making those assertions, all committed the sin of grievous false speech.

Tantric Buddhists believe that one becomes a Bodhisattva of the exalted stage after one has received the fourth initiation, cultivated the yab-yum method with a guru of the opposite sex, benefited from the guru's personal guidance, and experienced the state of the union of bliss and emptiness. According to them, the ground of vision achieved by this Bodhisattva allows him to understand the benefits of the body, the benefits of the mind, and the benefits of both the body and the mind. The benefits of the body consist of four fruits, namely the fruit of similar species,[9] the fruit of ripening,[10] the fruit produced by human effort,[11] and the fruit of undefilement.[12] The benefits of the mind are found at the

---

[9]   Fruit of similar species: S. *niṣyandaphala;* C. *dengliuguo* 等流果.
[10]   Fruit of ripening: S. *vipākaphala;* C. *yisoguo* 異熟果.
[11]   Fruit produced by human effort: S. *puruṣakāraphala;* C. *shiyongguo* 士用果.
[12]   Fruit of undefilement: C. *wuguoguo* 無垢果.

navel cakra, the heart cakra, the throat cakra, and the crown cakra. Furthermore, it is said:

> "Similar species" vanquishes white hair,
> "Ripening" grants strength,
> "That which is produced by human efforts" causes increase,
> "Undefilement" brings immortality.[13]

Not only do such assertions differ drastically from the true Buddhist Dharma, they have also misconstrued, misused, misassociated, and misallocated the terminology related to the states of Vijñaptimātratā in the knowledge-of-all-aspects, causing tantric practitioners to harbor serious misunderstandings about the Buddhist doctrines and to have fragmented knowledge and understanding as well as extensive misapprehension about the Buddha Dharma. Exoteric Buddhist practitioners also believe and accept those statements, as they are unaware of their fallacy; have fallen into the same predicament, they will suffer dire consequences. In fact, the "Buddha Dharma" preached by the ancient and contemporary tantric gurus is not the Buddha Dharma, but some "tantric Buddha Dharma" turned into a non-Buddhist philosophy and based on the gurus' own interpretations. All such false views will be explained and rectified in Chapter 14.

The purpose of the aforementioned tantric initiation is to enable the practitioner to personally realize the vast bliss and emptiness—to obtain the meritorious quality associated with Virtual Enlightenment[14] as well as the rewards consisting of the benefits of the body, the benefits of the mind, and the benefits of both the body and the mind, which will allow the practitioner to achieve a valid knowledge "exceeding" that of Buddha Śākyamuni. For this reason, those tantric gurus claim that the level of their fruition corresponds to half of the thirteenth ground (the "lower half" of the tantric Buddha ground)—according to them, they have

---

[13] Virūpa, *Daoguo* 道果, 301-303. Translated into English based on Stearns, Cyrus (trans. and ed.), *Taking the Result as the Path: Core Teachings of the Sakya Path with the Result Tradition* (Boston: Wisdom Publications, 2006), 42.

[14] Virtual Enlightenment: C. *dengjue* 等覺.

achieved the Buddhahood of the reward body by "realizing the vast bliss and emptiness and witnessing, amidst the bliss and emptiness of all saṃsāra and nirvāṇa, the absence of apprehension and abandonment as well as elimination and realization" (see *Path with the Result [Daoguo]* pp. 301-303). In fact, these statements are by no means the Buddha Dharma, for such views remain within the ground with which the mental consciousness connects—they have never entered the ground with which the mental faculty or the tathāgatagarbha connects and are related to the knowledge and concepts of common people and non-Buddhists. These fallacies will be explained and rectified in Chapter 14.

Such tantric "sages of Sublime Enlightenment"[15] are required to practice the four yogas during death: "the yoga of good rebirth, the yoga of body transference, the yoga of rebirth in another continent, and the yoga of powa—the yoga of transference of consciousness at death—in the path of Mahāmudrā" (see *Path with the Result [Daoguo]* pp. 304-312). These mistaken views will be addressed later.

The first initiation conferred during this fourth initiation is called ultimate initiation, as it allows practitioners to realize the "reality-suchness of the Buddha Ground":

> Furthermore, the so-called wisdom in the third initiation is, from the perspective of "using wisdom female consorts," the wisdom of the great bliss. The fourth initiation can be called ultimate initiation only if one understands that **the Dharma body is the non-arising and selfless emptiness-nature and if one cultivates the non-duality of bliss and emptiness**; such is the **reality-suchness**. Therefore, the last precept of the fourteen root infractions in Tantric Buddhism, which prohibits practitioners from slandering "female embodiments of wisdom," does not directly address the wisdom of the reality-suchness but relates to the nine postures of female

---

[15]   Sublime Enlightenment: C. *miaojiao* 妙覺.

consorts enjoying the great bliss.[16]

As indicated in the above passage, the reason why the third initiation is called secret wisdom initiation is because the female consort's vulva enables practitioners to realize the "wisdom" of the yab-yum practice. Hence, the third initiation, which is based on the female consort as its main entity, is known as the wisdom initiation. However, the third initiation merely focuses on the innate great bliss brought forth from the practice between the guru and the female consorts, on inducing the disciple's bliss by causing him to taste the red and the white bodhicitta issued from the guru and the female consort (the blending of the guru's semen and the consort's sexual fluid), and on explaining the key points about the cultivation and realization related to the yab-yum method. Given that the disciple does not personally engage in this practice, his understandings of this method and the bliss induced in him are both limited (indeed, his bliss is only triggered through tasting). As a result, he can neither truly take in the property of the non-duality of bliss and emptiness nor realize "the mind consisting of the reality-suchness of the Buddha Ground"; hence, this initiation still cannot be regarded as ultimate. It is only during the fourth initiation that he has the opportunity to personally practice with a guru of the opposite sex and to benefit from this guru's comprehensive guidance and explanations while he personally experiences this method. Only then will he, during the process in which he practices with a person of the opposite sex, be able to realize the "mind consisting of the reality-suchness of the Buddha Ground" and experience the meaning of the non-duality of bliss and emptiness through the inducement of bliss throughout his body.

Furthermore, both the woman and the vulva embody wisdom, because a woman's vulva enables practitioners to realize the

---

16   Yogi C. M. Chen (Chen Chien-ming 陳健民), *Qugongzhai quanji* 曲肱齋全集 [*The Complete Works of Yogi Chen*], vol. 1-5, ed. Xu Qinying 徐芹庭 (Taipei: Puxianwang rulai fojiaohui 普賢王如來佛教會, 1991), vol. 3, 109. Translated into English from Chinese.

Buddha's wisdom consisting of the non-duality of bliss and emptiness. Therefore, no one is allowed to deprecate the teaching that the female embodies wisdom. It is even said that this wisdom refers to the nine postures of female consorts enjoying the great bliss. Anyone who understands these contents is a wise person who has realized the "prajñā of bodhi."

According to tantric practitioners, this fourth initiation is the cause that enables them to realize the fourth joy. Furthermore, they equate the attainment of this state with the realization of the "reality-suchness of the reward body Buddha." However, the "reality-suchness" thus attained differs completely from the "reality-suchness" in "the eighth consciousness of the Buddha Ground is the reality-suchness" set forth by the World-Honored One in the exoteric sūtras. Based on the valid knowledge achieved through such "cultivation and realization," those tantric followers frequently claim to have realized the "reality-suchness of the Buddha Ground." At the same time, they deride the Exoteric Buddhist Bodhisattvas' cultivation and realization of the eighth consciousness (ālaya) and maturational consciousness by claiming that they pertain to the Causal Ground and that therefore the valid knowledge of realization achieved by those Bodhisattvas are nothing but elementary.

Just like unwise persons who arrogantly regard their bicycles as Porsche sports cars and therefore ridicule others' Harley motorcycles, which in fact they have never seen before, those tantric gurus, who misapprehend the attainment of the state of the fourth joy consisting of sexual pleasure in their schools as the "reality-suchness of the Buddha Ground" and who simply do not comprehend and have not realized the eighth consciousness, also ridicule Exoteric Buddhist Bodhisattvas by asserting that those Bodhisattvas' valid knowledge, which consists of realizing the eighth consciousness (ālaya) and the maturational consciousness, are elementary and that they are unable to realize the "reality-suchness of the Buddha Ground." The behavior of those gurus is as foolish as that of those unwise fools. Moreover, the unwise tantric practitioners who worship and adhere to those gurus with full obeisance and complete faith are even worse: They can indeed be said to be the most foolish persons in the world.

Based on these mistaken knowledge and views, ancient and contemporary tantric gurus have, beyond the sūtras preached by the Buddha, established the mind of feeling and cognition amidst the fourth joy consisting of sexual pleasure as the reality-suchness of the Buddha Ground. Consequently, they vehemently negate the eighth consciousness (ālaya) by denying its existence. As a result, the bodhi of prajñā that they practice and realize is by no means the Buddha Dharma, as it is completely different from the Buddha's teachings in the sūtras of the Three Vehicles. While the wise will find these tantric doctrines preposterous upon hearing them, those unwise tantric followers surprisingly adhere to them with unwavering faith and even uphold them with full devotion. It is just incredible how stubborn the habitual seeds issued from the long process of seed-transformation in past lifetimes due to wrong views can be!

3.5 The Internal Initiation

With respect to the internal initiation, Guru Padmasambhava says:

You can expand the drops through the actualization of an action seal. You should employ a sixteen-year-old female[1] with a thick lotus (vulva) and fat breasts; her waist must be so slim as to bring irresistible bliss to the males. Cause the body of your deity and that of the other's deity to appear clearly. A syllable can be seen in each of the three places; the red syllable *hri(h)* [啥] abides on the throne of the lotus moon. (After starting the co-practice, you should visualize that) a white syllable *ham* [杭] faces downward like mercury at the encephalon and flesh beneath the fontanelle at your crown; this syllable is surrounded by sixteen drops that are similar to mustard seeds. During the union between the Buddha-father Guru Vajradhara and the Buddha-mother (when the visualized guru deity and the female consort engage in sexual intercourse and bring forth the state of the union of bliss and emptiness), the red and the white nectar flows down from the top of the lotus sun located at the turban above your crown into your crown aperture (into the practitioner's crown). The inverted syllable *ham* becomes distinctive, which enhances the clear light of the red and the white [bodhicitta]. The red and the white [bodhicitta] fill up the sixteen drops, which descend to the throat and even to the heart. The eight drops that hold life abide therein, while the remaining eight drops descend to the navel. Among these eight, the four that subsist therein are the ones that hold life; the remaining four descend to the secret place. The two drops that subsist therein are the ones that hold life; the last two descend to the tip of the pestle and fuse with the green yellow syllable *phat* [怕] that craves for the self-arisen liberation. At this moment, the central

---

[1]   The use of underage girls in the yab-yum method is one of the most appalling and illegal practices of Tibetan Tantric Buddhism. No true Buddhist teaching condones such sexual exploitation of underage women.

channel within the body is filled up with drops; this is the profound method of the union on which the retention of the wind depends—the key to the vast bliss of the entire body. The deity who secretly cultivates the channel and the essential constituent (the central channel and the seeds) with Vajravārāhī (the female consort) simultaneously engages in the union (this also applies to yourself and the female consort, who must practice the union simultaneously with the visualized guru deity and the female consort); he thus practices without interruption until dawn (from night until dawn). He will grow in power and his sexual organ will become conspicuous; his channel and essential constituent will function in an orderly manner. Such is the main instruction. In front of (the female consort) endowed with the proper characteristics, empower your and the other's secret places (empower your and the female consort's sexual organs) and finally (perform) various deeds of greed (greed for sexual activity) through the union of the two sexual organs (through the union with the female consort's sexual organ) without the thought of common ordinary persons (without thinking that yourself and the female consort are common ordinary persons). (During the main practice,) you should take various actions to relax your body and mind and abide in the inherent purity free of conditions; this is a true teaching similar to plugging the water outlets in a pool. When it is in motion (when the mind is in motion and one is about to ejaculate), the novice should hold back upon the arising of bliss (he should hold back and remain motionless upon the arising of the blissful contact) and then move based on the knowing how much bliss he can take in (he should be well aware of the level of blissful contact that he can endure and move accordingly); when the bliss arises, it is essential that he (stops all his activities and) becomes motionless and relaxes his mind. He should apply the method of the tortoise: When the water of the pond is cold, the tortoise slowly moves towards the edge of the pond; when the sunshine is too hot, it slowly moves toward the center of the pond. This is the superior quintessential instruction. The expedient method: If your movement is too brutal, then it cannot be reverted, like a stone falling off from a cliff. You should practice according to the above metaphor: [the image of] the deity clearly appears in your body; keep your mind relaxed and without any attachment; it is essential to abide in the inherent purity. Four joys arise during the descending; another four joys arise during the ascending; and another four joys arise during the union. The descending of the sixteen drops from the crown to the throat constitutes the joy; it is the vase initiation, the unimpeded penetrating understanding of the union of the drops. The descending of the drops from the throat to the heart constitutes the supreme joy; it is the secret initiation, the unimpeded penetrating understanding of the union of emptiness and bliss. The descending of the drops to the navel constitutes the joy of absence; it is the unimpeded penetrating understanding of the third initiation, the abandonment of the attachment to joy, the elimination of the discrimination of the two attachments, the empty form (the fleshless form body of the visualized deity) akin to the cloudless sunny sky, and the manifestation of the Dharma body (when the mind of feeling and cognition remains immovable during the union of emptiness and bliss, it is the manifestation of the Dharma body). (The descending of the drops) to the secret place (while one enjoys the great bliss permanently without ejaculating) constitutes the innate joy; it is the fourth initiation, the unimpeded penetrating understanding of the innate wisdom of emptiness and bliss. Those of superior faculty can recognize the intrinsic entity of the Dharma body; if they can abide therein, then they will naturally possess all the functions of drawing-up and dispersal. Those of mid-level faculty should expand their abdomen with wind, be equipped with the body essentials, and stare at the syllable *ham* at their crown. At this moment, the purified portion [of the drops] can be reverted. Subsequently, they should, through the goat-shaking method, cause [a violent shaking motion] to pervade their entire body, thereby elevating [this bliss] into the four joys. The drops should be withheld at the tip of pestle without being leaked. (They should take in the great bliss by withholding the semen at the glans penis for a long duration and ensure that this great bliss does not induce ejaculation.) The drops ascend to the junction of the three channels where syllable *ah* can be found; this syllable is the prajñā Buddha-mother of the great bliss. These drops gather the first type of empty form, which is similar to a cloudless sunny sky; this allows you to gain unimpeded penetrating understanding of the view of supreme insight and **enter the First Ground by attaining the Mahāyāna Path of Vision**. At this moment, the knot at the central channel unravels, and **the ascending of the drops from this place to the navel marks the achievements of the Second Ground and the Third Ground respectively**. The meritorious quality associated with these achievements consists of the endowment of the pure and correct view, as asserted in the tantras. When the drops fill up the navel cakra, the sounds of the father and the mother abide on the navel; this allows you to comprehend the Buddha's twelve teachings without obstruction. Below the navel, the meritorious quality consists of the full endowment of the lotus lineage. Subsequently, the drops ascend to the heart, filling you with bliss; the channel at the heart opens and the wisdom of the Dharma body increases significantly. The clear lights, inner and outer alike, manifest the channels and essential constituents of the body, just as the four limbs have the ability to manifest the four continents. You become free from the practicing subject and the practiced object and **gain unimpeded penetrating understanding of the wisdom of the path. Afterward, the drops ascend to the throat and unlock the channel; this allows you to attain the achievement of the reward body,** gain mastery over all the Buddha's teachings and argumentations, and obtain unimpeded penetrating understanding of all the different languages. **The drops finally ascend to the great bliss cakra at the crown;** this allows you to directly realize the clear light of the Path of No More Learning, reach the lotus world, instantly perfect the Path to the Grounds, and **gain unimpeded penetrating understanding of the knowledge-of-the-aspects-of-paths and the views of the Ten Grounds. At this stage, the drops fill up the channel stretching from this place to the turban, causing the thirty-two knots of the central channel to unravel. Thereupon, the meritorious quality of elimination and realization are instantly perfected; this allows you to attain the primordial **stage of Samantabhadra Raja Tathāgata and directly realize the unsurpassed wisdom of the Sixteenth Ground.** The four joys that arise during the descending of the drops constitute the intensive accumulation of resources in all mundane paths. The ascending of the drops corresponds to the supramundane path; this allows you to become a Buddha in a single lifetime. It is essential to practice this profound path of females with concentrated diligence; you must, without fooling yourself, be genuinely and fully equipped with antidote, pure view, and diligence. To lose the bodhicitta while performing on a female (to lose the white bodhicitta—semen—while performing this yab-yum method on a female's body) constitutes a violation of the Precepts of Other-Liberation. To crave for one's bliss (if one only pursues one's own bliss and enjoyment without being mindful of whether the female has simultaneously reached orgasm) constitutes a violation of the Precepts of Bodhisattvas. To exterminate the spiritual life of all deities and sky-travelers constitutes a violation of the root precepts of Tantric Buddhism. Such persons will not gain any power from reciting mantras, will be abandoned by the deities and all sky-travelers, will not achieve their deeds, will wreck their efforts to protect the Dharma due to their own defilements, and will not succeed in any activities; therefore, you should not lose any drops (you should protect your semen from being lost). Any fellow practitioner who violates the precept must be expelled. My son! If you aspire to practice this tantric method, you should take loving care of your drops (semen) in the way that you would protect the Buddha's eyes. You should know how to generate the four joys in the right sequence. First, abide equally with the action seal (at the beginning, you should abide equally in orgasm with the female consort). (Next,) the drops descend from the crown to the throat, causing the bodily bliss to arise. Abandon the two attachments through the wisdom of joy (based on this great bliss, abandon the attachment to the self of persons and the attachment to self of phenomena), thus conforming to the view of the Two Vehicles (thus conforming to the ground of vision related to the Path to Liberation cultivated in the Two Vehicles). The bliss is enhanced (the bliss is intensified if the purified portion of the red and the white bodhicitta from both parties, which is drawn upward during orgasm, can ascend to the heart cakra). Eliminate the discrimination of self-attachment through the supreme joy, thus conforming to the view of Bodhisattva. The great bliss pervades the body when the drops arrive at the navel. Eliminate the attachment to the action seal through the wisdom of the absence of joy, thus conforming to the tantric view. Subsequently, the non-discrimination of bliss, the cause devoid of verbalization, gives rise to the innate joy when the drops arrive at the secret place. Eliminate the discrimination of the wisdom of joy pertaining to the first three initiations, thus conforming to the highest secret tantra—the view of holding the drops. Make observations in this fashion on the entity of bliss, take in (the nature) devoid of verbalization, see through the nature, and maintain that sensation. You should practice diligently in this way.[2]

This method, which is among **the quintessential instructions** found in Padmasambhava's *Dakini Teachings [Haimu shenshen yindao 亥母甚深引導]*, allows one to swiftly achieve the practice of the drops within one's body through an action seal—a real female consort. It is also known as internal initiation.

There are various designations for the four initiations within this internal initiation:

The vast arising of the innate correct wisdom depends entirely on this (on the yab-yum practice). The retention of an unembarrassed self, like a vase or chinaware, also depends on this. Keeping close with the sky-traveler of the three sources,

---

[2] Yogi C. M. Chen (Chen Chien-ming 陳健民), *Qugongzhai quanji 曲肱齋全集 [The Complete Works of Yogi Chen]*, vol. 1-5, ed. Xu Qinying 徐芹庭 (Taipei: Puxianwang rulai fojiaohui 普賢王如來佛教會, 1991), vol. 3, 553-56. Translated into English from Chinese.

with whom one has wondrous connections, also depends on this. Causing one to have pure faith also depends on this. The enhancement of the teachings also depends on this. I recall that when I was nineteen years old, I lived in Monastery Seduojin [色多緊寺]. I dreamed about a delightful young sramana[3] with a solemn appearance. Dressed perfectly, he held a treasure sword and a sūtra and was surrounded by four attending young girls. At that time, I thought that he was Bodhisattva Śāntideva and asked him to confer the Guhyasamāja[4] initiation on me. Thus, I received the four initiations in the correct sequence. Among the four attending females, the most graceful one kissed me and I fondled her breasts. I then embraced her and said: "This is the vase initiation." The emanation body of the main deity with a sword entered the state of meditative equipoise with the four girls, eliciting greed from anyone who watches them (the emanation body of the main deity entered and abided in sexual pleasure simultaneously with the four girls, causing anyone who watches them to crave for sexual pleasure). They engaged in sexual union and jointly released bodhicitta (they had sexual intercourse and released sexual fluid), filling up the kapāla (filling up the ritual cup made of a human skull). I tasted it again—it had the color and smell of borneol. I said: "This is the secret initiation." The emanation body gave me the girl, causing our bodies to coincide (causing the upper and lower parts of my body and the girl's to coincide intimately). I pressed her breasts and inserted [my penis] into her lotus, thereby generating the great bliss and releasing the drops (semen). I said: "Observe it! Observe it! This is the wisdom initiation." The recitation of the syllable *hum* caused the drops to ascend and bliss pervaded my body. I said: "This is the fourth initiation." ... It is also said: "Holding hands is the vase initiation, lustful speech is the secret initiation, fondling breasts is the wisdom initiation, and kissing lips is the fourth initiation; these are the four initiations within this initiation. ... The equal abiding of the guru father

---

3   Sramana: a male monastic; S. *śramaṇa*; C. *shamen* 沙門.
4   Guhyasamāja: C. *mijijingang* 密集金剛.

and the mother is the vase initiation; listening to the thrusting and the withdrawing motions of the guru father and the mother's pestle and lotus is the secret initiation; the descending of the drops that ensues is the wisdom initiation; the arising of the craving for sexual activity is the fourth initiation. These are the four initiations within the secret initiation. . . . Embracing a girl is the vase initiation; the mutual fondling of the lotus and the pestle is the secret initiation; the thrusting and the withdrawing motions are the wisdom initiation; the descending of the drops, coupled with the arising of great bliss, is the fourth initiation. These are the four initiations within the wisdom initiation. . . . The red and the white drops converge and ascend, filling up the four cakras one after another and thus giving rise to the four joys. These are the four initiations within the fourth initiation."[5]

The above records, which were translated by Yogi C. M. Chen, are the **quintessential instructions** given by a Tibetan tantric guru under the false identity of the patriarch of the Jonang School, Danalada (打那拉達, Tāranātha).

It is a challenging task to give a thorough account of the initiations that are performed properly, given the extreme intricacy of their rituals. Not only would such a presentation take up a lot of space, but relaying those rituals in detail would not be directly meaningful to the rectification of the tantric doctrines undertaken here. Hence, this publication will omit those details and solely focus on correcting the tantric doctrines. Readers who are interested in this topic may refer to *The Rituals of Initiation in the Generation Stage of the Kālacakra* [*Shilunjingang shengqicidi guandingyigui* 時輪金剛升起次第灌頂儀軌], which is listed in the bibliography at the back of this publication. They will be able to decipher the secret meanings on their own by relying on the indications provided in this

---

5   Yogi C. M. Chen (Chen Chien-ming 陳健民), *Qugongzhai quanji* 曲肱齋全集 [*The Complete Works of Yogi Chen*], vol. 1-5, ed. Xu Qinying 徐芹庭 (Taipei: Puxianwang rulai fojiaohui 普賢王如來佛教會, 1991), vol. 3, 618. Translated into English from Chinese.

book.

4. General Remarks on the Theory of Initiation

While the major types of initiation in Tantric Buddhism include the bonding initiations, which pertain to the Causal Ground, as well as the vase initiation, the secret initiation, the wisdom initiation, and the fourth initiation, people's diverse needs have led to the emergence of many other types of initiation. However, regardless of the types of initiation involved, all of them are underpinned, from beginning to end, by the theory of the non-duality of bliss and emptiness experienced in the yab-yum practice. In fact, to receive an initiation is to sow the causes and conditions for the future cultivation of the yab-yum method. Hence, **Tsongkhapa** of the Gelug School says: "*Practice internally the unsurpassed path and be externally concordant with the deeds of other-liberation; this is how you must guide disciples.*" (See *The Great Exposition of Secret Mantra [Mizong daocidi guanglun].*)

Having witnessed the misdeeds of the lamas in the Nyingma School as well as their licentious behavior and insatiable cravings for women, **Tsongkhapa** feverishly reformed Tibetan Tantric Buddhism and established the cultivation lineage of the Gelug School system. However, the Dharma-gate to attain Buddhahood in Tantric Buddhism entirely revolves around and firmly holds onto the theory of the non-duality of bliss and emptiness experienced amidst sexual pleasure. Tsongkhapa failed to reform this theory despite his aspirations to do so. This was not due to a lack of means, but rather because he was never aware of this theory's absurdity and the fact that it completely contradicts the Path to Liberation and the Path to Buddhahood. As a result, his reform of the tantric teachings was limited to raising the criteria of the real female consorts used by lamas in the actual practice (such as requiring that those females must have achieved the skills of the generation stage), as he was never involved in the slightest with the correction of those erroneous doctrines.

Being himself also deeply fascinated by the mistaken view of

349

the yab-yum practice in Tantric Buddhism, **Tsongkhapa** claims that one must internally practice the unsurpassed path of the non-duality of bliss and emptiness while being externally concordant with the deeds of other-liberation that are based on the non-duality of bliss and emptiness; according to him, this is the method that one must use to guide disciples in the cultivation of the secret doctrines. **Tsongkhapa** asserts that such a practice leads to the swift attainment of Buddhahood. **As a matter of fact, he has never negated the yab-yum practice or the methods of "the non-duality of bliss and emptiness" and of "the union of bliss and emptiness" and has never advocated that the lamas of the Gelug School must not cultivate the yab-yum practice with females. He merely added the requirement related to the skills of the generation stage and propounded that the lamas must abandon their precepts of monks before being allowed to use real female consorts in the yab-yum practice**—he has in fact not prohibited lamas from using real consorts in this practice. Given that his statements in *The Great Exposition of Secret Mantra* [*Mizong daocidi guanglun*] all revolve around the yab-yum practice and that this publication considers the yab-yum practice to be the central thought of the path of secret mantra, we can conclude that the core belief propagated by Tsongkhapa of the Gelug School is in no way different from that taught in the other major traditions of Tibetan Tantric Buddhism. It is completely unwise to claim that tantric practitioners perform the deeds of other-liberation when their cultivation methods consist of a Dharma-gate of practice based on licentious mental deeds and sexual misconduct.

With respect to the cultivation of the secret doctrines consisting of the yab-yum practice, Guru Padmasambhava opines that the action seal, which relies on the use of real female consorts, is "superior" to the wisdom seal, which resorts to the visualization of female consorts: "One who practices the unintermittent great bliss of deities must rely on a delightful woman with the proper characteristics. The superior method relies on the use of real females, whereas the mid-level method resorts to visualization."[1]

Yogi C. M. Chen shares the same view:

The bhikṣus who do not have access to the use of an action seal will stop their practice after reaching the second initiation, in which one visualizes a samaya consort; they will skip the stage of the third initiation, which relies on the use of a real consort seal, and directly practice the Mahāmudrā of the fourth initiation. The lay vajrasattvas have access to the use of an action seal (original note: the bhikṣus who practice the action seal should return their precepts of monks to the Buddha and declare that they will henceforth practice the action seal according to the secret doctrines; they should, in addition, leave the monastery); they can follow the proper order of cultivation by proceeding to the third initiation. When their practice reaches a mature stage, in which they experience the great bliss and the clear light glitters brilliantly during the third initiation, they will recognize the Mahāmudrā of clear light. Thereupon, they will formally obtain the fourth initiation and start to practice Mahāmudrā (start to cultivate the Mahāmudrā of the union of bliss and emptiness experienced in the yab-yum practice). Furthermore, they will proceed to the union with the illusory body. This method belongs to the correct practice of the Secret Mantra Vehicle and was advocated by Guru Tsongkhapa based on the approach of ancient people.[2]

The method that allows for the attainment of Buddhahood in this body, which is based on the lust experienced in the yab-yum practice, is not just reprehended by the enlightened Bodhisattvas in Exoteric Buddhism, who have indicated that both its theory and actual practice contradict the Path to Liberation and the Path to Buddhahood, it was in fact decried long ago by people with

---

[1]   Yogi C. M. Chen (Chen Chien-ming 陳健民), *Qugongzhai quanji* 曲肱齋全集 *[The Complete Works of Yogi Chen]*, vol. 1-5, ed. Xu Qinying 徐芹庭 (Taipei: Puxianwang rulai fojiaohui 普賢王如來佛教會, 1991), vol. 3, 552. Translated into English from Chinese.

[2]   Ibid., 727.

foresight within Tantric Buddhism:

> Furthermore, The *Achievement of Wisdom [Zhichengjiu* 智成
> 就*]* also says: "The bliss that arises from the two sexual organs
> is unvirtuously said to be reality. The supreme Buddha has
> never taught that this is the great bliss; all phenomena
> generated through causes and conditions cannot be called
> reality." Doesn't the claim that the third initiation connects
> with the innate meaning of reality contradict the above
> passage?[3]

Tsongkhapa is unwilling to concur with the above objection
and argues in favor of the yab-yum practice:

> The reply is as follows: "There is no fault." Those
> scriptures refer to the innate wisdom that is used to refute
> the heretics; this is the innate wisdom of the nature or the
> entity. Those passages affirm that the innate wisdom of the
> third initiation and so forth does not unimpededly connect with
> reality nor assert that there is no innate wisdom in the third
> initiation and so forth. As stated in the latter part of *The
> Tantra of the Voidness of Achievement [Wuchengjiu jing* 無成
> 就經 *]*:
>> Given that all those blisses,
>> Do not exist naturally,
>> The correct wisdom of all Sugatas,
>> Understands the nature.
>> As the most honorable among all blisses,
>> It is called "great bliss."
>> The great bliss is not impermanent,
>> It abides forever.
>
> **The above statements refute the blisses that are unreal,
> for the real bliss pertains to the Buddha Ground.**
> Consequently, if one cites those scriptures in order to refute
> the bliss that unimpededly connects with reality, then it should
> be asserted that no one on the path of training enjoys such

---

3   Tsongkhapa, *Mizong daocidi guang lun* 密宗道次第廣論, 389. Translated into
English from Chinese.

bliss. Therefore, the real bliss is known as the innate of the entity or the innate of the nature. In other words, this bliss operates spontaneously and unintermittedly in endless time to come without depending on any functions or any causes and conditions.[4]

Tsongkhapa cannot be regarded as a wise person given such profound fascination for the sexual pleasure experienced in the yab-yum practice. He has cunningly argued that the sexual pleasure within one's body corresponds to the innate bliss and is therefore not an impermanent phenomenon. Moreover, he has asserted that this bliss also exists within the bodies of all Buddhas and all sages in training and is therefore not an impermanent phenomenon, but a real and eternal one. He has further proclaimed that it is only when one's practice has reached the Buddha ground that one can cause this great bliss of the fourth joy consisting of sexual pleasure to exist permanently and thereby attain the fruition of permanent bliss. Hence, this state is considered in Tantric Buddhism to be that of the "reward body Buddha"—indeed, the "reward body Buddha" in Tantrism takes in the reward of sexual pleasure permanently. Surprisingly, there are tantric followers who faithfully adhere to the teachings of this "Most Honorable One" of the Gelug School—a lewd and ignorant man—and devote their entire lives to the assiduous practice of those doctrines. What an oddity of this Dharma-ending era!

Although sexual pleasure exists concomitantly with the physical body, it is neither a real dharma nor is it innate. Why do I say so? The reasons are as follows: (1) Sexual pleasure exists in dependence upon the mental consciousness (mind of feeling and cognition) and the form body of the desire realm. (2) It is the most rudimentary greed within the three realms. (3) It does not pervade all phenomena of the three realms. (4) It does not exist at all times. How does sexual pleasure exist in dependence upon the form body of the desire realm and the mental consciousness? The reasons are

---

[4]   Ibid., 389.

as follows: (1) Sexual pleasure is a contact-induced perception within the body—this bodily contact cannot arise without the existence of the form body of the desire realm. (2) Once sexual pleasure has arisen, the body consciousness comes into contact with this perception-induced sensation of sexual pleasure, so that there will be a blissful sensation for the humans of the desire realm to take in and cognize. There will be no sexual pleasure to speak of without the body-consciousness and mental consciousness (mind of feeling and cognition) taking in the perception-induced sensation of sexual contact. Given that sexual pleasure exists in dependence upon the perceiving nature of the body consciousness and the taking-in nature of the mental consciousness, and given that the mental consciousness relies on the five sense faculties of the form body to arise, the Buddha has stated that the mental consciousness (mind of feeling and cognition) possesses an other-dependent nature; consequently, sexual pleasure is a dharma that arises in dependence upon other dharmas with an other-dependant nature—it is the last one to arise within various other-dependent natures. How could it be said to be permanent? How could Tsongkhapa be hailed as "the Most Honorable One" when he is ignorant of such an elementary principle? How unwise are the proponents of the Gelug School!

Furthermore, sexual pleasure is the most rudimentary greed within the three realms. The Buddha has, in the four Āgamas, illustrated the eight gates to liberation:[5] Worldly beings can free themselves from the bondage to the desire realm by attaining the first concentration, from the bondage to the three heavens of the first concentration by attaining the second concentration, . . . and from the bondage to the neither perception nor non-perception heaven by attaining the absorption of cessation. These statements demonstrate that the mental consciousness is the most rudimentary bondage within the three realms. Anyone who eliminates the mistaken view that the mental consciousness is

---

[5] Eight gates to liberation: S. *aṣṭa-vimokṣa-mukha*; C. *ba jietuomen* 八解脫門.

permanent and indestructible will become liberated from the bondage of the view of eternalism. Those who cannot eliminate this mistaken view will never realize the absorption of cessation and, unable escape from the bondage to the three realms, will remain forever submerged in the bitter sea of cyclic existence, for the mental consciousness is the root of sentient beings' transmigration.

Given that the mental consciousness is not a permanent and indestructible mind—it is in fact an impermanent mind that arises in dependence upon other dharmas—sentient beings become entrapped in cyclic existence by holding onto the erroneous view that "the self" consisting of the mental consciousness is permanent and indestructible; therefore, the Buddha has frequently preached that this view should be eradicated. Since the erroneous view that "the self" consisting of the mental consciousness is permanent and indestructible constitutes the main cause behind the bondage to the three realms and should therefore, as the Buddha frequently taught, be eliminated, and since sexual desire exists in dependence upon the mental consciousness, it can be concluded that sexual desire is a dharma with an other-dependent nature that depends on other dharmas with an other other-dependent nature. Consequently, Tsongkhapa should not have claimed that the blissful contact amidst sexual desire is a permanent dharma.

Furthermore, only the great bliss that is devoid of pain and happiness and that is the quiescent nirvāṇa can be regarded as the real great bliss, for it is immutable. On the other hand, all sexual pleasures—including the contact-induced sensation of sexual pleasure in which tantric followers are able to abide for long durations by achieving the practice of the non-duality of emptiness and bliss—involve sensations; any involvement of sensations pertains to the sphere of the aggregate of sensations; the aggregate of sensations is a mutable and impermanent phenomenon; and a mutable phenomenon cannot be a permanent bliss. Indeed, given that a mutable blissful sensation induced by sexual contact sometimes exists and sometimes ceases, it cannot be said to be a permanent, immutable, and wondrous bliss. Therefore, Tsongkhapa's assertion that the non-duality of bliss and emptiness is "permanent and immutable" is incorrect. How could he call this impermanent and mutable bliss the most supreme of all blisses? How could it be dubbed the utmost bliss? It just does not make any sense. Tsongkhapa is surprisingly unaware of this error, which demonstrates that he is not a wise person.

Tibetan Tantric Buddhists regard the bliss induced by sexual desire during the yab-yum practice between a male and a female as a method that leads to the attainment of the ultimate Buddhahood. The following institutions and persons have all viewed the cultivation and realization of sexual pleasure during this yab-yum practice as the pillar of the tantric theory about the attainment of Buddhahood in this body as well as the Dharma-gate for the cultivation thereof: Beginning from the Tantric Buddhism in ancient India, followed by the Kadam School that was just introduced into China's Tibet, then the four major schools into which Tantric Buddhism has broken down, and subsequently Tsongkhapa, the founder of the Gelug School, which proclaims itself as the purest reformer. We can almost conclude that none of the tantric schools have been able to exclude themselves from the yab-yum practice. **Although the gurus of the Gelug School in Tantric Buddhism are mostly well aware of Tsongkhapa's fascination with the states of sexual desire experienced in the yab-yum practice, they deliberately conceal this fact from novice tantric practitioners in every way and deceive them by claiming that the Gelug School does not cultivate the yab-yum practice given Tsongkhapa's objection to this yab-yum method of sexual desire. Unbeknownst to the tantric learners, those gurus rely on such lies to lure them into the cultivation of tantras. Once those learners adhere to the tantric teachings with unwavering faith, those gurus will inform them in private that the Gelug School of Tantric Buddhism has in fact adopted the yab-yum practice as its core belief as well as the method to achieve Buddhahood. It is truly questionable to treat practitioners with such dishonesty.**

For instance, Chen Chunlong and Ding Guangwen, two proponents of the wanton practice of Tibetan Tantrism, argue cunningly in favor of Tsongkhapa by condemning others' endeavors to repudiate false doctrines while revealing the true Dharma:

> Our Buddhist community has seen, over the past few years, the emergence of persons with deep-seated prejudice who only value their own school, . . . they have attacked the tantric Kālacakra Vajra, Cakrasamvara, Hevajra, and so forth, all of which appear in the yab-yum form and have branded them as evil demons. **As a matter of fact, the great guru Tsongkhapa of the Gelug School in Tantric Buddhism forbade and rectified some of the bad habits in Tibet long ago. Over 80% of Tibetans belong to the Gelug School. Monks who violate the precept of sexual misconduct will immediately be demoted to lay practitioners and will no longer be accepted as monastics for the rest of their lives. These rules are stricter than those observed by Han Chinese.**[6]

However, these **deceitful** statements by Chen Chunlong and Ding Guangwen on their website constitute a flagrant lie to the public. **The truth is, Tsongkhapa has asserted that desire should not be abandoned,** and he himself does not practice abstinence from desire. For instance, in a previous passage cited in this section, Tsongkhapa insists that sexual pleasure is the permanent and indestructible great bliss and claims that the "meritorious quality" of the fourth initiation can only be achieved by cultivating with one's guru the state of the "non-duality of bliss and emptiness" amidst sexual pleasure. These proclamations demonstrate that Tsongkhapa approves of the yab-yum practice and that **Chen and Ding are simply liars.**

Tsongkhapa also advocates the necessity to use a beautiful girl aged fifteen or sixteen as the female consort during the

---

[6]   Translated into English from Chen Chunlong 陳淳隆 (Miaozhan 妙湛) and Ding Guangwen 丁光文's *Kongxing jian xinjiaodu de chanshi* 空性見新角度的闡釋《上下集》 *[An Explanation of the New Perspective on the View of Emptiness, vols. 1 & 2]*, retrieved from http://city080.mydreamer.com.tw/

performance of initiations on disciples. He has thus stated the following with respect to the rituals of initiation:

> With respect to the rules of creating the maṇḍala of samaya and entering the maṇḍala of wisdom during the practice of maṇḍala, *Abhaya's Vajra Rosary [Manlun]* says: "Once the painted maṇḍala has instantly become empty, visualize the maṇḍala that is the object of practice, together with the protection cakra, the hindrances that nail the demons," and so forth. With respect to the rituals related to family dependents, it says:
>> The female consort with wondrous beauty,
>> Is aged around fifteen or sixteen;
>> Nicely adorned with fragrances and flowers,
>> She enjoys pleasure in the maṇḍala **(she engages in sexual pleasure with the guru in the maṇḍala of initiation)**.
>> The Buddha-mother endowed with virtues,
>> Is empowered by the wise;
>> The wise exudes peacefulness and magnificence,
>> The Buddha abides in the realm of empty space.

This means that you should enter meditative absorption with an external seal (real female consorts are external seals; the two should dwell in orgasm simultaneously as well as one-pointedly and without distracting thoughts); if there is no external seal, then you should enter meditative concentration with a wisdom seal (the wisdom seal refers to a visualized female consort; the two should abide in orgasm simultaneously as well as one-pointedly and without distracting thoughts). Invoke the wisdom cakra with the joyous sounds of the correct practice. (The moans of pleasure made during sexual intercourse are hereby referred to as the joyous sounds of the correct practice; thinking that the sexual act of the yab-yum practice is a correct practice of the path to Buddhahood, Tsongkhapa views sexual moaning as "the joyous sounds of the correct practice.") First, make an offering by washing your feet (and then visualize that the Buddha-father and the Buddha-mother copulate with great bliss and thereby release the red and the white bodhicittas, which) enter your body. They are dissolved by the fire of desire (they drip down after being dissolved by your and the female consort's fire of desire) **and enter the lotus** (and move into the female consort's vulva) **through the vajra passageway** (through the urethra); **you release the wisdom cakra** (you ejaculate the drops—semen) **and enter the samaya cakra** (the two abide in orgasm simultaneously as well as one-pointedly and without distracting thoughts).[7]

Thus, the view of the Gelug School's **Tsongkhapa** is evident from his citation of this treatise, his concurrence with its statements, and his explications of its contents: He also asserts that it is more fitting to use a real female consort in the context of a formal tantric initiation. In this case, how could Tsongkhapa be said to oppose the use of real female consorts? How could he and the other gurus and disciples of the Gelug School be viewed as pure observers of the precepts? How could Tsongkhapa be regarded as a reformer when he thus propagates the path of secret mantra and has violated the precept of sexual misconduct, which is one of the Ten Major Precepts within the Precepts of Bodhisattvas? Tsongkhapa has in fact not forbidden the lamas of the Gelug School to cultivate the yab-yum method of sexual pleasure with women— real female consorts—instead, he has just tightened the restrictions for this practice. Furthermore, he advocates the necessity to cultivate and learn the yab-yum practice and regards it as the fundamental doctrine of the Gelug School. Anyone can verify that this mentality is extensively reflected in his *The Great Exposition of Secret Mantra [Mizong daocidi guanglun]*. How could Chen and Ding lie blatantly and continue to beguile sentient beings into cultivating Tsongkhapa's mistaken path? How malicious!

Sometimes **Tsongkhapa** squarely quotes tantras and concurs with their statements about the use of real female consorts—even as many as five:

Therefore, it is imperative to cultivate the yab-yum method

---

[7] Tsongkhapa, *Mizong daocidi guang lun* 密宗道次第廣論, 302-03. Translated into English from Chinese.

and to use women. **The guru Tsongkhapa himself acknowledged the necessity to use not just one woman, but at least five.** On the other hand, the Nyingma School claims that one is enough. Theoretically, why is it necessary to use five women? Because the number five denotes the Buddha-mothers in the five directions and the five wisdoms. Those numbers should be matched! Therefore, it is necessary to select lady sky-travelers with distinct properties: mother sky-travelers of the Vajra Division, mother sky-travelers of the Lotus Division, and so forth.[8]

Yogi C. M. Chen has, however, understated the truth. Why is that? Because, based on Tsongkhapa's statements previously cited in this chapter, not only does Tsongkhapa assert that the yab-yum practice is the basis of the path of secret mantra, but he also insists that the gurus of the Gelug School must use "nine female consorts" to confer the fourth initiation on their disciples. In other words, during a "proper" conferral of secret initiation, a truly "proper" tantric lama of the Gelug School must, after copulating with and then ejaculating into each of the nine female consorts one after another, collect the secretions issued from those sexual acts and use them as the nectar needed in the initiation. In addition, the lama must, during those sexual acts, allow the disciple to observe the lama's performance. Next, this lama must bestow those nine female consorts on the disciple and ask him to actually cultivate the yab-yum method with each of them under the lama's guidance. Therefore, Tsongkhapa has not forbidden monastics to use women; what he did was raise the criteria for the use of women in the yab-yum practice. For this reason, **Tsongkhapa has purely and simply remained a faithful practitioner of the tantric yab-yum practice as well as a devoted follower of the Shaktist method found in Hinduism.**

---

[8]   Yogi C. M. Chen (Chen Chien-ming 陳健民), *Qugongzhai quanji 曲肱齋全集 [The Complete Works of Yogi Chen]*, vol. 1-5, ed. Xu Qinying 徐芹庭 (Taipei: Puxianwang rulai fojiaohui 普賢王如來佛教會, 1991), vol. 1, 238-39. Translated into English from Chinese.

Furthermore, **Tsongkhapa** has advocated (as a matter of fact, all tantras issued from tantric gurus have advocated) the necessity of chanting a praise in order to extol the property of the great bliss pertaining to the sexual act as well as the fact that the sexual act enables practitioners to attain expediency and wisdom; only then is the disciple asked to enter the maṇḍala to receive the initiation:

> Next, in order to cause the disciple to enter the maṇḍala, you must first pray for the siddhi of maṇḍala as well as the empowerment from the words of truth by praising the nature of reality pertaining to the property of the great bliss, the expediency, and wisdom with nine praises such as the arising of empty space and so forth. . . . The song of the reality of the three purities is as follows:
>> The love among all cravings,
>> Is honorable, flawless, and permanent;
>> The World-Honored One has great cravings for joy,
>> I practice the nature of reality.
>> "Flawless" refers to the elimination of all hindrances and predispositions,
>> While "permanent" indicates that the three bodies throughout the boundless empty space are permanent.
>> Any desire to attain the siddhi can achieve the aim of craving all sentient beings,
>> And is therefore the great craving endowed with the non-conditioned great compassion. Since it generates joy through the method of signlessness,
>> It is called great joy.[9]

In the above passage, Tsongkhapa—a proponent of the Gelug School in Tibetan Tantric Buddhism—asserts that one must praise the "nature of reality" of the great craving, the great bliss, and so forth before entering the maṇḍala of initiation. In fact, "the great craving" and "the great bliss" related to sexual pleasure also constitute the core belief and final attainment of the Dharma-gate

---

[9] Tsongkhapa, *Mizong daocidi guang lun* 密宗道次第廣論, 322-23. Translated into English from Chinese.

of visualization propagated by Tsongkhapa. How could he be said to oppose the yab-yum practice given such teachings, practices, and realizations? Therefore, Chen and Ding are extremely deceitful to claim that Tsongkhapa forbids the disciples of the Gelug School to cultivate the yab-yum method.

Tsongkhapa also asserts that even if one is able to realize the innate joy (the sexual pleasure consisting of the fourth joy) by cultivating, during the fourth initiation, the yab-yum method with the guru or with nine female consorts under the guru's guidance, the innate joy thus attained can neither be said to be "permanent" nor be equated with "bliss," given that the practitioner has not been able to achieve the skill of abiding long-lastingly in the state of sexual pleasure:

> "There are two types of innate joy: temporary and permanent. The permanent innate joy is the best, for it is supreme, real, endless, and indestructible." **It is said to be permanent for being unintermittent and endless**. To view something that dwells for just one or two instants as permanent is to hold an unwholesome non-Buddhist view.[10]

Tsongkhapa's stance is evident from the above statements: One must be able to abide long-lastingly in the contact-induced sensation of the great bliss amidst the sexual pleasure consisting of the fourth joy and ensure that the contact-induced sensation of sexual pleasure experienced in orgasm remains "unintermittent and endless"; such a bliss "is said to be permanent." Given that Tsongkhapa has thus taught disciples that one attains the "permanent bliss" not just by enjoying the sexual pleasure consisting of the fourth joy together with the guru during the fourth initiation, but by additionally striving to dwell long-lastingly in this state of sexual pleasure, we can conclude that **Tsongkhapa indeed regards the cultivation of sexual pleasure as the main Dharma-gate of the Tantric Gelug School for the practice that leads to the attainment of Buddhahood in this body.** The above

---

[10] Ibid., 390.

statements are all recorded in his *The Great Exposition of Secret Mantra [Mizong daocidi guanglun]* and can be easily verified. It is useless for Chen and Ding to argue cunningly on Tsongkhapa's behalf.

Tsongkhapa further says:

As stated by *Lord of Speech [Yuzizai 語自在]* with respect to the seven branches: "Perfect reward, union, naturelessness of bliss, compassion, fullness, ceaselessness, and non-extinction, I agree with the meanings of the seven branches that are being practiced; they are praised by those who pervasively cultivate the wisdom of the correct, valid knowledge." The "perfect reward" body refers to the body adorned with auspicious marks and beauties; it also encompasses the Dharma body and the emanation body, for the three bodies are one identical entity. **"Union" signifies entering meditative absorption simultaneously with a female consort.** (In Tantric Buddhism, the term "meditative absorption" indicates the state of orgasm in which both the male and the female are caused to abide at the same time through the cultivation of the yab-yum method.) If only the reward body exists, then pāramitā (Mahāyāna) also teaches about it; our doctrine is superior to theirs because of this union. (Tantric Buddhism considers this great bliss of meditative absorption issued from the union between a male and a female to be superior to the pāramitā Mahāyāna principles.) What is Sumeru? It refers to the fact that one can achieve benefits for all sentient beings just with the nature of joy pervading the entire body. ("Pervading every part of one's body"—the great bliss that arises in all parts is said to "pervade Sumeru"; one can successfully achieve the great benefits of bringing welfare to all sentient beings with just the nature of joy that pervades the entire body.) The Buddha manifests meditative absorption in order to benefit and guide the sentient beings of the desire-realm who perform deeds of intense greed. (In order to benefit and guide the sentient beings of the desire realm who intensely crave sexual pleasure, "tantric Buddhas" manifest the state of meditative absorption consisting of abiding one-pointedly in sexual pleasure with a female consort.) A dense population of males and females created by a magician still cannot generate the great bliss; in contrast, the great bliss can be generated here (it does arise from this yab-yum practice) and is therefore called great bliss. The bodily bliss is to be taken in as bliss and the mental bliss as joy. The term "great" denotes the following attributes: vastest (this bliss is described as vast because it pervades the body), non-leaked (the drops—semen—are not leaked), wondrous (the fourth joy is superior to the orgasm of sexual pleasure experienced by worldly beings), and endless (this bliss is qualified as "endless" because it can be taken in any time throughout one's endless future lifetimes; the reward body Buddhas of Tantric Buddhism have been taking in this blissful contact of the fourth joy at all times—and will forever do so— ever since they attained Buddhahood). It is said to be "natureless" in order to highlight the fact that it is without a nature (the perception-induced sensation of sexual pleasure is said to be "without a nature" for being devoid of form and material) and detached from existences ("detached from existences" refers to the fact that one is detached from all existences consisting of worldly materials while taking in this bliss).[11]

However, **Tsongkhapa** is merely deceiving himself with the above statements rather than honestly facing the fallacy of the tantric doctrines. Indeed, the World-Honored One has never **"manifest[ed] meditative absorption in order to benefit and guide the sentient beings of the desire realm who perform deeds of intense greed."** In the sūtras of the Three Vehicles, the World-Honored One has never been seen to liberate sentient beings from cyclic existence with lascivious methods and by taking on a yab-yum form in which He enjoys sexual pleasure. Instead, He has preached in all sūtras that lust should be abandoned, for it is the most rudimentary form of greed within the three realms—He has thus asserted even in the authentic esoteric scripture, the *Śūraṃgama Sūtra [Lengyan jing 楞嚴經]*, in which He has

---

[11]   Ibid., 393.

vigorously underscored the pernicious effects of lust. Only fake sūtras that were compiled and created by a group of ancient tantric gurus over an extended period of time, such as *The Vairocanābhisaṃbodhi Sūtra [Dari jing]* and so forth, would preach the aforementioned misconceptions. Therefore, Tsongkhapa's teachings stem from his own imagination and do not conform to the truth.

Furthermore, contrary to the tantric doctrines, the Exoteric Buddhists sūtras do not state that the perfect reward body attained by the Buddha take on a form in which He receives the reward of taking bliss in while embracing and copulating with a female consort. Hence, the tantric assertion that the perfect reward bodies all take on the appearance of taking bliss in during the yab-yum copulation is based on the imagination of those gurus and is completely false.

Furthermore, the Path to Buddhahood does not hinge upon the state of the mental consciousness consisting of the non-duality of emptiness and bliss, which is based on sexual pleasure, but is instead achieved through the realization of the knowledge-of-general-aspect, the knowledge-of-specific-aspects, and the knowledge-of-all-aspects. If those tantric gurus do not want to be mocked as ignorant by the wise, then they should not blindly adhere to this heretical Shaktist method of sexual pleasure inherited from the Tantric Buddhism in ancient India, should not equate the fallacious sexual pleasure with the "great bliss of Buddhahood," as Tsongkhapa blindly does, and should not emulate Tsongkhapa's ignorant deeds by declaring that sexual pleasure forms the basis of the Dharma-gate of practice that leads to the achievement of Buddhahood.

With respect to the co-practice between a male and a female, Tsongkhapa's statements about "vastest," "union," "non-leaked," "wondrous," "endless," "natureless," "detached from existences" and so forth all serve for the purpose of unreasonable argumentation. They all conflict with the Buddha's tenets, contradict the Path to Liberation and the Path to Buddhahood in every way, and do not correspond to the Buddha Dharma in the least. Even those with limited Buddhist view and little Buddhist knowledge can understand the fallacy of those contents; how then could the tantric practitioners and gurus, with their self-declared "most superior faculty," believe in those elementary and mistaken teachings and even wrongly hail Tsongkhapa as the Most-Honorable One? How preposterous!

Tsongkhapa also asserts that tantric practitioners should not relinquish sexual desire—instead, they should take in and make use of sexual pleasure and enjoy women. He has urged his disciples not to be afraid of violating the precepts because of enjoying women:

> After invoking the main deity of the maṇḍala, place the umbrella elsewhere and utter the words that will please the disciples:
>> You have now become gurus of the maṇḍala,
>> Able to accept and abide by the mantras and tantras;
>> This is witnessed by all Buddhas, Bodhisattvas, and celestial beings.
>> Out of compassion for sentient beings,
>> You should follow the rituals of the maṇḍala,
>> Diligently and skillfully paint [a maṇḍala image] and build [an entire maṇḍala],
>> So that practitioners can learn the tantras.
>> Because of entering and seeing,
>> The supreme secret maṇḍala,
>> You will be freed from all sins.
>> You should now dwell blissfully, Adhering to this vehicle of the great bliss,
>> And you will be forever freed from future deaths
>> (you should now abide blissfully based on this method and according to this vehicle of the yab-yum great bliss; this will allow you to be forever freed from future births and deaths).
>> You will transcend the sufferings of the three existences,
>> And reach the limit of those three existences;

The Buddhas hold the vajra,
And now confer the initiation of longevity.
You will definitely be the lord,
On the throne of the Dharma-king in the three realms.
There is no sin in the three realms other than the sin of abandoning all desire (there is truly no sin in the three realms greater than the sin of relinquishing such desire; therefore, the tantric practitioners who abandon such desire for the yab-yum practice will commit the most grievous sin in the three realms).
Thus, you should never relinquish your desire (for this reason, you should never commit the deed of abandoning such desire for the yab-yum practice).
While enjoying sexual acts,
You should course in fearlessness (you should enjoy the desire for the yab-yum practice in an unbridled manner and without any fear);
You should eat the five meats and drink the five nectars,
As well as protect and keep all the other vows (as well as protect and keep all the other vows that were made during the process of learning Tantrism).
You should neither harm sentient beings,
Nor abandon the female treasures (nor abandon the female treasures—female consorts—of the yab-yum practice),
Nor give up the gurus (the tantric gurus).
It is difficult to violate the samaya precepts (the samaya precepts of the tantric yab-yum practice are not easily broken given the atrocity of the retribution entailed).
There is not the slightest expedient mind from this wisdom,
That should not be actualized (among the various expedient mental dharmas that arise from the practice and learning of this method, there is not one expedient, no matter how small, that should not be performed).
You are innocent and should have no fear (this

cultivation of the yab-yum method does not make you
guilty, and therefore, you should have no fear);
Just do as the Tathāgatas have instructed (just go
ahead and cultivate the yab-yum method freely as
taught by the tantric "Tathāgatas").
You should purify your mind and believe in the vajra
nature (you should believe and accept this vajra nature
with a pure mind),
And vow to abide by the endless bliss.
Starting with small pleasures,
You should attain the permanent nature of vajrasattva
(starting with the practice of very few pleasures, you
should eventually reach and abide in the vajrasattva's
permanent nature of the great bliss).
Furthermore, in order to increase the virtues of
those who have received initiation properly,
All Buddhas and Bodhisattvas are always mindful of
them with a pure mind as if they were their own sons;
The Dharma is thus.[12]

Tsongkhapa further says:

The object of desire here is called desire, a state of
vajrasattva; **"greed" refers to the aspirations to that desire**:
"There is no sin in the three realms other than the sin of
abandoning all desire." This points to the abandonment of
bodhicitta (material drops—semen). Hence, the teaching
states: "You should never give up your desire in the desired
state of vajrasattva."[13]

Tsongkhapa believes that the monastic lamas who engage in
the yab-yum practice with women do not transgress the precepts
and are not guilty as long as they do not abandon the bodhicitta—
as long as they do not ejaculate during sexual intercourse. These
statements signify that tantric practitioners commit the worst sin
by abandoning their desire: In the three realms, there is no sin

---

[12]   Tsongkhapa, *Mizong daocidi guang lun* 密宗道次第廣論, 409. Translated into
       English from Chinese.
[13]   Ibid., 410.

greater than the sin of relinquishing the desire for this yab-yum practice. Tsongkhapa further claims: **"Thus, you should never relinquish your desire,"** and instructs disciples: **"While enjoying sexual acts, you should course in fearlessness,"** thus exhorting the lay and the monastic disciples of the Gelug School to enjoy various types of women according to the tantric doctrines. How could Chen and Ding cunningly argue that those statements do not exist when they are clearly recorded in Tsongkhapa's *The Great Exposition of Secret Mantra [Mizong daocidi guanglun]*? How could they utter falsehoods to conceal Tsongkhapa's deeds? They are obviously dishonest, and therefore, their declarations are not credible in any way.

The other Tantric Buddhist schools even assert that one can enjoy sex with one's mother, daughters, sisters, aunts, and so forth (see the citations in Section 6 of Chapter 9). [14] Are those practitioners not telling the biggest lie in the world by claiming that they are able to attain Buddhahood while in fact they do not even conform to the morals of mankind with such incestuous and unethical behavior? Although the followers of the Gelug School do not use their mothers, daughters, sisters, or aunts as their female consorts, they do regard the sexual pleasure experienced during the yab-yum practice as the Dharma-gate to attain Buddhahood, as taught by Tsongkhapa. They even maintain that, for the fourth initiation to be proper, one must, during this ceremony, offer nine female consorts aged from twelve to twenty to the lama, so that he can have sex with them. The extent of their lust is evidenced by the fact that nine consorts are required instead of just one. Tsongkhapa has been advocating this practice given that he has himself not been able to avoid it even as a monastic. How then can the lay practitioners of the Gelug School eschew it? We can

---

14 The engagement in incestuous sexual relationships to satisfy one's religious cultivation is not only wholly illegal, but also morally wrong in all countries and societies. Such practices constitute a breach of major precepts and are strictly forbidden in the authentic Buddhism. Tantric Buddhism's explicit sanctification of unethical and criminal sexual exploitation of women should be taken as clear evidence of its corrupt and perverted nature.

conclude none of the gurus and disciples of the Gelug School—such as Tsongkhapa and so forth—have been able to abandon the lust for women as well as the various mistaken views and deeds preached in Tantrism. Therefore, the proclamations regarding the purity of the Gelug School and Tsongkhapa's reforms are all meaningless.

In the above teachings, **Tsongkhapa** exhorts tantric practitioners to enjoy women in the yab-yum practice without fear of transgressing the Buddhist precepts. This demonstrates that not only does Tsongkhapa not forbid the yab-yum practice in any way, but he even encourages others to cultivate it. We can, therefore, conclude that Chen and Ding either **are ignorant of the tantric doctrines** or **have deliberately and maliciously deceived the public.** How could such persons be qualified to openly propagate the "Buddha Dharma" on the Internet? The wise can definitely see through their behavior.

Furthermore, Chen and Ding argue that the Gelug School has prohibited all monks to enjoy women ever since Tsongkhapa forbade it long ago. That is, however, absolutely not the case. **Tsongkhapa actually insists that monastics can, and even must, enjoy women**, as evidenced by the assertions in his work:

> According to *Commentary on the Kālacakra Tantra [Shilunbenshi 時輪本釋]*, monastics transmit the third initiation exclusively through speech and are therefore allowed to confer initiations with wisdom seals. Abhaya's *Vajra Rosary [Manlun]* says: "**Supreme monastics who are not plagued by any obstructive conditions are allowed to perform real initiations.** (Supreme monastics without any obstructive conditions are allowed to perform actual initiations by relying on real female consorts; they do not need to resort to visualized consorts consisting of wisdom seals). Those who are afflicted by obstructive conditions or are not supreme monastics should transmit initiation with wisdom seals." Based on this guideline (this guideline applies to all initiations), the monastic ācāryas who confer secret initiations should also understand this principle (the monastics who confer the fourth

initiation on disciples should also understand this principle).[15]

Real initiations are performed by using actual female consorts instead of just relying on visualized ones to generate the sexual pleasure and sexual fluids needed for the initiations. It is clear from Tsongkhapa's assertions in the above passage that the monastics without obstructive conditions are not forbidden from enjoying women, as they are allowed to use real female consorts for the third and the fourth initiations. In fact, those with obstructive conditions are the ones who have failed to achieve the vase breathing technique and so forth in the generation stage. As a result, their incapacity to adequately control the timing of ejaculation will cause them to ejaculate before the nine female consorts with whom they perform sexual intercourse in the Buddhist maṇḍala during the fourth initiation have reached orgasm. It will, therefore, be impossible to extract a purified portion from the blended fluids, which means that those fluids cannot serve as nectar. Hence, the failure to achieve the vase breathing technique constitutes an obstructive condition. The monastic lamas without the aforementioned obstructive conditions should confer "actual initiations" by engaging in sexual intercourse with nine real female consorts during the fourth initiation. Tsongkhapa's statements can all be found in his writings; anyone can verify them and confirm that I have not accused him wrongfully. Consequently, Chen and Ding are deceitful and the proclamation on their website that "Tsongkhapa forbids the lamas of the Gelug School to enjoy female consorts" is completely false.

Furthermore, the erotic practice of the union of bliss and emptiness in Highest Yoga Tantra comprises four yogas (One-Pointed Yoga, Non-Proliferative Yoga, One-Taste Yoga, and Non-Meditation Yoga), which all consist of lustful states of the mental consciousness and have nothing to do with the "yoga" set forth in the Buddha Dharma. Indeed, the One-Pointed Yoga, Non-

---

[15] Tsongkhapa, *Mizong daocidi guang lun* 密宗道次第廣論, 390. Translated into English from Chinese.

Proliferative Yoga, One-Taste Yoga, and Non-Meditation Yoga preached by tantric gurus such as Tsongkhapa and so forth are just different terms established to designate the method whereby the mental consciousness abides in a state where it engages in the deed-contemplation of sexual bliss. Therefore, those yogas are all associated with the mundane sexual pleasure. Such a usage of "yoga" is an utter profanation of this sacred term.

Furthermore, tantric gurus have often claimed the following: "Only those who have abandoned all their desire are qualified to practice and realize Highest Yoga Tantra, a method to spiritually help those with the most superior faculty." The truth is, those who have relinquished all their desire no longer need this method, which consists of "abandoning desire through desire." Those with the most superior faculty can, upon hearing the related teachings, understand the faults entailed by having desire and can therefore abandon all their desire. In the Buddha's time, some heretics were even able to become great arhats upon hearing the Buddha's teachings about such faults and therefore did not have to eliminate their desire by performing lustful acts. A person who has to rely on libidinous deeds to get rid of his desire is absolutely not endowed with the most superior faculty—on the contrary, he possesses the most inferior faculty. In Tantric Buddhism, such lascivious practitioners with the most inferior faculty are surprisingly regarded as having the most superior faculty. No one in the world is more adept at stating the untruth than those tantric gurus!

Furthermore, having lust is a prerequisite for the practice of this method, for it causes the male's vajra pestle to become firm and generate a fluid (nectar) and also causes the female's lotus to generate a fluid (nectar), thus enabling both parties to practice together. If one of those two persons is unwilling to cooperate due to the lack of desire, then the other person cannot cultivate this yab-yum method; it is, therefore, clear that this method requires both practitioners to have desire. This concept is very obvious and easy to understand; how could the tantric gurus wrongly argue that this method is practiced without desire"? What an utter falsity!

Furthermore, those who adhere to this method and cultivate it "assiduously" cannot be said to be without any greed, for they are required to bring forth a greedy mind by extensively pondering over this sexual pleasure on a daily basis. For instance, a renowned tantric guru has written the following verses:

> The light of wisdom that stimulates people's potential
> Shoots directly into the lotus palace, inducing boundless bliss;
> Having caught a glimpse of some village girls,
> I felt unusually itchy and could not resist to scratch myself overtly. . . .
> The utter bliss in the empty space is the lotus house,
> It reaches the four directions due to the withdrawing and thrusting;
> Do not say that the upāsikā's [female lay practitioner] receptacle is small,
> It subsumes and stores the Dharma-realms of all Tathāgatas.[16]

The following is yet another endeavor to engage in sexual misconduct:

> The bottom of high heels has a fantastic function,
> Revealing it will trigger exhilarating joy:
> The legs stretch forward and the waist extends backward;
> The two banks of the brook are similar to high mounds.[17]

This guru further says:

> It is worrisome to communicate with a miss (young lady) by mail,
> Repeatedly fantasizing [about the yab-yum practice] is the most [fitting way to extinguish] yearnings;
> A lotus girl from the Akaniṣṭha Pure Land

---

16 Yogi C. M. Chen (Chen Chien-ming 陳健民), *Qugongzhai quanji* 曲肱齋全集 *[The Complete Works of Yogi Chen]*, vol. 1-5, ed. Xu Qinying 徐芹庭 (Taipei: Puxianwang rulai fojiaohui 普賢王如來佛教會, 1991), vol. 3, 311. Translated into English from Chinese.
17 Ibid., 312.

Has shown traces of herself in the human world and I might meet her.[18]

Yogi C. M. Chen has also written a poem titled "Drying the Pestle in the Sun (Exposing a Male's Private Parts in the Sun)":

It is used to moving to and fro amidst the low wet rocks (the vulva),
Hiding deeply in a deep secret place, unexposed;
I lie against the southern window of a mountain pavilion,
The almond flowers extending out of the wall get sunshine several times a day. (Original note: Sunshine contains Vitamin D, which fosters erections.)[19]

This author suggests that the males with a "short pestle" adopt a singular insertion during the yab-yum practice and depicts their sexual activities as follows:

Remember the benevolence of the father and the mother in śmaśāna,[20]
The vulva was shown once the demons had been subdued;
Guru Padmasambhava demonstrated the posture of a galloping horse,
I then realized that one can reach the water source through singular riding.
Riding in an inclined position with one leg will lengthen the pestle,
The positions can be swapped after a cycle;
Having left the perineum and now hanging beneath the lotus,
The vajra awakens and becomes more erect.[21]

This author also indicates the meaning of "the female with small feet and a plump lotus":

---

[18] Ibid., 315.
[19] Ibid., 316.
[20] Śmaśāna: In Sanskrit, lit. "charnel ground," "cemetery," or "forest of corpses"; Alt. śītavana; T. *dur khrod*; C. *shituolin/hanlin* 屍陀林/寒林).
[21] Yogi C. M. Chen (Chen Chien-ming 陳健民), *Qugongzhai quanji* 曲肱齋全集 [*The Complete Works of Yogi Chen*], vol. 1-5, ed. Xu Qinying 徐芹庭 (Taipei: Puxianwang rulai fojiaohui 普賢王如來佛教會, 1991), vol. 3, 308. Translated into English from Chinese.

The small feet are almost as tiny as a three-inch lotus,
Who can interpret the secret meaning contained therein?
The secret is to let her body incline forward when she walks,
Causing her lotus to be plump and her waist strong.
The small feet no longer exist nowadays,
Its fashionable replacement is high heels;
The mantis-like waist swings slowly and the body protrudes forward,
The tiny lotus brings forth the delightful Chan.[22]

For this great practitioner of Tantric Buddhism, the various features of women observed in his daily life all evoke sex. Those who are not aware of the contents of the esoteric doctrines are often befuddled by this type of assertions made by renowned tantric gurus: It is difficult to understand why those gurus enjoy so much talking about sex. In contrast, the wise and virtuous who understands that the yab-yum practice of sexual pleasure is what the esoteric doctrines, from beginning to end, are all about is not muddled by those statements and can stay away from the fallacious and preposterous tantric Dharma-gate based on sex. Therefore, all Buddhists should know the truth and carefully explore the absurdity of the tantric doctrines; they will then avoid being confused and will turn to the right path of Buddhism. If they do not believe my words and instead delve further into the cultivation of the tantric doctrines, then they will gradually enter this absurd and lustful path and will engage in sexual misconduct, degenerate, and even commit incestuous acts, break the precepts, perpetrate the sin of grievous false speech, and so forth. As a result, they will definitely fall into hell after death and endure measureless atrocious anguish for numerous kalpas therein. All Buddhist learners must beware of this fact if they wish to avoid future sufferings.

Furthermore, the aforementioned tantric teachings do not just apply to the males, but the females are also required to have

---

[22]   Ibid., 308.

desire, so that their vajra lotus can generate the fluid necessary for the practice. Clearly, those practitioners must all have desire. Based on the tantric assertion that only those without desire and who have relinquished all their desire are allowed to cultivate the yab-yum method with disciples of the opposite sex," none of those tantric lamas and gurus are qualified for this practice. Although they use the term "branch of subsequent mindfulness" to explain that their method does not consist of greed, they have in fact never veered away from greed.

The branch of subsequent mindfulness is as follows:

Indeed, we have greed, but we should not allow it to grow on afflictive emotions; instead, we should hitch it to emptiness-nature. Therefore, on one side there must be greed; on another side, there must be (sexual) bliss; and on yet another side it is necessary to still have "emptiness"; this is called a branch of subsequent mindfulness. The statement "nature of subsequent greed" can be found in the Chinese version of the hundred-syllable mantra; it means that one should follow the nature of "greed." But what is the nature of greed? It consists of emptiness and no-self. For this reason, vajrasattvas practice the nature of subsequent greed with the method of the Path of Desire, calling it the branch of subsequent mindfulness. . . . The branch of subsequent mindfulness refers to the ability to enter and exit the central channel at will while abiding in it; this is called subsequent mindfulness, for one follows the mind anywhere it goes! The branch of retention refers to the recognition that the winds are being retained in the central channel—hence the term "retention." The branch of mid-level goodness refers to the practice of the winds; the winds must pass through the central channel. As for the branch of retention, the winds do not just pass through the central channel but must also abide in it. Is it enough to abide in the central channel? Subsequent mindfulness is also necessary. What is the result of subsequent mindfulness? The winds will be able to arrive at the vajra pestle, which is located at the end of the central channel. The lower end of the central channel corresponds to the pestle in a male and to the conch channel (this usually refers to the cervix) in a female. At this stage of the practice, the winds can open the central channel by passing through it; once the central channel is opened, they must be able to abide in it. Next, they must be able to follow mindfulness anywhere it goes. So why do we need to practice the motions of entering and exiting during sexual intercourse? Because the entering and exiting motions of the vajra pestle in the lotus should be in harmony with the nature of "emptiness"—those entering and exiting motions should follow the mindfulness of greed. At this moment, one can invent and realize the emptiness-nature and achieve the samādhi of emptiness and bliss! One can attain the sixth branch—the branch of samādhi—by practicing well the "re-installment of emptiness" in the branch of subsequent mindfulness; by then, one will have entered concentration. Samādhi refers to the perfect enlightenment achieved at last, the highest level of concentration.[23]

The branch of subsequent mindfulness illustrated above refers to the ability to move through visualization the drops upward and downward at will within the central channel of one's body by following one's mindfulness during the yab-yum practice. This even includes the capacity to lower the drops to the lower end of the pestle by following one's mindfulness consisting of the craving for sexual pleasure, so as to induce the great bliss by connecting with the conch channel located at the lower end of the female's central channel. One should abide permanently in this great bliss without ejaculating and contemplate that all phenomena are empty while only this bliss is permanent and non-empty. If one is thus able to dwell eternally (long-lastingly) in the great bliss (the orgasm consisting of the fourth joy), then one is said "to abide permanently in the great bliss." One has achieved the branch of subsequent mindfulness if one is able to induce the great

---

23 Yogi C. M. Chen (Chen Chien-ming 陳健民), *Qugongzhai quanji* 曲肱齋全集 *[The Complete Works of Yogi Chen]*, vol. 1-5, ed. Xu Qinying 徐芹庭 (Taipei: Puxianwang rulai fojiaohui 普賢王如來佛教會, 1991), vol. 1, 248. Translated into English from Chinese.

bliss by thus following mindfulness everywhere within the central channel without ever ejaculating; this is known as the attainment of ultimate awakening in Tantric Buddhism, which means that this practitioner has become an ultimate tantric Buddha.

However, those without desire cannot even perform the third initiation, let alone engage in the real practice of the fourth initiation. For instance, **Tsongkhapa** says:

> Thus, try your best to retain the bodhicitta (make every possible effort to retain the bodhicitta—semen—and avoid its expulsion during the third initiation). If you cannot retain it any longer, then release it slowly. (If you cannot withhold ejaculation any longer, then instead of rapidly discharging everything at once, you should hold yourself back by abiding in orgasm and cause the semen to flow out slowly, so as to prolong the duration of the blissful contact.) Smell the odor coming from the arising of the water (from the arising of the sexual fluid) and collect it (smell the odor of the sexual fluid and collect this sexual fluid). Drink the great bodhicitta of samaya nature (during the secret initiation, the liquid resulting from the mixture of the semen ejaculated by the guru after he achieves orgasm simultaneously with the female consort and this female's sexual fluid is called great bodhicitta of samaya nature; to imbibe this sexual liquid is to **"drink the great bodhicitta of samaya nature"**) based on the real view (the view that the semen constitutes the basis for the births of all Buddhas).[24]

The above statements from **Tsongkhapa** demonstrate that the lamas of the Gelug School who confer initiation on others are also required to bring forth a desirous mind, so that they can copulate with female consorts in front of the Buddha's statue in the maṇḍala and subsequently obtain a "proper" sexual fluid that can serve as nectar when they perform the secret initiation on disciples. Therefore, how could those tantric lamas be regarded as "gurus who have abandoned all desire"? Hence, those lamas' assertions

---

[24] Tsongkhapa, *Mizong daocidi guang lun* 密宗道次第廣論, 390. Translated into English from Chinese.

are not reasonable because monastics who have attained the Path of Vision have forever relinquished all sexual deeds.

Furthermore, as stated by Yogi C. M. Chen:

> When you do not just rely on visualization but also use real ones—real women—then it is the third initiation. Why should we use a real woman instead of just visualizing one? Because, through visualization, his material condition ("material condition" refers to the semen ejaculated) will be deficient. If he uses a real one (female consort), his material condition will be very sufficient and he will have the asset—the asset to undergo sublimation, the resource needed. It is only by having the resource needed that he can truly practice and gain wisdom. For example, your dick might not have an erection if you visualize a woman or even extensively visualize her in every way. But if there is a real woman, then it will get a boner right away and can perform its real function (it will ejaculate the semen that will serve as nectar in the secret initiation).[25]

Therefore, it is hypocritical of those tantric masters to assert that gurus do not have a lustful mindset and that they merely use this method to confer initiation and assist others to learn and practice the Dharma-gate that leads to the attainment of Buddhahood in this body. In fact, those masters have long had libidinous thoughts, their extremely lustful intentions have well been reflected in their deeds, and they have fully taken in the sexual pleasure experienced in their practice.

After recording his own lustful deeds, the cravings that he had experienced, and so forth, a tantric guru maliciously attributed these occurrences to the last Dharma-king of the Jonang School, Tāranātha, who had refuted the yab-yum practice and propagated the doctrine of the tathāgatagarbha. The following text from this

---

[25]　Yogi C. M. Chen (Chen Chien-ming 陳健民), *Qugongzhai quanji* 曲肱齋全集 *[The Complete Works of Yogi Chen]*, vol. 1-5, ed. Xu Qinying 徐芹庭 (Taipei: Puxianwang rulai fojiaohui 普賢王如來佛教會, 1991), vol. 1, 238. Translated into English from Chinese.

guru attests to the lustfulness exhibited by tantric lamas:

> In this lifetime, I was born in a place called Angren [昂忍], in the north of Lhasa [拉薩]. I had two supporting seals (two action seals upon whom I depended for the yab-yum practice): One was Dengbagangqing [登巴綱傾], and the other Dejibazong [德幾巴宗]. When I traveled in India, I also encountered two (women): One was Nageli [那格里], a very beautiful lady sky-traveler from Manggeda [莽格打], and the other a lady sky-traveler from Jialijia [加里加]. I cultivated the Path of Desire (the Path of Desire of the yab-yum practice) numerous times with both. Although this was what I pursued with fondness through the power of my vow, I achieved my goal only during half of those encounters. Dejibazong met me when she was fourteen years old, and I was already thirty-eight. I conferred on her the initiation of Heruka Chakrasamvara [勝樂金剛] in the vajra garland. That night, after making an offering, I cultivated (the yab-yum practice) with her; we spent a long time together.
>
> When I was aged four or five, I experienced the joy of non-discrimination upon seeing a statue of the tantric union (a "Buddha statue" in the yab-yum copulation posture). During my formal visits to the greatly virtuous ones who had accomplished the union, I exhibited admiration towards their achievements and aspired to emulate their deeds. For this reason, after perusing the Sakya School's treatise *Path with the Result [Daoguo]*, the rituals conforming to the meanings of the third initiation, and Angzhaputi's [盎札菩提] *Dharma Category of Path with the Result [Daoguofalei 道果法類]*, I made up my mind, brought forth the delightful pure faith, felt chills running down my spine, and experienced the great bliss day and night without interruption.
>
> At the age of eight or nine, I did not need to memorize the words about the *Path of Desire in Chakrasamvara, Hevajra, Guhyasamaja*, and the tantra *Sanbuzha [三不札]*; in fact, I was able to recite them immediately and understood their meanings right away. Every time I read about the generative branch, the corresponding greed arose accordingly, and I

firmly resolved to cultivate the main practice of the path of the mother sky-traveler. Therefore, I deliberately engaged in sexual intercourses before accepting the precepts of monks and did not dare to forget the three visualizations.

In January of the year of rabbit, one night I dreamed about a woman with a sow head on her right ear. She told me: "Tame me (have intercourse with me) and you will extend your lifespan, expand your merit, and obtain great achievement." I asked her: "Will anyone who interconnects with you gain these results"? She replied: "These results are not definite for others, but they certainly are for you." Elated, I took her skirt off and had sex with her. Suddenly I woke up.

The next morning, a woman called Zheng-Cai came for the longevity initiation. After conferring the initiation and once the attendant went out, I kissed her and experienced the great bliss. The woman said: "I will stay at Eju Beach [俄據汀] tonight." I replied by setting up a rendezvous: "I have decided to go over there and have a chat with you tonight." I played with her lotus (her private parts) while I was talking. At that moment, my guru Xiangba [香巴] arrived. The woman and I panted and changed countenance; then the woman left. The guru detected my thoughts and spent the night with me, which prevented me from visiting the woman as promised. What a pity! The causes and conditions of the great bliss as well as those of benefiting sentient beings could not be perfectly fulfilled.

That year, I visited (had sex with) Ya-Zhu. I had numerous prophetic dreams about my wondrous connections with action seals. I first dreamed about a female who had applied yellow lead oxide on her skin and was wearing a fragrance of sandalwood. Afterward, I had several dreams about having sex with her (I dreamed for several consecutive nights about engaging in sexual intercourse with that woman); her lotus emitted fire and secreted milk (I dreamed that her vulva emitted fire and secreted milk). I sometimes saw in those dreams the state of abiding in the intrinsic Brahma thusness, a lamp, or magnificent brilliance. The next morning, I passed by Longna Temple [龍那寺] and stumbled upon the female of the dream. Her name was Cunzan [村攢]; she came with distant relatives. She was wearing new purple clothes and her hair was adorned with only a turquoise; she did not have any other ornaments. Smitten with her at first sight, I felt endless bliss. While I conferred initiation on her, we caressed each other in private (the woman and I fondled each other secretly), causing her joy to intensify and her countenance to change. She was exactly the woman in my dreams.

In my leisure time, I liked to look far into the distance from a platform and that woman often came to walk around the temple. One day she came alone, and I enticed her to a place without people. There, I embraced her and kissed her madly; she did indeed emit a fragrance of sandalwood. I proposed to meet up after dusk. She said: "I am a dirty fisherwoman and do not dare to accept your invitation." I replied: "Sky-travelers (female consorts) are neither defiled nor pure; the Highest-Yoga yogi (those who cultivate the yab-yum method) of Tantric Buddhism do not cling to the signs of defilement or purity." Having said that, I again kissed her lips and tongue and fondled the pistil of her lotus (caressed her private parts). At that moment, her sexual fluid gushed out; I collected it and drank it. Fearing that she might miss the appointment, I declared that I would go to her place. She replied: "My house is shabby and not livable; I will come along with the moon tonight; I promise."

That night, I set up a fur tent and waited for her. As expected, she came and brought along some offerings. After we made an offering together in a place without people, we each picked up the foods offered, chewed them, and fed them into each other's mouth. My body performed deeds of desire and my mouth uttered speeches of lust, all with abandon. When I slept with her, imbued with extreme bliss, I did not have time to grasp the main practice. Based on the practice of the generative branch, my drops (semen) flowed out several times and blended with her bodhi (the woman's sexual fluid). When her lotus palace became sticky (when it was sticky inside her vulva), I licked her lotus with my tongue. She knew that my drops (semen) possessed the power of blessing, and therefore, she also held my pestle in her mouth and sucked it as if she was extracting the essence (she also held my penis in her mouth and sucked it as if she was absorbing the essence). She was greedy to the point of being insatiable. My pestle (vajra pestle) remained strong and did not show any weakness. We went on until dawn, indulging in our desire. (We went on like this until daybreak, both indulging relentlessly in our desire.) At dawn, we urinated and imbibed each other's urine. The woman uttered cuckoo sounds while I performed (while I performed the sexual act). The heat in my body did not dissipate for three days; my mind was clear and bright, but my body inflamed. This was exactly the blazing fire and secreted milk of my previous dreams.[26]

In the above text maliciously attributed to Tāranātha, the tantric lama exhibited desire whenever he saw a woman and endeavored to have sexual intercourse with her. He was constantly preoccupied with having sex even in his dreams and also after awakening. After writing down his experience, he transmitted it secretly to his disciples and allowed it to be made public only during future generations. How could such a lama be deemed desireless? How could his statements be credible in any way?

This lama, who falsely assumed the identity of Tāranātha, was constantly preoccupied with sexual deeds even in his dreams:

Next, I conferred various initiations of sky-traveling sea. One night I dreamed about an extremely rare treasury mountain surrounded by three different zones in each of the four directions around it. Those areas were populated with multifarious celestial beings, humans, and animals, most of which were females. While I indulged in reverie (while I was fantasizing), I heard the vajra ācārya Zhibuba [知不巴] utter the following words: "I bestow on you all the women in this area

---

[26] Yogi C. M. Chen (Chen Chien-ming 陳健民), *Qugongzhai quanji 曲肱齋全集 [The Complete Works of Yogi Chen]*, vol. 1-5, ed. Xu Qinying 徐芹庭 (Taipei: Puxianwang rulai fojiaohui 普賢王如來佛教會, 1991), vol. 3, 605-7. Translated into English from Chinese.

of mine. Among them are the sixteen wondrous females whom you have previously enjoyed with abandon. Without contradicting the path, you can do whatever you want with them." I obeyed his order and **conspicuously performed with female animals, female bolos [波羅], female artisans, sows, bitches, and white female peacocks, thus experiencing each individual bliss** (thus taking in the sexual pleasure proper to each species). **Those animals had a human body with an animal head and were quite interesting.**

Later, when I asked Hevajra Gebapai [各巴派喜金剛] to confer initiation and cultivate the intensive practice, I dreamed about copulating with the female lords of fifteen villages (about copulating with the female lords of fifteen villages one by one), and subsequently with the ten servants belonging to each of those female lords. . . . Shortly thereafter, I took the precepts of monks, . . . One year later I took refuge in an Indian guru of great merit and benevolence, . . . In the night of the twenty-third, Yuyinduojisulüma [玉印多吉蘇縷媽], one of the twelve Tenma goddesses (the twelve goddesses of Tibet, among which the main deity is called Dorje Yudrönma [多傑玉燈媽]), visited my guru. According to her, she had previously made an offering with three sky-travelers of wisdom and three sky-travelers of action, and given that the guru was now going to confer initiation on a capable yogi, she planned to offer another mother sky-traveler of wisdom (a mother sky-traveler is a female consort) and to bring along another mother sky-traveler of action (a mother sky-traveler of action is a female consort who is willing to cultivate the yab-yum method with others) to my guru's place the next morning.

The following day, my guru set up a solemn maṇḍala. A day later, on the twenty-fifth, my guru entered the samādhi of infinite light behind the curtain, while I practiced the deity yoga in front of it. At dusk, a bright light suddenly flashed; it was Yulin who had arrived with an action seal (with a lady sky-travler of action). I only saw the action seal; she was a family dependent of Dalüjaba [打縷加巴], a female protector goddess from Guludou [古魯斗] who could speak the dialects of Tsang [後藏] and Bhutan [不丹]. She had loose hair and wore turquoise dangle earrings and colorful garment. She was twenty-eight or twenty-nine years old. With her peach skin, blush forehead, wet eyes, long eyebrows, beautiful and captivating looks, she possessed all the characteristics of the lotus lineage. Her name was Kanabao [卡那寶].

My guru bestowed an initiation on her (on the female). When he passed her over to me (when he gave me the woman after the initiation), he instructed me to visualize truly seeing male consorts and sky-travelers galloping throughout the empty space, each indulging in their desire (he instructed me to visualize truly seeing male consorts and mother sky-travelers copulate and gallop throughout the empty space, each indulging in his or her desire). As this caused me to burn intensely with lust, I embraced the woman. Upon riding on her (upon riding on the woman's body), my body was numb with bliss and had lost all sensations of pain and itchiness. I kissed her, eliciting her laughter; she panted and shivered. She was not wearing underwear. When my pestle had dried, I inserted it shallowly into her lotus, causing her to leap like a horse and to exhibit exhilarating joy. My guru advised me against penetrating deeply (My guru exhorted me not to penetrate deeply), asserting that the bliss will be doubled if one draws upward before penetrating deeply. We moaned with pleasure simultaneously during my impulsive intrusions. I withdrew and thrust, causing the woman to grind and bounce. We performed the motions of drawing-down, drawing-up, retention, and dispersion nine times each (see Chapter 9 for the meaning of this sentence) as if nothing had happened. The woman was extremely blissful; the channel of her lotus bounced randomly, like a fish blowing waves and whose heart jumps on the surface of the water. When she came into contact with my pestle, she was amazed and uttered cuckoo sounds. My body was also in an unusual state, feeling irresistible numbness and itchiness; I felt free to make all kinds of joyful sounds. When the pistil of the lotus and the channel of the pestle were in deep compatibility, one could see the appearance of a deity. My guru gave me the following instruction (at this moment, my guru, who was at the scene, gave the following instruction): "The woman whom you have tamed (the woman who had sex with you) can connect with you spiritually. **You should observe your sexual acts as well as the four properties of the emptiness and bliss that you have attained. If they cannot be demonstrated and yet are not a state of nothingness, then they will manifest naturally and unceasingly. You should well observe the great bliss on that ceaselessness and expose it candidly.**" This quintessential instruction from my guru is tantamount to Mahāmudrā (is equivalent to the Mahāmudrā of bliss and emptiness) and I was fortunate to experience it in person. Next, we proceeded with making an offering. My guru and I saw rotating diagrams of joy in motion on the woman's forehead; all the male consorts and sky-travelers came by to accept the offering. My guru sang the song of instructions, I the song of sensations, and the woman the song of Bhutan offering.

At midnight, before going to bed, my guru held my hand and said: "You have achieved the vow that you made in a previous lifetime; I shall now read the glorious verses to you." Having declared those words, he appeared extremely delighted. He stepped into his bedroom after reciting the verses. The woman and I connected with and entered the Mahāmudrā of the non-duality of bliss and emptiness the entire night. (The woman and I connected with and entered the Mahāmudrā of the non-duality of bliss and emptiness by having sex the entire night.) The sky-traveler of action (the sky-traveler—female consort) had a lady bring over some wine; we imbibed it with abandon. The two of us slept lightly and indistinctly saw in the empty space myriad pairs of male consorts and sky-travelers kissing and touching hands, [drinking wine from] clay cups [while the sky-travelers'] orange hair [floats in the air], playing with the lotus (the vulva), and activating the pestle (erecting the male's penis by playing with it); or abiding immovably in emptiness and bliss (or dwelling together in the pleasure of orgasm to experience the emptiness of the blissful contact while taking in the bliss one-pointedly, all without moving the body) in ecstasy; or indulging in the power of withdrawing and thrusting amid sounds and motions; or crying, laughing, panting, and roaring, all thunderously. We ignited our passion by fondling each other and proceeded in this fashion without interruption throughout the entire night (until dawn).

After daybreak, the following words emerged from the round, tranquil blue light on my right shoulder: "It is impossible to attain Buddhahood without connecting with the Path of Desire; I would be violating my vow if the opposite were true." The following words then emerged from the round, tranquil red light on my left shoulder: "It is impossible to purify one's desire without entering the lotus (one cannot purify one's desire without engaging the yab-yum practice by entering the vulva); I would be violating my vow if the opposite were true (I would be violating my vow if one could purify one's desire without engaging in the yab-yum practice by entering the vulva)." Therefore, I again performed sexual intercourse (this caused me to copulate with the woman again), retaining the drops in a slow and relaxed manner (withholding the semen—refraining from ejaculating—in a slow and relaxed way) and causing the bliss at the tip of my pestle to pervade my entire body (the bliss at the tip of the pestle gradually expanded, causing the sensation of bliss to pervade my body). Due to the relaxed and slow pace, I was able to retain the drops and avoid leakage without striving. The woman felt great bliss, which caused the channel of her lotus to extend

For two entire days and nights, until the twenty-seventh, we neither left the throne (the throne of the yab-yum practice) even for a brief instant nor urinated. We drank the few drops (the few drops of urine) that the other person occasionally leaked. The pestle and the lotus adhered to each other whenever the defiled portion spilled over (whenever the semen that is the defiled portion of the drops spilled over from the vulva). I then kissed the pistil of her lotus (I then kissed the clitoris of her lotus and so forth); it had a great taste, and we were both thrilled.

When the first morning light broke out, I searched for her channel (conch channel). It had the shape of a nipple and possessed two roots, just like a mung bean. One of the roots resembled a thorn with a white end. The other root, which was four-colored, had the length of four fingers; the heart of the flower, which was light red, had the shape of a concave nose and displayed the lines of a five-pronged pestle. The bliss was three hundred times more intense when we had sexual intercourse after the channel had reached the bottom of the pestle's hole (after the female's conch channel had been stretched into the pestle's hole). When there was no upward drawing (when the pure portion of the semen was not drawn upward) while the pestle abided in the lotus palace, the pestle became larger and stronger, its tip glittered, and its hole became round and emitted light upward. The woman said: "These are the signs that appear when the drops are neither drawn upward nor leaked." The pestle became small and soft when the drops were drawn upward, and I felt that everything had been thoroughly absorbed. The bliss intensified when the drops ascended to each of the cakras; when they reached the crown, I felt that my entire body was renewed and pervaded by bliss. **Bliss, luminosity, and thoughtlessness** arose simultaneously and I did not distinguish whether there was serenity; **the bliss was extremely intense and all discriminations had ceased**; this was due to the power of the winds.

The woman taught me the following: "Place your pestle in the lotus palace and retain, draw up, and disperse by way of mental retention; it is not necessary to use the winds." I acted according to her instruction and was no longer crazy about her channel (I was no longer crazy about the conch channel within her private parts). The frequent back and forth motions caused itchiness in the duct of my pestle and led to a profusion of fluids. I focused my attention on the chest; some of the fluids dripped on the mat, and laughter broke out.

At daytime, my guru tried to get in touch with me. The practice had persisted nearly three days. I drank four big buckets of wine and neither got drunk in the slightest nor needed to sleep at night. The pestle and the lotus still had some interaction (still performed a few inward and outward motions).

At the dawn of a given day, the great achiever Luheba [鲁

赫巴] came to my bedside and told me: "I am an emanation of Chakrasamvara." After hearing these words, I saw, on his crown, a deity with four faces and twelve arms embracing a Buddha-mother. Luheba gave me the following instruction: **"The cakras at the male's and female's secret places are the dwelling spots of the Chakrasamvara parents and so forth. They generate action seals, Dharma seals, and wisdom seals, which are all illusory bodies. The fundamental entity is the great bliss; all sentient beings are tamed by the opposite sex; yogis are tamed by the three seals; the fruition of Buddhahood is tamed by the Buddha-mothers possessed by the intrinsic mind and the blissful body. Be aware that this is all manifested by your mind, and therefore, you should resolve to practice in this lifetime."** I rejoiced at hearing these instructions, and the woman and I resumed fondling each other.

That night, after my guru had made an offering consisting of leftover food, I waited behind the curtain for him to finish his reading. A light and sound suddenly emerged and the one who brought me the seal (the action seal—the consort) instantly emanated into lightning and vanished. My bliss increased by the day during the two months that followed.

I stayed at the foot of Jingkare Mountain [静卡惹山] the following year. There was a cow farm nearby, where a female with purple red complexion gave me some milk. I felt better after drinking it and saw that Buddha Śākyamuni, who manifested as a monastic, embraced a Buddha-mother (Buddhist learners should not be duped: Such is the manifestation of a ghost or spirit). I had once taught the Dharma there and this sensation intensified by the day. After preaching the Dharma for three days, I moved to another cave at the right side of the mountain. The aforementioned woman and her companions brought over some robes. All I could do was peep at her—it was an inopportune time to interact with her given the multitude of persons present. At dusk, she came closer to me and, when people could not see us clearly, I could surreptitiously explore her lotus (I could furtively grope for her private parts) and gently kiss her cheeks. After her departure, as the praying mat was still wetted by her peony drops (her menstrual flow), I prostrated on the mat without a second thought to lick those drops and felt a blazing bliss. There was not a complete lack of wondrous conditions.

A few days later, I met Yenabanzou [耶那班走], who possessed the nature of a sky-traveler. She had previously lived with me for two months (she had lived and slept with me for two months) owing to the power of my vow from a previous lifetime, but back then her lustful bliss had not yet been pervasive (her sexual pleasure had not yet pervaded her body). It was pervasive when I saw her this time and her enlightenment level had increased manifold. I have recorded all this in detail in a separate biography. Afterward, I passed by places such as Raozhen [饒貞], Lü [縷], and so forth. Although there were signs of achievement, the causes and conditions required were not met. Those who had previously hindered me were hindering themselves at that point. It was really regretful.

When I passed by Yixiwangbo [移喜網波], I received the four-perfection initiation of Wujin [烏金]; my wisdom increased by the day. I gradually improved my chemistry with those with whom I previously did not get along. Several days later, I stayed in Duodu [多都]. A mother sky-traveler with bone ornaments brought an armful of food (held food balls previously offered to the "Buddhas" in the secret maṇḍala) and offered them to me. In the bright appearance of the moon's arising, I saw a wrathful female rākṣasa with a chest torn open. Inside her chest was a temple. In this temple, the lord of mother sky-travelers Sangwayixi [桑瓦移喜], who was naked, held a drum and a skull cup and leaned on kazhangjia [卡張加]. Surrounded by hordes of male and female family dependents, she conferred on me the initiation of the secret practice of Avalokitêśvara. Among the family dependents was a beautiful young girl. She kissed me madly and embraced me, causing me to feel blissful from the pestle all the way up to the crown (from my private parts to my crown aperture) and to breathe weakly. When my vajra (pestle) entered the center of the lotus, I attained the non-discriminative concentration (the meditative concentration in which one abides one-pointedly without discriminations or distracting thoughts). I observed the fundamental entity and naturally achieved the rest of the great bliss in this non-discriminative concentration. Next (after attaining this supreme bliss), I performed sexual intercourse once with each of those family dependents, young and old, and Sangwayixi taught me the great purification method of the Path of Desire.

Two years later, when I stayed in Dingji [丁吉] in the summer, I visited my root guru and received the Practice of Forbiddance together with Renqinwangben [仁親網本]. During the Extensive Initiation, I drank twelve bowls of rice wine and saw the appearance of various great achievers of India. I performed this ritual three times during the day and did not need to urinate at night. The great bliss generated by the blessing power of the initiation persisted for half a month without dispersing.

I remember that I took the precepts of monks at the age of eighteen. For five years, I neither rejoiced at the sight of women, nor behaved like young boys and girls who had never experienced sex. In fact, I never had any profound intent to masturbate. The mother sky-traveler Yeshe Tsogyal [27] prophesied: "Be forever subjugated by the Path of Desire until all cyclic existences are emptied." It was an instruction that I and others heartily accepted. Given that my wisdom grew every time I copulated (cultivated the yab-yum method) with an action seal, I vowed to **devote myself eternally and assiduously to this path** until all sentient beings are liberated. . . . (We will omit the other passages about the yab-yum practice that are far more obscene than the above contents.)

When I was thirty-seven years old, I practiced sitting meditation in Jibudaduan [幾不達端]. **I dreamed that I blended with the appearance of pure luminosity.** I felt that my fleshly body was not ordinary mind-made body; it arrived at the kingdom of Śambhalaḥ [28] and entered the Zhanbala

---

27 Yeshe Tsogyal: one of Padmasambhava's female consorts; C. *Yixicuojia* 移喜磋嘉.
28 Śambhalaḥ: a mythical kingdom in Tibetan Tantric Buddhism. C. *Xiangbala* 香巴拉.

Palace [戰巴拉殿]. While sitting on top of it, I saw female consorts and maids playing in another palace. This palace was made of treasures and decorated with suspended garlands of coral and amber, water animals, painted tiger veins, red jades, and multi-colored satin; the ground was covered with sand of gold; the jewels sparkled days and nights. The window frames were made of red sandalwood; the bamboo windows, which were adorned with corals, were translucent like vaiḍūrya and their chiffon cloth could shroud smoke. The lion throne had an embroidered mat; the corners of the throne were embedded with extremely bright and colorful precious jewels. On the embroidered mat was a damask-silk mattress decorated with flowers and birds. The back pad on this mattress was embroidered with swarms of dragons and dancing phoenixes; the knitting skill displayed in this work did not seem to be that of any female worker in the human world. The feet cushion beneath the throne, whose size was freely adjustable, was decorated with green blossoms and fresh flowers that seemed to be self-arisen. The king of Śambhalaḥ was named Diandengba [墊登巴]. Adorned with auspicious marks and beauties, he was of average stature; although he was one hundred years old, he had the appearance of a young boy. The new silk fabric of his sumptuous garment was richly embroidered with phoenixes and flying dragons. His crown was embedded with gold, jades, pearls, and bird ornaments. He kissed the cheeks of the concubine who accompanied him while playing with the jewelry that she was wearing from head to toe.

All those family dependents were also involved in homosexual love. I saw the king and the concubine sitting on the throne, each flanked by a person of the same sex who told them about various paths of desire, fueling their lust. Once they were both sexually aroused, the concubine took off her dress and the king untied his jade belt. The vajra was magnificent and brave; the lotus was plump and moist; thunderous laughter was heard amid sounds of adhesion and detachment. At that time, I shrank into the size of a snail through my mind-made body and dwelled between the king's pestle and the concubine's lotus. I personally witnessed the drops of the pestle descend into the lotus and the king abide in the great bliss without moving.

A few moments later, the king and the concubine adopted a cowgirl sex position. The withdrawing and lifting motions were performed numerous times. The pestle became firmer and more powerful and the drops were released again. This occurred three or four times; the libidinous fluid of the lotus spring blended with the drops, like milk mixing with water, drenching and moisturizing the petals of the lotus before spilling out. The pubic hair became bright and lovely, like grass moisturized by the long-awaited dew. **I woke up from the dream** with extreme bliss, (so it was just an absurd dream; how could there ever be any mind-made body to speak of?) Several days later, the blissful desire brewed without dispersing. This bliss was a hundred times more intense than any signs seen before. We will not elaborate further on this subject, as it is recounted in a biography specifically dedicated to this subject. (We will not provide any annotations for this paragraph; practitioners can ponder about the contents themselves).[29]

Not only does this lama, who has falsely assumed the identity of Danalada (Tāranātha) crave for beautiful women while he is awake, but he also yearns for this path in his dreams and even enjoys having sex even with female animals. He is mostly delighted by sexual contact. If we explore what he means by "realization," we will discover that he refers to nothing other than the sensation of the fourth joy amid sexual pleasure. He asserts that this sexual pleasure is "non-existent" by observing that it is formless and shapeless. Furthermore, he affirms that it is "not non-existent" by observing that the blissful sensation of this sexual pleasure truly exists. Hence, he believes that sexual pleasure is "neither existent nor non-existent" and that those who understand this concept

---

[29] Yogi C. M. Chen (Chen Chien-ming 陳健民), *Qugongzhai quanji* 曲肱齋全集 *[The Complete Works of Yogi Chen]*, vol. 1-5, ed. Xu Qinying 徐芹庭 (Taipei: Puxianwang rulai fojiaohui 普賢王如來佛教會, 1991), vol. 3, 612-24. Translated into English from Chinese.

have achieved "the view of the Middle Way." In addition, having observed the mind of feeling and cognition that takes in the bliss in this state, he is convinced that the blissful contact is generated by this mind of feeling and cognition; since the mind of feeling and cognition and the blissful contact are both devoid of material form and shape, he asserts that they are both endowed with the nature of "emptiness." He further observes that neither the mind of feeling and cognition nor the blissful contact differs from the emptiness-nature (the mind of feeling and cognition and the blissful contact are both empty due to their formlessness and shapelessness; such an emptiness differs from the emptiness-nature—the eighth consciousness—realized in Exoteric Buddhism; furthermore, as tantric practitioners mistakenly believe that the perceived portion of the tangible object from which the blissful sensation is derived is generated by the mind of feeling and cognition, they maintain that the sensation of the blissful contact does not differ from the mind of feeling and cognition) and concludes that the "emptiness-nature consisting of the mind of feeling and cognition" and the "emptiness-nature consisting of the blissful contact" are non-dual. This state is called "non-duality of emptiness and bliss." According to this lama, those who are able to realize it have achieved the ultimate Buddhahood of Tantric Buddhism, and the above method is known as the Dharma-gate of attaining Buddhahood in this body.

Such a practice and realization enable lamas to become great practitioners of Tibetan Tantrism. Therefore, the sight of any beautiful woman suffices to ignite the lust of the aforementioned author, spurring him to do everything he can to copulate with her to cultivate the yab-yum method. He fantasizes about obscene sex to the point of clinging to his desire at all times and even frequently sleeps with women in his dreams. Surprisingly unaware of his mistakes, he is mired in a dream within the big dream that is life itself. Taking a lot of pride in his acts, he secretly composed a text under the false identity of the Dharma-king of the Jonang School and turned it into some quintessential instructions that would be passed down to later generations. Such quintessential instructions can kill two birds with one stone: For one, they can achieve the goal of wrongfully slandering Tāranātha, the Dharma-king of the Jonang School who invariably fought against the yab-yum practice and Prāsaṅgika Madhyamaka throughout his entire life; in addition, they can help propagate the yab-yum practice taught in the four major schools. How could those tantric lamas be said to have abandoned all greed when the statements in this text testify to their boundless lust? Therefore, the tantric claim that "greed can be eliminated through greed" is completely baseless; it is merely a pretext coming from those with mistaken views who indulge in their desire. As a matter of fact, this practice is a fallacious method transmitted by demons that are born into the human world, who use it as a tool to mislead learners onto the wrong path and to thwart the propagation of the correct path of the Buddha Dharma.

Furthermore, even the arhats who have achieved the Path to Liberation according to the teachings of sound-hearer imparted by the Buddhas of the three times have forever abandoned all cravings and lust for persons of the opposite sex; how then could the Most Honorable One with Two Fulfillments, who has realized the Buddha Bodhi with perfection, possibly have, after attaining Buddhahood, a magnificent reward body in the yab-yum form, in which He embraces a woman and enjoys sexual pleasure while copulating with her? Thus, the view of tantric practitioners is utterly fallacious, yet none of them are aware of their errors and even falsely claim that Buddha Mahāvairocana—Buddha Śākyamuni's Dharma body—has enabled tantric practitioners to attain Buddhahood in this body by teaching them the yab-yum practice found in *The Vairocanābhisaṃbodhi Sūtra [Dari jing]*. Those tantric followers are in fact slandering the Buddha by uttering this extremely grotesque falsehood.

Furthermore, after achieving enlightenment, the veteran Bodhisattvas of Exoteric Buddhism advance in their practice by cultivating, in the right sequence, the knowledge-of-specific-aspects and the knowledge-of-all-aspects within prajñā. During this process, they must, amidst their four deportments, gradually eliminate all their desire related to the human world. How could those tantric gurus teach their disciples and so forth the opposite by urging them to act based on their desire? How could those lamas—gurus—frequently indulge in this path even in their dreams? Although I have manifested myself as a lay Buddhist for two successive lifetimes, I have not had sex dreams for twelve years since I became enlightened in this lifetime. I often remind myself that all desires for women are as poisonous as a snake or scorpion. All female practitioners should, after attaining enlightenment, also remind themselves that all desires for men are as poisonous as a snake or scorpion.

The bodhisattvas of Virtual Enlightenment manifest themselves as having wives and children only for the purposes of fulfilling relationships of past lifetimes, demonstrating that they have a perfect family as well as ideal socioeconomic status, and showing that they are fully endowed with a male's vajra signs—demonstrating that they are fully endowed with sexual capacities and are not impotent men or hermaphrodites, which means that they have abandoned all their desire not because they are impotent. They are in fact devoid of erroneous desire and do not have cravings even for their own wives; they did not get married and have children because of any desire. As Bodhisattvas already behave in this fashion, how could the Buddhas, who are pure to the point of having thoroughly extinguished the latencies of the two hindrances of all seeds, possibly have transmitted this practice, which contradicts the Path to Liberation, to tantric followers? How could the Buddhas possibly have preached a method of sexual pleasure that stands at odds with the Path to Buddhahood? How could Their real reward be a magnificent reward body in the yab-yum form, in which They permanently enjoy sexual pleasure while embracing and copulating with a woman? Clearly, the assertions made by those tantric gurus do not make any sense, which means that their teachings about "the elimination of desire through desire" is erroneous and not credible. The wide array of fallacious views found in the "sūtras" and tantras of Tantric Buddhism all conflict with the Path to Liberation and the Path to Buddhahood and are completely unrelated to the Buddha Dharma. How could they be regarded as the Buddha Dharma? How could Master Yinshun insist that Tantric Buddhism is a Buddhist tradition, when it is in fact a non-Buddhist faith that depends on Buddhism to exist, propagates heretical teachings, and is in essence absolutely not Buddhism?

CHAPTER 9

HIGHEST YOGA TANTRA: THE ACTUAL CULTIVATION OF THE YAB-YUM METHOD

1. Overview of Highest Yoga Tantra

According to *The Six Yogas of Nāropa [Naluo liufa]*, there are four classes of tantras: Highest Yoga Tantra, Yoga Tantra, Performance Tantra, and Action Tantra.

> There exists a fourfold division of tantras: (1) Highest Yoga Tantra, (2) Yoga Tantra, (3) Performance Tantra, and (4) Action Tantra. Other than in Highest Yoga Tantra, the practice of embracing a consort mother is not found in any of the other three lower tantras.[1]

"Highest Yoga Tantra" refers to the yab-yum method, whereas "embracing a mother consort" points to the Dharma-gate of the non-duality of bliss and emptiness, in which one embraces a woman in order to cultivate sexual pleasure with her.

In Tantric Buddhism, those who believe, accept, and adhere to the following concept without any doubt in their minds right upon hearing it, "The practice of sexual pleasure between a male and a female allows for the attainment of Buddhahood in this body," are "the ones with exactly the right capacity" for the Dharma-gate of Highest Yoga Tantra and are said to be "the greatly capable ones in Mahāyāna fully endowed with the supreme disposition." Only can such "greatly capable ones" believe, accept, and learn this yab-yum practice. Therefore, the Highest Yoga Tantra method of sexual pleasure, which is cultivated through the copulation between a male and a female, is a Dharma-gate learned by "those with great faculty" within Tantric Buddhism and so forth.

For example, **Tsongkhapa** says:

> **The ones with exactly the right capacity** for Highest Yoga are, as mentioned previously, those who have practiced the

---

[1] *Naluo liufa* 那洛六法 [*The Six Yogas of Nāropa*], narrated by Blo-Bzan-Grags-Pa Zam Lam [Daoran baluobu cangsangbu 道然巴羅布倉桑布], recorded by Lu Yizhao 盧以炤 (Taipei: Chenxi Wenhua Gongsi 晨曦文化公司, 1994), 51. Translated into English from Chinese..

common path and who have purified the continuum of the Mahāyāna disposition; they are the greatly capable ones in Mahāyāna fully endowed with the supreme disposition. The intention brought forth from their great compassion has fueled intense cravings as well as the vow to attain Buddhahood swiftly. In order to enter the Dharma-gate of Highest Yoga Tantra and quickly achieve Buddhahood, they must correctly understand the meanings of the tantras (understand the doctrines of the tantras) and proficiently study the two stages (the generation stage and the completion stage) and the various esoteric practices (the various esoteric Dharma-gates of practice such as the cultivation of the yab-yum method with persons of the opposite sex after the fourth initiation and so forth).[2]

Tsongkhapa has indicated in *The Great Exposition of Secret Mantra [Mizong daocidi guanglun]* that there exist four yogas in the Action and Performance Division—deity yoga, emptiness yoga, wind yoga, and recitation yoga—and that one must achieve the cultivation of these four methods before being able to learn the main practice that is Highest Yoga Tantra. The yogas of the Action and Performance Division are methods of the generation stage— the term "generation stage" denotes the fact that one must achieve the practices of this stage before being able to cultivate Highest Yoga Tantra with another person. Tsongkhapa has proclaimed that this Highest Yoga Tantra is a method of the Yoga Division in the **fruit tantra** and that those who learn the yab-yum method can attain Buddhahood in one lifetime:

> With respect to the subdivisions of the initiation rituals, you should understand the rituals of fire offering and of resource cakra, as well as the characteristics of the mantra chanter, the bell, the pestle, the big and small dippers, the skeleton stick, and so forth needed to cultivate these rituals—you should know how to make them and then how to use them and

---

[2] Tsongkhapa, *Mizong daocidi guang lun* 密宗道次第廣論, 154. Translated into English from Chinese.

so forth. Thus, these tools become ritual instruments through the power of initiation. By being skillful at the samaya precepts (by knowing the valid knowledge in "meditative concentration" related to the Dharma-gate of the non-duality of bliss and emptiness well), coming into contact with and pondering over the teachings, and ascertaining the right practice, **those with superior faculty will attain Buddhahood in this lifetime, those with mid-level faculty will attain Buddhahood after generating an intermediate state from** [the subtle discrimination of the body of] **other sentient beings, and those with inferior faculty will attain Buddhahood in the next rebirth.**[3]

After I published *Pingshi's Letter [Pingshi shujian 平實書箋]*, the lay Buddhist Chen Lü'an [陳履安] called me and said: "You should not have reprehended in *Pingshi's Letter [Pingshi shujian]* Tantric Buddhism for transmitting the yab-yum practice between a male and a female, given that this method does not even exist in Tantric Buddhism." The truth is, the yab-yum practice does exist in Tantric Buddhism, has been worshipped even by Tsongkhapa and other proponents of the Gelug School, which proclaims itself as the cleanest reformer, and has been constantly propagated up to this day.

So who are the people teaching this practice nowadays? It is not necessary to identify them one by one. We can get an idea of the overall situation from the fact that numerous female tantric practitioners have been requested by their male peers to help them achieve "the path to Buddhahood in this body" through the co-practice of the yab-yum method. Furthermore, given that a plethora of female practitioners as well as some of the nuns in Taiwan have cultivated the yab-yum method with their male gurus or have received a "proper" fourth initiation, we can conclude that the tantric yab-yum practice has never ceased to exist and is being

---

[3]   Ibid., 156.

disseminated in secret; its exponents do not dare to propagate it openly due to the establishment of the samaya precepts in Tantric Buddhism.

Furthermore, all tantric practitioners who have cultivated the yab-yum method with a guru of the opposite sex or have received the fourth initiation from a guru in the secret maṇḍala are not permitted to divulge any of those contents. Those facts must forever be kept secret between the tantric gurus and their disciples—male and female alike—and must never be disclosed to their spouses, especially if the cultivation occurred between a male guru and a female who has practiced Tantrism for a long time. Therefore, such inside information will never be exposed, unless under some special circumstances. In order to protect the fame of the female practitioners who have cultivated the esoteric doctrines for a long time and maintain peace in their families, we will omit the details related to those contemporary cases and will just cite the contents preached by the "great guru" Padmasambhava in the ancient times—they will suffice to prove the existence of this practice. Padmasambhava's teachings are illustrated in *Dakini Teachings [Haimu shenshen yindao 亥母甚深引導]*:

> Guru Padmasambhava says:
>
> Yeshe Tsogyal! You should listen carefully. I will teach you the practice of Vajravārāhī. Among these contents, the external calculation method encompasses the selection of proper dates and so forth, and the internal calculation method covers the establishment techniques of winds, channels, and drops—secrets such as the channels and so forth. You should first receive initiation to ripen yourself for the practice of the initial stage of Vajravārāhī. Next, cultivate, during the secret practice, the methods of the winds, the channels, the pure portion of the drops, and the descending of the self and other Vārāhīs; get to know the innate wisdom (the innate wisdom of sexual pleasure) on the wisdom of bliss and of emptiness. Understand all manifestations as the Dharma body. After ascertaining

the correct view, cultivate spontaneously the body of clear light in order to transform the contaminated into the uncontaminated and to enter the stage of Samantabhadra Rāja Tathāgata (to enter the fruition of "Samantabhadra Rāja Tathāgata" who embraces and copulates with a woman while naked, thus forever taking in the sexual pleasure consisting of the fourth joy). This is the teaching that I shall preach to you.

Yeshe Tsogyal recorded this teaching on yellow scrolls, placed these scrolls in a copper casket, and hid it in Sangshuang nazhe [桑爽那柘]. Later, the mantra holder Geji dengpu [歌吉登譜] retrieved it and hid it in Manaslu Mountain [孟餘山]. Jugu qugang zhebo [舉古取綱柘波] of the Nyingma School respectfully took it out and turned it into an object of offering. Finally, King Kutang [貢通王] transferred it to the palace, opened the case, and saw two yellow scrolls around ten centimeters in width and thirty centimeters in length. The contents, written in symbolic scripts, consisted of *Dakini Teachings [Haimu shenshen yindao 亥母甚深引導]*. . . .

> Guru Padmasambhava says:
> Among all the secret practices, the most secret one is to cultivate all dharmas in dependence upon the drops of the body. In the emptiness-nature without conditions, you become Hayagrīva Vajra with one face and two arms, . . . , three eyes and long and sharp fangs, red and yellow-colored erect hair, donning tiger, elephant or human skin, adorned with various beauties, . . . Vajravārāhī arises from the seed syllable at your heart; she is endowed with a black sow head at the vertex and utters sounds. She and the Buddha-father embrace each other and their crown cakra each contains three hundred and sixty *banzhazhage* [班札札格]. . . . Their mudrās appear in the following sequence: vajra, treasure, ax, lotus, and sword on the right and skull cup on the left; every pair of Buddha-father and Buddha-mother embrace each other fondly. . . . In brief, the vajra body is filled with myriad pairs of sky-

traveling father and mother—just like sesame pods opening up to unveil many of them embracing each other amidst sexual union. The sky-traveling warrior exhorts the vajra sky-traveling father and mother thus above his crown to pour down red and white nectar from their union, causing bliss to pervade his crown. The nectar blends into the central channel, pours into the throat, and finally arrives at the secret place, turning every cakra that it reaches; makes offerings in this fashion to all the pores in the body. Furthermore, hold the wind and push it upward, causing it to gush outward from the crown aperture; this is an offering to Guru Padmasambhava. Guru Padmasambhava Vajradhara then releases the red and white bodhicitta into the hearts of all sentient beings. Once purified, abide in the Buddha state of Guru Padmasambhava and transform into a light that blends into this guru's heart. This guru in turn transforms into a light that enters the spontaneous great radiance. . . . This is a secret practice that cannot be divulged. . . . The horse head that flows out from the compassion issued from the garland on my lotus head undergoes transformations in order to subdue sentient beings; this is the source of the attributes of my—Padmasambhava's—mental practice. For the sake of future sentient beings, I hope that the capable ones will encounter it as soon as possible.

Preliminary step: Empower your body so as to transform it into the bodies of the Buddha-father and Buddha-mother with a horse head. If the conditions manifest clearly, then Guru Padmasambhava will appear above your crown. By practicing naturelessness, you will be surrounded by sky-traveling family dependents. Bring forth the supreme bodhicitta and the seed syllable on the lotus sun will emit red light, burning up the three karmic predispositions of sentient beings. This light will revert and transform into a horse head with a red body that embraces Vajravārāhī; the pestle and the lotus will become united (the sexual organs of the two deities—the male with a horse head and the female with a sow head—will become united). Above the crown, Guru Padmasambhava will also act like the horse and the sow embracing each other (Guru Padmasambhava will embrace and copulate with a female consort in the same way that the horse and the sow engaged in sexual union; the sexual fluid that they will release due to the bliss generated will flow down into the practitioner's crown) and will confer the supreme initiation. . . .

Obeisance to the deity of secret speech: The secret practice that I cultivate is the most secret of all secrets. Lay the triangular ritual cakes[4] of five sky-travelers in a śmaśāna or a quiescent location, place a hawk feather on an arrow, and tie the following objects to this arrow: red damask silk, slices of red copper, conches, and so forth. These are the sky-travelers' objects of support. Adorn a rattan pole with three joints that is as solid as bamboo with five-colored—red and so forth—damask silk. Apply the blood (menstrual blood) of a virgin and yellow lead on one's neck. These are the support of the practice of worship. In the case of a monk, he should prepare a red robe, the mantra of the five female divisions of mother sky-travelers written with golden (ink) on a black paper, the blood (menstrual blood) of a lady sky-traveler aged sixteen and endowed with the proper characteristics, his own drops (semen), amrita that contains all five meats and five nectars (wine blended with all five meats and five nectars), five persons (five female consorts) and five treasures, and a skull cup in one single piece—for a female with normal functions. There, . . . (cultivate the activities of control based on the above teaching).

One's own cakra of great bliss (the tantric lamas without real female consorts at their disposal should practice the method of **"One's own cakra of great bliss"**): In order to enhance his uncontaminated wisdom, a powerful yogi should cultivate the methods of the winds, channels, and drops and receive a proper initiation. After completing the practice of inner fire, sit on a comfortable mat in a quiet place and visualize a Buddha-mother (female consort) of your choice. This is the

---

4   Ritual cake: a type of religious offering; T. *torma*; C. *shizi* 食子.

practice of the wisdom mother united with the mind. If she becomes real (if the visualized female consort truly appears in front of you), then simulate the following acts in the empty space: listening to her words, peeping at her appearance, pressing her breasts, and so forth. Based on the above, bliss is generated through an undetermined method. (Based on the above, you are free to use a method of your choice to generate your contact-induced sensation of sexual pleasure.) Your body becomes hot and sweaty and your pestle (sexual organ) releases cow saliva; at this moment, you should observe that the property is intrinsically empty. Through the shivering of your head, body, and so forth, instantly bring forth the Buddha's pride of the horse head. Visualize your pestle as a five-pronged pestle; the top of the red seed syllable will face downward, blocking the opening of the pestle. Perform by using your right hand as Vajravārāhī (use your right hand as the consort Vajravārāhī and induce sexual pleasure through masturbation), clearly show that your nature [pervades] your crown, your five cakras (in his body), and so forth, and cultivate in the same fashion as in the previous esoteric practice. Even if your life is at risk, do not release the drops (make sure that you do not ejaculate).

You should frequently bring forth such enthusiasm and masturbate slowly. When the bliss arises, the upper wind will abide in its original place and the middle wind will inflate your abdomen; look at the entity of luminosity and emptiness and shake your body. Masturbate again when the bliss subsides. When the bliss becomes unbearable, as if you were about to pass out, keep your body still, expand the middle wind outward, press the upper wind downward, lift the back wind upward (arch the back like a cat, contract the pelvic floor, and draw the wind upward from the root of the pestle to the Governing Vessel [督脈] at the back), exhale with long *hum* and short *hum*, and draw in the abdomen towards the back (pull in the abdomen towards the back and lift the wind upward). Repeat the above three times in a row without interruption (achieve orgasm three times in a row without interruption as highlighted above).

Furthermore, make an offering by performing in the five

cakras like a turtle (transfer the sexual pleasure to each of the vertically-aligned five cakras one after another, while abiding in orgasm to carefully and slowly take in the long-lasting pleasure; this constitutes an offering to yourself); all channels will vibrate when the bliss reaches the crown. The middle wind will expand the abdomen, and the drops (semen) will abide naturally without leaking. Afterward, draw upward (draw the pure portion of the semen upward) by making an empty sound, focus the mind and the eyes on the crown, and repeatedly draw upward. When the drops revert to their source (when the drops then descend to their source—the sexual organ), you can spread them to the entire body through fist methods such as goat shaking and so forth. Next, gradually repeat this practice. (Practice again this method of masturbation shortly afterward; when the sexual organ softens, resume the practice after a pause—your sexual power will be stronger than in the previous practice and your pleasure will consequently intensify—this is one of the quintessential instructions that tantric gurus must transmit to their male disciples; the females are not bound by this rule.)

For practitioners who are not yet familiar with the winds and the channels or whose "view" is not yet definite, when their drops are about to fall (when they are about to ejaculate), they should press the location between the anus and the genitals (perineum) with their index finger in order to slightly suppress the wind (in order to prevent ejaculation), while their minds focus on the syllable *ham* [罕] above their crowns. Subsequently, they should progressively suppress [the perineum] with the middle wind, inhale the upper wind and press downward, lift up the back wind with strength, and emit long and short *hum* sounds as if their bowels were about to break. Next, they should hold the vase wind to prevent the pure portion from leaking (this method prevents the pure portion of the semen from being ejaculated). By practicing diligently in this fashion (in order to induce great bliss), they can separate the pure and the defiled (they can separate the pure and the defiled portions thanks to this great bliss) and obtain firmness (and take in the bliss long-lastingly by avoiding softening).

By holding this practice spontaneously, a sky-traveling warrior can increase his merit and expand his lifespan. His body will become fresh like a boy's; he will not have any white hair, and his forehead will be without wrinkle. The red portion that he extracts from the other body (from the mother sky-traveler—female consort—who practices with him) must not be excessive (the extraction of the feminine performed on the consort's body in order to nourish the masculine must not be excessive); otherwise, the body (of the female consort) will become purple black. Therefore, he should know the capacity that can be sustained (by the female consort). This essential instruction must be accepted and upheld.[5]

The actual existence of the yab-yum practice between a male and a female within Tibetan Buddhism is substantiated by the above teachings by the founder of this faith, the "great guru" **Padmasambhava**, in *Dakini Teachings [Haimu shenshen yindao 亥母甚深引導]*. Chen Lü'an has simply lost his humanity by lying to me that this method does not exist in Tibetan Buddhism. In fact, such teachings were not just given by Padmasambhava, but were also imparted by Tsongkhapa; the readers who are interested in this topic will know that I am telling the truth by reading Tsongkhapa's *The Great Exposition of Secret Mantra [Mizong daocidi guanglun]*. Many gurus other than Padmasambhava and Tsongkhapa also preach this method, but they do not reveal it to the novice practitioners of Tantric Buddhism.

For instance, a guru has stated the following:

When the inner fire blazes and the white bodhicitta dissolves and moves upward and downward, one's greed arises naturally. Our greed has existed since beginningless time; it is deeply ingrained and therefore difficult to eradicate. If one can

---

[5]   Yogi C. M. Chen (Chen Chien-ming 陳健民), *Qugongzhai quanji 曲肱齋全集 [The Complete Works of Yogi Chen]*, vol. 1-5, ed. Xu Qinying 徐芹庭 (Taipei: Puxianwang rulai fojiaohui 普賢王如來佛教會, 1991), vol. 3, 529-39. Translated into English from Chinese.

utilize it skillfully, then it can be transformed into wisdom, just like water can be turned into nectar by adding nectar into it or like rigid iron can become gold if one spreads golden medicine over it. Practitioners who cultivate the bodhicitta for a long duration can transform the five poisons consisting of greed, anger, ignorance, arrogance, and doubt, which constitute the roots of eighty-four thousand afflictive emotions, into wondrous bodhicitta. The white bodhicitta (the semen of males) can benefit sentient beings. Those who do not understand the practice of embracing a female consort during the cultivation of inner fire regard it as a sexual act. Little are they aware that there is a profound meaning to it: **Having sexual intercourse without ejaculating and benefiting others one-pointedly** are entirely for the purpose of eliminating the karmic hindrances of sentient beings. If one can harbor the intention to benefit others, then his killing, robbing, hitting, and ranting all imply "wondrous bodhicitta and benefits of sentient beings." This wondrous doctrine is proper to the unsurpassed Tantric Buddhism and cannot be fathomed by elementary learners. Those people enjoy discussing about metaphysics and do not advocate actual practice, are their acts any different from elaborating on the neighbor's treasure? Could the treasure be obtained through such verbal elaborations?[6]

These brief passages from Guru Padmasambhava and other tantric masters suffice to demonstrate that this yab-yum practice does indeed exist in every tradition of Tibetan Tantric Buddhism. Not only does this preposterous method of sexual pleasure between a male and a female, which is based on sexual misconduct, truly exist, but it is precisely the main theory and Dharma-gate of actual practice of Tantric Buddhism. The tantric path would completely unravel and vanish if it were stripped of such a theory

---

[6] *Naluo liufa* 那洛六法 *[The Six Yogas of Nāropa]*, narrated by Blo-Bzan-Grags-Pa Zam Lam [Daoran baluobu cangsangbu 道然巴羅布倉桑布], recorded by Lu Yizhao 盧以炤 (Taipei: Chenxi Wenhua Gongsi 晨曦文化公司, 1994), 195. Translated into English from Chinese.

and Dharma-gate of sexual pleasure experienced amidst the non-duality of bliss and emptiness.

For these reasons, we can conclude that the statements made by the lay Buddhist Chen Lü'an are false. He deliberately deceived me in an effort to stop me from ever mentioning this fallacious tantric practice again. This event also tells us that he is in fact aware that this tantric theory—this Dharma-gate of practice—does not correspond to the true Buddha Dharma, and he therefore, fears that people might disparage Tantric Buddhism if they discover the truth; otherwise, he would not speak at length over the phone in order to untruthfully persuade me about the inexistence of this method in Tantric Buddhism.

In addition to the aforementioned examples, there exist similar teachings in other tantric sūtras, such as *The Vairocanābhisaṃbodhi Sūtra [Dari jing 大日經], The Compendium of Principles [Yiqie rulai zhenshi shedacheng xianzheng sanmei dajiaowang jing 一切如來真實攝大乘現證三昧大教王經], True Union Tantra [Jieho jing 結合經], The Vajra Rosary Tantra [Jinkangman jing 金剛鬘經], The Guhyasamāja Tantra [Jiemigenben jing 集密根本經], The Perfection of Wisdom in 150 Lines: The Samaya Sūtra about the Non-Empty Reality of Chakrasamvara [Liqi jing—Dalejingang bukongzhenshi sanmeiye jing 理趣經—大樂金剛不空真實三昧耶經], Compendium of Principles [Shezhenshi jing 攝真實經], The Tantra of the Second Observation [Dier guancha jing 第二觀察經], The Mahāmudrā Drop Tantra [Dayin kongdian jing 大印空點經], The Tantra of the Moon's Secret Drops [Yuemi kongdian jing 月密空點經], The Note-Taking Tantra [Zhana jing 札拏經]*, and so forth. The yab-yum practice is also set forth in *The Method of Mother Tantra [Muxu xiufa 母續修法]*, which is authored by Guru Kambalapada [毳衣] and Luoyiba [羅伊跋], *The Yab-Yum Method of Hevajra [Huanxi jingang shuangshen xiufa 歡喜金剛雙身修法]* by Commentator Ratnakarasanti, *The Method of the Selfless Mother [Wuwomu xiufa 無我母修法]* by Zhongbiba [種比跋], *The Method of Hevajra*

[Huanxi jingang xiufa 歡喜金剛修法] by Nanshengyue [難勝月], Vajra Tent *[Jingangmu 金剛幕]*, *The Guhyasamāja Tantra [Jimi 集密]*, *The Guhyasamāja Later Tantra [Jimi houxu 集密後續]*, *Commentary on the Clear Light of Reality [Zhenshi guangming lun 真實光明論]*, *Commentary on the Clear Union [Mingxian shuangyun lun 明顯雙運論]*, *Commentary on the Illuminating Torch [Mingju lun 明炬論]*, *The Compendium of Practice [Shexing lun 攝行論]*, *The Six Yogas of Nāropa [Naluo liufa 那洛六法]*, *Dakini Teachings [Haimu shenshen yindao 亥母甚深引導]*, *The Great Exposition of Secret Mantra [Mizong daocidi guanglun 密宗道次第廣論]*, *The Method of the Maṇi Tree [Monishu fa 摩尼樹法]*, *The Secret Biography of Tāranātha [Danalada mizhuan 打那拉達密傳]*, *Commentary on the Path of Desire [Tandao lun 貪道論]*, *A Guide to the Great Bliss [Dale yindaomen 大樂引導門]*, *Quintessential Instruction on the Retention of Drops [Mingdian bulou koujue 明點不漏口訣]*, *Quintessential Instruction on the Protection of Samaya [Shoufu sanmeiye koujue 守護三昧耶口訣]*, *Quintessential Instruction on Taking in Mudrā [Shouyong shouyin koujue 受用手印口訣]*, *Quintessential Instruction on Worship [Aijing koujue 愛敬口訣]*, *The Unique Quintessential Instruction on the Six Essentials of the Realization of Kālacakra Vajra [Shilun jingang zhengfen liuzhi fayao bugong koujue 時輪金剛證分六支法要不共口訣]*, and so forth. Furthermore, not only is this yab-yum practice taught in countless other tantras composed by ancient tantric gurus, but it is even extensively discussed in *The Great Exposition of Secret Mantra [Mizong daocidi guanglun]*, which is authored by Tsongkhapa, the founder of the Gelug School in Tibetan Tantric Buddhism, which proclaims itself as the "purest tradition." In brief, this method of sexual pleasure does truly exist and is set forth in innumerable esoteric sūtras and tantras of Tibetan Buddhism; only the elementary practitioners of this faith are unaware of its existence.

The tantric theory of attaining Buddhahood in this body entirely stems from this yab-yum method, which is practiced together by a male and a female. Moreover, the magnificent reward body obtained by those followers when they attain Buddhahood in the future will also take on the form of a "celestial being" of the desire-realm taking in pleasure in the yab-yum sitting sex position. Contrary to Chen Lü'an's assertion, this practice does exist because Milarepa of the Kagyu School in Tantric Buddhism also engaged in it. It is, therefore, unnecessary to dispute with Chen Lü'an over such an existence, as readers may refer to *The Hundred Thousand Songs of Milarepa* and so forth for further details. Moreover, many tantric gurus have untruthfully claimed in the tantras that Śākyamuni attained Buddhahood after cultivating this method; according to them, He did not preach it in the sūtras of the Three Vehicles but taught it after He manifested as an emanation body once He passed away.

Furthermore, those tantric gurus have unanimously maintained that it is impossible to become a Dharma body Buddha or a reward body Buddha without practicing this method, as evidenced by the following publication:

> The practice of Cakrasaṃvara is not limited to one version: The contents transmitted by Lama Marpa [末而幹], Lama Chokyi [秋既], and Lama Jueluoruo [覺洛若] are all different. The sixty-two forms of Chakrasaṃvara all have a maṇḍala. Both Cakrasaṃvara and Hevajra attach importance to the practice of inner fire with the objective of offering it to the countless Buddhas within one's body. However, **those who have failed to please their guru will not obtain any siddhi.** The practitioner should regard his body as a maṇḍala and offer the inner fire to the Buddhas; this is an essential point. Furthermore, he should cultivate the principle of the turning of all wheels in the maṇḍala. **One has no chance to attain Buddhahood if one cultivates the generative stage by itself without going through another practice.** In other words, **in order to achieve Buddhahood, it is indispensable to cultivate the yab-yum method;** the cultivation of inner fire in the main practice corresponds to the yab-yum cultivation. Therefore, one can attain Buddhahood only if one cultivates the main practice (the yab-yum practice) after completing the

generative stage.[7]

This publication further says:

> In ancient Tibet, the sūtras were mostly preached by lay
> practitioners; none of the monastics engaged in this activity.
> Hence, those who taught the sūtras all had family. **Lama
> Moerwo** (Marpa), **Milarepa's teacher, was a lay practitioner
> and his wife was a mother sky-traveler.** If one attains
> Buddhahood, then one's wife automatically becomes a mother
> sky-traveler. Indeed, if the wife has no chance of becoming a
> Buddha, then she will hinder her husband's practice of the
> Dharma out of fear that he might leave her once he attains
> Buddhahood. **In that case, no one would want to cultivate
> the method of Buddhahood. For this reason, a door of
> expediency was generously opened with the establishment
> of the yab-yum practice. It enables the husband and the
> wife to practice and become Buddhas together.** Thereafter,
> not only have the wives not obstructed their husbands from
> practicing the Dharma, but they have also joined them in their
> endeavors, hoping that both of them would become Buddhas.
> As a result, **the number of practitioners of the Dharma has
> naturally been able to increase by the day**. The Buddha came
> up with this expedient with thoughtful intention and through
> painstaking efforts spent in solitary pondering, hoping that
> people would practice the Dharma and free themselves from
> the ocean of suffering. Therefore, when you see a yab-yum
> statue, you should revere and understand the profound and
> secret intention of the Buddhas and Bodhisattvas and should
> not have any thought to slander them. This is essential.[8]

Thus, the lay Buddhist Chen Lü'an was just trying to fool me
when he dishonestly claimed that the yab-yum practice, which
leads to the attainment of Buddhahood in this body, does not exist

---

[7]   *Naluo liufa* 那洛六法 [*The Six Yogas of Nāropa*], narrated by Blo-Bzan-Grags-Pa
Zam Lam [Daoran baluobu cangsangbu 道然巴羅布倉桑布], recorded by Lu Yizhao
盧以炤 (Taipei: Chenxi Wenhua Gongsi 晨曦文化公司, 1994), 52. Translated into
English from Chinese.

[8]   Ibid., 63.

in Tibetan Buddhism. He further told me: "Many great tantric practitioners currently live in Taiwan. You should visit them, as they have all achieved high valid knowledge. In fact, they are very humble and have never proclaimed themselves as Buddhas, nor have they asserted that Buddhahood can be attained in this body. You should not level such false accusations against them." Who are the great tantric practitioners to which Chen was referring? He did not mention their names. I am not in a position to comment on them, given that they have declined to meet me after Chen invited them to do so. The fact is, not only do the tantric "sūtras" and tantras extensively mention the Dharma-gate of sexual pleasure— the yab-yum practice—but they also maintain that one can observe the non-duality of bliss and emptiness and become an ultimate Buddha by engaging in the union of bliss and emptiness amidst sexual pleasure. It is not true that no tantric guru has ever discussed this method, as the Dalai Lama also speaks about the existence of this practice in *Opening the Eye of New Awareness* [*Jiekai xinzhide aomi 揭開心智的奧秘*], which was published by Chung Sheng Publisher. Therefore, we can conclude that the statements made by the lay Buddhist Chen are deceitful.

Furthermore, there have been myriad cases in Tibetan Buddhism whereby in response to the Exoteric Buddhists who had corrected the false tantric views, the gurus in return accused them of being the ones with mistaken views. In the past, for instance, tantric followers exterminated the Jonang School and further deprecated it in various books and treatises after wrongfully vilifying it as a destroyer of the Dharma. In fact, for many generations of Dharma-kings in the Jonang School, starting from Dolpopa Sherab Gyaltsen, their apparent propagation of the Kālacakra teachings served as a cover-up to conceal their actual dissemination of the tathāgatagarbha doctrine. Based on this doctrine, they refuted the misconception upheld by the various tantric traditions that consisted of regarding the conscious mind in thoughtlessness as the reality-suchness of the Buddha Ground. Furthermore, those Dharma-kings banished the yab-yum practice and called for its abandonment. For this reason, the Jonang tradition was exterminated by the Gelug School, which falsely proclaimed that Tāranātha, the last Dharma-king of the Jonang School, cultivated the yab-yum method. Indeed, the followers of the Gelug School implicated Tāranātha in their misdeeds with a false biography titled *The Secret Biography of Tāranātha [Danalada mizhuan]*, in which he was wrongfully vilified as someone who approved and cultivated the yab-yum method. At that time, the proponents of the Gelug School further destroyed the carving plates preaching the view of other-emptiness stored in the monasteries of the Jonang School. They carved new plates containing the distortions they had made to the doctrines of the Jonang School and used those plates to replace the ones that they had destroyed by surreptitiously storing them among the other plates found in the monasteries of the Jonang School, so that they could be passed down to later generations. This is a historical fact that was deliberately omitted in the tantric history written under the command of the Gelug School. As a matter of fact, such instances in which Tantric Buddhists frame other traditions for their own wrongdoings and level false accusations against them have been widespread within Tantric Buddhism.

Here is another example:

> In the case of the unsurpassed vehicle, if a person obtains wisdom by cultivating the channels, winds, and drops for a hundred years and becomes truly pure, **then he will definitively achieve Buddhahood in this lifetime.** If he abides in this esoteric teaching but does not connect with the Prajñā Vehicle, then he is making an erroneous discrimination. Those who affirm the existence of the object consciousness, path consciousness, and omniscience are muddled by the teachings of Exoteric Buddhism. If the "path consciousness" did not exist, then one could not possibly attain Buddhahood; if one was unable to attain Buddhahood, then one would not have omniscience. This principle and so forth have been annotated by the Bodhisattvas and extensively delineated by the greatly skillful ones. It just does not make full sense for a person to claim that he has achieved the quiescence of

liberation while in fact he has not yet obtained the meritorious quality of the Prajñā Vehicle. To pretend that one can manifest one's meritorious quality in front of others while one does not have such quality is in fact a distortion of the truth. This is akin to the case in which one speaks about giving food to others while one does not have any food; isn't that a joke?[9]

Thus, as those tantric gurus are unaware of the fallacy of the misconceptions in which they are mired, they have criticized the Exoteric Buddhist practice for being inefficient and the valid knowledge attained by the Exoteric Buddhist Bodhisattvas through their practice for being elementary. In reality, not only are those gurus completely ignorant of the Buddha Dharma, but they have also fallen into heretical false views. They have, based on such "valid knowledge" in heretical doctrines, rebuked the Bodhisattvas of Exoteric Buddhism for not understanding the esoteric practice and have declared that the valid knowledge achieved by those Bodhisattvas is elementary. How preposterous! The plethora of such ridiculous instances makes it impossible to enumerate them all; not only were they extremely frequent in ancient times, but they are also extensively reflected in the writings of contemporary gurus. This fact is unknown to tantric practitioners in general; only those who possess the right knowledge and view of the Buddha Dharma can understand this truth.

---

9   Yogi C. M. Chen (Chen Chien-ming 陳健民), *Qugongzhai quanji* 曲肱齋全集 *[The Complete Works of Yogi Chen]*, vol. 1-5, ed. Xu Qinying 徐芹庭 (Taipei: Puxianwang rulai fojiaohui 普賢王如來佛教會, 1991), vol. 3, 477. Translated into English from Chinese.

2. The Buddhist Meditative Concentration in Tantric Buddhism: The Yab-Yum Practice

The "Buddhist meditative concentration" specific to Tantrism Buddhism is called Highest Yoga Tantra. Highest Yoga Tantra encompasses two different methods: (1) the Mahāmudrā of clear light, which belongs to the union of luminosity and emptiness; and (2) the yab-yum practice, which pertains to the union of bliss and emptiness in the Action Division. The method of the union of bliss and emptiness corresponds to the practice of the non-duality of bliss and emptiness; one cultivates it with one's own spouse or a tantric practitioner of the opposite sex after receiving the fourth initiation.

> The Mahāmudrā of clear light belongs to the union of luminosity and emptiness, while the action seal belongs to the union of bliss and emptiness; hence, the two are different. The former is the main target of this teaching. In the expedients consisting of the five poisons, the great ignorance corresponds to the great luminosity, and the great craving corresponds to the great bliss. Therefore, this method is the swiftest and most supreme, for it matches the sleep of the great ignorance with the clear light of Mahāmudrā.[1]

Please refer to the following publications for the practice and realization of the clear entity in the Mahāmudrā of clear light: *Commentary on the Three Statements of Dzogchen [Zhuiji sanyao 椎擊三要], The Great Perfection Yang Ti [Yangdui 仰兌], The Mahāmudrā of the Zhuba School [Zhubazong dashouyin 祝拔宗大手印], The Seven Points of Mind Training of Atiśha [Xiuxin qiyao 修*

---

[1] Yogi C. M. Chen (Chen Chien-ming 陳健民), *Qugongzhai quanji 曲肱齋全集 [The Complete Works of Yogi Chen]*, vol. 1-5, ed. Xu Qinying 徐芹庭 (Taipei: Puxianwang rulai fojiaohui 普賢王如來佛教會, 1991), vol. 3, 768. Translated into English from Chinese.

心七要], *Instructions on the Quintessential Teachings of the Great Perfection Yang Ti [Dayuanman zuishengxin zhongxin yindao lüeyao 大圓滿最勝心中心引導略要]*, and Khenpo Chacha's *Quintessential Instructions on Mahāmudrā [Chacha kanbu dashouyin kuojue 察察堪布大手印口訣]*. All of these writings maintain that one has realized the Mahāmudrā of clear light if one is able to abide long-lastingly in the firm belief that all phenomena are dependent arising and without their own nature, while one's mental consciousness (mind of feeling and cognition) dwells in thoughtlessness, without any attachment—without clinging to any state—and without discriminating any phenomena with verbal thinking. Those who have attained this state are said to have achieved the Path of Vision pertaining to the First Ground in Tantric Buddhism and are even regarded by some as having reached the ultimate Buddhahood. However, the truth is that those who practice in this fashion have not been able to realize the eighth consciousness (tathāgatagarbha)—they have not truly attained the Path of Vision. I will not elaborate further on this topic, as it is already illustrated at length in my *Commentary on the Chan Gong'ans [Gongan nianti 公案拈提]* series.

In summary, the theory of Highest Yoga Tantra, whose objective is to attain the union of bliss and emptiness, encompasses three stages: (1) the practice of the three bodies in the generation stage; (2) the union of bliss and emptiness in the completion stage; and (3) the union of the two truths in the completion stage. The practice of the generation stage consists of the visualization of the central channel and of the drops, which must be complemented by the visualization of deity yoga; in addition, one must cultivate the vase breathing technique and inner fire. Given that the cultivation and generation of these three methods aim to prepare for the actual practice of Highest Yoga Tantra, they constitute the generation stage of Highest Yoga Tantra and the training in these three domains is said to be included within the scope of Highest Yoga Tantra. In this chapter, "the union of bliss and emptiness in Highest Yoga Tantra" only refers to the latter two stages: the union of bliss and emptiness as well as the union of the two truths in the completion stage.

Tantric Buddhists have completely misunderstood prajñā. Indeed, they regard the various states of meditative concentration as prajñā. For instance, the Sakya School speaks of prajñā as the three meditative concentrations:

> The three meditative concentrations—which are the meditative concentration of the characteristic as a variety, the meditative concentration of the nature as emptiness, and the meditative concentration of the essence as their (the characteristic's and the nature's) unity. [2] The meditative concentration of the essence as their unity is further divided into three unions: the union of manifestation and emptiness on the objects, the union of luminosity and emptiness on the consciousness, and the union of bliss and emptiness on the body.[3]

One who has attained the meditative concentration of the characteristic as a variety is able to "perceive a variety of bliss, luminosity, true existence, and so forth on the characteristic of sensation."[4] In other words, one is able to observe, during the yab-yum practice, the following facts on the characteristic of the sensation of sexual pleasure: (1) Sexual pleasure induces different types of bliss at various parts of the body. (2) "The nature of luminosity" truly exists, which enables one to cognize and perceive the six sense objects and to take in the blissful sexual contact. The various types of "bliss" detected by the mind of feeling and cognition are not just imaginary states; instead, they truly exist and are tangible—the various blisses taken in on the body **truly exist** and are not unreal. The mind of feeling and cognition further observes that the "nature of luminosity (the nature of clear observation and discrimination)" experienced amidst various blisses is not imaginary, but truly exists; therefore, "luminosity"

---

2   Stearns, Cyrus (trans. and ed.), *Taking the Result as the Path: Core Teachings of the Sakya Lamdré Tradition* (Boston: Wisdom Publications, 2006), 26.
3   Virūpa, *Daoguo* 道果, 161. Translated into English from Chinese.
4   Ibid., 161.

truly exists. One has achieved "the meditative concentration of the characteristic as a variety" if one is able to directly observe the existence of these various characteristics during the yab-yum practice.

One who has attained the meditative concentration of the nature as emptiness is able to observe "the permanent existence of only emptiness after all manifestations of the nature are dissipated."[5] In order to achieve this objective, one must, during the yab-yum practice, concentrate on the ascending and descending of the drops as well as on the blissful contact that has arisen; at this moment, one must remain thoughtless and without the intention to take in any external states, thus dissipating all external states—not taking in any external states. While dwelling in this "great bliss—long-lasting bliss" of orgasm, one must further observe that all external phenomena are impermanent and will eventually disintegrate and that only this mind of feeling and cognition without distracting thoughts and this sexual pleasure are "everlasting and imperishable." Having thus inspected, one must abide in the nature of the mind of feeling and cognition and the sexual bliss and observe that this mind of feeling and cognition and sexual pleasure are truly the nature of "emptiness," for they are devoid of form and shape. One has achieved the meditative concentration of the nature as emptiness if one is able to make such direct observations on sexual pleasure.

The meditative concentration of the essence as their unity encompasses three unions:

> "The union of manifestation and emptiness on the objects" primarily arises on external objects; its property arises from non-discrimination. "The union of luminousity and emptiness on the consciousness" arises on the secret mind; its property arises from luminosity. "The union of bliss and emptiness on the body" arises on the internal body; its property arises from

---

[5]   Ibid., 161.

great bliss.[6]

In order to attain "the union of manifestation and emptiness on the objects" pertaining to the meditative concentration of the essence as their unity, one must primarily observe external objects instead of the mind of feeling and cognition itself or sexual pleasure: As all external phenomena are of material form and shape, they will inevitably disintegrate in the future—they are all dependent arising and without their own nature. One has achieved the union of manifestation and emptiness on objects pertaining to the meditative concentration of the essence as their unity if one can operate the following two items in parallel and perform the union thereof: this "view of dependent arising and without nature" and "the nature of emptiness of the mind of feeling and cognition and of sexual pleasure."

Below is a delineation of how to achieve "the union of luminosity and emptiness on the consciousness" pertaining to the meditative concentration of the essence as their unity. A secret mind consisting of the drops arises during the yab-yum practice; it radiates luminosity, untainted and entirely free from enervating defilements. This mind consisting of drops co-exists with the mind of feeling and cognition (mental consciousness) amidst the sexual pleasure of the yab-yum practice; the two operate in parallel and without conflict; they are both the "emptiness-nature" devoid of form and shape. One has achieved the union of luminosity and emptiness on the consciousness pertaining to the meditative concentration of the essence as their unity if one has thus observed and can comprehend the above principle.

In order to achieve "the union of bliss and emptiness on the body" pertaining to the meditative concentration of the essence as their unity, one must, during the yab-yum practice, induce the mental bliss consisting of the four joys through the bodily bliss. This mental bliss consisting of the four joys is generated by the internal body—it is not engendered by the external body, i.e., the

---

[6]   Ibid., 161-62.

rudimentary form body in the human world. In other words, this bliss arises from the nature of the intrinsic entity consisting of one's own mind (the mind of feeling and cognition without distracting thoughts). One has achieved the union of bliss and emptiness on the body within the meditative concentration of the essence as their unity if one is able to thus take in the various types of sexual pleasure in the body while taking in the great bliss—the fourth joy—of the mind of feeling and cognition.

The three meditative concentrations thus attained all fall within the scope of the mental consciousness. They do not touch on the realization of the eighth consciousness (tathāgatagarbha) or the mind consisting of the seventh consciousness (manas-consciousness); in fact, the practice and realization thereof have nothing to do with prajñā. The practice and realization of prajñā consists of the following: After realizing one's true mind, one must, based on the properties of this true mind, engage in the deed-contemplation of the Middle Way and preach the doctrines of the Middle Way. Only can such realization, observation, and teaching be called prajñā.

The direct observation of prajñā through the "three meditative concentrations" taught by the Sakya School, whose path is the most stringent and elaborate within Tibetan Buddhism, cannot even bring forth the knowledge-of-general-aspect, which is the most elementary wisdom within prajñā; how then could it generate the knowledge-of-specific-aspects and the knowledge-of-all-aspects within prajñā? With the Sakya School thus so, there is no need to mention "the practice and realization of prajñā" in the other schools.

Although the practice and attainment of Highest Yoga Tantra thus does not touch on the truth of the foremost meaning, those who aspire to practice the Highest Yoga Tantra of the union of bliss and emptiness must, before embarking on this cultivation, achieve the visualization of the drops, the visualization of the deity body, and the ability to move the winds upward and downward:

To embrace a female consort is for the benefit of sentient

beings. Nothing exceeds this practice when it comes to the wondrousness of the great path. This practice can transform greed into wisdom. Ordinary people do not understand it and regard it as a sexual act; they do not know that it is different from the normal sex between a man and a woman. **One has attained the innate wisdom and achieved the true path if one is able to withhold ejaculation when the drops descend to the gate of the secret place**; otherwise, one has not yet achieved the path. One will attain the quiescence of both the body and the mind if one is able to embrace a female consort without ejaculating. **The union of the male and female is to one-pointedly benefit sentient beings** (to benefit the persons of the opposite sex by earnestly bringing them happiness and causing them to understand the "emptiness-nature"), not for the sake of sexual pleasure; if one has this mindset, then the power of the channels, winds, and drops will come by naturally. Only those who can drive the winds into the central channel and move the drops upward and downward can be viewed as the yogis who cultivate the main practice. Such a definition of the consort mother (female consort) also exists in the second of the eight great divisions of the debating sūtras in Exoteric Buddhism: To embrace a consort mother is for the benefit of oneself and others, not for the sake of sexual pleasure. Moreover, a more efficient approach to steer sentient beings onto the correct path is to first delight them by partaking of their enjoyments and then to use this opportunity to guide them.[7]

A person will not violate the samaya precepts of Tantric Buddhism if he possesses the above skill and is therefore able to withhold ejaculation forever and take in the pleasure permanently while copulating with a person of the opposite sex. Therefore, the tantric gurus who have attained this skill can enjoy women whenever they want and can teach them the following concept

---

[7] *Naluo liufa* 那洛六法 [*The Six Yogas of Nāropa*], narrated by Blo-Bzan-Grags-Pa Zam Lam [Daoran baluobu cangsangbu 道然巴羅布倉桑布], recorded by Lu Yizhao 盧以炤 (Taipei: Chenxi Wenhua Gongsi 晨曦文化公司, 1994), 198-99. Translated into English from Chinese.

during the sexual act: Both the sensation of sexual pleasure and the mind of feeling and cognition that takes in this pleasure are called "emptiness-nature" for being empty of shape and sign. Those gurus thus benefit sentient beings by causing them to realize the emptiness-nature.

Even those who ejaculate after taking in the sexual pleasure during the copulation will not be breaking any samaya precepts as long as they have the ability to retract the semen into their abdomen after the ejaculation:

> Therefore, his sexual intercourse is not for the sake of sexual pleasure, but to benefit sentient beings; however, **this applies only if he does not ejaculate during the intercourse. Once he has gained the skill, then it will be fine for him to ejaculate, for he will be able to retract the semen after ejaculation.** There was a lama who lived in a cave of Ailunmu Mountain [愛倫姆山] in Mongolia. Because no one knew his last name, he was given the mountain's name: "Maerde [媽爾的] of Ailunmu." He lived in the cave for practice and many local women stayed there to sleep with him. The local men could not accept the lama's behavior and collectively filed a complaint with an official; however, the official was afraid of the lama's power and did not dare to accept the case. The local men then took their issue higher to the office of the commander-in-chief of Rehe [熱河] Province. After reading the accusation, the commander-in-chief secretly sent an inspector to investigate the case. Once the inspector had arrived at the cave, he staked it out by hiding in the nearby forest. As expected, he saw a woman enter the cave; he followed her into this shelter, hoping to surprise her and the lama by catching them in the act. To the inspector's disbelief, he could not find the woman inside the cave. It was because the lama had foreseen the arrival of the inspector and, after the woman entered the cave, had sent her away via another passage, causing the inspector to search in vain. Given that the inspector could not find the woman, Ailunmu deliberately asked the inspector about his purpose of visit. The inspector responded truthfully and invited the lama to return to the

office with him. Ailunmu agreed and followed the inspector to the office of the commander-in-chief. The commander-in-chief interrogated Ailunmu in the court: "You are a lama; why do you hide females in a cave and sleep with them? Do you know your guilt?" Ailunmu replied: "This is a method to practice the path; I do not know that it is forbidden." The commander-in-chief was furious and inflicted on him the punishment of kneeling on an iron chain. Ailunmu did not resist; he kneeled on the chain, while his body floated one meter above the ground to the great astonishment of the entire audience. The commander knew that Ailunmu would not surrender and therefore asked him: "How did you manage to do this?" Ailunmu replied: "It is my ability." The commander then asked: "Is a capable person allowed to infringe upon the law?" Ailunmu replied: "I have followed the inspector here because I abide by the law. Otherwise, you cannot make me come here." . . . Finally, the commander yielded, took Ailunmu as his teacher, and learned the Dharma with him. Eventually, the commander found out that Ailunmu did not take women in for the sake of enjoying sexual pleasure, but rather for the benefit of sentient beings. Consequently, he posted the following notice everywhere: "Lamas do not break the law by sleeping with women; local officials must not stop them from doing so or take the liberty to arrest them." Thereafter, Ailunmu continued to take women in as he did before. His disciples, seeing his acts, all emulated him by bringing in women in order to sleep with them. Ailunmu learned about this and asked them about their behavior. They replied: "We have just been emulating our teacher." Ailunmu said: "Very good indeed! All of you come with me." The disciples followed him to the front of the courtyard. Ailunmu filled a washbasin with boiled water and placed it under his crotch. He took off his underwear and squatted down to let the vapor of the boiled water steam his secret place. Shortly after, his semen flowed out like a thread that circled inside the washbasin without breaking off, with a length exceeding several *zhangs* [丈; one zhang equals 3.3 meters]. Thereupon, he retracted the semen into his abdomen without leaving any trace behind. Once he had completed this performance, he asked his disciples: "Can any of you do this?" By then, the disciples were all left stupefied; they shook their heads, speechless. Ailunmu told them: "If you do not have this capacity, then you should not harm yourself by having sex with women."[8]

This means that even monastic practitioners are allowed to cultivate the method of sexual pleasure with women if they have achieved the ability to release and retract the semen at will. Those who have attained this skill can even ejaculate for the sake of taking in the bliss of orgasm; all they need to do is retract the semen into their abdomen after ejaculation and they will not have violated any precepts. Therefore, the tantric lamas who have completed the practice of the drops and mastered the vase breathing technique are allowed to sleep with women. Furthermore, they will be "benefiting sentient beings" rather than "performing sexual intercourse" if they teach the women with whom they enjoy sexual pleasure about the practice and realization of the state of the fourth joy, which is experienced amidst the non-duality of bliss and emptiness. This concept is advocated by all the major traditions of Tibetan Tantric Buddhism:

> One should completely understand the principles related to the ascending and descending of all winds and so forth; otherwise, one will not be able to hear and obtain the unique Dharma of the Highest Tantra. Therefore, it is essential to hold this practice. If one does not cultivate the method to ascend and descend of all winds, then it is similar to aspiring to a tree with exuberant foliage without nourishing its roots— how could one obtain any good result?[9]

This concept is also asserted by **Tsongkhapa**. Readers who wish to learn more about this topic may refer to the extensive teachings in his *The Great Exposition of Secret Mantra [Mizong daocidi guanglun]*, which is hailed by the Gelug School of Tibetan

---

[8]   Ibid., 198-200.
[9]   Ibid., 295.

Tantric Buddhism as the most precious treasure with contents that are not easily transmitted to novice tantric practitioners.

Highest Yoga Tantra, which leads to the non-duality of bliss and emptiness, is practiced, first with the guru and then with the female consorts, during the fourth initiation under the guru's on-site guidance (as mentioned in the previous chapter, the Gelug School stipulates that, during the fourth initiation, the guru should, while practicing with nine female consorts, provide teachings to his disciple; subsequently, while the disciple practices with those nine female consorts, the guru should teach him about the details of this method). As for the female tantric practitioners, they should, after completing the fourth initiation, search for a male practitioner (who is known as the male consort) in order to cultivate the above method—the Highest Yoga Tantra that leads to "the non-duality of bliss and emptiness" or to "the union of bliss and emptiness," a method for assiduous practitioners that allows for the attainment of Buddhahood in this body. I will not elaborate further on it, as it will **be illustrated in detail and with examples in Section 6 of this chapter**.

3. The Attainment of the Rainbow Body through the Practice of Highest Yoga Tantra

The method of the rainbow body is briefly as follows:

But if you want to cremate this fleshly body because it remains behind after death, then that would not be correct; that would not called attaining Buddhahood in this body—not "in this body and in this life." Attaining Buddhahood in this body has two functions: It implies in both this life and this body; the attainment should not just be in this life, but also in this body. If one attains Buddhahood just in this life by becoming, for example, a Dharma body Buddha in the "state of death," then it will only be in this life—in this lifetime. If one becomes a reward body Buddha in the "intermediate state," then it will also be just in this lifetime, but not in this body. Why is it not in this body? Because one's form body will vanish, as it needs to be incinerated. That would not be right because it would not be in this body! It would be (attaining Buddhahood) just in this life, but not in this body. . . . Therefore, it is absolutely necessary to explain this samaya body clearly. Many of them did not expound it clearly and only spoke about becoming Buddha. For this reason, many people doubt about Milarepa's and Buddha Śākyamuni's attainment of Buddhahood. According to the reasoning of Tantric Buddhism, your fleshly body should not be cremated; instead, it should be emitting light. Aside from the great being Padmasambhava, many other persons have in reality also achieved Buddhahood in this fashion. If we do not explore this samaya body like most people, then we will think that many persons have already become Buddhas. However, we will find out after a careful investigation that they all became Buddhas in the intermediate state, for their bodies had to be incinerated. The great being Padmasambhava did not have cremation; all those who had achieved deathless yoga did not undergo cremation; Dangtong jiebo [盪通借波] was one of them. As for Milarepa, although

431

he possessed the true samādhi fire, he did not use it to burn his body. He became a Buddha in the intermediate state, not in this body; in other words, he did not attain Buddhahood in both this body and this life. In order to attain Buddhahood in both this life and this body, one should transform the entire samaya body into clear light—theoretically, that is. Examples of persons who have actually achieved this goal include the great being Padmasambhava, the patriarch Dangtong jiebo, and the two wives of Guru Padmasambhava—Mandarava [都那哇] and Yeshe Tsogyal [移喜磋嘉]. All of them left by flying away and did not die nor were cremated. Therefore, we can also achieve this feast by practicing assiduously. Marpa did not undergo cremation either. Moreover, each of his nine wives took turn to transform into light, with the first one transforming into light and entering the second one and so forth, until the last one transformed into light and entered Marpa, who then transformed into light himself.[1]

Those tantric Buddhists, who are in fact completely ignorant of the Path to Buddhahood, misapprehend the obtention of the rainbow body as the achievement of the ultimate Buddhahood. However, such tantric Buddhas have, after their attainment of "the ultimate Buddhahood," surprisingly no idea whatsoever about where the eighth consciousness (tathāgatagarbha) is in their bodies and are completely misunderstanding prajñā as well as the knowledge-of-all-aspects. Is such a proclamation of the ultimate Buddhahood not akin to the behavior of an arrogant elementary school student who scoffs at a professor of calculus for not knowing the four basic mathematical operations and brags that his achievement in mathematics exceeds that of this professor?

It is possible for all Buddhas to incinerate Their form bodies from the inside based on Their meritorious quality. Moreover, there have been a few westerners who, without learning the Taoist

---

[1] Yogi C. M. Chen (Chen Chien-ming 陳健民), *Qugongzhai quanji* 曲肱齋全集 *[The Complete Works of Yogi Chen]*, vol. 1-5, ed. Xu Qinying 徐芹庭 (Taipei: Puxianwang rulai fojiaohui 普賢王如來佛教會, 1991), vol. 1, 232. Translated into English from Chinese.

technique, had the merit of being endowed with the capability of the true samādhi fire and were able, upon death, to incinerate their own form bodies with the fire generated within their bodies. Furthermore, such instances are not uncommon in the Taoist legends. Therefore, there have been persons in the mundane world with the extraordinary ability to cremate their own corpses with the self-produced true samādhi fire both in ancient and modern times. Given that such a skill is definitely not specific to just a given tantric guru nor is it an extremely rare talent, it should by no means be viewed as evidence for Buddhahood.

Furthermore, a verification of the tale that Marpa's fleshly body did not undergo cremation, but instead directly transformed into a rainbow body—an unfounded rumor that has been perpetuated through many generations of ancient and modern tantric gurus—has shown this story to be actually false. Indeed, how could Marpa be endowed with such an extraordinary ability upon death when he had neither attained any skills of the four concentrations and four formless absorptions nor achieved any supernatural valid knowledge during his lifetime?

Even if there existed a guru within Tantric Buddhism truly endowed with such a supernatural ability and with the attainments of the rainbow body, he would be no different from a non-Buddhist with the same extraordinary power. Furthermore, the rainbow body is completely different from the reward body of the Buddha Ground; the two are just not comparable. Having all failed to understand and realize the eighth consciousness (tathāgatagarbha) in their own bodies, those gurus are unable to master the knowledge-of-general-aspect and the knowledge-of-all-aspects. Those who do not comprehend and have not attained the knowledge of general-aspect and the knowledge-of-all-aspects are not even Bodhisattvas of the Seventh Abiding; how then could they proclaim to have attained Buddhahood? It does not make any sense at all.

How could a Buddha not have the capacity to cremate Himself, when He has gained, after practicing for three great terms of asaṃkhya kalpas, an unimpeded penetrative understanding to the utmost degree of the five fields of knowledge? When our revered World-Honored One passed away, many persons attempted but failed to ignite perfumed firewood because Venerable Mahākāśyapa had not yet arrived. Once he had appeared, the Buddha burned Himself with a fire generated within His body and deliberately left behind relics of His fragmented body to scores of disciples, hoping that the sight thereof would slightly ease the feeling of longing that they might have for the Buddha. Those relics weighed a hefty forty-four dous [斗; one dou equals ten liters], far exceeding His form body's volume; this could never have been achieved by tantric "Buddhas."

Furthermore, as time goes by, the relics left behind by the World-Honored One of His fragmented body can continuously spawn new relics if their owner has karmic connections with the Buddha. This is a widely known fact among Buddhists, and I have also personally witnessed it. It is not a feat that only the tantric "Buddhas" are able to achieve once in a while.

How could the tantric "Buddhas" realize the supramundane wisdom of liberation when they cannot even perform such a mundane, uncontaminated, and compounded act? In fact, having all fallen into the sphere of the mental consciousness, they misapprehend the mental consciousness for the reality-suchness of the Buddha Ground. How could those tantric gurus understand and realize the wisdom of prajñā that even the arhats of Hīnayāna are not able to comprehend and attain? How could they realize the knowledge-of-specific-aspects without even being able to attain the knowledge-of-general-aspect within prajñā? Given their inability to realize the knowledge-of-specific-aspects, there is no need to mention the uncontaminated, uncompounded, as well as mundane and supramundane knowledge-of-all-aspects within prajñā, which is the ultimate nirvāṇa. Surprisingly, such tantric gurus in the stage of ordinary people dare to disparage the World-Honored One, Śākyamuni, by declaring that He has not achieved the ultimate Buddhahood. How extremely arrogant and unscrupulous!

The aforementioned text further says:

> One who has achieved the Great Perfection can also emit rainbow light by oneself without having to go through the union. However, this can only be accomplished by someone with great wisdom. Both Yin [陰] and Yang [陽] exist intrinsically within his body: The sunlight that he utilizes pertains to Yang, while the moonlight that he harnesses pertains to Yin; they resolve the problem together within the body. This can only be achieved after he completes the practice of Thod-Rgal [妥噶]. . . .

> Khregs-Chod [且卻] is the view of the Great Perfection in the stage of the Great Perfection. Thod-Rgal [妥噶] is the light of the Great Perfection. Why do I say that none of you have obtained the vajra chain? I can draw a picture for you to see. The light rings of the vajra chain sometimes manifest as many scattered small rings; sometimes these rings are connected with each other, sometimes they are connected into two chains, and sometimes the big rings connect with the small rings; these various connections are called vajra chain. This chain is white and transparent. As for the thread, it appears in its original color, without any other colors; this is called vajra chain. We can see it whenever we look at a bright spot. The vajra chain is a type of light—a light that arises from wisdom and therefore does not have a fixed shape. However, its basic fixed shape is, after all, a small ring. It is the light emitted by the nature and is not created by anything. In order to obtain it, one must understand the view of Khregs-Chod, and at the same time one must have received the guru's empowerment, causing one's channel to start undergoing some inner transformation. As for the light of Thod-Rgal, one must steer it slowly with the eyesight, so as to direct it from outside the body to inside it, until one can see it shine within the body. Those who possess this power can practice the method of "Attaining Buddhahood in Seven Days" taught in the

Great Perfection. If you truly have that power and cultivate it properly, then you will be able to transform all material substances inside your body into clear light. If you get used to the visualization of Chakrasamvara, then that vajra chain will take shape and resemble Chakrasamvara (and appear to take in the pleasure of the intercourse between a male and a female). The shape that it takes is sometimes similar to that of a pestle (vajra pestle); in this case, we are dealing with a more advanced stage. The five Dhyani Buddhas will gradually manifest therein. It is not just one ring, but at least many clusters of them; they are conspicuous and emit a light with original color—without any specific color. Those with the vajra chain and the view of Khregs-Chod will gradually have the opportunity to practice the Great Perfection. . . . With respect to the white retreat, it is the one that all of you usually perform; it is called white retreat because you can see the sunlight therein. As for the red retreat, one creates a dark room by closing all windows and curtains, but a lamp must be lit; with only one lamp, when one solely practices Thod-Rgal by facing this light, it is called red retreat. Because the lamp is red, one can, amidst the red light, slowly steer this red light into one's body; one must then absolutely practice the black retreat. The black retreat is as follows: There are many layers of walls; the layout of the different walls is such that air can penetrate. Once air has penetrated, light can absolutely not infiltrate—hence the designation "black retreat." The house for the black retreat must be built in a specific way so that air can penetrate, but light cannot infiltrate. However, sometimes a hole is opened. If the hole faces the east, then one can see the sun; if it faces the west, then one can see the moon. One can thus watch the descent of the moon and the rising of the sun. One then steers those lights into one's own body and uses them to transform the body by force; thus, the internal light and the external light transform it together while inside it. Consequently, this body becomes a body of light and does not need to go through cremation. . . .

What were the practices held by the Great Guru Padmasambhava? For a start, we should also accept the teachings of the Buddha Dharma; the first ritual that you must complete is that related to the Buddha's body. The inside of a Buddha's body, just like a bubble, is an empty nothingness without blood or flesh. Therefore, the first step of this practice is to transform one's fleshly body into a bubble (through visualization). The discussion here is not about the great enlightenment but only covers the first stage of this practice. Try to think of it in the following way: As long as my fleshly body becomes as transparent and lithe as a bubble, then it will float upward without hindrance. . . . By just practicing earnestly and diligently according to the criteria set forth by this ritual, you will be able to transform your solid form body into an extremely transparent, beautiful, and perfect object, meaning that you will not be far away from attaining the rainbow body. . . . Once you have completed this ritual, you can receive the first-level initiation and further visualize the Buddha's body instead of the aforementioned bubble. The inside of a Buddha's body is empty like a bubble, while the outside consists of the Buddha's five colors and vein decorations. You can also visualize a meditational deity—you must visualize it with whatever appearance to which it is assigned by the rituals. Everything must correspond perfectly to the body of this visualized deity without the slightest discrepancy. Thus, we can start off from the body of a veritable ordinary person and further visualize it as a deity's body, which is as transparent as emptiness on the inside and possesses all magnificence as well as the thirty-two marks of a Buddha on the outside. Once you have completed this visualization, you will not be far from attaining the imperishable rainbow body. In this deity's body, you must have a wisdom body—a form body composed of wisdom instead of flesh and blood. Given that you have completed the visualization of the bubble, your solid form body no longer exists. Consequently, to transform this bubble again, you need profound wisdom so as to transform it into the light of wisdom. You must visualize a lotus inside the heart cakra; once you have truly visualized this lotus successfully, it itself will protect you, preventing you from undergoing the next rebirth by falling into a womb. . . . The lotus symbolizes the womb; hence, the successful visualization of a lotus will enable you to avoid the rebirths from a womb, meaning that you will not have to go through the process of staying in a mother's uterus again. If you want to avoid the metamorphic rebirths, you must visualize a moon above the lotus and verify it. This moon is full and bright and emits a white light. Once you have successfully visualized such a moon, you will not have to undergo the metamorphic rebirths—processes that are similar to the transformation of a silkworm into a cocoon and further into a moth. In order to avoid the rebirths from moisture, we must visualize ourselves as standing atop a moon disc and chanting a mantra; furthermore, we must cause the uttered mantra to emit light and revert, thereby transforming this light into our deity. . . . With respect to the rebirths determined by the karma of previous lives, our eighth consciousness is precisely such seeds. However, we can avoid this type of rebirth as long as we can successfully visualize a syllable cakra called "seed," such as "*hum* [吽]" or "*hrih* [紇哩]." As long as you can successfully visualize this seed-syllable cakra, which represents the principle of the emptiness-nature in Buddhism, not only will you not take rebirth anywhere along with the eighth consciousness (original note: also called seed consciousness), but you also will actually attain a wisdom body instead of a rudimentary form body. Thus, you will be able to change the rebirths originally determined by the mental consciousness and take rebirth as a Buddha in the formless realm, which is above the heavens of the desire-realm and of the form-realm. In this fashion, you can also avoid the rebirths with a mind-made body. This seed-syllable cakra is endowed with the wisdom of the emptiness-nature; therefore, all you need to do is visualize it with a focused mind and your mental consciousness will be able to take rebirth in any place and definitely as a Buddha. . . . This body, which is called "wisdom body," is a fruition obtained from cultivating the second initiation; the first initiation includes the visualization of the Buddha's body from outside. During the second initiation, you must visualize, inside the channel cakra, a deity called "deity of wisdom" with an extremely subtle and wondrous body. This method of visualization is divided into three layers. First, one's body is originally composed of blood and flesh; this fleshly body transforms into a bubble body and further into a type of Buddha's body. Second, this intrinsic body, which is called "wisdom body," takes shape through a process of deep breathing and inner fire and has the function of exterminating other methods of rebirth. This is achieved during the second initiation. Such a wisdom body is constituted by red and white bodhicitta and none of the channel winds, breathing, and wisdom that it encompasses are made of rudimentary substances. Consequently, it is extremely easy to transform such a wisdom body into a rainbow body; it can be done without any obstruction and with all certainty; this is the second layer. The third layer is as follows. In such a wisdom body, the practitioner still maintains tiny "*hum* and *hrih*" or "*xie* [懈]." During your practice, not only does the entire universe emit light, but all the mountains, rivers, and lands, as well as all phenomena, also transform into light. This light enters the rudimentary fleshly body, causing the latter to transform into a wisdom body and further into a samādhi body. The seed-syllable cakra of the wisdom body must become as thin as fine hair and even completely dissolve into the noumenon body. Thus, you will have realized the so-called Dharma body, which is in fact empty. The rainbow body is in the sky; therefore, you need to first enter the sky in order to become like a rainbow and emit your light of rainbow body. Such is the "practice." First, you develop the usual bubble body, then a fleshly body named "samaya body," followed by the wisdom body, and finally the samādhi body. If you can attain these bodies one after another, then it will not be difficult for you to realize the rainbow body. . . . There should first be a central channel within the Buddha's body. . . . In the central channel, you must visualize inner fire below as well as the "*hum*" syllable and white bodhicitta above. . . . You must transform it with inner fire. . . In the case of a male, there is less tummo and more nectar; in the case of a female, there is more tummo and less nectar. This is why the third initiation is necessary. Indeed, in this initiation, the male and the female can help each other by exchanging inner fire and nectar, so as to enable the transformation. . . . In order to transform the body of an ordinary person into a rainbow body, not only is wisdom necessary, but one also needs to perform various types of visualization. The first channel cakra corresponds to the nervous system of the brain. When you practice the visualization of the "*hum*" syllable, you must transform this entire nervous system with inner fire, so that the system will dissolve into the crown cakra. The second channel cakra is tantamount to the breathing system consisting of the lungs and so forth; you must use inner fire to dissolve the breathing system into the throat cakra at the throat. In this process, you must control your breath, perform the visualization, and transform this system with inner fire. The circulatory system relates to the blood and the heart; therefore, we must use inner fire to dissolve the breathing system into the heart cakra. As a result, the blood and the heart will be extinguished, as will be the lung and the brain. Next, we must dissolve the digestive organs into the navel cakra—we must alter all the digestive organs such as the large and the small intestines and so forth through incineration. All the reproductive organs must be incinerated inside the reproduction cakra, so as to transform them into this channel cakra. Thus, what we will be in possession of will be these five channel cakras, instead of the five main organs and systems pertaining to ordinary beings. We will obtain the rainbow body once the various rudimentary organs have been transformed into the five main channel cakras. The transformations of the first four cakras occur during the second initiation, while the transformation of the reproductive organs is a matter of the third initiation. The purpose of the third initiation [original note: a practice with a person of the opposite sex] is to enhance the power of the transformation or of inner fire (the author might have meant to say "to enhance the power of the transformation into inner fire"), but one must not ejaculate; otherwise one will, again, be reborn in the body of an ordinary person. One must draw the semen upward so as to transform it into fire and subsequently use this fire power to dissolve any fleshly substances. This is the only way through which one can truly transform into a rainbow body. Guru Padmasambhava achieved this goal by practicing according to this method, which has been passed down to us, so that we can practice accordingly and have the opportunity to achieve the same goal. . . . The fruition of the rainbow body is related to the fifth body of the Buddha. The Buddha has five bodies: emanation body, incarnation body, noumenon body, innate body, and wisdom body of the great bliss. Among them, the wisdom body of the great bliss is precisely such a rainbow body. It is by abiding in the great bliss that the Buddha can enjoy this great bliss in the same way that a fleshly body enjoys it. Furthermore, the Buddha has realized the unsurpassed wisdom related to the Dharma body because wisdom is prajñā. The so-called achievement of realizing the great bliss signifies that the fleshly body generated by the Buddha has transformed into a rainbow body, which is of the highest shape and form. The rainbow light is such unsurpassed wisdom, and the rainbow color is of the highest shape and form—both have been blended into this wisdom body of the great bliss. The thorough realization— highest wisdom—that we have spoken about is precisely this kind of clear light. . . . The patterns and colors reflected by the rainbow in a cloudless sunny sky are an aspect of its possession of shape, while its light corresponds to wisdom. The fleshly body becomes the shape and form of the rainbow body, while its light corresponds to wisdom—the wisdom of the great bliss. Given that this is a rainbow from its outer appearance, there will be no death. Without death, one can save sentient beings endlessly. By being able to save sentient beings endlessly, one can perform compassion indefinitely. . . . This is the reason why Padmasambhava is imperishable. . . . If you make good use of the benefit generated from increasing the bodhi, then your bodhi will lift you upward. Therefore, the tummo must be strong and solid, just like a fire within one's body that incinerates everything and thereby causes such a form body to transform completely into clear light. Finally, if we manage to receive the four initiations and understand the theory of the principle of the emptiness-nature, then we can realize the Dharma body. One cannot realize the Dharma body without realizing the emptiness-nature; furthermore, one cannot become a rainbow body without realizing the Dharma body. Indeed, the rainbow body is in the empty sky, and if there is no empty sky, then the rainbow will not appear. In other words, our wisdom body of the great bliss must be achieved in a rainbow in the empty sky, with this empty sky symbolizing the Dharma body. In order to visualize and cultivate the Dharma body, one must practice the mode of emptiness through Mahāmudrā.[2]

Below is an identification of each of the errors contained in the above long passage:

1. The Buddha's body has nothing to do with the rainbow light, the sunlight and the moonlight, or Yin and Yang. It is obtained by accumulating meritorious quality through eliminating all latent seeds of afflictive hindrances, eliminating all latent ignorance of cognitive hindrances, benefiting sentient beings throughout three great terms of asaṃkhya kalpas by providing them with material welfare, and benefiting sentient beings through the propagation of the correct knowledge and views. The Buddha's body is absolutely not attained by cultivating non-Buddhist tantric methods such as Khregs-Chod, Thod-Rgal, and so forth without understanding or realizing the eighth consciousness (Dharma body) and by further misleading sentient beings with non-Buddhist mistaken views. Therefore, the claim made by tantric gurus that the practice and realization of the Mahāmudrā of the union of luminosity and emptiness or the Mahāmudrā of the union of bliss and emptiness lead to the achievement of the rainbow body is in fact unrelated to

---

2   Yogi C. M. Chen (Chen Chien-ming 陳健民), *Qugongzhai quanji* 曲肱齋全集 [*The Complete Works of Yogi Chen*], vol. 1-5, ed. Xu Qinying 徐芹庭 (Taipei: Puxianwang rulai fojiaohui 普賢王如來佛教會, 1991), vol. 1, 236, 267-68, 442-55. Translated into English from Chinese.

the Buddha Dharma, for those methods are in essence non-Buddhist.

2. As the visualization of the vajra chain and so forth neither relates to the elimination of the afflictive hindrances consisting of habitual seeds in the Path to Liberation nor the elimination of the cognitive hindrances consisting of the latent ignorance, the achievement of such visualization has nothing to do with the Buddha's wisdom consisting of omniscience and the knowledge-of-all-aspects. Given its irrelevance to the Buddha's wisdom, the visualization of the vajra chain is wholly unrelated to the obtainment of the Buddha's body, for the achievement of the magnificent reward body of the Buddha Ground results from the attainment of the knowledge-of-all-aspects.

3. Any method that involves steering sunlight, moonlight, red light, or any other forms of light into one's body to transform one's organs stems from erroneous thinking. One will never achieve the goal of transforming one's organs through this practice, given that such erroneous thinking is as delusional as the visualization of a deity's body. It is merely one's delusion to believe that one "has attained" this objective; although there is a perceived portion that can be seen by one's own mind of feeling and cognition, this portion is in fact tantamount to the manifested state of transposed substance involving the five sense objects in one's dream and hence is not a real dharma. Such a method is actually irrelevant to the Dharma-gate of practice of the Buddha Dharma, for it only results from heretical false thinking and does not lead to any valid knowledge in the Buddha Dharma.

Therefore, the establishment of the white and black retreats as well as their practice methods are actually senseless when it comes to the correct practice of the Buddha Dharma. The thought that one is steering various lights into one's body does not help one achieve any wisdom related to the doctrines of the Buddha Dharma nor does it help transform the fleshly organs within one's body into a body of light. The body of light belonging to the Bodhisattvas in the Akaniṣṭha Heaven, which is at the top of the form realm, is a reward body resulting from the practice and realization of the acquiescence to the non-arising of dharmas and from the fact that those Bodhisattvas were reborn in that heaven; it is a direct reward that is not obtained through visualization or meditative concentration.

Furthermore, the reason why the Buddha's body in the Akaniṣṭha Heaven is taller and larger than the body of the Bodhisattvas at or above the level of the First Ground is because it is a reward body resulting from the Buddha's perfection of the knowledge-of-all-aspects as well as from His immense meritorious quality. Such a reward body and its magnificence are not obtained through visualization. Therefore, the endeavors of those tantric Buddhists to transform their fleshly form bodies into five-colored rainbow bodies purely consisting of light by steering external light into their bodies through visualization are based on erroneous thinking.

4. The visualization that a Buddha's body appears in one's mind, that the inside of this body—just like the inside of a bubble—is empty of all objects, and that this body can float at will due to the fact that it is as light as a bubble is in fact completely unrelated to the magnificent reward body of a Buddha, for it has nothing to do with the wisdom of liberation or the wisdom of the Buddha Bodhi. Similarly, the visualizations of the lotus as well as of the moon and the light have also nothing to do with the magnificent reward body of the Buddha Ground, for it is not a correct practice of the Buddha Dharma. The same goes for the chanting of mantras—since it is also not a correct practice of the Buddha Dharma, it does not enable one to attain a magnificent reward body.

5. For those who aspire to free themselves from cyclic existence by avoiding the rebirths from a womb, the first objective that they should work on is to abandon the cyclic existence in the desire-realm by relinquishing all cravings for sexual pleasure, so that they can take rebirth in the form realm after death. It is not by experiencing, amidst sexual pleasure, the non-duality of bliss and emptiness in the union of bliss and emptiness that they can achieve

this goal. Experiencing even the slightest blissful sensation amidst sexual pleasure while claiming that one has no craving for the sexual act is a behavior that precisely goes against the realization of the magnificent reward body of the Buddha Ground. It is absolutely impossible to achieve such a body by practicing the Mahāmudrā of bliss and emptiness. Therefore, the endeavors of tantric Buddhists to attain a magnificent reward body of the Buddha Ground through the practice of the Mahāmudrā of luminosity and emptiness or of bliss and emptiness are based on erroneous thoughts.

6. No one has ever obtained a mind-made body through the rebirth from a womb, which demonstrates that the statements made by those tantric gurus are false. All three types of mind-made body result from meditative concentration (which is different from the meditative concentration consisting of the meditative absorption of the yab-yum practice set forth in Tantric Buddhism) and from the wisdom of the acquiescence to the non-arising of dharmas—not from the rebirth from a womb. How could those Tantric Buddhists bring forth the knowledge-of-the-aspects-of-paths by realizing the acquiescence to the non-arising of dharmas when they do not even understand the most elementary knowledge-of-general-aspect within prajñā? How could such persons obtain a mind-made body when they are totally ignorant of prajñā? How unwise of them to disparage the supreme mind-made body based on their erroneous view—misapprehension—thereof! The Bodhisattvas of the Ninth Ground possess all three types of mind-made body, but without perfection, for mind-made bodies are perfected only in the Buddha Ground. Indeed, they are achieved through the meritorious quality and wisdom accumulated during three great terms of incalculable eons and will exist forever after one's attainment of Buddhahood. Instead of being abandoned, as advocated by tantric Buddhists, those mind-made bodies should be sought after by all Bodhisattvas with diligence and devotion. Given that those tantric gurus do not comprehend the Buddha Dharma, their explications thereof, which are a complete nonsense,

have misled sentient beings to a very serious extent. It is difficult to imagine what their retributions will be after death.

7. It is impossible to achieve any valid knowledge in the Buddha Dharma through the visualization of seed syllables. Such visualization merely allows a practitioner to escape immediate disasters with the empowerment bestowed upon him by the supernatural powers of Dharma-protectors, Bodhisattvas, or Buddhas with whom he has karmic connections and to thereby cultivate the path with a sense of security. One can achieve valid knowledge in the Buddha Dharma only by earnestly seeking to realize the wisdom of liberation and the wisdom of the Buddha Bodhi; all tantric practitioners should be mindful of this fact. If they do not believe me, then they will still not understand the true doctrines of the Path to Liberation of Hīnayāna and the Path to Buddhahood of Mahāyāna after thirty years or even fifty years of practice. These well-intentioned predictions are made here for the wise practitioners of Tantric Buddhism to ponder.

8. With respect to the visualization and practices related to the central channel and the drops, the deity's body, the vase breathing technique, and inner fire, as well as the visualization of the seed syllables, bubbles, empty body, and so forth, none of these methods will enable one to generate a body of rainbow light by transforming one's fleshly form body into a body of light. The so-called "bubble-like body" is similar to, but in fact differs from, the celestial body obtained upon attaining the first concentration. I myself achieved the celestial body of the first concentration many years ago (soon after I became enlightened). In this state, the inside of the body is both cloud-like and fog-like (it is denser than fog, but lighter than a cloud in a sunny sky), without any internal or sex organs; the skin is akin to an extremely thin plastic wrap with capillary pores; the inside and the outside of the pores are connected and blissful sensation can be experienced in every single pore. This was all perceived by my mental eye instead of my physical eyes. After attaining this state, I experienced blissful contact in my chest cavity at all times and rejoiced greatly. Subsequently, this blissful contact gradually transformed as I

progressed in meditative concentration, naturally evolving to attain more advanced levels with the passage of time and without the need for me to exert any deliberate action.

All learners should know that the deity's body of the form realm is not achieved through visualization. In order to obtain it, one must abandon all cravings for the sexual contact of the desire-realm and must, on top of that, attain the meditative concentration of the form-realm. As for the magnificent reward body of the Buddha Ground, it also cannot be obtained through visualization. Instead, it is attained by achieving all samādhis consisting of meditative concentration in the three realms, perfecting the acquiescence to the non-arising of dharmas, and accumulating measureless meritorious quality. In other words, those who aspire to realize the magnificent reward body must attain the Madhyamaka within prajñā, the knowledge-of-all-aspects, and immeasurable samādhis consisting of meditative concentration (which differ from the samaya set forth in Tantric Buddhism) and must accumulate immeasurable meritorious quality. Such a practice of the Buddha Dharma is the sole correct path to cultivate and attain a magnificent reward body. To work on the visualization of Tantric Buddhism instead of this path is "an act of a person with erroneous thinking"; it is not the correct way to cultivate the Buddha Dharma.

9. The rainbow body is not a Buddha's body given that it has seven or five colors. Indeed, a Buddha's reward body is a body of golden light, not of seven colors. Based on my own valid knowledge, I have observed that ghosts and spirits have a liking for the light of the rainbow body, which results from their delusional imaginations. From my experience, I started to exhibit golden light upon realizing the wisdom of prajñā; this golden light subsequently became interwoven with intense white light due to my attainments in meditative concentration. The golden light gradually intensified as my wisdom of prajñā progressed with the passage of time; meanwhile, the white light also intensified by the day, as my meditative concentration kept on improving owing to my

continuous elimination of afflictive emotions, but there was no intertwining of multifarious seven-colored or five-colored light.

The above personal experience has allowed me to gradually comprehend the different stages and contents of the Buddhist path. I was able to gain this progressive understanding through the knowledge-of-the-aspects-of-paths, which I obtained through the practice and realization of the knowledge-of-all-aspects. Furthermore, as I gradually comprehended the correct principle to obtain the celestial body of the form realm through my cultivation and attainments in meditative concentration, I became aware that the statements made by tantric Buddhists with respect to the practice and realization of the rainbow body are delusional. All wise learners should ponder this assertion carefully. It is absolutely vital that they do not neglect the fact that their losses will outweigh their gains if they fall into those erroneous tantric views, waste their precious time by mistakenly embarking in the cultivation of non-Buddhist doctrines, achieve nothing from lifelong endeavors, and even commit the hell-destined sin of grievous false speech.

10. It is in fact impossible to achieve a rainbow body through the method preached by tantric practitioners, for this Dharma-gate of practice is based on erroneous thinking. Even if there was a technique that allows them to truly attain a rainbow body, it would still be a heretical method, for the rainbow body is neither the magnificent reward body of the Buddha Ground nor the mind-made body of Bodhisattvas. The statement, based on such erroneous thinking, that Padmasambhava's methods of imperishable yoga, imperishable rainbow body, and so forth correspond to the Buddha Dharma is deceitful and absolutely meaningless to the practice of the Buddha Dharma.

11. Furthermore, if Padmasambhava had truly obtained a rainbow body before his death, then given the claim made by tantric Buddhists that a rainbow body is achieved by transforming fleshly organs into a body of light, a non-material body—a case that differs from the attainment of the celestial body of the form realm by the Exoteric Buddhist Bodhisattvas while still having a

rudimentary form body of the desire-realm—Padmasambhava should have been devoid of a fleshly body before his death, as his fleshly body would have been transformed into a body of light. However, based on textual evidence, Padmasambhava enjoyed women and cultivated the yab-yum method of sexual pleasure even in his old age. Those truly endowed with a rainbow body are definitely without a fleshly body and therefore cannot engage in the yab-yum Dharma-gate of sexual pleasure with the women in the desire-realm's human world.

As Padmasambhava "benefited women" in his entire life by frequently cultivating the yab-yum method with them, it is obvious that he had a fleshly body—instead of a rainbow body—during those sexual encounters. Therefore, the assertion that Padmasambhava had long achieved a rainbow body conflicts with other facts about his life, does not conform to the truth, and is simply illogical. If Padmasambhava had indeed maintained his fleshly body and transformed it into a rainbow body only during death, then this theory would be contradicted by the above citation about the cultivation of the rainbow body.

Furthermore, the only way to diminish the material quality of a fleshly form body is through incineration; no incineration is possible without fire. Such is the law of materiality that governs all objects without exception. Thus, a fleshly body can only be incinerated with inner or outer fire. This law applies to everyone, even to those who have become Buddhas—They must incinerate their bodies with the inner fire manifested with Their own supernatural power, given that the fleshly body is a rudimentary form dharma of the desire-realm. Based on these correct reasonings, we can conclude that the statements made by Tantric Buddhists about Padmasambhava's imperishable rainbow body are nothing but unfounded rumors, which, with the passage of time, have been turned into an overhyped legend with distorted facts aimed at duping sentient beings and generating the faith thereof. There is in fact no such a thing as a rainbow body.

12. The proponents of Tantrism such as Padmasambhava and so forth cannot even attain the celestial body of the form realm pertaining to the first concentration, yet they pretentiously assert that they are able to obtain the magnificent reward body of the Buddha Ground in the form of a rainbow body. Such an assertion must be false and not credible. Why is that? Because all Buddhas have, without any doubt, fully attained each and every one of the four concentrations and four formless absorptions, which are the basic practices and realizations leading to the achievement of Buddhahood. Although many heretics had realized the four concentrations and four formless absorptions, such attainments were all negated by the Buddha, who declared that those states did not correspond to nirvāṇa.

Given that Padmasambhava incessantly engaged in sexual activities during his entire life, taught others to dedicate their lives to the diligent practice of masturbation, and even had sex with a **little girl** raised by a monkey, we can conclude that he had not been able to attain the first concentration before his death—indeed, in order to attain the first concentration, one must eliminate the greed that one experiences in one's mind for the sexual act of the desire-realm. Padmasambhava could not possibly have attained the first concentration given that he did not exterminate his greed of the desire-realm and actively pursued the unsurpassed sexual pleasure—the fourth joy—during his entire life. In addition, based on his biography and his writings about the various Dharma-gates of practice, it is obvious that he had not extinguished his greed of the desire-realm and had not attained the first concentration.

It just does not make sense to proclaim that someone has achieved all samādhis consisting of meditative concentration when he has not even attained the most elementary meditative concentration in the three realms. It does not make sense to declare that someone has obtained the celestial body of the first concentration when he has not even attained the samādhi consisting of the first concentration. It also does not make any sense to pretend that someone has been able to attain a dharma—

such as a rainbow body— that is superior to the celestial body of the first concentration when he has not even attained such a celestial body. It just does not make sense to claim that the rainbow body that someone has obtained is superior to the emanation body, the magnificent reward body, and the Dharma body of the Buddhas in Exoteric Buddhism when he has failed to achieve the celestial body of the first concentration. Consequently, the allegations made by those tantric gurus that Padmasambhava had attained a rainbow body and achieved Buddhahood are nothing but superstitious tales based on sheer fiction and are therefore not credible in the slightest.

13. The proclamations frequently made by tantric gurus about their realization of the Dharma body are mere falsehoods. The Dharma body corresponds in fact to the eighth consciousness: In the Causal Ground, the Dharma body is known as the eighth consciousness-ālaya; the Dharma body in the stage of no-learning within the Path to Liberation is called the eighth consciousness-maturational consciousness; in the Buddhahood of the ultimate Fruition Ground, the Dharma body is known as the eighth consciousness-immaculate consciousness, or renamed the reality-suchness, but it remains in essence the eighth consciousness. Although the eighth consciousness in the stage of no-learning within the Path to Liberation is called ninth consciousness for convenience, its entity remains that of the original eighth consciousness—its name has changed, but not its entity. Although the eighth consciousness in the ultimate Buddhahood can also be called tenth consciousness, it remains in essence the eighth consciousness; its name has changed to "tenth consciousness," but its entity is still that of the eighth consciousness, and therefore, this does not mean that a Buddha has ten consciousnesses.

None of the tantric gurus have realized the mind consisting of the eighth consciousness, starting from Maitripa, Candrakīrti, Virūpa, and so forth in the Tantric Buddhism of ancient India, followed by Atiśa, Padmasambhava, Yeshe Tsogyal, Tsongkhapa, Khedrup Je, Marpa, Milarepa, Gampopa, and so forth in Tibet, through to today's Dalai Lama, Yinshun, all the great Dharma-kings, Yogi C. M. Chen, Kalu, Dzongsar, and so forth. Given that they have not realized the body of the eighth consciousness, they are all ordinary persons who have not attained the Dharma body. Moreover, they engage in empty talks about the practice and realization of the Dharma body and regard the rainbow body as the Dharma body; how then could the various doctrines transmitted in Tantric Buddhism be said to be the Buddha Dharma given such extensive misunderstandings of the Buddha Dharma? How could those gurus have supplanted the Buddha Dharma with non-Buddhist doctrines that have nothing to do with the Buddha Dharma and further claimed that such doctrines are superior to the true Buddha Dharma of Exoteric Buddhism? One cannot help but sigh with pity at hearing such distortions of the truth!

Tantric Buddhists have declared that their practice of the rainbow body is superior to the Taoist methods after comparing the two:

> The tantric method is drastically different from it (original note: the Taoist practice). One must first cultivate the clear light of metaphor and the clear light of meaning through the illusory body; subsequently, one will achieve the illusory body after performing the union. With respect to its nature, the spiritual consciousness does not need to exit from the body, and there is no such distinction as the Yin spirit and the Yang spirit. One will become a deity's body with the achievement of the illusory body; even one's samaya body will becomes a deity's body, but it will do so without breaking away from the fleshly body. With respect to the achievements of lower level, the visualized deity's body can be seen by oneself but not by others; furthermore, it only manifests in meditative concentration and in dreams and does not appear in states of distraction. With respect to the achievements of middle level, the deity's body can be seen by both oneself and others. However, those

without karmic connections or wisdom cannot see their deity's bodies. Furthermore, their bodies remain physical ones. As for the achievements of higher level, all persons, regardless of whether they have karmic connections or wisdom, can see themselves as a deity's bodies; furthermore, their bodies are similar to the rainbow light and can be penetrated by hand without obstruction, just like Padmasambhava's body (These statements are deceitful—whenever tantric Buddhists proclaim that there are persons who can see the various attainments of visualization achieved by their gurus, those persons are actually all deceased; since ancient times, no one has been able to identify a contemporary guru with a visualized celestial rainbow body that can actually be seen and verified by others; thus, the assertions made by tantric Buddhists about past and modern gurus with such an attainment are nothing but groundless and overhyped statements based on distorted facts). Therefore, the illusory body is obtained simultaneously with the external samaya body.[3]

This text further says :

> How was the great being Padmasambhava able to manifest the attainment of Buddhahood in a lifetime? The hand of the Tibetan king penetrated through Padmasambhava's entire body while touching it, as if it were passing through a rainbow body.[4]

However, Padmasambhava's rainbow body was not real; the wise should know that his so-called rainbow body is merely a terminology based on fictitious, distorted facts. As previously

---

3   Yogi C. M. Chen (Chen Chien-ming 陳健民), *Qugongzhai quanji 曲肱齋全集 [The Complete Works of Yogi Chen]*, vol. 1-5, ed. Xu Qinying 徐芹庭 (Taipei: Puxianwang rulai fojiaohui 普賢王如來佛教會, 1991), vol. 1, 469. Translated into English from Chinese.

4   Yogi C. M. Chen (Chen Chien-ming 陳健民), *Qugongzhai quanji 曲肱齋全集 [The Complete Works of Yogi Chen]*, vol. 1-5, ed. Xu Qinying 徐芹庭 (Taipei: Puxianwang rulai fojiaohui 普賢王如來佛教會, 1991), vol. 3, 247. Translated into English from Chinese.

mentioned, such a body completely contradicts the law of the form dharma in the three realms, given that Padmasambhava could still cultivate the yab-yum method by engaging in sexual activities with women.

Furthermore, even though a visualized rainbow body may, upon its achievement, be seen by one with the divine eye, this case is similar to that in which one's thoughts are known to a mind reader; the supernatural power lies with the mind reader, not with the one whose thoughts are being read. The theory of the rainbow body is no different. As for Yogi C. M. Chen's assertion that the rainbow body that can be seen by all, it is obvious, based on textual evidence and real facts, that no one has been able to achieve such a body up until now. Given that this is true of all the ancient and modern tantric gurus, we can conclude that the rainbow body set forth in Tantrism is a fictitious dharma without any real, verifiable substance. Furthermore, the existence of a rainbow body is illogical and contradicts the Buddhist teachings. Therefore, instead of blindly believing in those tantric assertions, the wise should ponder rationally in order to avoid going astray without knowing it.

All learners should know that the rainbow body "achieved" through visualization and the control of the winds is unreal, for it is an internal perceived portion issued from one's own visualization and is neither related to the celestial body nor to the Buddha's body. Both the rainbow body and the Buddha's body attained through visualization are set forth by Tantric Buddhists based on their erroneous thinking.

The practice and attainment of the rainbow body are established by *The Vairocanābhisaṃbodhi Sūtra [Dari jing]*. This text falsely pretends to be about the truth of the foremost meaning, while its contents do not even touch on it. As its statements differ completely from the Buddha's teachings in all sūtras of the Three Vehicles, we can conclude that it does not contain the Buddha's words, but is instead a fabrication of the tantric gurus during the late period of Buddhism in ancient India. *The Vairocanābhisaṃbodhi Sūtra* has established the following basis for the practice of the rainbow body:

> He ascends into the sky through *siddhi* like one who is
> unafraid of illusions;
> His ensorcellments by means of the net of magical
> arts are like Indra's net;
> Just like all the people in a gandharva city (i.e.,
> mirage),
> So too is the secrecy (i.e., invisibility) of his body,
> being neither of the body nor of consciousness.
> **Again, just as in a dream while asleep one may visit**
> **the palaces of the gods,**
> **Without forsaking this body and without [actually]**
> **going there,**
> **So too in yogic dreams, for him who dwells in**
> **mantra practices,**
> **His physical appearance born of meritorious actions**
> **is like a rainbow.** [5]

The above teaching from a tantric "Buddha" demonstrates that the so-called rainbow body is merely issued from one's internal perceived portion and that there is no actual physical form body or appearance of light for others to see. Indeed, this "sūtra" itself compares this body to the state in which one visits celestial palaces in a dream and asserts that this body is "achieved" through mantra practices in yogic dreams. Furthermore, the five-colored and the seven-colored rainbow lights are impure, given that both are interwoven with various mundane lights and that they result from the desire experienced during the yab-yum practice; therefore, they should not be sought after by practitioners.

Under the influence exerted by the mistaken tantric knowledge and views, a five-colored banner has been established as the official symbol of Buddhism by its followers. Such an

---

[5] *The Vairocanābhisaṃbodhi Sūtra*, translated by Rolf W. Giebel (Berkeley, CA: Numata Center for Buddhist Translation and Research, 2005), 133-134. [CBETA, T18, no. 848, 38a26-b13.]

establishment actually results from the imputation—which is itself based on erroneous views—that consists of dividing all phenomena into five categories, such as the five elements, five colors, five Buddhas, five Buddha-mothers, five Taras, five wisdoms, five Bodhisattvas, and so forth. Thus, the tantric Buddhas are of five-colored, and so are the Bodhisattvas, the rainbow body, and so forth; any phenomenon that falls within the reach of Tantric Buddhism will end up being five-colored. Even the four wisdoms of Buddhahood have, within Tantric Buddhism, been converted to five wisdoms with the addition of "the wisdom of the property of the dharma-realm" atop those wisdoms of Buddha. Although "the wisdom of the property of the dharma-realm" is in fact attained in the stage of the Path of Vision, the Bodhisattvas' lowest level of practice and realization, tantric practitioners have wrongly dubbed it the fifth wisdom unique to the "Buddhas" of Tantric Buddhism—that which is not possessed by any Buddha of Exoteric Buddhism.

Assigning also five colors to the official banner of Buddhism due to the above imputation—which is based on misconceptions—is in fact a delusional act issued from the erroneous views and knowledge of Tantric Buddhism and therefore has nothing to do with the Buddha Dharma. A Buddha's light has never been of five colors, nor has a Bodhisattva's light, but both the tantric Buddhas and bodhisattvas are five-colored. Thus, the "Bodhisattva Mañjuśrī" in Tantric Buddhism has various aspects, such as black Mañjuśrī, red Mañjuśrī, and so forth; these phenomena are all disguised emanations from ghosts and spirits and have always been unrelated to the correct Buddhist Dharma. All learners should be aware of this fact.

Furthermore, as stated by Tsongkhapa:

> As stated in Guhyasamāja Tantra *[Jimi]*:
> One will obtain the non-dual wisdom,
> After arising from the true limit.
> This statement explains the meanings of **the rainbow-like body and entering the clear light in the stage of the union**: The entity cannot be divided into two;

before the entry into the wisdom of clear light, the two apprehensions do not exist given that the three appearances have been purified, but it does not mean that there is no appearance of the body at that moment. If this was not the case, then it would not make sense to assert that the empty form has obtainment and that immutable bliss does not have obtainment. The so-called "having obtainment" requires the manifestation of various appearances, for it is also necessary for the various appearances to manifest before one obtains the immutable bliss of sages. Therefore, one should know that although [the physical body] exists at that time, it is non-existent before the attainment of the non-conceptual wisdom; these principles do not conflict with each other.[6]

Tsongkhapa's statement "the rainbow-like body and entering the clear light in the stage of the union" is based on erroneous thinking. Indeed, the visualization that one enters clear light while cultivating the Dharma-gate of the non-duality of bliss and emptiness—which is practiced between a male and a female—is definitely based on one's delusion and fantasy. Clear light is an imaginary state of the "self" consisting of the mind of feeling and cognition—it results from the visualization performed by the mind of feeling and cognition. Moreover, as this state of clear light exists within the mind of feeling and cognition—not beyond it—how then could the mind of feeling and cognition dissolve itself, through the method of visualization, into the state of clear light that this mind of feeling and cognition has itself visualized? This demonstrates that the mind of feeling and cognition's visualization of entering the clear light in this fashion is imaginary: The mind of feeling and cognition seems to have entered the state of clear light, but in

---

6   Yogi C. M. Chen (Chen Chien-ming 陳健民), *Qugongzhai quanji 曲肱齋全集 [The Complete Works of Yogi Chen]*, vol. 1-5, ed. Xu Qinying 徐芹庭 (Taipei: Puxianwang rulai fojiaohui 普賢王如來佛教會, 1991), vol. 1, 573. Translated into English from Chinese.

reality it has not. This is similar to the fact that there seems to be various states for one to enter in a dream, but those states are merely internal perceived portions manifested by the eighth consciousness, which are identical to the manifested states of transposed substance in a dream—there are no corresponding states of the three realms with their own nature and functions that have actually materialized beyond the dream. All Buddhist learners should know this principle in order to avoid the mistake made by the ancient and modern tantric gurus that consists of **making a dream within the big dream that is life**.

Furthermore, based on **Tsongkhapa**'s assertions in the above passage, the rainbow body is attained from the union of bliss and emptiness amidst the ultimate bliss of sexual pleasure consisting of the fourth joy experienced during the yab-yum practice between a male and a female, which means that the rainbow body is in essence achieved through both visualization and sexual pleasure. We can, therefore, conclude that the rainbow body is in essence a phenomenon of the desire-realm: As a phenomenon that does not transcend the human world, it naturally cannot transcend any of the six heavens of the desire-realm, given that the inhabitants of those heavens have less sexual desire than the sentient beings of the human world. Thus, how could the states of those who have attained the rainbow body transcend the form realm and the formless realm when they do not even reach the level of the heaven of the first concentration? Those who have realized a phenomenon that does not transcend the desire-realm do not even have the slightest understanding of the fruition of liberation attained by sound-hearer arhats, yet they claim that the persons who "have attained" the rainbow body transcend the states of all Buddhas in Exoteric Buddhism. As such, are they not as ignorant as an elementary school student who proclaims that his more proficient in arithmetic than all professors of mathematics? The wise should, upon hearing this analysis, choose the right path from the wrong one in order to bring forth the mundane wisdom and build up the correct knowledge and view of the Buddha Dharma.

4. The Yab-Yum Practice of Sexual Pleasure: A Method That Has Never Been Preached in the Avataṃsaka Sūtra

Ancient and contemporary tantric gurus have frequently asserted that yab-yum practice, which is cultivated between a male and a female, is taught in the *The Flower Garland Sūtra [Avataṃsaka Sūtra, 華嚴經]* of Exoteric Buddhism. According to them, as the Buddha did not teach it before passing away, it was expounded by Padmasambhava, a "Buddha" who appeared later in this world. Those gurus have thus "legitimized" Esoteric Buddhism. However, this assertion does not conform to the truth because this method appeared only after the 8th or 9th century and is not found in any Exoteric sūtras. Professor Chen Yujiao (陳玉蛟, who later became a monastic named Master Shirushi) says:

> Highest Yoga Tantra emerged around the 8th century in India. Before then, the Mahāyāna treatises of Exoteric Buddhism conserved their integrality; it was almost impossible to detect a trend towards the complete integration of the practice system of Tantric Buddhism. In the 7th century, Śāntideva, who is renowned for putting the exalted teachings into practice, merely cited some mantras in his famous *Śikṣāsamuccaya [Xuechu jiyao 學處集要]* without touching on the practice of Esoteric Buddhism as a whole. By the time of King Dharmapala's [達磨波羅王] reign in the 9th century, Vikrama śīla vihāra [Chaojie si 超戒寺] was built and both Exoteric Buddhism and Esoteric Buddhism were propagated. Thereafter, Esoteric Buddhism flourished by the day. The (Esoteric Buddhist) scholars of that time who wrote treatises about both Exoteric Buddhism and Esoteric Buddhism, however, generally handled these two systems separately, viewing them as independent entities. Rarely did they integrate these two philosophies into one single path with a

determined sequence of practices: connecting Exoteric Buddhism and Esoteric Buddhism with bodhicitta by starting with the three refuges and the three trainings; achieving meditative concentration by observing the precepts, obtaining supernatural power through meditative concentration, (further) practicing the union of wisdom and expediency; and finally advancing into the Secret Mantra Vehicle and attaining the complete enlightenment by swiftly perfecting the collections of merit and wisdom through the unique practice (the yab-yum practice, which is cultivated between a male and a female). With respect to such cultivation of the path with a determined sequence of practices that integrates both Exoteric Buddhism and Esoteric Buddhism, it was very difficult to find a treatise of this nature other than (before the publication of) *Lamp for the Path to Enlightenment [菩提道燈, Bodhipathapradīpa]* and *Commentary on the Difficult Points of the Lamp for the Path to Enlightenment [Nanchushi 難處釋]*.[1]

Therefore, the yab-yum practice in Tantric Buddhism originated in the following way: After the Shaktist philosophy found in Hinduism was later incorporated into Tantric "Buddhism," it underwent a long process of evolution that saw its tenets being compiled and rearranged, resulting first in the emergence of invocation methods such as secret mantras, rituals, and so forth in *The Adamantine Pinnacle Sūtra [Jingangding jing 金剛頂經]*, before the yab-yum practice, which is cultivated between a male and a female and allows for the attainment of Buddhahood in this body, was set forth in *The Vairocanābhisaṃbodhi Sūtra [Dari jing]*. In order to enhance the credibility of this method, the proponents of Tantric Buddhism further composed *A Brief History of Padmasambhava's Manifestation [Lianhuasheng yinghua shilue 蓮花生應化史略]*, which hails Padmasambhava as an emanation body Buddha originating from Buddha Amitabha, who Himself is

---

[1] Chen Yujiao 陳玉蛟 (ed.), *Adixia yu putidao dengshi 阿底峽與菩提道燈釋 [Atiśa and Commentary on the Lamp for the Path to Enlightenment]* (Dongchu Publisher 東初出版社, 1991), 53. Translated into English from Chinese.

the emanation of a lotus in the human world. However, the story of Padmasambhava's metamorphic birth is full of inconsistencies and cannot be trusted by the wise. This topic will be elaborated later.

We can affirm that the **Tantric path is indeed non-Buddhist** based on the timing when those tantras appeared in the human world as well as the sequence whereby they appeared, based on the fact that the methods taught in those tantras contradict in all respects and to a large extent the doctrines of the Three-Vehicles, and based on the accounts given by the great practitioners of Secret Mantra in the past as well as in the present. These facts also allow us to ascertain that the yab-yum practice is a Dharma-gate that indeed did not exist in the early stages of Tibetan Buddhism. Drawn later from the philosophy of Shaktism, which is a branch of Hinduism and Brahmanism, this practice infiltrated into Buddhism and has now become the tantric Dharma-gate of the "unsurpassed esoteric doctrine" that leads to the attainment of Buddhahood in this body. Tantric practitioners cannot deny—yet refuse to acknowledge—these facts, which are substantiated by the contents of the various tantras in ancient India as well as by the sequence whereby those tantras appeared in this world.

The learners and gurus of Tantric Buddhism frequently assert that the yab-yum Dharma-gate of sexual pleasure was set forth long ago in the *Avataṃsaka Sūtra* and therefore insist that this yab-yum tantric method cultivated between a male and a female is definitely the Buddha Dharma and will doubtlessly enable practitioners to attain Buddhahood in this body. However, the deeds of Bodhisattva Vasumitra [婆須蜜多] that are recounted in the *Avataṃsaka Sūtra* consist of steering sentient beings onto the Path to Buddhahood by taking advantage of their cravings for stunning beauties. Unlike those tantric gurus, Bodhisattva Vasumitra did not preach about the mental consciousness (mind of feeling and cognition), the union of bliss and emptiness, or the non-duality of bliss and emptiness. Instead, what she taught was the eighth consciousness (tathāgatagarbha)—the ālaya-consciousness.

This topic will be discussed in Section 11 of this chapter.

Some learners accuse me of wrongfully defaming Tantric Buddhism, given that they have never heard their gurus mention about the yab-yum method despite many years of practice. This is because their gurus refrained from teaching them this method during the cause initiation, the first initiation, and the second initiation after having observed that their causes and conditions are not yet mature. The objective of those gurus is to prevent these disciples, whose intention towards the path has not yet become steadfast, from doubting this practice due to a lack of faith or even from divulging this method and thereby hindering the future propagation of the tantric path. Such a precaution is based on a tacit understanding among tantric gurus. Therefore, those who accuse me of denigrating Tantric Buddhism are elementary practitioners who are unaware of the fundamental principle and Dharma-gate of practice that underpin this religion. Why is that? If my statements truly constituted groundless slanders of Tantric Buddhism, then could all the Dharma-kings and lamas—gurus—of the four major Tibetan tantric schools have turned a blind eye to my acts and allowed me to "defame" them without restraint in my publications? How could it be possible that no one has been willing to step forward to clarify the truth and stop my "misdeeds"? It would not make any sense.

As a matter of fact, "the great tantric practitioners who propagate the Dharma in Taiwan" mentioned by the lay Buddhist Chen Lü'an have all remained completely silent. None of them have been able to step forward to refute my assertions and proclaim, as Chen Lü'an pretends, that the yab-yum practice of sexual pleasure cultivated between a male and a female indeed does not exist in Tantric Buddhism. As none of them have the courage to discuss the Dharma with me in person, they are unable to deny the existence of this method openly and can only acknowledge it in silence.

If the gurus are certain that this practice does not exist in Tantric Buddhism, then they should deny its existence in public in order to protect the reputation of Tantric Buddhism and to prevent people from looking at tantric lamas in a peculiar way. On the other hand, if those gurus are convinced that the yab-yum practice indeed benefits sentient beings by enabling them to attain the fruitions of liberation and of Buddhahood, then they should, based on morality and courage, step forward to protect the "unsurpassed esoteric method" of Tibetan Tantrism, the method that leads to the attainment of Buddhahood in this body. If they have verified that this yab-yum practice indeed does not exist in Tantric Buddhism, then in the face of my groundless slander insisting on the existence of such erroneous views and deeds, they should join forces and attack me collectively—together, they should sign an open statement with their real names requesting to debate the Dharma with me, instead of individually using aliases to hurl all types of personal attacks and unfounded slander at me on the Internet.

If those great tantric practitioners have ascertained that the yab-yum practice of Tantric Buddhism is indeed **an unsurpassed esoteric method that truly benefits sentient beings,** but surprisingly do not have the courage to step forward to openly defend the authenticity of this highest great tantric method in the face of my scathing condemnation and destructive acts, then they are not qualified to learn, practice, or propagate the esoteric teachings, for they are selfish and unwilling to forsake their own interests for the benefit of the Dharma. On the contrary, if they have confirmed that the tantric theory of **attaining Buddhahood through the Path of Desire** is mistaken, then they should repent thoroughly and correct their actions for their and others' sake. Only then will they conform to **the vow that they made when they learned Esoteric Buddhism, which consists of extensively benefiting sentient beings**. How can they observe everything in silence and deliberately ignore these important facts? Such a cowering approach is not typical of those who cultivate the tantric path, as it stands in stark contrast to the aggressive and lofty stance invariably adopted by tantric gurus when they preach the Dharma.

Stringent rules have always been imposed on learners in the tantric training environment. Even after they have entered the

Dharma-gate, they must continue to diligently serve their gurus and consult those gurus on all matters:

> However, after encountering a knowledgeable mentor, one must consult him frequently in order to make progress. A guru with achievements on the path will never take the initiative to impart his teachings, but will always teach the disciple only when the latter asks him questions. This is an indisputable stipulation in Tantric Buddhism.[2]

Generally speaking, it is impossible for tantric learners to receive a "proper" secret initiation if they have failed to please their gurus.

If those practitioners cannot obtain a "proper" secret initiation, then they are even less likely to receive the guidance imparted through the actual cultivation of the yab-yum method during the fourth initiation and to subsequently perform the unsurpassed esoteric yab-yum method that allows for the attainment of Buddhahood in this body. The only exception to this rule concerns women (and also men) coveted by male lamas or female gurus due to their stunning appearance or the particular vibes that they display. In such instances, the practitioners will be taught the yab-yum practice by their gurus—lamas—without resorting to the pleasing method, as those gurus will view those encounters as opportunities to frequently get together with the women of their liking. A plethora of tantric gurus thus offer to transmit the unsurpassed yab-yum esoteric method to disciples due to the important that they attach to physical appearance. Instead of being isolated cases, those instances remain widespread in today's Taiwan (they involve both monastic lamas and lay gurus; however, their names will not be disclosed for privacy reasons and in order to avoid double victimization, unless those lamas continue to

---

[2]   *Naluo liufa* 那洛六法 *[The Six Yogas of Nāropa]*, narrated by Blo-Bzan-Grags-Pa Zam Lam [Daoran baluobu cangsangbu 道然巴羅布倉桑布], recorded by Lu Yizhao 盧以炤 (Taipei: Chenxi Wenhua Gongsi 晨曦文化公司, 1994), 292. Translated into English from Chinese.

propagate the erroneous tantric path).

Such events are frequently heard from the parties involved; they do not need to be relayed by unrelated persons and are by no means exaggerated stories aimed at causing fear and horror. As a matter of fact, it is difficult for tantric learners in general to hear about this yab-yum method. If they have never heard about it, then we can conclude that they are either elementary practitioners or have been unable to please their gurus. Upon hearing me identify the fallacies of the yab-yum method, such practitioners declare that my acts consist of deprecating Tantric Buddhism and rebuke me by asserting that I "must go to hell to endure the related retribution." Little do they know that the tantric gurus are actually the ones who have been destroying the Buddhist doctrines and who will inevitably go to hell to suffer the related retribution for long kalpas (this mostly applies to the proponents of Prāsaṅgika Madhyamaka in the Gelug School, such as the Dalai Lama and so forth).

Those elementary tantric practitioners have been vehemently defending Tibetan Tantric Buddhism in public, as they are unaware of its true essence and have failed to grasp, in accordance with the truth, the fact that Tantric Buddhism has been seriously damaging the essence of the true Buddhist doctrines. By all appearances, they seem to be protecting the Buddha Dharma; in fact, they have been helping Tantric Buddhism destroy the true Buddha Dharma. Through such "defense of the Buddha's true doctrines," they have actually been writing "an application letter to enter hell," which will grant them the right to abide therein long-lastingly after death to suffer the related retribution. How utterly pitiful!

A tantric guru has taught the following:

> The Tantra of Secrets [Mimi jing 秘密經] says: "There are four objects in the world that are not to be abandoned: (1) flower, (2) alcohol, (3) sexual intercourse, and (4) precious object (the sexual fluid issued from the copulation between a guru and his female consort)." The first three items do not

seem to be virtuous at first glance, but they can be turned into unsurpassed wondrous objects of offering to the Buddhas through the empowerment of a powerful person—this is the so-called natural achievement by effort. There are two types of flower: external and internal. External flower refers to the flowers as we know them, whereas internal flower is found in a woman (this refers to the vulva, whose metaphor is the lotus). If one makes good use of a woman's flower, then one will obtain immense benefit; otherwise, endless harm will be entailed. You will understand the related secret once you have mastered the required skill; I will not discuss this topic any further. . . . The so-called sexual intercourse here has nothing to do with the normal sex between a male and a female. Someday, you will grasp the secret meaning contained therein.[3]

Similar statements are extensively found in the tantric sūtras. How could those elementary tantric learners be unaware of those facts and assert that my revelation of the existence of this Dharma-gate in Tantric Buddhism constitutes a denigration of its doctrines? Not only is this method adopted in the Nyingma, Kagyu, and Sakya schools, but it also exists in the Gelug School, which proclaims itself to be the purest reformer. In *The Great Exposition of Secret Mantra* [*Mizong daocidi guanglun*], Tsongkhapa also advocates this "yab-yum practice that leads to the attainment of Buddhahood," which is cultivated between a male and a female. As those elementary learners have not truly entered the Dharma-gate of Tantric Buddhism, they do not know that this religion conceals filthy methods and fallacious theories. Consequently, in response to my repudiation of the false teachings and articulation of the true doctrines, which are meant to save them from straying onto the demonic path, they disparaged me as a demonic heretic who destroys the Buddha Dharma. What a complete distortion of the truth!

The yab-yum method has been playing a major role since "the late period of Buddhism" in ancient India, which was characterized

---

[3]   Ibid., 290-91.

by the prevalence of Tantric Buddhism in the Pala Dynasty. This continued to be the case when this method was introduced into the Kadam School in Tibet and when the Kadam School subsequently split into the four main traditions consisting of Nyingma, Kagyu, Sakya, and Gelug (later, even the Jonang School, which relied on the view of other-emptiness about the tathāgatagarbha to refute the yab-yum practice and was therefore disavowed by the four main traditions, had no choice but to secretly teach this true doctrine of the tathāgatagarbha—the view of other-emptiness—under the guise of this yab-yum practice, i.e., by relying on the outward propagation of Kālacakra as a cover). After the yab-yum practice was introduced into the Tantric Buddhism of Tibet, it invariably acted as the primary practice of this religion as well as the final goal that followers strived to attain with methods such as visualization, the vase breathing technique, inner fire, and so forth. Even today, it continues, without exception, to be the main practice of the "Buddha Dharma" disseminated by the Gelug School of Tibetan Tantric Buddhism throughout the world.

However, the yab-yum practice is not unconditionally approved by all tantric gurus in today's Taiwan. For instance, Guru Zheng Liansheng (鄭蓮生) says:

> Although the yab-yum practice allows one to attain Buddhahood in this body, hardly anyone dares to teach it or has the ability to cultivate it in this Dharma-ending era (in fact, it is still being taught and practiced by many in secret), as no one can meet its excessively stringent criteria. For instance, a male practitioner is required, during the practice of the winds and channels, to draw the uncompounded true wind from his sexual organs upward to his crown and then backward, and then upward again, until he gains full control of himself and is able to avoid leaking (ejaculating). He is also required to bring forth the drops in a special place of retreat and is not allowed to leak (ejaculate) in an extremely cold or hot environment. As for the female practitioner, after her drops—red bodhicitta—have vaporized, she must be able to move them upward and

downward as well as release and retract them, while remaining unperturbed by stimulation. Furthermore, she must be able to assist the male in his practice by steering her drops into his body and must then be able to retract them. Such a capability is that of a mother sky-traveler and is therefore beyond the wildest dreams of an ordinary person.[4]

The above passage demonstrates that not all the gurus within Tantric Buddhism agree that the yab-yum practice should be widely disseminated. Regardless of whether this method is based on any correct view and understanding, we may conclude from the above stipulations about the required skills that it is extremely difficult nowadays to find a person in Tantric Buddhism fully equipped with such abilities, not to mention finding one who can propagate this method. Even if there was truly such a capable person in Tantric Buddhism, who could steer his drops into the body of his female counterpart with his true winds through the yab-yum method—due to the fact that the two sexual organs are unified—thereby helping this female to attain the state of the union of bliss and emptiness and giving him the possibility to teach her the principle of the non-duality of bliss and emptiness, this method would remain non-Buddhist—it still could not be considered to be a Buddhist Dharma-gate of practice because it has absolutely nothing to do with the Path to Liberation of Hīnayāna or the Path to Buddhahood of Mahāyāna.

In summary, the yab-yum Dharma-gate in Tantric Buddhism teaches about the union of bliss and emptiness and the non-duality of bliss and emptiness, both of which are centered on the mental consciousness (mind of feeling and cognition) and are entirely unrelated to the wisdom of prajñā and to the wisdom of liberation pertaining to the Dharma of the Two Vehicles. Within the prajñā of the Buddha Bodhi, this practice is deemed a non-Buddhist method of "the ground associated with the mental consciousness." As for the teachings of Bodhisattva Vasumitra that are set forth in the

---

[4]   Ibid., 348.

Avataṃsaka Sūtra, they consist of the Dharma of the eighth consciousness (tathagatagarbha) and therefore differ drastically from those preached in the aforementioned tantric path. Therefore, tantric followers are said to have ascribed the yab-yum practice to the *Avataṃsaka Sūtra* of Exoteric Buddhism based on their mistaken knowledge and views. Such far-fetched distortion of the truth is by no means the authentic Buddha Dharma.

5. The Selection of a Female with Suitable Characteristics as a Prerequisite for the Yab-Yum Practice

Any male tantric practitioner who aspires to cultivate the yab-yum method must first select a woman with suitable characteristics, known as a "female consort." If a female has completed the practice of the generation stage and the fourth initiation and has cultivated the union of bliss and emptiness as well as the non-duality of bliss and emptiness by engaging in the yab-yum practice with a male, then she is deemed as a Buddha-mother or mother sky-traveler.

The Sakya School states the following with respect to how to select a female consort with suitable characteristics:

> i. The females with the features of a beast: . . . ii. The females with the features of a conch: . . . iii. The females with the features of an elephant: . . . iv. The females with lines: . . . v. The females with various characteristics: . . . In addition, there are the ones who are so-called endowed with the lineage of the females with the features of a lotus: . . .[1]

With respect to the various features of female consorts, please refer to the discussion about the path initiation in Section 8.3.3. Those details will not be reiterated here.

As stated by **Tsongkhapa**:

> The female consort with wondrous beauty,
> Is aged around fifteen or sixteen;
> Nicely adorned with fragrances and flowers,
> She enjoys pleasure in the maṇḍala.
> The Buddha-mother endowed with virtues,

---

[1] Virūpa, *Daoguo* 道果, 275-76. Translated into English from Chinese.

Is empowered by the wise;
The wise exudes peacefulness and magnificence,
The Buddha abides in the realm of empty space.[2]

The above passage also stipulates that the practitioner must select a girl "**with wondrous beauty . . . aged around fifteen or sixteen**" and must adorn her with "fragrances and flowers" before enjoying sexual pleasure with her in front of a Buddha's statue inside the maṇḍala; hence, **Tsongkhapa** has said: "The female consort with wondrous beauty . . . enjoys pleasure in the maṇḍala."

As stated, furthermore, by Yogi C. M. Chen:

> Theoretically, why is it necessary to use five women? Because the number five denotes the Buddha-mothers in the five directions and the five wisdoms. Those numbers should be matched! Therefore, it is necessary to select lady sky-travelers with distinct properties: mother sky-travelers of the Vajra Division, mother sky-travelers of the Lotus Division, and so forth.[3]

The purpose of, thus, selecting females with varied personalities and sexual organs is to enable practitioners to experience the different natures exhibited by women amidst the union of bliss and emptiness as well as the distinct features of every process; this will allow those practitioners to understand the correlation between the responses of diverse women and the differences among the various processes of the union of bliss and emptiness and to thereby fully gain the **wisdom** of differences related to the yab-yum practice.

Female consorts and lady sky-travelers are generally required to be beautiful and poised, as advocated by Tsongkhapa. However, *The Six Yogas of Nāropa [Naluo liufa]* does not take physical

---

2 Tsongkhapa, *Mizong daocidi guang lun* 密宗道次第廣論, 303. Translated into English from Chinese.

3 Yogi C. M. Chen (Chen Chien-ming 陳健民), *Qugongzhai quanji* 曲肱齋全集 [*The Complete Works of Yogi Chen*], vol. 1-5, ed. Xu Qinying 徐芹庭 (Taipei: Puxianwang rulai fojiaohui 普賢王如來佛教會, 1991), vol. 1, 238. Translated into English from Chinese.

appearances into consideration and regards the female's sexual organ as the only factor that needs to meet specific criteria:

One can cause the four joys to arise one after another by merging the inner fire at the navel and the wind and by moving the merged entity upward and downward; such is the principle of causes and conditions. As for the principle of external causes and conditions, begin by completing the above practices; after you have become powerful, **travel the world to find an exceptional woman. To qualify as such, she must be endowed with special sexual power**. Having found her, first ensure that she receives initiation and observes all the precepts well. However, her practice cannot be achieved if she does not understand the rituals; therefore, it is necessary for her to thoroughly comprehend the meanings of the rituals and to subsequently **cultivate** (the yab-yum method) **assiduously four times a day**. If one cultivates the bodhicitta well, then one will feel **one-pointedly blissful** (one will enjoy bliss one-pointedly) **during the practice, without being mindful of anything else**. If one clearly understands the rituals, then the path of joy will be extremely delightful. Women who are endowed with special sexual power can exhibit sixty-four types of attractiveness, which are normally hidden, but will become completely manifest during sexual intercourse. At this moment, one will definitely bring forth the mind of the view of emptiness as well as each of the four minds of joy. . . . The women endowed with sixty-four types of sexual power differ from normal women; they can exhibit the sixty-four types of sexual power one by one during sexual intercourse. In addition, they clearly understand each one of them; otherwise, we can conclude that they are definitely fake mother sky-travelers. If a practitioner who knows the main practice performs sexual intercourse with a fake mother sky-traveler, then he will definitely fall to hell. Therefore, it is imperative that practitioners understand both the generative branch and the main practice and frequently engage in introspection in order to check whether they are doing the right thing and whether the paths of the generative branch and of the main practice have been brought forth. Furthermore, it is mandatory that they carefully check the states that they have experienced against those that are set forth in the sūtras (tantric sūtras). During the practice, it would be good for practitioners to be aware of the level that they have reached. *The Cakrasamvara's Tantra for the Cultivation of the Path [Shanglewang zhi xiudao jing 上樂王之修道經]* (this is a tantric sūtra) says: "With respect to those who claim to have attained yoga when in fact they have not, as well as those who pretend to have obtained wisdom when in fact they have not, if such persons (if such persons who are thus devoid of the meritorious quality of the main practice) engage in sexual intercourse with women and proclaim that they possess great meritorious quality and great yoga, then they will definitely fall to hell." Therefore, before performing sexual intercourse, you must observe the counterpart's vulva to find out whether she is a demoness or a mother sky-traveler. If you cannot ascertain that she is a mother sky-traveler, then you must never recklessly engage in sexual union with her, so as to avoid perpetrating an egregious sin. During the process of finding a suitable woman, disregard her physical appearance and be only mindful of whether she is a mother sky-traveler.[4]

The criteria of a true female consort or mother sky-traveler are briefly as follows: In terms of valid knowledge in the practice of the Dharma, she must have completed the generation stage and the stage of the main practice; in addition, she must be able to steer the winds into her counterpart's body, so as to help him master the skill of the drops and the vase breathing technique and even help him achieve the cultivation and realization of the union of bliss and emptiness as well as the non-duality of bliss and emptiness during the yab-yum practice. Only then can she assume the role of a

---

[4] *Naluo liufa 那洛六法 [The Six Yogas of Nāropa]*, narrated by Blo-Bzan-Grags-Pa Zam Lam [Daoran baluobu cangsangbu 道然巴羅布倉桑布], recorded by Lu Yizhao 盧以炤 (Taipei: Chenxi Wenhua Gongsi 晨曦文化公司, 1994), 205-6. Translated into English from Chinese.

mother sky-traveler. This is also asserted by Guru Zheng Liansheng (his statements will not be cited here; see Section 4 of this chapter).

However, as the cultivation of the yab-yum method between tantric gurus and their disciples of the opposite sex has become rampant nowadays, the gurus do not even observe whether the persons of the opposite sex with whom they practice possess the skills of a mother sky-traveler; in other words, those counterparts do not need to meet the requirements stipulated in the tantras as long as they are beautiful or handsome. Thus, the Dharma-gate that leads to the attainment of Buddhahood in this body is actually based on cravings for gorgeous persons—the yab-yum practice that allows for the attainment of Buddhahood in this body is merely a pretext used by those gurus for their endeavors.

Padmasambhava has asserted the following in the article "Observing the Characteristics of Mother Seals" in *The Profound Guidance for Vajravārāhī [Haimu shenshen yindao]*:

> With respect to the instructions related to the observation of a mother seal's characteristics, *The Lotus Root Tantra [Lianhua benxu 蓮花本續]* says: "She must be fully equipped with the internal, external, and secret characteristics, have supreme wisdom and profound faith in the Buddha Dharma, show respect for yoga practitioners, never become tired of the great bliss, and so forth."
>
> 1. External characteristics: She must be good-looking, young, and delightful; her body must emit a nice fragrance; her face must resemble a peach flower; her waist must be slim and seductive; her height must be appropriate; her eyes must be thin and long, distinctly white and black, and with rosy contours; her hair must be black, lustrous, and smooth like silk; her teeth must be white and without gaps in between; she must have a propensity to look sideways; her face must be full of greed and people cannot help but feel affection for her at first sight. Her waistband must curl to the right; she stretches out her left foot first when she

walks; as a Buddha-mother endowed with the lotus lineage, her lips are similar to the petals of a lotus and she has a rosy complexion. Glanced at from behind, she seems to be lowering her head; looked from the front, she appears to be raising her head; looked from the side, her waist seems to be crooked, but is in fact very slim. Her body is rather wide below her waist and she seems to be drawing a lotus on the ground when she walks. Such is a person endowed with the lotus lineage. Internal characteristics inferred from external ones: To have a mole at the forehead is the feature of a body vajra mother; to have a mole at the throat is the feature of a speech vajra mother; to have a mole at the chest is the feature of a mind vajra mother; to have a mole at the eyebrows and at the navel is the feature of a mother of meritorious quality and action. The female with three straight striations in all those areas also belongs to this category. These are internal characteristics inferred from external ones.

2. Internal characteristics: The consort mother must be a person of few words, with a big heart and little jealousy. She must be able to accept esoteric doctrines with adamant faith. She is frugal and does not crave the yogi's wealth and treasures. She must be tactfully submissive, exceptionally caring, and able to resist temptations.

3. Secret characteristics: Her lotus (vulva) must be extremely tight and warm. Her lotus palace (cervix) must be plump, protruding, and skillful at keeping the vajra pestle (penis) within it. She must have small hips, a wide pelvis, inward-curling flesh, and tightly adhering flesh at the lotus palace. Her flower embryo must be plump; upon being touched by the pestle, she reacts as if she were in an unbearable condition and utters sweetly seductive sounds. Any slight thrusting and drawing motion will cause her body to tremble and her lotus to become warm and wet.

4. Characteristics of reality: She must exhibit great faith and understanding towards the yogi; her immense wisdom enables her to distinguish between the Dharma and the non-Dharma; her magnanimity allows her to accept the

esoteric practice; she can keep secrets, does not deprecate the yogi (the one who cultivates the yab-yum practice with her), respects him, and is able to behave according to the teachings. Her proficiency at the action (her good knowledge of sexual skills) can enhance the yogi's bliss (can enhance the bliss of the male who engages in the cultivation and realization of the yab-yum method). One experiences bliss upon seeing and touching her. In fact, one's body feels blissful just by slightly getting close to her; this allows the yogi to easily approach bliss and emptiness and his mind to easily connect with the intrinsically undefiled property (here, "the intrinsically undefiled property" refers to the mind of feeling and cognition and the sensation of sexual pleasure, which are both free from material defilements due to being shapeless and formless). Even when she abides in the state of correct thought, her yearning persists while she practices the non-arising with the yogi. (Even when this woman dwells in the state of thoughtlessness amidst the great bliss, her yearning for her counterpart persists while she cultivates this "non-arising" dharma with him). She maintains a blissful mind at all times, cultivates shame, embarrassment, and diligence, and readily serves the yogi upon all his requests. Her manner of speech is delightful and her demeanor is always graceful. She is driven and makes efforts with respect to all Buddhist deeds ("Buddhist deeds" refers to the various activities of Tantric Buddhism as well as the yab-yum practice).[5]

In some traditions, practitioners are even allowed to use their mothers, sisters, or daughters as yoginis—the counterparts of their yab-yum practice.

---

[5] Yogi C. M. Chen (Chen Chien-ming 陳健民), *Qugongzhai quanji* 曲肱齋全集 [*The Complete Works of Yogi Chen*], vol. 1-5, ed. Xu Qinying 徐芹庭 (Taipei: Puxianwang rulai fojiaohui 普賢王如來佛教會, 1991), vol. 3, 540-42. Translated into English from Chinese.

Among these, some sections of the tantric texts (original note: renowned ones) are cited occasionally, such as those that permit the use of any female—mother, sister, or daughter—as yogini. Some of those sections either interpret the meanings out of their context or are ignorant of the secret meanings, making those publications a severe threat to the correct Dharma.[6]

Although the above text condemns those who interpret some meanings out of their context, it advocates the following deed:

Reciprocal observation of mother and daughter:
The mother resembled a village girl when she was young,
But this was not the case after she aged;
The basic matter is achieved through reverse and reciprocal observation,
Isn't this normal for the daughter?[7]

The above passage is about the cultivation of the yab-yum method between a mother and a daughter.

In order to practice the Highest Yoga Tantra of bliss and emptiness, it is even acceptable to use female animals:

One should, in order to attain Buddhahood, couple great bliss with great emptiness. There are two types of coupling: vertical and horizontal. Vertical coupling concerns the four joys from top to bottom: The first joy is to eliminate the emptiness of past lifetimes; the second joy is to eliminate the emptiness of this current lifetime; the third joy is to eliminate the emptiness of future lifetimes; and the fourth joy is to eliminate the emptiness of the thusness of the three times. The elimination of the three times enables one to attain the

---

6   *Fojiao chanding* 佛教禪定 [*Buddhist Meditation*], vol. 2, narrated by Yogi C. M. Chen, recorded by Kangdi Paulo 康地保羅, translated by Wuyouzi 無憂子 (Taipei: Puxianwangrulai yinjinghui 普賢王如來印經會, 1991), 430. Translated into English from Chinese.

7   Yogi C. M. Chen (Chen Chien-ming 陳健民), *Qugongzhai quanji* 曲肱齋全集 [*The Complete Works of Yogi Chen*], vol. 1-5, ed. Xu Qinying 徐芹庭 (Taipei: Puxianwang rulai fojiaohui 普賢王如來佛教會, 1991), vol. 3, 306. Translated into English from Chinese.

immortal rainbow body. Thus, the method of longevity only exists in Secret Mantra. As for horizontal coupling, it unites the great bliss of the Buddhas in the ten directions (it aggregates the bliss consisting of the sexual contact of the fourth joy experienced by "all the Buddhas" in the ten directions) into one body and thereby attains the highest and the greatest achievement. Such coupling neither involves Yin or Yang nor resorts to the use of dragons and tigers, but completely hinges on the power of the concurrent application of tranquility and insight; externally, it uses all kinds of greedy methods, greedy thoughts, and greedy deeds, as well as all afflictive emotions of greed—the more the better. The more intense the bliss (blissful contact) is, the larger is the emptiness and hence the greater is the achievement. Having many tigers is a good thing, but having dragons is also great. **The biographies of ancient venerables recount the use of animals; one should use all the animals that can bring forth the great bliss.**[8]

In order to induce the bliss needed for the practice of the non-duality of bliss and emptiness as well as of the union of bliss and emptiness, it is even acceptable to use female corpses or female ghosts:

> With respect to the immutable secret meaning, one should know that it is incorrect to view oneself, the male consort, and the sky-traveler as separate, for they are in fact one single entity of the Dharma body. Indeed, one's mind consisting of the mental consciousness and the sky-traveler are undifferentiable. The channel is the male consort, and all thoughts consisting of discriminations are the female consort; they all flow out from the Dharma body. By knowing this essence, **one can attain the meritorious quality consisting of the supreme and the common** [consisting of the supreme and

---

[8] Yogi C. M. Chen (Chen Chien-ming 陳健民), *Qugongzhai quanji 曲肱齋全集* [*The Complete Works of Yogi Chen*], vol. 1-5, ed. Xu Qinying 徐芹庭 (Taipei: Puxianwang rulai fojiaohui 普賢王如來佛教會, 1991), vol. 1, 470. Translated into English from Chinese.

of the common siddhis] **even by practicing with a female corpse in the charnel ground or with a female ghost**.[9]

When a person encounters a female consort with whom he aspires to cultivate the yab-yum method, he should seek her consent by expressing his intention with various codes. Therefore, he must be familiar with the method to invoke female consorts:

> When one knows well that there is a connection (when one is certain that the other person is a female consort with whom one can connect), one should chant the following mantra: "*Ha ri ni sa siddhi pala hung* [哈惹尼沙悉地趴拉啥]," blow (one's) index finger with the mantra, and tap oneself three times to express one's intention. If a female consort with suitable characteristics touches her vertex with her hand, then she implies: "You can be my guru"; if she touches her crown of five Buddhas, then she implies: "You can be my adornment"; if she touches her eyes, then she implies: "You can be my eyes"; if she touches her throat, breasts, heart, and so forth, then she agrees to let the other person be her male consort [or "he agrees to act as the other person's male consort"]. (In this case, the male practitioner agrees to act as the male consort of the female practitioner). If she touches her navel and the intersection of the three channels, then she implies that she "can provide bliss" (she is willing to bring happiness to her counterpart by cultivating the yab-yum method with him); if she touches some foods and drinks, then she implies: "I can offer myself for your enjoyment."[10]

One should also understand the meanings of the following reactions from the other party after one has expressed one's intention through the mantra of invocation:

> If the female turns her back to me after I have tapped myself, then she expresses "rejection"; if she tears off the hair on

---

9   Yogi C. M. Chen (Chen Chien-ming 陳健民), *Qugongzhai quanji 曲肱齋全集 [The Complete Works of Yogi Chen]*, vol. 1-5, ed. Xu Qinying 徐芹庭 (Taipei: Puxianwang rulai fojiaohui 普賢王如來佛教會, 1991), vol. 3, 537. Translated into English from Chinese.

10 Ibid., 542.

her head or the fine hair on her body, then she implies: "I will leave you right away"; if she touches her lips or tongue, then she implies: "I will have an argument with you"; if she touches her teeth, then she implies: "I will eat you"; if she touches her fingernails and teeth, then she implies: "I will peel off your skin"; if she breaks off a branch or a blade of grass with her hands, then she implies: "I will take away your life"; if she touches her hips and feet, then she implies: "I will subdue you." One should comprehend the above responses, whether they are good or bad. If the response is good, then one should take the woman as a mother sky-traveler and rely on her. If the response is bad, then one should abandon her.[11]

Before invoking a female consort, one should be well aware of the "incongruous characteristics." One should not ask a woman with incongruous characteristics to be one's female consort, so as to avoid future disasters:

With respect to meat-eating rākṣasīs, blazing forms, and semen-seizing mothers, a tantra says: "The seven aspects such as meat-eating mother, blood-drinking mother, marrow-sucking mother, semen-seizing female ghost, and so forth."
The traits of a meat-eating mother: She has an extremely dark body, a masculine voice, very long eyelashes, thick eyebrows, and coarse skin; her promiscuity is reflected by the profusion of her sexual fluid; she enjoys using crude and filthy language and her speeches are deceitful; furthermore, she is stingy and greedy. If one relies on her, then one's achievements will be destroyed; not only will one be unable to enhance the two siddhis, but one's power of meditative concentration will weaken (original note: anyone who cultivates yoga (the yab-yum method) with her will die in fifty days).
The characteristics of a blood-drinking red mother: Her body is dark red like blood; she has dark red eyelashes, eyes that are often dry, a huge belly, and hairy underarms; she

---

11   Ibid., 542-543.

craves alcoholic beverages; her rākṣasa feet are like those of a sparrow; she vomits fire. Anyone who relies on her will be stripped of one's achievement of lordship (original note: Any practitioner who cultivates yoga with her will die in twenty-three days and fall to the unintermittent hell).

The characteristics of a marrow-sucking and bone-biting mother: Her body is dark blue and her skin has dark spots; she has thick, black, and spiking hair; her eyes are fierce like those of a sparrow; according to her, after she dreams about fire or ghosts, she stretches out her right foot first when walking; she is ferocious and belligerent and destroys others' achievements (original note: Any practitioner who cultivates yoga with her will die in twenty days).

The characteristics of a semen-seizing mother: Her face and body are grey; she is attracted to defiled and filthy objects; whenever she engages in sexual intercourse with a male, she is reluctant to stop this activity; although she has beautiful teeth, her breath smells like feces; she has big and piercing eyes. A male practitioner's reliance on her will shorten his lifespan, bring about many illnesses, undermine his bodily force, and cause his offspring to be dumb and mute.

The characteristics of a mara mother: She displays extreme cleverness; she has heavy footsteps, coarse flesh, and a large and protruding black face; she belongs to the lineage of demonesses and should be relinquished.

The characteristics of a mother of the rākṣasī lineage: She has blue flesh, small eyes, and big cheekbones; her skin is without fine wrinkles; she relishes false speeches and hence should be abandoned.

The characteristics of a human-eating rākṣasī mother: Small pits can be seen on her left underarm; she exhibits debauchery during the action (during sexual intercourse); she has very sharp canines, and both her eyes and nose are red. She should be abandoned.

The characteristics of a yakṣiṇī mother with ghost sons: She has flat heels and a very distracted mind and should be abandoned. The characteristics of a hungry ghost mother: She is debauched and has a very distracted mind; she has much jealousy and much greed and should be discarded. The characteristics of a mother of evil hindrances: She displays tremendous dexterity in performing mistaken activities (sexual intercourse) and inflicts evil hindrances; she is to be abandoned.

A practitioner's reliance on the aforementioned mothers will shorten his lifespan and undermine his wealth and meritorious quality. Therefore, those mothers should be relinquished. When one observes a mother action seal, it is essential to inspect if she has any defects. Yogis with sharp capacity, spurred by past vows and wholesome faculties, will naturally encounter a mother seal endowed with all the proper characteristics. It is difficult for a person with little merit to encounter such a female. Even if he does stumble across one, her lineage and characteristics will not fully meet the requirements—for instance, she may relish lowly behavior, have coarse flesh, or suffer from old age and humpback; she may be fond of eating, enjoy perpetrating misdeeds, and show no faith in the Buddha Dharma; her body may be mostly gray or blue gray. Consequently, all yogis who cultivate the profound Vajra Vehicle must carefully observe the characteristics of action seals. In summary, (the selected female consort) should be good-looking, young, and delightful; she should have few desires and should attach little importance to the yogi's wealth (she should not crave financial rewards from the male practitioner); she should make effort at Buddhist activities, have great faith, and be devoid of stinginess, greed, and jealousy; her bodily, verbal, and mental deeds must exhibit great delicacy.

One should select a female between thirteen and twenty-five years old, who is fully endowed with the essence (who still possesses the essence of sexual fluid). If one's drops, which are part of one's aggregates and realms, are fully preserved, then one will naturally have the opportunity to encounter a consort mother with whom one gets along. The internal channel and the bodhi (the internal channel and the semen) are originally the nature of the consort father and consort mother. If one does not lose one's bodhi (one's semen), then one will naturally encounter an internal mother sky-traveler as well as an external mother consort, bring forth the secret emptiness and bliss, enjoy food, drinks, and wealth in this lifetime, and hold the true nature. It is, thus, essential to fully preserve the bodhi (to ensure that the semen is not lost).[12]

Despite dedicating their entire life to the assiduous practice of this theory and Dharma-gate of Highest Yoga Tantra, a process through which they make use of many females, those tantric gurus are in fact unable to attain Buddhahood, for they are using this mistaken view as a pretext for their sexual misconduct, as evidenced by the following publication:

> **Two verses about the secret offerings made by a woman reincarnated from a magical crow:**
> Once freed, one will bask in the light of benevolence,
> The love and compassion bestowed by the Buddha thus perdure;
> The girl next door from the proper lineage accompanied me for the secret offering,
> She has transmigrated from a magical crow and lives close to the maṇḍala. . . .
> Her beautiful face has largely blossomed,
> I can smell the scent of roses;
> She is of the wondrous age of thirteen,
> I have won the race to own her.[13] . . .
> I rejoice at the idea that I have abandoned all attachment,
> And let the encounters come by without intentionally seeking them;
> The girl next door asked for union last night,
> The good news has arrived this morning from afar.[14] . . .

---

12 Yogi C. M. Chen (Chen Chien-ming 陳健民), *Qugongzhai quanji* 曲肱齋全集 *[The Complete Works of Yogi Chen]*, vol. 1-5, ed. Xu Qinying 徐芹庭 (Taipei: Puxianwang rulai fojiaohui 普賢王如來佛教會, 1991), vol. 3, 543-45. Translated into English from Chinese.

13 Ibid., 305.

14 Ibid., 309.

I fed a crow for over twenty years,
It has reincarnated as a human and we came across each other;
The virtuous girl next door untied her hair bun and offered her unopened lotus,
Who would have recognized that she was the crow that I fed?[15] . . .
The azuki bean was unexpectedly cut open long ago;
She discreetly came along with her sisters;
Although she was shy and reluctant to practice,
She exhorted her sisters to perform several times.[16] . . .
A Danish woman's arrival:
I dreamt that I saw a little dragonfly,
It brushed against the meditation mat and flew away;
Today I was happy to encounter a Danish woman;
Surprisingly, she was as large as a duckweed. (This is a complaint about the Danish woman's sexual organ being large and loose.)[17] . . .
I unexpectedly encountered love in my old age,
Sky-travelers from all directions descended upon my home;
I engaged in sexual union with a youthful teenage girl several times,
This girl next door is the reincarnation of a crow.[18] . . .
Who calls me with the loudest voice?
The light of a giant clam shines through the window;
It is unusual to witness the descent of a sky-traveler,
The concentration of the union of bliss and emptiness persists.
Having company, the vajra remains full of vigor,
The precious pestle becomes erect forever;
The palace of lotus is immersed in elation the entire night,
The bright moonlight shines on the bodies.

---

15   Ibid., 310.
16   Ibid., 312.
17   Ibid., 312.
18   Ibid., 315.

I am able to perform various postures such as flying seagull and galloping horse,
Only because the palace of lotus and my channel are not connected;
Once the two are intertwined and intoxicated,
The other person becomes flabby like soft cotton.[19] . . .
I recall that, in the sacred maṇḍala, the woman rolled around to foster the secret [practice], so that I could move [the winds] within my channel:
When I unexpectedly moved [the winds] within the exalted channel,
She tightly embraced my vajrasattva chest,
And became euphoric without the motion of thrusting and withdrawing,
Fascinated and with her eyes closed, she connected with the true emptiness.[20]

This tantric practitioner has tamed a plethora of women throughout his entire life. The above examples are likely just the tip of the iceberg, as many such cases have not been recorded. How could one possibly become an ultimate Buddha with such behavior that violates the precept of sexual misconduct, which is one of the ten grave precepts? How could one claim that this is the union of bliss and emptiness as well as the non-duality of bliss and emptiness?

In some cases, nine-year-old girls are used to achieve the union of bliss and emptiness through the pursuit of blissful contact:

The first awakening of love began early;
The nine year-old girl next door is akin to a fresh plum blossom,
But she already understands the meaning of love;

---

19   Ibid., 314.
20   Ibid., 314.

She has offered her undefiled lotus to me several times.[21,22]

Guru Padmasambhava also perpetrated similar acts; anyone can verify this fact, as those occurrences are recounted in *A Brief History of Guru Padmasambhava's Manifestation [Lianhuasheng dashi yinghua shilue 蓮花生大師應化史略]* and so forth. Few people within Tantric Buddhism possess as much integrity as Yogi C. M. Chen; given the considerable number of females that Chen has tamed, it goes without saying that those with a dishonorable personality who use the tantric Dharma-gate of attaining Buddhahood in this body as a pretext to attain their goals have slept with even more women. Any tantric practitioner can understand my statements by pondering over them. Therefore, those with foresight within Tantric Buddhism should be mindful of this issue, so as to prevent more women from falling prey to their misdeeds as well as to protect underage girls from also becoming their victims and living a life of regret.

Furthermore, it is necessary for the males who cultivate the yab-yum practice to enhance their sexual power and fortify their sperm by consuming meat; otherwise, they will not be able to maintain a long-lasting erection, as required by the unsurpassed esoteric method consisting of the non-duality of bliss and emptiness:

> Anyone who must further practice Highest Yoga Tantra and perform the action seal of a female consort (cultivate the yab-yum method with a real female consort) must eat meat. The hormones found in meat can better fortify the drops than the vitamins contained in vegetables. This is the secret of

---

[21] The use of underage girls in sexual yoga is one of the most appalling and illegal practices of Tibetan Tantric Buddhism. This demonstrates that this faith is by no means the authentic Buddhism.

[22] Yogi C. M. Chen (Chen Chien-ming 陳健民), *Qugongzhai quanji 曲肱齋全集 [The Complete Works of Yogi Chen]*, vol. 1-5, ed. Xu Qinying 徐芹庭 (Taipei: Puxianwang rulai fojiaohui 普賢王如來佛教會, 1991), vol. 3, 315. Translated into English from Chinese.

dependent arising and is also completely scientific.[23]

Given that the tantric Dharma-gate of Highest Yoga Tantra, which allows for the attainment of Buddhahood in this body, hinges, from beginning to end, on the blissful contact of sexual intercourse, male practitioners must enhance their sexual capacity by ingesting meat during the cultivation of the unsurpassed esoteric method in the completion stage; the goal is to avoid early ejaculation and ensure that the female practitioners who cultivate this method with them will reach orgasm. Indeed, a male guru can enhance his sexual capability by eating special foods; as a result, he will be able to extend the duration of his sexual acts, enjoy the blissful contact for a longer period of time as he abides long-lastingly in a state in which he withholds ejaculation, and cause the female to also attain orgasm. Therefore, both parties will be able to achieve a higher "state of realization"—the fourth joy—during sexual union. This is the reason why the Dalai Lama and other gurus held onto their cravings for meat—among others, red meat (beef)—during their visit to Taiwan despite the wide array of world-renowned vegetarian delicacies on this island. The wise can identify himself the fallacies of the tantric practice.

---

[23]   Ibid., 221.

6. Overview of the Actual Practice Known as "Union of Bliss and Emptiness"

Not only is the union of bliss and emptiness a philosophy preached in all the major traditions of Tantric Buddhism, but it in fact constitutes the fundamental belief of all the tantric schools. Although this method is no longer transmitted by the tantric traditions in Japan, it can still be found in their root sūtras. As for all the Tibetan tantric lineages, this yab-yum Dharma-gate, which is cultivated between a male and a female, is the final objective of all their practice theories and Dharma-gates of actual cultivation; none of those traditions can be disassociated from this method. A comprehensive citation of all those contents will likely bore readers, while a discussion of selected teachings from the major schools will enable readers to understand that the same principles, with the exception of slight variations in the details, also apply to the other traditions. This section will quote and summarize the teachings from the various traditions. First, we will cite **Tsongkhapa**'s statements:

> As stated in *Abhaya's Vajra Rosary [Manlun]*:
> The auspiciousness of the union of wisdom,
> Correctly manifests reality;
> From the full-lotus vajra position,
> The mind enters the maṇi.
> . . . . This means that, among the four joys, the innate wisdom is established as this wisdom. The moment it arises is when the bodhicitta has reached the vajra maṇi, but has not yet been expulsed (when the semen has arrived at the glans penis due to orgasm and is about to be discharged). The full-lotus vajra position refers to the moment when one abides in the maṇi and when nasal breathing ceases. (The full-lotus vajra position refers to the moment when one experiences immense blissful contact while one moves the semen to the glans penis and withholds it through the practice of the winds, causing the blissful contact to be intense and unintermittent—to the point

that one can hardly endure, which causes nasal breathing to cease). According to Guru Lawapa, the timing whereby the innate wisdom arises and its property are as previously mentioned; all four joys arise from the supreme joy, the joy of absence, and the stages between them. Guru Saraha also says that the innate wisdom is the third initiation. If a guru confers initiation on female disciples, then the "vajra place" (a male's penis) should be understood as the lotus (should be understood as a female's vulva). This is as stated in the section "The Third Initiation" of *Oral Teachings of Mañjuśrī* [*Miaojixiang koushoulun* 妙吉祥口授論]:

> From the union of vajra in the realm of empty space,
> Those endowed with the correct eyes can bring forth the great bliss;
> If one can renounce the joy of desire amidst the correct joy,
> Then one will see the middle of two extremes and will become free and steadfast.
> The lotus emptiness ("the lotus emptiness" denotes the fact that the inside of a lotus is empty of all objects) and vajra ("vajra" denotes the fact that the penis is erect and firm) maṇi (the glans penis glows like a jewel when the penis is erect) are treasures (this phrase refers to the emptiness-nature of a female's vulva and the treasure consisting of the male's vajra maṇi),
> The union of the lotus and treasure in the full-lotus position (the moment when one attains extreme bliss and when one's nasal breathing ceases temporarily due to the union of the lotus and the vajra maṇi),
> If, at that moment, one sees the mind enter the maṇi (if one can, at that moment, withhold ejaculation while witnessing the bodhicitta—semen—enter the glans penis and forever abide in this state of great bliss),
> Then one will understand that this bliss is precisely the wisdom (then one will comprehend that this bliss and emptiness consitutute the wisdom of realizing the Buddha Dharma).
> This is the path that fulfills the various stages (this is

the Dharma-gate of practice that fulfills the various
stages of the "Buddha Dharma"),
Preached in common by the supreme gurus (this
supreme and wondrous Dharma-gate is preached in
common by the most supreme teachers in Buddhism).
Both the states of greed and without greed are
without attainment (one must abide in the great bliss
and observe that one is without attainement whether
one is craving this bliss or free from such craving, for the
blissful contact is formless and shapeless),
But the wondrous wisdom manifests for a brief
instant therein (during the instant in which the great
bliss arises once one has attained the fourth joy, the
wondrous wisdom manifests within this great bliss);
One must receive this wisdom for eight dual hours,
A day, a month, a year, a kalpa, or a thousand kalpas
(those who learn the Tantric Buddha Dharma should
receive this great bliss and wisdom properly for eight
dual hours a day, for an entire day, for an entire month,
or even for an entire year, a kalpa, a thousand kalpas).
While this is taken in for only a brief moment during a
proper initiation (during a proper reception of secret
initiation, one takes in such happiness only during the
instant in which one tastes the "nectar"), one must,
during the main practice, take it in for long durations,
such as eight dual hours and so forth (when one
engages in the actual practice and cultivates with a
person of the opposite sex, one should take this bliss in
for extended periods of time—for even as long as eight
consecutive dual hours—"and so forth" refers to the fact
that one should take this bliss in for an entire day, an
entire month, an entire year, an entire kalpa, or even a
thousand kalpas).[1]

---

[1] Yogi C. M. Chen (Chen Chien-ming 陳健民), *Qugongzhai quanji* 曲肱齋全集 *[The Complete Works of Yogi Chen]*, vol. 1-5, ed. Xu Qinying 徐芹庭 (Taipei: Puxianwang rulai fojiaohui 普賢王如來佛教會, 1991), vol. 3, 383-84. Translated into English from Chinese.

In other words, **Tsongkhapa asserts** that, in order to realize the "wisdom of prajñā" pertaining to Buddhahood, one must move one's bodhicitta (one's drops—semen) into the maṇi (the glans penis, which is located at the tip of one's penis) while adopting the "full-lotus vajra position" during the yab-yum union. Moving the bodhicitta into this location allows one to take in the great bliss. Furthermore, one can bring forth the great bliss consisting of the fourth joy by abiding long-lastingly in the state in which one withholds the semen and maintains it on the brink of being expulsed through the practice of the winds. The wisdom related to this great bliss is called "innate wisdom," or simply "wisdom."

In the above passage, the term "full-lotus vajra position" used by Tsongkhapa does not designate a sitting posture in Chan meditation. Instead, it refers to the moment in which the semen induces the great bliss as it is on the brink of being expulsed, but is withheld in the maṇi (glans penis) **through the practice of the winds and inner fire, while the practitioner himself takes in this great bliss properly—this bliss is so intense that it interrupts his nasal breathing to cease temporarily.**

In the case of a conferral of secret initiation on a female, the guru should, in his teachings to the female, indicate that the expression "vajra place" refers to the lotus (a woman's sexual organ) and that the term "maṇi" in "the mind enters the maṇi" designates the clitoris of the lotus. Furthermore, the male guru should give the following instructions to his female disciple during this secret initiation: One can bring forth the greatest blissful contact by taking in the drops and orgasm after gathering them at the clitoris; in this state, one should take in the fact that this sexual pleasure has the property of being empty of all material form—hence, this sexual pleasure is called emptiness-nature—in addition, the mind of feeling and cognition amidst this sexual pleasure is also not a metarial form dharma and is therefore also the emptiness-nature; this sexual pleasure—this contact-induced perception of happiness—and this mind of feeling and cognition that takes in this happiness are in fact non-dual, for they both result from the same mind of feeling and cognition—hence the expression "non-duality of bliss and emptiness."

Thus, during his sexual intercourse with a female disciple, the male guru should, through the use of various expedients, cause the female disciple to maintain her orgasm for a long duration. Furthermore, while her orgasm persists, he should teach her the methods that will allow her sexual pleasure to perdure, and he must tell her that one can attain the union of bliss and emptiness by experiencing without interruption this perception-induced sensation of the "emptiness-nature." The guidance thus given by the male guru to his female disciple during the actual practice constitutes the contents of the fourth initiation.

After a female disciple has received this fourth initiation from a male guru or a male disciple has received this initiation from a female guru, he or she must, **as stipulated by Tsongkhapa**, find opportunties to put those teachings into practice. In those instances, the cultivation does not last just one or two hours, as is in the case during the fourth initiation performed with the guru. Instead, one must, during a proper practice of this method, dwell long-lastingly in the perception-induced sensation of sexual pleasure and bring forth the thoughts that "the perception-induced sensation of sexual pleasure is the emptiness-nature" and that "the mind of feeling and cognition amidst this blissful sensation is the emptiness-nature." Upon firmly maintaining these two "views of the emptiness-nature," one must bring forth the notions that "the mind of feeling and cognition and the emptiness-nature are non-dual" and that "sexual pleasure and the emptiness-nature are non-dual," before abiding in the state of "the non-duality of bliss and emptiness" while maintaining one's orgasm for an extensive period of time. To thus dwell in the union of bliss and emptiness of the fourth joy is the proper way to cultivate the non-duality of bliss and emptiness as well as the union of bliss and emptiness. If those who can thus abide in the orgasm consisting of the fourth joy and in this "correct view of the emptiness-nature" for a long time without regression are willing to further their practice with dedicated efforts, so as to attain the state in which their blissful contact pervades their bodies and their five cakras are filled with great bliss, then they have achieved the ultimate Buddhahood, "the complete and perfect enlightenment."[2] Given that the tantric "Buddhas" enjoy this **reward of great bliss**, the fruition of Buddhahood that they have attained is called "reward body Buddha" or "Dharma body Buddha". This Dharma-gate is precisely the Dharma-gate of Highest Yoga Tantra that leads to the attainment of Buddhahood in this body, which is found in all the traditions of Tantric Buddhism.

The "proper" way for a tantric disciple to cultivate Highest Yoga Tantra after receiving the fourth initiation is to select a date and a venue to again engage in the yab-yum practice with a female consort (in the case of a female practitioner, she must practice with a male consort whose strong body enables him to have prolonged erections—this will allow the female to take in sexual pleasure for a long duration) or a guru of the opposite sex and take in the state of the union of bliss and emptiness for an extended period of time;. In fact, the correct way to take in the union of bliss and emptiness during the cultivation of Highest Yoga Tantra is to dedicate at least eight dual hours a day to this practice. Hence, Tsongkhapa says: "One must, during a proper practice, **take it in for long durations, such as eight dual hours and so forth**." The words "and so forth" stand for an entire day, month, year, kalpa, or thousand kalpas. Such is the proper way to practice Highest Yoga Tantra **according to Tsongkhapa,** the Most Honorable One of the Gelug School.

Tsongkhapa believes that such desire should not be abandoned, for they underpin the "Path to Buddhahood." In order to obtain the guru's personal guidance during the fourth initiation, one must offer one's body to the guru (one must cultivate the yab-yum method with the guru) after prostrating oneself in front of him:

Guru Dari Jiaba [答日迦跋] says: "Next, one must prostrate

---

oneself at the eastern gate **with one's head pressed against the ground for some time and offer one's body to the guru."** . . . Because of entering it (because of entering the state of the union of bliss and emptiness), one will henceforth abide joyously in the human or celestial world, even without realizing the bodhi. As stated in *Abhaya's Vajra Rosary [Manlun]*: "It is said that one will definitely enjoy the bliss of good transmigrations, as one becomes free from bad transmigrations by absolutely refraining from perpetrating sinful deeds. Since you have entered and seen it, you will definitely have no death henceforth, for you have entered this Vajrayāna of the great bliss endowed with the nature of the great liberation."[3]

Why is it necessary for the receivers of the fourth initiation to offer their form bodies to the guru? The reason is because this initiation contains myriad details that are difficult to transmit orally. It is definitely tough for the disciple to understand them accurately and precisely if the guru does not explain them on-site during the co-practice and instead conveys them by relying solely on his memory and imagination. Therefore, the disciple must offer his form body to his guru. It is indeed difficult for a guru who does not cultivate this method with his disciple to delineate every single detail of the initiation; his possible omissions might prevent the practitioner from fully taking in the true secret meanings of the Highest Yoga Tantra's yab-yum method that he is trying to highlight. Hence, it is necessary for the practitioner to offer his body to the guru. In fact, tantric gurus frequently use the above reason as a pretext to request good-looking disciples of the opposite sex to offer their bodies to them. In case the disciples do not believe their assertions, they will quote the above arguments from Tsongkhapa in order to persuade those practitioners to give in to their demands.

Tsongkhapa claims that one "can escapte all sins such as killing

---

3   Tsongkhapa, *Mizong daocidi guang lun* 密宗道次第廣論, 410. Translated into English from Chinese.

and so forth" by thus entering the maṇḍala to receive the fourth initiation. However, the truth is that those who have received this initiation have not dissociated themselves from their past sins of killing in the slightest, given that the fourth initiation does not obliterate them. The sin of killing has two components: the sin of precept-violation and the sin of crime-nature. One eradicates the sin of precept-violation by repenting every day in front of a Buddha's statue until one sees auspicious signs, whereas the sin of crime-nature is obliterated only when the perpetrator suffers the related retribution in future lifetimes. It is, therefore, impossible to write those sins off by entering the maṇḍala of the fourth initiation.

Furthermore, if a tantric learner cultivates the method of the fourth initiation with his guru in the maṇḍala, then both the guru and the disciple will commit the grievous sin of sexual misconduct, which will definitely cause them to fall to hell where they will suffer excruciating sheer anguish for countless lifetimes. Moreover, from worldly standards, such sexual misconduct between a teacher and his disciple is **an act that violates the generally accepted principles of ethics** and is therefore not tolerated by society. As those tantric learners are unable to behave morally, it would be nonsensical to believe that they are qualified to practice the profound prajñā and the unsurpassed knowledge-of-aspects pertaining to the truth of the foremost meaning. Therefore, they are simply fooling themselves and others by affirming that Highest Yoga Tantra leads to the attainment of Buddhahood.

It is completely impossible for the tantric gurus and receivers of the fourth initiation who cultivate such erroneous deeds to ever achieve the following state set forth by Tsongkhapa, "Because of entering it, one will henceforth abide joyously in the human or celestial world, even without realizing the bodhi." Why is that? By engaging in sexual misconduct with one's guru in the maṇḍala, one will definitely suffer the proper retribution of anguish in hell; subsequently, one will need to endure the residual retribution first in the path of hungry ghosts and then in the path of animals before one can return to the human world. As a human, one will, during the first five hundred years, suffer from the remaining retribution, which consists of being reborn in peripheral regions with physical handicaps—blindness, deafness, and mutism. Such retributions are set forth in the Mahāyāna sūtras; how could Tsongkhapa turn a blind eye to these teachings and continue to harm tantric practitioners with this Dharma-gate of deceitful esotericism? Why would those tantric learners choose to believe Tsongkhapa's fallacious assertions instead of reading the Buddha's words in the sūtras?

One has exhibited the disposition for hell with the transgression of a grave precept—with the aforementioned erroneous views and deeds related to the practice of the fourth initiation in the maṇḍala as well as the cultivation, after the initiation, of Highest Yoga Tantra with a guru or a tantric practitioner of the opposite sex other than one's own spouse. How could Tsongkhapa deceive sentient beings with the statement, "one will definitely enjoy the bliss of good transmigrations," when it will actually be difficult for the aforementioned perpetrator to avoid long kalpas of sufferings in hell? With respect to such sexual misconduct and misdeeds that wreck the Buddhist doctrines, how could Tsongkhapa fool sentient beings with the assertion, "Since you have entered and seen it, you will definitely have no death henceforth, for you have entered this Vajrayāna of the great bliss endowed with the nature of the great liberation"? This statement, which indeed distorts the truth, thoroughly contradicts the Buddha's thoughts and extensively damages the Buddha Dharma. How could those practitioners enter the great liberation when they are not even able to keep their human bodies for the next lifetime? How could this method be called "Vajrayāna of great bliss"? Those who engage in this yab-yum practice solely based on fallacious views and behavior seek to attain bliss in this current lifetime as well as liberation in future litimes; however, they end up committing a sin that will generate excruciating sheer agony for countless lifetimes to come. How utterly ignorant!

Vajra Guru Gangkar has transmitted the following practice of the union of bliss and emptiness to his disciple Yogi C. M. Chen:

> "Action Seal of the Other's Body" in Chapter 9 of *Dakini*
> *Teachings [Haimu shenshen yindao]* says:
> Obeisance to the Honorable Bhagavān Heruka:
>> In order to enhance the dependent arising
>> of the vajra essence,
>> The body should be transformed into an
>> immutable vajra,
>> With the most supreme tantric practice,
>> This teaching is from Vajravārāhī.
>> Such a profound method is transmitted
>> orally,
>> May the capable disciples obtain this
>> quintessential instruction,
>> Which should be guarded as a secret, a top
>> secret, an utmost secret within the samaya
>> precepts.
>
> In order to enhance the view of wisdom as well as to
> strengthen the winds, the channels, and the drops of
> the Vajrayāna practitioners, these capable
> practitioners who do not regress from the drops should
> be given the following instructions: You should cultivate
> diligently with action seals who are endowed with the
> proper characteristics and abide in this bliss. In
> summary, there are five items: 1. the initial observation
> of the action seal, 2. the invocation, 3. the ripening, 4.
> the practice, and 5. the instruction about the
> meritorious quality and fruition.
>
>> 1. The initial observation of the action seal: *Tantra of*
>> *the Rotating Lotus [Lianhuaxuanxu 蓮花旋續]* says:
>> "She must be fully endowed with internal, external,
>> and secret characteristics. If she has separate
>> great faith in the Buddha, she must also have faith
>> in yogis, never become tired of the great bliss, and
>> so forth."
>>> i. External characteristics: She must be good-
>>> looking, young, and delightful; her body must
>>> emit a nice fragrance; her complexion must be

fair with rosy undertones; her waist must be slim; her figure must be proportioned properly; her eyes must be long and distinctly white and black, and the area underneath her eyes is preferably rosy; her hair must be lustrous and smooth like silk; her teeth must be white and without gaps in between; she must have a propensity to look sideways; her face must be full of greed; she must appear as if she does not dare to look at others. Her waistband must curl to the right; when she walks, she must stretch out her left foot first and move on the ground like a rotating lotus. She walks naturally and draws five types of beautiful seal with her footsteps. She is obsessed with love and people feel blissful upon seeing her. These are the general characteristics.

ii. The other types of action seals include the Buddha-mother endowed with the lotus lineage: Her lips resemble the petals of a lotus; her fingers are snow white; her hair is black and smooth; her flesh is rosy. Looked at from behind, she seems to be lowering her head; looked at from the front, she appears to be raising her head; looked at from the side, she appears to be turning her body sideways; her waist is slim, but the area beneath it is rather wide; she seems to be drawing a lotus on the ground when walking. These features are those of a female endowed with the lotus lineage.

iii. Internal characteristics inferred from external ones: If a female has a bright spot on her forehead, then she is a body vajra; if she has a bright spot on her throat, then she is a speech vajra; if she has a bright spot on her heart, then she is a mind vajra; if she has a bright spot on her eyebrows or her navel, then she is a mother of meritorious quality and action; if she has three straight striations in the five aforementioned areas, then she is also included in this category.

iv. Internal characteristics: She must be a person of few words, with a big heart and little jealousy. She must be able to accept the esoteric doctrines with adamant faith. She has few cravings for the practitioner's wealth, accepts other people's advice, and can resist temptations.

v. Secret characteristics: Her lotus must be tight, warm, plump, protruding, and skillful at keeping the pestle tightly within it. She must have small hips, a wide pelvis, inward-curling flesh, and tightly adhering flesh at the lotus opening. Her flower embryo must be plump; upon being touched by the pestle, she reacts as if this condition was unbearable for her lotus and utters sounds of shame. The slight thrusting and withdrawing motion excites her body and causes the inside of her lotus to become warm and wet.

vi. Observation of reality: She must have faith in Tantric Buddhism and in particular in its practitioners. Her immense wisdom enables her to distinguish between the Dharma and the non-Dharma. She is magnanimous and accepts the esoteric doctrines. She speaks with caution, does not deprecate the yogi, respects him, perfoms her tasks according to his instructions, serves him well, and can enhance his bliss.

vii. The female who induces bliss in those who see and touch her: Due to the nourishing function inside her body, the yogi who slightly gets close to her will experience bliss in his body and his mind will also easily connect manifest the intrinsically undefiled property. Her mind remains stable even if she does not hold the correct view; while practicing with the yogi, she is able to bring forth bliss and her mind remains close to the yogi's; she possesses immense conscience and shame; she serves the yogi diligently upon request. Her manner of speech is delightful and her demeanor is always graceful. She makes extreme efforts with respect to all Buddhist deeds.

2. The invocation: (This section is omitted here because its contents do not differ from Padmasambhava's teachings in Section 9.5).

3. The ripening: After obtaining an action seal (having found a female consort), ripen her by conferring the profound secret initiation on her, preach the profound path of liberation, and be able to set forth the benefits generated by practicing the various stages of the third initiation, which should by no means be amalgamated with the false mundane views, so as to steer her into the Buddha Dharma. If she has a narrow mindset, then help broaden it; furthermore, cause this action seal to bring forth a definitive understanding of the action, explain the profound expedient Path of Desire (explain to this female consort the profound expedient Path of Great Desire related to the yab-yum practice), and rely on physical substance (material drops—your semen) and the power of mantra to cause her to become an action seal receptacle (to cause this female consort to become an action seal who is fit to cultivate the yab-yum method with the male practitioner). Thereafter, you should know that all sacred and ordinary phenomena arise from the non-regression of the drops. The quintessential instruction related to such non-regression and enhancement is as follows: In a

quiet thatched shed into which people cannot peek, invoke the consort father and consort mother. Next, cause the action mother endowed with the suitable characteristics to wash and adorn her body (cause the mother sky-traveler of action endowed with the proper characteristics to wash her body and adorn it in different ways), apply perfume, and carry a sachet. Extend your feet to her naked legs; the two of you should embrace and kiss each other. Hold her head with your wrists, caress her body, search her lips and tongue with your tongue, press her breasts, stare at her secret place, and cause her to hold your pestle and perform the bliss-generating expedients as much as she can (cause the female to hold the penis of the male tantric practitioner and try her best to perform various deeds—to induce the male practitioner's happiness through various expedients). If you experience the discrimination of desire while performing the action, then you should know that greed is devoid of a real property and results from the spontaneous operation of all dharmas as thus. Recognize the intrinsic aspect on the greed that you have not eliminated and abide in the fundamental meditative concentration. If the greed is of an ordinary type, then it should be immediately and thoroughly eradicated. Practice diligently and manifest the expedient of bliss.

Subsequently, the one who has been empowered by himself and others should generate a supreme mind directed toward enlightenment for the first time. He should visualize that all phenomena are empty and that a bed—a lotus sun disc—manifests in the empty space. On the disc appears a meditational deity with one face and two arms; the practitioner should directly observe the arising of this deity. Next, he should visualize the void of conditions in his secret place. A secret pestle (a male's penis) appears amidst the void of conditions; on this pestle (penis) appears a syllable *hum* [ᵒ༔], which transforms into a five-pronged pestle. In the empty space arises a blue syllable *hum* with its head pointing inwards; on the pointed opening of this syllable lies a red and yellow syllable *phat* [呸] pointing outwards. The Buddha-mother instantly transforms into Vajravārāhī. (The female consort instantly becomes Vajravārāhī upon the completion of this visualization). Endowed with one face, two arms, and all the beauties, she is extremely blissful and delighted. With her protruding breasts and plump secret lotus, she is blissful beyond herself.

Once the void of conditions has arisen in the secret place, a lotus with four leaves appears amidst this void of conditions. In this lotus arises a flower embryo adorned with a syllable *ah*. Visualize every cakra of the body as a pair of consort father and consort mother (one should visualize a pair of consort father and female consort engaged in sexual intercourse at each of the five cakras located in the consort's central channel), just like in the esoteric practice (this visualization is identical to that of the esoteric method mentioned in the previous paragraph). Afterward, hit down with the Buddha-father's pestle from atop the syllable *ah* at the embryo of the lotus (hits down with your penis from atop the syllable *ah* at the clitoris). After performing in this fashion for a brief moment, abide in the fundamental meditative concentration of intrinsic purity that is free from proliferations and shake your body like a sheep (thus causing the blissful contact to reach a climax); it then comes down in torrents due to this bliss (this great bliss causes the semen to gush down). You should keep it from flowing out, just like a farmer digging a ditch with a hoe to steer the water (at this moment, you should use your penis to prevent the semen and the consort's sexual fluid from flowing out, just like a farmer digging a ditch with a hoe to steer the water), for it can only enter the ditch and descend upon each of the cakras as an offering to the four sky-travelers (as it can only be steered into the ditch and descend into each of the cakras as an offering to the four sky-traveler consort fathers and Buddha-mothers). The esoteric practice is thus: Shake your body when it moves to each cakra and most importantly prevent the drops from being expulsed (it is essential to keep the sexual fluid from flowing out). Subsequently, when the bliss descends to the secret place, visualize it as before and offer it to the sky-travelers in the secret cakra. (Finally, move the blissful contact downward into the genitalia in order to bring forth the great bliss once again; observe it as before and offer it to the consort fathers and mother sky-travelers in the secret cakra).

The skillful ones can stop the leaking like plugging the water outlets of a pool; the best ones can hold it on the entity of the intrinsic view free from the net of all conceptual proliferations; the mid-level ones can hold it with the winds: The holding of the ascending winds is similar to a leaked vase; the holding of the descending winds enables the winds that exit downward to ascend; and the holding of the central winds occurs at the navel cakra and causes a slight outward expansion. With respect to visualization, those with superior faculty visualize the view that all phenomena are intrinsically pure; those with mid-level faculty visualize a syllable *ham* [罕] above their crown similar to a stake used to fasten horses; those with inferior faculty visualize that the guru—consort father—above their crown is bright and clear like a crystal.

Novice practitioners may ejaculate immediately. In this case, they should know the channel essential and press it with three fingers aligned like a staircase (original note: They should press their perineum, which is the area between their external genitalia and their anus, or their nose tip; the so-called nose tip here refers to the tip of the pestle, given that the pestle designates the lower nose). Those who are adept at reversing the fluids—they are similar to the water that activates the waterwheel, which in turn activates the water—should visualize a syllable *hum* in their pestle, use it to hook the pure portion of the syllable *ah* in the lotus, chant a long *hum* sound, retract it into the pestle, and offer it to the deities at the secret place (after chanting a long *hum* sound, they should rely on the practice of the winds to retract the semen and sexual fluid from the vulva into their own genitalia and visualize that they offer this semen and sexual fluid to the deities in their genitalia). Next, they should suck this *hum* up, move it up along the central channel all the way into the guru above their crown, and offer it to the great being Padmasambhava as well as the father and the mother, as if they were making an offering to Vajradhara.

Here, the body essentials are as follows: Withdraw the four continents into Sumeru (original note: "The four continents" refers to the four limbs; "withdraw into Sumeru" means "withdraw into one's back"). Just like a dragon bumping against Sumeru, the sun and the moon should be facing the sky (original's note: you should stare upward). Roll your tongue and place it against the palate; press your chin against your Adam's apple. If the different parts of the body do not experience bliss (during the sexual intercourse), then you should generate it by shaking your body.

The speech essentials are as follows: Chant a long *hum* and ensure that it comes out in an uninterrupted breath. Furthermore, practice the visualization of the "body essentials and wind essentials" at each of the individual cakras; if you encounter difficulties during this practice, then practice the three essentials simultaneously at each cakra. Afterward, you should sit in the posture of a fox and practice the fist seal of drawing the drops upward (practice the fist seal of extracting the drops and drawing them upward); in other words, sit with your legs comfortably positioned, place your fists in front of yourself on the bed, abide in warm breaths during the practice, observe the great being Guru Padmasambhava above your crown, visualize that the empty space is shaking, hold a long warm breath before exhaling it completely, and then inhale a short breath and exhale it at will. After performing this practice four or five times, your body will swing naturally and bliss will arise. This is called the natural method of drawing upward, steering, and dispersion, which constitutes the wind essentials without exertion.

The last step is the dedication of meritorious quality. Make the vast resolution to make efforts at cultivating the vase breathing technique and fix your mind on the intrinsic property; this is in accordance with the esoteric practice of the five lineages of sky-traveler. This is a sequence of the path concordant with the generation and completion stages, which relies on the consort motherseal to bring joy to the consort father and consort mother. . . . The teachings imparted by Gangkar Dalŭ's [貢噶打縷] about mother sky-travelers and those given by the Most Honorable Rinchen [仁親] about celestial ladies are as follows:

> i. Having contact, ii. listening to her voice, iii. smelling her fragrance, iv. touching her body, v. taking in the supreme flavor (taking in the taste of sexual fluid with one's mouth), vi. embracing her, vii. kissing her lips, and viii. entering her lotus. Another text stipulates that one should touch the eight petals of the lotus before entering it; this constitutes an offering to the eight-mother sky-travelers. Next, one should touch the outside of her anus this constitutes an offering to the goddess of the defense. Only then can one enter the lotus and perform this method of slow performance. Given that males ejaculate easily while females do not bring forth bliss easily, a slow performance is recommended. Indeed, this can help avoid early ejaculation and will give the female enough time to attain bliss.

Note: The method of drawing upward is composed of six branches: i. pulling the abdomen inward toward the back, ii. pulling the anus up, iii. pressing the chin against the Adam's apple, iv. placing the tongue against the palate, v. staring upward, and vi. exhaling the upper wind or pressing the perineum with the finger. The performance of these six methods before ejaculation will definitely prevent any leakage. . . . In addition, the aforementioned path of slow performance is concomitant with the emergence of the five sense objects. Having touched the female, one will further see the arising of the five secret sense objects. After engaging (engaging in sexual intercourse) for a long time, the female's face will turn red, which will render her more beautiful; her laughter will be amazing, her voice will become graceful, and her lotus will turn wet and soniferous upon being touched.

For those whose lotus is too dry, apply banana flesh as instructed in my book titled *The Dharma Treasury of Clear Light [Guangming facang 光明法藏]*; this will definitely make the lotus soniferous. It is rare to come across a lotus that emits the scent of musk. In fact, women of good lineages release a special fragrance, not necessarily that of musk. Upon being touched, the female generates saliva at the root of her tongue; furthermore, the palace of her lotus becomes watery with a drinkable fluid; the [sensation of the] five sense objects amidst this contact is even more profound and blissful, and you must absolutely perform along with the emptiness-nature. Therefore, it is necessary to practice slowly and calmly so that you have enough time to engage in introspection.

During the observation of the form, inspect whether the emptiness-nature exists or not after the arising of the bliss. Such introspection is necessary. If the emptiness-nature does not exist, then you must perform along with it. It is only through such non-duality of form and emptiness, of sound and emptiness, of odor and emptiness, of flavor and emptiness, and of tactile object and emptiness that one can achieve the "non-duality of bliss and emptiness." **This is the objective of the action seal, of which one must absolutely be aware.**

Furthermore, with respect to the sixty-four methods of full-lotus position. . . . Among these sixty-four methods, there are eight basic ones: 1. getting close for fondling, 2. kissing, 3. drawing with fingers, 4. playful biting, 5. lotus-fondling, 6. uttering sounds, 7. rubbing of the body, and 8. cowgirl position; each of these encompasses eight subordinate ones that add up to a total of sixty-four:

1. Getting close for fondling: i. stealing the jade: peeking at the female's face, walking close enough to the female so that the two person's shoulders brush each other, and massaging her breasts; ii. pretending to reject the other person: flirting with mellow words; iii. erotic attraction: getting close for fondling and biting each other's lips and tongue; iv. sexual arousal: holding the female's neck and kissing her madly by making noise; v. intertwined rattan: stepping on the female's instep with one foot and holding her waist with the other foot; vi. cherry-picking: lifting her neck with the hand and sucking her lips; vii. entry: sleeping together with the abdomens tightly stuck and holding each other's waist with the legs; viii. blending of water and milk: entry of the pestle into the lotus.

2. Kissing: Kissing the female on eight locations— mouth, throat, breasts, underarms, waist, nose, cheekbones, and lotus.

3. Drawing with the finger: i. silk of the lotus root: drawing lightly and subtly with the finger on the lips, breasts, and so forth, so as to cause a fine line to appear vaguely; ii. half-moon: pressing

slightly more deeply into the breasts and throat with the fingernails, so as to cause a curved line to appear; iii. maṇḍala: pressing the female's body with all five fingers when she swings her body due to itchiness; iv. lingering love: drawing a long line at the navel and the tailbone area; v. light gauze: drawing the aforementioned lines with an inclination; vi. karma [jiemo 羯摩]: drawing a cross-shaped pestle on her bust point and below her chin; vii. plum flower: making an imprint at the breasts and so forth with the five fingernails; viii. small lotus: drawing the shape of a lotus at the breasts and so forth.

4. Playful biting: i. spring color: extreme blushing due to lust; ii. touching the lips: making light teeth marks on her lips; iii. coral: kissing her cheeks with one's lips closed; iv. drops: biting each other with incisors, as if both persons sported long, sharp, and protruding teeth; v. pearl garland: making continuous teeth marks at her waist, shoulder, throat, and eyebrows; vi. dazzling cloud: making teeth marks randomly on her body, like a cloud wandering in the empty space without an originally fixed location; vii. lotus pearls: making teeth marks on her underarms; viii. coquetry: tickling her ticklish areas such as the earlobes and so forth.

5. Lotus-fondling: i. wave-spitting: pressing one's abdomen against her body and playing with one's pestle beside her lotus; ii. frivolousness: holding the root of the pestle and inserting its upper half into the lotus; iii. deep entry: plunging the male's pestle like inserting a phurpa (puba 蒲巴, Vajrakila dagger) while the female lies supine with her legs extended; iv. partial acceptance: making the thrusting and withdrawing motions whenever it pleases the female and then

remaining motionless after a deep insertion; v. crying and laughing: making sudden withdrawals and insertions; vi. getting drunk: making several shallow insertions followed by one deep insertion, and vice versa; vii. tacit understanding: moving up and down in sync; viii. fulfillment of the vow: making one gradual insertion of half of the pestle followed by one sudden insertion of the entire pestle.

6. Uttering sounds: making sounds similar to weeping, sighing, complaining, panting, moaning, *awada* [阿哇打], *wana ada* [哇那阿打], little liberation, and *awa juewa* [阿哇爵哇] (original note: Guru Gangkar has, in his reply, affirmed his unawareness of the above terms); these are respectively similar to the sounds of pigeon, cuckoo, *halida* [哈里打], heron, bee, goose, spring bird, and *bawajia* [巴哇嫁]. All of these sounds should be uttered from the abdomen.

7. Rubbing of the body: It is identical to the aforementioned "kissing" (original note: It involves the same locations); in particular, use the hand to massage the female's fists, palms, elbows, waist, face, and so forth. The female's utterance of any of the aforementioned eight sounds reflects her greed, which means that she will definitely experience great bliss; if her tone is cold, then massage her for a long period of time.

8. Cowgirl position: This applies to the case where the male has a body that is too large and heavy for the female to bear; therefore, the two should perform the action in the reverse position. The female should perform the following, just like a man: i. running: performing swift thrusting and withdrawing motions; ii. pressing: dwelling for a long period of time and then exiting slowly; iii. spinning: performing wheel-like spinning motions [this applies to the female] while the legs of both

persons are entangled; iv. filtering: moving slightly from beneath [this applies to the male] while the legs of the female are entangled; v. flatness: taking a rest [this applies to the male]; vi. shuttle: remaining immobile [this applies to the male] while the female performs slowly; vii. intoxication: fully extending one's arms and legs [this applies to the male]; viii. playing hard to get: performing in the sitting position with the female turning her back to the male.

The above sixty-four deeds should be performed at will in order to connect with emptiness and bliss.

The above contents briefly highlight the connection with emptiness and bliss: This practice should indeed be performed slowly so that **the arising of bliss occurs concurrently with the connection with emptiness**. For instance, if you are unable to view emptiness in the initial stage of "getting close for fondling," then stop the practice immediately, repent, and try again. If you are unable to view emptiness in either one of the first two stages, then you should halt all the stages that follow. It is imperative to **bring forth bliss through every physical contact and connect with emptiness in every moment**; this will allow you to enhance the bliss step by step in an orderly fashion while you try your best to connect with the emptiness. The manuscripts only contain the way to obtain bliss, but rarely give earnest instructions on how to generate emptiness from bliss and how to cultivate bliss based on emptiness, which are methods that practitioners should be aware of. Therefore, I have no choice but to hereby complement the teachings of ancient sages. It is to be known that one can forsake bliss, but not emptiness. Bliss causes one to easily fall onto the plane of common beings, while emptiness definitely leads to the realization of bodhi; by all means be cautious about it.

With respect to the myriad mentions in this book

about "the medicines that can expose a woman's secret channel," I once accompanied Rinpoche Palpung Khyentse to a large pharmacy and verified the medicines sold there one by one. I discovered that in Beiping [北平, currently named Beijing (北京)], the same medicine can bear different Mandarin and Tibetan names. The translated manuscripts contain many errors and should not be used; using them will definitely be ineffective. Therefore, for the channels to connect, it is necessary to adopt various postures and try them out one by one. Given that the female's channel is undersized and is, for every woman, found in a different location of the body, both parties (the lower ends of the central channels—the sexual organs—belonging to both parties) will, during the union, inevitably become inseparable like dogs (like in the state in which dogs are inseparable after copulation; see the original note at the end of this quotation). Despite such sensations of inseparability, the two do not need to truly remain inseparable; this is evidence that the two channels are indeed interconnected. I am speaking from my personal experience of practicing with my wife.

The situation, however, is different when it comes to practicing with other women. I cultivated this method with a female from the monastery with remarkable tantric skills who was granted by Guru Gangkar; her channel was found in a location that was different from my wife's, which corroborates my previous statement. Once the channels are interconnected, the red bodhicitta of the female can flow out easily; this is one possible way of verification. The texts do not mention about postures; even if they do, few explanations are provided. With respect to the postures that are more likely to induce orgasm in the different types of females, the practitioner himself must derive all the relevant knowledge from every practice of union during which he tries out various postures to see if they fit the females and has to reach the following agreement with her: She must praise him whenever and wherever she experiences bliss; this will allow the practitioner to explore and ascertain which posture suits her best and to therefore perform it frequently.

The practitioners must be aware of the following: The bliss is definitely intense when the channels are interconnected; at this moment, one is prone to ejaculation and it is, therefore, necessary to carefully draw the semen upward. *Transcript of A Guide to the Great Bliss through the Lower Opening [Xiamen dale yindao chaoben 下門大樂引導鈔本]* depicts the following four postures:

1. The male embraces the female's neck while the female embraces the male's waist; the pestle shuttles upward and downward; the channel appears on the left side of the lotus.

2. The female lies supine with her head positioned on a high pillow; her feet are placed on the male's shoulder; the male performs intercourse by holding her from beneath; the channel appears from the top and bottom of the lotus.

3. The female's legs are placed on the elbows of the male's folded arms; the male performs intercourse by holding her from below her waist; the channel emerges from the left and right sides of the lotus.

4. The female extends her legs to the male's breasts; the male wraps the female's waist with one leg and extends his other leg straight; he embraces the female's lower body; the channel appears at the center of the lotus.

These four types of female belong respectively to the vajra lineage, the lotus lineage, the beast lineage, and the elephant lineage. With respect to this topic, I personally believe that each lineage of females exhibits specific characteristics and we may not meet all the lineages. We cannot limit ourselves to these four postures if we wish to explore the channel of the particular woman with whom we have the karmic connections to cultivate this method. As a matter of fact, the teachings in the manuscripts are questionable, for they speak about left and right or top and bottom without giving specific instructions. One should explore the channel with postures that allow for "the concordance of the pestle and the lotus from all directions" until one obtains the perception-induced sensation of interconnection. Many of the books about sexual skills delineate over thirty different postures; the recent ones also feature many photographs. However, one had better rely on the actual practice with a sexual partner. Indeed, to believe everything that the books say is worse than not having any books at all.

Furthermore, each of the secret manuscripts also highlights a plethora of secret mantras, secret medicines, and secret magic symbols that can be used to entice lady sky-travelers. Although I do not dare to say that those methods are "ineffective," I do believe that they are neither easily applicable nor completely efficacious. The best method is to observe the precepts so as to invoke the Dharma-protectors who safeguard the esoteric doctrines and who will direct lady sky-travelers over to the practitioner. This method actually worked during my stay in Dege [德格]: The woman that the Dharma-protectors guided to me emitted light when she showed up and her arrival was announced by a Dharma-protector: "The sky traveker has come." It is not necessary to observe the sky-traveler's appearance, for one beholds her light well before seeing her face. After seeing her, one can naturally unite with her without having to seduce her. When she leaves, there is no entanglement or any mundane harassment involved. This is the way the Dharma-protectors guard the path.

A superior practitioner is able to connect with a lady sky-traveler by cultivating the related method; he can protect his drops and be fully endowed with the bodhicitta. As for the female, she comes by automatically to make an offering, as she has asserted in her vows. During the cultivation, this superior practitioner experiences even greater responses such as seeing the sun and the moon, abiding in proper meditative concentration, or connecting with the Mahāmudrā. After the female leaves, there will be no worldly harassment whatsoever. It is unnecessary to entice her with medicines, money, or food and drink. These are the special effects brought forth by the lady sky-traveler's automatic arrival.

A supreme practitioner is able to practice various visualizations related to the non-duality of bliss and emptiness, thereby causing the clear entity of Mahāmudrā to manifest naturally; in addition, he is fully endowed with the power for various actions of great compassion and is able to bring forth the meritorious quality related to the achievement of the deity. As a deity, he automatically has a Buddha-mother. There will be a prediction before he encounters her; when she arrives, he will feel a strong sense of familiarity upon seeing her. Whether they meet via a long-distance visit or a spontaneous gathering, the male practitioner will not face any obstructions in his practice and will experience sheer emptiness and bliss. After this practice, which will not be discovered by anyone, he will perceive and sense the abrupt progress of his enlightenment. These result from the practitioner's perfect observance of the precepts, profound meditative concentration, and advanced wisdom, as well as from all his meritorious qualities. In summary, given that this law of causality always prevails, if the practitioner is filled up with drops, proficient in the practice of the winds, and able to match his wisdom with the four joys and four emptinesses of the tantric practice, then he will definitely benefit from the help of a lady sky-traveler.[4] (Original note: When the two channels interconnect, the pure young lady will shake her body violently like a female dog and, rendered mellow by the great bliss, will roll all over the bed; the pestle and the lotus will be inseparably intertwined.)[5]

Furthermore, tantric practitioners who wish to cultivate this method must first master the winds in the channel of the five cakras:

Therefore, one should adopt the principle of the yab-yum practice, which is to rely on the practice of the winds to untie the channel at the external layer of the secret cakra and then to use the pervasive winds to open the channel at the external layer of the heart cakra. Once the channel at the external layer of the heart cakra is opened, the winds can easily enter the central channel. Next, one must break through the lower area with fire (original note: inner fire) and wash the upper area with water (original note: drip drops from the crown cakra) to open the heart cakra layer by layer. Therefore, in order to open the five cakras, one should first open the heart cakra; by contrast, one should begin the practice from one's secret place—hence the importance of cultivating the union. If you do not cultivate the union, then it will be difficult for you to open the channel at the external layer of the secret place. Consequently, the testicle is said to be the aggregation of semen! This is where all the semen is formed. **One should practice herein every day** and slowly untie it through the samādhi power of the emptiness-nature as well as through the practices of the winds and the union.[6]

---

[4] Yogi C. M. Chen (Chen Chien-ming 陳健民), *Qugongzhai quanji* 曲肱齋全集 *[The Complete Works of Yogi Chen]*, vol. 1-5, ed. Xu Qinying 徐芹庭 (Taipei: Puxianwang rulai fojiaohui 普賢王如來佛教會, 1991), vol. 3, 279-303. Translated into English from Chinese.

[5] Ibid., 306.

[6] Yogi C. M. Chen (Chen Chien-ming 陳健民), *Qugongzhai quanji* 曲肱齋全集 *[The Complete Works of Yogi Chen]*, vol. 1-5, ed. Xu Qinying 徐芹庭 (Taipei: Puxianwang

If one does not cultivate tantrism with the objective of mastering the winds in the channel of the five cakras, then one will be unable to withhold the winds at the edge of the maṇi without leaking them during the yab-yum practice—one will be incapable of maintaining orgasm for a long period of time and will definitely ejaculate. Consequently, one will not be able to follow Tsongkhapa's instruction, "one must, during a proper practice, take it in for long durations, such as eight dual hours and so forth," nor bring forth the "wisdom to maintain the intensity and long duration of this blissful contact." As a result, this practitioner will be one who has not attained the great bliss and will therefore never become a "tantric Buddha." For this reason, those who aspire to cultivate the yab-yum practice must first complete the cultivation of the generation stage before being able to receive the fourth initiation and perform the yab-yum practice with others. Hence, it is said:

> Life is to the mind what the pistil is to the lotus; if a practitioner's mind is adamant on the outside, then in the inside "none of the Buddhas in the mind" can leave. **The Buddhas that one has invited have filled up the inside; they will stay firmly and will never be able to exit**. As the saying goes: "The water will not leak out if there is no hole." If a follower can practice with determination, then even though he is about to ejaculate when he embraces a consort mother, he can, just as fast as clapping his hands, prevent his semen from leaking by shutting the semen gate. **One who does not ejaculate while having sexual intercourse with a consort mother will definitely attain Buddhahood**. As the Buddhas within his body will never be able to leave, he will at this moment bring forth the yoga mind: One pore becomes one world, one world becomes one Buddha's maṇḍala, and one becomes Bodhisattva Mañjuśrī with a body whose immunity is unparalleled; in every world, one is preaching sūtras to sentient beings, thus liberating them one by one. Such a practice of

rulai fojiaohui 普賢王如來佛教會, 1991), vol. 1, 235. Translated into English from Chinese.

visualization yields immeasurable meritorious quality. Once a practitioner's semen has exited from the semen gate, it will be very difficult to retract it. Therefore, when one practices the mind of joy and moves the semen downward after melting it, one should not lower it too much; otherwise, one might not be unable to resist expulsing it. As for moving the semen upward back to the crown in order to bring forth the mind of the joy of union at the cakra of the great bliss, it is fine to do it slowly—the semen is the safest in that location, given that there is no hole to discharge it. . . . The fusion of the red and the white (the fusion of the white bodhicitta—the male's semen—and the red bodhicitta—the female's sexual fluid) causes the mind of the joy of union to arise. When it arises, one should not think of anything except the fact that "all phenomena are empty; the consort mother and myself are also empty."[7]

Those who wish to practice this Highest Yoga Tantra must first cultivate, in the generation stage, the method of the central channel and the drops, the vase breathing technique, and inner fire; tantric male practitioners must further focus on improving their sexual organs through a method called sword-making:

Pepper and ginger foster contraction and dispersion,
Growing in humid lowlands, they are strongly effective;
The use of medicines should comply with the wondrous principles,
The use of cnidium is set forth in *Shadowy Attic of the Two Plums [Shuangmei yingge 雙梅影閣]*.
(Original note: As pepper causes skin contraction, it is, in Tantrism, applied on the lotus to make it contract; given that ginger disperses cold and humidity, washing the pestle with cnidium helps eliminate the humidity and strengthen the pestle—from Ye Dehui's [葉德輝] *Shadowy Attic of the Two*

---

7   *Naluo liufa 那洛六法 [The Six Yogas of Nāropa]*, narrated by Blo-Bzan-Grags-Pa Zam Lam [Daoran baluobu cangsangbu 道然巴羅布倉桑布], recorded by Lu Yizhao 盧以炤 (Taipei: Chenxi Wenhua Gongsi 晨曦文化公司, 1994), 188-89. Translated into English from Chinese.

Plums [Shuangmei yingge 雙梅影閣].)[8]

It is also said:

When it is too dry, it is akin to a newly polished sword,
If it is too wet, then it is similar to crossing over a large river;
The best is when it is wet and about to dry,
The two compose a song of spring king with a stringless instrument.
(Original note: If the lotus is too dry, then one should insert a small quantity of banana therein; see my publication *Dharma Treasury of Clear Light [Guangming facang]*.)[9]

In the Sakya School, the quintessential instruction about this actual practice is guarded secretly and is only orally transmitted by the guru. *Taking the Result as the Path: Core Teachings of the Sakya Lamdré Tradition* describes it briefly as follows:

The quintessential instruction includes five key points: descent, retention, reversal, dispersion, and preservation.

Descent: First, cultivate the four joys so as to become familiar with them. The causes that give rise to the four joys are the four instants—they are divided into four types based on the different time periods. The four fruitions of joy that they generate are divided into four categories based on four distinct perception-induced sensations. Furthermore, the four instants correspond to the perception-induced sensations that are the distinguishing subject, whereas the four joys consist of the levels that are the distinguished object. The first instant, "the instant of various aspects," occurs in linkage with various things such as seeing form and so forth; during this time period, all perception-induced sensations that are generated are

---

8   Yogi C. M. Chen (Chen Chien-ming 陳健民), *Qugongzhai quanji 曲肱齋全集 [The Complete Works of Yogi Chen]*, vol. 1-5, ed. Xu Qinying 徐芹庭 (Taipei: Puxianwang rulai fojiaohui 普賢王如來佛教會, 1991), vol. 1, 313. Translated into English from Chinese.
9   Ibid., 306.

called "wisdom of joy." In the second instant, "the instant of ripening," due to the joining in equal portions of the two tastes consisting of *bola* (a seed-syllable) and *kakkola*, bliss is intensified compared to the previous practice and becomes more supreme; during this time period, all perception-induced sensations that are generated are called "wisdom of supreme joy." In the third instant, "the instant of rubbing," based on rubbing seals such as stirring and so forth, one internally brings forth joy while being externally free from the discrimination bound by forms and appearances; during this time period, all perception-induced sensations that are generated are called "wisdom of joy free from joy." The fourth instant, "the instant free from all aspects," manifests the non-discrimination of both the nine realms' pure portion and the joy of characteristics or the non-discrimination of the discriminative reflections; during this time period, all perception-induced sensations that are generated are the innate wisdom of the obliteration of both bliss and non-doubt.

Retention: This key point is extensively explained as follows. Use a thoroughly pure consort endowed with the wisdom of real entity as your support. While she is at a suitable distance, learn from her "form": Cause your drops to descend by igniting your rudimentary fire of passion and move them within the subtle channels. Practice bliss without regressing; it is important to protect its moment of extension. . . . (Original note: The actual practice is omitted here.) Those who learn from "sound". . . . (Original note: The actual practice is omitted here.) Furthermore, those who learn from "odor". . . . (Original note: The actual practice is omitted here.) Furthemore, those who learn from "flavor". . . . (Original note: The actual practice is omitted here.) Furthermore, those who learn from "tactile object". . . . (Original note: The actual practice is omitted here.) In the same way, the so-called "descent and expansion," "expansion and retention," and "retention and reversal in the right sequence" of the drops occur in linkage; given that there are many deeds but little bliss, this is called "first instant—wisdom of joy." Furthermore, the joining in equal portions of the two tastes consisting of *bola* and *kakkola* ignites the fire of passion and causes the drops to descend; meditate on the bliss, protect the moment in which the cavity opens, and withhold the secret pestle; this is called "second instant—wisdom of supreme joy." These two instants, which are characterized by the descent of the drops and the intensity of the bliss, are known as the "warmth of the blazing drops"; they are extremely difficult to retain. Furthermore, the non-conceptual bliss will arise if you slightly perform the thrusting and withdrawing motions. While the drops descend as previously mentioned, meditate on the bliss and non-conceptuality, withhold the secret pestle, and carefully relinquish the secrecy of the second withholding; this is called the "third instant—joy free from joy," which is also known as the "warmth of the moving drops of joy."

Reversal: When the drops are difficult to retain, preserve them by reversing the upper winds or by means of the "six actions" that arise from beneath and so forth. If they are easily preserved, then preserve them during the fourth instant. Before the third instant, the drops must not be reversed because the bliss is easily lost. . . . (Original note: The actual practice is omitted here). . . . then it will be difficult to retain the drops. Signs that allow you to verify that the drops have been growing: Your anus experiences numbness, heaviness, and astringency; your feces, urine, and so forth sometimes come forth and sometimes do not come forth as well as sometimes stop and sometimes do not stop. Omens that the drops will be retained: You feel that your hair is sparse and loose (original note: erect) and you keep having tears due to yawning. The generation in accordance with the truth from practicing with a female endowed with a proper lotus in her lower body: You must perform the three applications—the equanimity of the body and speech, the equanimity of empowerment, and the equanimity of the desired objects—on the support consisting of a thoroughly pure consort; the empowerment should be on her channels. Based on the union of the pestle and the lotus. . . . (Original note: The actual practice is omitted here). . . . a meditative concentration free from the retention of bliss arises. Sustain this meditative concentration and protect the moment in which the cavity opens and so forth. Those who protect it by means of the "six actions": (1) drying up the ocean around Mount Sumeru, which means pulling the abdomen inward towards the spine; (2) bringing the four continents under control, which means bending the fingers of the four limbs; (3) placing the tongue in its own place, which means placing the tongue against the palette; (4) raising the sublime sense organs upward, which means staring upward. The above four points are the actions of the body. . . .

Dispersion: With respect to the girdle that binds the winds, bind your waist with both hands as if you were fastening a girdle with the motion of a spinning wooden wheel rotating back and forth at the level of your waist. Furthermore, while sitting in the full lotus position with arms akimbo, swing your upper body back and forth in the four directions like a child playing around. This is "the fourth instant—the warmth of the stabilizing drops of the innate joy," which does not need to be protected with assiduity.

Preservation: This topic will be omitted here (readers may refer to the statements by Padmasambhava and Guru Gangkar cited earlier), as it will be explained during the discussion about how to preserve the drops from leaking. The condensed expedient path consists of three parts:

1. Preparation: Adapt the demeanor of preparation, with the sun in the right hand and the moon in the left hand. Cross both hands and cover the two knees. Train with nine long *hū* and short *hū* forward and purify the left and the right three times each; this training is performed three times. The quintessential instruction says:

Three exhalations and three inhalations,
The wheel and so forth are purified;

> On the third day and so forth,
> It will enter the cavity of the secret place
> in an undetected way.

The meaning of these verses is as follows: First, nourish the basic constituent well with the essence of food. Leave your house and go to an elevated area. Adopt a full-lotus position and hold your fists firmly, with a mandala of the sun wheel in the right palm and a mandala of the moon wheel in the left palm. Cross both hands and cover your knees with them; these are the body essentials. As for the mind essentials, direct all the pure portions of the lower body or the secret place upward in the reverse direction through the central channel, like steering water through empty tubes. With respect to the speech essentials, just like in the actual training with long *hū* and short *hū*, utter three times in the central channel, followed by three times on the right, three times in the middle, three times on the left, and three times in the middle. This adds up to nine times in the central channel and six times in the right and left channels—a total of fifteen times. Furthermore, steer the breath with the nostrils: Exhale three times and inhale three times—this adds up to a total of six times. Understand this training in accordance with the truth. Preserve the energy of the basic constituent (seeds—semen) for three days and so forth; this is the purification of the wheel. If a practitioner can perform this exercise for three days, then he will be able to direct the basic constituent into the cavity of the secret place in an undetected way and gain mastery over the lower winds. Those who are extremely skillful at subduing the winds can achieve this training by practicing in this fashion for half a day. Anyone who experiences headache, nausea, or stagnated heat at the heart during this exercise should slightly slow down the pace and nourish the (body's) basic constituent well. Those who cannot urinate or defecate or experience pain and so forth in doing so can get rid of these symptoms by doing a handstand. This is a key point.

2. The main practice: After performing the empowerment and so forth, slightly constrict the anus, intensely suck both middle fingers, and stare upward; this will retain the drops. Or speak while panting strongly and perform the other physical methods of redemption; this will also retain the drops. The meanings of these statements are as follows: The benefit is limited if, during the empowerment of the pestle, the lotus, and so forth, one just performs the equanimity of the body and speech and the equanimity of the desired object in the various stages of observing the forms and so forth of the pure female consort. Indeed, one must join *bola* and *kakkola* in equal portions; **with the shaking and rubbing as well as the slow entries and withdrawals, the fire of passion will cause the drops to descend, causing one to become blissful beyond oneself.** However, due to the preservation of the drops.... (Original note: The actual practice is omitted here. See the contents cited previously). . . . when one's body and mind abide in a relaxed, slow, and magnanimous state, the drops will be retained. Furthermore, speak while panting strongly and rely on other physical redemptions to halt the upper winds. Those who experience limited bliss while performing in this fashion should withdraw and thrust. Those who become blissful beyond themselves should retain [retain the drops]; this is called the descent of the drops followed by the retention and then the

expansion thereof.

3. Conclusion: Subsequently, the conclusion takes place when the drops do not undergo any transformation. In order to simultaneously "reverse" and "disperse" the drops, direct them to the navel, heart, throat, and crown—in this order—with the crying of an elephant, the howling of a tiger, the retching of a beast, and the sniffing of a fox; spread them throughout the body with the seal of liberation. The meanings of these statements are as follows: Sit in the full lotus position while performing this practice after the equal entry. Contemplate the fact that the drops are being drawn from the secret place up to the navel; focus the mind on the navel. The speech consisting of "the crying of an elephant" means that one directs the drops with the crying of an elephant consisting of the *he* sound and moves one's focus from the navel to the heart. The speech consisting of "the howling of a tiger" means that one directs the drops with the howling of a tiger consisting of *uhu* and moves one's focus from the heart to the throat. The speech consisting of "the retching of a beast" means that one directs the drops with the retching sound consisting of *haha* and moves the focus of one's consciousness from the throat to the crown. The speech consisting of "the sniffing of a fox" means that one directs the drops with the sniffing sound of a fox consisting of *hahe* and practices the liberation seal in accordance with the truth by shaking one's head and spreading the drop throughout the body.

The common practice of the extensive and condensed expedient paths: The four types of unskillfulness among the key points in the quintessential instruction about the loss of the drops:

1. If the practitioner is not skillful in the descent, then the drops will be quickly lost; 2. if he is not skillful in retention, then the bliss will be short-lived; 3. if he is not skillful in reversal, then the drops will fuse with water; and 4. if he is not skillful in the dispersion, then illness will ensue.

The four skills that should be used as the antidote to those types of unskillfulness: 1. The skill in descent is the turtle-like movement—the generation of the four joys in the correct sequence; 2. the skill in retention is the three actions of body and one action of speech; 3. The skill in reversal is the four actions of animal, namely the crying of an elephant and so forth; 4. the skill in dispersion is the liberation seal of the lion. Three actions of the body means. . . . (Original note: The actual practice is omitted here.) One action of the speech means speaking while panting strongly. Furthermore, the binding of the waist with the winds and so forth are the same as in the extensive path.[10]

It is not necessary to expound each of the secret meanings contained in the above passage from *Taking the Result as the Path: Core Teachings of the Sakya Lamdré Tradition,* as readers can comprehend them simply by pondering carefully over the views and knowledge obtained from the previous explanations found in this book. Furthermore, I do not need to explicate this topic, as readers can refer to the detailed illustrations thereof in Padmasambhava's *The Profound Guidance for Vajravārāhī [Haimu shenshen yindao]* as well as in the quintessential instruction of actual practice transmitted by Guru Gangkar to Yogi C. M. Chen. Only one of those teachings will be cited here; readers can use it to infer the meanings of the rest. Yogi C. M. Chen has stated the following with respect to the practice of retention" amidst form, sound, odor, flavor, and tactile object set forth in the above text:

Cultivate the non-duality of form and emptiness when you see

---

10   Virūpa, *Daoguo* 道果, 280-89. Translated into English from Chinese.

the good looks of a mother sky-traveler (when you engage in the yab-yum practice with her). Cultivate the non-duality of sound and emptiness when you hear the wondrous sounds of a mother sky-traveler (when you engage in the yab-yum practice with her). Cultivate the non-duality of odor and emptiness when you smell the scent of musk emitted by the lotus palace (by the sexual fluid in the lotus palace) of a mother sky-traveler. Cultivate the non-duality of flavor and emptiness when you suck the nectar (saliva and sexual fluid) of a lady sky-traveler through kissing. Cultivate the non-duality of tactile objects and emptiness when you embrace, kiss, rub, and press the entire body of a lady sky-traveler. Avoid the union when you experience the slightest loss in the samādhi of emptiness—indeed, bliss and emptiness must be non-dual.[11]

Readers can infer the whole picture of this practice from the above example.

Tantric male and female practitioners should, when they cultivate this method together, perform the following visualization in order to realize the clear light:

Concentrate one-pointedly on the non-duality and indivisibility of emptiness and bliss when you embrace a consort mother, and you will naturally attain the Path of Vision. It is good to practice emptiness and bliss every day with immutable one-pointedness. Practice at least fifteen minutes each time and gradually extend the duration of practice after becoming familiar with this method (according to Tsongkhapa, one should practice eight dual hours every day). It is also fine to enter samādhi one-pointedly if emptiness and bliss do not come by together—if the blissful mind comes by on its own. The combination of emptiness and bliss gives rise to the wisdom of the non-duality and indivisibility of emptiness and bliss. When

---

[11]   *Fojiao chanding* 佛教禪定 [*Buddhist Meditation*], vol. 1, narrated by C. M. Chen, recorded by Kangdi Paulo 康地保羅, and translated by Wuyouzi 無憂子, (Taipei: Puxianwangrulai yinjinghui 普賢王如來印經會, 1991), vol. 2, 678. Translated into English from Chinese.

bliss comes by, the second discrimination to be made is "all phenomena are empty"; practice the illusion in the empty space. A seed syllable will suddenly appear within this illusion; its arising is similar to the abrupt jumping of a fish from the ocean. This syllable will immediately transform into the deity on which one normally meditates; this is precisely the clear light.[12]

In contrast to the Path of Vision in Exoteric Buddhism, which consists of bringing forth the wisdom of prajñā through the realization of the eighth consciousness (tathāgatagarbha), the Path of Vision in Tantric Buddhism is attained through the perception-induced sensations of the mental consciousness amidst the sexual contact of the yab-yum practice. Thus, the states of this practice constitute the core contents of the aforementioned deed-contemplation. After completing such deed-contemplation, one should, through moving the winds, draw the drops upward and lower them into the sexual organ, so that they can be fused with the female consort; this is known as "the full-lotus vajra position." There exist four types of full-lotus vajra position:

1. The full-lotus vajra position through the channel: Use the finger to repeatedly explore the lower tip of the central channel located within the *baaga* 拔阿嘎 [vulva] of the action seal (consort); it protrudes like a wheat straw (this refers to the protrusion at the cervix, which is known as the conch channel). Enter the emptiness of your own vajra (original note: pestle), while your vajra penetrates into the *baaga* of the action seal (while your vajra pestle penetrates into the consort's vulva); perform by interconnecting the two.

2. The full-lotus vajra position through the winds: Winds exit from within your and the action seal's (the consort's) *dhūtī* (central channel), like a long and fragrant blue smoke. At

---

[12] *Naluo liufa* 那洛六法 [*The Six Yogas of Nāropa*], narrated by Blo-Bzan-Grags-Pa Zam Lam [Daoran baluobu cangsangbu 道然巴羅布倉桑布], recorded by Lu Yizhao 盧以炤 (Taipei: Chenxi Wenhua Gongsi 晨曦文化公司, 1994), 207. Translated into English from Chinese.

the juncture of the two channels (the two channels interconnect within the vulva), the two winds fuse and abide, dense and swirling.

3. The full-lotus vajra position through the drops: A wind exits from within the consort's (the action seal's) *dhūtī* (central channel), like a long and fragrant blue smoke; it then ascends and enters your *dhūtī*, before reaching the channel cakra at your crown. A wind from within your *dhūtī* (descends to the tip of the vajra pestle and) also exits like a long and fragrant blue smoke; it further enters the consort's *dhūtī* (from the connection point located at the lower extreme) and ascends to the channel cakra at the consort's crown. White drops with the size of mustard seeds descend from your crown, while red drops also the size of mustard seeds drip down from the consort's crown. The red and the white (drops) converge at the juncture of the two winds, which is located at the lower tips of the male and the female's *dhūtīs* (the *dhūtīs* of the father and the mother—the male and the female who practice together); the red and the white unite and thus abide.

4. The full-lotus vajra position through emptiness and bliss: The blissful nature of the true water drips from your mental consciousness and central channel. This nature, from which even a minute particle is unobtainable, transforms into the nature of the Dharma body; concentrate one-pointedly thereon.[13]

Those who cultivate this yab-yum practice should first understand how to find the channel:

Inspection of the channel in different locations:
The location of the secret conch channel differs in every female.
One may begin exploring from the center;

---

[13] Yogi C. M. Chen (Chen Chien-ming 陳健民), *Qugongzhai quanji* 曲肱齋全集 [*The Complete Works of Yogi Chen*], vol. 1-5, ed. Xu Qinying 徐芹庭 (Taipei: Puxianwang rulai fojiaohui 普賢王如來佛教會, 1991), vol. 3, 136-37. Translated into English from Chinese.

It is fitting to know the meaning of the cowgirl position,
So that the two channels [interconnect and the sexual organs]
emit fragrance during the intertwining.[14]

And:

A mother sky-traveler's wisdom channel of the great bliss is
known as the conch channel of wisdom. It is located in the lotus
palace at the lower extreme of her central channel. Its end is
thin and short, but one can, by taking various medicines,
extend it until it penetrates into the pestle. When the central
channels of the Buddha-father and the Buddha-mother unite,
the **winds shakta and shakti are exchanged through the
lotus, the pestle, and the drops, while the four emptinesses
and four joys fuse into one taste in the great samādhi of
non-duality, which fosters the attainment of Buddhahood.**
In this way, the yoga of the completion stage can be said to
integrate the Buddha's body with more perfection.[15]

The method to extend the conch channel is as follows:

First, make offerings to all the deities from the outside of
the lotus,
Then prostrate before the anus to worship Mother
Protector;
After pleasing all the consorts,
The marvelous conch channels will naturally extend.[16]

Tantric practitioners are able to achieve "the vajra path" by
cultivating this non-duality of emptiness and bliss based on sexual
pleasure; hence, it is said they should pursue the "Path of Vision"
by dedicating their entire lives to the practice of the "union of

---

14   Ibid., 307.
15   *Fojiao chanding* 佛教禪定 [*Buddhist Meditation*], vol. 1, narrated by C. M. Chen,
     recorded by Kangdi Paulo 康地保羅, and translated by Wuyouzi 無憂子, (Taipei:
     Puxianwangrulai yinjinghui 普賢王如來印經會, 1991), vol. 2, 678. Translated into
     English from Chinese.
16   Yogi C. M. Chen (Chen Chien-ming 陳健民), *Qugongzhai quanji* 曲肱齋全集 [*The
     Complete Works of Yogi Chen*], vol. 1-5, ed. Xu Qinying 徐芹庭 (Taipei: Puxianwang
     rulai fojiaohui 普賢王如來佛教會, 1991), vol. 3, 307. Translated into English from
     Chinese.

emptiness and bliss." They can even cause their "state of realization to be more profound and advanced" if they are able to withhold ejaculation for a long duration:

> Hence, the withholding of ejaculation generates immense power. The descent of the seminal drops from the crown carries a powerful effect. Therefore, when they arrive at the navel, the practitioner should cause the semen to promptly reverse upward by bringing forth a reluctant mind (a mind that is unwilling to take in the bliss of ejaculation); this is the method of upward reversal. It is exceptionally difficult for novice practitioners to reverse their semen upward, as they would normally ejaculate. Hence, they should, in all cases, stay away from women; otherwise, they will definitely ejaculate. After practicing for a long time, they will gain the power to reverse their semen upward and will be able to tame women. Indeed, by achieving the practice of the mind, they will be able to retract and release the semen at will. Once the semen has reversed upward, it should be dispersed towards the various channels; you must definitely be aware that if the semen is not dispersed upon its reversal, then you will immediately suffer from a serious illness. It is vital that you never tame a woman when the wind is about to melt into the central channel after transforming your consciousness; otherwise, your practice will be futile. If you do not tame any woman, then your wind will naturally melt into your central channel. At this moment, avoid bringing forth a desirous mind (a mind that is keen to ejaculate) and instead just visualize that the drops ascend gradually to the crown. Such a practice of visualization will cause the semen to reverse upward. Practice visualization only in your mind without actually getting close to women. After practicing in this fashion for a long time, your drops will naturally disperse upon reversing upward. You will then be qualified to approach women with such skills of retraction and dispersion.
>
> How is it possible to cause the drops to descend and move upward in the reverse direction without getting close to women? The method to disperse semen is as follows. Visualize yourself as a Buddha while sitting in the full-lotus vajra

position and make the Tarjani seal (original note: make a fist while stretching out the forefinger and the little finger) with both hands; cross your hands in front of your chest, with the left hand inside and the right hand outside. Stare upward and see a clear and distinct syllable *hum* [ༀ] on your crown; chant the syllable *hum* twenty-one times. During chanting, exert great force with the hands, feet, and entire body, so as to cause all vase winds to ascend and definitely enter the central channel from a location near the waist. Next, make each hand into a fist and swing both of them downward and sideways to the left and right three times. After this swinging, while keeping both hands in a fist, use them to push the legs downward with strength three times. After this pushing down of the legs, position both hands, which are still in a fist, on the legs and twist the upper body to the left and the right three times, as if you were making greetings with joined palms to the left and to the right. After this twisting of the body, the semen will be dispersed to all the channels of the body, and you will sweat profusely. If you practice in this fashion three or four times a day, then your body will become strong and completely free from all illnesses. As for the way to practice wisdom, bring forth the four joyful minds from the top to the bottom, then repeat this process by inverting the sequence. You will experience immense bliss if you do not ejaculate when the drops reach the gateway of the secret place. Amidst the bliss, bring forth the thought that "My death denotes impermanence; all phenomena are empty"; this is the wisdom of the non-duality of emptiness and bliss. **The great joy that one experiences while embracing a consort mother is precisely bliss; the thought "My death denotes impermanence; all phenomena are empty" is emptiness and luminosity; emptiness in bliss and bliss in emptiness constitute "the non-duality and indivisibility of emptiness and bliss** (original note: "The non-duality and indivisibility of emptiness and bliss" is also known as "the non-duality of bliss and luminosity"). Only those who achieve the non-duality and indivibility of emptiness and bliss can attain the Path of

Vision.[17]

It is important to note four key points with respect to the method uniquely found in Tantrism that aims to attain Buddhahood through the union of two truths—"emptiness and bliss" or "bliss and emptiness":

> 1. **The unreal**: During the descent, you should observe that the great bliss is unreal; 2. **the vastness**: During the retention, you should observe that the great bliss is empty like the sky; 3. **the oneness**: During the extraction, you should observe that emptiness and bliss are one and non-dual; and 4. **the spontaneous functioning**: After the dispersal, abide in the spontaneous functioning of the noumenon.[18]

With respect to "the unreal," a tantric practitioner performs the following deed-contemplation during the yab-yum practice after he causes his drops and winds to fuse with those of his female counterpart in their sexual organs, moves them upward to all five cakras in the female's central channel, gathers the drops and winds and moves them to all five cakras in his own central channel, and then lowers them to the tip of his pestle (for the female, the cervix or clitoris) to induce sexual pleasure (or one of the four joys, as tantric practitioners call it): Although one can rely on the practice of the winds to withhold ejaculation and elevate any sexual pleasure among the four joys that has descended to the tip of the pestle to the state of ultimate bliss, such a state of sexual pleasure is in fact unreal; it is an impermanent phenomenon destined to disintegrate and cease; owing to this deed-contemplation, one will no longer crave for sexual pleasure.

---

17 *Naluo liufa 那洛六法 [The Six Yogas of Nāropa]*, narrated by Blo-Bzan-Grags-Pa Zam Lam [Daoran baluobu cangsangbu 道然巴羅布倉桑布], recorded by Lu Yizhao 盧以炤 (Taipei: Chenxi Wenhua Gongsi 晨曦文化公司, 1994), 201-3. Translated into English from Chinese.

18 Yogi C. M. Chen (Chen Chien-ming 陳健民), *Qugongzhai quanji 曲肱齋全集 [The Complete Works of Yogi Chen]*, vol. 1-5, ed. Xu Qinying 徐芹庭 (Taipei: Puxianwang rulai fojiaohui 普賢王如來佛教會, 1991), vol. 3, 172. Translated into English from Chinese.

With respect to "the vastness," the tantric practitioner performs the following deed-contemplation in the state in which he properly and one-pointedly takes in the greatest sexual pleasure: Given that the mental state of his blissful sensation is as vast and boundless as empty space, the bliss therein is said to be endlessly vast; this is called retention.

With respect to "the oneness," when the tantric practitioner takes in the extreme bliss after lowering the drops to the tip of the pestle, he should contemplate that this bliss is the one and only greatest bliss in the world. Furthermore, he should contemplate that this bliss is brought forth by the mind of feeling and cognition that visualizes the drops, and therefore, this sexual pleasure and the emptiness-nature consisting of the mind of feeling and cognition are in fact non-dual. Given that this mind of feeling and cognition abides long-lastingly, one-pointedly, and without distracting thoughts in the state of great bliss, where this mind of feeling and cognition neither discriminates nor has any thoughts of duality, the emptiness-nature consisting of the mind of feeling and cognition and the great bliss are non-dual—hence the expression "non-duality of emptiness and bliss," which is a state of oneness.

The so-called "spontaneous functioning" refers to the following: After taking in the great bliss for a long period of time during the yab-yum method, the tantric practitioner disperses the wind that is gathered at the lower end of the central channel to his entire body. He temporarily dissociates himself from the bliss of sexual contact but maintains the innate joy, and causes his mind of feeling and cognition to dwell in the "noumenon" that he "has realized" through the yab-yum practice. He thus abides spontaneously and without moving in this state of thoughtlessness; this is known as spontaneous functioning.

However, the aforementioned deed-contemplation of "the unreal" conflicts with Tsongkhapa's teaching about "the permanent and immutable great bliss" set forth by Tsongkhapa, for something that is said to be unreal cannot be the "permanent and immutable great bliss."

536

Such deed-contemplation of the "unreal" does not enable practitioners to attain the fruition of liberation, but merely allows mundane people to realize the impermanence of the world and life in general. In order to realize the fruition of liberation, one must first eliminate one's self-view. Even if all the ancient and contemporary tantric gurus and their disciples could observe, in accordance with the truth and through a deed-contemplation performed amidst sexual pleasure, that this sexual pleasure is empty, illusory and impermanent, they would still remain roped by their self-view for the following reasons: They would not have eliminated the view that "the mental consciousness (mind of feeling and cognition) is permanent and imperishable"; the mental consciousness (mind of feeling and cognition) is said, in all Three Vehicles of the Buddha Dharma, to be a mutable phenomenon included among the five aggregates; the Mahāyāna doctrine defines it as a phenomenon with an other-dependent nature; and according to the four Āgamas, the conception that "the mental consciousness (mind of feeling and cognition) is permanent and imperishable" is an erroneous view of eternalist non-Buddhists, a "self-view" of ordinary sentient beings.

This "one and only" bliss is not truly unique, for this practice method—this great bliss consisting of sexual pleasure—is also found in some of the sects belonging to non-Buddhist traditions such as Hinduism and Brahmanism; moreover, such tantric great bliss was in fact incorporated into Buddhism after being drawn from those non-Buddhist traditions. In addition, this method of the great bliss consisting of sexual pleasure counts among the teachings set forth in various Chinese writings such as *The Classic of the Plain Girl [Sunujing 素女經]*, *Master Dongxuan [Dongxuanzi 洞玄子]*, *Secrets of the Jade Chamber [Yufangmijue 玉房秘訣]*, and so forth that have been propagated until this day. In brief, this great bliss transmitted in Tibetan Tantrism is not truly "unique," as it is also disseminated in non-Buddhist faiths such as Hinduism, Brahmanism, and so forth.

Furthermore, such sexual pleasure is precisely the

fundamental cause behind the cyclic existence of sentient beings within the desire-realm. In other words, if one does not abandon the cravings for this sexual pleasure, then one will never become free from the fetters of the desire-realm and will definitely continue to transmigrate, life after life, within this realm; how then could one escape from the cyclic existence within the three realms? Such bliss cannot be said to be "one and only" because the preservation thereof is always inevitably accompanied by various sufferings in the desire-realm—those who seek to take this bliss in and preserve it must constantly transmigrate within the human world of the desire-realm, which is forever associated with various sufferings such as impermanence and so forth. Furthermore, this bliss is not permanent because one is sometimes dissociated from it; it is an impermanent phenomenon—it always exists with impermanence and cannot be equated with oneness.

It is only through the Path to Liberation in the Buddha Dharma that one can eliminate the sufferings related to the cyclic existence in the three realms, but none of the "great tantric practitioners," ancient and modern alike, have been able to realize this path. This bliss, which transcends cyclic existence is described as "one and only" for being proper to Buddhism. Indeed, only the great Path to Buddhahood in the Buddha Dharma allows practitioners to bring forth the great mundane and supramundane wisdom; it does not just enable these practitioners to attain the Path to Liberation realized in Hīnayāna, but it also allows them to realize the knowledge-of-all-aspects that the arhats who do not convert to Mahāyāna are unable to attain. Although the Mahāyāna practitioners of the Path to Buddhahood have the capacity to transcend this world, they follow their vows and remain in this world to rescue sentient beings. Such wisdoms of liberation and of the Buddha Bodhi are "one and only," because they only exist in Mahāyāna and are not possessed by non-Buddhists, tantric gurus and disciples, or the arhats who do not convert to Mahāyāna. Hence, it is said that "only the self is unique and honorable" in the three realms—only "the self consisting of the eighth consciousness" is unique and honorable. This oneness does not refer to the uniqueness of the practice and realization of sexual pleasure set forth by tantric practitioners for the following reasons: All sentient beings of the desire-realm can experience the contact-induced realization of sexual pleasure; non-Buddhists also have the ability to take in this great bliss without ejaculating after lowering their drops to the tip of the pestle; and those non-Buddhists can also realize the mind of feeling and cognition amidst the "great bliss" consisting of sexual pleasure—it is not uniquely attained by Tibetan tantric practitioners and hence cannot be said to be "one and only."

With respect to the term "spontaneous functioning" in the Mahāyāna Buddha Dharma, the Bodhisattvas who have personally realized the eighth consciousness (tathāgatagarbha) can directly observe at all times and in all places that this tathāgatagarbha exists in all sentient beings and operates spontaneously in accordance with the conditions—that it functions spontaneously amidst all mundane conditions in reaction to all phenomena by operating its own mental concomitants. All ancient and contemporary truly enlightened persons in the Chan School have been able to realize the nature of the tathāgatagarbha whereby it spontaneously operates its own mental concomitants in accordance with the conditions. In every sentient being, the tathāgatagarbha also operates spontaneously in accordance with the conditions in reaction to this being's mind consisting of the seven consciousnesses without the slightest exertion or disorder, even in the states of deep sleep, unconsciousness, or thorough death.

The tathāgatagarbha remains unperturbed and always operates spontaneously according to the conditions amidst the turbulence of the six sense objects in this world; only can an operator who always functions in this fashion—spontaneously in accordance with the conditions—be regarded as a truly spontaneous operator. Conversely, the "wisdom of sexual misconduct" obtained by tantric gurus through their deed-contemplation amidst sexual pleasure can by no means be said to be a spontaneous operator because it definitely ceases along with the mental consciousness in the five states such as deep sleep and so forth. A phenomenon that arises and ceases can never be deemed as a spontaneous operator, for it does not exists at all times without interruption.

The mind of feeling and cognition that perceives the sensations of pain and happiness can absolutely not be said to be a spontaneous operator because it inevitably takes in the sensations of pain and pleasure induced by all phenomena consisting of the six sense objects. Only those who do not take such sensations in can function spontaneously in accordance with the conditions. Indeed, anyone who takes in such sensations will definitely exhibit detestation or craving towards the states consisting of such sensations, which means that he will definitely bring forth the intention of either continuing to take in such contact-induced sensations or getting away from them, which in turn means that he will definitely make a decision with respect to the six sense objects—this will cause a temporary cessation of his mind of feeling and cognition's nature of spontaneous functioning in accordance with the conditions; in that case, his mind of feeling and cognition will not be a spontaneous operator that functions at all times in accordance with the conditions.

Based on this correct reasoning, we can conclude that the union of bliss and emptiness experienced during the yab-yum practice between a male and a female, as propagated in Tibetan Tantric Buddhism, has nothing to do with the dharma that functions spontaneously in accordance with the conditions set forth in the Buddha Dharma, for the mind of feeling and cognition that operates during that union cannot function spontaneously amidst all phenomena. Hence, this method is absolutely not the true Buddha Dharma.

It is truly unnecessary for those Tibetan tantric gurus to brag that such a preposterous method of sexual misconduct is their exclusivity and disparage the doctrines preached by the various schools of Exoteric Buddhism as being non-ultimate for being bereft just of this practice. Why do I say so? Because this practice is in fact completely unrelated to the bodhi of the Three Vehicles—"the unreal," "the vastness," "the oneness," and "the spontaneous functioning" observed through deed-contemplation amidst sexual contact have nothing to do with the Buddha Dharma. Those tantric gurus have merely been using those Buddhist terms to actually propagate a method of Shaktism, which is a branch of Brahmanism.

Even after striving in this "practice" for three countless kalpas, one will still fail to connect with the true bodhi of the Three Vehicles, will still remain entangled in the views and false realizations of non-Buddhists, and will still misapprehend non-Buddhist doctrines as the practice and realization of the Buddha Dharma. Tantric practitioners should explore this issue rationally and in-depth to avoid falling into the cultivation of non-Buddhist doctrines and becoming great sinners who destroy the Buddha Dharma despite dedicating their bodies, minds, and financial resources to the assiduous practice of this Buddha Dharma.

The fallacy of the doctrines taught in Tantric Buddhism can be attributed to their erroneous basis: The visualizations, the deity yoga, the vase breathing technique, the bonding initiations, the vase initiation, the secret initiation, the fourth initiation, and finally the actual practice based on the quintessential instructions of the fourth initiation that those gurus have established have all been connected and integrated into one complete system by the theory of the yab-yum practice—each of those methods is in essence related to the yab-yum practice; for instance, the purpose of the practice and realization of the generation stage is purely to prepare for the actual cultivation of the yab-yum method.

In light of the fallacious basis of Tibetan Buddhism, it goes without saying that the various methods that follow are totally unrelated to the true Buddha Dharma. However, those tantric gurus have turned the non-Buddhist states of the yab-yum practice and the secret initiation method into valid knowledge in the Buddha Dharma by using the terminology related to the fruitions of practice and realization found in the Buddhist sūtras to describe those non-Buddhist states. As a result, it is very common to see tantric gurus proclaim their attainments of the First Ground, the Tenth Ground, or even the Buddha Ground and use such achievements to disparage the valid knowledge of the Exoteric Buddhists who practice in accordance with reality as being elementary.

The truth is, those tantric gurus have completely failed to understand the true meanings of the Buddha Dharma—they have misconstrued the Buddha Dharma of all Three Vehicles. Based on erroneous views that stem from their misapprehension, they have belittled the Exoteric School as being a Dharma-gate of "the practice on the casual ground," while hailing their own school as being a Dharma-gate of "the practice on the Fruition Ground." The skills displayed by those gurus in their secret tantras and speeches to defend, with strained and unreasonable arguments, misconceptions that distort the truth are simply unsurpassed in this Sahā world. All tantric practitioners should explore this practice rationally, truly understand the fallacy of the tantric doctrines, and return to the right path as soon as possible.

Although I propagated the Kālacakra Tantra when I acted as the Dharma-king of the Jonang School in a past lifetime, it was in fact a disguise to conceal my actual teachings of the tathāgatagarbha through the view of other-emptiness. After observing the circumstances, **I had no choice but to proceed in this fashion.** Based on the doctrine of the eighth consciousness (tathāgatagarbha) known as "Madhyamaka of the view of other-emptiness," I secretly refuted the yab-yum method transmitted in all the major tantric lineages and refused to actually cultivate this method myself. However, with the passage of time, those tantric Buddhists gradually found out about our deeds and objectives. The Gelug School could no longer tolerate our existence and eventually used its political power to exterminate our doctrines through the hands of the Sakya School and the Dabu School.

Now that times have changed and the tantric theocracy in Tibet has declined in power, its people should no longer blindly believe in the tantric doctrines nor approve of this old theocratic institution. Instead, they should follow the trend of the modern society and adjust their view on the Tibet "government" in exile and on the Dalai Lama based on the concept set forth by the Buddha about the separation of the state and religion. They should, based on the essence of the tantric doctrines, decide whether they should continue to learn the Buddha Dharma by adhering to Tibetan Tantric Buddhism, whether they should continue to worship the Dalai Lama, who propagates those esoteric doctrines, whether they should continue to believe and accept the teachings of the "Buddha Dharma" imparted by the Dalai Lama, whether they should relinquish the non-Buddhist doctrines set forth in the tantras of Tibetan Tantric Buddhism and re-embrace the teachings of the Three-Vehicle sūtras found in Exoteric Buddhism. As a matter of fact, the contemporary gurus of the Jonang School should no longer preach the practice of Kālacakra Tantra, for they do not need this disguise anymore. Instead, they should directly and exclusively disseminate the doctrine of the tathāgatagarbha known as "the Madhyamaka of the view of other-emptiness."

However, the Jonang School's doctrine of the tathāgatagarbha—the Madhyamaka of the view of other-emptiness—has been falsified and distorted by the Fifth Dalai Lama of the Gelug School and his successors for many generations based on the views issued from this school's misunderstandings. It is now very difficult to find the correct doctrine of the tathāgatagarbha— the Madhyamaka of the view of other-emptiness—that was propagated by the Jonang School.[19]

The Kālacakra practice is briefly as follows:

Although we have learned and familiarized ourselves with the following contents, listening to them one more time is

---

[19]   This is no longer the case with the publication in 2006 of *Mountain Doctrine,* which is authored by Döl-bo-ba Shay-rap-gyel-tsen and translated by Jeffry Hopkins, as well as the publication in 2018 of its Mandarin rendition *Shan Fa* (山法 *Mountain Doctrine*) in Taiwan.

beneficial for one's cultivation of the Dharma, for it will allow them to remain deeply engraved in the continuum of our minds.

1. and 2.: "Individual aggregation" (the branch of individual withdrawal—pratyāhara) consists of visualizing that a deity with empty form who embraces a Buddha-mother appears at the forehead opening of the central channel, while "individual stabilization" (the branch of tranquil reflection—dhyāna) consists of enhancing stability. Among the six branches, these two can cause different active winds to become suitable for the practice.

3. The third stage is as follows: Vitality blocks the left and the right channels, causing the winds to abide in the central channel; therefore, the "yoga of the branch of vitality" (the branch of mid-level goodness—praṇayāma) primarily consists of bringing together the low wind and vitality. This practice corresponds to the methods of vajra chanting (*om ah hum* 嗡啊吽) and of vase winds, both of which have already been mentioned.

4. The fourth stage is "the branch of retention (dharāṇā)." Practice this branch once you are able to steer the winds into the central channel and cause this wind to somewhat abide therein. The branch of retention consists of stabilizing the winds at the center of the central channel—causing the winds to dwell there with great stability.

5. The fifth one is "the branch of recollection (anusmṛti)." The practitioner performs sexual intercourse with a female consort endowed with one of the three types of property. The formal designation (for female consort) is "(action) seal"; she is a real person who is invoked through her karmic connections with the practitioner in a past lifetime. The wisdom seal is an image visualized by the practitioner—he performs sexual intercourse with this female consort in his visualization. The grand seal refers to Kālacakra's consort Natsog Yum [那错由姆]; her body is an empty form. Practitioners with inferior capacity engage in sexual intercourse with a real female consort; those with mid-level capacity have sex with a wisdom seal; and the ones with superior capacity perform sexual union with the grand

seal Natsog Yum (this assertion contradicts those made by Padmasambhava and Tsongkhapa, who believe that the supreme scenario is to have sexual intercourse with a real female consort). When a practitioner who cultivates the branch of recollection engages in sexual union with one of the three types of female consort mentioned above, the white bodhi at his crown cakra will melt and drip to the tip of his glans penis, where it needs to be withheld; the practitioner will thus experience the **immutable great bliss**. If you wish to practice with an action seal instead of a wisdom seal, you must meet the following criteria: (i) you must have received training on the ordinary path; (ii) you must have received a perfect initiation; (iii) you must observe and protect the vows and precepts; and (iv) the male and the female must have the same level of spiritual realization—one person's level of realization cannot exceed that of the other person; for example, if the male practitioner has achieved the liberation of the mind in the completion stage, then for this practice to be proper, his female consort must have attained the same level. When both parties have the same level of realization, **the male practitioner can enhance the female's realization through this yab-yum practice, and vice versa, thus allowing both parties to swiftly become Buddhas.** It is imperative that you understand the objective of this Dharma-gate of co-practice—this sexual intercourse between a male and a female—which is a profound Dharma-gate passed down from Vajradhara. Milarepa has highlighted the key points as follows: "During the union, you should cultivate visualization through the channels, winds, and drops. The practitioner should practice with the action seal (a woman or male consort of the human world) at a suitable occasion, but only after fully meeting all the various criteria. One who cultivates unduly without being qualified will fall to hell." Allegedly, the retribution for such an improper co-practice is to remain entrapped in hell for all eternity. I have already spoken extensively about this branch of recollection. As a matter of fact, I could spend many days analyzing this topic in detail given the wide scope of its contents. One approach to this practice is to gaze at Kālacakra's Buddha-mother Natsog Yum: This method enables the practitioner to experience the innate great bliss and to ignite his inner fire. After this inner fire has melted the white bodhi at the crown cakra, the white bodhi will flow through the various cakras, allowing the practitioner to experience the four joys at those cakras: joy, supreme joy, transcendent joy, and innate joy. The above is a delineation of the first five branches. The practitioner who achieves the proper valid knowledge in the first five branches can attain the branch of samādhi—the last of the six yoga branches of Kālacakra.

6. The unique perfection of all phenomena and the mind's emptiness-nature: This corresponds to the realization of the emptiness-nature, the sixth branch of Kālacakra—the branch of samādhi. There is another way to understand the branch of samādhi: The perfection of the emptiness-nature of all phenomena is manifested through the deity body of the Buddha-mother Natsog Yum—the Buddha-mother's nature is wisdom—whereas the unsurpassed immutable great bliss is manifested through the deity body of Kālacakra. Therefore, the perfection of the wisdom of emptiness embodied by the Buddha-mother and the **mind of the unsurpassed immutable great bliss** represented by Kālacakra are also known as the branch of samādhi of Kālacakra. You must be mindful of the following: The copulation between a deity and a Buddha-mother is nothing like mundane sexual intercourse, as it symbolizes the union of wisdom and expediency—Kālacakra embodies expediency, whereas the Buddha-mother Natsog Yum represents wisdom. The immutable great bliss arises from the sexual intercourse between the practitioner and one of the three types of female consort and subsequently intensifies infinitely. The above is a brief introduction to the six-

branch yoga of Kālacakra and here ends my explanation.[20]

However, such a practice remains in essence a non-Buddhist Shaktist method. It is opposed by many sects within Brahmanism, as they believe that those who engage in it will never connect with liberation—instead, they will be bound by lust. In contrast to some of the non-Buddhists within Brahmanism, tantric gurus are not aware that this method will definitely cause its practitioners to fall into the cyclic existence within the desire-realm—as a matter of fact, they will inevitably fall to the demonic path and eventually, after a long period of time, to hell owing to the sin of sexual misconduct or even of adultery. Those who denigrate the authentic Buddhist doctrine and the truly enlightened worthies and sages to protect the erroneous teachings of Tantrism will definitely and instantaneously fall to hell after death to suffer unintermittent anguish for long kalpas with hardly any opportunity to escape. Consequently, all tantric practitioners should face up to this problem to avoid entering the wrong path by adhering to the tantric misconceptions and becoming the demon's family dependents for countless lifetimes to come with hardly any chance of escape.

According to **Tsongkhapa,** one should further visualize the subtle characteristics after realizing the non-duality of bliss and emptiness during the yab-yum practice:

> Next, practice the method of maṇḍala within the subtle characteristics. *Four Hundred and Fifty Verses [Sibai wushi lun 四百五十論]* says:
>
>> Also practice your subtle characteristics,
>> Abide at the apex of the consort's nose (visualize that your mind dwells at the clitoris of the female consort's sexual organ),

---

[20] Gawang, Jida (嘎旺 · 吉達) and *Shilun benxu zhu* 時輪本續註 *[Commentary on the Kālacakra Tantra]*, translated into Chinese by Cui Zhongzhen 崔忠鎮 (Taiwan: Shilun yijing yuan 時輪譯經院, 1989, first edition), 220-222. Translated into English from Chinese.

And realize the cakra of nengren [能仁輪].

In other words, visualize that the emblem of the lord deity at the apex of the consort's nose has the size of a wheat grain and practice the method of maṇḍala within this emblem. According to Shrī Phalavajra (祥米金剛), this refers to the apex of the secret place (the tip of the sexual organ, i.e., glans penis or clitoris) belonging to either the father or the mother. According to Commentator Yaozu Jingang (藥足金剛), practice maṇḍala within the emblem located in the vajra maṇi vase. Practice at the upper apex of the nose if you are drowsy; this is my teaching. If you become drowsy while practicing within the emblem located in the consort's lotus (sexual organ), then practice by visualizing that the central prong of your five-pronged vajra takes the shape of a hook, which is hooked to the apex of the consort's nose. Hence, there is no fixed location of practice. Commentator Yaozu states that the seed of your mind emits light to invoke the Buddhas. Subsequently, it melts into bodhicitta and descends to the secret place (sexual organ) and becomes an emblem; practice therein. *Clusters of Quintessential Instructions [Jiaoshousui lun 教授穗論]* also teaches these meanings as well as the aforementioned descent of the subtle drops, which are found at the navel, to the secret place (sexual organ); practice maṇḍala therein. The yoga location of these two subtle characteristics refers to the apex of the nose (glans penis or clitoris) belonging to either the vajra (the male's sexual organ) or the lotus (the female's sexual organ)—either one is acceptable. Although *Commentary of the Illuminating Torch [Mingju lun 明炬論]* clearly affirms that one should practice in the subtle drops and within the consort's lotus (the female's sexual organ), both secret places (the sexual organs of the male and the female) are in fact the same.[21]

Such is the visualization of the subtle characteristics set forth by

---

[21] Tsongkhapa, *Mizong daocidi guang lun 密宗道次第廣論*, 482. Translated into English from Chinese.

Tsongkhapa, the Most Honorable One of the Gelug School.

Next, one must visualize each of the five great vajras into a Buddha's body, based on the visualization of the five Dhyani Buddhas coupled with the practice of Highest Yoga Tantra:

> The most important element in the esoteric doctrines is the five Dhyani Buddhas. In order to attain Buddhahood in this body through the cultivation of the five Dhyani Buddhas, one should first transform them into the five great vajras. Therefore, the method of Chakrasamvara that I have mentioned should be coupled with these five great vajras and practiced at each of the five cakras.[22]

In reality, the Path to Buddhahood has nothing to do with the five Dhyani Buddhas. The endeavors to achieve the ultimate Path to Buddhahood through the visualization of the five Dhyani Buddhas are unrelated to the true Buddha Dharma; such a method is in fact an establishment of ancient and contemporary tantric gurus based on their thinking. Why do I say so? Because the World-Honored One has never taught this method; in addition, such visualization does not allow practitioners to connect in the slightest with the knowledge-of-general-aspect, the knowledge-of-specific-aspects, and the knowledge-of-all-aspects within prajñā. In fact, the Path to Buddhahood hinges upon the wisdom of prajñā and is definitely not achieved through the visualization of the five Dhyani Buddhas or the transformation of the visualized five Dhyani Buddhas into the five vajras. The five vajras are merely an internal perceived portion manifested by one's own mind, and the visualization thereof is unrelated to the practice, realization, or experience of the intrinsic entity of the practitioner's own mind.

Furthermore, the allocation of the five great vajras to the five cakras also stems from those tantric practitioners' erroneous

---

[22]　Yogi C. M. Chen (Chen Chien-ming 陳健民), *Qugongzhai quanji* 曲肱齋全集 *[The Complete Works of Yogi Chen]*, vol. 1-5, ed. Xu Qinying 徐芹庭 (Taipei: Puxianwang rulai fojiaohui 普賢王如來佛教會, 1991), vol. 1, 246. Translated into English from Chinese.

thinking, as it is in fact impossible to generate the five great vajras by performing visualization on the five cakras. In fact, the five Dhyani Buddhas that a practitioner has visualized are only his internal perceived portion—one will not actually obtain five Dhyani Biddhas upon achieving the visualization thereof. As those five Dhyani Buddhas merely emanate from one's imagination and do not truly exist, it goes without saying that the five great vajras visualized from the five Dhyani Buddhas that one has visualized are also a fantasy of one's mind of feeling and cognition. Therefore, the endeavors to visualize the five Dhyani Buddhas as the five vajras and to thus achieve the practice of the five vajras are based on delusional thinking and are completely meaningless to the practice and realization of the Buddha Dharma.

Even if the five Dhyani Buddhas or five great vajras that one has visualized were truly an external perceived portion that can be seen by all, they still would have nothing to do with the attainment of Buddhahood. Indeed, the achievement of Buddhahood hinges upon the wisdom of prajñā rather than upon "visualized images." The wisdom of prajñā refers to the wisdom of ultimate reality that is brought forth after one has realized the eighth consciousness—the fundamental dharma, the dharma-realm of all phenomena—and experienced its properties. As a matter of fact, the method of visualization taught in Tantric Buddhism neither enables one to become a Buddha nor allows one to realize the most elementary wisdom of prajñā at the level of the Path of Vision. Tantric practitioners should be wise enough to distinguish between right and wrong and be aware of where they are heading.

Contrary to the lay Buddhist Chen Lü'an's declaration that the yab-yum method, which is cultivated between a male and a female, does not exist within Tantric Buddhism and that Tantric Buddhists have never spoken about the attainment of Buddhahood in this body, the Kālacakra teachings actually assert that this practice leads to the attainment of the ultimate Buddhahood, as evidenced by the following passage:

What follows is an outline of the contents that I have taught in the class over the past few weeks: First, I. A. & B., The Basis; next, II. A. & B., The Discussion about the Vows and Precepts; III. The Correct Path of Practice. A. The Generation Stage, and B. The Completion Stage. Now I will explain the attainment of true enlightenment through the Dharma-gate of Kālacakra in the chapter "Manifesting the Virtue of Fruition." The first step is the training on the ordinary path: The practitioner must nurture his mind of deliverance, bodhicitta, and the correct view of Madhyamaka before receiving the initiation. Next, he must cultivate the generation stage: First, the coarse (original note: yoga) stage, followed by the subtle (original note: yoga) stage. Once he has achieved proper valid knowledge in the generation stage, he must proceed to the completion stage, whose contents are the six-branch yoga. In the completion stage, he must concentrate on the six cakras—namely, the reproductive cakra, the navel cakra, and so forth. Meanwhile, he must gradually build up the white bodhi; at the same time, he must cause the red bodhi to descend through these cakras in the right sequence. During this entire process, the expulsion (original note: leakage) of the bodhicitta is forbidden. Consequently, the active winds and the substances that make up one's body will gradually disappear; eventually, the red and the white bodhicittas will also vanish. As a result of this method, the practitioner will attain the body of empty form, which has the colors of a rainbow. The Vajra Buddha has been extremely kind to unveil this profound tantric practice to sentient beings. It is indeed similar to alchemical agents that can transform stones, copper, and other cheap metals into precious gold. Through this method, a practitioner can transform a coarse physical form body tormented by illnesses and pain by melting its various material components (original note: elements), this method also enables him to convert his "primordial mind" and "primordial body" into a deity or a Buddha-mother (original note: into the essence of a deity or of a Buddha-mother). In this physical form body, the active winds can bring forth mental twistings such as anger, attachment, and so forth.

These active winds will be melted and extinguished during the process of conversion. It is very important to understand the meanings of "primordial mind" and "primordial body." The primordial mind (original note: or stream of consciousness] is the most subtle type of mind, which has always been with us. The primordial body is the most subtle vitality; it accompanies the primordial mind and has also been always with us. These are the items that will be transformed into a deity—a deity's body is exclusively composed of the mind (original note: mind or consciousness) and wind. To help you understand, try to conceive a person who has always lived in Seattle; you may say that he is just like an aborigine or a native of Seattle. Separately, another person comes to Seattle as a visitor; you may call him an adventitious resident of Seattle. Similarly, each of us has a mental consciousness and vitality that have always been with us; they are primordial. Most of the elements in our body—for instance, the senses, most of the factors that constitute the mental consciousness, the coarse physical body, and so forth—are merely temporary aggregations in the short process of life. As mentioned before, during the process of death, these elements will peel off and the various senses will go into hiding; the most subtle primordial mind and wind will manifest after the dark period of the death process. In other words, **the most subtle mind and wind**—and not the other aggregates—**are the ones that will proceed from this life onto the next one.** Upon reaching the pinnacle of the tantric path, you will realize the empty form body pertaining to the deity or Buddha-mother and will immediately and directly witness that **the essence of all phenomena is the mental consciousness of the immutable great bliss. You—the practitioner—will thus achieve the perfect true enlightenment** and realize "the perfection of the seven branches," more formally known as "the kiss of the seven branches," which refers to the sexual intercourse between a deity and a Buddha-mother. In addition, the practitioner will also attain the Buddha's fourfold body: emanation body, reward body, dharma body of wisdom, and dharma body of nature. Having become a Buddha, he will have endless power to benefit sentient beings—he will be able to rescue them by instantly generating countless emanation bodies that pervade this world.[23]

Such statements about the attainment of Buddhahood in this body and in this life—specifically, the attainment of the ultimate Buddhahood—are not just made found in the Kālacakra Tantra, but in all the Tibetan tantric traditions; this is a fact that cannot be denied by the lay Buddhist Chen Lü'an. Padmasambhava taught the yab-yum practice in the same fashion; readers may refer to the citations in Section 1 of this chapter. Not only did Padmasambhava teach the yab-yum method, but he repeatedly cultivated it himself in this manner, as evidenced by his biography. We will not reiterate the details here.

Below is the proper way of practice **set forth by Padmasambhava**:

At that moment, you should think that all sacred and ordinary causes of phenomena are generated from the perfection of the drops; hence, you should cultivate the quintessential instruction related to the enhancement of the drops. In a quiet thatched shed into which people cannot peek, invoke the male consorts and mother sky-travelers after making her wash and adorn her body, apply perfumed oil on herself, and carry a sachet. Next, extend your feet to the legs of the consort mother endowed with the proper characteristics; the two of you should embrace and kiss each other; caress her lips and tongue with your hands and rub her breasts. Another option is to observe the other person's lotus or pestle (another option is to admire the other person's sexual organ), place the pestle on her hand (place the penis on the consort's hand), and make every effort to demonstrate the bliss-generating expedients

---

[23] Gawang, Jida (嘎旺・吉達) and *Shilun benxu zhu* 時輪本續註 *[Commentary on the Kālacakra Tantra]*, translated into Chinese by Cui Zhongzhen 崔忠鎮 (Taiwan: Shilun yijing yuan 時輪譯經院, 1989, first edition), 226. Translated into English from Chinese.

(make the consort understand the various methods that can induce blissful contact at the male's sexual organ). If you experience desire while performing the action (if you bring forth the mind that craves for orgasm while performing the deed of sexual intercourse), then you should thoroughly comprehend that its nature consists of a wondrous use pertaining to a dharma of the dharma body (you should thoroughly understand that the nature of the mind that craves for ejaculation—orgasm—consists of a wondrous use pertaining to a dharma of the dharma body). You will thus get to know the nature—the intrinsic aspect—on the greed (you will thus get to know the nature of the mind on the greed) and will abide in the intrinsic aspect (and will firmly regard the mind of feeling and cognition that is taking in the bliss as the intrinsic aspect, the nature of the intrinsic entity); all ordinary desire will then automatically be eradicated (you will thus be able to destroy all ordinary desire). This is expedient that manifests the great bliss through desire (this is a Dharma-gate of expediency that manifests the great bliss through desire) and **should therefore be cultivated assiduously.** Furthermore, the one who has been empowered by himself and others should generate a supreme mind directed towards enlightenment for the first time. He should visualize that all phenomena are empty and that a bed—a lotus sun disc—appears in the empty space. On the disc appears Hayagrīva Vajra with one face and two arms, as mentioned in the generation stage. Next, from your secret place (from your sexual organ) appears a syllable *hum* [呼], which transforms into a five-pronged pestle. A blue syllable *hum* with its head pointing inwards appears in one of the gaps between the prongs; on the pointed tip of the pestle lies a red and yellow syllable *phat* [呸] pointing outwards. The Buddha-mother instantly transforms into Vajravārāhī; she has one face and two arms, is endowed with all the beauties, and is extremely blissful and delighted. With her protruding breasts, which are squeaking and plump (original note: This refers to the protrusion of her nipples), she is blissful beyond herself. Observe the void of conditions at the secret place and see the lotus with four petals; in this lotus arises a flower embryo adorned with the syllable [what follows is a Sanskrit word that is omitted here]. In all the channel cakras belonging to your Buddha-father and Buddha-mother, visualize all consort fathers and consort mothers simultaneously engaged in the same esoteric practice (visualize all Buddha-fathers and Buddha-mothers engaged in the same type of esoteric practice, which consists of sexual intercourse). Afterward, hit down with the pestle (break in with the penis and perform sexual intercourse fiercely) from atop the syllable (what follows is a Sanskrit word that is omitted here) at the embryo of the lotus. Settle down slightly (slow down slightly and settle down when the utmost bliss arises); while you abide in the intrinsic fundamental meditative concentration free from proliferations (while you abide in the state of thoughtlessness during the orgasm of sexual pleasure), continue to shake your body like a sheep, ensure that your entire body shivers (enhance the sexual pleasure), and visualize the drops pour down in torrents (you should, during the ejaculation, visualize that the semen pours down majestically in torrents). Just like a farmer digging a ditch with a hoe to steer the water, you should keep it (the semen) from flowing out, spread it to the entire body, and cause it to descend upon each of the cakras (furthermore, you should use your penis, just like a farmer digging a ditch with a hoe to steer the water, to keep the sexual fluid from flowing out and visualize that you extract the pure portion—the wind portion—of this sexual fluid, draw it upward, and spread it to the entire body, before causing it to descend into the five cakras of the central channel), just like in the esoteric practice. You should swing your body while it descends to each cakra; it is essential that the action does not cause the drops to leak (it is essential that the various movements of sexual intercourse do not cause the semen to leak). Subsequently, when the drops descend to the secret place, visualize that they are being offered to the Buddha-father and mother sky-traveler at the secret place; perform as in the previous practice. (Subsequently, while you visualize that the drops descend into the sexual organ, you should also visualize that you offer this blissful sensation to the Buddha-father and Buddha-mother within this sexual organ; the method of offering is the same as the one performed while taking in the bliss during your practice with the female consort). At this moment, the holding skill is similar to the skill to plug water outlets in a pool. The holders with superior faculty abide in the entity of Tathāgata consisting of the limit that is free from the net of all conceptual proliferations (abide in the entity of the mind of feeling and cognition in the state of thoughtlessness induced by the orgasm of sexual pleasure). The holders with mid-level faculty focus on the winds: They must hold the ascending winds; the lower winds are similar to a *jebi* chicken vase that does not leak any wind; holding the lower winds in this fashion will naturally cause them to hover. Moreover, the central winds (original note: the winds that are neither masculine nor feminine) can be held firmly, for the holding thereof causes the navel to slightly expand outward. Furthermore, with respect to the skillful holders of the visualization method, there are also those with superior, mid-level, or inferior faculty. The holders with superior faculty observe the intrinsically pure view of "the limit that is free from the net of all conceptual proliferations." Those with mid-level faculty visualize a syllable *ham* [罕] at the top like a stake used to fasten horses. Those with inferior faculty visualize that the guru—consort father—and consort mother appear on their crown, internally and externally clear and transparent like crystal light. Novice practitioners of the action (the action seals that have just begun to learn the yab-yum method) who discharge immediately (who ejaculate right after they engage in sexual intercourse) should press their perineum with three fingers aligned like a staircase and withhold it (and prevent the semen from being released). Those who are adept at drawing upward in the reversed direction have skills that are similar to those to extract water from a well. They visualize that the heart of a syllable *hum* in their pestle, which is akin to a hook, is used to hook the pure portion of the red syllable (what follows is a Sanskrit word that is omitted here) in the lotus palace of the mother action seal; they chant a long *hum* sound, absorb it into the pestle (original note: they draw it upward with all their might), and offer it to all the deities at the secret place (they offer the sexual fluid that has been drawn upward to the deity fathers and mothers within the sexual organ). Next, they absorb it into the navel, heart, throat, and crown through the continuum of the central channel path. Having offered it to all the deities, they cause it to exit from the Brahmā aperture and offer it to Guru Vajradhara, Master Padmasambhava, and all the Buddha-fathers and Buddha-mothers on the crown. At this moment, the body essentials are as follows: You should withdraw all four continents (the four continents refer to the four limbs) into Mount Sumeru (original note: like a snake coiled around Sumeru), stare upward, place your tongue against the palate, and press your chin against your Adam's apple. Shake your entire body, chant a long *hum* sound, and draw it upward by exhaling fully without interruption. While drawing it upward, perform the three essentials—body essentials, wind essentials, and visualization essentials—simultaneously at each cakra; keep drawing upward. In case there is difficulty in drawing upward, then perform the three essentials simultaneously at each cakra three times. Next, you should perform the sitting posture of a fox's son after you dissociate yourself from the mother seal (after your body is dissociated from that of the consort). Draw upward and disperse (disperse to every part of the body). The body essentials of this method are as follows: Sit with the legs comfortably positioned. . . .[24]

Padmasambhava has further expounded the quintessential instruction related to the yab-yum practice as follows:

The game of sexual union contains eight basic methods; each basic method encompasses eight subordinate methods, forming a total of sixty-four postures. The eight basic methods are as follows: 1. getting close for fondling, 2. kissing, 3. drawing with fingers 4. playful biting 5. lotus-fondling 6. uttering sounds, 7. rubbing of the body, and 8. cowgirl position.

---

[24] Yogi C. M. Chen (Chen Chien-ming 陳健民), *Qugongzhai quanji* 曲肱齋全集 [*The Complete Works of Yogi Chen*], vol. 1-5, ed. Xu Qinying 徐芹庭 (Taipei: Puxianwang rulai fojiaohui 普賢王如來佛教會, 1991), vol. 3, 545-47. Translated into English from Chinese.

1. "Getting close for fondling" includes eight subordinate methods: i. stealing the jade: first, peeking at the female's face, followed by bringing forth a joyous mind; the male and the female's bodies coincidentally brush each other when the two walk together; ii. pretending to reject the other person: massaging her breasts; iii. erotic attraction: uttering mellow words while the male and the female's shoulders brush each other; iv. sexual arousal: getting close for fondling and biting each other's lips and tongue; v. intertwined rattan: circling the female's neck tightly with the hand and kissing her madly by making noise; vi. cherry-picking: standing up in order to step on the female's insteps, holding her waist, grabbing her neck, and sucking her lips; vii. entry: kissing and holding each other's waist while sleeping together; viii. blending of water and milk: entry of the pestle into the lotus palace.

2. "Kissing" consists of kissing each other in eight different locations: mouth, throat, breasts, underarms, waist, nose, cheekbones, and lotus.

3. "Drawing with the finger" includes eight subordinate methods aimed at stimulating sexual desire and straightening the female's pores: i. silk of the lotus root: drawing lightly on the lips, breasts, and so forth, so as to only cause a fine line to appear; ii. half-moon: pressing slightly more deeply into the breasts, throat, and so forth with the finger, so as to cause a curved line to appear; iii. maṇḍala: pressing the female's body with all five fingers when she swings her body shyly and restlessly due to itchiness; iv. lingering love: drawing with the hand on the navel and tailbone area; v. light gauze: drawing inclined lines on the aforementioned areas; vi. karma [jiemo 羯摩]: drawing a cross-shaped pestle on her bust point and below her chin; vii. plum flower: making an imprint at the breasts and so forth with the five fingernails; viii. small lotus: drawing the shape of a lotus petal at the breasts and so forth.

4. "Playful biting": i. spring color: extreme blushing due to cravings; ii. touching the lips: making light teeth marks on

her lips; iii. coral: kissing her cheeks with one's lips closed; iv. dimples: manifesting teeth garlands on the cheeks; v. drops: biting each other with one or two teeth, as if both persons sported long, sharp, and protruding teeth; vi. pearl garland: making continuous teeth marks at her waist, throat, eyebrows, and face; vii. dazzling cloud: making teeth marks randomly on her breasts, back, and so forth, like a cloud in the empty space without a fixed location; viii. lotus pearls: drawing with fingernails on her underarms and then making teeth marks there. In summary, in order to cause the female to experience the greed and joy of a sparrow and a hinny, make imprints, if possible, with your teeth and nails simultaneously on her ticklish areas—for instance, under her ears, on her neck, on her underarms, on her breasts, in her secret lotus, and around her waist and her back.

5. "Lotus-fondling" includes eight subordinate methods: i. wave-spitting: pressing the abdomen against the pestle and flicking from an inclined angle the petals on the surface of the lotus; ii. frivolousness: holding the root of the pestle with the hand and inserting the other half of the pestle into the lotus; iii. deep entry: plunging the male's pestle like inserting a phurpa [*puba* 蒲巴, Vajrakila dagger] and abiding down there while the female lies supine with her legs extended; iv. partial acceptance: slightly making the thrusting and withdrawing motions whenever it pleases the female and then remaining motionless after entering deeply; v. crying and laughing: making sudden withdrawals and insertions; vi. getting drunk: making several shallow insertions followed by one deep insertion, and vice versa; vii. tacit understanding: moving up and down in sync; viii. fulfillment of the vow: making one gradual insertion followed by one deep and sudden insertion of half of the pestle.

6. "Uttering sounds" (The female consort's moaning) includes eight subordinate methods: making sounds similar to weeping, sighing, panting, moaning, *awada* [阿哇打], *wala ada*

[哇拉阿打], little liberation, and *awa juewa* [阿哇爵哇]; these are respectively similar to the sounds of pigeon, cuckoo, *halida* [哈里打], heron, bee, goose, spring bird, and *bawajia* [巴哇嫁]. All of these sounds should be uttered from the abdomen (should be uttered directly from the abdomen and should not be faked with the mouth).

7. "Rubbing of the body" includes eight subordinate methods: It is identical to the aforementioned "kissing"; in particular, use the hand to massage the female's fists, palms, elbows, waist, face, and so forth, as mentioned previously. If the female utters any of the eight sounds, then it reflects her greed, which means that she will definitely experience great bliss; if her tone is cold, then she will definitely experience bliss if you massage her for a long period of time.

8. Cowgirl position: This applies to the case where the male has a body that is too large and heavy for the female to bear; therefore, taming should be done in a reversed position. The female should perform the following, just like a man: i. running: performing swift thrusting and withdrawing motions; ii. pressing: dwelling for a long period of time and then exiting slowly; iii. spinning: performing wheel-like spinning motions with the abdomen [this applies to the female] while the legs of both persons are entangled; iv. filtering: moving slightly from beneath [this applies to the male] while his legs and heels are entangled; v. flatness: taking a rest [this applies to the male]; vi. shuttle: remaining immobile [this applies to the male] while the female performs slowly; vii. intoxication: fully extending the arms and legs [this applies to the male]; viii. playing hard to get: performing at the top in the sitting position with her back turned to the male [this applies to the female].

Perform the above sixty-four postures at will (according to your preferences) in order to connect with emptiness and bliss . . . .

Below is an extract of the sixteen postures found in *A Guide to the Great Bliss* [*Dale yindaomen* 大樂引導門]: You should know the expediency of every posture, given the differences among the various lineages of channels in the lotus. There are primarily four lineages, which encompass a total of sixteen postures:

1. Vajra lineage: The father embraces the mother's neck while the mother embraces the father's waist; the pestle shuttles upward and downward; the channel appears on the left side of the lotus.

2. Lotus lineage: The female lies supine with her neck positioned on a high pillow; her feet are placed on her shoulder; the father performs intercourse by holding her tightly from beneath; the channel appears either at the top or at the bottom of the lotus.

3. Beast lineage: The female's legs are placed on the elbows of the father's folded arms; the father performs intercourse by holding her from below her waist; the channel emerges from the left and right sides of the lotus.

4. Elephant lineage: The mother extends her legs to the father's breasts; the male holds the mother by circling her with one leg and extends his other leg straight; he embraces the mother's lower body with his hand; the channel appears at the center of the lotus. In the particular case where a secret fist seal is performed with the pestle on the female, bounce the pestle lightly on the surface of the lotus (vulva) and then insert it into the lotus; you will find the channel everywhere. With respect to the performance of the action once the channel is found, the best channel is both long and fine. A short and coarse channel denotes that it has not yet been opened; in this case, one can open it (one can unlock the entrance of the consort's conch channel) by applying the following items on the pestle (by having sex after applying the following items on the penis): a red flower (original note: the Tibetan name signifies

"bird apprehension"), the root of a plant (a plant name in Tibetan, whose meaning is unclear), red honey, ice block of milk, the pestle of a white dog (the penis of a white dog), angelica, a plant (another plant name in Tibetan, whose meaning is unclear), *guanzhong* [管仲], Chinese red pepper, *zhujing* [硃京], and goat milk.[25]

Guru Padmasambhava has given another quintessential instruction:

The four sitting postures of celestial beings induce the thoughtlessness of bliss and luminosity; the four sitting postures of demi-gods generate luminosity; the four sitting postures of humans engender bliss; and the four sitting postures of beasts bring forth thoughtlessness.

1. The four sitting postures of celestial beings: i. Beautiful posture: The female lies supine with her legs placed behind her head; she embraces her own upper legs with her arms while the father kneels on her. ii. Non-action: The female lies supine and embraces her legs with her arms from the inner side of her knees while her legs are raised vertically with the heels on top; the father performs the action while embracing the mother's head. iii. Abiding in the supine position: Same posture as ii., except that the female's toes are on top instead of her heels; the father performs the action while embracing her waist. iv. All views: The female lies supine with her upper body in a slightly lower position; the father performs the action while his hands are placed on the left and the right sides of her ears; he places a pillow under her neck; the female extends her arms from the inner side of her knees and embraces the male's waist; the male opens up his knees and kneels down to perform the action. While implementing the above four methods, it is

---

[25] Yogi C. M. Chen (Chen Chien-ming 陳健民), *Qugongzhai quanji 曲肱齋全集 [The Complete Works of Yogi Chen]*, vol. 1-5, ed. Xu Qinying 徐芹庭 (Taipei: Puxianwang rulai fojiaohui 普賢王如來佛教會, 1991), vol. 3, 596-600. Translated into English from Chinese.

necessary to exert force with the four limbs and support the female's hips with a pillow. While the female's upper winds spiral and press downward, the father performs the action slowly on top of her.

2. The four sitting postures of demi-gods: i. The mother lies supine, raises her legs vertically, and embraces her legs with her arms; the father lies prone and extends his legs. ii. The mother can lie in a supine or lateral posture; she places her left leg on the father's right shoulder, embraces the father's waist with her right leg, supports her right leg with her left arm, and embraces the father with her right arm; the male raises his upper body and performs the action; he can also perform the action while he extends his legs and embraces the mother's neck with his arms, causing her lotus to protrude. iii. The father opens up his knees and kneels; the mother sits on his lap, embraces his legs, and performs the action by opening up her knees. iv. The ritual mother either kneels or lies on the side that stretches from her left foot to her right underarm; the father embraces her hips with his arms, while the mother embraces the father's hips with her arms from outside her thighs towards the inner side; the father performs the action with his legs extended. During the implementation of the above four methods, the mother lifts and contracts her lower opening and the father rotates his pestle to the left before plunging it into the lotus.

3. The four sitting postures of humans: i. The Buddha-mother lies supine and places her folded legs on the father's shoulder; the father opens up his knees and kneels, allowing the mother to sit in his embrace; the father embraces the mother's neck with his arms, while the mother embraces the inner side of the father's knees; she can lie in either a supine or prone position. ii. The female lies supine with her legs around the father's waist; the father sits in a full-lotus position and embraces the female's underarms; the female holds the male's ankle bones; she can lie in a supine or prone position. iii. The female lies on her side with her

left hip into the floor; she folds her legs and opens up her knees; the male and the female embrace each other on either the right or the left side. iv. The female lies supine, raises her legs and bends her feet downward, with the center of her soles at the father's waist, while the father embraces the mother's waist with his arms; furthermore, the mother opens up her knees and kneels, while the father embraces her hips with his arms; she can lie in a lateral or supine position. During the implementation of the above four methods, the Buddha-mother lifts her left side while the father performs the action by lifting his right side.

4. The four sitting postures of animals: i. The posture of the garuda:[26] The female stands on her feet, slouches, and pushes her hips backward; she supports her thighs from the inner side with her arms and opens up her plump place; the father kneels behind her, embraces her shoulder with his arms, leans his body forward, and extends his neck upward. ii. The posture of the lion: The female lies on her right side with her hips facing outward; the father performs the action from her back and embraces her under her waist; the female crosses her arms to raise her upper body and extends her legs; the upper bodies of the male and female are laterally dissociated from each other. iii. The posture of the elephant: The female bends her waist downward while her four limbs press into the floor; the male performs the action by embracing her hips from her back. iv. The posture of the turtle: The mother lies prone, while the father opens up his knees and kneels; the female positions her hips between the male's legs, while the father embraces the female's thighs with his arms (original note: When the female lies prone, she should retract her legs like a turtle, bend her thighs, and support her hips with a pillow; the male can then embrace her thighs). While implementing the above four methods, the female should

---

[26] Garuda: a mythical "golden-winged bird," often depicted as an eagle-like one with a human-like head and torso; S. *garuḍa*; T. *khyung/mkha' lding*; C. *jinchiniao* 金翅鳥.

expel her lower winds while the father should lean forward before starting to exert strength.

5. The four sitting postures of beasts: i. The proud and upright posture: The male sits in the lotus position and embraces the female's waist; the female places her legs behind the male's waist and embraces the male's neck with her arms. ii. The blazing deed: The male lies supine while the female rides on top of him; the father embraces the bones of her hips with his arms and performs the action in an upward motion; the mother slightly lowers her head, presses her hands into the floor, and rotates her lower body left and right. iii. The fierce loquat: The female lies supine on her hips, lowers her neck, opens up and bends her knees, and embraces her legs with her arms from the outer side; the father extends his legs and makes a vajra passing-through with his hands, pressing on the female's neck. iv. Dragon-like sporting: The upper bodies of the father and mother are dissociated and outward-facing; they embrace each other's hips with their arms and sport at leaning their bodies forward and backward as in a salutation (original note: This exercise should be performed in the lotus sitting posture and not the supine position). During the implementation of the above four methods, the male pushes upward while the female spins her body. Although myriad sitting postures are involved, the key is visualization.[27]

Tantric gurus have thus used Buddhist terminology to designate the postures that allow them to enjoy sexual pleasure in the yab-yum practice and have claimed that this method leads to the attainment of the ultimate Buddhahood in this body and this life. As a result, they have inflated their school tenets by proclaiming that they constitute "a Dharma-gate of the Fruition Ground." Given their possession of such a yab-yum method, which

---

[27] Yogi C. M. Chen (Chen Chien-ming 陳健民), *Qugongzhai quanji 曲肱齋全集 [The Complete Works of Yogi Chen]*, vol. 1-5, ed. Xu Qinying 徐芹庭 (Taipei: Puxianwang rulai fojiaohui 普賢王如來佛教會, 1991), vol. 3, 600-602. Translated into English from Chinese.

enables tantric practitioners to achieve the "ultimate Buddhahood" in one lifetime, they have denigrated the practitioners of the various Exoteric Buddhist traditions and have deemed the practices of those traditions as a "Dharma-gate of the Causal Ground." Whenever Exoteric Buddhist Bodhisattvas or patriarchs become enlightened and achieve the valid knowledge in prajñā pertaining to the Seventh Abiding, of the three stages of worthiness, or even of the First Ground and so forth, those gurus will deliberately imply that those valid knowledge are "elementary," for they pertain to "the practice of the Causal Ground"; furthermore, they will teach their disciples that the Dharma-gate of Tibetan Buddhism, in contrast, involves "practices and realizations of the Fruition Ground" because they enable them to attain the ultimate Buddhahood in this body.

As a matter of fact, while those tantric gurus have not even attained the wisdom of prajñā pertaining to the stage of the Seventh Abiding, which is realized by the Exoteric Buddhists who have just become enlightened, they have designated the various stages of the states of sexual pleasure cognized during the yab-yum practice with Buddhist terminology related to prajñā and various fruitions and have deceived Buddhist disciples by claiming that they have realized the wisdom of the First Ground, the Eighth Ground, or even the Buddha Ground. Clearly, such a tantric faith is by no means Buddhism—the views, assertions, practices, and realizations found therein do not correspond in any way to the practices and realizations set forth in the Buddhist sūtras and Dharma; instead, they consist of practices and realizations related to various states cultivated in non-Buddhist Shaktism in which one craves for sexual pleasure.

In Exoteric Buddhism, all enlightened persons cultivate the path with honesty—they would never dare to proclaim that they have become enlightened or achieved some attainments if they have not truly done so. They fulfill their tasks with candor and only speak about the doctrines about which they are entitled to speak and about the attainments that they have truly achieved. They would never dare to fool others with the valid knowledge that they have not achieved or by replacing the Buddha Dharma with non-Buddhist doctrines. By contrast, ancient and contemporary tantric gurus have replaced the Buddha Dharma with their valid knowledge in non-Buddhist doctrines and have used them to disparage the valid knowledge in the Buddha Dharma attained by truly enlightened Exoteric Buddhists by branding them as elementary; they have thus relied on false speeches to elevate themselves above the truly enlightened Bodhisattvas of Exoteric Buddhism in order to dupe both exoteric and esoteric learners. Not content with uttering those assertions, they have widely disseminated their tantric publications, misleading current and future generations of learners around the world into perpetrating with them the sins of grievous false speech and of destroying the true Buddhist doctrine—sins that will cause one to undergo excruciating sheer anguish in hell for numerous kalpas to come. The price that those followers must pay to enjoy fame, offerings, and respect for one lifetime is to endure abominable sheer agony throughout long kalpas for countless lifetimes to come—to die would be better than undergo such atrocious sufferings that no one can bear coming into contact with and taking in even once. How utterly unwise! Those who are still learning Tantric Buddhism **must absolutely be particularly mindful of this fact**.

Furthermore, female tantric practitioners who are requested by their gurus to cultivate this yab-yum practice with them so as to benefit the "spiritual cultivation" of those gurus or who aspire to receive the fourth initiation from their gurus should first ask their gurus to prove that they have completed the practice of the generation stage (the visualization of the drops in the central channel, the vase breathing technique, and the skill to move upward, move downward, expulse and retract the semen). If a tantric lama or guru—either male or female—refuses to certify that he or she has achieved the practice of the generation stage, then the disciple should by no means accept the role of male or female consort as requested by this guru, which consists of providing his or her form body for the guru to cultivate the method of the union of bliss and emptiness. The same goes for the disciple who aspires to receive the fourth initiation from the guru if he or she does not want to be fooled. If the guru cannot prove on the spot that he has completed the generation stage (which means, for example, that he is able to retract the released fluid into his lower body and so forth), then the disciple should definitely reject the guru's request to cultivate the yab-yum practice with him, for he is not yet qualified to seek another person's form body for practice and his request to his disciple to co-practice the yab-yum method simply results from his cravings for his disciple's beautiful appearance. These words are addressed to those who still exhibit adamant faith in the tantric doctrines, for these are issues that they will definitely encounter given the nature of those tenets.

To those who have not yet embarked on the learning of Tibetan Buddhism, we must honestly tell them that they should not cultivate the yab-yum method even with a person who has completed the practice of the generation stage for the following reasons: Such a Dharma-gate of "practice" has absolutely nothing to do with the practice and realization of the Buddha Dharma; the "prajñā" or "wisdom" that those tantric followers have realized is by no means the wisdom of prajñā found in the Buddha Dharma; and the fruitions that they have attained consist in fact of various states counterfeited by those gurus—they are purely non-Buddhist doctrines and have therefore completely nothing to do with the fruitions that are cultivated and realized in Buddhism. Those who practice according to this tantric method will end up propagating non-Buddhist tenets during their lifetime—they will be wrecking the true Buddhist doctrine by replacing the Buddha Dharma with these non-Buddhist tenets—after death, such persons will have to bear the retribution related to the grievous sin of destroying the true Buddhist doctrine. The wise should not behave in this fashion and commit an act that only the unwise would enjoy perpetrating.

The contents attained amidst the four joys during the yab-yum practice are as follows:

"Stone, Pan, donkey, smallness, and leisure, these five terms constitute the gate of the sex demon." One who is fully endowed with the characteristics of these five words is most likely a demon. This is mundane love! As for supramundane love, there must be four joys because the way of copulation is different. Both entering and exiting involve happiness. In this practice, the joy and the supreme joy are different, as are the supreme joy and the discriminative joy, as well as the discriminative joy and the innate joy. The joy is similar to the joy of common beings—ordinary people only have this joy. The supreme joy connects with emptiness; in this state, one experiences a feeling of vastness and smoothness; he is no longer just a body performing sex, but he actually feels the following: "How vast and smooth!" That is precisely the supreme joy. The discriminative joy arises after the supreme joy when one generates the "wisdom of specific knowledge." At that moment, one brings forth "various theories." Only this thing can help a person unleash his wisdom! The author of the renowned *Broad Comments on the Historical Facts in Zuozhuan* [*Donglai boyi* 東萊博議] completed this work during his honeymoon. This was the period when he attained the discriminative joy, which enabled him to write such a text. The innate joy is even less likely to be realized by ordinary people. What is the innate joy? It has existed since beginningless time throughout past lifetimes. How can we prove that it comes from past lifetimes? I recall that when I was a baby, my mother , who was very busy, sometimes left me in the care of my aunt. (At that time,) I was only one-month old, but did the movement on my aunt's body as if I was "fucking." My aunt said: "This kid has barely been born for a month but already knows how to do it." Why is that? This is something innate. Therefore, innate joy is even harder to attain than the previous joys. One achieves the highest authenticity upon realizing the innate joy—this is when one attains innocence! One will exude innocence. Why does a boy's dick have an erection during sleep? That is the innate joy! He has neither masturbated nor been seduced or turned on. That is the innate joy! Therefore, such is the extent to which one should revert when it comes to reverting to the state of a child. The child only manifests this state while asleep, whereas that (the fourth joy of the yab-yum practice) does not just emerge during sleep. That is truly the joy of a child, which is the innate joy. Such explanations of the four joys cannot be found in any publication and no one else has had such an experience. This is all from my own experience and has all been realized by myself. This is not an ordinary situation. "How could one do nothing during leisure time?" The joy is associated with the initial emptiness; the supreme joy is associated with the vast emptiness; the discriminative joy is associated with the great emptiness; and the innate joy is associated with the thorough emptiness. After attaining the thorough emptiness, one can further realize the Dharma body Buddha.[28]

If these tantric methods had any truth to them, then all persons would realize the joy and the associated initial emptiness on their wedding night. Based on the tantric doctrines and fruitions of practice and realization, one will become an exalted one of the First Ground just by taking in sexual pleasure after getting married, comprehending that this sexual pleasure and one's mind of feeling and cognition are in fact a non-dual entity, and maintaining the co-existence of this knowledge and the blissful sensation. Since over 70% of the pedestrians outside are married, all we would need to do is print out the above knowledge and disseminate it for free, so that all those married persons could attain the joy. If so, then we could assert that sages of the First Ground are all over the place. How exhilarating! That would denote a flourishing era of Buddhism. In that case, the tantric gurus would no longer need to step out to propagate the Dharma; they would just need to inform the public about the aforementioned principle by widely circulating publications about it. Those who are mindful of it and who

---

[28] Yogi C. M. Chen (Chen Chien-ming 陳健民), *Qugongzhai quanji* 曲肱齋全集 *[The Complete Works of Yogi Chen]*, vol. 1-5, ed. Xu Qinying 徐芹庭 (Taipei: Puxianwang rulai fojiaohui 普賢王如來佛教會, 1991), vol. 1, 342. Translated into English from Chinese.

experience it carefully on their wedding night would all become sages of the First Ground the next day. It would then be unnecessary for any monastic monks to sustain the true Dharma within Buddhism. The ability of Tantric Buddhists to invent such a grand method deserves our "utmost appreciation and admiration"!

The tantric writing *The Profound Inner Reality [Zhamo nangdun—shenshen neiyi 扎莫囊敦—甚深內義]*[29] says:

> Once the winds, channels, and drops are purified, the non-dual wisdom of bliss and the mind devoid of greed and so forth will arise, like the moon in the water, during the time interval between the departure of the supreme joy and the arrival of the joy of absence. One will become free from the views of reality and non-reality, experience the unleaked, immutable supreme bliss, and **attain the First Ground** by instantly eliminating a thousand or eight hundred karmic winds. This meaning and analysis conform to the three treatises of Bodhisattvas.[30]

Is this method, which enables one to attain the First Ground without relinquishing mundane happiness—the sexual pleasure of the desire-realm—as well as the cravings thereof not the most wondrous "Buddha Dharma" in this world? Given that this method enables one to achieve the fruition of the First Ground while enjoying the pleasures of this world, it is, therefore, no surprise that most of the senior practitioners as well as all the Dharma-kings and so forth within Tibetan Tantric Buddhism indulge in the

---

29   T. *zab mo nang don*. The title of this major work authored by Rangjung Dorje, the third Karmapa of the Nyingma School, is translated as *The Profound Inner Reality* or *The Profound Inner Principles*. Please see Karl Brunnhölzl, *Luminous Heart: The Third Karmapa on Consciousness, Wisdom, and Buddha Nature* (Ithaca, NY: Snowlion Publications, 2009) and Callahan, Elizabeth, *The Profound Inner Principles* (Boston: Snow Lion, 2014). The passages of *zab mo nang don* cited in this book are all taken from Yogi C. M. Chen's *Qugongzhai quanji* 曲肱齋全集.

30   Yogi C. M. Chen (Chen Chien-ming 陳健民), *Qugongzhai quanji* 曲肱齋全集 *[The Complete Works of Yogi Chen]*, vol. 1-5, ed. Xu Qinying 徐芹庭 (Taipei: Puxianwang rulai fojiaohui 普賢王如來佛教會, 1991), vol. 3, 330-31. Translated into English from Chinese.

cultivation of this method and delightfully comply with the Tsongkhapa's instruction to "cultivate the yab-yum practice assiduously for eight dual hours every day" as well as the exhortation by Padmasambhava, Virupa, Rangjung Dorje, and so forth to "perform the yab-yum method for infinite lifetimes to come." As this method leads to the swift attainment of Buddhahood through the enjoyment of sexual pleasure days and nights, it is not surprising that many Westerners and Tibetan tantric followers flock to this practice with great enthusiasm.

However, the wise will, upon hearing about this method, immediately wonder about the following: How could such a practice, which binds one to the desire-realm, enable one to achieve the fruition of the First Ground when it does not even emancipate one from the fetters of the desire-realm? How could it help one obtain the fruition of liberation? How could it lead to the various fruitions starting from the First Ground through to Buddhahood when its contents have completely nothing to do with the wisdom of prajñā set forth in the Buddhist sūtras? It is, therefore, no surprise that none of the great tantric practitioners have, up to this day, dared to come to me for a private doctrinal debate, not to mention having the courage to engage in a public one with me. I have made the above statements with the intention of urging tantric practitioners to revert quickly to the true Buddhist Dharma instead of indulging further in this fallacious method. It is also my goal to warn those who are about to embark on this practice against going astray: Not only will they lose both their dignity and wealth, but they will also incur the much bigger loss of going to hell by perpetrating the sins of breaking the precepts and wrecking the Dharma. Hence, they should absolutely not take this matter lightly.

BIBLIOGRAPHY

BUDDHIST SCRIPTURES & TANTRIC TEXTS

CBETA (Chinese Buddhist Electronic Text Association). http://www.cbeta.org.

Da piluzhena chengfo shenbian jiachi jing. 大毘盧遮那成佛 神變加持經 *[The Vairocanābhisaṃbodhi Sūtra].* T18, no. 848.

Jixiang jimi daxuwang 吉祥集密大續王 *[Guhyasamāja Tantra].* Translated into Chinese by Baofachen Rinchenquzha 寶法 稱・仁欽曲札. Hong Kong: Fojiao cihui fuwu zhongxin 佛教慈慧服 務中心, 1997.

Jingangding yiqie rulai zhenshi shedacheng xianzheng dajiaowang jing. 金剛頂一切如來真實攝大乘現證大教王經 *[The Adamantine Pinnacle Sūtra: The Compendium of the Truth of All the Tathāgatas and the Realization of the Great Vehicle, Being the Scripture of the Great King of Teachings].* T 18, no. 865.

Lengyan jing 楞嚴經 *[The Śūraṃgama Sūtra].* T19, no. 945.

Two Esoteric Sutras: The Adamantine Pinnacle Sutra [and] *The Susiddhikara Sutra.* Translated from Chinese (Taishō Volume 18, Numbers 865, 893) by Rolf W. Giebel. Berkeley, CA: Numata Center for Buddhist Translation and Research, 2001.

The Śūraṅgama Sūtra: A New Translation, with Excerpts from the Commentary by Venerable Master Hsüan Hua. Burlingame, CA: Buddhist Text Translation Society, 2009.

The Vairocanābhisaṃbodhi Sūtra (Taishō ed., Vol. 18, No. 848). Translated from Chinese by Rolf W. Giebel. Berkeley, CA: Numata Center for Buddhist Translation and Research, 2005.

PRIMARY SOURCES

Chen, Chien-ming (Yogi C. M. Chen 陳健民). *Fojiao chan ding* 佛教禪定 *[Buddhist Meditation].* Volume 1 & 2. Narrated by Yogi C. M. Chen. Recorded by Kangdi Paulo 康地保羅. Translated by

Wuyouzi 無憂子. Taipei: Puxianwang rulai yinjinghui 普賢王如來印經會, 1991.

Chen, Chien-ming (Yogi C. M. Chen 陳健民). *Qugongzhai quanji 曲肱齋全集 [The Complete Works of Yogi Chen].* Volume 1-5. Edited by Xu Qinying 徐芹庭. Taipei: Puxianwang rulai yinjinghui 普賢王如來印經會, 1991.

Gewei Luojue 楊堅葛威洛 and Gunqian Dianbei Nima 袞謙滇貝尼瑪. *Shengqi cidi shilunji 生起次第釋論集 [A Collection of Articles on the Generation Stage]*, translated into Chinese by Fahu 法護, first edition. Taipei: Nantian shuju 南天書局, 1998.

Naluo liufa 那洛六法 [The Six Yogas of Nāropa]. Narrated by Blo-Bzan-Grags-Pa Zam Lam (Daoran baluobu cangsangbu 道然巴羅布倉桑布), recorded by Lu Yizhao 盧以炤. Taipei: Chenxi Wenhua Gongsi 晨曦文化公司, 1994.

Taking the Result as the Path: Core Teachings of the Sakya Path with the Result Tradition. Translated and edited by Cyrus Stearns. Boston: Wisdom Publications, 2006.

The Hundred Thousand Songs of Milarepa. Translated and annotated by Garma C. C. Chang. Boston: Shambhala Publications, 1962.

Tsong-ka-pa. *Tantra in Tibet: The Great Exposition of Secret Mantra. Vol. 1.* Translated & edited by Jeffrey Hopkins. Introduced by H.H. Tenzin Gyatso, the Fourteenth Dalai Lama. London: George Allen & Unwin, 1975.

Tsong-ka-pa. *The Yoga of Tibet: The Great Exposition of Secret Mantra, Vol. 2 and 3.* Translated and edited by Jeffrey Hopkins. Introduced by H.H. Tenzin Gyatso, the Fourteenth Dalai Lama. London: George Allen & Unwin, 1975.

Tsong-ka-pa. *Mizong daocidi guanglun 密宗道次第廣論 [The Great Exposition of Secret Mantra].* Translated into Chinese by Fazun 法尊法師. Taipei: Miaojixiang chubanshe 妙吉祥出版社, 1986.

Tsong-ka-pa. *A Lamp to Illuminate the Five Stages: Teachings on Guhyasamāja Tantra.* Translated by Gavin Kilty. Boston: Wisdom Publications, 2013.

Tsong-ka-pa (as Tsong Khapa Losang Drakpa). *Great Treatise on the Stages of Mantra (Sngags rim chen mo): (Critical Elucidation of the Key Instructions in All the Secret Stages of the Path of the Victorious Universal Lord, Great Vajradhara). Creation Stage. Chapters XI-XII. The Creation Stage.* Introduced and translated by Thomas Freeman Yarnall. Edited by Robert A. F. Thurman. New York: The American Institute of Buddhist Studies, Columbia University Center for Buddhist Studies, Tibet House US, 2013.

Virūpa (Biwaba 畢瓦巴). *Daoguo: Jingangju jizhu* 道果—金剛句偈註 *[Path with the Result: Commentary on the Vajra Lines].* Explicated by Sakya Paṇḍita 薩迦班智達. Translated into Chinese by Fahu 法護. Jilong: Dazang wenhua chubanshe 大藏文化出版社, 1992.

OTHER WORKS

Brunnhölzl, Karl. *In Praise of Dharmadhātu: Nāgārjuna and the Third Karmapa, Rangjung Dorje.* Ithaca, NY: Snow Lion Publications, 2007.

Brunnhölzl, Karl. *Luminous Heart: The Third Karmapa on Consciousness, Wisdom, and Buddha Nature.* Ithaca, NY: Snowlion Publications, 2009

Brunnhölzl, Karl. *When the Clouds Part: The Uttaratantra and Its Meditative Tradition as a Bridge between Sūtra and Tantra.* Boston & London: Snow Lion Publications, 2014.

Buswell Jr., Robert E., and Donald S. Lopez Jr. *The Princeton Dictionary of Buddhism.* Princeton, NJ: Princeton University Press, 2014.

Callahan, Elizabeth. *The Profound Inner Principles.* Boston: Snow Lion, 2014.

Chen, Chunlong 陳淳隆 (Miaozhan 妙湛) and Ding Guangwen 丁光文. *Kongxing jian xinjiaodu de chanshi* 空性見新角度的闡釋《上下集》 *[An Explanation of the New Perspective of the View of Emptiness, vols. 1 & 2]*, retrieved from http://city080.mydreamer.com.tw/

Cozort, Daniel. *Highest Yoga Tantra*. Boston: Snow Lion Publications, 1986.

Cook, Francis. *Three Texts on Consciousness Only*. Berkeley, CA: Numata Center for Buddhist Translation and Research, 1999.

Gyalva Wensapa Lobzang Dondrup. "Handprints of the Profound Path of the Six Yogas of Naropa: A Source of Every Realization" in *The Practice of the Six Yogas of Naropa*. Translated, edited, and introduced by Glenn H. Mullin. Ithaca, NY: Snow Lion Publications, 2006.

Laird, Thomas 湯瑪斯·賴爾德. *Xizang de gushi: yu dalailama tan xizanglishi* 西藏的故事: 與達賴喇嘛談西藏歷史 [*The Story of Tibet: Conversations with the Dalai Lama*]. Translated into Chinese by Zhuang An-qi 莊安祺. Taipei: 聯經出版社 Linking Publishing, 2008.

Maitreya. *Middle Beyond Extremes: Maitreya's Madhyāntavibhāga with Commentaries by Khenpo Shenga and Ju Mipham*. Translated by Dharmachakra Translation Committee. Ithaca, NY: Snow Lion, 2006.

Maerba 馬爾巴. *Mizong qigong* 密宗氣功 [*The Practice of Internal Energy in Tantric Buddhism*]. Translated by Yu Wanzhi 余萬治 and Wanguo 萬果. Taipei: Baitong tushu 百通圖書, 1998.

Padmasambhava. *The Tibetan Book of the Dead: The Great Liberation by Hearing in the Intermediate States*. Revealed by Terton Karma Lingpa. Translated by Gyurme Dorje. Edited by Graham Coleman and Thupten Jinpa. Introduced and commented by H.H. the Dalai Lama. New York: Penguin Books, 2005.

Tsongkhapa. *Tantric Ethics*. Translated by Gareth Sparham. Somerville, MA: Wisdom Publications, 2005.

Xiao, Pingshi 蕭平實. *Ganlu fayu* 甘露法雨 [*The Ambrosial Dharma Rain*]. Taipei: True Wisdom Publishing Center, 2001.

Xiao, Pingshi 蕭平實. *Zongmen daoyan—gongan nianti (vol. 3)* 宗門道眼—公案拈提 (第三輯) [*Commentaries on the Chan Gong'an Collection: The Essence of the Path to Buddhist Enlightenment, Part 3 of 7*]. Taipei: True Wisdom Publishing Center, 1999.

Xiao, Pingshi 蕭平實. *Zongmen zhengdao—gongan nianti (vol. 5)* 宗門正道―公案拈提（第五輯）*[Commentaries on the Chan Gong'an Collection: The Essence of the Path to Buddhist Enlightenment, Part 5 of 7]*. Taipei: True Wisdom Publishing Center, 2001.

Xiao, Pingshi 蕭平實. *Wo yu wuwo* 我與無我 *[Self and Non-Self]*. Taipei: True Wisdom Publishing Center, 2001.

Xiao, Pingshi 蕭平實. *Xiejian yu fofa* 邪見與佛法 *[False Views versus the Buddha Dharma]*. Taipei: True Wisdom Publishing Center, 2001.

Xiao, Pingshi 蕭平實. *Zongtong yu shuotong* 宗通與說通―成佛之道 *[The Way to Buddhahood: Mastering and Skillfully Articulating the Essence of Buddhist Enlightenment]*. Taipei: True Wisdom Publishing Center, 2001.

Yinshun 印順, *Yi fofa yanjiu fofa* 以佛法研究佛法 *[A Study of the Buddha Dharma Based on the Buddha Dharma]*. Taiwan: Zhengwen chubanshe 正聞出版社, 1972.

Zangmi xiufa midian 藏密修法秘典 *[A Secret Book on the Practices of Tibetan Tantra]*, vol. 1-5. Edited by Lü Tiegang 呂鐵鋼. Beijing: Huaxia chuban she 華夏出版社, 1995.

CHARTS: THE CULTIVATION STAGES OF THE

TWO PATHS WITHIN THE BUDDHA BODHI

The Cultivation Stages of the Two Paths within the Buddha Bodhi

The joint cultivation of these two paths is the one and only way to attain Buddhahood

		The Great Bodhi: Path to Buddhahood		The Two Lesser Vehicles Bodhi: Path to Liberation
Distant Pāramitās ▲	Path of Accumulation	Ten Faiths: Bodhisattvas accumulate faith in the Buddha Dharma. This will take one to ten thousand eons to accomplish.		
		First Abiding: Bodhisattvas accumulate virtues of charitable giving, primarily material goods.	Extensively practicing the six *pāramitās* before achieving awakening to the True Mind.	Practitioners eliminate the three fetters to attain the first fruition of liberation.
		Second Abiding: Bodhisattvas accumulate virtues of precept observance.		
		Third Abiding: Bodhisattvas accumulate virtues of forbearance.		
		Fourth Abiding: Bodhisattvas accumulate virtues of diligence.		
		Fifth Abiding: Bodhisattvas accumulate virtues of meditative absorption.		
		Sixth Abiding: Bodhisattvas accumulate virtues of *prajñā* by studying and familiarizing themselves with the Middle Way of *prajñā* and eliminating the view of self during the Path of Preparation.		Practitioners attain the second fruition of liberation by reducing greed, aversion, and delusion.
First Faith to Tenth Dedication	Path of Vision	Seventh Abiding: Bodhisattvas awaken to the True Mind and gain direct comprehension of *prajñā*, thereupon realize directly the inherently pure nirvana.		
		Eighth Abiding: Starting from this stage, bodhisattvas gain direct comprehension of the Middle Way of *prajñā* in all phenomena, and gradually eliminate their dispositional hindrances.	Extensively practicing the six *pāramitās* after achieving awakening to the True Mind.	Practitioners attain the third fruition of liberation by eliminating the five lower fetters.
		Tenth Abiding: Bodhisattvas see the Buddha-nature with the physical eye and attain direct comprehension of the illusoriness of the world.		
		First Practice to Tenth Practice. While extensively cultivating the six *pāramitās*, bodhisattvas rely on their insights into the Middle Way of *prajñā* to directly comprehend the aggregates, sense-fields, and elements are illusory like mirages. Upon completing the Tenth Practice, they will have fully accomplished the direct comprehension of these phenomena being like mirages.		
		First Dedication to Tenth Dedication: Bodhisattvas study and familiarize themselves with the knowledge-of-all-aspects and eliminate dispositional hindrances, except the last portion of afflictions associated with mentation. Upon completing the Tenth Dedication, they will have attained direct comprehension of the bodhisattva path being like a dream.		

Near Pāramitās ▲	Path of Vision	First Ground: Upon completing the Tenth Dedication, bodhisattvas will have realized a portion of the knowledge-of-the-aspects-of-paths, consisting of personal and direct realization of each of the eight consciousnesses, which enables them to perceive the five aspects of dharmas, the three natures, the seven facets of the ultimate truth, the seven intrinsic natures [of the *Tathāgatagarbha*], and the two types of no self. They enter the Stage of Proficiency (First Ground) after bravely making the ten inexhaustible vows. Also, they have forever subdued the dispositional hindrances without eliminating them completely. While they can attain liberation from saṃsāra through wisdom at this point, they purposely retain the last portion of afflictions associated with mentation to nourish future rebirths out of their great vows. The principal cultivation of the First Ground consists of the *pāramitā* of Dharma teaching as well as the Hundred Dharmas. The cultivation of the First Ground is completed when bodhisattvas attain direct comprehension of the six sense-objects being like images in a mirror.
First Ground to Seventh Ground	Path of Cultivation	Second Ground: Bodhisattvas enter the Second Ground when they have completed their cultivation of the First Ground and realized an additional portion of the knowledge-of-the-aspects-of-paths. Cultivation of this stage focuses on the *pāramitā* of precept observance and the knowledge-of-all-aspects. Upon completing the Second Ground, bodhisattvas will have attained direct comprehension of the first seven consciousnesses being like light and shadows. Thereupon, they will be able to adhere to precepts in a way that is both pure and natural. Third Ground: Bodhisattvas advance to the Third Ground after having realized an additional portion of the knowledge-of-the-aspects-of-paths upon completing the Second Ground. The principal cultivation of the Third Ground includes the *pāramitā* of forbearance, the four concentrations and the four formless absorptions, the four boundless minds, as well as the five supernatural powers. While bodhisattvas on the Third Ground can realize the fruition of twofold liberation, they deliberately choose not to; instead, they purposely retain the last portion of afflictions associated with mentation to nourish future rebirths. Upon completing the Third Ground, bodhisattvas will have attained direct comprehension of all voices of Dharma teaching being like echoes in a valley and achieved the mind-made body attained through the taintless and wondrous *samādhi*. Fourth Ground: Bodhisattvas advance to the Fourth Ground after having realized an additional portion of the knowledge-of-the-aspects-of-paths on the Third Ground. The principal cultivation of this stage is the *pāramitā* of diligence, for which bodhisattvas extensively and tirelessly teach and guide sentient beings who have karmic connections with them in this and other worlds. They will also continue their cultivation of the knowledge-of-all-aspects. Upon completing the Fourth Ground, bodhisattvas will have attained direct comprehension of their own mind-made bodies generated during *samādhi* being like the moon reflected in the water. Fifth Ground: Bodhisattvas advance to the Fifth Ground after having realized an additional portion of the knowledge-of-the-aspects-of-paths on the Fourth Ground. The *pāramitā* of meditative absorption and the knowledge-of-all-aspects constitute the principal cultivation of the Fifth Ground. Bodhisattvas will also eliminate the desire for nirvāṇa possessed by adherents of the lesser vehicles. Upon completing the Fifth Ground, they will have attained direct comprehension of all bodhisattvas' mind-made bodies and emanation bodies being like the effects of conjuring.	Bodhisattvas undertake the four levels of intensified effort before entering the First Ground, to eradicate the manifestation of all afflictive hindrances and attain the fourth fruition of liberation. The last portion of afflictions associated with mentation, however, is purposely retained to nourish future rebirths. Upon entering the First Ground, bodhisattvas will have put an end to delimited existence (*paricchedajarāmaraṇa*) and will proceed to eliminate the habitual seeds of afflictive hindrances, as well as the higher afflictions of beginningless ignorance. →

	Path of Cultivation	
Near Pāramitās ▲ First Ground to Seventh Ground	**Sixth Ground**: Bodhisattvas advance to the Sixth Ground after having realized an additional portion of the knowledge-of-the-aspects-of-paths on the Fifth Ground. The principal cultivation of the Sixth Ground is the *pāramitā of prajñā*: relying on the knowledge-of-the-aspects-of-paths they have acquired, bodhisattvas directly comprehend that each of the twelve factors of dependent arising as well as the mind-made and emanation bodies are all transformations of one's mind of True Suchness, and therefore are "seemingly but not truly existent." Having accomplished the contemplation of the subtle characteristics of these dharmas, they acquire the ability to spontaneously realize the meditative absorption of cessation without any added effort. Thereupon, they become Mahāyāna adepts (*aśaikṣa*) of twofold liberation. **Seventh Ground**: After attaining direct comprehension of the transformations of one's own mind of True Suchness being "seemingly but not truly existent" on the Sixth Ground, bodhisattvas attain an additional portion of the knowledge-of-the-aspects-of-paths and advance to the Seventh Ground. The cultivation of the Seventh Ground focuses on continued learning of the knowledge-of-all-aspects and the *pāramitā* of skillful means. Additionally, bodhisattvas contemplate again all the subtle characteristics of each of the twelve factors of dependent arising from the perspectives of transmigration and the extinction of transmigration, whereby they achieve mastery of skillful means and the ability to enter the meditative absorption of cessation in a single thought. Upon completing the Seventh Ground, bodhisattvas will have attained direct comprehension of the nirvana they have realized being as illusory as a *gandharva's* city.	Upon completing the Seventh Ground, bodhisattvas will have eliminated the last portion of afflictions associated with mentation that has been purposely retained. They will also have thoroughly eliminated all tainted habitual seeds of afflictive hindrances associated with the aggregates of form, sensation, and perception.
Great Pāramitās ▲ Eighth Ground to Virtual Enlight-enment	**Eighth Ground**: Having attained the contemplation of the extremely subtle characteristics at the Seventh Ground, bodhisattvas realize an additional portion of the knowledge-of-the-aspects-of-paths and advance to the Eighth Ground. The principal cultivation of the Eighth Ground concentrates on the continued learning of the knowledge-of-all-aspects and the *pāramitā* of vows. Upon completing the Eighth Ground, bodhisattvas will be able to spontaneously bring forth the exclusively signless contemplation at all times and hence can manipulate physical objects or mental images at will. Also, they will have realized the mind-made body attained through correct realization of dharma characteristics. **Ninth Ground**: Bodhisattvas advance to the Ninth Ground after having realized an additional portion of the knowledge-of-the-aspects-of-paths on the Eighth Ground. The principal cultivation of the Ninth Ground consists of the *pāramitā* of strength as well as continued learning of the knowledge-of-all-aspects. Upon completing the Ninth Ground, bodhisattvas will have mastered the four unhindered knowledges and realized the mind-made body attained without added effort and in accordance with the classes of beings to be delivered.	Bodhisattvas gradually and spontaneously eliminate the taintless habitual seeds of afflictive hindrances associated with the aggregates of formation and consciousness, as well as the higher afflictions of cognitive hindrances.

	Path of Cultivation	Tenth Ground: Bodhisattvas advance to the Tenth Ground after having realized an additional portion of the knowledge-of-the-aspects-of-paths on the Ninth Ground. The principal cultivation of the Tenth Ground is the knowledge-of-all-aspects, namely, the *pāramitā* of omniscience. Upon completing the Tenth Ground bodhisattvas will be able to generate the cloud of great Dharma wisdom and manifest the various meritorious qualities contained therein. They will also become a "designated bodhisattva."	
Perfect Pāramitās		Virtual Enlightenment: After having realized the portion of the knowledge-of-the-aspects-of-paths cultivated on the Tenth Ground, bodhisattvas advance to the stage of Virtual Enlightenment. At this stage, they cultivate the knowledge-of-all-aspects and perfectly realize the acquiescence to the non-arising of dharmas (*anutpattikadharmakṣānti*) pertaining to this stage. They will also perfect the thirty-two majestic physical features and immumerable associated good marks unique to Buddha by cultivating and accumulating enormous amount of virtues over a hundred eons.	
	Path of Ultimate Realization	Sublime Enlightenment: Bodhisattvas have thoroughly eliminated all habitual seeds of afflictive hindrances and all latent cognitive hindrances, as well as permanently eradicated the ignorance that leads to transformational existence. They will manifest birth in the human world, realize the great nirvana, and perfect the four kinds of wisdom of Buddha. After displaying physical death in the human world, their reward-bodies will permanently reside in the highest heaven of the form-realm to continue to teach and guide bodhisattvas on or above the First Ground coming from all worlds. Having accomplished the ultimate fruition of Buddhahood, they will generate numerous emanation bodies to perpetually teach and guide sentient beings.	Bodhisattvas bring transformational existence (*parinamiktjarāmaraṇa*) to a complete end and attain the great nirvana.

Perfect Ultimate Fruition of Buddhahood
Respectfully composed by Buddhist disciple Xiāo Píngshí (Feb. 2012)

CHINESE PUBLICATIONS OF THE VENERABLE XIAO PINGSHI

Available from True Wisdom Publishing Center
(http://books.enlighten.org.tw/zh-tw/)

1. *Signless Buddha-Mindfulness*
   《無相念佛》

2. *Stages in Cultivating Buddha-Mindfulness Samādhi*
   《念佛三昧修學次第》

3. *Chan: Before and After Enlightenment (2 Vols.)*
   《禪—悟前與悟後》上下冊

4. *Treasury of the Wisdom-Eye that Sees the Correct Dharma—Collection of Protecting the Dharma*
   《正法眼藏—護法集》

5. *Ascertaining the True Reality of Life*
   《生命實相之辨正》

6. *An Easy Way to Identify True versus False Enlightenment*
   《真假開悟之簡易辨正法佛子之省思—合訂本》

7. *Perfect Harmony between Chan and Pure Land*
   《禪淨圓融》

8 *Commentaries on the Chan Gong'an Collection: The Correct Eye of Buddhist Enlightenment (vol. 1)*
   《宗門正眼》公案拈提第一輯

9. *The Undeniable Existence of the Tathāgatagarbha*
   《真實如來藏》

10. *Entering the Dharma-Door of Buddha-Mindfulness*

   《如何契入念佛法門》

11. *Commentaries on the Chan Gong'an Collection: The Dharma-Eye of Buddhist Enlightenment (vol. 2)*

   《宗門法眼》公案拈提第二輯

12. *Letters of Xiao Pingshi*

   《平實書箋》

13. *An Exposition on the Laṅkāvatāra Sūtra (10 vols.)*

   《楞伽經詳解》共十輯

14. *Commentaries on the Chan Gong'an Collection: The Essence of the Path to Buddhist Enlightenment (vol. 3)*

   《宗門道眼》公案拈提第三輯

15. *Awakening to the True Mind versus Entering the First Ground*

   《明心與初地》

16. *Commentaries on the Chan Gong'an Collection: The Lineage Holders of Buddhist Enlightenment (vol. 4)*

   《宗門血脈》公案拈提第四輯

17. *The Way to Buddhahood: Mastering and Skillfully Articulating the Essence of Buddhist Enlightenment*

   《宗通與說**通**—成佛之道》

18. *Wrong Views versus the Buddha Dharma*

   《邪見與佛法》

19. *Ambrosial Dharma Rain*

   《甘露法雨》

20. *Commentaries on the Chan Gong'an Collection: The Correct Path to Buddhist Enlightenment (vol. 5)*

《宗門正道》公案拈提第五輯

21. *Self and Non-Self*

《我與無我》

22. *Behind the Façade of Tibetan Tantra (4 vols.)*

《狂密與真密》共四輯

23. *Commentaries on the Chan Gong'an Collection: The Correct Meaning of Buddhist Enlightenment (vol. 6)*

《宗門正義》公案拈提第六輯

24. *The Contemplation of Non-Self in Mahāyāna Buddhism*

《大乘無我觀》

25. *The Crises of Buddhism*

《佛教之危機》

26. *The Secrets of the Heart Sūtra*

《心經密意》

27. *The Shadow of the Lamp*

《燈影》

28. *Commentaries on the Chan Gong'an Collection: The Implicit Truth of Buddhist Enlightenment (Part 7 of 7 vols.)*

《宗門密意》公案拈提第七輯

29. *Entering the Dharma-Door of Non-Duality*

《入不二門》

30. *True versus False Enlightenment*

《真假開悟》

31. *A Discourse on the Awakening of Mahayana Faith (6 vols.)*

《起信論講記》共六輯

32. *Mastery of the Universal Gateway*

《普門自在》

33. *The Correct Meaning of the Consciousness-Aggregate*

《識蘊真義》

34. *A Discourse on the Sūtra on Upāsaka Precepts (8 vols.)*

《優婆塞戒經講記》共八輯

35. *The Correct Meaning of the Āgamas: Exploring the Origin of the Consciousness-Only Doctrine (7 vols.)*

《阿含正義—唯識學探源》共七輯

36. *The Dull Bird and the Bright Tortoise*

《鈍鳥與靈龜》

37. *A Discourse on the Vimalakīrti Sūtra (6 vols.)*

《維摩詰經講記》共六輯

38. *In Accord with Conditions*

《隨緣》

39. *A Discourse on the Śrīmālādevī Siṃhanāda Sūtra (6 vols.)*

《勝鬘經講記》共六輯

40. *Mastering the Essence of the Diamond Sūtra (9 vols.)*

《金剛經宗通》共九輯

41. *A Discourse on the Śūraṃgama Sūtra (15 vols.)*

《楞嚴經講記》共十五輯

42. *The Supra-Consciousness that Transcends Time and Space*

《第七意識與第八意識？—穿越時空「超意識」》

43. *Textual Research on the Chaste Lady Kāśyapa: A Critique of Lü Kai-Wen's "An Analysis of Buddhist Discourses on Rebirth"*

《童女迦葉考》—論呂凱文〈佛教輪迴思想的論述分

析〉之謬

44. *Mastering the Essence of the Reality Prajñāpāramitā Sūtra (8 vols.)*

《實相經宗通》共八輯

45. *A Discourse on the Lotus Sūtra (25 vols.)*

《法華經講義》共二十五輯

46. *A Discourse on the Buddha Treasury Sutra (21 vols.)*

《佛藏經講義》共二十一輯

47. *A Discourse on the Great Drum Sutra (6 vols.)*

《大法鼓經講義》共六輯

Cultivation Centers of The True Enlightenment Practitioners Association

CULTIVATION CENTERS OF THE TRUE ENLIGHTENMENT PRACTITIONERS ASSOCIATION

Taipei Lecture Hall

9F, No. 277, Sec. 3, Chengde Rd.,
Taipei 103, Taiwan, R.O.C.

Tel.: +886-2-2595-7295

(Ext. 10 & 11 for 9F; 15 & 16 for 10F;
18 & 19 for 5F; and 14 for the
bookstore on 10F.)

Daxi Patriarch Hall

No. 5-6, Kengdi, Ln. 650, Xinyi Rd.,
Daxi Township, Taoyuan County 335,
Taiwan, R.O.C.

Tel.: +886-3-388-6110

Taoyuan Lecture Hall

10F, No. 286 & 288, Jieshou Rd.,
Taoyuan 330, Taiwan, R.O.C.

Tel.: +886-3-374-9363

Hsinchu Lecture Hall

2F-1, No. 55, Dongguang Rd.,
Hsinchu 300, Taiwan, R.O.C.

Tel.: +886-3-572-4297

Taichung Lecture Hall

13F-4, No. 666, Sec. 2, Wuquan W.
Rd., Nantun Dist., Taichung 408,
Taiwan, R.O.C.

Tel.: +886-4-2381-6090

Jiayi Lecture Hall

8F-1, No. 288, Youai Rd., Jiayi 600,
Taiwan, R.O.C.

Tel.: +886-5-231-8228

Tainan Lecture Hall

4F, No. 15, Sec. 4, Ximen Rd., Tainan
700, Taiwan, R.O.C.

Tel.: +886-6-282-0541

Kaohsiung Lecture Hall

5F, No. 45, Zhongzheng 3rd Rd.,
Kaohsiung 800, Taiwan, R.O.C.

Tel.: +886-7-223-4248

Hong Kong Lecture Hall

Unit E1, 27th Floor, TG Place, 10
Shing Yip Street, Kwun Tong,

Kowloon, Hong Kong

Tel: +852-2326-2231

Website of the True Enlightenment
Practitioners Association:

http://www.enlighten.org.tw

Website of the True Wisdom
Publishing Co.:

http://books.enlighten.org.tw

Readers may download free
publications of the Association from
the above website.